# A Back Pain Bibliography

# A Back Pain Bibliography

Compiled and Edited for the Back Pain Association by

**BARRY WYKE** M.B., B.S., M.D.

*Director of the Neurological Unit, Royal College of Surgeons of England. Member of Research Committee, Back Pain Association; Member of International Association for the Study of Pain; Member of Society for Back Pain Research; Formerly Member of Executive Committee, Back Pain Association; Member of Working Group on Back Pain, Department of Health and Social Security, London*

With a Foreword by the late
SIR ALAN PARKS M.A., M.D., M.Ch., F.R.C.P., P.R.C.S.

PUBLISHED ON BEHALF OF
THE BACK PAIN ASSOCIATION
by

LLOYD-LUKE (Medical Books) LTD.
49 NEWMAN STREET · LONDON
1983

FILMSET, PRINTED AND BOUND IN ENGLAND BY
HAZELL WATSON AND VINEY LTD
AYLESBURY, BUCKS

ISBN 0 85324 193 7

# Foreword by
The late President of the
Royal College of Surgeons of England

That there should be an Association entitled "Back Pain" is testimony enough to the fact that there is an unsolved problem of considerable magnitude. Pain of the type dealt with here can be acute and agonising or constant, of low key, yet demoralising. Not only is the painful episode itself extremely unpleasant, it engenders a sense of insecurity and uncertainty which is in itself a permanent disability. The victim always fears a recurrence of his symptoms and may limit activities and change his mode of work for fear of yet another attack. Treatment is hindered by the difficulties of making a definite diagnosis, and also by the fact that pain, being an individual experience, can never be exactly equated with an observed pathological process. The need for research into causes, prevention and treatment must be obvious to all.

The present publication aims to give information which is immediately accessible to the research worker, so that he can ascertain what has already been achieved and develop ideas as to which field is most likely to yield fruitful progress. It is therefore a most valuable contribution to research which will ultimately help individual sufferers and relieve society as a whole of a social and economic burden.

*October 1982*                                    ALAN PARKS

# The Back Pain Association

The Back Pain Association is a Registered Medical Charity whose aims are to promote research into the causes, treatment and prevention of back pain, and to foster educational and training programmes designed to reduce the incidence of this widespread disability, by raising and disbursing funds for these purposes. Consonant with these objectives, the Association has sponsored the preparation of this Bibliography by Professor Barry Wyke as a contribution to the needs of research workers in the field of back pain throughout the world, the publication of which has been assisted by generous grants from the Department of Health and Social Security in the United Kingdom and from the Foundation for Chiropractic Education and Research in the United States of America.

Because of the vast size of the economic, industrial, social and domestic problems posed by the problems of back pain throughout the world, more funds are everywhere needed to facilitate research in this field; and the Back Pain Association would give whole-hearted support to the creation of similar organisations by interested parties in other countries. Further information regarding this matter, and the research and educational activities of the Back Pain Association, may be obtained from the Executive Director, Back Pain Association, 31–33 Park Road, Teddington, Middlesex, TW11 0AB, England.

# Preface

In recent years, statistical studies in a number of industrialised societies have shown that back pain—defined as pain experienced in the posterior surface of the body anywhere between the occiput and the coccyx—is (after headache) the most frequently encountered painful complaint in general clinical practice. The same studies also show that back pain—and especially pain in the lumbosacral region (so-called "low back pain")—is the principal cause of occupational, social and domestic disablement in such societies, some four out of five individuals having such a complaint at some time in their lives. Thus in the United Kingdom some 3·4 million medical consultations per annum are the result of the occurrence of back pain, and it is estimated that the annual loss of industrial output from this cause amounts to some £220 million; while in the United States the cost of treatment of and compensation to sufferers from back pain involves an expenditure of some $14 billion per year.

Nevertheless, in spite of the immensity and universality of the problem presented by back pain the fact remains that its differential diagnosis, treatment (whether surgical, medical or manipulative) and prevention remain in a very unsatisfactory state everywhere in the world. But increasing recognition of the socio-economic (let alone the humanitarian) consequences of this situation in a number of countries over the last decade has at last led to realisation of the fact that traditional empirical approaches to this vast problem have largely failed, and that urgently necessary improvements in the diagnosis, treatment and prevention of back pain will only arise from scientifically-orientated research aimed principally at delineating the various mechanisms by which this disabling complaint may be produced—a fact that has been officially recognised by designation of back pain research as an area of special importance

ix

by the Department of Health and Social Security and the Medical Research Council in Great Britain and by the National Institutes of Health in the United States of America.

Promotion of such research is one of the principal objectives of the Back Pain Association, in furtherance of which the Association has commissioned the publication of this Bibliography (with financial assistance from the Department of Health and Social Security in the United Kingdom and the Foundation for Chiropractic Education and Research in the United States), since a basic requirement of all workers embarking on research into back pain is access to pertinent multidisciplinary investigations that have already been published. Perhaps because of the wide range of disciplines that bear on this problem, no comprehensive international bibliography of the literature relating to back pain research is yet in existence, nor do computer-stored references derived from particular disciplines provide adequate coverage of the whole field for research workers: it is therefore hoped that the present work (and its later Supplements) will go some way towards meeting this basic need.

This Bibliography has been compiled with the assistance of a number of British scientific and medical departments currently engaged in research into various aspects of back pain, who have generously made their individual reference indices available to the Editor and his assistants—chiefly, the Department of Human Biology at the University of Surrey, the Spinal Research and Spinal Treatment Units of the Royal National Orthopaedic Hospital, the Department of Community Medicine at Guy's Hospital, the Department of Rheumatology at the Westminster Hospital and the Neurological Unit of the Royal College of Surgeons of England. The Editor, and the Back Pain Association, are also extremely grateful to the Librarians of the Royal College of Surgeons of England, the Royal Society of Medicine and the British Medical Association for their co-operation in this project, and especially to Mrs. Phillipa Lane, L.S.A. and Mrs. K. M. Suggate (Society of Indexers) for their invaluable assistance in compiling and arranging the bibliographic material. Above all the Editor is deeply indebted to his Secretary, Mrs. Marguerite Holman, for her devoted efforts in preparing the material for publication. Thanks are also due to the Publisher, Mr. Douglas Luke (of Messrs. Lloyd-Luke), for his assistance and advice in the preparation of this work.

It should be pointed out that the references included in this

Bibliography are deliberately selective, being chosen because of their research relevance, or their historical significance, or because they represent contrasting or controversial contributions to the literature of the subject from workers in different countries. Emphasis has been placed on publications in the English language; and the titles of those issued in other languages have been translated (by the Editor) into English. The entries are arranged alphabetically by authors in research categories according to a classification system (outlined in the following Classification and Contents Table) designed for the purpose by the Editor. The present volume presents references published up to the end of 1979—later references will be included in smaller Supplements that will be issued at three-year intervals in order to provide workers in the field of back pain research with a continuously updated source of access to the relevant literature. The Editor would welcome submission of entries from readers that are thought to be appropriate for inclusion in such Supplements.

BARRY WYKE

Royal College of Surgeons of England,
Lincoln's Inn Fields,
London WC2A 3PN,
England
*September 1982*

# Classification and
# Table of Contents

### Section One: BASIC SCIENCES

— ligaments, fasciae, aponeuroses, cartilage and
    fibro-adipose tissues
— muscles and tendons
— meninges and cerebrospinal fluid
— nerves, nerve roots and spinal cord
— blood vessels and blood supply

## Section Two: CLINICAL ASPECTS

*Section One*

# BASIC SCIENCES

# REGIONS OF BACK

## (a) Cervical

ADAMS, C. B. T. & LOGUE, V. (1971). Studies in cervical spondylotic myelopathy. *Brain*, **94:** 557–594.

AHLGREN, P. & FOG, J. (1968). Atlanto-epistrophical subluxation in rheumatoid arthritis. *Acta Rheum.*, **14:** 210, 221.

AHO, A., VARTIANEN, O. & SALO, O. (1955). Segmentary antero-posterior mobility of the cervical spine. *Ann. Med. Int. Fenn.*, **44:** 287–289.

ALDER, E. & LAVIS, S. (1956). Clinical evaluation of X-ray findings in the cervical spine. *Act. Med. Orient. (Tel Aviv)*, **15:** 129–136.

ALLEN, K. L. (1952). Neuropathies caused by bony spurs in the cervical spine with special reference to surgical treatment. *J. Neurol. Neurosurg. Psychiat.*, **15:** 20–36.

ANDERSON, R. E. & SHEALY, C. N. (1970). Cervical pedicle erosion and rootlet compression caused by a tortuous vertebral artery. *Radiology*, **96:** 537–538.

ANDERSON, W. F. (1964). Cervical spine studies in older people. *Rheumatism*, **20:** 7–12.

AZOUZ, E. M. & WEE, R. (1974). Spondylosis of the cervical vertebrae. *Radiology*, **111:** 315–318.

BAGCHI, A. K. (1973). Cervical spondylosis as an ecological problem. *J. Indian Med. Ass.*, **60:** 382–383.

BAILEY, D. K. (1952). The normal cervical spine in infants and children. *Radiology*, **59:** 712–719.

BAILEY, R. W. (1975/6). *The Cervical Spine.* Lea and Febiger; Philadelphia.

BALAU, J. & HUPFAUER, W. (1974). The differential diagnosis of injuries of the atlanto-axial region in childhood. *Arch. Orthop. Unfall-Chir.*, **78:** 343–355.

BALL, J. & MEIJER, K. A. E. (1964). On cervical mobility. *Ann. Rheum. Dis.*, **23:** 429–438.

BARDFIELD, R. & STREDA, A. (1973). Ankylosing spondylo-arthritis of the cervical spine in association with juvenile chronic polyarthritis (the relevance of age). *Radiol. Diag., (Berlin)*, **14:** 81–87.

BARRATT, J. G. (1974). Enlargement of cervical intervertebral foramina by coiling of the vertebral artery. *Australas. Radiol.*, **18:** 171–174.

BASTIN, J. M. & THOMAS, J. D. (1973). Acquired blocks and vertebral fusions in cases of degenerative discopathy and joint aging. *Rec. Rheum. Mal. Osteoartic.*, **40:** 443–446.

BAUZE, R. J. (1975). The mechanism of forward dislocation in the human cervical spine. *J. Bone Joint Surg.*, **57B:** 253–254.

BECHAR, M. (1971). Cervical myelopathy caused by narrowing of the cervical spinal canal. *Clin. Radiol.*, **22:** 63–68.

BEETHAM, M. D. (1971). Whiplash injuries of the cervical spine. *Aust. J. Physiother.*, **17:** 77.

BELLAMY, R., LIEBER, A. & SMITH, S. D. (1972). Congenital spondylolisthesis of the sixth cervical vertebra. *J. Bone Joint Surg.*, **56A:** 405–407.

BERNSTEIN, S. A. (1975). Acute cervical pain associated with soft-tissue calcium deposition anterior to the interspace of the first and second cervical vertebrae. *J. Bone Joint Surg.*, **57A:** 426–428.

BHATTACHARYYA, S. K. (1974). Fracture and displacement of the odontoid process in a child. *J. Bone Joint Surg.*, **56A:** 1071–1072.

BLAND, J. H. (1965). Study of roentgenologic criteria for rheumatoid arthritis of the cervical spine. *Amer. J. Roent.*, **95:** 949–954.

BOCK, W. J. (1975). Fenestration of cervical spinal canal before and after fusion operation. *Neurochirurgia*, **18:** 12–15.

BOYLE, A. C. (1971). The rheumatoid neck. *Proc. Roy. Soc. Med.*, **65:** 1161–1165.

BRAAKMAN, R. (1967). Unilateral facet interlocking in the lower cervical spine. *J. Bone Joint Surg.*, **49B:** 249.

BRAAKMAN, R. (1973). Mechanisms of injury to the cervical cord. *Paraplegia*, **10:** 314–320.

BRACKETT, C. E. (1973). The posterior midline approach to a cervical disc. *J. Neurosurg.*, **38:** 668–671.

BRADSHAW, P. (1957). Some aspects of cervical spondylosis. *Quart. J. Med.*, **26:** 117–208.

BRAIN, R., & WILKINSON, M. (Eds.) (1967). *Cervical Spondylosis and Other Disorders of the Cervical Spine*. Heinemann; London.

4

Brain, W. R. (1963). Some unsolved problems of cervical spondylosis. *Brit. Med. J.*, **1:** 771–777.

Brain, W. R., Northfield, D. & Wilkinson, M. (1952). The neurological manifestations of cervical spondylosis. *Brain*, **75:** 187–225.

Brendler, S. J. (1968). Human cervical myotomes: functional anatomy studies at operation. *J. Neurosurg.*, **28:** 105–111.

Brewerton, D. A. (1964). The conservative treatment of the painful neck. *Proc. Roy. Soc. Med.*, **57:** 163–165.

British Association of Physical Medicine (1966). Pain in the neck and arm: a multicentre trial of the effects of physiotherapy. *Brit. Med. J.*, **1:** 253–258.

Bulos, S. (1974). Dysphagia caused by cervical osteophyte: report of a case. *J. Bone Joint Surg.*, **56B:** 148–152.

Burke, D. C. & Berryman, D. (1971). The place of closed manipulation in the management of flexion-rotation dislocations of the cervical spine. *J. Bone Joint Surg.*, **53B:** 165–182.

Burrows, E. H. (1963). Sagittal diameter of the spinal canal in cervical spondylosis. *Clin. Radiol.*, **14:** 77–86.

Burwood, R. J. & Watt, I. (1974). Assimilation of the atlas and basilar impression: a review of 1,500 skull and cervical spine radiographs. *Clin. Radiol.*, **25:** 327–333.

Carlioz, H. & Dubousset, J. (1973). Instability between the atlas and axis in the child. *Rev. Chir. Orthop.*, **59:** 291–307.

Carmel, W. & Kramer, F. J. (1968). Cervical cord compression due to exostosis in a patient with hereditary multiple exostoses. *J. Neurosurg.*, **28:** 500–503.

Cattell, H. A. & Filtzer, D. L. (1965). Pseudosubluxation and other normal variations in the cervical spine in children: a study of one hundred and sixty children. *J. Bone Joint Surg.*, **47A:** 1295–1309.

Cevansir, B. & Baserer, N. (1972). Cervical osteophytes: clinical and radiological findings. *J. Otolaryngol. Soc. Australia*, **3:** 359–361.

Chaco, J. (1974). Cervical spondylosis and pseudomyotonia. *Scand. J. Rehab. Med.*, **6:** 99–101.

Chakravorty, B. G. (1967). Arterial supply of the cervical spinal cord and its relation to the cervical myelopahty in spondylosis. *Ann. Roy. Coll. Surg. Engl.*, **45:** 232–251.

CHAND, K. (1972). Cervical spine and rheumatoid arthritis. *International Surgery*, **57**: 721–726.

CHESNEY, M. O. (1952). Radiography of the cervical and upper thoracic vertebrae. *Radiography*, **18**: 243–251.

CHRISMAN, O. D. & GERVAIS, R. F. (1962). Otologic manifestations of cervical syndrome. *Clin. Orthop.*, **24**: 34–39.

CLOWARD, R. B. (1959). Cervical diskography. *Ann. Surg.*, **150**: 1052–1064.

CLOWARD, R. B. (1960). The clinical significance of the sinuvertebral nerve in relation to the cervical disc syndrome. *J. Neurol. Neurosurg. Psychiat.*, **23**: 321–326.

COLACHIS, S. C. & STROHM, B. R. (1965). Radiographic studies of cervical spine motion in normal subjects: flexion and hyperextension. *Arch. Phys. Med.*, **46**: 753–760.

COLACHIS, S. C., STROHM, B. R. & GANTER, E. L. (1973). Cervical spine motion in normal women: radiographic study of effect of cervical collars. *Arch. Phys. Med. Rehab.*, **54**: 161–169.

COPE, S. & RYAN, G. M. S. (1959). Cervical and otolith vertigo. *J. Laryngol. Otol.*, **63**: 113–120.

COPPOLA, A. R. (1974). Disease of the cervical spine and nerve root pain. *Virginia Med. Month.*, **101**: 199–201.

CORRIGAN, A. B. (1969). Radiological changes in rheumatoid cervical spines. *Aust. Radiol.*, **13**: 370–375.

COVENTRY, M. B. (1970). Calcification in a cervical disc with anterior protrusion and dysphagia. *J. Bone Joint Surg.*, **52A**: 1463–1466.

CRANDALL, P. H. (1966). Cervical spondylotic myelopathy. *J. Neurosurg.*, **25**: 57–66.

DANZIGER, J. (1973). Arteriovenous malformation of the cervical cord. *Sth. Afr. Med. J.*, **47**: 1413–1416.

DANZIGER, J. (1975). Congenital absence of a pedicle in a cervical vertebra. *Clin. Radiol.*, **26**: 53–56.

DANZIGER, J. (1975). The widened cervical intervertebral foramen. *Radiology*, **116**: 671–674.

DAVIES, D. M. (1960). Epidemic cervical myalgia. *Lancet*, **1**: 1275–1277.

DEE, R., ANDREW, J., SWEETMAN, D. R. & WILLIAMS, R. A. (1969). Separate dens with subluxation and paraplegia treated by occipito-cervical fusion. *Proc. Roy. Soc. Med.*, **62**: 581–583.

DUFJES, F. (1972). Occipitocervical spondylodesis for atlanto-axial instability with neurological changes in rheumatoid conditions. *Acta. Orthop. Belg.*, **38**: 40–46.

DURBIN, F. C. (1956). Spondylolisthesis of the cervical spine. *J. Bone Joint Surg.*, **38B**: 734–735.

DUTTON, C. B. & RILEY, C. H. (1969). Cervical migraine—not merely a pain in the neck. *Amer. J. Med.*, **47**: 141–148.

ECTORS, P. & BREMEN, J. (1971). Management of cervical spine trauma: eleven years' experience. *Lyon. Chir.*, **67**: 429–434.

ELLIS, S. C. (1975). Massive swelling of the head and neck. *Anaesthesiology*, **42**: 102–103.

FELDMAN, F. & SEAMAN, W. B. (1969). The neurological complications of Paget's disease in the cervical spine. *Amer. J. Roent.*, **105**: 375–382.

FENLIN, J. M. (1971). Pathology of degenerative disease of the cervical spine. *Orthop. Clin. Nth. Amer.*, **2**: 371–387.

FERLIC, D. C. (1963). The nerve supply of the cervical intervertebral disc in man. *Bull. Johns Hopkins Hosp.*, **113**: 347–387.

FIELDING, J. W. (1957). Cineradiography of the normal cervical spine. *J. Bone Joint Surg.*, **39B**: 585.

FIELDING, J. W. (1957). Cineroentgenography of the normal cervical spine. *J. Bone Joint Surg.*, **39A**: 1280–1288.

FIELDING, J. W. (1964). Normal and selected abnormal motion of cervical spine from C2–C7, based on cineroentgenography. *J. Bone Joint Surg.*, **46A**: 1779–1781.

FIELDING, J. W. (1973). Selected observations on the cervical spine in the child. In *Current Practice in Orthopaedic Surgery*, **5**: 31–55. Ed. by J. P. Ahstrom. C. V. Mosby Co.; Saint Louis.

FIELDING, J. W. & GRIFFIN, P. P. (1974). Os odontoideum: an acquired lesion. *J. Bone Joint Surg.*, **56A**: 187–190.

FIELDING, J. W. & RATZAN, S. (1973). Osteochondroma of the cervical spine. *J. Bone Joint Surg.*, **55A**: 640–641.

FIELDING, J. W. & REDDY, K. (1969). Atlanto-axial rotatory deformity. *J. Bone Joint Surg.*, **51A**: 1672–1673.

FINEMAN, S. (1963). The cervical spine: transformation of the normal lordotic pattern into a linear pattern in the neutral posture. *J. Bone Joint Surg.*, **45A**: 1179–1183.

FLEISCHLI, D. J. (1967). Lytic lesion in a cervical vertebra. *J. Amer. Med. Ass.*, **201**: 192–193.

7

FRANCIS, C. C. (1955). Variations in the articular facets of the cervical vertebrae. *Anat. Rec.*, **122**: 589–609.

FRANCIS, C. C. (1956). Certain changes in the aged male white cervical spine. *Anat. Rec.*, **125**: 783–787.

FRANKS, A. S. (1968). Cervical spondylosis presenting as the facial pain of temporomandibular joint disorder. *Ann. Phys. Med.*, **9**: 193–196.

FRIED, L. C. (1973). Atlanto-axial fracture-dislocations: failure of posterior C1 to C2 fusion. *J. Bone Joint Surg.*, **55B**: 490–496.

FRIEDENBERG, Z. B. & MILLER, W. T. (1963). Degenerative disease of the cervical spine. *J. Bone Joint Surg.*, **45A**: 1171–1178.

FUNK, F. F. (1975). Injuries of the cervical spine in football. *Clin. Orthop.*, **109**: 50–58.

GANGULY, D. N. & ROY, K. K. S. (1964). A study on the cranio-vertebral joint in man. *Anat. Anz.*, **114**: 433–452.

GARBER, J. N. (1964). Abnormalities of the atlas and axis vertebrae. *J. Bone Joint Surg.*, **46A**: 1782–1791.

GARGANO, F. P., MEYER, J., HOUDEX, P. V. & CHARYULU, K. K. N. (1974). Transverse axial tomography of the cervical spine. *Radiology*, **113**: 363–367.

GAUFIN, L. M. (1975). Cervical spine injuries in infants: problems in management. *J. Neurosurg.*, **42**: 179–184.

GELBERMAN, R. H. & OLSON, C. O. (1974). Benign osteoblastoma of the atlas: case report. *J. Bone Joint Surg.*, **56A**: 808–810.

GOFF, C. W., ALDES, J. H. & ALDEM, J. O. (1964). *Traumatic Cervical Syndrome and Whiplash*. Lippincott; Philadelphia.

GOLDING, D. N. (1969). Cervical and occipital pain as presenting symptoms of intracranial tumour. *Ann. Phys. Med.*, **10**: 1–6.

GRACZYK, M. (1973). Lesions in the osseous-articular system of the upper extremities and cervical spine caused by mechanical vibration. *Bull. Inst. Mar. Med., Gdansk*, **24**: 63–72.

GRAY, L. P. (1956). Extralabyrinthine vertigo due to cervical muscle lesions. *J. Laryngol. Otol.*, **70**: 352–360.

GREENBERG, A. D. (1968). Transoral decompression of atlanto-axial dislocation due to odontoid hypoplasia. *J. Neurosurg.*, **28**: 266–269.

GRIFFITHS, E. R. (1974). Growth problems in cervical injuries. *Paraplegia*, **11**: 277–289.

GUKELBERGER, M. (1972). The uncomplicated post-traumatic cervical syndrome. *Scand. J. Rehab. Med.*, **4**: 150–153.

HANSON, T. A., KRAFT, J. P. & ADOCK, D. W. (1973). Subluxation of the cervical vertebrae due to pharyngitis. *Southern Med. J.*, **66**: 427–429.

HARALSON, R. H. (1969). Posterior dislocation of the atlas on the axis without fracture. *J. Bone Joint Surg.*, **51A**: 561–566.

HARMENING, H., PANNENBORG, E. & HEIRINGHOFF, F. W. (1973). On the treatment of lumbar and cervical syndromes with obstruction of inter-vertebral foramina. *Fortschr. Med.*, **91**: 1367–1369.

HARRIS, R. D. & HECHT, H. L. (1969). The notched inferior lamina. *Amer. J. Roentgenol.*, **3**: 511–514.

HARTHAN, J. T. (1975). A comparative study of five commonly used cervical orthoses. *Clin. Orthop.*, **109**: 97–102.

HARVIANEN, S., LAHTI, P. & DAVIDSSON, L. (1972). On cervical injuries: a radiographic analysis. *Acta Chir. Scand.*, **138**: 349–355.

HASUE, M. (1974). Cervical spine injuries in children. *Fukushima J. Med. Sci.*, **20**: 115–123.

HASUE, M., ITO, R. & SUZUKI, N. (1972). Circulatory dynamics of the epidural space in cervical and lumbar disc lesions. *Clin. Orthop.*, **89**: 129–138.

HEKSTER, R. E. (1972). The combination of occipitalization of the atlas with atlanto-axial dislocation due to an extravertebral (inflammatory) process in the head-neck region. *Phys. Neurol. Neurochir.*, **75**: 85–93.

HENTZER, L. & SCHALIMTZEK, M. (1971). Fractures and subluxations of the atlas and axis. *Acta Orth. Scand.*, **42**: 251–258.

HERTEL, G. (1973). The width of the cervical spinal canal and the size of the vertebral bodies in syringomyelia: a statistical comparative study. *Europ. Neurol.*, **9**: 168–182.

HILL, R. C. J. (1960). The cervical disc syndrome. *J. Bone Joint Surg.*, **42B**: 860.

HIRSCH, C. (1967). Structural changes in the cervical spine. *Acta Orthop. Scand. Suppl.*, **109**: 7–77.

HIRSCH, C. & ZOTTERMAN, Y. (1973). *Cervical Pain.* Pergamon Press; Oxford.

HODGKINSON, A. (1970). Neck pain localisation by cervical disc stimulation and treatment by anterior interbody fusion. *J. Bone Joint Surg.*, **52B**: 789.

9

HODGSON, L. (1969). Cervical spondylosis. *J. West Pacif. Orthop. Ass.*, **6:** 117–140.

HOHL, M. (1964). Normal motions in the upper portion of the cervical spine. *J. Bone Joint Surg.*, **46A:** 1777–1779.

HOHL, M. & BAKER, H. R. (1964). The atlanto-axial joint. *J. Bone Joint Surg.*, **46A:** 1739–1752.

HUNTER, G. A. (1968). Non-traumatic displacement of the atlanto-axial joint: a report of seven cases. *J. Bone Joint Surg.*, **50B:** 44–51.

HYYPPÄ, S. E., LAASONEN, E. M. & HALONEN, V. (1974). Erosion of cervical vertebrae caused by elongated and tortuous vertebral arteries. *Neuroradiology*, **7:** 49–51.

ISDALE, I. C. & CONLON, P. W. (1971). Atlanto-axial subluxa ion: a six year follow-up report. *Ann. Rheum. Dis.*, **30:** 387–389.

JACKSON, B. T. (1967). Headaches associated with disorders of the cervical spine. *Headache*, **6:** 175–179.

JACOBS, B. (1975). Cervical fractures and dislocations (C3–C7). *Clin. Orthop.*, **109:** 18–32.

JANETOS, G. P. (1966). Paget's disease of the cervical spine. *Amer. J. Roent.*, **97:** 655–657.

JIROUT, J. (1971). Patterns of changes in the cervical spine on lateroflexion. *Neuroradiology*, **2:** 164–166.

JIROUT, J. (1972). Mobility of the cervical vertebrae in lateral flexion of the head and neck. *Acta Radiol.*, **13:** 919–927.

JIROUT, J. (1972). The effect of mobilisation of segmental blockade on the sagittal component of the reaction on lateroflexion of the cervical spine. *Neuroradiology*, **3:** 210–215.

JIROUT, J. (1972). Changes in the sagittal component of the reaction of the cervical spine to lateroflexion after manipulation of movement restriction. *Česk. Neurol.*, **35:** 175–180.

JIROUT, J. (1973). Suprasegmental effect of ante- and retroflexion. *Česk. Neurol.*, **36:** 72–76.

JIROUT, J. (1974). The dynamic dependence of the lower cervical vertebrae on the atlanto-occipital joints. *Neuroradiology*, **7:** 249–252.

JOHNSON, C., PENRY, J. B. & BURWOOD, R. J. (1972). An unusual presentation of cervical block vertebrae. *Australas. Radiol.*, **16:** 63–65.

JOHNSON, P. H. (1974). Cervical disc syndrome. *J. Arkansas Med. Soc.*, **71:** 128.

JONES, D. M. (1957). Pain of cervical origin. *J. Bone Joint Surg.*, **39B:** 157–158.

JONES, D. M. (1967). Cineradiographic studies of abnormalities of the high cervical spine. *Arch. Surg.*, **94:** 206–213.

JUHL, J. H. (1962). Roentgenographic variations in the normal cervical spine. *Radiology*, **78:** 591–597.

KADRI, N. (1973). Cervical spondylitis. *Paediatr. Indones.*, **13:** 134–144.

KANSHEPOLSKY, J., AGNEW, D., ECHOLS, C. & HODAK, J. (1973). The missing cervical spine pedicle. *Bull. Los Angeles Neurol. Soc.*, **38:** 85–90.

KESSLER, L. A. (1973). Delayed, traumatic dislocation of the cervical spine. *J. Amer. Med. Ass.*, **224:** 124–125.

KEUTER, R. (1970). Vascular origin of cranial sensory disturbances caused by pathology of the lower cervical spine. *Acta Neurochir.*, **23:** 229–245.

KIWERSKI, J., CHROSTOWSKA, T. & MAKOWSKI, J. (1974). On the reasons and the mechanism of trauma to the cervical spine. *Chir. Narzod. Ruchu Ortop. Pol.*, **39:** 1–6.

KLINE, D. G. (1966). Atlanto-axial dislocation simulating a head injury: hypoplasia of the odontoid. *J. Neurosurg.*, **24:** 1013–1016.

KONO, R. (1974). Clinical significance of sagittal air myelopathy on the cervical spinal region: especially clinical studies on cervical spondylotic myelopathy. *J. Jap. Orthop. Ass.*, **48:** 581–602.

KOSOY, J. (1974). Audiovestibular findings with cervical spine trauma. *Texas Med.*, **70:** 66–71.

KOTTKE, F. J. & LESTER, R. G. (1958). Use of cineflurography for evaluation of normal and abnormal motion in the neck. *Arch. Phys. Med.*, **39:** 229–231.

KOVACS, A. (1974). Observation of the cervical segment of the spinal canal by an extension device. *Acta Radiol.*, **15:** 33–42.

KRAUSOVA, L. & LEWITT, K. (1965). The mechanism and measuring of the mobility in the cranio-cervical joints during lateral inclinations. *Acta Univ. Carol. Med., Suppl.* 21: 123–126.

KRUSEN, E. M. (1968). Cervical pain syndromes. *Arch. Phys. Med. Rehab.*, **49:** 376–382.

KULOWSKI, J. (1972). Spontaneous anterior dislocation of the atlas. *Missouri Med.*, **69:** 805–808.

LALLI, J. J. (1972). Cervical vertebral syndromes. *J. Am. Osteopath. Ass.*, **72:** 121–128.

LANGFITT, T. W. & ELLIOTT, F. A. (1967). Pain in the back and legs caused by cervical spinal cord compression. *J. Amer. Med. Ass.*, **200**: 382–385.

LAVARDE, G. (1973). Isolated fractures of the articular processes of the cervical spine. *J. Chir. (Paris)*, **105**: 241–248.

LEVINE, R. A. (1970). Cervical spondylosis and dykinesias. *Neurology*, **20**: 1194–1199.

LEWITT, K. & KRAUSOVA, L. (1963). Measurements of intervertebral and dorsal flexion of the cranio-cervical junction. *Česk. Neurol.*, **26**: 371–376.

LI, C. P. & PAULL, D. (1971). A new head rotation method for cervical spine radiography. *Radiology*, **98**: 568.

LOBO, M. (1974). A modified oblique view of the cervical spine. *Radiography*, **40**: 113–114.

LOURIE, J., SHENDE, M. C. & STEWART, D. H. (1973). The syndrome of central cervical soft disc herniation. *J. Amer. Med. Ass.*, **226**: 302–305.

McCUE, C. M. (1973). Cervical aortic arch. *Amer. J. Dis. Child.*, **125**: 738–742.

McKEEVER, F. M. (1968). Atlanto-axial instability. *Surg. Clin. Nth. Amer.*, **48**: 1375–1390.

McKIBBIN, B. (1973). The early management of cervical spine injuries. *Resuscitation*, **2**: 241–248.

MacNAB, I. (1964). Acceleration injuries of cervical spine. *J. Bone Joint Surg.*, **46A**: 1797–1799.

MacNAB, I. (1975). Cervical spondylosis. *Clin. Orthop.*, **109**: 69–77.

MARAR, B. C. (1974). The pattern of neurological damage as an aid to the diagnosis of the mechanism in cervical-spine injuries. *J. Bone Joint Surg.*, **56A**: 1648–1654.

MARAR, B. C. (1974). Hyperextension injuries of the cervical spine. The pathogenesis of damage of the spinal cord. *J. Bone Joint Surg.*, **56A**: 1655–1662.

MARAR, B. C. (1975). Fracture of the axis arch: "hangman's fracture" of the cervical spine. *Clin. Orthop.*, **106**: 155–165.

MARAR, B. C. & BALACHANDRANDRAN, N. (1973). Non-traumatic atlanto-axial dislocation in children. *Clin. Orthop.*, **92**: 220–226.

MARKS, R. L. (1973). Nonpenetrating injuries of the neck and cerebrovascular accident. *Arch. Neurol.*, **28**: 412–414.

MAROTZKY, H. J. (1972). Isometric energy determinations in the cervico-cranial system in young and old people. *Arch. Orthop. Unfall-Chir.*, **74:** 42–62.

MARVEL, J. P. (1971). The clinical syndrome of cervical disc disease. *Orthop. Clin. Nth. Amer.*, **2:** 419–433.

MASSARE, C., BARD, M. & TRISTANT, H. (1974). Cervical discography: speculative observations on the technique and on the indications in our experience. *J. Radiol. Electrol.*, **55:** 395–399.

MATHEWS, J. A. (1974). Atlanto-axial subluxation in rheumatoid arthritis: a five-year follow-up study. *Ann. Rheum. Dis.*, **33:** 526–531.

MED, M. (1973). Articulations of the cervical vertebrae and their variability. *Folia Morphol. (Prague)*, **21:** 324–327.

MEIJERS, K. A. (1973). Treatment of dislocations in the cervical spine in rheumatoid arthritis and ankylosing spondylitis, complicated by signs of cord compression. *Ann. Rheum. Dis.*, **32:** 88–89.

MEIKLE, J. A. & WILKINSON, M. (1971). Rheumatoid involvement of the cervical spine. *Ann. Rheum. Dis.*, **30:** 154–161.

MICHIE, I. (1968). Neurological syndromes associated with cervical and cranio-cervical anomalies. *Arch. Neurol.*, **18:** 241–247.

MILES, W. A. (1974). Discogenic and osteoarthritis disease of the cervical spine. *J. Natl. Med. Ass.*, **66:** 300–304.

MINAGI, H. & GRONNER, A. T. (1969). Calcification of the posterior longitudinal ligament: a cause of cervical myelopathy. *Amer. J. Roent.*, **105:** 365–369.

MOLINA, F., RAMCHARAN, J. & WYKE, B. D. (1976). Structure and function of articular receptor systems in the cervical spine. *J. Bone Joint Surg.*, **58B:** 255–256.

MOURGES, G. DE, FISCHER, L., JARSAILLON, B. & MACHENAUD, A. (1973). Fractures of the posterior arch of the axis, and of the pedicles, arches and laminae based on 21 observations. *Rev. Chir. Orthop.*, **59:** 549–564.

MUNRO, D. (1961). Treatment of fractures and dislocations of the cervical spine, complicated by cervical cord and root injuries. *New Eng. J. Med.*, **264:** 573–582.

MURONE, I. (1974). The importance of the sagittal diameters of the cervical spinal canal in relation to spondylosis and myelopathy. *J. Bone Joint Surg.*, **56B:** 30–36.

NAGASHIMO, G. (1972). Cervical myelopathy due to ossification of the posterior longitudinal ligament. *J. Neurosurg.*, **37:** 653–660.

NATHAN, F. R. AND BICKEL, W. H. (1968). Spontaneous axial

subluxation in a child as the first sign of juvenile rheumatoid arthritis. *J. Bone Joint Surg.*, **50A:** 1675–1678.

NEUWIRTH, E. (1952). Headache and facial pains in cervical discopathy. *Ann. Int. Med.*, **37:** 75–83.

NEWILL, R. G. (1963). Epidemic cervical myalgia. *J. Coll. Gen. Pract.*, **6:** 344–347.

NEWTON, T. H. (1958). Cervical intervertebral disc calcification in children. *J. Bone Joint Surg.*, **40A:** 107–113.

NICHOLSON, J. T. (1968). Anomalies of the occipito-cervical articulation. *J. Bone Joint Surg.*, **50A:** 295–304.

NIELSEN, P. B. (1965). Asymptomatic vertical fracture of a cervical vertebra. *Acta Orthop. Scand.*, **36:** 250–256.

NIEMINEN, R. (1973). Fractures of spinous processes of the lower cervical spine. *Ann. Chir. Gynaec. Fenn.*, **62:** 328–333.

NIEMINEN, R. (1974). Fractures of the articular processes of the lower cervical spine. *Ann. Chir. Gynaec. Fenn.*, **63:** 204–211.

NORRIS, C. W. (1974). Head and neck pain: T-M joint syndrome. *Laryngoscope*, **84:** 1466–1478.

NURICK, S. (1972). The pathogenesis of the spinal cord disorder associated with cervical spondylosis. *Brain*, **95:** 87–100.

NURICK, S. (1972). The natural history and the results of surgical treatment of the spinal cord disorder associated with cervical spondylosis. *Brain*, **95:** 101–108.

OBERSON, R., FOROGLOU, G. & ZANDER, E. (1972). Myelography and vertebral angiography in traumatic lesions of the cervical spine. *Z. Unfall-Med. Berufskr.*, **65:** 3–10.

O'CONNELL, J. E. A. (1956). Discussion on cervical spondylosis. *Proc. Roy. Soc. Med.*, **49:** 202–208.

ODOM, G. L., FINNEY, W. & WOODHALL, B. (1958). Cervical disk lesions. *J. Amer. Med. Ass.*, **166:** 23–28.

OKUBO, J. (1973). Study of the upper cervical spine by means of panoramic tomography. *Bull. Tokyo Med. Dent. Univ.*, **20:** 105–119.

ORNILLA, E., ANSELL, B. M. & SWANNELL, A. J. (1972). Cervical spine involvement in patients with chronic arthritis undergoing orthopaedic surgery. *Ann. Rheum. Dis.*, **31:** 364–368.

OSGOOD, C., MARTIN, L. G. & ACKERMAN, E. (1973). Fracture-dislocation of the cervical spine with ankylosing spondylitis: report of two cases. *J. Neurosurg.*, **39:** 764–769.

OTRICH, G. C. (1968). The temporomandibular syndrome. *Illinois Med. J.*, **133**: 705–706.

PAGE, C. P., STORY, J. L. & WISSINGER, J. P. (1973). Traumatic atlanto-occipital dislocations. *J. Neurosurg.*, **39**: 394–397.

PALLIS, C., JONES, A. M. & SPILLANE, J. D. (1954). Cervical spondylosis: incidence and implications. *Brain*, **77**: 274–289.

PATTERSON, F. P. (1973). Instability of the upper cervical spine. *J. Bone Joint Surg.*, **55B**: 456–457.

PATZAKIS, M. J., KNOPF, A., ELFERING, M., HOFFER, M. & HARVEY, J. P. (1974). Posterior dislocation of the atlas on the axis: a case report. *J. Bone Joint Surg.*, **56A**:1260–1262.

PERCY, E. C. (1969). Extension injury to the cervical spine. *Canad. Med. Ass. J.*, **101**: 626–628.

PEROVIC, M. N., KOPITS, S. E. & THOMPSON, R. C. (1973). Radiological evaluation of the spinal cord in congenital atlanto-axial dislocation. *Radiology*, **109**: 713–716.

PETRIE, J. G. (1964). Flexion injuries of cervical spine. *J. Bone Joint Surg.*, **46A**: 1800–1806.

PHILLIPS, D. G. (1975). Upper limb involvement in cervical spondylosis. *J. Neurol. Neurosurg. Psychiat.*, **38**: 386–390.

POLGA, J. P. & CRAMER, G. G. (1974). Cleft anterior arch of atlas simulating odontoid fracture. *Radiology*, **113**: 341.

PROLO, D. J., RUNNELS, J. B. & JAMESON, R. M. (1973). The injured cervical spine: immediate and long-term immobilization with the halo. *J. Amer. Med. Ass.*, **224**: 591–594.

PURSER, D. W. (1970). Rheumatoid arthritis of the cervical spine. *Physiotherapy*, **56**: 445–448.

PUT, T. (1969). The therapeutic value of cirnarizarine in cervicobrachial and ischial syndromes. *Arzteinmittelforschung*, **19**: 1868–1869.

QUADERY, L. A. (1974). Myelopathy in cervical spondylosis. *Lancet*, **2**: 1453.

RAJU, G. C. (1975). Congenital lesions of the craniospinal axis. *Indian J. Paediat.*, **42**: 112–115.

RANA, N. A., HANCOCK, D. O., TAYLOR, A. R. & HILL, A. G. S. (1973). Atlanto-axial subluxation in rheumatoid arthritis. *J. Bone Joint Surg.*, **558**: 458–470.

RANA, N. A., HANCOCK, D. O., TAYLOR, A. R. & HILL, A. G. S. (1973). Upward translocation of the dens in rheumatoid arthritis. *J. Bone Joint Surg.*, **55B**: 471–477.

RAWKINS, M. D. (1954). Diagnosis of herniation of intervertebral discs in the cervical spine. *Brit. J. Phys. Med.*, **17**: 219–223.

RAWLINGS, M. S. (1960). The "Straight Back" syndrome: a new cause of pseudo-heart disease. *Amer. J. Cardiol.*, **5**: 333–338.

REYMOND, R. D., WHEELER, P. S., PEROVIC, M. & BLOCK, B. (1972). The lucent cleft, a new radiographic sign of cervical disc injury or disease. *Clin. Radiol.*, **23**: 188–192.

RIGAMONTI, L., GHINDINI, O., MOLINARI-TOSATTI, P., SALVI, S., DIMONDA, V., CERNIC, F. & RICAMONTI, D. (1972). Fracture-dislocations of the cervical vertebrae: treatment and results in eight cases. *Archivio Scienze Mediche*, **129**: 1–10.

RILEY, G. (1954). Cervical spondylosis. *J. Bone Joint Surg.*, **36B**: 681.

ROBINSON, H. S. (1966). Rheumatoid arthritis, atlanto-axial subluxation and its clinical presentation. *Can. Med. Ass. J.*, **94**: 470–477.

ROOSEN, K., RÖMER, F. & SCHULZ, S. (1973). Myeloscintography and Pantopaque-myelography in traumatic avulsion of cervical roots: a diagnostic study. *Fortschr. Geb. Roentgen.*, **118**: 728–730.

ROSENBERG, D., LONGIN, B., DUQUESNEL, C., BERAUD, C. & MONNET, P. (1970). Calcification of intervertebral discs in the child (based on six observations). *Rev. Neurol. (Paris)*, **123**: 181–186.

ROSSIER, A. B., WERNER, A., WILDI, E. & BERNI, J. (1968). Contribution to the study of late cervical syringomyelic syndromes after dorsal or lumbar traumatic paraplegia. *J. Neurol. Neurosurg. Psychiat.*, **31**: 99–105.

ROTHMAN, R. H. (1975). The acute cervical disk. *Clin. Orthop.*, **109**: 59–68.

ROTHMAN, R. H., MARVEL, J. P. & BAKER, R. (1971). The conservative treatment of cervical disc disease. *Orthop. Clin. Nth. Amer.*, **2**: 435–441.

ROUSSEAU, J. (1969). Radiological and clinical study of 16 cases with congenital malformation of the cervico-occipital joint. *Ann. Radiol.*, **12**: 499–521.

RYAN, G. M. S. & COPE, S. (1955). Cervical vertigo. *Lancet*, **2**: 1355–1358.

SATOYOSHI, E., DOI, Y. & KINOSHITA, M. (1972). Pseudomyotonia in cervical root lesions with myelopathy. *Arch. Neurol.*, **27**: 307–313.

SCHATZKER, J., RORABECK, C. H. & WADDELL, J. P. (1971). Fractures of the dens (odontoid process): an analysis of 37 cases. *J. Bone Joint Surg.*, **53B:** 392–405.

SCHIFF, D. C. (1973). The arterial supply of the odontoid process. *J. Bone Joint Surg.*, **55A:** 1450–1456.

SCHNEIDER, D. (1973). Traumatic cervical vertebral lesions with particular reference to the bony injuries. *Arch. Orthop. Unfall-Chir.*, **75:** 133–120.

SCHOENING, H. A. & HANNAN, V. (1964). Factors related to cervical mobility: Part 1. *Arch. Phys. Med. Rehab.*, **45:** 602–609.

SCHUTT, C. H. & D¯HAN, F. C. (1968). Neck injury to women in automobile accidents. *J. Amer. Med. Ass.*, **206:** 2687–2692.

SCOTT, M. (1966). Lower extremity pain simulating sciatica: tumours of the high thoracic and cervical cord as causes. *J. Amer. Med. Ass.*, **160:** 528–534.

SCOVILLE, W. B. (1966). Type of cervical disk lesions and their surgical approaches. *J. Amer. Med. Ass.*, **196:** 479–481.

SEIDEL, K. & SATERNUS, K. S. (1972). Anatomico-myelographic studies of traumatic lesions in cervical vertebral preparations. *Arch. Orthop. Unfall-Chir.*, **74:** 10–20.

SELECKI, B. R. (1969). The effects of rotation of the atlas on the axis: experimental work. *Med. J. Aust.*, **1:** 1012–1015.

SELECKI, B. R. (1970). Cervical spine and cord injuries. Mechanisms and surgical implications. *Med. J. Aust.*, **1:** 838–840.

SEMMES, R. E. & MURPHEY, F. (1941). The syndrome of unilateral rupture of the sixth cervical intervertebral disk with compression of the seventh cervical nerve root: a report of four cases simulating coronary disease. *J. Amer. Med. Ass.*, **121:** 1209–1214.

SERRE, H. & SIMON, L. (1966). Atlanto-axial dislocation in rheumatoid arthritis. *Rheumatism (April)*: 53–58.

SEUR, N. H. (1972). Subtraction in cervical pneumomyelography and an application of RISA myelography. *Radiol. Clin. Biol.*, **41:** 387–396.

SHAFAR, J. (1966). The syndrome of the third neurone of the cervical sympathetic system. *Amer. J. Med.*, **40:** 97–109.

SHAHRESTANI, E. & CLOWARD, R. B. (1972). Treatment of cervical disc pains without nerve root involvement. *J. Western Pacific Orthop. Ass.*, **9:** 40–48.

SHAPIRO, R. (1973). The differential diagnosis of traumatic lesions of the occipito-atlanto-axial segment. *Radiol. Clin. Nth. Amer.*, **11:** 505–526.

SHERK, H. H. & NICHOLSON, J. T. (1970). Fractures of the atlas. *J. Bone Joint Surg.*, **52A:** 1017–1024.

SHERK, H. H. & NICHOLSON, J. T. (1971). Comparative anatomy and embryology of the cervical spine. *Orthop. Clin. Nth. Amer.*, **2:** 325–341.

SHERK, H. H. & NICHOLSON, J. T. (1972). Cervico-occulo-acusticus syndrome: case report of death caused by injury to abnormal cervical spine. *J. Bone Joint Surg.*, **54A:** 1776–1778.

SHERK, H. H., SHUT, L. & CHUNG, S. (1974). Iniencephalic deformity of the cervical spine with Klippel-Feil anomalies and congenital elevation of the scapula: report of three cases. *J. Bone Joint Surg.*, **56A:** 1254–1259.

SHRAGO, G. G. (1973). Cervical spine injuries: association with head trauma. A review of 50 patients. *Amer. J. Roentgenol.*, **118:** 670–673.

SILBERSTEIN, C. E. (1965). The evolution of degenerative changes in the cervical spine and an investigation into the joints of Luschka. *Clin. Orthop.*, **40:** 184–204.

SIM, F. H., SVIEN, H. J., BICKEL, W. H. & JANES, J. M. (1974). Swan-neck deformity following extensive cervical laminectomy. *J. Bone and Joint Surg.*, **56A:** 564–580.

SIMONS, D. J., DAY, E., GOODELL, H. & WOOLFF, H. G. (1943). Experimental studies on headache: muscles of the scalp and neck as sources of pain. *Res. Pub. Ass. Nerv. Ment. Dis.*, **23:** 228–244.

SINGER, W. D. (1975). Occlusive vertebrobasilar artery disease associated with cervical spine anomaly. *Amer. J. Dis. Child.*, **129:** 492–495.

SINGH, S. (1965). Variations of the superior articular facets of atlas vertebrae. *J. Anat.*, **99:** 565–571.

SIWE, S. A. (1931). The cervical part of the ganglionated cord, with special reference to its connections with the spinal nerves and certain cerebral nerves. *Amer. J. Anat.*, **48:** 479–497.

SMEULERS, J. (1975). Cervical arthosis in a young man subjected to electric shock during imprisonment. *Lancet*, **1:** 1249–1250.

SMITH, G. R. (1975). Visualization of the posterolateral elements of the upper cervical vertebrae in the anteroposterior projection. *Radiology*, **115:** 219–220.

SMITH, P. H., BENN, R. T. & SHARP, J. (1972). Natural history of rheumatoid cervical luxations. *Ann. Rheum. Dis.*, **31**: 431–439.

SMITH, R. A. & ESTRIDGE, M. N. (1962). Neurologic complications of head and neck manipulations. *J. Amer. Med. Ass.*, **182**: 528–531.

Soo, Y. S. & ANG, A. H. (1973). The value of the lateral cervical myelogram in the evaluation of cervical spondylosis. *Australas. Radiol.*, **17**: 371–374.

Soo, Y. S. & SACHDEV, A. S. (1972). The value of Pantopaque (Iodophendylate) myelography in cervical spondylosis. *J. Western Pacific Orthop. Ass.*, **9**: 32–39.

SOUTHWICK, W. O. (1964). The normal cervical spine. *J. Bone and Joint Surg.*, **46A**: 1767–1777.

SOUTHWICK, W. O. & ROBINSON, R. A. (1957). Surgical approaches to the vertebral bodies in the cervical and lumbar regions. *J. Bone and Joint Surg.*, **39A**: 631–643.

SPENCE, K. F. (1970). Bursting atlantal fracture associated with rupture of the transverse ligament. *J. Bone and Joint Surg.*, **52A**: 543–549.

SPILBERG, I. & LIEBERMAN, D. M. (1972). Ankylosing hyperostosis of the cervical spine. *Arth. Rheum.*, **15**: 208–212.

SPURLING, R. G. (1956). *Lesions of the Cervical Intervertebral Disk.* Springfield, Ill.; Thomas.

SPURLING, R. G. & SCOVILLE, W. B. (1944). Lateral rupture of the cervical intervertebral discs: a common cause of shoulder and arm pain. *Surg. Gynec. Obst.*, **78**: 350–358.

SPURLING, R. G. & SEGERBERG, L. H. (1953). Lateral intervertebral disk lesions in the lower cervical region. *J. Amer. Med. Ass.*, **151**: 354–359.

STAMM, T. T. (1955). Manipulation and cervical spondylosis. *Lancet*, **1**: 355–356.

STEEN, B. (1966). The function of certain neck muscles in different positions of the head with and without loading of the cervical spine. *Acta. Morph. Neurol. Scand.*, **6**: 301–310.

STEIN, A. & KALK, F. (1974). Selective conservatism in the management of penetrating wounds of the neck. *Sth. Afr. J. Surg.*, **12**: 31–40.

STEVENS, J. C. (1971). Atlanto-axial subluxation and cervical myelopathy in rheumatoid arthritis. *Quart. J. Med.*, **40**: 391–408.

STEVENSON, J. G. (1975). Cervical venous hums. *New Eng. J. Med.*, **292**:212.

STEWART, D. Y. (1962). Current concepts of the 'Barre syndrome' or the post-cervical sympathetic syndrome. *Clin. Orth.*, **24**: 40–48.

STOFFT, E. (1973). On the morphology of the superficial suspensory apparatus of the spinal cord in the cervical vertebral column. *Radiologie*, **13**: 531–540.

STRACHAN, W. E. (1972). Surgical treatment of cervical spondylosis. *Bristol Med. Chir. J.*, **87**: 59–60.

STUART, E. (1972). Persistent dislocation of cervical vertebrae 5 and 6. *Nursing Times*, **68**: 1376–1378.

SUKOFF, M. H. (1972). Transoral decompression for myelopathy caused by rheumatoid arthritis of the cervical spine. *J. Neurosurg.*, **37**: 493–497.

SUNDERLAND, S. (1974). Mechanisms of cervical nerve root avulsion in injuries of the neck and shoulder. *J. Neurosurg.*, **41**: 705–714.

SUTRO, C. J. (1970). Posterior paravertebral ossification in the cervical region in a Caucasian patient. *Bull. Hosp. Joint Dis.*, **31**: 111–113.

SUZUKI, T. (1972). Cervical air myelography and its significance in cervical spondylosis. *J. Jap. Orthop. Ass.*, **46**: 125–138.

SWINDON, D. R., HAMILTON, E. B. D., MATHEWS, J. A. & YATES, D. A. H. (1972). Vertical subluxation of the axis in rheumatoid arthritis. *Ann. Rheum. Dis.*, **31**: 359–363.

TAKAHASHI, K. (1968). Headache caused by cervical spondylosis. *Clin. Neurol.*, **11**: 643.

TAREN, J. A. & KAHN, E. A. (1962). Anatomic pathways related to pain in face and neck. *J. Neurosurg.*, **19**: 116–121.

TCHANG, S. P. K. (1974). The cervical spino-laminar line. *J. Canad. Ass. Radiol.*, **25**: 224–226.

THAMBYRAJAH, K. (1972). Fractures of the cervical spine with minimal or no symptoms. *Med. J. Malaya*, **26**: 244–249.

THAWLEY, S. E. (1974). Air in the neck. *Laryngoscope*, **84**: 1445–1453.

THERON, J & DJINDJIAN, R. (1973). Cervicovertebral phlebography using catheterization. *Radiology*, **108**: 325–331.

THISTLE, H. G. (1969). Neck and shoulder pains: evaluation and conservative treatment. *Med. Clin. Nth. Amer.*, **53**: 511–524.

THOMPSON, S. M. (1960). Dislocation of the cervical spine. *J. Bone Joint Surg.*, **42B:** 858.

THORSON, J. (1972). Neck injuries in road accidents: incidence of acute injuries and sequelae among in-patients. *Scand. J. Rehab. Med.*, **4:** 110–113.

TINDALL, G. T. & WILKINS, R. H. (1969). Management of cervical disc disease. *Southern Med. J.*, **62:** 33–40.

TOGLIA, J. U. (1972). Vestibular and medico-legal aspects of closed cranio-cervical trauma. *Scand. J. Rheum. Med.*, **4:** 126–132.

TONDURY, G. (1943). On the anatomy of the cervical vertebral column: does it reveal uncovertebral joints? *Zeitschr. Anat. Entwgesch.*, **112:** 448–459.

TOWNSEND, E. H. & ROWE, M. L. (1952). Mobility of the upper cervical spine in health and disease. *Paediatrics*, **10:** 567–573.

TREVOR-JONES, R. (1970). Spondylosis of the cervical spine. *Sth. Afr. Med. J.*, **44:** 752–756.

TULI, S. M. (1974). Tuberculosis of the cranio-vertebral region. *Clin. Orthop.*, **104:** 209–212.

TURNBULL, I. M. (1966). Blood supply of cervical spinal cord in man. *J. Neurosurg.*, **24:** 951–965.

VAN DER MEER, P. (1965). Rheumatoid arthritis and the cervical spine. *Acta. Rheum. Scand.*, **11:** 81.

VAN KERCKHOVE, H. (1970). Involvement of the lateral atlanto-axial joints as first and late symptoms of rheumatoid arthritis. *Acta. Rheum. Scand.*, **16:** 197–210.

VAUGHAN, B. (1968). Lateral tomography of atlanto-axial joint in rheumatoid disease. *Australas. Radiol.*, **12:** 58–60.

VERBIEST, H. (1973). The management of cervical spondylosis. *Clin. Neurosurg.*, **20:** 262–294.

VERBIEST, H. (1973). Anterolateral operations for fractures or dislocations of the cervical spine due to injuries or previous surgical interventions. *Clin. Neurosurg.*, **20:** 334–366.

VILEAUNU, C. (1972). Observations on the morphological characteristics of the cervical vertebrae. *Acta Anat.*, **81:** 148–157.

VILEAUNU, C. (1974). Aspects of ontogenetic evolution of the osteo-vasculo-nervous space relationships at the level of the cervical intervertebral canal in man. *Ant. Anz.*, **136:** 412–416.

VILEAUNU, C. (1975). Morphofunctional peculiarities of the transverse processes of the axis: considerations of their pathogenetic significance. *Acta. Anat.*, **92:** 301–309.

21

VINES, F. S. (1969). The significance of 'occult' fractures of the cervical spine. *Amer. J. Roentgenol.*, **107**: 493–504.

VOGELSANG, H. (1973). Cervical intervertebral discitis after discography. *Neurochirurgia*, **16**: 80–83.

VOGELSANG, H., ZEIDLER, H., WITTENBORG, A. & WEIDNER, A. (1973). Rheumatoid cervical luxations with fatal neurological complications. *Neuroradiography*, **6**: 87–92.

WALDRON, R. L. & WOOD, E. H. (1973). Cervical myelography. *Clin. Orthop.*, **97**: 74–89.

WALTZ, T. A. (1967). Physical factors in the production of the myelopathy of cervical spondylosis. *Brain*, **90**: 395–404.

WATANUKI, A. (1973). The effect of the sympathetic nervous system on cervical spondylosis: an experimental study. *J. Jap. Orthop. Ass.*, **47**: 963–974.

WAYLONIS, G. W. (1968). Electromyographic findings in chronic cervical radicular syndromes. *Arch. Phys. Med. Rehab.*, **49**: 407–412.

WEIR, D. C. (1975). Roentgenographic signs of cervical injury. *Clin. Orthop.*, **109**: 9-17.

WEISS, M. H. & KAUFFMANN, B. (1973). Hangman's fracture in an infant. *Amer. J. Dis. Child.*, **126**: 268–269.

WENER, L., DI CHIRO, G. & GARGOUR, G. W. (1974). Angiography of cervical cord injuries. *Radiology*, **112**: 597–604.

WERNE, S. (1955). Spontaneous atlas dislocation. *Acta. Orthop. Scand.*, **25**: 32–43.

WERNE, S. (1959). The possibilities of movement in the craniovertebral joints. *Acta. Orthop. Scand.*, **28**: 165–173.

WHALEN, J. P. & WOODRUFF, C. L. (1970). The cervical prevertebral fat stripe. *Amer. J. Roentgenol.*, **109**: 445–451.

WHALEY, K. (1968). Fatal sub-axial dislocation of cervical spine in rheumatoid arthritis. *Brit. Med. J.*, **2**: 31.

WHITE, A. A. (1975). Biomechanical analysis of clinical stability in the cervical spine. *Clin. Orthop.*, **109**: 85–96.

WILKINSON, H. A. (1969). Roentgenographic correlations in cervical spondylosis. *Amer. J. Roentgenol.*, **105**: 370–374.

WILKINSON, M. (1960). The morbid anatomy of cervical spondylosis and myelopathy. *Brain*, **93**: 589–617.

WILKINSON, M. (1967). The relationship of cervical vertebral disease to spinal cord disorder. *Modern Trends Neurol.*, **4:** 255–268.

WILKINSON, M. (1970). Cervical spondylosis. *Practitioner*, **204:** 537–545.

WILSON, P. J. (1967). Painful sensory disturbance in cervical dermatomes after head injury. *Lancet*, **2:** 1391–1392.

WING, L. W. (1974). Cervical vertigo. *Aust. N.Z. J. Surg.*, **44:** 275–277.

WIRSCHING, M. (1972). On the relations of the pattern, severity and location of cervical vertebral column lesions to the mechanics of injury. *Arch. Orthop. Unfall-Chir.*, **74:** 63–90.

WISNIEWSKI, M., TOKER, C., ANDERSON, P. J., HUANG, Y. P. & MALIS, L. I. (1973). Chondroblastoma of the cervical spine: a case report. *J. Neurosurg.*, **38:** 763–766.

WITEK, J. (1963). Functional-anatomical radiological studies of the atlanto-axial joint. *Fol. Med. Cracow.*, **5:** 577–610.

WOESNER, M. E. & MITTS, M. G. (1972). The evaluation of cervical spine motion below C2: a comparison of cineroentgenographic and conventional roentgenographic methods. *Amer. J. Roentgenol.*, **115:** 148–154.

WOLF, B. S., KHILANANI, M. & MALIS, L. I. (1956). Sagittal diameter of bony cervical canal and its significance in cervical spondylosis. *J. Mt. Sinai Hosp.*, **23:** 283–292.

WOLFF, H. D. (1972). On persistent pain in the vertebral column (vertebral blocking and its manual treatment). *Verh. Dtsch. Ges. Rheumatol.*, **2** *(Suppl. 2)*: 215–226.

WONG, M. L. (1974). Cervical mycobacterial disease. *Trans. Amer. Acad. Ophth. Otolar.*, **78:** 175–187.

WOOD, W. G., ROTHMAN, L. M. & NUSSBAUM, B. E. (1975). Intramedullary neurilemoma of the cervical spinal cord. *J. Neurosurg.*, **42:** 465–468.

WOODS, W. W. & COMPERE, W. E. (1969). Electronystagmography in cervical injuries. *Internat. Surg.*, **51:** 251–258.

WORTZMAN, G. (1968). Rotatory fixation of the atlanto-axial joint. *Radiology*, **90:** 479–487.

WYKE, B. D. (1958). The surgical physiology of facial pain. *Brit. Dent. J.*, **104:** 153–168.

WYKE, B. D. (1968). Neurology of facial pain. *Brit. J. Hosp. Med.*, **1:** 45–65.

WYKE, B. D. (1973). Structural and functional aspects of arthrokinetic reflexogenic systems in the cervical spine. *Proc. Int. Symp. Exper. Clinical. Neurobiol., Košice.* p. 59.

WYKE, B. D. (1975). The neurological basis of movement: a developmental review. In *Movement and Child Development.* p.p. 19–33. Ed. by K. S. Holt. Heinemann; London.

WYKE, B. D. (1976). Neurological aspects of the diagnosis and treatment of facial pain. In *Scientific Foundations of Dentistry.* p.p. 278–299. Ed. by B. Cohen and I. Kramer. Heinemann; London.

WYKE, B. D. & MOLINA, F. (1972). Articular reflexology of the cervical spine. *Proc. 6th Int. Congr. Phys. Med., Barcelona:* p. 4.

YATES, D. A. (1969). Cervical spine. *Brit. Med. J.*, **2:** 807–809.

YUTAKA, O., HIROYUKI, A., YUTAKA, S., KEIRO, O., SINUSUKE, H. & SYOTARA, M. (1967). Posterior paravertebral ossification causing cervical myelopathy. *J. Bone Joint Surg.*, **49A:** 1314–1328.

ZALIS, A. W. (1970). Electrophysiologic diagnosis of cervical nerve root avulsion. *Arch. Phys. Med. Rehab.*, **51:** 708–710.

ZEITER, W. J. & HOUSE, F. B. (1946). Cervical periarthritis: diagnosis and treatment. *Arch. Phys. Med.*, **27:** 162–165.

ZIMMERMAN, H. B. & FARRELL, W. J. (1970). Cervical vertebral erosion caused by vertebral artery tortuosity. *Amer. J. Roentgenol.*, **108:** 767–770.

ZINGESSER, L. H. (1973). Radiological aspects of anomalies of the upper cervical spine and craniocervical junction. *Clin. Neurosurg.*, **20:** 220–231.

*(b) Thoracic*

ABBOTT, K. H. & RETTER, R. H. (1956). Protrusions of thoracic intervertebral disks. *Neurology*, **6:** 1–10.

BASTIN, J. M. & THOMAS, J. D. (1973). Acquired blocks and vertebral fusions in cases of degenerative discopathy and of joint ageing. *Rev. Rheum. Mal. Osteoartic.*, **40:** 443–446.

BYWATERS, E. G. (1974). Rheumatoid discitis in the thoracic region due to spread from costovertebral joints. *Ann. Rheum. Dis.*, **33:** 408–409.

CHESNEY, M. O. (1952). Radiography of the cervical and upper thoracic vertebrae. *Radiography*, **18:** 243–251.

CHESTERMAN, P. J. (1964). Spastic paraplegia caused by sequestrated thoracic intervertebral disc. *Proc. Roy. Soc. Med.*, **57**: 87–88.

DAVIS, P. R. (1957). Studies on the functional anatomy of the human vertebral column, with special reference to the thoracic and lumbar region. *Ph.D. Thesis, Univ. Lond.*

GRANT, A. P. & KEEGAN, D. A. J. (1968). Rib pain—a neglected diagnosis. *Ulster Med. J.*, **37**: 162–169.

HARRIS, J., CARTER, A. R., GLICK, E. N. & STOREY, G. O. (1974). Ankylosing hyperostosis: 1. Clinical and radiological features. *Ann. Rheum. Dis.*, **33**: 210–215.

HOHMANN, P. (1968). Degenerative changes in the costotransverse joints: a contribution to the diagnosis, pathogenesis and clinical features of arthroses and insertion ligaments of the costotransverse joints in relation to vertebral aspects of the disease. *Zeitschr. Orthop.*, **105**: 217–229.

JIROUT, J. (1963). Mobility of the thoracic spinal cord under normal conditions. *Acta Radiol.*, **1**: 729–735.

JOHNSON, A. (1959). Rib lesions in rheumatoid disease. *J. Bone Joint Surg.*, **41B**: 237.

KUS, W. M. & KOKOSZCZYNSKA-LESZEK, I. (1973). Histiocytosis of the Xth thoracic vertebra. *Chir. Narzad. Ruchu. Ortop. Pol.*, **38**: 361–364.

LACSAY, A. (1973). Degenerative changes in the constotransverse and costovertebral joints. *Fortschr. Rontgenstr.*, **119**: 108–111.

LANGLAND, N. & ROAAS, A. (1971). Spondylitis psoriatica. *Acta Orthop. Scand.*, **42**: 391–396.

LAWRENCE, M. S. (1967). Thoracic outlet compression syndrome. *J. Iowa Med. Soc.*, **57**: 561–566.

NEUGEBAUER, H. (1970). A measuring device for estimations of range of back movement. *Zeitschr. Orthop.*, **108**: 395–406.

NIZZOLI, V. & TESTA, C. (1968). A case of calcification in the spinal arachnoid giving rise to spinal cord compression. *J. Neurol. Sci.*, **7**: 381–384.

PEPPER, H. W. (1973). Extrapleural mass with neurologic signs. *Chest*, **64**: 345–346.

PEROT, P. & MUNRO, D. D. (1969). Transthoracic removal of midline thoracic disc protrusions causing spinal cord compression. *J. Neurosurg.*, **31**: 452–458.

PIERCE, D. S. (1972). Long-term management of thoracolumbar

fractures and fracture dislocations. *A.A.O.S. Instructional Course Lectures*, **21**: 102–107.

PLAUE, R. (1972). Relations between breadth, depth and level of thoracic and lumbar vertebral bodies. *Fortschr. Geb. Roentgenstr.*, **116**: 469–472.

PLAUE, R. (1972). Characteristics of fractures of the thoracic and lumbar vertebral bodies: Part 1: compression tests on macerated specimens. *Zeitschr. Orthop.* **110**: 159–166.

PLAUE, R. (1972). Characteristics of fractures of the thoracic and lumbar vertebral bodies. Part 2: compression tests on fresh cadaveric vertebrae. *Zeitschr. Orthop.*, **110**: 357–362.

REEVES, D. L. & BROWN, H. A. (1968). Thoracic intervertebral disc protrusion with spinal cord compression. *J. Neurosurg.*, **28**: 24–28.

RICHARDSON, A. T. (1975). The painful shoulder. *Proc. Roy. Soc. Med.*, **68**: 731–736.

ROBERTS, M., RINAUDO, P. A., VILINSKAS, J. & OWENS, G. (1974). Solitary sclerosing plasma-cell myeloma of the spine: case report. *J. Neurosurg.*, **40**: 125–129.

ROSE, D. L. & NOVAK, E. N. (1966). The painful shoulder: the scapulocostal syndrome in shoulder pain. *J. Kansas Med. Soc.*, **67**: 112–114.

ROSENBERG, D., LONGIN, B., DUQUESNEL, C., BERAUD, C. & MONNET, P. (1970). Calcification of the intervertebral discs in the child (based on six cases). *Rev. Neurol. (Paris)*, **123**: 181–186.

ROSS, C. A. & VYAS, U. S. (1972). Thoracic outlet syndrome due to congenital anomalous joint of the first thoracic rib. *Canad. J. Surg.*, **15**: 186–190.

SCALISE, L., STANCATI, G. & VENA, P. (1973). Two cases of intradural meningioma. *Clin. Ortopaedica*, **24**: 187–193.

SCOTT, M. (1956). Lower extremity pain simulating sciatica: tumors of the high thoracic and cervical cord as causes. *J. Amer. Med. Ass.*, **160**: 528–534.

SELLER, H. (1973). The discharge pattern of single units in thoracic and lumbar white rami in relation to cardiovascular events. *Pflüger's Arch.*, **343**: 317–330.

SHELDON, P. J. (1972). A retrospective survey of 102 cases of shoulder pain. *Rheumat. Phys. Med.*, **11**: 422–427.

SHORE, L. R. (1931). A report on the nature of certain bony spurs arising from the dorsal arches of the thoracic vertebra. *J. Anat.*, **65:** 379–387.

SIMEONE, F. A. (1971). The modern treatment of thoracic disc disease. *Orthop. Clin. Nth. Amer.*, **2:** 453–462.

SIMON, W. H. (1975). Soft tissue disorders of the shoulder. Frozen shoulder, calcific tendinitis and bicipital tendinitis. *Orthop. Clin. Nth. Amer.*, **6:** 521–539.

STANGER, J. K. (1947). Fracture dislocation of the thoracolumbar spine, with special reference to reduction by open and closed operations. *J. Bone Joint Surg.*, **29:** 107–118.

STEGMAN, D. & MEAD, B. T. (1970). The chest wall twinge syndrome. *Nebraska State Med. J.*, **55:** 528–533.

STEINBROCKER, O. (1947). The shoulder-hand syndrome: associated painful homolateral disability of shoulder with swelling and atrophy of hand. *Amer. J. Med.*, **3:** 402–407.

STUNDLER, A. (1929). *Diseases and Deformities of Spine and Thorax.* St. Louis, Miss.; C. V. Mosby.

TAYLOR, T. K. F. (1964). Thoracic disc lesions. *J. Bone Joint Surg.*, **46B:** 788.

TAYLOR, T. K. F. (1970). Thoracic and abdominal pain originating in the vertebral axis: some aspects of physical diagnosis. *Northwest Med.*, **69:** 679–685.

THIEBAUT, F. & ISCH, C. (1952). Electromyographic study of suspension equilibrium. *C.R. Soc. Biol.*, **146:** 1385–1387.

TOMSICK, T. A., LEBOWITZ, M. E. & CAMPBELL, C. (1974). The congenital absence of pedicles in the thoracic spine. *Radiology*, **111:** 587–589.

TOVI, D. & STRANG, R. R. (1960). Thoracic intervertebral disk protrusion. *Acta. Clin. Scand., Suppl.* **267:** 1–14.

VASILEV, V., OVCHAROV, V. & MALINOV, G. (1971). Age-related changes in the thoracic intervertebral discs of humans. *Nauchni Tr. Vissh. Med. Inst. Sofia*, **50:** 15–24.

VELEANU, C., GRUN, U., DIACONESCU, M. & COCOTA, E. (1972). Structural peruliarities of the thoracic spine: their functional significance. *Acta Anat.*, **82:** 97–107.

VITEK, J. J. (1973). Thoracic bifurcation of the common carotid artery. *Neuroradiol.*, **5:** 133–139.

VRETTOS, X. C. & WYKE, B. D. (1974). Articular reflexogenic systems in the costovertebral joints. *J. Bone Joint Surg.*, **56B:** 382.

WEINBERG, H., NATHAN, H., MAGORA, F., ROBIN, G. C. T. & AVIAD, I. (1972). Arthritis of the first costovertebral joint as a cause of thoracic outlet syndrome. *Clin. Orthop.*, **86:** 159–163.

WHITE, A. A. (1969). Analysis of the mechanics of the thoracic spine in man. An experimental study of autopsy specimens. *Acta Orthop. Scand., Suppl.* **127:** 1–105.

WHITE, A. A. & HIRSCH, C. (1971). The significance of the vertebral posterior elements in the mechanics of the thoracic spine. *Clin. Orthop.*, **81:** 2–14.

WILLIAMS, R. (1954). Complete protrusion of a calcified nucleus pulposus in the thoracic spine. *J. Bone Joint Surg.*, **36B:** 597–600.

WYKE, B. (1970). The neurological basis of thoracic spinal pain. *Rheumat. Phys. Med.*, **10:** 356–367.

WYKE, B. D. (1975). Morphological and functional features of the innervation of the costovertebral joints. *Folia morph., Prague*, **23:** 296–305.

YOUNG, M. H. (1973). Long-term consequences of stable fractures of the thoracic and lumbar vertebral bodies. *J. Bone Joint Surg.*, **55B:** 295–300.

### (c) Lumbosacral

ADKINS, E. W. O. (1955). Lumbo-sacral arthrodesis after laminectomy. *J. Bone Joint Surg.*, **37B:** 208–223.

ALLEN, M. L. AND LINDEN, M. C. (1950). Significant roentgen findings in routine pre-employment examination of the lumbosacral spine. *Amer. J. Surg.*, **80:** 762–766.

BARCERO, P. (1959). Anatomy, physiology and biomechanics of the lumbosacral region. *Rev. Esp. Reum.*, **8:** 233–251.

BARNETT, A. G. & CONNOLLY, E. S. (1975). Lumbosacral nerve root avulsion. *J. Trauma*, **15:** 532–535.

BARR, J. (1950). Low back pain and sciatica. *J. Bone Joint Surg.*, **32B:** 514–517.

BHALLA, S. K. & SIMMONS, E. H. (1968). Electrolytic reaction to dissimilar metals as a cause of sciatica. *Canad. J. Surg.*, **11:** 52–56.

BOUCHARD, C., TRANIER, J. & CHAUVET, J. (1972). Sciatica and surgical treatment in 458 cases. *Ann. Med. Intern.*, **123:** 587–591.

BOUDIN, G., GODLEWSKI, S. & MARAGAL, M. (1973). Aneurysmal

sciatica in the syndrome of the painful buttock. *Sem. Hôp. Paris*, **49:** 3509–3514.

BRAILSFORD, J. F. (1929). Deformities of the lumbosacral region of the spine. *Br. J. Surg.*, **16:** 562–627.

BRECK, L. W., HILLSMAN, J. W. & BASOM, W. C. (1944). Lumbosacral roentgenograms of 450 consecutive applicants for heavy work. *Ann. Surg.*, **120:** 88–93.

BREIG, A. & MARIONS, O. (1963). Biomechanics of the lumbosacral nerve roots. *Acta Radiol. (Diagn.)*, **1:** 1141–1160.

BREMNER, R. A. & EDIN, M. B. (1958). Manipulation in the management of chronic low backache due to lumbosacral strain. *Lancet*, **1:** 20–21.

BREMNER, R. A. & SIMPSON, M. (1959). Management of chronic low backache due to lumbosacral strain. *Lancet*, **2:** 949–950.

BROWN, L. T. (1937). The mechanics of lumbosacral and sacro-iliac joints. *J. Bone Joint Surg.*, **19A:** 770–775.

BROWN, T., HANSEN, R. J. & JORRA, A. J. (1957). Some mechanical tests on the lumbosacral spine with particular reference to the intervertebral discs: preliminary report. *J. Bone Joint Surg.*, **39A:** 1135–1164.

CAPENER, N. (1944). Sciatica—an anatomical and mechanical study of the lumbosacral region. *Ann. Rheum. Dis.*, **4:** 29–36.

CAUCHOIX, J., BENOIST, M., TAUSSIG, G., *et al.* (1969). Sciatica and the "horse-tail" syndrome in pseudospondylolisthesis. *Sem. Hôp. Paris*, **45:** 2017–2022.

CHABOT, J. (1969). A posterior neuralgia: sciatica. *Consultations journalières en rheumatologie:* 141–148.

CIHAK, R. (1970). Variations of lumbosacral joints and their morphogenesis. *Acta. Univ. Carol. Med. Prague*, **16:** 145–165.

CLEVELAND, M., BOSWORTH, D. M. & THOMPSON, F. R. (1948). Pseudarthrosis in the lumbosacral region. *J. Bone Joint Surg.*, **30A:** 302–311.

COLE, J. P., LESSWING, A. L. & COLE, J. R. (1968). An analysis of the lumbosacral dermatomes in man. *Clin. Orthop.*, **61:** 241–247.

COOMES, E. N. (1961). A comparison between epidural anaesthesia and bed-rest in sciatica. *Br. Med. J.* **5218:** 20–24.

CRAIG, W. M. & WALSH, M. N. (1941). Neuro-anatomical and physiological aspects and significance of sciatica. *J. Bone Joint Surg.*, **23A:** 417–434.

DANFORTH, M. S., PROVIDENCE, R. L. & WILSON, P. D. (1925). The anatomy of the lumbosacral region in relation to sciatic pain. *J. Bone Joint Surg.*, **7A:** 109–160.

DAY, M. H. (1962). The anatomy of the lumbosacral plexus with particular reference to the blood supply. *Ph.D.Thesis, Univ. Lond.*

DELMAS, A. & PINEAU, H. (1970). The surface of the lumbar apophyseal joints. *Compt. Rend. Ass. Anat.*, **148:** 353–356.

ERDMAN, H. (1956). Support of the vertebral column at the pelvic brim. In *Die Wirbelsäule in Forschung und Praxis*, pp. 51–62. Ed. Junghanns, H. Stuttgart; Hippokrates-Verlag.

FENOGLIO, V., PISANI, P. C. & BARALE, I. (1968). Lumbosciatalgias of the yellow ligaments in hypertrophy. *Minerva Ortop.*, **19:** 656–668.

FERGUSON, A. B. (1934). The clinical and roentgenolographic interpretation of lumbosacral anomalies. *Radiology*, **22:** 548–558.

FLAX-JAFFE, H. J. (1973). Evaluation of lumbosacral disability. *Bol. Ass. Med., Puerto Rico*, **65:** 292–294.

FORD, L. T. & GOODMAN, F. G. (1966). X-ray studies of the lumbosacral spine. *Southern Med. J.*, **59:** 1123–1128.

FORREST, J. S. & BROOKS, D. L. (1972). Cyclic sciatica of endometriosis. *J. Amer. Med. Ass.*, **222:** 1177–1178.

FRIEDMAN, M. M., FISCHER, F. J. & VAN DENMARK, R. D. (1946). Lumbosacral roentgenograms of 100 soldiers: a control study. *Amer. J. Roentgenol.*, **55:** 292–298.

GARDNER, E., PEDERSEN, H. E. & BLUNCK, F. R. J. (1955). The anatomy of lumbosacral posterior primary divisions and sinuvertebral nerves with an experimental study of their function. *Anat. Rec.*, **121:** 297.

GOLDTHWAIT, J. E. (1911). The lumbosacral articulation. An explanation of many cases of "lumbago", "sciatica" and paraplegia. *Boston. Med. Surg. J.*, **164:** 365–372.

GOULD, N. (1974). Back-pocket sciatica. *New Eng. J. Med.*, **290:** 633.

GOWERS, W. R. (1904). Lumbago: its lessons and analogies. *Br. Med. J.*, **1:** 117–121.

GRAHAM, C. E. (1974). Backache and sciatica: a report of 90 patients treated by intradiscal injection of chymopapain (discase). *Med. J. Austr.*, **1:** 5–8.

GREENE, L. B. & ARMSTRONG, W. E. (1967). Radiographic measurement of the lumbosacral angle. *Arch. Phys. Med.*, **48:** 240–243.

GRIEVE, G. P. (1970). Sciatica and the straight-leg-raising test in manipulative treatment. *Physiotherapy*, **56:** 337–346.

HAGGART, G. E. & GRANNIS, W. R. (1953). Management of low back pain and sciatic pain. *Am. J. Surg.*, **85:** 339–346.

JIROUT, J. (1957). The normal mobility of the lumbosacral spine. *Acta Radiol.*, **47:** 345–348.

KEON-COHEN, B. (1968). Abnormal arrangement of the lower lumbar and first sacral nerves within the spinal canal. *J. Bone Joint Surg.*, **50B:** 261–265.

KREYENBÜHL, H. W. & HESSLER, C. (1973). A variation of the sacrum on the lateral view. *Radiology*, **109:** 49–52.

LACKUM, H. L. VON (1924). The lumbosacral region: an anatomical study and some clinical observations. *J. Amer. Med. Ass.*, **82:** 1109–1114.

LANGLOH, N. D., JOHNSON, E. W. & JACKSON, C. B. (1972). Traumatic sacro-iliac disruptions. *J. Trauma*, **12:** 931–935.

LANIER, R. R. (1954). Some factors to be considered in the study of lumbosacral fusion. *Am. J. Phys. Anthrop.*, **12:** 363–371.

LEIKKONEN, O. (1959). Low back pain and sciatica with special reference to secondary lumbosacral insufficiency. *Acta. Orthop. Scand., Suppl.* **40:** 1.

LOUYOT, P., MONTAUT, J., POUREL, J., STAAL, D. & PICARD, L. (1973). Late results of operated cases of sciatica of discal origin. *Rev. Rheum. Mal. Osteoartic.*, **40:** 171–178.

LUMSDEN, R. M. & MORRIS, J. M. (1968). An in vivo study of axial rotation and immobilisation at the lumbosacral joint. *J. Bone Joint Surg.*, **50A:** 1591–1602.

MANDELL, A. J. (1960). Lumbosacral intervertebral disc disease in children. *Calif. Med.*, **93:** 307–308.

MATHUR, T. N. (1956). Sciatica in brucellosis. *J. Amer. Med. Ass.*, **160:** 993.

MITCHELL, G. A. G. (1934). The lumbosacral junction. *J. Bone Joint Surg.*, **16A:** 233–254.

MITCHELL, G. A. G. (1936). The significance of lumbosacral transitional vertebrae. *Br. J. Surg.*, **24:** 147–158.

MITCHELL, G. A. G. (1937). Lumbosacral strain. *Arch. Phys. Ther.*, **18:** 56.

NEWMAN, P. H. (1965). A clinical syndrome associated with severe lumbosacral subluxation. *J. Bone Joint Surg.*, **47B:** 472–481.

PAILLAS, J. E., WINNINGER, J. & LOUIS, R. (1969). Role of lumbosacral malformations in sciatica and lumbar pain. A study of 1500 radio-clinical records including 500 proved disc herniae. *Presse Méd.*, **77**: 853–855.

PHEASANT, H. C. & SWENSON, P. C. (1942). The lumbosacral region: a correlation of the roentgenographic and anatomical observations. *J. Bone Joint Surg.*, **24A**: 299–306.

REDMAN, J. F. (1973). Congential absence of the lumbosacral spine. *Southern Med. J.*, **66**: 770–771.

RUNGE, C. F. (1954). Roentgenographic examination of the lumbo-sacral spine in routine pre-employment examination. *J. Bone Joint Surg.*, **36A**: 75–84.

SCHAM, S. M. (1974). Manipulation of the lumbosacral spine. *Clin. Orthop.*, **101**: 146–450.

SCHMIDT, W. & SMITH, J. L. (1939). The sciatic syndrome and its management. *Arch. Phys. Ther.*, **20**: 494–500.

SELLER, H. (1973). The discharge pattern of single units in thoracic and lumbar white rami in relation to cardiovascular events. *Pflüger's Arch.*, **343**: 317–330.

SHAKHNOVSKAYA, E. I. (1974). Role of anterior disc displacement in the origin of the pain syndrome of lumbosacral localization. *Sov. Med.*, **8th Aug.**: 22–27.

SHERRINGTON, C. S. (1892). Notes on the arrangement of some motor fibres in the lumbosacral plexus. *J. Physiol.*, **13**: 621–772.

SMITH, M. S. & WRIGHT, V. (1958). Sciatica and the intervertebral disc: an experimental study. *J. Bone Joint Surg.*, **40A**: 1401–1418.

SOUTHWICK, W. L. & ROBINSON, R. A. (1957). Surgical approaches to the vertebral bodies in the cervical and lumbar regions. *J. Bone Joint Surg.*, **39A**: 631–643.

SOUTHWORTH, J. D. & BERSACK, S. R. (1950). Anomalies of the lumbosacral vertebrae in 550 individuals without symptoms referable to the low back. *Amer. J. Roentgenol.*, **64**: 624–634.

SPLITHOFF, C. A. (1946). Chronic lumbar backache. *Arch. Phys. Med.*, **27**: 116–117.

SPLITHOFF, C. A. (1953). Lumbosacral junction: roentgenographic comparison in patients with and without backaches. *J. Amer. Med. Ass.*, **152**: 1610–1613.

SPURLING, R. G. (1953). *Lesions of the Lumbar Intervertebral Disc.* Springfield, Ill.: Thomas.

STECKLER, R. M. & EPSTEIN, B. S. (1969). Seat belt trauma to the lumbar spine: an unusual manifestation of the seat belt syndrome. *J. Trauma*, **9:** 508–513.

STEINDLER, A. (1940). Interpretation of sciatic radiation and syndrome of low back pain. *J. Bone Joint Surg.*, **22A:** 28–34.

SYMPOSIUM (1968). Low back pain and sciatic pain. *J. Bone Joint Surg.*, **50A:** 167–210.

TABOR, E. (1968). A statistical study of anomalies of the lumbar and lumbosacral spine: Radiological findings in 7500 orthopaedic patients. *J. Radiol.*, **49:** 713–718.

TAKADA, N. (1973). Studies on the ageing process of the lumbar discs and facets, especially the histological changes. *J. Jap. Orth. Ass.*, **47:** 333–349.

THOMPSON, I. M. (1974). Sacral agenesis. *Paediatrics*, **54:** 236–238.

THORNTON, B., HANSEN, R. J. & YORRA, A. J. (1957). Some mechanical tests on the lumbosacral spine with particular reference to the intervertebral discs. *J. Bone Joint Surg.*, **39A:** 1135–1164.

TILLEY, P. (1970). Is sacralization a significant factor in lumbar pain? *J. Amer. Osteopathic Ass.*, **70:** 238–241.

TRIBOLET, N. DE & OBERSON, R. (1974). Variations and anomalies of the caudal cistern. *Schweiz. Med. Wschr.*, **104:** 459–464.

TROTTER, M. & LETTERMAN, G. S. (1944). Variations of the female sacrum: their significance in continuous caudal analgesia. *Surg. Gynec. Obst.*, **78:** 419–424.

TSIV'IAN IAL. & SHVETS, A. I. (1973). Characteristics of lumbosacral lordosis in man. *Arkh. Anat. Gistol. Embriol.*, **64:** 103–105.

WEIS, E. B. (1975). Stresses at the lumbosacral junction. *Orthop. Clin. Nth. Amer.*, **6:** 83–91.

WETZEL, N. (1968). The enigma of sciatica. *Med. Clin. Nth. Amer.*, **52:** 183–188.

WILLIAMS, P. C. (1965). *The Lumbosacral Spine, Emphasising Conservative Management*. New York; McGraw Hill.

WILLIS, T. A. (1963). Lumbosacral retrodisplacement. *Amer. J. Roentgenol.*, **90:** 1263–1266.

WILLIS, T. A. (1963). The lumbosacral vertebral column in man: its stability of form and function. *Amer. J. Anat.*, **32:** 95–123.

WINNINGER, J. (1969). Malformation of the lumbosacral spine and determination of the appearance of lumbar and lumbosciatic pain (1000 cases): medicolegal incidence. *Med. Leg. Dommage Corp.*, **2:** 65–67.

## (d) Sacro-iliac

ALBEE, F. H. (1934). A study of the anatomy and clinical importance of the sacro-iliac joint. *J. Amer. Med. Ass.*, **53**: 1273–1276.

BONJEAN, DEJUSSIEU & BISCH. (1955). A sacro-iliac joint ligament not previously described. *J. Med. Bordeaux*, **132**: 597–599.

BORELL, U. & FERNSTRÖM, I. (1957). The movements at the sacro-iliac joints and their importance to changes in the pelvic dimensions during parturition. *Acta Obst. Gyn. Scand.*, **36**: 42–57.

BROOKE, R. (1923). The sacro-iliac joint. *J. Anat.*, **58**: 299–305.

BROWN, L. T. (1937). The mechanics of the lumbosacral and sacro-iliac joints. *J. Bone Joint Surg.*, **19A**: 770–775.

CARTER, M. E. & LOEWI, G. (1962). Anatomical changes in normal sacro-iliac joints during childhood and comparison with the changes in Still's disease. *Ann. Rheum. Dis.*, **21**: 121–134.

CHUNG, S. M. K. & BORNS, P. (1973). Acute osteomyelitis adjacent to the sacro-iliac joint in children; report of 2 cases. *J. Bone Joint Surg.*, **55A**: 630–634.

COHEN, A. S., McNEILL, J. M., CALKINS, E., SHARP, J. T. & SCHUBART, A. (1967). The normal sacro-iliac joint: analysis of 88 sacro-iliac roentgenograms. *Amer. J. Roentgenol.*, **100**: 559–563.

COLACHIS, S. C., WORDEN, F. E., BECHTOL, C. O. & STROHM, B. R. (1963). Movements of the sacro-iliac joint in the adult male: a preliminary report. *Arch. Phys. Med.*, **44**: 490–498.

DONKER, E. DE, THYES, A. & VAN GAVER, P. (1953). The sacro-iliac joint. *Acta Ortho. Belg.*, **19**: 7–40.

DIHLMANN, W. (1963). Typical strain damage to the anterior part of the iliosacral joint capsule and its ligaments. *Fortschr. Roentgenst.*, **99**: 667–681.

DIHLMANN, W. (1964). Developmental abnormalities of the transverse iliac joints on the basis of so-called osteochondritis sacri. *Fortschr. Roentgenstr.*, **101**: 285–295.

DIHLMANN, W. (1967). Roentgen diagnosis of the sacro-iliac joints and their near vicinity. *Fortschr. Roentgenstr.*, Suppl. **97**: 1.

DIHLMANN, W. & MULLER, G. (1973). Sacro-iliac observations in hyperparathyroidism (radiology, histomorphology). *Radiologie*, **13**: 160–163.

DIXON, A. ST. J. & LIENCE, E. (1961). Sacro-iliac joint in adult rheumatoid arthritis and psoriatic arthropathy. *Ann. Rheum. Dis.*, **20:** 247–251.

DOWNING, C. H. (1946). Sacro-iliac syndrome. *J. Amer. Osteopath. Ass.*, **46:** 149–153.

FALLET, G. H., WETTSTEIN, P., OTT, H., RADI, I. & MOSIMANN, U. (1972). Radiological study of the sacro-iliac joints in seronegative rheumatoid polyarthritis. *Schweiz. Med. Wschr.*, **100:** 1610–1616.

FEFFER, H. L. & ADAMS, J. P. (1958). Sacro-iliac changes associated with dysfunction of the spine. *Southern Med. J.*, **51:** 986–993.

FREIBURG, A. H. (1937). Sciatic pain, and its relief by operation on muscle and fascia. *Arch. Surg.*, **34:** 337–350.

FREIBURG, A. H. & VINKE, T. H. (1934). Sciatica and the sacro-iliac joint. *J. Bone Joint Surg.*, **16A:** 126–136.

FRIEDENBERG, S. B. (1966). Dislocation of the sacro-iliac joint. *Am. J. Orthop.*, **8:** 90–95.

FRIGERIO, N. A., STOWE, R. R. & HOWE, J. W. (1974). Movement of the sacro-iliac joint. *Clin. Orthop.*, **100:** 370–377.

GRAY, H. (1938). Sacro-iliac joint pain. *Intern. Clinics*, **2:** 54–96.

HERSHEY, C. D. (1943). The sacro-iliac joint and pain of sciatic radiation. *J. Amer. Med. Ass.*, **122:** 983–986.

HEYMAN, W. C. (1968). Considerations of a diagnostic test for sacro-iliac lesions. *J. Amer. Osteopath. Ass.*, **67:** 1013–1017.

ILLOUZ, G. & COSTE, F. (1964). The "tripod sign" in clinical examination of the sacro-iliac joints. *Presse Méd.*, **72:** 1979–1980.

JAJIC, I. (1968). Radiologic changes in the sacro-iliac joints and spine of patients with psoriatic arthritis and psoriasis. *Ann. Rheum. Dis.*, **27:** 1–6.

JOHANNSEN, A. (1974). Radiological and scintigraphical examination of the sacro-iliac joints in the diagnosis of sacro-iliitis. *Dan. Med. Bull.*, **21:** 246–250.

JOHNSON, J. W. (1964). Sacro-iliac strain. *J. Amer. Osteopath. Ass.*, **63:** 1015–1029.

JONES, R. (1938). Sacro-iliac joint pain. *Intern. Clincs*, **2:** 54–96.

KAULIG-BEYER, J. & KAULIG-BEYER, W. (1965). On disorder of the sacro-iliac joints. *Beitr. Orthop. Trauma*, **12:** 29–35.

KIDOKORO, Y. (1968). Study on changes in shape of the lower lumbar intervertebral foramina in loading and unloading conditions. *J. Jap. Orthop. Ass.*, **42:** 217–231.

LICHMBLAV, S. (1962). Dislocation of the sacro-iliac joint. *J. Bone Joint Surg.*, **44A**: 192–198.

LÖVGREN, O. & DOWEN, S. A. (1969). Strontium (85SR) scintigrams of the sacro-iliac joint. *Acta Rheum. Scand.*, **15**: 327–333.

LUSSKIN, H. & SONNENSCHEIN, H. (1927). Low back sprain: the sacro-iliac syndrome. *Amer. J. Surg.*, **3**: 534–549.

MACDONALD, G. R. & HUNT, T. E. (1952). Sacro-iliac joints. *Canad. Med. Ass. J.*, **83**: 316–319.

MCFARLAND, H. R. (1963). Differential diagnosis of sacro-iliac joint disease. *J. Lancet*, **83**: 316–319.

MALAWISTA, S. E., SEEGMILLER, J. E., HATHAWAY, B. E. & SOKOLOFF, L. (1965). Sacro-iliac gout. *J. Amer. Med. Ass.*, **194**: 954–956.

MANGIONE, F. (1958). On the morphology and significance of the sacro-iliac joint. *Archiv. Ital. Anat. Embr.*, **63**: 21–46.

METZ, B. (1970). Arthosis of the sacro-iliac joint and indications for its arthrodesis. *Zeit. Orthop.*, **107**: 315–334.

MILLER, R. F. (1970). Subluxation of the sacro-iliac joint. *Lancet*, **1**: 193–194.

MOSS, L. (1970). Subluxation of the sacro-iliac joint. *Lancet*, **1**: 412–413.

NAKAGWA, T. (1966). A study of the distribution of nerve filaments over the ilio-sacral joint and its adjacent region. *J. Jap. Orth. Ass.*, **419–430**.

NEWTON, D. R. L. (1957). Clinical aspects of sacro-iliac disease. *Proc. Roy. Soc. Med.*, **50**: 850–853.

NORMAN, G. R. (1968). Sacro-iliac disease and its relationship to lower abdominal pain. *Amer. J. Surg.*, **116**: 54–56.

PACE, J. B. & HENNING, C. (1972). Episacro-iliac lipoma. *Amer. Fam. Phys.*, **6**: 70–73.

PITKINS, H. C. & PHEASANT, H. C. (1936). Sacro-arthrogenetic telalgia. *J. Bone Joint Surg.*, **18A**: 111–133; 365–374; 706–716; 1008–1017; and **19A**: 169–184.

REINHARD, W. H. (1954). Tuberculosis of the sacro-iliac joint and its treatment. *Chirurg.*, **25**: 82–84.

RICHARDS, A. (1951). New radiological and surgical thoughts on the sacro-iliac joint. *Réun. Chirug. Orth.*, **37**: 152–165.

RIGAUD, DEJUSSIEU, WANGERMEZ, C., BONJEAN & BISCH, C. (1957). Concerning the physiology of the sacro-iliac joints. *J. Méd. Bordeaux Sud-ouest*, **134**: 206–210.

RONDIER, J., DELRIEU, F., EVRARD, J., CAYLA, J., MENKS, C. J., AMOR, B. & DELBARRE, F. (1974). Infectious sacro-iliitis due to common organisms: 12 cases. *Rev. Rheum.*, **41**: 11–24.

RUSSELL, A. S., LENTLE, B. C. & PERCY, J. C. (1975). Investigation of sacro-iliac disease: comparative evaluation of radiological and radionucleide techniques. *J. Rheumatol.*, **2**: 45–51.

RUSSELL, J. G. B. (1965). Gas in the sacro-iliac joint in pregnancy. *J. Obst. Gyn. Br. Comm.*, **72**: 797–798.

SASHIN, D. (1930). A critical analysis of the anatomy and the pathologic changes of the sacro-iliac joints. *J. Bone Joint Surg.*, **12A**: 891–910.

SCALABRINO, R. (1970). The sacro-iliac joints in ulcerative colitis and in certain rheumatic diseases. *Rev. Rheum.*, **37**: 151–154.

SCHONBERGER, M. VON & HELLMICH, K. (1974). Sacro-iliac shift and fibrositis. *Zeit. Allgemeinmed.*, **50**: 1097–1098.

SCHUNKE, G. B. (1938). The anatomy and development of the sacro-iliac joint in man. *Anat. Rec.*, **72**: 313–331.

SOLONEN, K. A. (1957). The sacro-iliac joint in the light of anatomical, roentgenological and clinical studies. *Acta. Orthop. Scand., Suppl.* **27**: 1.

STAMM, T. T. (1955). Sacro-iliac strain. *Br. Med. J.*, **2**: 833.

STRANGE, F. G. ST. C. (1963). Prognosis in sacro-iliac tuberculosis. *Br. J. Surg.*, **50**: 561–571.

THOMPSON, M. (1957). Discussion on the clinical and radiological aspects of sacro-iliac disease. *Proc. Roy. Soc. Med.*, **50**: 847–850.

TÖNNIS, D. (1970). Degenerative changes in the iliosacral joints: their symptoms and treatment. *Beitr. Orthop. Traumat.*, **17**: 680–682.

TÖNNIS, D., HÖRDEGEN, K. AND BÄR, H. W. (1970). Causes of iliosacral joint irritation: their symptoms and treatment. *Arch. Orthop. Unfall-Chir.*, **68**: 358–369.

TRAVELL, W. & TRAVELL, J. (1942). Techniques for reduction and ambulatory treatment of sacro-iliac displacement. *Arch. Phys. Therap.*, **23**: 222.

TROTTER, M. (1964). Accessory sacro-iliac articulations in skeletons. *Am. J. Phys. Anthrop.*, **22**: 137–142.

VAN LAERE, M., VEYS, E. M. & MIELANTS, H. (1972). Strontium 87m scanning of the sacro-iliac joints in ankylosing spondylitis. *Ann. Rheum. Dis.*, **31**: 201–206.

VAN ROOYEN, A. J. L. (1956). The iliosacral joint and its role in the female pelvis. *Sth. Afr. Med. J.*, **30**: 442–447.

WATT, I. (1971). Septic abortion and sacro-iliitis. *Proc. Roy. Soc. Med.*, **64**: 55–56.

WEISL, H. (1952). Movements of the sacro-iliac joints. *J. Anat.*, **86**: 489–490.

WEISL, H. (1954). The ligaments of the sacro-iliac joint examined with particular reference to their function. *Acta Anat.*, **20**: 201–213.

WEISL, H. (1954). The articular surfaces of the sacro-iliac joint and their relation to the movement of the sacrum. *Acta Anat.*, **22**: 1–14.

WEISL, H. (1954). The movements of the sacro-iliac joint. *Acta Anat.*, **23**: 80–91.

WILKINSON, M. & MEIKLE, J. A. K. (1966). Tomography of the sacro-iliac joints. *Ann. Rheum. Dis.*, **25**: 433–440.

WRIGHT, R., LUMSDEN, K. & LUNTZ, M. H. (1965). Abnormalities of the sacro-iliac joints and uveitis in ulcerative colitis. *Quart. J. Med.*, **34**: 229–236.

YEOMAN, W. (1928). The relation of arthritis of the sacro-iliac joint to sciatica, with an analysis of 100 cases. *Lancet*, **2**: 1119–1122.

YERGASON, R. M. (1932). A diagnostic sign in examination of affections of the sacro-iliac joint: chair test. *J. Bone Joint Surg.*, **14A**: 116–117.

### (e) Coccygeal

BOHM, E. & FRANKSSON, C. (1959). Coccygodynia and sacral rhizotomy. *Chir. Scand.* **116**: 268–274.

CAMERON, H. U. (1975). Coccygodynia. *Can. Med. Ass. J.*, **112**: 557–558.

FARA, M. (1973). The human tail. *Acta Chir. Plast.*, **15**: 184–189.

HOLMES, I. (1975). Coccygodynia. *Am. Med. Ass. J.*, **112**: 1166.

JONES, P. H. & LOVE, J. G. (1958). Tight filum terminale. *Arch. Surg.*, **73**: 556–566.

LETHÉ, P. (1962). Radiological study of the normal pelvis: unpublished observations. *J. Belg. Radiol.*, **45**: 659–681.

LEWITT, E. (1967). The coccyx and lumbago (sacral pain). *Manuelle Méd.*, **4**: 2.

PAAVOLAINEN, P. & SUNDELL, B. (1973). Sacrococcygeal chereloma. *Duodecim.*, **89**: 1329–1336.

# 2

# ANATOMY AND DEVELOPMENT

## (a) General

BELL, J. & BELL, C. (1826). *The Anatomy and Physiology of the Human Body.* 6th Ed.; London.

CRUVEILHIER, J. (1862). *Textbook of Descriptive Anatomy,* 4th Ed., Vol. 1. Paris; Asselin.

GARDNER, E., PEDERSEN, H. E. & BLUNCK, C. F. J. (1955). "The anatomy of lumbosacral posterior primary divisions and sinuvertebral nerves, with an experimental study of their function." *Anat. Rec.*, **121**: 297.

GARDNER, E. D. (1963). "The development and growth of bones and joints." *J. Bone Joint Surg.*, **45A**: 856–862.

GESELL, A. & AMATRUDA, C. S. (1941). *Developmental Diagnosis: Normal and Abnormal Child Development.* New York; Hoeber.

HABOUSH, E. J. (1942). "An anatomical explanation of traumatic low back pain." *J. Bone Joint Surg.*, **24**: 123–134.

HADLEY, L. A. (1961). "Anatomico-roentgenographic studies of the posterior spinal articulations." *Am. J. Roentgenol.*, **86**: 270–276.

HARRIS, H. A. (1939). "Anatomical and physiological basis of physical training." *Brit. Med. J.*, **2**: 939–943.

HASSE, C. & SCWARCK, W. (1873). "Studies on the comparative anatomy of the vertebral column, particularly in man and mammals." In *Anatomische Studien*, pp. 21–171. Ed. Hasse, C. Leipzig; Engelman.

HOLLINSHEAD, W. H. (1965). "Anatomy of the spine: points of interest to orthopaedic surgeons." *J. Bone Joint Surg.*, **47A**: 209–215.

INMAN, V. T. & SAUNDERS, J. B. DE C. M. (1947). "Anatomico-physiological aspects of injuries to the intervertebral disc." *J. Bone Joint Surg.*, **29A**: 461–475.

LE DOUBLE, A. F. (1912). *Treatise on Variations in the Vertebral Column of Man.* Paris; Masson.

MORRIS, H. (Ed.) (1893). *A Treatise on Human Anatomy.* London; Churchill.

POIRIER, P. & CHARPY, A. (1899). *Textbook of Human Anatomy.* Paris; Masson.

REITH, P. (1959). "Pathologic and anatomic factors in back pain." *J. Med. Ass. Georgia,* **48:** 516–517.

SCHMORL, G. (1929). "On the pathological anatomy of the vertebral column." *Klin. Wochenschrift,* **8:** 1243–1249.

SCHMORL, G. & JUNGHANNS, H. (1932). *Records and Atlas of Normal and Pathological Anatomy in Typical Radiographs.* Leipzig; Thieme.

THAGE, O. (1965). "The myotomes L2–S2 in man." *Acta Neurol. Scand.,* **13:** 241–243.

TOUDURY, G. (1953). "Development of the spinal column." *Rev. Chir. Orth.,* **39:** 553–569.

TROUP, J. D. G. (1970). "Functional anatomy of the spine." *Brit. J. Sports Med.,* **5:** 27–34.

WILLIS, T. A. (1932). "Backache—an anatomical consideration." *J. Bone Joint Surg.,* **14:** 267–272.

WOOD, S. (1972). "Anatomical aspects of some vertebral anomalies." *S. Afr. J. Physiol.,* **28:** 10–15.

### (b) Topographical Anatomy (Morphology)

ALLBROOK, D. (1962). "Some problems associated with pelvic form and size in the Ganda of East Africa." *Royal Anthropological Instit.,* **92:** 102–114.

AMSTUTZ, H. C. & SISSONS, H. A. (1969). "The structure of the vertebral spongiosa." *J. Bone Joint Surg.,* **51B:** 540–550.

ANDERSON, R. J. (1883). "Observations on the diameters of human vertebrae in different regions." *J. Anat.,* **17:** 341–344.

BARGERO, P. (1959). "Anatomy, physiology and biomechanics of the lumbosacral region." *Rev. Esp. Reum.,* **8:** 233–251.

BEIGHTON, P. (1968). "X-linked recessive inheritance in the Ehlers-Danlos syndrome." *Brit. Med. J.,* **3:** 409–411.

BENASSY, J. (1970). "Metamerical topography of the cord and its roots." *Paraplegia,* **8:** 75–79.

BOWSHER, D. (1962). "The topographic projection of fibres from the anterolateral quadrant of the spinal cord to the subdiencephalic brain stem in man." *Psychiat. Neurol., Basel,* **143:** 75–99.

BRODAL, A. (1969). *Neurological Anatomy in Relation to Clinical Medicine*, 2nd Ed. London; Oxford University Press.

CALVÉ, J. & GALLAND, M. (1930). "The intervertebral nucleus pulposus. Its anatomy, physiology and pathology." *J. Bone Joint Surg.*, **12:** 555–578.

COCKSHOTT, W. P. (1958). "Anatomical anomalies observed in radiographs of Nigerians." *West African Medical Journal*, **7:** 179–184.

CYRIAX, E. F. (1919). "On certain absolute and relative measurements of human vertebrae." *J. Anat.*, **54:** 305–308.

DAVIS, P. R. (1957). "Studies on the functional anatomy of the human vertebral column, with special reference to the thoracic and lumbar region." *Ph.D. Thesis, University of London.*

DELMAS, A. & DUPREUX (1953). "Spinal curves and intervertebral foramina." *Rev. Rheumat.*, **20:** 25.

DELMAS, A., NDJAGA-MBA, M. & VANNARETH, T. (1970). "The articular cartilage of L4–L5 and L5–S1." *Compt. Rend. Assoc. Anat.*, **147:** 230–234.

DELMAS, A. & PIWNICA, A. (1957). "Determination of the functional axes of the lumbar vertebrae." *Arch. Anat. Path.*, **35:** 11–19.

DOMISSE, G. R. (1975). "Morphological aspects of the lumbar spine and lumbrosacral region." *Orthop. Clin. Nth. Amer.*, **6:** 163–175.

EPSTEIN, B. S. (1966). "An anatomic, myelographic and cinemyelographic study of the dentate ligaments." *Amer. J. Roentgenol.*, **98:** 04–712.

EPSTEIN, B. S., EPSTEIN, J. A. & LAVINE, L. (1964). "The effect of anatomic variations in the lumbar vertebrae and spinal cord on cauda equina and nerve root syndromes." *Amer. J. Roentgenol.*, **91:** 1055–1065.

FRIBERG, S. (1948). "Anatomical studies on lumbar disc degeneration." *Acta Orthop. Scand.*, **17:** 224–230.

FRIBERG, S. & HIRSCH, C. (1949). "Anatomical and clinical studies on lumbar disc degeneration." *Acta Orthop. Scand.*, **19:** 222–242.

GOLDTHWAIT, J. E. & OSGOOD, R. B. (1905). "A consideration of the pelvic articulations from an anatomical, pathological and clinical standpoint." *Boston Med. Surg. J.*, **152:** 593–601, 634–638.

HARRIS, J. (1973). "Hand measurements in ankylosing spondylitis." *Ann. Rheum. Dis.*, **32:** 140–142; **31:** 534–535.

HARRIS, R. I. & McNAB, I. (1954). "Structural changes in lumbar intervertebral discs: their relationship in low back pain and sciatica." *J. Bone Joint Surg.*, **36B:** 304–322.

HASEBE, K. (1913). "The vertebral column of the Japanese." *Zeit. Morphol. Anthrop.*, **15:** 259–380.

HIRSCH, C. & SCHAJOWICZ, F. (1953). "Studies on structural changes in lumbar annulus fibrosus." *Acta Orthop. Scand.*, **22:** 184–231.

HOUSTON, C. S. & ZALESKI, W. A. (1967). "The shape of vertebral bodies and femoral necks in relation to activity." *Radiology*, **89:** 59–66.

IMHAUSER, G. (1952). "Morphological development of the transitional lumbosacral vertebra and its correlation with hip joint and vertebral column." *Fortschr. Roentgen.*, **76:** 770–774.

JAYSON, M. I. V., HERBERT, C. M. & BARKS, J. S. (1973). "Intervertebral discs: nuclear morphology and bursting pressures." *Ann. Rheum. Dis.*, **32:** 308–315.

JONSSON, B. (1969). "Morphology, innervation and electromyographic study of the erector spinae." *Arch. Phys. Med.*, **50:** 638–641.

JONSSON, B. (1970). "Topography of the lumbar part of the erector spinae muscle: an analysis of the morphologic conditions precedent for insertion of EMG electrodes into individual muscles of the lumbar part of the erector spinae muscle." *Zeit. Anat. Entwickl.-Gesch.*, **130:** 177–191.

KAPLAN, E. B. (1970). "Antero-posterior width of the vertebral bodies." *Bull. Hosp. Joint Dis.*, **31:** 197–198.

KEYES, D. C. & COMPERE, E. L. (1932). "The normal and pathological physiology of the nucleus pulposus of the intervertebral disc: an anatomical, clinical and experimental study." *J. Bone Joint Surg.*, **14:** 897–938.

KLUGE, A. (1955). "Intervertebral foramina of the lower cervical vertebra and its surroundings. A topographic and anatomic study." *Beit. Klin. Chir.*, **191:** 494–505.

KOS, J. & WOLF, J. (1972). "The intervertebral menisci and their possible rôle in vertebral blockages." *Annales Med. Physique*, **15:** 203–218.

KRENZ, J. & TROUP, J. D. G. (1973). "The structure of the pars interarticularis of the lower lumbar vertebrae and its relation to the aetiology of spondylosis: with a report of a healing fracture in the neural arch of a fourth lumbar vertebra." *J. Bone Joint Surg.*, **55B:** 735–741.

KRENZ, J. & TROUP, J. D. G. (1974). "The structure of the pars interarticularis in the lower lumbar region of the vertebral column." *Zeit. Orthop.*, **112**: 853–856.

KUBIK, S. & MUNTENER, M. (1969). "The topography of the spinal nerve roots. The influence of the development of the dural sac, as well as of the curvature and movements of the vertebral column, on the course of the spinal nerve roots." *Acta Anat.*, **74**: 119–168.

LANDMESSER, W. E. & HEUBLEIN, G. W. (1953). "Measurement of the normal interpedicular space in the child." *Connecticut Med. J.*, **17**: 310–313.

LANIER, V. S., McKNIGHT, H. F. & TROTTER, M. (1944). "Caudal analgesia: and experimental and anatomical study." *Amer. J. Obst. Gynec.*, **47**: 633–641.

LEGER, W. (1959). "The form of the vertebral column, with studies of its effects on the pelvis and the upright posture together with a contribution on the value of full-length radiography of the vertebral column." *Zeitschrift Orthopädie*, **91**: 1–108.

LETHÉ, P. (1961). "The human sacro-iliac joint: mechanical and microscopic study of an intrinsic ligament." *C.R. Assoc. Anat.*, **107**: 441–460.

LETHÉ, P. (1962). "Microscopic study of a part of the posterior vertebral arch." *Anat. Anz.*, **109**: 685–704.

LETTERMAN, G. S. & TROTTER, M. (1944). "Variations of the male sacrum: their significance in caudal analgesia." *Surg. Gynec. Obstet.*, **78**: 551–555.

LEWIN, T., MOFFETT, B. & VIDIK, A. (1962). "The morphology of the lumbar synovial joints." *Acta Morph. Néerl.-Scand.*, **4**: 299–319.

LEWIN, T. & REICHMAN, S. (1968). "Anatomical variations in the S-shape contour of the lumbar articular processes with special reference to subluxation." *Acta. Morph. Néerl.-Scand.*, **7**: 179–184.

LEWIN, T. & REICHMAN, S. (1968). "Bony contacts between the tips of the articular processes and adjacent parts of the vertebral arch in the lumbar spine in young individuals." *Acta Morph. Néerl.-Scand.*, **7**: 185–193.

LUYENDIJK, W. (1963). "Canalography: roentgenological examination of the peridural space in the lumbosacral part of the vertebral canal." *J. Belg. Radiol.*, **46**: 236–252.

LUYENDIJK, W. & VOORTHISEN, A. E. VAN (1966). "Contrast examination of the spinal epidural space." *Acta Radiol.*, **5:** 1051–1066.

McCOY, C. H. (1938). "X-ray studies of differences in straight and curved spines." *Res. Quart.*, **9:** 50–57.

MAGNUS, R. (1924). *Body Posture.* Berlin; Springer.

MALCOLMSON, P. H. (1935). "Radiologic study of the development of the spine and pathologic changes of the intervertebral disc." *Radiology*, **24:** 98–104.

MANGIONE, F. (1958). "On the morphology and significance of the sacroiliac joint." *Arch. Ital. Anat. Emb., (Firenze)*, **63:** 21–46.

MED, M. (1972). "Articulations of the thoracic vertebrae and their variability." *Folia Morphol., Prague*, **20:** 212–215.

MED, M. (1973). "Articulations of the cervical vertebrae and their variability." *Fol. Morphol., Prague*, **21:** 324–327.

NATHAN, H. (1968). "Compression of the sympathetic trunk by osteophytes of the vertebral column in the abdomen: an anatomical study, with pathological and clinical considerations." *Surgery*, **63:** 609–625.

NAYLOR, A. & SMARE, D. L. (1935). "Fluid content of the nucleus pulposus as a factor in the disk syndrome." *Br. Med. J.*, **2:** 975–976.

NOMURA, I. (1971). "A study of the topographic anatomy of the venous system of the lumbar region through an anterior approach to the lumbar spine." *J. Jap. Orthop. Assoc.*, **45:** 1987–1097.

PLAUE, R., GERNER, H. J. & PÜHL, W. (1973). "The characteristics of fractures of the thoracic and lumbar vertebral bodies." *Z. Orthop.*, **111:** 139–146.

POLÁČEK, P. (1956). "Morphological changes in the innervation of the joints in laboratory animals under experimental functional and pathological conditions." *Acta Chir. Orthop. Traumatol. Česk.*, **23:** 286–292.

RABEY, G. (1974). "Analytical anatomy of the human head and neck." *J. Anat.*, **119:** 379.

ROCKWELL, H., EVANS, F. G. & PHEASANT, H. C. (1938). "The comparative morphology of the vertebrate spinal column: its form related to function." *J. Morphol.*, **63:** 87–117.

RUSSELL, J. G. B. (1966). "Moulding of the pelvic outlet." *J. Obstet. Gynec.*, **76:** 817–820.

SCHLÜTER, K. (1960). "Form and structure of normal and pathological variations of the vertebrae." *Verh. Deutsch. Orthop. Ges.*, **63**: 357–368.

SCHUNKE, G. B. (1938). "The anatomy and development of the sacro-iliac joint in man." *Anat. Rec.*, **72**: 313–331.

SIBTHORPE, E. M. (1958). "A radiological survey on the measurements of specimens of the female pelvis in Uganda." *J. Obstet. Gynec.*, **64**: 600–605.

SIM, G. P. G. (1973). "Vertebral contour in spondylolisthesis." *Brit. J. Radiol.*, **46**: 250–254.

SIMRIL, W. A. & THURSTON, D. (1955). "The normal interpediculate space in the spines of infants and children." *Radiology*, **64**:

SLIM, G. P. (1973). "Vertebral contour in spondylolisthesis." *Brit. J. Radiol.*, **46**: 250–254.

SNIDJERS, C. J. (1972). "The form of the spine related to the human posture." *Agressollogie*, **13B**: 5–14.

SYLVEN, B., PAULSEN, S., HIRSCH, C. & SNELLMAN, O. (1951). "The ultrastructure of bovine and human nuclei pulposi." *J. Bone Joint Surg.*, **33A**: 333–340.

TAILLARD, W. (1971). "The microscopic anatomy of spondylolysis." *Rév. Chir. Orthop.*, **57**: 106.

TAYLOR, J. (1972). "Development of the intervertebral disc." *J. Bone Joint Surg.*, **54B**: 193–194.

TIMM, H. (1970). "Comparative description of the form and mobility of the vertebral column by means of plastic curve templates." *Manuelle Medizin*, **8**: 140–150.

TULSI, R. S. (1972). "Vertebral column of the Australian aborigine: selected morphological and metrical features." *Zeit. Morph. Anthrop.*, **64**: 117–144.

VELENEAU, C. (1972). "Comments on the morphological characteristics of the cervical vertebrae." *Acta Anat.*, **81**: 148–157.

VELENEAU, C. (1975). "Morphofunctional peculiarities of the transverse processes of the axis: considerations of their pathogenic significance." *Acta Anat.*, **92**: 301–309.

VELENEAU, C., GRUN, U., DIACONESCU, M. & COCOTA, E. (1972). "Structural peculiarities of the thoracic spine: their functional significance." *Acta Anat.*, **82**: 97–107.

VERBIEST, H. (1975). "Pathomorphologic aspects of developmental lumbar stenosis." *Orthop. Clin. Nth. Amer.*, **6**: 177–196.

VERNON-ROBERTS, B. & PIRIE, C. J. (1973). "Healing trabecular microfractures in the bodies of lumbar vertebrae." *Ann. Rheum. Dis.*, **32:** 406–412.

WAGSTAFFE, W. W. (1874). "On the mechanical structure of the cancellous tissue of bone." *St. Thomas's Hosp. Rep.*, **5:** 193–214.

WALMSLEY, R. (1953). "The development and growth of the intervertebral disc." *Edinb. Med. J.*, **60:** 341–364.

WALSKI, A. (1972). "Investigations on the anatomy of the isthmus of the neural arch in lumbar vertebrae of pre-school children." *Chir. Narz. Ruchu. Ortop. Pol.*, **37:** 25–33.

WHALEN, J. P. & WOODRUFF, C. L. (1970). "The cervical prevertebral fat stripe." *Amer. J. Roentgenol.*, **109:** 445–451.

WILLIS, T. A. (1931). "The separate neural arch." *J. Bone Joint Surg.*, **13:** 709–721.

WILLIS, T. A. (1941). "Anatomical variations and roentgenographic appearances of low back pain in relation to sciatic pain." *J. Bone Joint Surg.*, **23:** 410–416.

## *(c) Embryology and Genetics: Developmental Abnormalities*

ANGEVINE, J. B. (1973). "Clinically relevant embryology of the vertebral column and spinal cord." *Clin. Neurosurg.*, **20:** 95–113.

AZOUZ, E. M. & WEE, R. (1974). "Spondylolysis of the cervical vertebrae." *Radiology*, **111:** 315–318.

BANTA, J. V. & NICHOLAS, O. (1969). "Sacral agenesis." *J. Bone Joint Surg.*, **51A:** 693–703.

BARDEEN, C. R. (1905). "The development of the thoracic vertebrae in man." *Am. J. Anat.*, **4:** 163.

BARDEEN, C. R. (1905). "Studies of the development of the human skeleton." *Am. J. Anat.*, **4:** 265.

BARTSOCAS, C. S., KIOSSOGLOU, K. A. & PAPAS, C. V. (1974). "Costovertebral dysplasia." *Birth Defects.*, **10:** 221–226.

BLECK, E. E. (1974). Spondylolisthesis: acquired, congenital or developmental." *Dev. Med. Child Neurol.*, **16:** 680–982.

BOMBELLI, R. (1953). "The development of the lumbar segment of the vertebral column in the foetus." *Arch. Orthop.*, **66:** 634–645.

BULL, J., EL GAMMAL, T. & POPHAM, M. (1969). "A possible genetic factor in cervical spondylosis." *Brit. J. Radiol.*, **42:** 4–16.

BUTLER, J. M. (1946). "Short leg backache." *Lancet*, **66:** 10–11.

CHEN, L. T. (1975). "The development of the vertebral bone marrow of human foetuses." *Blood*, **46:** 389–408.

DAY, M. H. (1964). "The blood supply of the lumbar and sacral plexuses in the human foetus." *J. Anat.*, **98:** 105–116.

DIAMOND, L. S. (1970). "A family study of spondylo-epiphyseal dysplasia." *J. Bone Joint Surg.*, **52A:** 1587–1594.

DI CHARO, G., HARRINGTON, T. & FRIED, L. C. (1973). "Microangiography of the human fetal spinal cord." *Amer. J. Roentgenol.*, **118:** 193–199.

DURBIN, F. C. (1956). "Spondylolisthesis of the cervical spine." *J. Bone Joint Surg.*, **38B:** 734–735.

EHRENHAFT, J. L. (1943). "Development of the vertebral column as related to certain congenital and pathological changes." *Surg. Gynec. Obst.*, **76:** 282–292.

FAWCETT, E. (1907). "On the completion of ossification of the human sacrum." *Anat. Anz.*, **30:** 414–421.

FRANCESCHINI, P. (1974). "The autosomal recessive form of spondylocostal dysostosis." *Radiology*, **112:** 673–675.

GESELL, A. & AMATRUDA, C. S. (1945). *The Embryology of Behavior*. New York; Harper.

GJORUP, P. A. (1964). "Dorsal hemivertebra." *Acta Orthop. Scand.*, **35:** 117–125.

GOVONI, A. F. (1971). "Developmental stenosis of a thoracic vertebra resulting in narrowing of the spinal canal." *Amer. J. Roentgenol.*, **112:** 401–404.

HAARDICK, H. (1956). "The development of the proportions of the body through limited growth of the elements of the skeleton." *Acta Anat.*, **27** (Suppl. 26): 5–99.

HASSAN, S. Z. & WILLIAMS, J. R. (1973). "Spread of radio-opaque solution in the epidural space of a human neonate." *J. Reproduc. Med.*, **10:** 31–34.

HIBBS, R. A. & SWIFT, W. E. (1929). "Developmental abnormalities at the lumbosacral juncture causing pain and disability: a report of one hundred and forty-seven patients treated by the spine fusion operation." *Surg. Gynec. Obst.*, **48:** 604–612.

HINCK, V. C. & SACHDEV, N. S. (1966). "Developmental stenosis of the cervical spine canal." *Brain*, **89:** 27–36.

HOLMES, I. (1975). "Coccydynia." *Can. Med. Ass. J.*, **112:** 1166.

HORAN, F. R. & BEIGHTON, P. H. (1973). "Recessive inheritance of generalized joint hypermobility." *Rheumatol. Rehab.*, **12:** 47–49.

IGNELZI, R. J. & LEHMAN, R. A. W. (1974). "Lumbosacral agenesis: management and embryological implications." *J. Neurol. Neurosurg. Psychiat.*, **37**: 1273–1276.

INGELMARK, B. E. & LEWIN, T. (1968). "Asymmetries and deviations of the skeletal axis, particularly in relation to scoliosis." In *Die Wirbelsäule in Forschung und Praxis*, Vol. 40., pp. 83–95. Ed. H. Junghanns. Stuttgart; Hippokrates Verlag.

INGELMARK, B. E. & LINDSTROM, J. (1963). "Asymmetries of the lower extremities and pelvis and their relations to lumbar scoliosis: a radiographic study." *Acta Morph. Néerl.-Scand.*, **5**: 221–234.

KARMANSKI, J., KARMANSKI, W., STOKLOSA, E. & BLUSZCZ, A. (1973). "Studies on the blood vessels of the ischiadic nerve in human fetuses." *Folia morph., (Warsz.)*, **32**: 323–330.

KIRKALDY-WILLIS, W. H., PAINE, K. W. E., CAUCHOIX, J. & McIVOR, G. (1974). "Lumbar spinal stenosis." *Clin. Orthop.*, **99**: 30–50.

KLEIN, K. K. (1969). "A study of the progression of the lateral pelvic asymmetry in 585 elementary, junior and senior high school boys." *Amer. Correct. Ther. J.*, **23**: 171–174.

KLEIN, K. K. (1970). "Asymmetries in the pelvis and legs and their implications in knee injury." *Amer. Correct. Ther. J.*, **24**: 93–95.

KLEIN, K. K. (1973). "Progression of pelvis tilt in adolescent boys from elementary through high school." *Arch. Phys. Med. Rehab.*, **54**: 57–59.

KLEIN, K. K. & BUCKLEY, J. C. (1966). "Asymmetries of growth in the pelvis and legs of growing children: a preliminary report." *J. Ass. Phys. Med. Rehab.*, **20**: 112–117.

KLEIN, K. K. & BUCKLEY, J. C. (1968). "Asymmetries of growth in the pelvis and legs of growing children." *Amer. Correct. Ther. J.*, **22**: 53–55.

KLEIN, K. K., REDLER, I. & LOWMAN, C. L. (1968). "Asymmetries of growth in the pelvis and legs of children." *J. Amer. Osteop. Ass.*, **68**: 153–156.

LANIER, R. R. (1939). "The presacral vertebrae of American white and negro males." *Amer. J. Phys. Anthrop.*, **25**: 341–420.

LEWIN, T., REICHMANN, S. & ENGSTRÖM, G. (1972). "The postnatal development of the lumbar neuro-central epiphyseal cartilages." *Acta Morphol. Néerl.-Scand.*, **9**: 165–178.

LINDAHL, O. & MOVIN, A. (1968). "Measurement of the deformity in scoliosis." *Acta Orthop. Scand.*, **39**: 291–302.

LINDSTRÖM, J. A. (1971). "A diabetic embryopathy: the caudal regression syndrome." *Birth Defects*, **7**: 278–279.

MAITLAND, G. D. (1961). "Some observations on sciatic scoliosis." *Aust. J. Physiother.*, **7**: 84–87.

MALINSKÝ, J. (1959). "The ontogenetic development of nerve terminations in the intervertebral discs of man." *Acta Anat.*, **38**: 96–113.

MANNING, C. W. (1976). "Scoliosis." *Br. J. Hosp. Med.*, **15**: 49–55.

MEHTA, M. H. (1973). "Radiographic estimation of vertebral rotation in scoliosis." *J. Bone Joint Surg.*, **55B**: 513–520.

MINKOWSKI, M. (1922). "On early movements. Reflex and muscular reactions in the human fetus and their relation to the fetal nerve and muscle system." *Schweiz. Med. Wochenschr.*, **52**: 721–724.

MUTCH, J. & WALMSLEY, R. (1956). "The aetiology of cleft vertebral arch in spondylolisthesis." *Lancet*, **1**: 74–77.

NATHAN, H. (1962). "Osteophytes of the vertebral column: an anatomical study of their development according to age, race and sex, with considerations as to their etiology and significance." *J. Bone Joint Surg.*, **44A**: 243–264.

NATHAN, H. & SCHWARTZ, A. (1962). "Inverted pattern of development of thoracic vertebral osteophytosis in situs inversus and in other instances of right descending aorta." *Radiol. Clin.*, **31**: 150–158.

NICHOLS, P. J. R. (1960). 'Short-leg syndrome." *Brit. Med. J.*, **1**: 1863–1865.

NOBACK, C. R. & ROBERTSON, G. C. (1951). "Sequence of appearance of ossification centers in the human skeleton during the first five prenatal months." *Am. J. Anat.*, **89**: 1–28.

NOZAKI, K. (1955). "On the innervation, especially the sensory innervation, of the periosteum and the area surrounding it in the earlier stage of human embryo." *Archiv. Histol. Jap.*, **9**: 269–281.

PEACOCK, A. (1951). "Observations on the prenatal development of the intervertebral disc in man." *J. Anat.*, **85**: 260–274.

PETERSEN, D. (1967). "On developmental abnormalities of the vertebral column in dysmelic children." *Z. Orthop.*, **102**: 386–395.

POPOVA-LATKINA, N. V. (1956). "Development of intervertebral cartilages in the embryonal period in man." *Trns. Astrakh. Med. Inst.*, **12**: 9–18.

PRADER, A. (1947). "The early embryonic development of the

human intervertebral disc." *Zeit. Anat. Inst. Universität Zürich:* 68–83.

REICHMANN, S. (1971). "The postnatal development of form and orientation of the lumbar intervertebral joint surfaces." *Z. Anat. Entwickl.-Gesch.*, **133:** 102–123.

REICHMANN, S. (1971). "Longitudinal growth of the lumbar articular processes with reference to the development of clefts." *Z. Anat. Entwickl.-Gesch.*, **133:** 124–134.

REICHMANN, S. & LEWIN, T. (1971). "The development of the lumbar lordosis: a post mortem study on excised lumbar spines." *Arch. Orthop. Unfall-Chir.*, **69:** 275–85.

REICHMANN, S. & LEWIN, T. (1971). "Growth processes in the lumbar neural arch." *Z. Anat. Entwickl.-Gesch.*, **133:** 89–101.

RUSH, W. A. & STEINER, H. A. (1946). "A study of lower extremity length inequality." *Amer. J. Roentgenol.*, **56:** 616–623.

SCHEUERMANN, H. (1934). "Roentgenologic studies of the origin and development of juvenile kyphosis, together with some investigations concerning the vertebral epiphyses in man and animals." *Acta Orthop. Scand.*, **5:** 162–220.

SEVER, L. E. (1974). "A case of meningomyelocele in a kindred with multiple cases of spondylolisthesis and spina bifida occulta." *J. Med. Genet.*, **11:** 94–96.

SICURANZA, B. J., RICHARDS, B. J. & TISDALL, L. H. (1970). "The short leg syndrome in obstetrics and gynecology." *Amer. J. Obstet. Gynec.*, **107:** 217–219.

SIDEL, K. & SAERNUS, K. S. (1972). "Myelographic anatomical studies in injured cervical vertebral column preparations." *Arch. Orthop. Unfall-Chir.*, **72:** 10–20.

SKOGLUND, S. (1960). "On the postnatal development of postural mechanisms as revealed by electromyography and myography in decerebrate kittens." *Acta Physiol. Scand.*, **49:** 299–317.

SOGOMY, B. (1961). "Blood supply of the foetal spine." *Acta Morph. Hungarica*, **8:** 261–274.

TONDURY, G. (1958). "*Developmental History and Development Defects of the Vertebral Column.*" Stuttgart; Thieme.

VELEANU, C. (1974). "Aspects of ontogenetic evolution of the osteo-vascular nervous space relationships at the height of the cervical intervertebral canal in man." *Anat. Anz.*, **136:**

VERBEIST, H. (1954). "A radicular syndrome from developmental narrowing of the lumbar vertebral canal." *J. Bone Joint Surg.*, **36B:** 230–237.

WYBURN, G. M. (1944). "Observations on the development of the human vertebral column." *J. Anat.*, **78:** 94–102.


### (d) Maturation and Ageing

ALLBROOK, D. B. (1956). "Changes in lumbar vertebral body height with age." *Amer. J. Phys. Anthrop.*, **14:** 35–39.

ANDERSON, M. & GREEN, W. T. (1965). "Growth of the normal trunk in boys and girls during the second decade of life." *J. Bone Joint Surg.*, **47A:** 1554; 1564.

ATKINSON, P. H. (1967). "Variation in trabecular structure of vertebrae with age." *Calcif. Tissue Res.*, **1:** 24–32.

BARSON, A. J. (1970). "The vertebral level of termination of the spinal cord during normal and abnormal development." *J. Anat.*, **106:** 489–497.

BICK, E. M. & COPEL, J. W. (1950). "Longitudinal growth of the human vertebra: a contribution to human osteogeny." *J. Bone Joint Surg.*, **32A:** 803–814.

BIJLSMA, F. & PEEREBOOM, J. W. C. (1972). "The ageing pattern of intervertebral discs." *Gerontologica*, **18:** 157–168.

BLOUNT, W. P. (1973). "Scoliosis treatment: skeletal maturity evaluation." *Minn. Med.*, **56:**

BOHATRICHUK, F. (1955). "The ageing vertebral column: macro and historadiographical study." *Br. J. Radiol.*, **28:** 389–404.

BRANDIVER, M. E. (1970). "Normal values of the vertebral body and intervertebral disc index during growth." *Amer. J. Roentgenol.*, **110:** 618.

BRANDNER, M. (1972). "Normal values of the vertebral body and intervertebral disc index in adults." *Am. J. Roentgenol. Radium Ther. Nucl. Med.*, **114:** 411–414.

CARLSON, I. E., ALSTON, W. & FELDMAN, D. J. (1964). "Electromyographic study of ageing in skeletal muscle." *Amer. J. Phys. Med.*, **43:** 141; 145.

CASSUCIO, C. (1962). "An introduction to the study of osteoporosis: biochemical and biophysical research in bone ageing." *Proc. Roy. Soc. Med.*, **55:** 663–668.

CORBIN, K. B. & GARDNER, E. D. (1937). "Decrease in number of myelinated fibers in human spinal roots with age." *Anat. Rec.*, **68:** 63–74.

DRAGIEV, M. & MILENKOV, H. (1974). "Age conditioned changes of the lumbar intervertebral disks in humans." *Folia Med. (Plovdiv)*, **16:** 207–211.

EDER, M. (1960). "The structural organization of the vertebral bone marrow." *Virchows Arch. Path. Anat.*, **333:** 509–522.

FISCHER, E. (1970). "Major variations in regions of the vertebral column and lower extremities with age in male and female." *Z. Orthop.*, **107:** 624–626.

FISCHER, E. (1970). "Major variations in regions of the vertebral column and lower extremities with age in male and female." *Z. Orthop.*, **107:** 638–642.

FISCHER, E. & GIERE, W. (1970). "Major variations in regions of the vertebral column and lower extremities with age in male and female." *Z. Orthop.*, **107:** 620–624.

FISCHER, E. & VOLCK, H. (1970). "Major variations in regions of the vertebral column and lower extremities with age in male and female." *Z. Orthop.*, **107:** 627–637.

FRANCIS, C. C. (1956). "Certain changes in the aged male white cervical spine." *Anat. Rec.*, **125:** 783–787.

GOODING, C. A. & NEUHAUSER, E. B. D. (1965). "Growth and development of the vertebral bodies in the presence and absence of normal stress." *Am. J. Roentgenol.*, **93:** 388.

GOWER, W. E. & PEDRINI, V. (1969). "Age related variations in proteinpolysaccharides from human nucleus pulposus, annulus fibrosus and costal cartilage." *J. Bone Joint Surg.*, **51A:** 210.

GRAHAME, R. & HOLT, P. J. L. (1969). "The influence of ageing on the *in vitro* elasticity of human skin." *Gerontologia*, **15:** 21–129.

HALLEN, P. (1958). "Hexosamine and ester sulphate content of the human nucleus pulposus at different ages." *Acta Chem. Scand.*, **12:** 1869–1872.

HAPPEY, F. (1972). "A study of the changes in collagen and allied polysaccharides and protein in ageing of the human intervertebral disc." *Symposium—Arthritis and Rheumatism Research Council, London*.

HAPPEY, F., PEARSON, C. H., NAYLOR, A. & TURNER, R. L. (1969). "The ageing of the human intervertebral disc." *Gerontologia*, **15:** 174–188.

HIRSCH, C., PAULSON, S., SYLVEN, B. & SNELLMAN, O. (1953).

"Biophysical and physiological investigations on cartilage and other mesenchymal tissues. VI. Characteristics of human nuclei pulposi during ageing." *Acta Orthop., Scand.*, **22:** 175–183.

HOLT, K. (Ed.). (1975). *Movement and Child Development.* London; Heinemann.

ISRAEL, H. (1973). "Progressive enlargement of the vertebral body as part of the process of human skeletal ageing." *Age and Ageing,* **2:** 71–79.

KIEFFER, S. A., STADLAN, E. M., MOHANDAS, A. & PETERSON, H. O. (1969). "Discographic-anatomical correlation of developmental changes with age in the intervertebral disc." *Acta Radiol., (Diagn.),* **9:** 733–739.

KNUTTSON, R. (1961). "Growth and differentiation of the postnatal vertebrae." *Acta Radiol,* **55:** 401–404.

McKERN, T. W. & STEWART, T. D. (1957). "Skeletal age changes in young American males, analysed from the standpoint of identification." *HQM Res. & Dev. Command. Tech. Rep. EP—45.* Massachusetts; Nattick.

MORGAN, B. (1973). "Ageing and osteoporosis—in particular spinal osteoporosis." *Clin. Endocrinol. Metabol.,* **2:** 187–201.

MUKOYAMA, M. (1973). "Age changes in the internodal length in the human spinal roots—nerve teasing study." *Nagoya J. Med. Sci.,* **36:** 17–27.

MURAYAMA, K. (1972). "Biochemical studies on the age-related variations of human intervertebral discs." *J. Jap. Orthop. Ass.,* **46:** 81–104.

NAYLOR, A., HAPPEY, F. & McCRAE, T. P. (1954). "The collagenous changes in the intervertebral disc with age and their effect on its elasticity—an X-ray crystallographic study." *Brit. Med. J.,* **2:** 570–573.

NEUGEBAUER, H. (1973). "Kyphometric study of 9,000 schoolchildren in Austria." *Z. Orthop.,* **111:** 633–639.

OCHA, J. & MAIR, W. G. P. (1966). "The normal sural nerve in man. II. Changes in the axons and Schwann cells due to ageing." *Acta neuropathol., Berlin,* **13:** 217–239.

PEERBOOM, J. W. (1970). "Age dependent changes in the human intervertebral disc: fluorescent substances and amino-acids in the annulus fibrosus." *Gerontologia,* **16:** 352–367.

PLAUE, R. (1974). "The behaviour of fractures of the thoracic and lumbar vertebral bodies. 6. Discussion—some theoretical fracture models." *Z. Orthop.*, **112:** 1071–1077.

PROBERT, J. C. (1973). "Growth retardation in children after megavoltage irradiation of the spine." *Cancer*, **32:** 634–639.

RITCHIE, J. H. & FAHRINI, W. H. (1970). "Age changes in lumbar intervertebral discs." *Canad. J. Surg.*, **13:** 65–71.

SCHWARTZ, L., BRITTEN, R. H. & THOMPSON, L. F. (1928). "Studies in physical development and posture." *Public Health Bulletin*, p. 179.

SHERK, H. H. & NICHOLSON, J. T. (1971). "Comparative anatomy and embryology of the cervical spine." *Orthop. Clin. Nth. Amer.*, **2:** 325–341.

SYLVEN, B. (1951). "Mucoid in discs at different ages." *Acta Orthop. Scand.*, **20:** 275.

TONDBURY, G. (1955). "The anatomy and development of the vertebral column, with special reference to changes of the intervertebral disks induced by age." *Schweiz. Med. Wschr.*, **85:** 825–827.

TULSI, R. S. (1971). "Growth of the human vertebral column: an osteological study." *Acta Anat., Basel*, **79:** 570–580.

VASILEV, V., OVCHARV, V. & MALINOV, G. (1971). "Age-related changes in the thoracic intervertebral discs of humans." *Nauchni Tr. Vissh. Med. Inst., Sofia*, **50:** 15–24.

WEAVER, J. K. & CHALMERS, J. (1966). "Cancellous bone: its strength and changes with ageing and an evaluation of some methods for measuring its mineral content. I. Age changes in cancellous bone." *J. Bone Joint Surg.*, **48A:** 289–299.

WEI, J. K. & ARNOLD, J. S. (1972). "Variations in osteoid pattern with age in human vertebrae." *Okajimas Folia Anat. Jap.*, **49:** 157–173.

WILSON, A. K. (1969). "The lumbosacral angle: criterion for employability." *Rocky Mountain Med. J.*, **66:** 38–42.

WYKE, B. D. (1975). "The neurological basis of movement: a developmental review." In *Movement and Child Development*, pp. 19–33. Ed. K. S. Holt. London; Heinemann.

## (e) Evolution and Comparative

ALLBROOK, D. B. (1954). "Characteristics of the East African vertebral column." *J. Anat.*, **88**: 599.

ALLBROOK, D. B. (1955). "The East African vertebral column." *Amer. J. Phys. Anthrop.*, **13**: 489–514.

ALLBROOK, D. B. (1956). "The skeletal anatomy of the back in East Africans." *East Afr. Med. J.*, **33**: 9–13.

BENZIAN, S. R., MAINZER, F. & GOODING, C. A. (1971). "Pediculate thinnings: a normal variant at the thoraco-lumbar junction." *Brit. J. Radiol.*, **44**: 936–939.

CLIFFORD, E. C. (1960). "Compilation of anthropometric measures on U.S. Navy pilots." *Naval Air Material Centre—Air Crew Equipment Laboratory*, NAMC/ACEL 437.

GASKELL, J. F. & GREEN, H. L. H. (Eds.) (1933). *The Evolution of the Vertebral Column.* Cambridge; Cambridge University Press.

GOFF, C. W. (1955). "Postural evolution related to backache." *Clin. Orthop.*, **5**: 8–16.

SCHULTZ, A. H. (1955). "The position of the occipital condyles and of the face relative to the skull base in primates." *Am. J. Phys. Anthrop.*, **13**: 97–120.

SILBERSTEIN, C. E. (1965). "The evolution of degenerative changes in the cervical spine and an investigation into the joints of Luschka." *Clin. Orthop.*, **40**: 184–203.

TOBIAS, P. V. (1959). "Studies on the occipital bone in Africa, IV. Components and correlations of occipital curvature in relation to cranial growth. *Human Biol.*, **31**: 121–137.

TODD, T. W. & PYLE, S. I. (1928). "A quantitative study of the vertebral column by direct and roentgenologic methods." *Amer. J. Phys. Anthrop.*, **12**: 321–338.

TONDURY, G. (1952). "New results in the study of the evolutionary physiology of the spine." *Arch. Orthop. Unfall*, **45**: 313.

## (f) Histology (including Histochemistry and Electron Microscopy)

ARNIM, S. S. (1935). "A method of preparation of serial sections of teeth and surrounding structures in the rat." *Anat. Rec.*, **62**: 321–330.

BROMLEY, R. G., DOCKUM, N. L., ARNOLD, J. S. & JEE, W. S. S.

(1966). "Quantitative histologic study of human vertebrae." *J. Geront.*, **21:** 537–543.

BUTLER, W. F. (1974). "Comparison on the effects of two sources of hyaluronidase on tissue sections using visual estimates and microdensitometric measurements." *Histochem. J.*, **6:** 117–120.

CIARPAGLINI, L. & FUSI, G. (1955). "Histochemical and radiographic studies of the vertebrae in old subjects." *Sperimentale*, **105:** 29–131.

CLAYDEN, E. C. (1952). "A discussion on the preparation of bone sections by the paraffin wax method with special reference to the control of decalcification." *J. Med. Lab. Technol.*, **10:** 103–123.

COPIUS PEREBOOM, J. W. (1973). "Some biochemical and histochemical properties of the age pigment in the human intervertebral disc." *Histochemie*, **37:** 119–130.

DRAGIEV, M. & KITOV, D. (1971). "Histologic and some histochemical changes of the lumbar vertebral discs in patients with discogenic sciatica." *Folia Medica (Plovdiv)*, **13:** 259–265.

FRANCOIS, R. J. (1969). "Microradiographic and histological study of vertebral osteophytes." *Pathol. Europeae*, **4:** 193–208.

GHADIALLY, N. & ROY, S. (1966). "Ultrastructure of synovial membrane." *Ann. Rheum. Dis.*, **25:** 318–326.

GOTTE, L., STERN, P., ELSDEN, D. F. & PARTRIDGE, S. M. (1963). "The chemistry of connective tissues: the comparison of elastin from three bovine tissues." *Biochem. J.*, **87:** 344–351.

HIRANO, S. (1972). "Electron microscopic studies on back muscles in scoliosis." *J. Jap. Orthop. Ass.*, **46:** 47–62.

HOLMES, W. (1943). "Silver staining of nerve axons in paraffin sections." *Anat. Rec.*, **86:** 157–187.

HOSOKAWA, O. (1964). "The histological study of the type and distribution of the sensory nerve endings in human hip joint capsule and ligament." *J. Jap. Orthop. Ass.*, **38:** 887–901.

JOWETT, R. L., FIDLER, M. W. & TROUP, J. D. G. (1975). "Histochemical changes in the multifidus in mechanical derangements of the spine." *Orthop. Clin. Nth. Amer.*, **6:**

JUNG, A. & BRUNSCHWIG, A. (1932). "Histological investigations of the innervation of the joints of the vertebral bodies." *Presse Méd.*, **40:** 316–317.

LANDON, D. N. (1966). "Electron microscopy of muscle spindles." *In Control and Innervation of Skeletal Muscle.* Ed. B. L. Andrew. Edinburgh; Livingstone.

LEVER, J. D. & FORD, E. H. R. (1958). "Histological, histochemical and electron microscopic observations on synovial membrane." *Anat. Rec.*, **132**: 524–534.

LEWIS, P. R. & SHUTE, C. C. D. (1964). "Demonstration of cholinesterase activity with the electron microscope." *J. Physiol.*, **175**: 5P–7P.

MORIN, F., KENNEDY, D. T. & GARDNER, E. D. (1966). "Spinal afferents to the lateral reticular nucleus: an histological study." *J. Comp. Neurol.*, **126**: 511–522.

NAYLOR, A. (1958). "Changes in the human intervertebral discs with age." *Proc. Roy. Soc. Med.*, **51**: 573–576.

PAUSTY, I. (1975). "Leaching of glycosaminoglycans from tissues by the fixatives formalin saline and formalin cetrimide." *Histochem. J.*, **7**: 361–365.

POLÁČEK, P. (1966). *Receptors of the Joints.* Brno; Purkinyĕ University Press.

PRAESTHOLM, J. & ØLGAARD, K. (1972). "Comparative histological investigation of the sequelae of experimental myelography using Sodium Methiodal and Meglumine Iothalamate." *Neuroradiology*, **4**: 14–19.

RICHARDSON, K. C. (1960). "Studies on the structure of autonomic nerves in the small intestine correlating the silver impregnated image in light microscopy with the permanganate fixed ultra-structure in electron microscopy." *J. Anat.*, **94**: 457–472.

RONCORONIL, I. (1953). "Histochemical study of the intervertebral discs." *Monit. Zool. Ital.*, **62**: 407–410.

STORTI, E. (1973). "The histochemistry of fibrinolysis in haemophilic synovial membranes." *Acta Haematol., Basel.* **49**: 142–153.

SULEMANA, C. A. & SUCHENWIRTH, R. (1972). "Topical differentiation in the histological localization of enzymes in the skeletal musculature. Studies on 5 skeletal muscles from cadavers without neuromuscular diseases." *J. Neurol. Sci.*, **16**: 433–444.

TAKADA, N. (1973). "Studies on the ageing process of the lumbar discs and facets, especially of the histological changes." *J. Jap. Orthop. Ass.*, **47**: 333–349.

THAGE, O. (1965). "The quadriceps syndrome: an electromyographic and histological evaluation." *Acta Neurol. Scand.*, **41** (Suppl. 13): 245–249.

TSUKADA, K. (1938). "Histological studies on the human intervertebral disc: histological findings in the fetus." *Mitt. Med. Akad. Kioto*, **24:** 1057–1091; 1172–1174.

TSUKADA, K. (1939). "Histological studies on the human intervertebral disc: changes with age." *Mitt. Med. Akad. Kioto.*, **25:** 1–29; 207–209.

VERNON-ROBERTS, B., PIRIE, C. J. & TRENWITH, V. (1974). "Pathology of the thoracic spine in ankylosing hyperostosis." *Ann. Rheum. Dis.*, **33:** 281–288.

WEI, J. K. & ARNOLD, J. S. (1970). "Staining osteoid seams in thin slabs of undecalcified trabecular bone." *Stain. Techn.*, **45:** 193–198.

WELLER, R. O., BRUCKNER, F. E. & CHAMBERLAIN, M. A. (1970). "Rheumatoid neuropathy: a histological and electrophysiological study." *J. Neurol. Neurosurg. Psychiat.*, **33:** 592–604.

WHITEHOUSE, W. J., DYSON, E. D. & JACKSON, C. K. (1971). "The scanning electron microscope in studies of trabecular bone from a human vertebral body." *J. Anat.*, **108:** 481–496.

WINKELMANN, R. K. & SCHMITT, R. W. (1957). "A simple silver method for nerve axoplasm." *Proc. Staff Meetings Mayo Clinic*, **32:** 217–222.

WINKELMANN, R. K. & SCHMIT, R. W. (1957). "Factors relating to the staining of nerve axoplasm with concentrated silver solutions." *Proc. Staff Meetings, Mayo Clin.*, **32:** 222–226.

WINKELMANN, R. K. & SCHMIT, R. W. (1959). "Histochemical investigations of a silver method for axons." *J. Histochem.*, **7:** 86–92.

WYKE, B. D. (1967). "The neurology of joints." *Ann. Roy. Coll. Surg. Engl.*, **41:** 25–50.

WYKE, B. D. (1972). 'Articular neurology: a review." *Physiotherapy*, **58:**94–99.

WYKE, B. D. (1975). "Morphological and functional features of the innervation of the costovertebral joints." *Fol. Morphol., Prague*, **23:** 296–305.

WYKE, B. D. (1976). "Neurological aspects of low back pain." In *The Lumbar Spine and Back Pain*, pp. 189–256. Ed. M. I. V. Jayson. London; Pitman Medical.

WYKE, B. D. (1979). "The neurology of the cervical spine." *Physiotherapy*, **65:** 72–76.

WYKE, B. D. & POLÁČEK, P. (1973). "Structural and functional characteristics of the joint receptor apparatus." *Acta Chir. Orthop. Traum. Česk., Prague*, **40:** 489–497.

YAMAMOTO, T. (1925). "The detailed histology of bone marrow." *Vichows Arch. Path. Anat.*, **258:** 62–107.

# 3

# INDIVIDUAL TISSUES

### (a) Skin and Subcutaneous Tissues

BEARDWELL, A. (1969). "Familial ankylosing vertebral hyperstosis with tylosis." *Ann. Rheum. Dis.*, **28:** 518–523.

BISHOP, G. H. (1946). "Neural mechanisms of cutaneous sense." *Physiol. Rev.*, **26:** 77–102.

BOURLAND, A. & WINKELMANN, R. K. (1966). "Study of cutaneous innervation in congenital anaesthesia." *Archiv. Neurol., Chicago*, **14:** 223–227.

BURTON, C. & MAURER, D. D. (1974). "Pain suppression by transcutaneous electronic stimulation." *IEEE Trans. Biomed. Eng.*, **21:**81–88.

EDELBERG, R. (1973). "Local electrical response of the skin to deformation." *J. Appl. Psychol.*, **34:** 334–340.

EDELBERG, R. & WRIGHT, D. J. (1964). "Two galvanic skin response effector organs and their stimulus specificity." *Psychophysiology*, **1:** 39–47.

GRAHAME, R. & BEIGHTON, P. (1969). "Physical properties of the skin in the Ehlers-Danlos syndrome." *Ann. Rheum. Dis.*, **28:** 246–251.

GRAHAME, R. & HOLT, P. J. L. (1969). "The influence of ageing on the in vivo elasticity of human skin." *Gerontologia*, **15:** 121–129.

GREENWOOD, B. M. (1966). "Capillary resistance and skin-fold thickness in patients with rheumatoid arthritis: effect of corticosteroid therapy." *Ann. Rheum. Dis.*, **25:** 272–277.

HERTZMAN, A. B. & FLATH, F. (1963). "The continuous simultaneous registration of sweating and blood flow in a small skin area." *Aerospace Med.*, **34:** 710–713.

IVES, D. R. (1973). "Urticaria pigmentosa with spinal osteoporosis." *Proc. Roy. Soc. Med.*, **66:** 175–176.

JAJIC, I. (1968). "Radiologic changes in the sacro-iliac joints and spine of patients with psoriatic arthritis and psoriasis." *Ann. Rheum. Dis.*, **27:** 1–6.

KEEGAN, J. J. (1943). "Dermatome hypalgesia associated with

herniation of intervertebral disc." *Arch. Neurol. Psych.*, **50:** 67–83.

KEEGAN, J. J. (1944). "Neurosurgical interpretation of dermatome hypalgesia with herniation of the lumbar intervertebral disc." *J. Bone Joint Surg.*, **26A:** 238–248.

KENNEDI, R. M., GIBSON, T., EVANS, J. H. & BARBENEL, J. C. (1975). "Tissue mechanics." *Phys. Med. Biol.*, **20:** 699–717.

KENSHALO, D. R. (Ed.). (1968). *The Skin Senses.* Springfield, Illinois; Thomas.

KORR, I. M., WRIGHT, H. M. & CHACE, J. A. (1964). "Cutaneous patterns of sympathetic activity in clinical abnormalities of the musculoskeletal system." *Acta Neurovegetativa*, **25:** 589–606.

KORR, I. M., WRIGHT, H. M. & THOMAS, P. E. (1961). "Effects of experimental myofascial insults on cutaneous patterns of sympathetic activity in man." *Acta Neurovegetativa*, **23:** 329–355.

LIM, R. K. S. (1968). "Cutaneous and visceral pain and somesthetic chemoreceptors. In *The Skin Senses*, Ed. by D. R. Kenshalo, pp. 458–464. Springfield, Illinois; Thomas.

LIM, R. K. S., GUZMAN, F. & RODGERS, D. W. (1962). "Note on the muscle receptors concerned with pain." In *Symposium on Muscle Receptors*, pp. 215–219. Ed. by D. Barker. Hong Kong; Hong Kong University Press.

McCONKEY, B., FRASER, G. M. & BLIGH, A. S. (1965). "Transparent skin and osteoporosis—a study in patients with rheumatoid disease." *Ann. Rheum. Dis.*, **24:** 219–223.

MALINOVSKÝ, L. (1966). "Some problems connected with the evaluation of skin receptors and their classification." *Folia Morph., Prague*, **15:** 18–25.

MELZACK, R. & EISENBERG, H. (1968). "Skin sensory afterglows." *Science*, **159:** 445–447.

MELZACK, R. & WALL, P. D. (1962). "On the nature of cutaneous sensory mechanisms." *Brain*, **85:** 331–356.

RANDALL, W. C. (1946). "Sweat gland activity and changing patterns of sweat secretion on the skin surface." *Am. J. Physiol.*, **147:** 391–398.

RIDGE, M. D. & WRIGHT, V. (1966). "Rheological analysis of connective tissue—a bio-engineering analysis of the skin." *Ann. Rheum. Dis.*, **25:** 509–515.

SHEALY, C. N. (1974). "Transcutaneous electrical stimulation for control of pain." *Clin. Neurosurg.*, **21:** 269–277.

SINCLAIR, D. C. (1967). *Cutaneous Sensation*. London; Oxford University Press.

TAUB, A. (1964). "Local segmental and supraspinal interaction with a dorsolateral spinal cutaneous afferent system." *Exper. Neurol.*, **10**: 357–374.

TREGEAR, R. T. (1966). *Physical Function of Skin*. London; Academic Press.

WEDDELL, G. (1941). "The pattern of cutaneous innervation in relation to cutaneous sensibility." *J. Anat., Lond.*, **75**:346–368.

WEDDELL, G., PALMER, E. & PALLIE, W. (1955). "Nerve endings in mammalian skin." *Biol. Rev.*, **30**: 159–195.

WEST, L. J., NIELL, K. C. & HARDY, J. D. (1952). "Effects of hypnotic suggestion on pain perception and galvanic skin response." *Archiv. Neurol. Psychiat.*, **68**: 549–560.

WINKELMANN, R. K. (1960). *Nerve Endings in Normal and Pathologic Skin: Contributions to Anatomy of Sensation*. Springfield, Illinois; Thomas.

WOOLLARD, H. H., WEDDELL, G. & HARPMAN, J. A. (1940). "Observations on the neurohistological basis of cutaneous pain". *J. Anat., Lond.*, **74**: 413–440.

WRIGHT, H. M. (1965). "Measurement of the cutaneous circulation." *J. Appl. Physiol.*, **20**: 696–702.

WRIGHT, H. M., KORR, I. M. & THOMAS, P. E. (1960). "Local and regional variations in cutaneous vasomotor tone of the human trunk." *Acta Neuroveg.*, **22**: 32–52.

## (b) Bones

ANDREWS, F. M. (1973). "Bone pain." *Ann. Rheum. Dis.*, **54**: 245–246.

ARNOLD, J. S. (1973). "Amount and quality of trabecular bone in osteoporotic vertebral fractures." *Clin. Endocr. Metabol.*, **2**: 221–228.

AZUMA, H. (1964). "Intraosseous pressure as a measure of hemodynamic changes in bone marrow." *Angiology*, **15**: 396–406.

BEARDWELL, A. (1969). "Familial ankylosing vertebral hyperostosis with tylosis." *Ann. Rheum. Dis.*, **28**: 518.

BICK, E. (1951). "Ring apophysis of the human vertebra." *J. Bone Joint Surg.*, **33A**: 783–787.

BLOEM, J. J. & KUYPERS, P. J. (1970). "A patient with an osteo-arthritic spur, intermittent claudication and low back pain." *J. Cardiovasc. Surg.*, **11**: 249–251.

BONE, R. C. (1974). "Evaluation and correction of dysphagia producing cervical osteophytosis." *Laryngoscope*, **84**: 2045–2050.

BORISOV, B. K. (1974). "Weight parameters of adult human skeleton." *Health Phys.*, **27**: 224–229.

BOSWORTH, D. M., FIELDING, J. W., DEMAREST, L. & BANAQUIST, M. (1955). "Spondylolisthesis: a critical review of a conservative series of cases treated by arthrodesis." *J. Bone Joint Surg.*, **37A**: 767–786.

BROWN, H. P. & WICKSTROM, J. K. (1971). "Paget's disease of the atlas and axis." *J. Bone Joint Surg.*, **53A**: 1441–1444.

CARTILIDGE, N. E. F., McCOLLUM, J. P. K. & AYYAR, R. D. A. (1972). "Spinal cord compression in Paget's disease." *J. Neurol. Neurosurg. Psychiat.*, **35**: 825–828.

CAVE, P. (1958). "Butterfly vertebrae." *Brit. J. Radiol.*, **31**: 503–506.

DOYLE, F., BROWN, J. & LACHANCE, C. (1970). "Relation between bone mass and muscle weight." *Lancet*, **1**: 391–393.

DYSON, E. D., JACKSON, C. K. & WHITEHOUSE, W. J. (1970). "Scanning electron microscope studies of human trabecular bone". *Nature*, **225**: 957–959.

EVANS, F. G. (1957). *Stress and Strain in Bones*. Springfield, Illinois; Thomas.

EVANS, F. G. & VINVENTELLI, R. (1969). "Relation of collagen fiber orientation to some mechanical properties of human cortical bone." *J. Biomechanics*, **2**: 63–71.

FROST, H. M. (1964). *The Laws of Bone Structure*. Springfield, Illinois; Thomas.

GALANTE, J., ROSTOKER, W. & RAW, R. D. (1970). "Physical properties of trabecular bone". *Calcif. Tissue Res.*, **5**: 236–246.

GARDNER, E. D. (1963). "The development and growth of bones and joints." *J. Bone Joint Surg.*, **45A**: 856–862.

KECK, S. W. AND KELLY, P. J. (1965). "The effect of venous stasis on intraosseous pressure and longitudinal bone growth in the dog." *J. Bone Joint Surg.*, **47A**: 539–544.

KINOSITA, R., OHNO, S., & BIERMAN, H. R. (1959). "Observations on regenerating bone marrow tissue *in situ*." *Proc. Amer. Ass. Cancer Res.*, **2**: 125.

KLENERMAN, L. (1966). "Cauda equina and spinal cord compression in Paget's disease." *J. Bone Joint Surg.*, **48B:** 365–370.

McNAB, I. (1964). "Acceleration injuries of cervical spine." *J. Bone Joint Surg.*, **46A:** 1797–1799.

MOFFAT, N. A. (1973). "Spondylitis following urinary tract instrumentation". *J. Urol.*, **110:** 339.

POLÁČEK, P. (1955). "Innervation of the periosteum, bone and bone marrow". *Acta Clin. Orthop. Traumatol. Česk.*, **22:** 201–203.

PUGH, J. W. (1974). "Quantitative studies of human subchondral cancellous bone. Its relationship to the state of its overlying cartilage." *J. Bone Joint Surg.*, **56A:** 313–321.

SHAW, N. E. (1963). "Observations on the intramedullary blood flow and marrow-pressure in bone". *Clin. Sci.*, **24:** 311–318.

SHIM, S. S. & PATTERSON, F. P. (1967). "A direct method of qualitative study of bone blood circulation." *Surg. Gynec. Obst.*, **125:** 261–268.

SMITH, J. W. & WALMSLEY, R. (1959). "Factors affecting the elasticity of the bone." *J. Anat.*, **93:** 503–523.

SWANSON, S. A. V. & FREEMAN, M. A. R. (1966). "Is bone hydraulically strengthened?" *Med. Biol. Eng.*, **4:** 433–438.

THOMPSON, B. H. (1974). "Dominantly inherited periodic bone pain." *Birth Defects*, **10:** 245–248.

WAGSTAFFE, W. W. (1874). "On the mechanical structure of the cancellous tissue of bone." *St. Thomas' Hosp. Rev.*, **5** (N.S.): 193–214.

WOOD, A. E. (1973). "Dietary osteomalacia and bone pain in the elderly." *J. Irish Med. Assoc.*, **66:** 241–243.

## (c) Joints

BADGLEY, C. E. (1941). "The articular facets in relation to low back pain and sciatic radiation." *J. Bone Joint Surg.*, **23A:** 481–496.

BALLER, W. ROPES, M. W. & WAINE, H. (1940). "The physiology of articular structures." *Physiol. Rev.*, **20:** 272–312.

BARNETT, C. H., DAVIES, D. V. & McCONAILL, M. A. (1961). *"Synovial Joints—Their Structure and Mechanics*. London; Longmans, Green.

BLAND, J. H. (1974). "Cholesterol in connective tissue of joints." *Scand. J. Rheumatol.*, **3**: 199–203.

BOREADIS, A. G. & GERSHON-COWEN, J. (1956). "Luschka joints of the cervical spine." *Radiology*, **66**: 181–187.

BOSSERS, G. TH.M. (1972). "Columotomy in severe Bechterew kyphosis." *Acta Orthop. Belg.*, **38**: 47–54.

CARTER, C. & SWEETNAM, R. (1958). "Familial joint laxity and recurrent dislocation of the patella." *J. Bone Joint Surg.*, **40B**: 644–648.

CARTER, C. & WILKINSON, J. (1954). "Persistent joint laxity and congenital dislocation of the hip." *J. Bone Joint Surg.*, **46B**: 40–45.

CAVE, A. J. E. (1930). "On fusion of the atlas and axis vertebrae." *J. Anat.*, **64**: 337–343.

CAVE, A. J. E. (1934). "On the occipito-atlanto axial articulations." *J. Anat.*, **68**: 416–423.

CAVE, A. J. E., GRIFFITHS, J. D. & WHITLEY, M. M. (1955). "Osteoarthritis deformans of the Luschka joints." *Lancet*, **2**: 176–179.

CEDELL, C. A. & WIBERG, G. (1970). "Long-term results of laminectomy in spondylolisthesis". *Acta Orthop. Scand.*, **40**: 773–776.

DAVIS, P. R. (1955). "The thoraco-lumbar mortice joint." *J. Anat.*, **89**: 370–377.

DAVIS, P. R. (1961). "The thoraco-lumbar mortice joint in West Africans." *J. Anat.*, **95**: 589–593.

DONISCH, E. W. & TRAPP, W. (1971). "The cartilage endplates of the human vertebral column." *Anat. Record.*, **169**: 705.

DOWSON, D. (1973). "Lubrication and wear of joints." *Physiotherapy*, **59**: 104–106.

DOYLE, J. R. (1960). "Narrowing of the intervertebral disc space in children." *J. Bone Joint Surg.*, **42A**: 1191–1200.

EMMINGER, E. (1971). "Vertebral facet joints. Facet joints and their meniscoid structures from the point of view of pathology." *3rd Int. Congr. Manual Med., Monaco.*

FISHER, A. G. T. (1923). "Some researches into the physiological principles underlying the treatment of injuries and diseases of the articulations." *Lancet*, **2**: 541–548.

FREEMAN, M. A. R. (1969). "Some mechanical properties of articular cartilage." *J. Bone Joint Surg.*, **51B**: 576.

FROMMER, J. (1975). "The study of joints in gross anatomy." *J. Dent. Educ.*, **39:** 299–300.

GARDNER, E. D. (1948). "The nerve supply of diarthrodial joints." *Stanford Med. Bull.*, **6:** 367–373.

GARDNER, E. D. (1950). "Physiology of movable joints." *Physiol. Rev.*, **30:** 127–176.

GARDNER, E. D. (1953). "Blood and nerve supply of joints." *Standford Med. Bull.*, **11:** 203–209.

GARDNER, E. D. (1953). "Physiological mechanisms in movable joints." *Amer. Acad. Orthop. Surg.*, **10:** 251–261.

GARDNER, E. D. (1954). "Physiology of the nerve supply of joints." *Bull. Hosp. Joint Dis.*, **15:** 35–44.

GARDNER, E. D. (1956). "Nerves and nerve endings in joints and associated structures of monkey (Macaca mulatta)." *Anat. Rec.*, **124.**

GARDNER, E. D. (1960). "The nerve supply of muscles. joints and other deep structures." *Bull. Hosp. Joint. Dis.*, **21:** 153–161.

GARDNER, E. D. (1963). "The development and growth of bones and joints." *J. Bone Joint Surg.*, **45A:** 856–862.

GARDNER, E. D. (1963). "Physiology of joints." *J. Bone Joint Surg.*, **45A:** 1061–1066.

GARDNER, E. D. (1969). "Pathways to the cerebral cortex for nerve impulses from joints." *Acta Anat., Basel*, **73:** 203–216.

GHORMLEY, R. K. (1933). "Low back pain with special reference to the articular facets." *J. Amer. Med. Ass.*, **101:** 1773–1777.

GLOOBE, H. & NATHAN, H. (1970). "The costovertebral joint: anatomical observations in various mammals." *Anat. Anz.*, **127:** 22–31.

GODWIN-AUSTEN, R. B. (1969). "The mechanoreceptors of the costovertebral joints." *J. Physiol.*, **202:** 737–753.

GOLDTHWAIT, J. E. & OSGOOD, R. B. (1905). "A consideration of the pelvic articulations from an anatomical, pathological and clinical standpoint." *Boston Med. Surg. J.*, 593–601; 634–638.

HELAL, B. & KARADI, B. S. (1968–9). "Artificial lubrication of joints." *Ann. Phys. Med.*, **9:** 334–340.

HOLT, P. J. L. (1969). "Joints and their diseases—management of rheumatoid arthritis." *Brit. Med. J.*, **3:** 514–518.

HOLZMANN, H. (1974). "Joint involvement in psoriasis." *Arch. Dermatol. Forsch.*, **250:** 95–107.

HORWITZ, T. & SMITH, R. M. (1940). "An anatomical, pathological and roentgenological study of the intervertebral joints of the lumbar spine and of the sacro-iliac joints." *Amer. J. Roentgenol.*, **43:** 173–186.

JANECKI, C. J., NELSON, C. S. & DOHN, D. F. (1972). "Intrasacral cyst: report of a case and review of the literature." *J. Bone Joint Surg.*, **54A:** 423–428.

KARPOVICH, P. V. HERDEN, E. L. & ASA, M. M. (1960). "Electro-goniometric study of joints." *U.S. Armed Forces Med. J.*, **11:** 424–450.

KELLGREN, J. H. (1939). "Some painful joint conditions and their relation to osteoarthritis." *Clin. Sc.*, **4:** 193–205.

MACDONALD, G. R. & HUNT, T. E. (1952). "Sacro-iliac joints." *Canad. Med. Ass. J.*, **83:** 316–319.

MCEWAN, C. (1943). "The genesis of pain from the joints." *Res. Pub. Ass. Nerv. Ment. Dis.*, **23:** 244–251.

MASI, R. (1973). "Joint scan in haemophilic arthropathy." *J. Nucl. Biol. Med.*, **17:** 104–107.

MORRIS, H. (1879). *The Anatomy of the Joints in Man.* London; Churchill.

NATHAN, H. (1959). "The para-articular processes of the thoracic vertebrae." *Anat. Rec.*, **133:** 605–618.

NATHAN, H., WEINBERG, H., ROBIN, G. C. & AVIAD, I. (1964). "The costovertebral joints: anatomical-clinical observations in arthritis." *Arthr. Rheum.*, **7:** 228–240.

OROFINO, C., SHERMAN, M. S. & SCHECHTER, D. (1960). "Luschka's joint—a degenerative phenomenon." *J. Bone Joint Surg.*, **42A:** 853–858.

POLÁČEK, P. (1954). "The innervation of fat cells of the joint capsule and its environs." *Morphol. Česk.*, **2:** 190–198.

POLÁČEK, P. (1956). "Morphological changes in the innervation of the joints in laboratory animals under experimental functional and pathological conditions." *Acta Clin. Orthop. Traumatol. Česk.*, **23:** 286–292.

POLÁČEK, P. (1966). "Receptors of the joints." *Acta Univ. Brno*, **23:** 1–107.

RADIN, E. L. (1972). "The physiology and degeneration of joints." *Seminars on Arthritis and Rheum.*, **2:** 245–257.

REICHMANN, S. (1972). "Tomography of the lumbar intervertebral joints." *Acta Radiol.*, **12:** 641–659.

REICHMANN, S. (1973). "Radiography of the lumbar intervertebral joints." *Acta Radiol.*, **14**: 161–170.

SCOTT, J. T. (1969). "Joints and their diseases—management of gout." *Brit. Med. J.*, **8**: 456–457.

SEMLACK, K. & FERGUSON, A. B. (1970). "Joint stability maintained by atmospheric pressure." *Clin. Orthop.*, **68**: 294–300.

SILBERSTEIN, C. E. (1965). "The evolution of degenerative changes in the cervical spine and an investigation into the joints of Luschka." *Clin. Orthop.*, **40**: 184–284.

SOLOMON, S. D. (1970). "Joints and joint fluid." *New Eng. J. Med.*, **282**: 1050.

STRAVINO, V. D. (1972). "The synovial system." *Am. J. Phys. Med.*, **51**: 312–320.

SWANSON, S. A. & FREEMAN, M. A. (1969). "Mechanisms of human joints." *Science J.*, **5**: 72.

TONDURY, G. (1972). "Functional anatomy of the small joints of the spine". *Ann. Med. Phys.*, **15**: 173–191.

UNSWORTH, A. (1973). "Some new evidence on human joint lubrication." *Ann. Rheum. Dis.*, **32**: 587–588.

UNSWORTH, A., DOWSON, D., & WRIGHT, V. (1971). "Cracking joints." *Ann. Rheum. Dis.*, **30**: 348–358.

VAN LAERE, M., VEYS, E. M. & MIELANTS, H. (1972). "Strontium 87m scanning of the sacro-iliac joints in ankylosing spondylitis." *Ann. Rheum. Dis.*, **31**: 201–206.

WILLIAMS, M. & STUTZMAN, L. (1959). "Strength variations through the range of joint motion." *Phys. Therapy Rev.*, **39**: 145–152.

WRIGHT, J. (1944). "Mechanics in relation to derangements of the facet joints of the spine." *Arch. Phys. Ther.*, **25**: 201–206.

WRIGHT, V. (1971). "The lubrication and stiffness of joints." *Mod. Trends Rheumatol.*, **2**: 30–45.

WRIGHT, V. (1972). "Joint mechanics." *Physiotherapy*, **58**: 367–370.

WRIGHT, V. & JOHNS, R. J. (1960). "Physical factors concerned with the stiffness of normal and diseased joints." *Bull. Johns Hopkins Hosp.*, **106**: 215–231.

WRIGHT, V, LONGFIELD, M. D. & DOWSON, D. (1969). "Joint stiffness: its characteristics and significance." *Biomed. Eng.*, *(Jan)*: 1–9.

WYKE, B. D. (1967). "The neurology of joints." *Ann. Roy. Coll. Surg. Eng.*, **41**: 25–50.

WYKE, B. D. (1972). "Articular neurology: a review." *Physiotherapy*, **58**: 94–99.

WYKE, B. D. & MOLINA, F. (1972). "Articular reflexology of the cervical spine." *Proc. 6th Int. Congr. Phys. Med.*, Barcelona. p. 4.

YOUNG, J. (1940). "Relaxation of the pelvic joints in pregnancy." *J. Obst. Gyn. Brit. Emp.*, **47**: 493–524.

ZACCHEO, D. & REALE, E. (1956). "Research on the articulations between the articular processes of human vertebrae." *Arch. Ital. Anat.*, **61**: 1–16.

## (d) Intervertebral Discs

ABBOTT, K. H. & RETTER, R. H. (1956). "Protrusions of thoracic intervertebral discs." *Neurology*, **6**: 1–10.

ABDULLAH, A. F., DITTO, E. W., BYRD, E. B. & WILLIAMS, R. (1974). "Extreme lateral lumbar disc herniations: clinical syndrome and special problems of diagnosis." *J. Neurosurg.*, **41**: 229–234.

ABEL, M. S. & HARMON, P. H. (1960). "Oblique motion studies and other non-myelographic roentgenographic criteria for diagnosis of traumatized or degenerated lumbar intervertebral discs." *Amer. J. Surg.*, **99**: 717–726.

ALBERT, J. (1950). "Intervertebral disc lesions in children and adolescents." *J. Bone Joint Surg.*, **32A**: 97–102.

ALLEN, K. (1952). "Neuropathies caused by bony spurs in the cervical spine with special reference to surgical treatment." *J. Neurol. Neurosurg. Psychiat.*, **15**: 20–36.

AMBRUS, L. & PAPATHEODOROU, C. (1973). "Trauma and lumbar disc herniation in childhood." *Calif. Med.*, **119**: 66–68.

AMLINSKY, J. & JELINEK, J. (1955). "Vascularisation of lumbar intervertebral discs of man." *Česk. Morfol.*, **3/4**: 358–367.

ANDERSON, T. (1967). *Debunking the Disc. Ethical Implications.* Glasgow; St. Andrews Press.

ARIMA, T. (1970). "A study on the water content in the intervertebral disc." *J. Jap. Othop. Ass.*, **44**: 571–587.

ARMSTRONG, J. R. (1964). "Lumbar disc lesions." *Physiotherapy*, **50**: 284.

ARMSTRONG, J. R. (1967). *Lumbar Disc Lesions. 3rd Ed.* Edinburgh; Livingstone.

ARONSON, H. A. & DUNSMORE, R. H. (1963). "Herniated upper lumbar discs." *J. Bone Joint Surg.*, **45A:** 311–317.

BARR, J. S. (1937). "Sciatica caused by intervertebral disc lesions." *J. Bone Joint Surg.*, **19A:** 323–342.

BARR, J. S. (1947). "Ruptured intervertebral disc and sciatic pain." *J. Bone Joint Surg.*, **29A:** 429–437.

BARR, J. S. (1951). "Protruded discs and painful backs." *J. Bone Joint Surg.*, **33B:** 3–4.

BARR, J. S., KUBIK, C. S., MOLLOY, M. K., MCNEILL, J. M., RISEBOROUGH, E. J. & WHITE, J. C. (1967). "Evaluation of end results in treatment of ruptured intervertebral discs with protrusion of nucleus pulposus." *Surg. Gynec. Obst.*, **125:** 250–256.

BARR, J. S. & MIXTER, W. J. (1941). "Posterior protrusion of the lumbar intervertebral discs." *J. Bone Joint Surg.*, **23A:** 444–456.

BARTELINK, D. K. (1957). "The role of abdominal pressure in relieving the pressure on the lumbar intervertebral discs." *J. Bone Joint Surg.*, **39B:** 718–725.

BEADLE, O. A. (1931). "The Intervertebral Discs." *M.R.C. Special Report Series, No. 161.* London; H.M.S.O.

BIDWELL, R. E. & WHITTAKER, C. K. (1968). "Herniated nucleus pulposus in a 10 year old girl." *Missouri Med.*, **65:** 113–115.

BIJILSMA, F. & PEEREBOOM, J. W. C. (1972). "The ageing pattern of human intervertebral discs." *Gerontologia*, **18:** 157–168.

BOGORODINSKI, D. K. (1974). "Neurological complications of osteochondrosis of the lower lumbar intervertebral disks." *Sov. Med.*, (Aug.): 5–9.

BORGESSEN, S. E. & VANG, P. S. (1974). "Herniation of the lumbar intervertebral disk in children and adolescents." *Acta Orthop. Scand.*, **45:** 540–549.

BRADFORD, F. K. & SPURLING, R. G. (1945). *The Intervertebral Disc.* 2nd Ed. Springfield, Illinois; Thomas.

BRAGDON, F. H. & SHAFTER, W. A. (1951). "Herniation of the lumbar intervertebral disk. A ten year follow-up study." *Penn. Med. J.*, **54:** 350–351.

BRAILSFORD, J. F. (1955). "Lesions of the intervertebral discs: some personal reflections." *Br. J. Radiol.*, **28:** 415–431.

BROWDER, J. & WATSON, R. (1945). "Lesions of the cervical

intervertebral disc: clinicopathological study of 22 cases." *N.Y. St. J. Med.*, **36**: 730–737.

BROWN, M. D. (1971). "The pathophysiology of disc disease." *Orthop. Clin. Nth. Amer.*, **2**: 359–370.

BULOS, S. (1973). "Herniated intervertebral lumbar disc in the teenager." *J. Bone Joint Surg.*, **55B**: 273–278.

BUTLER, W. F. (1963). "The annulus fibrosus of the intervertebral disc of the newborn cat." *Res. Vet. Sci.*, **4**: 454–458.

BUTLER, W. F. (1967). "Age changes in the nucleus pulposus of the non-ruptured intervertebral disc of the cat." *Res. Vet. Sci.*, **8**: 151–156.

BUTLER, W. F. (1968). "Histological changes in the ruptured intervertebral disc of the cat." *Res. Vet. Sci.*, **9**: 130–135.

CAILLIET, R. (1974). "Evaluation and management of lumbar discogenic disease." *Maryland State Med. J.*, **23**: 51–52.

CAILLIET, R. (1975). "Lumbar disc disease." *Modern Geriatrics, June:* 2–18.

CAILLIET, R. (1975). "Lumbar discogenic disease: why the elderly are more vulnerable." *Geriatrics*, **30**: 73–76.

CHRISMAN, O. D., MITTNACHT, A. & SNOOK, G. A. (1964). "A study of the results following rotatory manipulation in the lumbar intervertebral disc syndrome." *J. Bone Joint Surg.*, **46A**: 517–524.

CLOWARD, R. B. (1963). "Lesions of the intervertebral disks, and their treatment by interbody fusion methods: the painful disk." *Clin. Orthop.*, **27**: 51–77.

CLOWARD, R. B. & BUZIAD, L. L. (1952). "Discography: technique, indications and evaluation of the normal and abnormal intervertebral disc." *Amer. J. Roentgenol.*, **68**: 552–564.

COPE, J. T. & GREEN, J. P. (1972). "Lumbar disc problems." *Brit. Med. J.*, **3**: 285–286.

COPIUS PEEREBOOM, J. W. (1973). "Some biochemical and histochemical properties of the age pigment in the human intervertebral disc." *Histochemie*, **37**: 119–130.

CORNAH, M. S., MEACHIM, G. & PARRY, E. W. (1970). "Banded structures in the matrix of human and rabbit nucleus pulposus." *J. Anat.*, **107**.

COVENTRY, M. B. (1969). "Anatomy of the intervertebral disc." *Clin. Orthop.*, **67**: 9–15.

COVENTRY, M. B., GHORMLEY, R. G. & KERNOHAN, J. W. (1945).

"The intervertebral disc, its microscopic anatomy and pathology. Parts 1 and 2." *J. Bone Joint Surg.*, **27A**: 105–112; 233–247.

DEPALMA, A. F. & ROTHMAN, R. H. (1970). *The Intervertebral Disc.* Philadelphia; Saunders.

DEPALMA, A. F., ROTHMAN, R. H., LEVITT, R. L. & HAMMOND, N. S. (1972). "The natural history of severe cervical disc degeneration." *Acta Orthop. Scand.*, **43**: 392–396.

DICKSON, I. R., HAPPEY, F., PEARSON, C. H., NAYLOR, A. & TURNER, R. L. (1967). "Decrease in the hydrothermal stability of collagen on ageing in the human intervertebral disk". *Nature*, **215**: 50–52.

DIXON, A. F. (1955). "Notes on the vertebral epiphyseal discs." *J. Anat.*, **55**: 38–39.

DOLL, G. (1944). "Further notes on the structure and function of the intervertebral joints." *Brit. J. Radiol.*, **17**: 255.

DRAGIEV, M. & MILKENOV, H. (1974). "Age conditioned changes of the lumbar intervertebral disks in humans." *Folia Med. (Plovdiv)*, **16**: 126.

ECKERTS, C. & DECKER, A. (1947). "Pathological studies of the intervertebral discs." *J. Bone Joint Surg.*, **29**: 447–454.

EMME, R. E. & MURPHY, F. (1941). "Syndrome of unilateral rupture of the sixth cervical intervertebral disk with compression of the seventh cervical nerve root. A report of four cases with symptoms simulating coronary disease." *J. Am. Med. Ass.*, **121**: 1209–1214.

FITZGERALD, R. T. D. (1972). "Lumbar disc problems." *Br. Med. J.*, **4**: 116.

GOODING, C. A. & NEUHAUSER, E. B. D. (1965). "Growth and development of the vertebral bodies in the presence and absence of normal stress." *Amer. J. Roentgenol.*, **93**: 388.

GORDON, E. E. (1961). "Natural history of the intervertebral disc." *Arch. Phys. Med.*, **61**: 760–763.

GREGG, G. (1974). "The commonest lumbar disc—L3!" *Brit. J. Sports Med.*, **8**: 69–73.

HALEY, J. C. & PERRY, J. H. (1950). "Protrusions of intervertebral discs: study of their distribution, characteristics and effects on the nervous system." *Amer. J. Surg.*, **80**: 394–404.

HALL, D. A. (1973). "Protein polysaccharide relationships in tissues subjected to repeated stress throughout life. II. The intervertebral disc." *Age and Ageing*, **2**: 218–224.

HALLEN, A. (1962). "The collagen and ground substance of human intervertebral disc at different ages." *Acta Chem. Scand.*, **16:** 705–710.

HAPPEY, F., HORTON, W. G., MACRAE, T. P. & NAYLOR, N. (1955). "The human intervertebral disk." *Nature*, **175:** 1032–1033.

HARDY, W. G., LISSNER, H. R., WEBSTER, J. E. & GURDJIAN, E. S. (1958). "Repeated loading tests of the lumbar spine. A preliminary report." *Surgical Forum*, **9:** 690–695.

HARRIS, R. I. & MACNAB, I. (1954). "Structural changes in lumbar intervertebral discs: their relationship in low back pain and sciatica." *J. Bone Joint Surg.*, **36B:** 304–322.

HIRSCH, C. & NACHEMSON, A. (1954). "New observations on the mechanical behaviour of lumbar discs". *Acta Orthop. Scand.*, **23:** 254–283.

HOAG, J. M. & ROSENBERG, P. (1953). "Physics of the intervertebral disc". *J. Am. Osteopath. Assoc.*, **52:** 326–334.

HOEN, T. I., ANDERSON, R. K. & CLARE, F. B. (1948). "Lesions of the intervertebral disks". *Surg. Clin. Nth. Amer.*, **28:** 456–466.

HORTON, W. G. (1958). "Further observations on the elastic mechanism of the intervertebral disc." *J. Bone Joint Surg.*, **40B:** 552–557.

JACKSON, R. K. (1972). "Lumbar disc problem". *Br. Med. J.*, **3:** 403.

JAYSON, M. I. V. & BARKS, J. S. (1973). "Structural changes in the intervertebral disc." *Ann. Rheum. Dis.*, **32:** 10–15.

JAYSON, M. I. V., HERBERT, C. M. & BARKS, J. S. (1973). "Intervertebral discs: nuclear morphology and bursting pressures." *Ann. Rheum. Dis.*, **32:** 308–315.

JOPLIN, R. J. (1935). "The intervertebral disc: embryology, anatomy, physiology and pathology." *Surg. Gynec. Obst.*, **61:** 591–599.

KEET, P. C. (1975). "The lumbar disc and its imitators." *Sth. Afr. Med. J.*, **49:** 1169–1176.

KERR, A. S. (1972). "Problem of recurrent lumbar intervertebral disc lesion." *J. Neurol. Neurosurg. Psychiat.*, **35:** 919.

KIEFFER, S. A., STADLAN, E. M., MOHANDAS, A. & PETERSON, H. O. (1969). "Discographic anatomical correlation of development changes with age in the intervertebral disc." *Acta Radiol. (Diagn.)*, **9:** 733–739.

LANCASTER, R. P. (1954). "Some interesting and unusual disc problems." *J. Bone Joint Surg.*, **36B:** 343.

LANNIN, D. R. (1954). "Intervertebral disc lesions in the teenage group." *Minn. Med.*, **37:** 136–137.

LEVY, L. F. (1967). "Lumbar intervertebral disc disease in Africans." *J. Neurosurg.*, **26:** 31–34.

LITTLE, K. (1972). "Interaction between the intervertebral disc and vertebrae." *J. Bone Joint Surg.*, **54B:** 194.

MANDELL, A. J. (1960). "Lumbosacral intervertebral disc disease in children." *Calif. Med.*, **93:** 307–308.

MARKOLF, K. L. & MORRIS, J. M. (1974). "The structural components of the intervertebral disc: a study of their contributions to the ability of the disc to withstand compressive forces." *J. Bone Joint Surg.*, **56A:** 675–685.

MARSHALL, L. L. (1971). *The Lumbar Disc.* Angus and Robertson; Sydney.

MARTINI, G. & SARACCO, C. (1965). "Report on healing in intervertebral discopathy." *Minerva Orthop.*, **16:** 664–665.

MASSARE, C., BENOIST, M. & CAUCHOIN, J. (1973). "Diagnosis of lumbar and lumbosacral disc herniations: value of discography." *Rev. Chir. Orthop.*, **59:** 61–67.

MASSARE, C. & BERNAGEAU, J. (1972). "Indications for discography: report on 1200 discographies." *J. Radiol. Electrol. Med. Nucl.*, **53:** 429–431.

MATTHEWS, J. A. (1975). "Symposium on lumbar intervertebral disc lesions. 1. A rheumatologist's point of view." *Rheumatology and Rehab.*, **14:** 160–161.

MENELAUS, M. B. (1964). Discitis—an inflammation affecting the intervertebral discs in children." *J. Bone Joint Surg.*, **46B:** 16–23.

MIRKIN, L. (1970). "The lumbar disk on the level." *J. Bone Joint Surg.*, **52B:** 189.

MURLEY, A. H. G. (1972). "Lumbar disc problems." *Br. Med. J.*, **3:** 529.

NACHEMSON, A. (1959). "Measurement of intradiscal pressure." *Acta Orthop. Scand.*, **28:** 269–289.

NACHEMSON, A. (1960). "Lumbar intradiscal pressure: experimental studies on postmortem material." *Acta Orthop. Scand.* **43:** 1–104.

NACHEMSON, A. (1962). "Some mechanical properties of the lumbar intervertebral discs." *Bull. Hosp. Joint. Dis.*, **23:** 130–143.

NACHEMSON, A. (1963). "The influence of spinal movements on the lumbar intradiscal pressure and on the tensile stresses in the annulus fibrosus." *Acta Orthop. Scand.*, **33**: 183–207.

NACHEMSON, A. (1965). "In vivo discometry in lumbar discs with irregular nucleograms." *Acta Orthop. Scand.*, **36**: 418–434.

NACHEMSON, A. (1966). "The load on lumbar disks in different positions of the body." *Clin. Orthop.*, **45**: 107–122.

NACHEMSON, A. (1966). "Mechanical stresses on lumbar discs." *Curr. Pract. Orthop. Surg.*, **3**: 208–224.

NACHEMSON, A. (1972). "The mechanical properties of the lumbar intervertebral discs and their clinical implications." *J. Bone Joint Surg.*, **54B**: 195.

NACHEMSON, A. & ELFSTROM, G. (1970). "Intravital dynamic pressure measurements in lumbar discs: a study of common movements, manoeuvres and exercises." *Scand. J. Rehab. Med., (Suppl.)*, **1**: 3–40.

NACHEMSON, A., LEWIN, T., MAROUDAS, A. & FREEMAN, M. A. R. (1970). "In vitro diffusion of dye through the end plates and the annulus fibrosus of human intervertebral discs." *Acta Orthop. Scand.*, **41**: 589–607.

NACHEMSON, A. & MORRIS, J. M. (1963). "Lumbar discometry: lumbar intradiscal pressure measurements in vivo." *Lancet*, **1**: 1140–1142.

NACHEMSON, A. & MORRIS, J. M. (1964). "In vivo measurements of intradiscal pressure." *J. Bone Joint Surg.*, **46A**: 1077–1092.

NASHOLD, B. S. & HRUBEC, Z. (1917). *Lumbar Disc Disease: A 20 Year Clinical Follow up Study*. St. Louis; C. V. Mosby Company.

NAYLOR, A. (1958). "Changes in the human intervertebral discs with age." *Proc. Roy. Soc. Med.*, **54**: 573–576.

NAYLOR, A. (1970). "The structure and function of the intervertebral disc." *Orthopaedics (Oxford)*, **3**: 7–22.

NAYLOR, A., HAPPEY, F. & MACRAE, T. P. (1954). "The collagenous changes in the intervertebral disc with age and their effect on its elasticity: an X-ray crystallographic study." *Brit. Med. J.*, **2**: 570–573.

NAYLOR, A., HAPPEY, F., TURNER, R. L., SHENTALL, R. D., WEST, R. D. C. & RICHARDSON, C. (1975). "Enzymic and immunological activity in the intervertebral disk." *Orthop. Clin. Nth. Amer.*, **6**: 51–58.

NAYLOR, A. & SMARE, D. L. (1953). "Fluid content of the nucleus pulposus as a factor in the disk syndrome." *Brit. Med. J.*, **2:** 975–976.

ODOM, G. L., FINNEY, W. & WOODHALL, B. (1958). "Cervical disk lesions." *J. Amer. Med. Ass.*, **166:** 23–28.

PARKE, W. W. & SCHIFF, D. C. M. (1971). "Applied anatomy of the intervertebral disc." *Orthop. Clin. Nth. Amer.*, **2:** 309–324.

PEACOCK, A. (1952). "Observations on the postnatal structure of the disc in man." *J. Anat.*, **86:** 162–179.

PENNYPACKER, J. (1949). "Lesions of the lumbar intervertebral disc." *J. Bone Joint Surg.*, **31B:** 635–636.

PETERSON, H. O. & KIEFFER, S. A. (1972). "Radiology of intervertebral disk disease." *Seminars in Roentgenology*, **7:** 260–276.

PURKE, W. W. & SCHIFF, D. C. (1971). "The applied anatomy of the intervertebral disc." *Orthop. Clin. Nth. Amer.*, **2:** 309–324.

RABINOVITCH, R. (1961). *Diseases of the Intervertebral Disc and Its Surrounding Tissues.* Springfield, Illinois; Thomas.

RISSANEN, P. (1964). "Comparison of pathologic changes in intervertebral discs and interspinous ligaments of the lower part of the lumbar spine in the light of autopsy findings." *Acta Orthop. Scand.*, **34:** 51–65.

ROBERTS, F. (1944). "Nature and function of intervertebral disc." *Brit. J. Radiol.*, **17:** 54–59.

ROBLES-MARIN, J. (1974). "Study of disk nutrition." *Rev. Chir. Orthop.*, **60:** 349–363.

ROCCO, H. D. & EYRING, E. J. (1972). "Intervertebral disk infections in children." *Amer. J. Dis. Child.*, **123:** 448–451.

RONCORONI, G. (1953). "Histochemical study of the intervertebral discs." *Monit. Zool. Ital.*, **62:** 407–410.

ST. CLAIR STRANGE, J. (1966). "Debunking the disc." *Proc. Roy. Soc. Med.*, **59:** 952–956.

SASHIN, D. (1931). "Intervertebral disc extensions into the intervertebral bodies and the spinal cord." *Arch. Surg.*, **22:** 527–547.

SCOVILLE, W. B. (1966). "Types of cervical disk lesions and their surgical approaches." *J. Amer. Med. Ass.*, **196:** 479–481.

SIMEONE, F. A. (1971). "The modern treatment of thoracic disc disease." *Orthop. Clin. Nth. Amer.*, **2:** 453–462.

SMITH, J. R. & WRIGHT, V. (1958). "Sciatica and the intervertebral disc: an experimental study." *J. Bone Joint Surg.*, **40A:** 1401–1418.

SMITH, N. R. (1931). 'The intervertebral discs." *Brit. J. Surg.*, **18:** 358–375.

SOUTER, W. A. & TAYLOR, T. K. F. (1970). "Sulphated acid mucopolysaccharide metabolism in the rabbit intervertebral disc." *J. Bone Joint Surg.*, **52B:** 371–384.

STEVEN, F. S., KNOTT, J., JACKSON, D. S. & PODRAZKY, K. (1969). "Collagen-protein polysaccharide interactions in human intervertebral disc." *Biochem. Biophys. Acta*, **188:** 307–313.

SYLVEN, B. (1951). "Mucoid in discs at different ages." *Acta Orthop. Scand.*, **20:** 275.

TAYLOR, J. (1972). "Development of the intervertebral disc." *J. Bone Joint Surg.*, **54B:** 193–194.

THORNTON-BROWN, J., HANSEN, R. J. & YORRA, A. J. (1957). "Some mechanical tests on the lumbosacral spine with particular reference to the intervertebral disc." *J. Bone Joint Surg.*, **39A:** 1135–1164.

TODD, T. W. & PYLE, S. I. (1928). "Dimensions of intervertebral discs." *Am. J. Phys. Anthrop.*, **12:** 321–337.

TONDURY, G. (1955). "Anatomy and development of the spine with special reference to the changes of the intervertebral disc with age." *Schweiz. Med. Wschr.*, **85:** 825.

TROUP, J. D. G. (1961). "Disc lesion." *J. Coll. Gen. Pract.*, **4:** 101–105.

TROUP, J. D. G. (1961). "The significance of disc lesions." *Lancet*, **2:** 43–45.

TSIV'IAN, I. A. L., RAIKHINSHTEIN, V. K. H., MOTOV, V. P. (1972). "Results of the clinical study of pressure within intervertebral lumbar discs." *Orthop. Traumatol.*, **33:** 31–35.

VASILEV, V., OVCHAROV, V. & MALINOV, G. (1971). "Age-related changes in the thoracic intervertebral discs of humans." *Nauchni Tr. Vissh. Med. Inst., Sofia*, **50:** 15–24.

VIRGIN, W. J. (1951). "Experimental investigations into the physical properties of the intervertebral disc." *J. Bone Joint Surg.*, **33B:** 607–611.

VIRGIN, W. J. (1958). "Anatomical and pathological aspects of the intervertebral disc." *Indian J. Surg.*, **20:** 113–119.

WALMSLEY, R. (1953). "The development and growth of the intervertebral disc." *Edinburgh Med. J.*, **60:** 341–364.

WEISS, S. R. & RASKIND, R. (1968). "The teenage lumbar disk syndrome". *Intern. Surg.*, **49:** 528–533.

WIBERG, G. (1949). "Back pain in relation to the nerve supply of the intervertebral disc." *Acta Orthop. Scand.*, **19:** 211–221.

WILKINSON, M. (1975). "Symposium on lumbar intervertebral disc lesions. 2. A neurological perspective." *Rheum. Rehab.*, **14:** 162–163.

### (e) Ligaments, Fasciae, Aponeuroses, Cartilage and Fibro-adipose Tissues

BAILEY, H. L. & KATO, F. (1972). "Paravertebral ossification of the cervical spine." *Southern Med. J.*, **65:** 189–192.

BARNETT, C. H. (1954). "The structure and function of fibrocartilage within vertebral joints." *J. Anat.*, **88:** 363–368.

BASMAJIAN, J. V. (1961). "Weightbearing by ligaments and muscles." *Canad. J. Surg.*, **4:** 166–170.

BASMAJIAN, J. V. (1974). "The unsung virtues of ligaments." *Surg. Clin. Nth. Amer.*, **54:** 1259–1267.

BEAMER, Y. B., GARNER, J. T. & SHELDEN, C. H. (1973). "Hypertrophied ligamentum flavum: clinical and surgical significance." *Arch. Surg.*, **106:** 289–292.

BEATTY, R. A., SUGAR, O. & FOX, T. A. (1968). "Protrusion of the posterior longitudinal ligament simulating herniated lumbar intervertebral disc." *J. Neurol. Neurosurg. Psychiat.*, **31:** 61–66.

BECK, W. C. & BERHEISER, S. (1954). "Prominent costal cartilages (Tietze's syndrome)." *Surgery*, **35:** 762–765.

BILLEWICZ, W. Z., KEMSLEY, W. F. F. & THOMSON, A. M. (1962). "Indices of adiposity". *Br. J. Prev. Soc. Med.*, **16:** 183–188.

BONJEAN, DE JUSSIEU & BISCH (1955). "A previously undescribed ligament of the sacro-iliac joint." *J. Med. Bordeaux*, **132:** 597–599.

BREIDAHL, P. (1969). "Ossification of the posterior longitudinal ligament in the cervical spine: 'The Japanese disease' occurring in patients of British descent." *Australas. Radiol.*, **13:** 311–313.

BROWN, H. A. (1937). "Low back pain, with special reference to dislocation of intervertebral disc and hypertrophy of ligamentum flavum." *West. J. Surg.*, **45:** 527–531.

BURMAN, M. (1952). "Tear of the sacrospinous and sacrotuberous ligaments." *J. Bone Joint Surg.*, **34A:** 331–339.

DUNCAN, A. W. (1973). "Calcification of the anterior longitudinal vertebral ligaments in Hodgkin's disease." *Clin. Radiol.*, **24:** 394–396.

EPSTEIN, B. S. (1966). "An anatomic, myelographic and cinemyelographic study of the dentate ligaments." *Amer. J. Roentgenol.*, **98:** 704–712.

EVANS, J. H. (1969). "Biochemical study of human ligamentum flavum." *J. Anat.*, **105:** 188–189.

FIELDING, J. W. (1974). "Tears of the transverse ligament of the atlas: a clinical and biochemical study." *Br. J. Radiol.*, **47:** 1683–1691.

FORCIER, P. & HORSEY, W. J. (1970). "Calcification of the posterior longitudinal ligament at the thoracolumbar junction." *J. Neurosurg.*, **6:** 684–685.

GERRIER, Y. & COLIN, R. (1954). "Occipital pains: the role of the second cervical nerve and the dentate ligament." *Montpellier Med.*, **46:** 151–153.

GOLUB, B. S. & SILVERMAN, B. (1969). "Transforaminal ligaments of the lumbar spine." *J. Bone Joint Surg.*, **51A:** 947–956.

HIRAMATUS, Y. & NOBECHI, T. (1971). "Calcification of the posterior longitudinal ligament of the spine among Japanese." *Radiology*, **100:** 307–312.

HIRSCH, C., PAULSON, S., SYLVEN, B. & SNELLAN, O. (1953). "Biophysical and physiological investigations on cartilage and other mesenchymal tissues. VI. Characteristics of human nuclei pulposi during ageing." *Acta Orthop. Scand.*, **22:** 175–183.

HO, R. W. & CHACE, J. A. (1959). "Lumbar facet study." *J. Amer. Osteopath. Ass.*, **59:** 257–265.

INOUE, H. (1973). "Three dimensional observation of collagen framework of intervertebral discs in rats, dogs and humans." *Arch. Histol. Jap.*, **36:** 39–56.

KOCZOCIK-PRZEDLEPSKA, J., SWIDERSKI, G., WALSKI, A., GRUSZCYNSKI, W. & KOWALSKA, H. (1973). "Electromyographic and thermometric studies and assessment of motor and sensory excitability in patients with low back pains." *Pol. Tyg. Lek.*, **28:** 315–317.

KOHLER, R. (1962). "Contrast examination of lumbar interspinous ligaments." *Acta Orthop. Scand.* (Suppl. **55**): 1.

KORR, I. M., WRIGHT, H. M. & THOMAS, P. E. (1961). "Effects of experimental myofascial insults on cutaneous pattern of sympathetic activity in man." *Acta Neurovegetativa*, **23:** 329–355.

KRAFT, G. L. & LEVINTHAL, D. H. (1951). "Facet synovial impingement: new concept in etiology of lumbar vertebral derangement." *Surg. Gynec. Obst.*, **93**: 439–443.

LENOCH, F. (1970). "Disturbances of nourishment of the articular cartilage and its relation to the development of osteo-arthritis." *Rev. Czech. Med.*, **16**: 113–117.

LEWIT, K. (1971). "Ligament pain and anteflexion headache." *Europ. Neurol.*, **5**: 365–378.

LUDWIG, K. S. (1952). "The alar ligament of the odontoid process in man." *Zeit. Anat. Entwgesch.*, **116**: 442–444.

MEACHIM, G. (1972). "Meshwork patterns in the ground substance of articular cartilage and nucleus pulposus." *J. Anat.*, **111**: 219–227.

MENDELSOHN, R. A. & SOLA, A. (1958). "Electromyography in herniated lumbar discs." *Arch. Neurol.*, **79**: 142–145.

MENSOR, M. C. & FENDER, F. A. (1941). "The ligamentum flavum: its relationship to low back pain." *Surg. Gynec. Obst.*, **73**: 822–827.

MUKHERJEE, D. P. (1974). "The physical properties and molecular structure of ligamentum nuchae elastin." *Biomed. Eng.*, **13**: 2447–2459.

MULLIGAN, J. H. (1957). "The innervation of the ligaments attached to the bodies of the vertebrae." *J. Anat.*, **91**: 455–463.

NACHEMSON, A. L. & EVANS, J. H. (1968). "Some mechanical properties of the third human lumbar interlaminar ligament." *J. Biomechanics*, **1**: 211–220.

NAFFZIGER, H. C., INMAN, V. & SAUNDERS, J. B. DE CM. (1938). "Lesions of intervertebral disc and ligamenta flava: clinical and anatomical studies." *Surg. Gynec. Obst.*, **66**: 288–299.

NAGASHIMO, G. (1972). "Cervical myelopathy due to ossification of the posterior longitudinal ligament." *J. Neurosurg.*, **37**: 653–660.

NAKAJIMA, H. (1969). "A study on the dynamic aspect of facet syndrome with consideration for therapy." *J. Jap. Orthop. Ass.*, **43**: 629–643.

NAKANISHI, T. (1974). "Symptomatic ossification of the posterior longitudinal ligament of the cervical spine." *Neurology*, **24**: 1139–1143.

NAKANISHI, T., MANNEN, T. & TOYOKURA, Y. (1973). "Asymptomatic ossification of the posterior longitudinal ligament of the

81

cervical spine: incidence and roentgenographic findings." *J. Neurol. Sci.*, **19:** 375–381.

OPPENHEIMER, A. (1937). "Diseases affecting the intervertebral foramina." *Radiology*, **28:** 582–592.

OPPENHEIMER, A. (1938). "Diseases of the apophyseal articulations." *J. Bone Joint Surg.*, **20A:** 285–312.

OPPENHEIMER, A. (1941). "Longitudinal fissures in vertebral articular processes." *J. Bone Joint Surg.*, **23A:** 280–282.

PALACIOS, E., BRACKETT, C. E. & LEARY, D. J. (1971). "Ossification of the posterior longitudinal ligament associated with a herniated intervertebral disc." *Radiol.*, **100:** 313–314.

PERCY-LANCASTER, R. (1969). "Pelvic arthopathy." *Sth. Afr. Med. J.*, **43:** 551–557.

PICKETT, J. C. (1941). "Role of fascia in low back pain." *South Surg.*, **10:** 738–746.

POPOVA-LATKINA, N. V. (1956). "Development of intervertebral cartilages in the embryonal period in man." *Trud. Astrakh. Med. Inst.*, **12:** 9–18.

PUTTI, V. & LOGROSCINO, D. (1938). "Anatomy of vertebral apophyseal arthritis." *Chir. Org. Movimento*, **22:** 317–353.

RADIN, E. L., PAUL, I. L., SWANN, D. A. *et al.* (1971). "Lubrication of synovial membrane." *Ann. Rheum. Dis.*, **30:** 322–325.

RALSTON, H. J., MILLER, M. R. & KASAHARA, M. (1960). "Nerve endings in the human fasciae, tendons, ligaments, periosteum and joint synovial membrane." *Anat. Rec.*, **136:** 137–148.

RAMANI, P. S. (1975). "Role of ligamentum flavum in the symptomatology of prolapsed lumbar intervertebral discs." *J. Neurol. Neurosurg. Psychiat.*, **38:** 550–557.

RAMSEY, R. H. (1966). "The anatomy of the ligamenta flava." *Chir. Orthop.*, **44:** 129–140.

RISSANEN, P. (1960). "The surgical anatomy and pathology of the supraspinous and interspinous ligaments of the lumbar spine with special reference to ligament ruptures." *Acta Orthop.* Scand. (Suppl. **46**): 1–100.

RISSANEN, P. (1962). " 'Kissing-spine' syndrome in the light of autopsy findings." *Acta Orthop. Scand.*, **32:** 132–139.

RISSANEN, P. (1964). "Comparison of pathologic changes in intervertebral disc and interspinous ligaments of the lower part of the lumbar spine in the light of autopsy findings." *Acta Orthop. Scand.*, **34:** 54–65.

ROOFE, P. G. (1940). "Innervation of annulus fibrosus and posterior longitudinal ligament." *Arch. Neurol. Psychiat.*, **44:** 100–103.

SAPPEY, P. (1866). "Studies of the vessels and nerves of fibrous and fibro–cartilaginous tissues." *Compt. Rend. Acad. Sci.*, **62:** 116–118.

SCAPINELLI, R. (1960). "The interspinous ligaments of man and their apophyseal attachments: structural changes in relation to age." *Archiv. Ital. Anat.*, **65:** 364–416.

SHEALY, C. N. (1974). "The role of the spinal facets in back and sciatic pain." *Headache*, **14:** 101–104.

SHEALY, C. N. (1974). "Facets in back and sciatic pain." *Minn. Med.*, **57:** 199–203.

SILVER, P. H. S. (1954). "Direct observations on changes in tension in the supraspinous and interspinous ligaments during flexion and extension of the vertebral column in man." *J. Anat.*, **88:** 550–551.

SINCLAIR, D. C., FEINDEL, W. H., WEDDELL, G. & FALCONER, M. A. (1948). "The intervertebral ligaments as a source of referred pain." *J. Bone Joint Surg.*, **30B:** 514–521.

SINGH, S. (1965). "Variations of the superior articular facets of atlas vertebrae." *J. Anat.*, **99:** 565–571.

STILWELL, D. L. (1957). "The innervation of tendons and aponeuroses." *Amer. J. Anat.*, **100:** 289–317.

STILWELL, D. L. (1957). "Regional variations in the innervation of deep fasciae and aponeuroses." *Anat. Rec.*, **127:** 635–653.

STOFFT, E. (1971). "Dimensions of the intervertebral joints in man and animals." *Verh. Anat. Ges.*, **66:** 489–497.

STOFFT, E. (1973). "The morphology of the suspensory apparatus of the spinal cord in the cervical region of the vertebral column." *Radiologie*, **13:** 531–540.

STOFFT, E., WIEBECKE, K. & MULLER, G. (1969). "Flaval ligaments of the human spine." *Verh. Anat. Ges.*, **63:** 363–371.

SYLVEN, B., POULSON, J., HIRSCH, C. & SNELLMAN, O. (1951). "Biophysical and physiological investigation on cartilage and other tissues." *J. Bone Joint Surg.*, **33A:** 333–340.

TRACZUK, H. (1968). "Tensile properties of human lumbar longitudinal ligaments." *Acta Orthop. Scand. (Suppl. 115)*: 9–19; 44–69.

TRAVELL, J. & RINZLER, S. H. (1952). "The myofascial genesis of pain." *Postgrad. Med.*, **11:** 425:434.

TRIAS, A. (1961). "Effects of persistent pressure on the articular cartilage." *J. Bone Joint Surg.*, **43B:** 376–386.

Voss, A. C. (1972). "Ossification of the ligamentum flavum." *Fortschr. Röntgenstr.*, **117:** 226–227.

WATERS, R. L. & MORRIS, J. M. (1973). "An *in vitro* study of normal and scoliotic interspinous ligaments." *J. Biomechanics*, **6:** 343–348.

WEIGHTMAN, B. O., FREEMAN, M. A. R. & SWANSON, S. A. (1973). "Fatigue of articular cartilage." *Nature*, **244:** 303–304.

WEISL, H. (1952). "The ligaments of the sacro-iliac joint examined with particular reference to their function." *Acta Anat.*, **20:** 201–213.

WEISL, H. (1954). "The articular surfaces of the sacro-iliac joint and their relation to the movement of the sacrum." *Acta Anat.*, **22:** 1–14.

WHITNEY, C. (1926). "Asymmetry of vertebral articular processes and facets." *Amer. J. Phys. Anthrop.*, **9:** 451–455.

## (f) Muscles and Tendons

ADAMS, R. D. (1969). "Pathological reactions of the skeletal muscle fibre in man." In *Disorders of Voluntary Muscle*. 2nd Ed. pp. 143–202. Ed. by J. N. Walton. London; Churchill.

ADRIAN, E. D. (1925). "The spread of activity in the tenuissimus of the cat and in other complex muscles." *J. Physiol.*, **60:** 301–315.

ALLEN, C. E. L. (1948). "Muscle action potentials used in the study of dynamic anatomy." *Br. J. Phys. Med.*, **11:** 66–73.

ALSTON, W., CARLSON, K. E., FELDMAN, D. J., GRIMM, Z. & GERONTINOS, E. (1966). "A quantitative study of muscle factors in the chronic low back syndrome." *J. Amer. Geriat. Soc.*, **14:** 1041–1047.

ANDERSON, B. J. G., JONSSON, B. & ORTENGREN, B. (1974). "Myoelectric activity in individual lumbar erector spinae muscles in sitting. A study with surface and wire electrodes." *Scand. J. Rehab. Med.*, **3:** 91–108.

ANDREW, B. L. (1966). *Control and Innervation of the Skeletal Muscle*. Edinburgh; Livingstone.

ANSARI, K. A., WEBSTER, D. & MANNING, N. (1972). "Spasmodic torticollis and L-dopa." *Neurology*, **22:** 670–674.

BARNETT, C. H. & COBBOLD, A. F. (1969). "Muscle tension and joint mobility." *Ann. Rheum. Dis.*, **28**: 652–654.

BASMAJIAN, J. V. (1960). "Electromyography of postural muscles." *Anat. Rec.*, **136**: 160.

BASMAJIAN, J. V. (1961). "Weightbearing by ligaments and muscles." *Canad. J. Surg.*, **4**: 166–170.

BASMAJIAN, J. V. (1974). *Muscles Alive: Their Functions Revealed by Electromyography.* 3rd Ed. Baltimore; Williams and Wilkins.

BEARN, J. (1961). "Function of certain shoulder muscles in posture and in holding weights." *Ann. Phys. Med.*, **6**: 100–104.

BEARN, J. (1961). "The significance of the activity of the abdominal muscles in weight lifting." *Acta Anat.*, **45**: 83–89.

BEARN, J. G. (1961). "An electromyographic study of the trapezius, deltoid, pectoralis major, biceps and triceps muscles during static loading of the upper limb." *Anat. Rec.*, **140**: 103–107.

BEEVOR, C. (1904). *Croonian Lectures on Muscular Movements.* London; Macmillan.

BENTELEV, A. (1961). "Changes in tone of the spinal muscles in man." *Sechenor Physiol. J.*, **47**: 393–398.

BORS, E. (1926). "The numerical relationships between nerves and muscle bundles." *Anat. Anz.*, **60**: 415–416.

BRENDSTRUP, P., JESPERSEN, K. & ASBOE-HANSEN, G. (1957). "Morphological and chemical tissue changes in fibrositic muscles." *Ann. Rheum. Dis.*, **16**: 438–440.

BUCHTHAL, F., GULD, C. & ROSENFALCK, P. (1954). "Action potential parameters in normal human muscle and their dependence on physical variables." *Acta Physiol. Scand.*, **32**: 200–218.

BUCHTHAL, F. & MADSEN, A. (1950). "Synchronous activity in normal and atrophic muscles." *Electroenceph. Clin. Neurophysiol.*, **2**: 425–444.

BUCHTHAL, F., PINELLI, P. & ROSENFALCK, P. (1954). "Action potential parameters in normal human muscle and their physiological determinants." *Acta Physiol. Scand.*, **32**: 219–229.

BUGYI, B. (1971). "Examination of the lower spinal musculature in heavy workers." *Int. Arch. Arbeitsmed.*, **28**: 265–270.

CAILLIET, R. (1975). "Therapeutics when muscle spasm strikes your patients." *Patient Care*: 4–15.

CAMPBELL, E. D. R. & GREEN, B. A. (1965). "An attempt to

measure spasticity objectively and the effect on these measurements of 'carispodal'." *Ann. Phys. Med.*, **8:** 4–11.

CAMPBELL, E. J. M., AGOSTONI, E. & NEWSOM DAVIS, J. (1970). *The Respiratory Muscles: Mechanics and Neural Control.* 2nd Ed. London; Lloyd-Luke.

CAMPBELL, E. J. M. & GREEN, J. H. (1953). "The expiratory function of the abdominal muscles in man." *J. Physiol.*, **120:** 409–418.

CASELLA, C. (1950). "Tensile force in total striated muscle, isolated fibre and sarcolemma." *Acta Physiol. Scand.*, **21:** 380–401.

CHACO, J. (1974). "Cervical spondylosis and pseudomyotonia." *Scand. J. Rehab. Med.*, **6:** 99–101.

CLEMMAESEN, M. (1951). "Some studies on muscle tone." *Proc. Roy. Soc. Med.*, **44:** 637–646.

COBB, S. (1925). "Review on the tonus of skeletal muscle." *Physiol. Rev.*, **5:** 518–550.

COOPER, S. & ECCLES, J. (1930). "The isometric responses of mammalian muscles." *J. Physiol.*, **69:** 377–385.

DEVRIES, H. A. (1965). "Muscle tonus in postural muscles." *Am. J. Phys. Med.*, **44:** 52–53.

DOYLE, F., BROWN, J. & LACHANCE, C. (1970). "Relation between bone mass and muscle weight." *Lancet*, **1:** 391–393.

EBERSTEIN, A. & GOODGOLD, J. (1968). "Slow and fast twitch fibers in human skeletal muscle." *Amer. J. Physiol.*, **215:** 535–541.

EBLE, J. N. (1961). "Reflex relationships of paravertebral muscles." *Amer. J. Physiol.*, **200:** 939–943.

ECCLES, J. C. & SHERRINGTON, C. S. (1930). "Number and contraction values of individual motor units examined in some muscles of the limbs." *Proc. Roy. Soc.*, **106B:** 326–357.

EDWARDS, R. G. & LIPPOLED, O. C. J. (1956). "The relation between force and integrated electrical activity in fatigued muscle." *J. Physiol.*, **132:** 677–681.

ELFTMAN, H. (1939). "The function of muscles in locomotion." *Am. J. Physiol.*, **125:** 357–366.

ELFTMAN, H. (1966). "Biomechanics of muscle, with particular application to studies of gait." *J. Bone Joint Surg.*, **48A:** 363–377.

ETEMADI, A. A. (1963). "Observations on the musculature and innervation of the human back." *M. Sc. Thesis—University of London.*

ETEMADI, A. A. (1974). "Extensor power of different parts of the erector spinae musculature in man." *Anat. Anz.*, **135:** 164–177.

FLOYD, W. F. & SILVER, P. H. S. (1951). "Function of erector spinae in flexion of the trunk". *Lancet*, **1:** 133–134.

FLOYD, W. F. & SILVER, P. H. S. (1951). "Further observations concerning erector spinae function in trunk flexion." *J. Anat.*, **85:** 433.

FLOYD, W. F. & SILVER, P. H. S. (1952). "Patterns of muscle activity in posture and movement." *Physiotherapy*, **45.**

FLOYD, W. F. & SILVER, P. H. S. (1955). "The function of the erector spinae muscles in certain movements and postures in man." *J. Physiol.*, **129:** 184–203.

FOUNTAIN, F. P., MINEAR, W. L. & ALLISON, R. D. (1966). "Function of longus colli and longissimus cervicis muscles in man." *Arch. Phys. Med.*, **47:** 665–669.

GARDNER, E. D. (1960). "The nerve supply of muscle, joints and other deep structures." *Bull. Hosp. Joint Dis.*, **21:** 153–161.

GOLDING, D. N. (1975). "The musculoskeletal features of Wilson's disease: a clinical, radiological and serological surgery." *Ann. Rheum. Dis.*, **34:** 201.

HAFNER, R. H. V. (1952). "The relation of the hamstring muscles and movements of the spine." *Proc. Roy. Soc. Med.*, **45:** 139–142.

HARDY, R. H. (1959). "A method of studying muscular activity during walking." *Med. Biol. Illustr.*, **9:** 158–163.

HEEROLL-NIELSEN, K. (1964). "Muscular asymmetry in normal young men." *Danish Nat. Ass. Infantile Paralysis. Comm. No. 78.*

HELLEBRANDT, P. A. (1939). "Variations in intramuscular pressure during postural and phasic contractions of human muscle." *Am. J. Physiol.*, **126:** 247–253.

HELLEBRANDT, P. A. & HOLTZ, S. J. (1956). "Mechanisms of muscle training in man." *Phys. Ther. Rev.*, **36:** 371–383.

HENCHE, P. (1947). "Investigations on the structure and function of living, isolated cross-striated muscle fibres of mammals." *Acta Phys. Scand.*, **15** (Suppl. **48**): 1.

HILL, A. V. (1922). "The maximum work and mechanical efficiency of human muscles and their most economical speed." *J. Physiol.*, **56:** 19–41.

HILL, A. V. (1951). "The mechanics of voluntary muscle." *Lancet*, **2:** 947–951.

HOPKINS, A. P. (1974). "Spinal myoclonus." *J. Neurol. Neurosurg. Psychiat.*, **37**: 1111–1115.

HOUTZ, S. J. (1964). "Influence of gravitational forces on function of lower extremity muscles." *J. App. Physiol.*, **19**: 999–1004.

HOUTZ, S. J., LEBOW, M. J. & BEYER, F. R. (1957). "Effect of posture on strength of the knee flexor and extensor muscles." *J. Appl. Physiol.*, **11**: 475–480.

HUXLEY, A. T. & TAYLOR, R. E. (1958). "Local activation of striated muscle fibres." *J. Physiol.*, **144**: 426–441.

JOHNSON, M. A., POLGAR, J., WEIGHTMAN, D. & APPLETON, D. (1973). "Data on the distribution of fibre types in thirty-six human muscles: an autopsy study." *J. Neurol. Sci.*, **18**: 111–129.

KALDESTAD, E. (1973). "Myalgia." *J. Norweg. Med. Ass.*, **32**: 2364–2367.

KAPPLER, R. E. (1973). "Role of psoas mechanism in low-back complaints." *J. Amer. Osteopath. Ass.*, **72**: 794–801.

KARLSSON, E. & JONSSON, B. (1965). "Function of the gluteus maximus muscle." *Acta Morph. Néerl. Scand.*, **6**: 161–169.

KARPOVICH, P. V. (1965). *Physiology of Muscular Activity.* 6th Ed. Philadelphia; W. B. Saunders.

LAMY, H. (1904). "Role of the spinal muscles in normal walking in man." *Rev. Neurol., Paris*, **12**: 906–907.

LAUBACH, B. L. & MCCONVILLE, J. T. (1966). "Muscle strength: flexibility and body size of adult males." *Research Quarterly*, **37**: 384–392.

LOWMAN, C. L. (1932). "The relation of the abdominal muscles to paralytic scoliosis." *J. Bone Joint Surg.*, **14A**: 763.

MAYER, L. & GREENBERG, B. B. (1942). "Measurements of the strength of trunk muscles." *J. Bone Joint Surg.*, **24A**: 842–856.

NACHEMSON, A. (1966). "Electromyographic studies on the vertebral portion of the psoas muscle: with special reference to the stabilizing function of the lumbar spine." *Acta Orthop. Scand.*, **37**: 177–190.

NACHEMSON, A. (1968). "The possible importance of the psoas muscle for stabilization of the lumbar spine." *Acta Orthop. Scand.*, **39**: 47–57.

OKADA, M. (1972). "An electromyographic estimation of the relative muscular load in different human postures." *J. Human Ergon.*, **1**: 75–93.

OKADA, M., KOGI, K. & ISHII, M. (1970). "Loading capacity of the erectores spinae muscles in static work." *J. Anthrop. Soc. Nippon*, **78:** 99–110.

PANSINI, A. (1955). "The fine structure of the musculotendinous organs of Golgi." *Quad. Anat. Prat.*, **10:** 217.

PANSINI, F. (1888). "The terminations of nerves in tendons of vertebrates." *Boll. Soc. Nat. Napoli, (Series 1)*, **2:** 135.

PERRY, S. V. (1967). "Contractile processes in striated muscle." *J. Clin. Phys.*, **50:** 60–70.

PETERSEN, I. & KUGELBERG, E. (1949). "Duration and form of action potential in normal human muscle." *J. Neurol. Neurosurg. Psychiat.*, **12:** 124–128.

PHALEN, G. S. & DICKSON, J. A. (1961). "Spondylolisthesis and tight hamstrings." *J. Bone Joint Surg.*, **43A:** 505–512.

RAPER, A. J., THOMPSON, W. T., SHAPIRO, W. & PATTERSON, J. L. (1966). "Scalene and sternomastoid muscle function." *J. Appl. Physiol.*, **21:** 497–502.

RETSLAFF, E. W. (1974). "The piriformis muscle syndrome." *J. Am. Osteopath. Ass.*, **73:** 799–807.

SIMON, W. H. (1975). "Soft tissue disorders of the shoulder. Frozen shoulder, calcific tendinitis and bicipital tendinitis." *Orthop. Clin. Nth. Amer.*, **6:** 521–539.

SIMONS, D. J., DAY, E., GOODELL, H. & WOOLFF, H. G. (1943). "Experimental studies on headache: muscles of the scalp and neck as sources of pain." *Res. Pub. Assoc. Nerv. Ment. Dis.*, **23:** 228–244.

SLIJPER, E. J. (1946). "The vertebral column and spinal musculature of mammals." *Verh. Aked. Wet.*, **42:** 1.

STILWELL, D. L. (1957). "The innervation of tendons and aponeuroses." *Amer. J. Anat.*, **100:** 289–317.

VOSS, H. (1963). "Studies of the absolute and relative numbers of muscle spindles in developing muscle groups (scalene and spinal muscles) in man." *Anat. Anz.*, **112:** 276–279.

WEBER, A., HERZ, R. & REISS, I. (1963). "On the mechanism of the relaxing effect of fragmented saxoplasmic reticulum." *J. Gen. Physiol.*, **46:** 679–702.

WIRSCHING, B. (1972). "Structure and function of the prevertebral and hyoid musculature." *Arch. Orthop. Unfall-Chir.*, **73:** 286–307.

ZELLWEGER, K. (1972). "Spinal muscular atrophy with autosomal dominant inheritance." *Neurology*, **22:** 957.

## (g) Meninges and Cerebrospinal Fluid

BENINI, A. (1973). "The vertical course of lumbar and sacral nerve roots as a cause of sciatica." *Neurochirurgia*, **16:** 1–8.

BERNELL, W. R., KEPES, J. J. & CLOUGH, C. A. (1973). "Subarachnoid haemorrhage from malignant schwannoma of cauda equina." *Texas Med.*, **69:** 101–104.

BORGESEN, S. E. & VANG, P. S. (1973). "Extradural pseudocysts: a cause of pain after lumbar disc operation." *Acta Orthop. Scand.*, **44:** 12–20.

BORGHI, G. (1973). "Extradural spinal meningiomas." *Acta Neurochir.*, **29:** 195–202.

BRIDGE, C. J. (1959). "Innervation of spinal meninges and epidural structures." *Anat. Rec.*, **133:** 553–562.

BURKE, W. J. (1973). "A case of cauda equina tumour presenting with stupor and papilloedema." *Proc. Austr. Assoc. Neurol.*, **9:** 95–97.

DU BOULAY, G. (1966). "Pulsatile movements in the cerebrospinal fluid pathways." *Brit. J. Radiol.*, **39:** 255–262.

DU BOULAY, G. (1972). "Further investigations on pulsatile movements in the cerebrospinal fluid pathways." *Acta Radiol.*, **13:** 496–523.

FRASER, A. R. A., RATZAN, K., WOLPERT, S. M. & WEINSTEIN, L. (1973). "Spinal subdural empyema." *Arch. Neurol.*, **28:** 235–238.

GILLAND, O., TOURTELLOTTE, W. W., O'TAUMA, L. & HENDERSON, W. G. (1974). "Normal cerebrospinal fluid pressure." *J. Neurosurg.*, **40:** 587–593.

GOMEZ, D. G. (1974). "The spinal cerebrospinal fluid absorptive pathways." *Neuroradiol.*, **8:** 61–66.

GORDON, S. L. & YUDELL, A. (1973). "Cauda equina lesion associated with rheumatoid spondylitis." *Ann. Intern. Med.*, **78:** 555–557.

GRUMME, T., BINGAS, B. & KNUPLING, R. (1972). "Meningocoele after lumbar intervertebral disc operations." *Acta Neurochir.*, **27:** 177–187.

HALABURT, H. (1973). "Leptomeningeal changes following lumbar myelography with water-soluble contrast media (meglumine iothalamate and methiodal sodium)." *Neuroradiology*, **5:** 70–76.

HEILBRUN, M. P. & DAVIS, D. O. (1973). "Spastic paraplegia

secondary to cord constriction by the dura: case report." *J. Neurosurg.*, **39**: 645–647.

HEINDEL, G. G., FERGUSON, J. P. & KUMARASAMY, T. (1974). "Spinal subdural empyema complicating pregnancy: case report." *J. Neurosurg.*, **40**: 654–656.

HOWLAND, W. J. & CURRY, J. L. (1966). "Experimental studies of pantopaque arachnoiditis." *Radiol.*, **87**: 253–261.

KAPLAN, E. B. (1947). "Recurrent meningeal branch of the spinal nerves." *Bull. Hosp. Joint. Dis.*, **8**: 108–109.

KEOGH, A. J. (1974). "Meningeal reactions seen with myodil myelography." *Clin. Radiol.*, **25**: 361–365.

McLENNAN, J. E., McLAUGHLIN, W. T. & SKILLICORN, S. A. (1973). "Traumatic lumbar nerve root meningocoele: a case report." *J. Neurosurg.*, **39**: 528–532.

MARTINS, A. N., WILEY, J. K. & MYERS, P. W. (1972). "Dynamics of the cerebrospinal fluid and the spinal dura mater." *J. Neurol. Neurosurg. Psychiat.*, **35**: 468–473.

MILLER, P. R. & ELDER, F. W. (1968). "Meningeal pseudocysts (meningocele spurius) following laminectomy: report of ten cases." *J. Bone Joint Surg.*, **50A**: 268–276.

MILSOAVLJETIČ, B. & POPOVIČ, V. (1971). "Transdural herniation of arachnoid after laminectomy for protruded lumbar disc." *Minerva Neurochir.*, **15**: 100–102.

NIZZOLI, V. & TESTA, C. (1968). "A case of calcification in the spinal arachnoid giving rise to spinal cord compression." *J. Neurol. Sci.*, **7**: 381–384.

PETERSON, D. I. (1975). "Myelopathy associated with Marateaux-Larny syndrome." *Arch. Neurol.*, **32**: 127–129.

PIERCE, D. S. (1972). "Long term management of thoracolumbar fracture dislocations." *Amer. Assoc. Orthop. Surg. Instr. Course Lectures:* **21**: 102–107.

REITAN, H. (1941). "On movements of fluid inside the cerebrospinal space." *Acta Radiol. Scand.*, **22**: 762–779.

ROGOFF, E. E., DECK, M. D. F. & D'ANGIO, G. (1974). "The second sac: a complicated factor in regimens based on intrathecal medications." *Amer. J. Roentgenol.*, **120**: 568–572.

RUNTAN, H. (1941). "Movements of fluid inside the cerebrospinal space." *Acta Radiol.*, **22**: 762–779.

SEVER, L. E. (1974). "A case of meningomyelocele in a kindred with multiple cases of spondylolisthesis and spina bifida occulta." *J. Med. Genet.*, **11**: 94–96.

SUNDERLAND, S. (1974). "Meningeal neural relations in the inter-vertebral foramen." *J. Neurosurg.*, **40**: 756–763.

TARLOV, I. M. (1970). "Spinal perineural and meningeal cysts." *J. Neurol. Neurosurg. Psychiat.*, **33**: 833–843.

TRIBOLET, N. DE & OBERON, R. (1974). "Variations and anomalies of caudal cistern." *Schweiz. Med. Wschr.*, **104**: 459–464.

## (h) Nerves, Nerve Roots and Spinal Cord

ANDERSON, R. E. & SHEALY, C. N. (1970). "Cervical pedicle erosion and rootlet compression caused by a tortuous vertebral artery." *Radiology*, **96**: 537–538.

BALE, P. M. (1973). "A congenital intraspinal gastro-enterogenous cyst in diastenatomyelia." *J. Neurol. Neurosurg. Psychiat.*, **36**: 1011–1017.

BECHAR, M., BERKS, J. W. F. & PENNING, L. (1972). "Intradural arachnoid cysts with scalloping of vertebrae in the lumbosacral region: case report and review of literature." *Acta Neurochir.*, **26**: 275–283.

BENASSY, J. (1970). "Metamerical topography of the cord and its roots." *Paraplegia*, **8**: 75–79.

BENINI, A. (1973). "Vertical course of lumbar and sacral nerve roots as a cause of sciatic disorders." *Neurochirurgia*, **16**: 1–8.

BRIHAYE, J. & RETIF, J. (1969). "The monoradicular pain component in tumours of the cauda equina." *Acta Orthop. Belg.*, **35**: 679–686.

BROCHER, J. E. (1970). *"Disorders of the Spine and Their Differential Diagnosis."* Stuttgart; Thieme Verlag.

DI CHIRO, G., HARRINGTON, T. & FRIED, L. C. (1973). "Micro-angiography of human fetal spinal cord." *Amer. J. Roentgenol.*, **118**: 193–199.

DI CHIRO, G. & WENER, L. (1973). "Angiography of the spinal cord: review of contemporary techniques and applications." *J. Neurosurg*, **39**: 1–29.

EMME, R. E. & MURPHEY, F. (1941). "Syndrome of unilateral rupture of the sixth cervical intervertebral disk with compression of the seventh cervical nerve root. Report of four cases with symptoms simulating coronary disease." *J. Amer. Med. Ass.*, **121**: 1209–1214.

FOERSTER, O. (1936). "Symptomatology of disorders of the spinal cord." In *Handbuch der Neurologie.* Vol. 5. pp. 1–403. Edited by E. Bumke and O. Foerster. Berlin; Springer.

HALDEMAN, S. & MEYER, B. J. (1970). "The effect of experimental constriction on the structure of the sciatic nerve." *Sth. Afr. Med. J.*, **44**: 888–892.

HALDEMAN, S. & MEYER, B. J. (1970). "The effect of constriction on the conduction of the action potential in the sciatic nerve." *Sth. Afr. Med. J.*, **44**: 903–906.

HARRIS, W. R., WORTZMAN, G., RATHBUN, J. B. & HUMPHREY, J. G. (1973). "Lumbo-sacral nerve root avulsion." *J. Bone Joint Surg.*, **55B**: 662.

HAWK, W. A. (1936). "Spinal compression caused by ecchondrosis of the intervertebral fibrocartilage with a review of the literature." *Brain*, **59**: 204–224.

HENSON, R. A. & PARSONS, M. (1967). "Ischaemic lesions of the spinal cord." *Quart. J. Med.*, **36**: 205–222.

HERTEL, G. (1973). "The width of the cervical spine canal and the size of the vertebral bodies in syringomyelia: a statistical comparative study." *Europ. Neurol.*, **9**: 168–182.

HEWITT, W. (1970). "The intervertebral foramen." *Physiotherapy*, (August): 332–336.

HOLMES, J. & SWORN, B. R. (1946). "Lumbo-sacral root pain." *Brit. Med. J.*, **1**: 946–948.

HOLT, S. & YATES, P. O. (1966). "Cervical spondylosis and nerve root lesions." *J. Bone Joint Surg.*, **48B**: 407–423.

HORACK, H. M. (1967). "Cervical root syndrome." *Med. Clinics Nth. Amer.*, **51**: 1027–1034.

HOVELACQUE, A. (1925). "The sinu-vertebral nerve." *Ann. Anat. Path.*, **2**: 435–443.

HUTTON, S. R. (1973). "Subcutaneous lumbar 'rhizolysis'." *Med. J. Aust.*, **2**: 1027.

HYNDMAN, O. R. (1944). "Physiology of the spinal cord." *Arch. Phys. Ther.*, **25**: 123–124.

IRVING, D. (1974). "The numbers of limb motor neurones in the individual segments of the human lumbo-sacral spinal cord." *J. Neurol. Sci.*, **21**: 203–212.

JIMENEZ, J., EASTON, J. K. M. & REDFORD, J. B. (1970). "Conduction studies of the anterior and posterior tibial nerves." *Arch. Phys. Med.*, **51:** 164–169; 179.

KAISER, R. A. (1949). "Obturator neurectomy for coxalgia—an anatomical study of the obturator and the accessory obturator nerves." *J. Bone Joint Surg.*, **31A:** 815–819.

KEEGAN, J. J. (1955). "Relations of the nerve roots to abnormalities of lumbar and cervical portions of the spine." *Arch. Phys. Med.*, **36:** 246–276.

KELLY, D. L., GOLDRING, W. & O'LEARY, J. L. (1965). "Average evoked somato-sensory responses from exposed cortex in man." *Archiv. Neurol., Chicago*, **13:** 1–19.

KEON-COHEN, B. (1968). "Abnormal arrangement of the lower lumbar and first sacral nerves within the spinal canal." *J. Bone Joint Surg.*, **50B:** 261–265.

KEUTER, E. J. (1970). "Vascular origin of cranial sensory disturbances caused by pathology of the lower cervical spine." *Acta Neuroclin.*, **23:** 229–245.

KIMMEL, D. L. (1961). "Innervation of spinal dura mater and of the posterior cranial fossa." *Neurology*, **11:** 800.

KOBAYASHI, H. (1973). "Studies of symptomatology and radiology of cervical spondylotic myelopathy." *J. Jap. Orthop. Ass.*, **47:** 495–514.

KUBIK, S. (1966). "Topography of the spinal nerve roots. Part I." *Acta Anat.*, **63:** 324–345.

KUBIK, S. & MUNTENER, M. (1969). "Topography of the spinal nerve roots. Part II." *Acta Anat.*, **71:** 449–468.

KUGELBERG, E. (1946). "Injury activity and trigger zones in human nerves." *Brain*, **69:** 310–324.

LANGFITT, T. W. & ELLIOTT, F. A. (1967). "Pain in the back and legs caused by cervical spinal cord compression." *J. Amer. Med. Ass.*, **200:** 382–385.

LAZORTHES, G. (1972). "The posterior branches of the spinal nerves and the plane of the posterior vertebral joints." *Ann. Med. Phys.*, **15:** 192–202.

LINDAHL, O. (1966). "Hyperalgesia of the lumbar nerve roots in sciatica." *Acta Orthop. Scand.*, **37:** 367–374.

LINDAHL, O. & REXED, B. (1951). "Histologic changes in spinal nerve roots of operated cases of sciatica." *Acta Orthop. Scand.*, **20:** 215–225.

LOUIS, R., LAFFONT, J., CONTY, C. R. & ARGÈME, M. (1967).

"Mobility of the spinal cord." *Compt. Rend. Assoc. Anat.*, **138**: 817–827.

LUSCHKA, H. VON (1850). "*The Nerves of the Human Spinal Cord.*" Tübingen; Laupp.

MADIGAN, R. (1974). "Cervical cord compression in hereditary multiple exostosis." *J. Bone Joint Surg.*, **56A**: 401–404.

MALCOLM, D. S. (1951). "A method of measuring reflex times applied to sciatica and other conditions due to nerve root compression." *J. Neurol. Neurosurg. Psychiat.*, **14**: 15–24.

MANELFE, C., TREIL, J., LESTRADE, M., FARDOU, H. & ROULLEAU, J. (1973). "Enlargement of the anterior epidural space in relation to the lumbosacral junction: its interpretation in radiculography." *J. Radiol. Electrol. Med. Nucl.*, **54**: 864–865.

MARCHISELLO, P. M. (1975). "Comment on the 'battered' root problem." *Orthop. Clin. Nth. Amer.*, p. 309.

MARSHALL, A. (1973). "Multiple bilateral percutaneous 'rhizolysis'." *Med. J. Aust.*, **2**: 868.

MARSHALL, J. (1952). "Studies of ischaemic and postischaemic paraesthesiae in normal subjects and in sciatica." *J. Neurol. Neurosurg., Psychiat.*, **15**: 242–245.

MARTIN, S. H. & BLOEDAL, J. R. (1973). "Evaluation of experimental spinal cord injury using cortical evoked potentials." *J. Neurosurg.*, **39**: 75–811.

MARTINI, G. & SARACCO, C. (1965). "Chronaxie and accommodation in intervertebral disc disease." *Minerva Orthop.*, **16**: 664–665.

MAURICE-WILLIAMS, R. S. (1974). "Drop attacks from cervical cord compression." *Brit. J. Clin. Pract.*, **28**: 215–216.

MAYER, R. F. & MAUDSLEY, C. (1965). "Studies in man and cat of the significance of the 'H' wave." *J. Neurol. Neurosurg. Psychiat.*, **28**: 201–211.

MEHLER, W. R., FREEMAN, M. E. & NAUTA, W. J. H. (1960). "Ascending axon degeneration following anterolateral cordotomy: an experimental study in the monkey." *Brain*, **83**: 718–750.

MEINECKE, R. (1973). "The mechanism of the nerve root syndrome." *Zeit. Artztl. Fortbild.*, **67**: 908–911.

MIDDLETON, G. S. & TEACHER, J. H. (1911). "Injury of the spinal cord due to rupture of the intervertebral disc during muscular effort." *Glasgow Med. J.*, **76**: 1–6.

MIXTER, W. J. & BARR, J. S. (1934). "Rupture of the intervertebral disc with involvement of the spinal cord." *New Engl. Med. J.*, **211:** 210–214.

MIYAKAWA, T. (1974). "Ultrastructure of the sural nerve in chronic polyneurotherapy associated with Adie's syndrome." *Acta Neuropathol.*, **29:** 181–186.

MUKOYAMA, M. (1973). "Age changes in the internodal length in the human spinal roots—nerve teasing study." *Nagoya J. Med. Sci.*, **36:** 17–27.

MUNRO, D. (1961). "Treatment of fractures and dislocations of the cervical spine, complicated by cervical cord and root injuries." *New Engl. J. Med.*, **264:** 573–582.

NAGASHIMO, G. (1972). "Cervical myelopathy due to ossification of the posterior longitudinal ligament." *J. Neurosurg.*, **37:** 653–660.

NASHOLD, B. S. (1972). "The effects of stimulating the dorsal columns of man." *Med. Progr. Technol.*, **1:** 89–91.

NASHOLD, B. S., SOMJEN, G. & FRIEDMAN, H. (1972). "Paraesthesiae and E.E.G. potentials evoked by stimulation of the dorsal funiculi in man." *Exper. Neurol.*, **36:** 273–287.

NATHAN, P. W. & SMITH, H. C. (1959). "Fasiculi proprii of the spinal cord: a review of present knowledge." *Brain*, **82:** 610–668.

NIEMINEN, R. (1973). "Fractures of spinous processes of the lower cervical spine." *Ann. Chir. Gyn. Fenn.*, **62:** 328–333.

NIZZOLI, V. & TESTA, C. (1968). "A case of calcification in the spinal arachnoid giving rise to spinal cord compression." *J. Neurol. Sci.*, **7:** 381–384.

NURICK, S. (1972). "The pathogenesis of the spinal cord disorder associated with cervical spondylosis." *Brain*, **95:** 87–100.

NURICK, S. (1972). "The natural history and the results of surgical treatment of the spinal cord disorder associated with cervical spondylosis." *Brain*, **95:** 101–108.

OCHOA, J. & MAIR, W. G. P. (1966). "The normal sural nerve in man. II. Changes in the axons and Schwann cells due to ageing." *Acta Neuropath., Berlin*, **13:** 217–239.

O'CONNELL, J. E. A. (1955). "Involvement of the spinal cord by intervertebral disk protrusions." *Brit. J. Surg.*, **63:** 225–247.

OUAKINE, G. (1973). "Anastomotic connections between the eleventh nerve and the posterior root of the first cervical nerve in humans." *J. Neurosurg.*, **38:** 189–197.

OUDENHOVEN, R. C. (1974). "Articular rhizotomy." *Surg. Neurol.*, **2:** 275–278.

PALLIE, W. (1959). "The intersegmental anastomoses of posterior spinal rootlets and their significance." *J. Neurosurg.*, **16**: 188–196.

PALLIE, W. & MANUEL, J. K. (1968). "Intersegmental anastomoses between dorsal spinal rootlets in some vertebrates." *Acta Anat.*, **70**: 341–351.

PARKER, A. J. (1974). "Traumatic occlusion of segmental spinal veins." *J. Trauma*, **14**: 868–872.

PEARSON, A. A., SAUTER, R. W. & BASS, J. J. (1963). "Cutaneous branches of the dorsal (primary) rami of the cervical nerves." *Am. J. Anat.*, **112**: 169–180.

PECKER, J., SIMON, J., BOU-SALAH, A. & PIVAULT, C. (1974). "Fusion of spinal nerve roots in gun-shot wounds: diagnostic problems." *Nouv. Press. Med.*, **3**: 1155–1156.

PEDERSEN, H. E., BLUNCK, C. F.J. & GARDNER, E. (1954). "The anatomy of the lumbosacral posterior rami and meningeal branches of spinal nerves (sinu-vertebral nerves): with an experimental study of their functions.' *J. Bone Joint Surg.*, **38A**: 377–391.

PEIRIS, O. A. (1974). "Conduction in the fourth and fifth lumbar and first sacral nerve roots." *N.Z. Med. J.*, **80**: 502–503.

PEMBREY, M. E. (1972). "Discordant identical twins and neural tube defects." *Practitioner*, **209**: 709–712.

PEROVIC, M. N., KOPITS, S. E. & THOMPSON, R. C. (1973). "Radiological evaluation of the spinal cord in congenital atlanto-axial dislocation." *Radiology*, **109**: 713–716.

PINAU, H. & DELMAS, A. (1969). "Variations in the diameter of the spinal canal and variation in the number of lumbar vertebrae." *Arch. Anat. Path.*, **17**: 269–273.

POMERANZ, B. (1973). "Specific nociceptive fibers projecting from spinal cord neurones to the brain. A possible pathway for pain." *Brain Res.*, **50**: 447–451.

PRENTICE, W. B., KIEFFER, S. A., GOLD, L. A. & JOHNSON, R. G. (1975). "Myelographic characteristics of metastasis to the spinal cord and cauda equina." *Amer. J. Roentgenol.*, **118**: 681–689.

PRICE, D. D. (1975). "Spinal cord coding of graded non-noxious and noxious temperature increases." *Exp. Neurol.*, **48**: 201–221.

RALSTON, H. J. (1965). "The organisation of the substantia gelatinosa Rolandi in the cat lumbosacral cord." *Zeit. Zellforsch.*, **67**: 1–23.

RANSON, S. W. & CLARK, S. L. (1959). *The Anatomy of the Nervous System.* 10th Ed. Philadelphia: Saunders.

REES, W. S. (1975). "Multiple bilateral percutaneous rhizolisis." *Med. J. Australia*, **1**: 536–537.

REID, J. D. (1960). "Ascending nerve roots." *J. Neurol. Neurosurg. Psychiat.*, **23**: 148–155.

REID, J. D. (1960). "Effects of flexion-extension movements of the head and spine upon the spinal cord and nerve roots." *J. Neurol. Neurosurg. Psychiat.*, **23**: 214–221.

RENGACHARY, S. S., MURPHY, D. & KEPES, M. (1973). "Spondylitic cord compression with focal destructive vertebral lesions." *J. Kansas Med. Soc.*, **74**: 82–84.

REXED, B. (1944). "Contributions to the knowledge of the post-natal development of the peripheral nervous system in man." *Acta Psychiat.*, (Suppl. **33**): 1–206.

REXED, B. (1954). "A cytoarchitectonic atlas of the spinal cord in the cat." *J. Comp. Neurol.*, **100**: 297–379.

REXED, B. & WENNSTROM, K. G. (1959). "Arachnoidal proliferation and cystic formation in the spinal nerve root pouches of man." *J. Neurosurg.*, **16**: 73–84.

ROBLES, J. (1968). "Brachial plexus avulsion." *J. Neurosurg.*, **28**: 434–438.

ROMANES, G. J. (1951). "The motor cell columns of the lumbosacral spinal cord of the cat." *J. Comp. Neurol.*, **94**: 313–364.

ROSSIER, A. B., WARNER, A., SILDI, E. & BERNI, J. (1968). "Contribution to the study of the late cervical syringomyelic syndromes after dorsal or lumbar traumatic paraplegia." *J. Neurol., Neurosurg. Psychiat.*, **31**: 99–105.

ROTH, M. (1965). "Caudal end of the spinal cord. I. Normal pneumographic features." *Acta Radiol.*, **3**: 177–188.

ROTH, M. (1965). "The caudal end of the spinal cord. II. Abnormal pneumographic features: lumbar intumesence artery syndrome and spinal dysraphism." *Acta Radiol.*, **3**: 297–304.

ROTHMAN, R. H. (1975). "Comment on the 'battered root' problem." *Orthop. Clin. Nth. Amer.*, 310.

ROTHMAN, R. H., JACOBS, S. R. & APPLEMAN, W. (1970). "Spinal epidural cysts. A report of five cases." *Clin. Orthop.*, **71**: 186–192.

SALAMON, G., LOUIS, R. & GUERINEL, G. (1966). "The lumbosacral dural sheath: a radio-anatomical study." *Acta Radiol.*, **5**: 1107–1123.

SCHEIBEL, M. E. & SCHEIBEL, A. B. (1966). "Spinal motoneurones, interneurones and Renshaw cells: a Golgi study." *Archiv. Ital. Biol.*, **104:** 328–353.

SCHEIBEL, M. E. & SCHEIBEL, A. B. (1968). "Terminal axonal patterns in cat spinal cord. II. The dorsal horn." *Brain Res.*, **9:** 32–58.

SCOTT-CHARLTON, W. & ROEBUCK, D. J. (1972). "The significance of posterior primary divisions of spinal nerves in pain syndromes." *Med. J. Austr.*, **2:** 945–948.

SEARS, T. A. (1964). "The fibre calibre spectra of sensory and motor fibres in the intercostal nerves of the cat." *J. Physiol.*, **172:** 150–161.

SELECKI, B. R. (1970). "Cervical spine and cord injuries: mechanisms and surgical implications." *Med. J. Aust.*, **1:** 838–840.

SELZER, M. & SPENCER, W. A. (1969). "Convergence of visceral and cutaneous afferent pathways in the lumbar spinal cord." *Brain Res.*, **14:** 331–348.

SELZER, M. & SPENCER, W. A. (1969). "Interactions between visceral and cutaneous afferents in the spinal cord: reciprocal primary afferent fiber depolarization." *Brain Res.*, **14:** 349–366.

SEMMER, R. E. & MURPHEY, F. (1941). "The syndrome of unilateral rupture of the 6th cervical intervertebral disc with compression of the 7th cervical nerve root. Report of 4 cases simulating coronary disease." *J. Amer. Med. Ass.*, **121:** 1209–1214.

SHATSKY, S. (1974). "Spinal cord injury research." *J. Neurosurg.*, **41:** 518–519.

SIWE, S. A. (1931). "The cervical part of the ganglionated cord, with special reference to its connections with the spinal nerves and certain cerebral nerves." *Amer. J. Anat.*, **48:** 479–497.

SPRAGUE, J. M. & HA, H. (1964). "The terminal fields of dorsal root fibers in the lumbo-sacral cord of the cat, and the dendritic organization of the motor nuclei." In *Organization of the Spinal Cord.* pp. 120–152. Edited by J. C. Eccles and J. P. Schadé. Amsterdam; Elsevier.

STILWELL, D. L. (1956). "The nerve supply of the vertebral column and its associated structures in the monkey." *Anat. Rec.*, **125:** 139–169.

STOOKEY, B. (1938). "Compression of the spinal cord due to ventral extradural cervical chondromas." *Arch. Neurol. Pysch.*, **20:** 275–291

STOOKEY, B. (1940). "Compression of spinal cord and nerve roots by herniation of the nucleus pulposus in the cervical region." *Arch. Surg.*, **40**: 417–432.

SWIFT, T. R. (1970). "Involvement of peripheral nerves in radical nerve dissection." *Am. J. Surg.*, **119**: 694–698.

SYKES, M. T. (1973). "Unmyelinated fibers in the human L4 and L5 ventral roots." *Brain Res.*, **63**: 490–495.

SZENTÁGOTHAI, J. (1964). "Neuronal and synaptic arrangement in the substantia gelatinosa Rolandi." *J. Comp. Neurol.*, **122**: 219–239.

TEWNE, E. B. & REICHERT, F. L. (1931). "Compression of lumbo-sacral nerve roots of spinal cord by thickened ligamenta flava." *Ann. Surg.*, **94**: 327–336.

THAGE, O. (1965). "The myotomes L2–S2 in man." *Acta Neurol. Scand.*, **41**: 241–243.

VRETTOS, X. C. & WYKE, B. D. (1974). "Articular reflexogenic systems in the costovertebral joints." *J. Bone Joint Surg.*, **56B**: 382

WAGMAN, I. H. & PRICE, D. D. (1969). "Response of dorsal horn cells of M. Mulatta to cutaneous and sural nerve A and C fiber stimuli." *J. Neurophysiol.*, **32**: 803–817.

WATANUKI, A. (1973). "The effect of sympathetic nervous system on cervical spondylosis. An experimental study." *J. Jap. Orthop. Ass.*, **47**: 963–974.

WIBERG, G. (1949). "Back pain in relation to the nerve supply of the intervertebral disc." *Acta Orthop. Scand.*, **19**: 211–221.

WILKINSON, H. A. (1971). "Nerve root entrapment in traumatic extradural arachnoid cyst." *J. Bone Joint Surg.*, **53A**: 163–166.

WILKINSON, M. (1967). "The relationship of cervical vertebral disease to spinal cord disorder." *Modern Trends Neurol.*, **4**: 255–268.

WILSON, C. B. (1969). "Significance of the small lumbar spinal canal: cauda equina compression syndromes due to spondylosis." *J. Neurosurg.*, **31**: 499–506.

WOODHALL, B. (1947). "Anatomicophysiological aspects of injuries to the intervertebral disc." *J. Bone Joint Surg.*, **29**: 470–475.

ZULCH, K. J. (1970). "The pathogenesis of 'intermittent spino-vascular insufficiency' (spinal claudication of Déjerine) and other vascular syndromes of the spinal cord. *Vasc. Surg.*, **4**: 116–136.

## (i) Blood Vessels and Blood Supply

ABRATE, M., QUAINI, L. & BAIOTTI, G. (1967). "Rheography of the lower extremities in patients with intervertebral disc hernia." *Minerva Orthop.*, **18:** 9–11.

AHO, A. J., AURANEN, A. & PESONEN, K. (1969). "Analysis of cauda equina symptoms in patients with lumbar disc prolapse: preoperative and follow-up clinical and cystometric studies." *Acta Chir. Scand.*, **135:** 413–420.

AMATO, V. P. & BOMBELLI, R. (1959). "The normal vascular supply of the vertebral column in the growing rabbit." *J. Bone Joint Surg.*, **41B:** 782–795.

AMINOFF, M. J. (1974). "Clinical features of spinal vascular malformations." *Brain*, **97:** 197–210.

AMINOFF, M. J. (1974). "The pathophysiology of spinal vascular malformalities." *J. Neurol. Sci.*, **23:** 255–263.

AMINOFF, M. J. (1974). "The prognosis of patients with spinal vascular malformities." *Brain*, **97:** 211–218.

AMLINSKY, J. & JELINEK, J. (1955). "Vascularisation of lumbar intervertebral discs of man." *Česk. Morfol.*, **3/4:** 358–367.

ANDERSON, R. E. & SHEALY, C. N. (1970). "Cervical pedicle erosion and rootlet compression caused by a tortuous vertebral artery." *Radiology*, **96:** 537–538.

ANDERSON, R. K. (1951). "Diodrast studies of the vertebral and cranial venous systems to show their probable role in cerebral metastases." *J. Neurosurg.*, **8:** 411–422.

ARNOLDI, C. C. (1972). "Intravertebral pressures in patients with lumbar pain: preliminary communication." *Acta Orthop. Scand.*, **43:** 109–117.

ASSEM, W. M. (1974). "Late development of subclavian artery false aneurysm." *Arch. Surg.*, **109:** 844.

ATLAS, P. (1974). "Multiple anomalous venous systemic connections in a case of atrial septal defect associated with right aortic arch and spine deformities." *Cardiology*, **59:** 268–275.

BALLA, J. I. & LANGFORD, K. H. (1967). "Vertebral artery compression in cervical spondylosis." *Med. J. Aust.*, **1:** 284–286.

BARRATT, J. G. (1974). "Enlargement of cervical intervertebral foramina by coiling of the vertebral artery." *Austral. Radiol.*, **18:** 171–178.

BATSON, O. V. (1940). "The function of the vertebral veins and their role in the spread of metastases." *Annals Surg.*, **112:** 138–149.

BATSON, O. V. (1957). "The vertebral vein system." *Amer. J. Roentgenol.*, **78:** 195–212.

BATSON, O. V. (1960). "The Valsava manoeuvre and the vertebral vein system." *Angiology*, **11:** 443–447.

BEIGHTON, P. (1968). "X-linked recessive inheritance in the Ehlers-Danlos syndrome." *Brit. Med. J.*, **3:** 409–411.

BILBAO, J. M. (1975). "Compression of the cauda equina due to a necrobiotic granuloma of ligamentum flavum." *Can. J. Neurol. Sci.*, **2:** 135–138.

BILLINGS, K. J. & WERNER, L. G. (1972). "Aneurysmal bone cyst of the first lumbar vertebra." *Radiology*, **104:** 19–20.

BIRKELAND, I. W. & TAYLOR, T. K. F. (1969). "Major vascular injuries in lumbar disc surgery." *J. Bone Joint Surg.*, **51B:** 4–19.

BLAND, J. E., PERRY, M. O. & CLARK, K. (1967). "Spasm of internal carotid artery." *Ann. Surg.*, **166:** 987–989.

BLAU, J. N. & LOGUE, V. (1961). "Intermittent claudication of the cauda equina: an unusual syndrome from central protrusion of a lumbar intervertebral disc." *Lancet*, **1:** 1081–1086.

BLOEM, J. J. & KUPERS, P. J. (1970). "A patient with an osteoarthritic spur, intermittent claudication and low back pain." *J. Cardiovasc. Surg.*, **11:** 249–251.

BOHMIG, R. (1930). "The blood vessel supply to the intervertebral discs." *Archiv. Klin. Chir.*, **158:** 374.

BOUDIN, G., GODLEWSKI, S. & MARAVAL, M. (1973). "Sciatic aneurysms, or the syndrome of the 'beaten buttock'." *Sem. Hôp. Paris*, **49:** 3509–3514.

BRANEMARK, P. I. (1961). "Experimental investigation of microcirculation in bone marrow." *Angiology*, **12:**293–306.

BREE, R. L. (1974). "Extramedullary haemotopoiesis in the spinal epidural space." *J. Can. Ass. Radiol.*, **25:** 297–299.

BRISH, A., LERNER, M. A. & BRAHAM, J. (1969). "Intermittent claudication from compression of cauda equina by a narrowed spinal canal." *J. Neurosurg.*, **21:** 207–211.

BROMAG, P. R. "Spinal thrombophlebitis after hypotensive anaesthesia." *N.Z. Med. J.*, **80:** 519–520.

BROOKES, M. (1958). "The vascular architecture of tubular bone in the rat." *Anat. Rec.*, **132:** 25–47.

BROOKES, M. (1960). "Sequelae of experimental partial ischaemia of long bones of the rabbit." *J. Anat. Lond.*, **94:** 552–561.

BROOKES, M. (1960). "The vascular reaction of tubular bone to ischaemia in peripheral occlusive vascular disease." *J. Bone Joint Surg.*, **42B:** 110–125.

BROOKES, M., ELKIN, A. C., HARRISON, R. G. & HEALD, C. B. (1961). "A new concept of capillary circulation in bone cortex." *Lancet*, **1:** 1078–1081.

BROOKES, M. & HARRISON, R. G. (1957). "The vascularization of the rabbit femur and tibio-fibula." *J. Anat.*, **91:** 61–72.

BROWN-GRANT, K. & CUMMING, J. D. (1962). "A study of the capillary blood flow through bone marrow by the radio-isotope depot clearance technique." *J. Physiol.*, **162:** 21–29.

BUCKNILL, T., JACKSON, J. W., KEMP, H. B. S. & KENDALL, B. E. (1973). "Hemangioma of a vertebral body treated by a ligation of the segmental arteries: report of a case." *J. Bone Joint Surg.*, **55B:** 534–539.

BULCKLEY, B. H. (1973). "Ankylosing spondylitis and aortic regurgitation. Description of the characteristic cardiovascular lesion from study of eight necropsy patients." *Circulation*, **48:** 1014–1027.

CAUCHOIX, J., BENOIST, M. & TAUSSIG, G. (1969). "Sciatica and the syndrome of the cauda equina due to pseudo-spondylolisthesis." *Sem. Hôp. Paris*, **45:** 2017–2022.

CHAKRAVORTY, B. G. (1967). "Arterial supply of the cervical spinal cord and its relation to the cervical myelopathy in spondylosis." *Ann. Roy. Coll. Surg. Eng.*, **45:** 232–251.

CLARK, K. (1969). "Significance of the small lumbar spinal canal: cauda equina compression syndromes due to spondylosis. Part 2. Clinical and surgical significance." *J. Neurosurg.*, **31:** 495–498.

CONSTANTIN. P. & LUCRETIA, C. (1971). "Relations between the cervical spine and vertebral arteries." *Acta Radiologica*, **11.**

CROCK, H. V. (1960). "The arterial supply and venous drainage of the vertebral column of the dog." *J. Anat.*, **94:** 88–99.

CROCK, H. V., YOSHIZAWA, H. & KAMIE, S. K. (1974). "Observations on the venous drainage of the human vertebral body." *J. Bone Joint Surg.*, **55B:** 528–533.

CUMMING, J. D. (1962). "A study of blood flow through bone marrow by a method of venous effluent collection." *J. Physiol.*, **162:** 13–20.

CUMMING, J. D. & NUTT, M. E. (1962). "Bone marrow blood flow and cardiac output in the rabbit." *J. Physiol.*, **162**: 30–34.

CUTTER, I. S. & JOHNSON, C. A. (1935). "Studies on capillary fragility: a device for the study of capillary haemorrhage." *J. Amer. Med. Ass.*, **105**: 505.

DALLDORF, G. & RUSSELL, H. (1935). "Effect of cevitamic acid injections on capillary resistance." *J. Amer. Med. Ass.*, **104**: 1701–1702.

DANZIGER, J. (1973). "Arteriovenous malformation of the cervical cord." *Sth. Afr. Med. J.*, **47**: 1413–1416.

DAY, M. H. (1962). "The anatomy of the lumbosacral plexus with particular reference to the blood supply." *Ph.D. Thesis, University of London.*

DAY, M. H. (1964). "The blood supply of the lumbar and sacral plexuses in the human foetus." *J. Anat.*, **98**: 105–116.

DEPREUX, R., FONTAINE, M. & DESCAMPES, C. (1954). "Study of arterial vascularization of the spine." *Sem. Hôp. Paris*, **30** (Suppl.): 33–34.

DiCHIRO, G., HARRINGTON, T. & FRIED, L. C. (1973). "Micro-angiography of the human foetal spinal cord." *Amer. J. Roentgenol.*, **118**: 193–199.

DiCHIRO, G. & WENER, L. (1973). "Angiography of the spinal cord: a review of contemporary techniques and applications." *J. Neurosurg.*, **39**: 1–29.

DICK, W. C., JASANI, M. K. & BOYLE, J. A. (1968). "Study of capillary resistance in rheumatoid arthritis with special reference to the effects of long-term low dosage oral cortico-steroid therapy." *Acta Rheum. Scand.*, **14**: 265–275.

DILENGE, D. (1972). "Spinal angiography." *Union Med. Canada*, **101**: 1159–1163.

DILENGE, D. (1973). "An angiographic study of the meningo-rachidian venous system." *Radiol.*, **108**: 333–337.

DiPALMA, J. R. & FOSTER, F. I. (1942). "The segmental and ageing variations of reactive hyperaemia in human skin." *Amer. Heart J.*, **24**: 332–344.

DiPALMA, J. R., REYNOLDS, S. R. H. & FOSTER, F. I. (1941). "Measurement of the sensitivity of the smallest blood vessels in human skin: responses to graded mechanical stimuli in normal skin." *J. Clin. Invest.*, **20**: 333–343.

DOMMISSE, G. F. (1974). "The blood supply of the spinal cord: a critical vascular zone in spinal surgery." *J. Bone Joint Surg.*, **56B**: 225–235.

DRINKER, C. K. & DRINKER, K. R. (1916). "A method of maintaining an artificial circulation through the tibia of the dog, with a demonstration of the vasomotor control of the marrow vessels." *Amer. J. Physiol.*, **40**: 514–521.

ECKENHOFF, J. E. (1970). "The physiologic significance of the vertebral venous plexus." *Surg. Gynec. Obst.*, **131**: 72–78.

ECKENHOFF, J. E. (1971). "The vertebral venous plexus." *Canad. Anaesth. Soc. J.*, **18**: 487–495.

EDELSON, R. N., CHERNIK, N. L. & POSNER, J. B. (1974). "Spinal subdural hematomas complicating lumbar puncture: occurrence in thrombocytopenic patients." *Arch. Neurol.*, **31**: 134–137.

EHNI, G., CLARK, K., WILSON, C. B. & ALEXANDER, E. (1969). "Significance of the small lumbar spinal canal: cauda equina compression syndromes due to spondylosis." *J. Neurosurg.*, **31**: 490–519.

EPSTEIN, B. S. & DAVIDOFF, L. M. (1943). "Roentgenologic diagnosis of dilation of the spinal cord veins." *Amer. J. Roentgenol.*, **49**: 476–479.

EPSTEIN, H. C. (1970). "The vertebral venous plexus as a major cerebral venous outflow." *Anaesthesiology*, **32**: 332–342.

EVANS, W. E. (1974). "Arteriovenous fistula following disc surgery." *Vasc. Surgery*, **8**: 33–35.

FERGUSON, W. R. (1950). "Some observations on the circulation in foetal and infant spines." *J. Bone Joint Surg.*, **32A**: 640–648.

FICHERA, A. P. & CELANDER, D. R. (1969). "Effect of osteopathic manipulative therapy on autonomic tone as evidenced by blood pressure changes and activity of the fibrinolytic system." *J. Amer. Osteopathic Ass.*, **68**: 1036–1038.

FORMAN, A. R. (1975). "Ocular findings in patients with arteriovenous malformations of the head and neck." *Amer. J. Ophthalmol.*, **79**: 626–633.

FREIDBERG, G. (1973). "Cauda equina compression secondary to swollen nerve roots in narrow lumbar canal." *Lahey Clinic Fndtn. Bull.*, **22**: 65–67.

GARDNER, E. D. (1953). "Blood and nerve supply of joints." *Stanford Med. Bull.*, **11**: 203–209.

GARGANO, F. P., MEYER, J. D. & SHELDON, J. J. (1974). "Transfemoral ascending lumbar catheterization of the epidural veins in lumbar disk disease." *Radiology*, **111**: 329–336.

GEDDESM, E. W. (1970). "Complete subluxation of the fifth lumbar vertebra with cauda equina lesion." *Proc. Mine Med. Ass.*, **49**: 191–192.

GELMAN, M. I. (1974). "Cauda equina compression in acromegaly." *Radiology*, **112**: 357–360.

GILLILAN, L. A. (1970). "Veins of the spinal cord." *Neurology*, **20**: 860–868.

GLASS, B. A. & ILGENFRITZ, H. C. (1954). "Arteriovenous fistula secondary to operation for ruptured intervertebral disc." *Ann. Surg.*, **140**: 122–127.

GORDON, A. L. & YUDELL, A. (1973). "Cauda equina lesion associated with rheumatoid spondylitis." *Ann. Intern. Med.*, **78**: 555–557.

GREENWOOD, B. M. (1966). "Capillary resistance and skin-fold thickness in patients with rheumatoid arthritis—effect of corticosteroid therapy." *Ann. Rheum. Dis.*, **25**: 272–277.

GRNJA, V., ALLEN, W. E., OSBORN, D. J. & KIER, E. L. (1974). "Sacral neurofibrosarcoma: an angiographic evaluation." *J. Neurosurg.*, **40**: 767–771.

GROH, P., HOFFMAN, K. T. & SIMONIS, G. (1973). "Arteriovenous iliac fistula after lumbar spinal operations." *Zeit. Orthop.*, **111**: 224–229.

HARBISON, S. P. (1954). "Major vascular complications of intervertebral disc surgery." *Ann. Surg.*, **140**: 342–348.

HARRIS, H. A. (1941). "A note on the clinical anatomy of the veins with special reference to the spinal veins." *Brain*, **64**: 291–300.

HARZER, K. & TONDURY, G. (1966). "The behaviour of the vertebral artery in the senile cervical vertebral column." *Fortschr. Röntgenstr.*, **104**: 687–699.

HASSLER, O. (1970). "The human intervertebral disc: a microangiographical study on its vascular supply at various ages." *Acta Orthop. Scand.*, **40**: 765–772.

HASUE, M., ITO, R. & SUZUKI, N. (1972). "Circulatory dynamics of the epidural space in cervical and lumbar disk lesions." *Clin. Orth.*, **89**: 129–138.

HEINDEL, C. C. (1975). "Spinal arteriovenous malformation with hypogastric blood supply." *J. Neurosurg.*, **42**: 462–464.

HENRIQUES, C. Q. & CHIR, M. (1962). "The veins of the vertebral column and their role in the spread of cancer." *Ann. Roy. Coll. Surg. Eng.*, **31**: 1–22.

HENSON, R. A. & PARSONS, M. (1967). "Ischaemic lesions of the spinal cord." *Quart. J. Med.*, **36**: 205–222.

HERDT, J. R., SHIMKIN, P. M., OMMAYA, A. K. & DI CHIRO, G. (1972). "Angiography of vascular spinal tumours." *Amer. J. Roentgenol.*, **115**: 165–170.

HERLIHY, W. F. (1947). "Revision of the venous system: the role of the vertebral veins." *Med. J. Aust.*, **1**: 661–672.

HERLIHY, W. F. (1948). "Experimental studies on the internal vertebral venous plexus." In *Essays in Biology*, pp. 151–163. Ed. by G. Phillips. B. D. Wyke and W. F. Herlihy. Sydney; Australian Medical Publishing Company.

HERZIG, E. & ROOT, W. S. (1959). "Relation of sympathetic nervous system to blood pressure of bone marrow." *Amer. J. Physiol.*, **196**: 210.

HEWITT. R. L. (1974). "Penetrating vascular injuries of the thoracic outlet." *Surgery*, **76**: 715–722.

HOLSCHER, E. C. (1968). "Vascular and visceral injuries during lumbar disc surgery." *J. Bone Joint Surg.*, **50A**: 383–393.

HORTON, R. E. (1961–62). "Arteriovenous fistula following operation for prolapsed intervertebral disc." *Brit. J. Surg.*, **49**: 77–80.

HUTCHINSON, E. C. & YATES, P. O. (1956). "The cervical portion of the vertebral artery." *Brain*, **79**: 319–331.

JENNET, W. B. (1956). "Study of 25 cases of compression of the cauda equina by prolapsed intervertebral discs." *J. Neurol. Neurosurg. Psychiat.*, **19**: 109–116.

JOFFE, R., APPLEBY, A. & ARJONA, V. (1966). "Intermittent ischaemia of the cauda equina due to stenosis of the lumbar canal." *J. Neurol. Neurosurg. Psychiat.*, **29**: 315–318.

JOHNSON, R. W. (1927). "A physiological study of the blood supply of the diaphysis." *J. Bone Joint Surg.*, **9**: 153–184.

KARMINSKI, J., KARMINSKA, W., STOKOLOSA, E. & BLUSZCS, A. (1973). "Studies of the blood vessels of the ischiadic nerve in human fetuses." *Folia morph.*, **32**: 323–330.

KAVANAGH, G. J., SVIEN, H. J. & HOLMAN, C. B. (1968). "Pseudo-claudication syndrome produced by compression of the cauda equina." *J. Amer. Med. Ass.*, **206**: 2477–2481.

KECK, S. W. & KELLY, P. J. (1965). "The effect of venous stasis on

intraosseous pressure and longitudinal bone growth in the dog."
*J. Bone Joint Surg.*, **47A**: 539–544.

KENDALL, B. E. & ANDREW, J. (1972). "Neurogenic intermittent claudication associated with aortic seal from the anterior spinal artery complicating coarctation of the aorta: case report." *J. Neurosurg.*, **37**: 89–94.

KERY, L., VISKELETY, T. & WOUTERS, H. W. (1971). "Experimental studies of the effect of venous stasis on bone, cartilage and the intervertebral disc." *Rev. Chir. Orthop.*, **57**: 99–108.

KEUTER, E. J. (1970). "Vascular origin of cranial sensory disturbances caused by pathology of the lower cervical spine." *Acta Neuroclin.*, **23**: 229–245.

KINOSITA, R., OHNO, S. & BIERMAN, H. R. (1959). "Observations of regenerating bone marrow tissue in situ." *Proc. Amer. Ass. Cancer Res.*, **2**: 125.

KINSELLA, T. D. (1974). "Cardiovascular manifestations of ankylosing spondylitis." *Can. Med. Ass. J.*, **111**: 1309–1311.

KLENERMAN, L. (1966). "Cauda equina and spinal cord compression in Paget's disease." *J. Bone Joint Surg.*, **48B**: 365–370.

LABAN, M. N., JOHNSON, H. E. & VERDON, T. A. JR. (1969). "Blood volume following spinal cord injury." *Arch. Phys. Med. Rehab.*, **50**: 439–441.

LACAPERE, J., DRIEUX, H. & KRIEGEL, A. (1952). "Vascularisation of the vertebral body." *Rev. Rheum.*, **19**: 477–482.

LEBKOWSKI, J., POLOCKI, B., BORUCKI, Z., DUDEK, H., SZPAKOWICS, P. & TOMCZYK, H. (1973). "Determination of the level of prolapsed intervertebral disk in ischialgia by means of an electric thermometer." *Pol. Tyg. Lek.*, **28**: 907–908.

LEPAGE, J. R. (1974). "Transferred ascending lumbar catheterization of the epidural veins." *Radiology*, **111**: 337–339.

LOGINOVA, I. (1971). "Comparative characteristics of blood supply to vertebral venous plexuses in man and dog." *Arkh. Anat. Gi. Tol. Embriol.*, **59**: 50–55.

LOMOREUX, J. (1975). "Cervical venous reflex: a normal variant of radionuclide cerebral blood flow study in nuclear medicine." *Amer. J. Roentgenol., Radium Ther. Nucl. Med.*, **124**: 276–280.

LOWMAN, R. M., GRNJA, V., PECK, D. R., OSBORN, D. & LOVE, L. (1972). "The angiographic patterns of the primary retroperitoneal tumours: the role of the lumbar arteries." *Radiology*, **104**: 259–268.

McAllister, V. L. (1975). "Symptomatic vertebral haemangiomas." *Brain*, **98:** 71–80.

McCue, C. M. (1973). "Cervical aortic arch." *Amer. J. Child.*, **125:** 738–742.

MacNab, I. (1958). "The blood supply of tubular and cancellous bone." *J. Bone Joint Surg.*, **40A:** 1433–1434.

Martin, V. M. (1973). "Lymphosarcomatous arthropathy." *Ann. Rheum. Dis.*, **32:** 162–166.

Matthews, W. B. (1974). "Cauda equina syndrome in ankylosing spondylitis." *Brit. Med. J.*, **1:** 517.

Maury, M., Nocolle, M. H., Skoda, A. & Francois, N. (1972). "Discal herniation and syndromes of the conus and cauda equina." *Rev. Chir. Orthop.*, **58:** 247–261.

Mehalič, T. (1974). "Vertebral artery injury from chiropractic manipulation of the neck." *Surg. Neurol.*, **2:** 125–129.

Michelson, K. (1967). "Pressure relationship in the bone marrow vascular bed." *Acta Physiol. Scand.*, **71:** 16–29.

Moiel, R., & Ehni, G. (1968). "Cauda equina compression due to spondylolisthesis with intact neural arch: report of two cases." *J. Neurosurg.*, **28:** 262–265.

Muller, R. (1951). "Protrusion of thoracic intervertebral disks with compression of the spinal cord." *Acta Med. Scand.*, **139:** 99–104.

Nagler, W. (1973). "Mechanical obstruction of vertebral arteries during hyperextension of neck." *Brit. J. Sports Med.*, **7:** 92–97.

Nagler, W. (1973). "Vertebral artery destruction by hyperextension of the neck." *Arch. Phys. Med. Rehab.*, **54:** 237–240.

Nathan, M. H. & Blum, L. (1960). "Evaluation of vertebral venography." *Amer. J. Roentgenol.*, **83:** 1027–1033.

Nicola, G. C. & Nizzoli, V. (1974). "Intermittent claudication in the lower limbs due to total stenosis of the lumbar canal." *Neurochirurgia*, **17:** 48–57.

Nizzoli, V., Solime, F., Reggiani, R. & Nicola, G. C. (1970). "Bilateral obstruction of the vertebral arteries." *Europ. Neurol.*, **3:** 28–37.

Nomura, I. (1971). "A study on the topographic anatomy of the venous system of the lumbar region through anterior approach to the lumbar spine." *J. Jap. Orthop. Ass.*, **45:** 1087–1097.

Pear, B. L. (1972). "Spinal epidural hematoma." *Amer. J. Roentgenol.*, **115:** 155–164.

POLLEY, E. H. (1955). "Innervation of blood vessels in striated muscle and skin." *J. Comp Neurol.*, **103**: 253–267.

PRENTICE, W. B., KIEFFER, S. A., GOLD, L. H. A. & BJORNSON, R. G. (1973). "Myelographic characteristics of metastasis to the spinal cord and cauda equina." *Amer. J. Roentgenol.*, **118**: 681–689.

RAMANI, P. S. & SENGUPTA, R. P. (1973). "Cauda equina compression due to tabetic arthropathy of the spine." *J. Neurol. Neurosurg. Psychiat.*, **36**: 260–264.

RAPPAPORT, I. (1973). "Congenital arteriovenous fistulas of the head and neck." *Arch. Otolaryngol.*, **97**: 350–353.

REDISCH, W., MESSINA, E. J., HUGHES, G. & McEWEN, C. (1970). "Capillaroscopic observations in rheumatic diseases." *Ann. Rheum. Dis.*, **29**: 244–253.

ROBERTS, W. C. (1974). "Combined mitral and aortic regurgitation in ankylosing spondylitis. Angiographic and anatomic features." *Amer. J. Med.*, **56**: 237–243.

ROBSON, P. N. & TIBBS, D. J. (1957). "Aneurysm complicating traumatic spondylolisthesis." *J. Bone Joint Surg.*, **39B**: 498–501.

ROSENFELD, M. (1972). "Sciatica due to epidural venous anomalies: Study of L5–S1 sciatica nine years after operation." *Rev. Rheum. Mal. Osteoartic.*, **39**: 47–49.

ROSENKRANZ, W. (1971). "Ankylosing spondylitis: cauda equina syndrome with multiple spinal arachnoid cysts." *J. Neurosurg.*, **34**: 241–243.

ROTH, M. (1965). 'The caudal end of the spinal cord. II. Abnormal pneumographic features: lumbar intumescence artery syndrome and spinal dysraphism." *Acta Radiol.*, **3**: 297–304.

RUSSELL, M. L., GORDON, D. A., ORGYZLO, M. A. & McPHEDRAN, R. S. (1973). "The cauda equina syndrome of ankylosing spondylitis." *Ann. Int. Med.*, **78**: 551–554.

SALDINO, R. M., WHITE, A. A. & PALUBINSKAS, A. J. (1971). "Arterio-venous fistula: a complication of lumbar disc surgery." *Radiology*, **98**: 565–567.

SCHATZKER, J. & PENNAL, G. F. (1968). "Spinal stenosis, a cause of cauda equina compression." *J. Bone Joint Surg.*, **50b**: 606–618.

SCHIFF, D. C. (1973). "The arterial supply of the odontoid process." *J. Bone Joint Surg.*, **55**: 1450–1456.

SCHLESINGER, E. B. & TAVERAS, J. M. (1953). "Factors in the

production of cauda equina syndromes in lumbar discs." *Trans. Amer. Neurol. Assoc.*, **78**: 263–365.

SCHWARTZ, G. A. & GEIGER, J. K. (1956). "Posterior inferior cerebellar artery syndrome of Wallenberg after chiropractic manipulation." *Arch. Int. Med.*, **97**: 352–354.

SELLER, B. (1973). "The discharge pattern of single units in thoracic and lumbar white rami in relation to cardiovascular events." *Pflüger's Arch.*, **343**: 317–330.

SHAW, N. E. (1963). "Observations on the intramedullary blood flow and marrow pressure in bone." *Clin. Sci.*, **24**: 311–318.

SHEA, J. D., GIOFFRE, R., CARRION, H. & SMALL, M. P. (1973). "Autonomic hyperreflexia in spinal cord injury." *Southern Med. J.*, **66**: 869–872.

SHEPHARD, R. H. (1959). "Diagnosis and prognosis of cauda equina syndrome produced by protrusion of the lumbar disc." *Brit. Med. J.*, **2**: 1434–1439.

SHIM, S. S. & PATTERSON, F. P. (1967). "A direct method of qualitative study of bone blood circulation." *Surg. Gynec. Obst.*, **125**: 261–268.

SILVER, R. A., SCHUELE, H. L. STACK, J. K., *et al.* (1969). "Intermittent claudication of neurospinal origin." *Arch. Surg.*, **98**: 523–529.

SINGER, W. D. (1975). Occlusive vertebrobasilar artery disease associated with cervical spine anomaly." *Amer. J. Dis. Child.*, **129**: 86.

SLOWICK, F. A., CAMPBELL, C. J. & KETTELKAMP, D. B. (1968). "Aneurysmal bone cyst: an analysis of thirteen cases." *J. Bone and Joint Surg.*, **50A**: 1142–1151.

SMITH, R. F. (1973). "Arteriovenous fistula and chronic congestive heart failure following intervertebral disk surgery." *Southern Med. J.*, **66**: 1310–1313.

SOMOGY, B. (1964) "Blood supply of the foetal spine." *Acta Morph.*, **8**: 261–274.

SPANOS, N. C. & ANDREWS, J. (1966). "Intermittent claudication and lateral lumbar disc protrusion." *J. Neurol. Neurosurg. Psychiat.*, **29**: 273–277.

STANLEY, R. J. (1975). "Neurosurgical treatment of arteriovenous malformations of the trunk and limbs by transcatheter arterial embolisation." *Radiology*, **115**: 609–612.

STEVENSON, J. G. (1975). "Cervical venous hums." *New. Engl. J. Med.*, **292**: 212.

STOKES, J. M. (1968). "Vascular complications of disc surgery." *J. Bone Joint Surg.*, **50A**: 394–399.

STYCZYNSKI, T., ZARSKI, S. & KOZINA, W. (1972). "The vertebro-radicular conflict in lumbar spine and the blood flow to lower extremities in the light of an observed case." *Rheum.*, **10**: 81–85.

SUH, T. H. & ALEXANDER, L. (1939). "Vascular system of the human spinal cord." *Arch. Neurol. Psych.*, **41**: 659–677.

SWEETMAN, B. J. (1975). "Capillary resistance and back pain." *Rheumatol. Rehab.*, **14**: 1–6.

SZEPEZI, K., VIZELETY, T. & WOUTERS, H. W. (1970). "Experimental studies of the effect of ischaemia of the intervertebral disc." *Rev. Chir., Orthop.*, **56**: 471–480.

TARZY, B. J., GARCIA, C. R., WALLACH, E. E., ZWEIMAN, B. & MYERS, A. R. (1972). "Rheumatic disease, abnormal serology and oral contraceptives" *Lancet*, **2**: 201–503.

TAYLOR, A. R. (1960). "Fallacies in the interpretation of Queckenstedt's test." *Lancet*, **2**: 1001–1004.

TAYLOR, H. & WILLIAMS, E. (1962–3). "Arteriovenous fistula following disk surgery." *Brit. J. Surg.*, **50**: 47–50.

TENG, P. & PAPATHEODOROU, C. (1963). "Lumbar spondylosis with compression of cauda equina." *Arch. Neurol.*, **8**: 221–229.

TISSINTON TATLOW, W. F. & BAMMER, H. G. (1957). "Syndrome of vertebral artery compression." *Neurology*, **7**: 331–340.

TRISKA, H. (1964). "On the effect of acute changes of volume in the abdomen on intra-abdominal pressure and venous reflex." *Klin. Med.*, **19**: 281–298.

TURNBULL, M., BRIEG, A., & HASSLER, O. (1966). "Blood supply of cervical spinal cord in man." *J. Neurosurg.*, **24**: 951–965.

TURNEY, J. P. (1952). "A cauda equina lesion due to spondylolisthesis." *Brit. Med. J.*, **2**: 1028–1029.

VAN WIERINGEN, A. (1968). "An unusual cause of occlusion of an anterior spinal artery." *Europ. Neurol.*, **1**: 363–374.

VERBIEST, H. (1973). "Neurogenic intermittent claudication in cases with absolute and relative stenosis of the lumbar vertebral canal, in cases with narrow lumbar vertebral foramina and in cases with both entities." *Clin. Neurosurg.*, **20**: 204–214.

VITEK, J. J. (1973). "Thoracic bifurcation of the common carotid artery." *Neuroradiology*, **5**: 133–139.

VITOVEK, J. (1974). "Spontaneous fistula between abdominal aorta and vena lumbalis quarta on the left side." *Česk. Radiol.*, **28**: 39–42.

WAGGONER, G. & PENDERGRASS, E. P. (1932). "Intrinsic circulation of the vertebral column." *Amer. J. Roentgenol.*, **27**: 818–826.

WEBER, A. (1953). "The morphological basis of arterial sensibility." *Acta Neuroveg., Wien*, **7**: 32–39.

WEINBERG, P. E. (1973). "Traumatic vertebral arteriovenous fistula." *Surg., Neurol.*, **1**: 162–167.

WEISS, R. A. & ROOT, W. S. (1959). "Innervation of the vessels of the marrow cavity of certain bones." *Amer. J. Physiol.*, **197**: 1255–1257.

WENER, L., DI CHIRO, G. & GARGOUR, G. W. (1074). "Angiography of cervical cord injuries." *Radiology*, **112**: 597–604.

WILEY, A. M. & TRUETA, J. (1959). "The vascular anatomy of the spine and its relationship to pyogenic vertebral osteomyelitis." *J. Bone Joint Surg.*, **41B**: 7961809.

WILKINSON, I. M. (1972). "Arteries of the head and neck in giant cell arteritis: a pathological study to show the pattern of arterial involvement." *Arch. Neurol.*, **27**: 378–391.

WILLIS, T. A. (1949). "Nutrient arteries of the vertebral bodies." *J. Bone Joint Surg.*, **31A**: 538–540.

WILSON, P. J. E. (1962). "Cauda equina compression due to intrathecal herniation of an intervertebral disc." *Brit. J. Surg.*, **49**: 423–426.

WRIGHT, H. M. (1965). "Measurement of the cutaneous circulation." *J. Appl. Physiol.*, **20**: 696–702.

YAMADA, H., OHYA, M., OKADA, T. & SHIOZAWA, Z. (1972). "Intermittent cauda equina compression due to narrow spinal canal." *J. Neurosurg.*, **37**: 83–88.

ZIELONKA, J. S. (1974). "Alterations in spinal cord blood flow during local hypothermia." *Surg. Forum*, **25**: 434–436.

ZULCH, K. J. (1970). "The pathogenesis of 'intermittent spinovascular insufficiency' (spinal claudication of Déjerine) and other vascular syndromes of the spinal cord." *Vasc. Surg.*, **4**: 116–136.

# 4

# PHYSIOLOGY AND BIOCHEMISTRY

## (a) General

ARIMA, T. (1970). "A study on the water content in the intervertebral disc." *J. Jap. Orthop. Ass.*, **44:** 571–587.

ASTRAND, P. O. & RADAHL, K. (1970). *Text-Book of Work Physiology*. New York; McGraw Hill.

COTTON, F. S. (1934). "Centre of gravity in man." *Am. J. Phys. Anthrop.*, **18:** 401–405.

GOWER, W. E. & PEDRINI, V. (1969). "Age related variations in proteinpolysaccharides from human nucleus pulposus, annulus fibrosus and costal cartilage." *J. Bone Joint Surg.*, **51A:** 1154–1162.

HAMILTON, W. F., WOODBURY, R. A. & HARPER, H. T. (1936). "Physiological relationships between intrathoracic, intraspinal and arterial pressures." *J. Amer. Med. Assoc.*, **107:** 853–856.

HARRIS, H. A. (1939). "Anatomical and physiological basis of physical training." *Brit. Med. J.*, **2:** 939–943.

INMAN, V. T. & SAUNDERS, J. B. (1947). "Anatomicophysiological aspects of injuries to the intervertebral disc." *J. Bone Joint Surg.*, **29A:** 461–475.

KAMON, E. (1974). "Instrumentation for work physiology." *Trans. N.Y. Acad. Sci.*, **36:** 625–639.

LEHTONEN, A., VILJANTO, J. & KARKAINEN, J. (1967). "The mucopolysaccharides of herniated human intervertebral discs and semilunar cartilages." *Acta Chir. Scand.*, **133:** 303–306.

LLOYD, D. P. C. (1960). "Spinal mechanisms involved in somatic activities." In *Handbook of Physiology*. Ed. by J. Field, H. W. Magoun, and V. E. Hall. Vol. II. pp. 929–949. Washington; American Physiological Society.

MCMICHAEL, J. & MCGIBBON, J. P. (1939). "Postural changes in the lung volume." *Clin. Scand.*, **4:** 175–183.

MARGARIA, R., EDWARDS, H. T. & DILL, D. B. (1933). "The possible mechanisms of contracting and paying the oxygen debt and the role of lactic acid in muscular contraction." *Am. J. Physiol.*, **106:** 689–715.

MATTHEWS, B. H. C. (1928). "A new electrical recording system for physiological work." *J. Physiol.*, **65**: 225–242.

WYKE, B. D. (1976). "Neurological aspects of low back pain." In *The Lumbar Spine and Back Pain*, pp. 189–256. Ed. M. I. V. Jayson. London; Sector Publishing Co.


*(b) Normal (including Developmental)*

ALLEN, T. H., KRZYWICKI, H. J., NORTH, W. S. & NIMS, R. M. (1960). "Human body volumeter based on water displacement." *U.S. Army Medical Research and Nutr. Lab., Project No. 6-60-11-001. Report No. 250.*

ASMUSSEN, E. & NIELSEN, M. (1949). "Studies on the initial changes in respiration at the transition from rest to work and from work to rest." *Acta Physiol. Scand.*, **16**: 270–285.

BARCERO, P. (1959). "Anatomy, physiology and biomechanics of the lumbosacral region." *Rev. Esp. Reum.*, **8**: 233–251.

BEHNKE, A. R., FEEN. B. G. & WELHAM, W. C. (1942). "The specific gravity of healthy men." *J. Amer. Med. Assoc.*, **118**: 495–498.

BERNARDI, G., HAPPEY, F. & NAYLOR, A. (1957). "Mucopolysaccharides from cartilage and nucleus pulposus." *Nature*, **180**: 1341–1342.

BIANCHI, C. P. & SHANES, A. M. (1959). "Calcium influx in skeletal muscle at rest, during activity and during potassium contracture." *J. Gen. Physiol.*, **42**: 803–825.

BIJLSMA, F. & PEEREBOOM, J. W. C. (1972). "The ageing pattern of human intervertebral discs." *Gerontologica*, **18**: 157–168.

BLAIR, E. & HICKAM, J. B. (1955). "Effect of change in body position on lung volume and intrapulmonary gas mixing in normal subjects." *J. Clin. Invest.*, **34**: 383–389.

BLAND, J. H. (1974). "Cholesterol in connective tissue of joints." *Scand. J. Rheumatol.*, **3**: 199–203.

BOYLE, P. J. & CONWAY, E. J. (1941). "Potassium accumulation in muscles and associated changes." *J. Physiol.*, **100**: 1–63.

BULLARD, R. W. (1962). "Continuous recording of the sweat rate by resistance hygrometry." *J. Appl. Physiol.*, **17**: 735–737.

BUSH, H. D., HORTON, W. G., SMARE, D. L. & NAYLOR, A. (1956).

"Fluid content of the nucleus pulposus as a factor in the disc syndrome." *Brit. Med. J.*, **2**: 81–83.

CAMPBELL, E. J. M. & GREEN, J. H. (1953). "The expiratory function of the abdominal muscles in man: an E.M.G. study." *J. Physiol.*, **120**: 409–418.

CASSUCIO, C. (1962). "An introduction to the study of osteoporosis: biochemical and biophysical research in bone ageing." *Proc. Royal Soc. Med.*, **55**: 663–668.

COOTE, J. H. (1975). "Physiological significance of somatic afferent pathways from skeletal muscles and joints, with reflex effects on the heart and circulation." *Brain Res.*, **87**: 139–144.

CRAIG, A. B. (1960). "Effects of position on expiratory reserve volume of the lungs." *J. Appl. Physiol.*, **15**: 59–61.

DABEK, J. T. (1974). "In vivo measurement of spinal calcium." *Clin. Sci. Mol. Med.*, **47**: 22–23P.

DALLY, J. F. H. (1908). "An inquiry into the physiological mechanisms of respiration with special reference to the movement of the vertebral column and diaphragm." *J. Anat. Physiol.*, **43**: 93–114.

DAVIS, P. R. (1966). "Using E.C.G., the cardiac costs of the bent stoop methods of lifting." *Ergonomics*, **9**: 431.

DICKSON, I. R., HAPPEY, F., PEARSON, C. H., NAYLOR, A. & TURNER, R. L. (1967). "Decrease in the hydrothermal stability of collagen on ageing in the human intervertebral disk." *Nature*, **215**: 50–52.

DICKSON, I. R., HAPPEY, F., PEARSON, C. H., NAYLOR, A. & TURNER, R. L. (1967). "Variations in the protein components of human intervertebral disk with age." *Nature*, **215**: 52–53.

EMES, J. H. (1975). "The proteoglycans of the human intervertebral disc." *Biochem. J.*, **145**: 549–586.

EVANS, F. G. & LISSNER, H. R. (1959). "Biomechanical studies on the lumbar spine and pelvis." *J. Bone Joint Surg.*, **41A**: 278–290.

EYRING, E. J. (1967). "The biochemistry and physiology of the intervertebral disk." *Clin. Orthop.*, **67**: 16–28.

FOA, P. P. (1943). "Studies on innervation of bone marrow: physiology." *Univ. Hosp. Bull., Ann. Arbor.*, **9**: 19–21.

GALANTE, J. O. (1967). "Tensile properties of the human lumbar annulus fibrosus." *Acta Orthop. Scand.* (Suppl. **100**): 1–91.

GARDNER, E. D. (1950). "Physiology of movable joints." *Physiol. Rev.*, **30**: 127–176.

GARDNER, E. D. (1953). "Physiological mechanisms in movable

joints." *Amer. Acad., Orthop. Surg. Instructional Course Lect.*, **10:** 251–261.

GARDNER, E. D. (1954). "Physiology of the nerve supply of joints." *Bull. Hosp. Joint. Dis.*, **15:** 35–44.

GARDNER, E. D. (1963). "Physiology of joints." *J. Bone Joint Surg.*, **45A:** 1061.

GEUBELLE, F. & GOFFIN, C. (1962). "Respiratory studies in children. IV. Lung volumes and body positions in children." *Acta Paediatrica*, **51:** 255–260.

GITELSON, S. & MANN, K. J. (1959). "The influence of body build and posture on the expiratory reserve volume." *Israel Med. J.*, **18:** 71–81.

HALL, D. A. (1973). "Protein polysaccharide relationships in tissues subjected to repeated stress throughout life. II. The intervertebral disc." *Age and Ageing*, **2:** 218–224.

HALL, F. G. & SALZANO, J. (1959). "Maximal inspiratory and expiratory stroke volumes in human subjects as related to posture." *J. Aviation Med.*, **30:** 167–172.

HALLEN, A. (1958). "Hexosamine and ester sulphate content of the human nucleus pulposus at different ages." *Acta Chem. Scand.*, **12:** 1869–1872.

HALLEN, A. (1962). "The collagen and ground substances of human intervertebral discs at different ages." *Acta Chem. Scand.*, **16:** 705–710.

HAMILTON, W. F. & MORGAN, A. B. (1932). "Mechanisms of the postural reduction in vital capacity in relation to orthopnoea and storage of blood in the lungs." *Amer. J. Physiol.*, **99:** 526–532.

HELLEBRANDT, F. A. (1939). "Variations in intramuscular pressure during postural and phasic contractions of human muscle." *Amer. J. Physiol.*, **126:** 247–253.

HELLEBRANDT, F. A. & FRANSEN, F. B. (1943). "Physiological study of the vertical stance in man." *Physiol. Rev.*, **23:** 220–255.

HERZIG, E. & ROOT, W. S. (1959). "Relation of sympathetic nervous system to blood pressure of bone marrow." *Amer. J. Physiol.*, **196:** 1053–1056.

HURTADO, A. & FRAY, W. W. (1933). "Studies of total pulmonary capacity and its subdivisions. III. Changes with body posture." *J. Clin. Invest.*, **12:** 825–832.

JACKSON, B. T. (1974). "The normal lymphographic appearances of the lumbar lymphatics." *Clin. Radiol.*, **25:** 175–186.

JACKSON, B. T. (1974). "Lumbar lymphatic crossover." *Clin. Radiol.*, **25**: 187–193.

JACKSON, B. T. (1974). "The lumbar lymphatics: a lymphographic study." *Ann. Roy. Coll. Surg. Engl.*, **54**: 3–15.

JONES, F. P. & O'CONNELL, D. N. (1958). "Posture as a function of time." *J. Physiol.* **46**: 287–251.

JONES, L. (1955). *The Postural Complex.* Springfield, Illinois; Thomas.

JONES, P. F., GRAY, F. E., HANSON, J. A. & O'CONNELL, D. N. (1959). "An experimental study of the effect of head balance on patterns of posture and movement in man." *J. Physiol.*, **47**: 247–258.

KARPOVICH, P. V. (1965). *Physiology of Muscular Activity.* 6th Ed. Philadelphia: Saunders.

KURODA, E., KUSSOURAS, V. & MULSUM, J. H. (1970). "Electrical and metabolic activities and fatigue in human isometric contraction." *J. Appl. Physiol.*, **29**: 358–367.

LAGNEAU, D., NAMUR, M. & PETIT, J. M. (1960). "Influence of body position on lung volume in the normal man." *Arch. Int. Physiol.*, **68**: 596–607.

LEWIS, B. M., LIN, T. H., NOE, F. E. & KOMISARUK, R. (1958). "The measurement of pulmonary capillary blood volume and pulmonary membrane diffusing capacity in normal subjects: the effects of exercise and position." *J. Clin. Invest.*, **37**: 1061–1070.

LIM, T. P. & LUFT, U. C. (1959). "Alterations in lung compliance and functional residual capacity with posture." *J. Appl. Physiol.*, **14**: 164–166.

LINDERHOLM, H. (1963). "Lung mechnics in sitting and horizontal postures studied by body plethysmographic methods." *Amer. J. Physiol.*, **204**: 85–91.

LIVINGSTONE, J. L. (1928). Variations in the volume of the chest with changes in posture." *Lancet*, **1**: 754–755.

LLOYD, W. F. & SANDOVER, J. (1974). "Apparatus for the study of the effects of impulsive forces on man." *J. Physiol.*, **238**: 4–6.

MARCELLE, R. & PETIT, J. M. (1963). "Influence of body posture on pulmonary resistance." *Rev. Franc. D'Etud. Clin. Biol.*, **8**: 694–696.

MAY, J. & WRIGHT, H. B. (1961). "Heights and weights of business men." *Trans. Assoc. Ind. Med. Offs.*, **11**: 143–149.

MORENO, F. & LYONS, H. A. (1961). "Effect of body posture on lung volumes." *J. Appl. Physiol.*, **16**: 27–29.

MURAYAMA, K. (1972). "Biochemical studies on the age-related variations of human intervertebral disc." *J. Jap. Orthop. Ass.*, **46**: 81–104.

NAIMARK, A. & WASSERMAN, K. (1962). "The effect of posture on pulmonary capillary blood flows in man." *J. Clin. Invest.*, **41**: 949–954.

NAYLOR, A., HAPPEY, F., TURNER, R. L., SHENTALL, R. D., WEST, D. C. & RICHARDSON, C. (1975). "Enzymic and immunological activity in the intervertebral disc." *Orthop. Clin. Nth. Amer.*, **6**: 51–58.

NORDGREN, B. (1972). "Arthropometric measures and muscle strength in young women." *Scand. J. Rehab. Med.*, **4**: 165–169.

PANKOVICH, A. M. & KORNGOLD, L. (1967). "A comparison of the antigenic properties of nucleus pulposus and cartilage protein polysaccharide complexes." *J. Immunol.*, **99**: 431–437.

PEARSON, C. H. (1972). "Lysosomal ensymes and degradation of the proteoglycans of the human intervertebral disc." *Biochem. J.*, **129**: 44–45.

PEARSON, C. H., HAPPEY, F., SHENTALL, R. D., NAYLOR, A. & TURNER, R. J. (1969). "The non-collagenous proteins of the human intervertebral disc." *Gerontologia*, **15**: 189–202.

PEEREBOOM, J. W. (1970). "Age dependent changes in the human intervertebral disc: Fluorescent substances and amino acids in the annulus fibrosus." *Gerontologia*, **16**: 352–367.

PODRAZKY, V., STEVEN, F. S., JACKSON, D. S., WEISS, J. B. & LEIBOVICH, S. J. (1971). "Interaction of tropocollagen with protein polysaccharide complexes: an analysis of the tonic groups responsible for interaction." *Biochem. Biophys. Acta*, **229**: 690–697.

RIGAUD, DEJUSSIEU, WANGERMEZ, C., BONJEAN, & BISCH, C. (1957). "Observations on the physiology of the sacro-iliac joints." *J. Med. Bordeaux Sud-Ouest*, **134**: 206–210.

RILEY, R. L., PERMUTT, S., SIAD, S., GODFREY, M., CHENG, T. O., HOWELL, J. B. & SHEPHERD, R. H. (1959). "Effect of posture on pulmonary dead space in man." *J. Appl. Physiol.*, **14**: 339–340.

ROBERTS, T. D. M. (1967). *Neurophysiology of Postural Mechanisms*. London: Butterworth.

RONNHOLM, N. (1962). "Physiological studies on the optimum rhythm of lifting work." *Ergonomics*, **5**: 51–52.

SEMLAK, K. & FERGUSON, A. B. (1970). "Joint stability maintained by atmospheric pressure: an experimental study." *Clin. Orthop.*, **68**: 294–300.

SHERR, C. J. & GOLDBERG, B. (1973). "Antibodies to a precursor of human collagen." *Science*, **180**: 1190–1191.

SOUTER, W. A. & TAYLOR, T. K. F. (1970). "Sulphated acid mucopolysaccharide metabolism in the rabbit intervertebral disc." *J. Bone Joint Surg.*, **52B**: 371–384.

STAINIER, L. & GEUBELLE, F. (1963). "The time factor and the influence of body position and blood flow on the lung volumes of healthy children." *Ann. Paediat.*, **201**: 389–398.

STEVENS, F. S., JACKSON, D. S. & BROADY, K. (1968). "Proteins of the human intervertebral disc: the association of collagen with a protein fraction having an unusual amino acid composition." *Biochem. Biophys. Acta*, **160**: 435–446.

STEVENS, F. S., KNOTT, J., JACKSON, D. S. & PODRAZKY, V. (1969). "Collagen-protein-polysaccharide interactions in human intervertebral disc." *Biochem. Biophys. Acta*, **188**: 307–313.

SVANBERG, L. (1957). "Influence of posture on lung volumes, ventilation and circulation in normals: a spirometric-bronchospirometric investigation." *Scand. J. Clin. Lab. Invest.*, **9**: 1–195.

SYLVEN, B., PAULSON, S., HIRSCH, C. & SNELLMAN, O. (1951). "Biophysical and physiological investigation on cartilage and other mesenchymal tissues." *J. Bone Joint Surg.*, **33A**: 33–340.

TRISKA, H. (1964). "On the effect of acute changes of volume in the abdomen on intra-abdominal pressure and venous reflux." *Klin. Med.*, **19**: 281–298.

VON DER MARK, K., CLICK, E. V. & BORNSTEIN, P. (1973). "The immunology of procollagen. 1. Development of antibodies to determinants unique to the proal chain." *Arch. Biochem. Biophys.*, **156**: 356–364.

WADE, O. L. (1954). "Movements of the thoracic cage and diaphragm in respiration." *J. Physiol.*, **124**: 193–212.

WADE, O. L. & GILSON, C. (1951). "Effect of posture on diaphragmatic movement and vital capacity in normal subjects, with a note on spirometry as an aid in determining radiologic chest volumes." *Thorax*, **6**: 103–126.

WAGONER, G. W. (1926). "Studies on intra-abdominal pressure. 1.

Negative intra-abdominal pressure as a normal condition." *Amer. J. Med. Sci.*, **171**: 697–707.

WILSON, W. J. (1927). "The influence of posture on the volume of the reserve air." *J. Physiol.*, **64**: 54–64.

WYKE, B. D. (Ed.) (1974). *Ventilatory and Phonatory Control Systems: An International Symposium.* London; Oxford University Press.

WYKE, B. D. (1976). "Neurological aspects of low back pain." In *The Lumbar Spine and Back Pain*, pp. 189–256. Ed. M. I. V. Jayson. London: Sector Publishing Co.

YAMAMOTO, S., MIYAJIMA, M. & URABE, M. (1960). Respiratory neuronal activities in spinal afferents of cat." *Jap. J. Physiol.*, **10**: 509–517.

YOSHITAKE, J. (1963). "The postural influence on lung volumes of normal and obese subjects." *Kyushu J. Med. Sci.*, **14**: 305–315.

*(c) Pathophysiology*

AMINOFF, M. J. (1974). "The pathophysiology of spinal vascular malformities." *J. Neurol. Sci.*, **23**: 255–264.

BARACH, A. L. & BECK, G. L. (1954). "Ventilatory effects of head-down position in pulmonary emphysema." *Amer. J. Med.*, **16**: 55–60.

BHALLA, S. K. & SIMMONS, E. H. (1968). "Electrolytic reaction to dissimilar metals as a cause of sciatica." *Canad. J. Surg.*, **11**: 52–56.

BROWN, M. D. (1971). "The pathophysiology of disc disease." *Orthop. Clin. Nth. Amer.*, **2**: 359–370.

BRUNSCHWIG, A. & JUNG, A. (1932). "The importance of the periarticular innervation in the pathological physiology of sprained joints." *J. Bone Joint Surg.*, **14B**: 273.

CITRIN, D. L. (1973). "Ventilatory function and transfer factor in ankylosing spondylitis." *Scott. Med. J.*, **18**: 109–113.

CRAIG, W. & WALSH, M. N. (1941). "Neuroanatomical and physiological aspects and significance of sciatica." *J. Bone Joint Surg.*, **23**: 417–434.

FARROW, R. C. (1961). "Shoulder pain and stiffening." *Physiotherapy*, **47**: 326–329.

FISHER, A. G. T. (1923). "Some researches into the physiological principles underlying the treatment of injuries and diseases of the articulations." *Lancet*, **2:** 541–548.

FLLOYD, W. F. & SANDOVER, J. (1974). "Apparatus for the study of the effects of impulsive forces on man." *J. Physiol.*, **238:** 4–6.

GRIMBY, G. (1974). "Partitioning of the contributions of rib cage and abdomen to ventilation in ankylosing spondylitis." *Thorax*, **29:** 179–184.

GUTTMAN, L. (1940). "Topographic studies of disturbances of sweat secretion after complete lesions of peripheral nerves." *J. Neurol. Psychiat.*, **3:** 197–210.

HAUGE, B. N. (1973). "Diaphragmatic movement and spirometric volume in patients with ankylosing spondylitis." *Scand. J. Respir. Dis.*, **54:** 38–44.

HENDRY, N. G. C. (1958). "The hydration of the nucleus pulposus and its relation to intervertebral disc derangement." *J. Bone Joint Surg.*, **40B:** 132–144.

HEVER, F. (1930). "Physiology in scoliosis of the vertebral column." *Zeit. Orth. Chir.*, **52:** 513–533.

KENDALL, M. J. (1963). "Haematology and biochemistry of ankylosing spondylitis." *Brit. Med. J.*, **2:** 235–237.

KENDALL, M. J. (1973). "Serum immunoglobulins in ankylosing spondylitis." *Brit. Med. J.* **2:** 172.

KENDALL, M. J. (1973). "Synovial fluid in ankylosing spondylitis." *Ann. Rheum. Dis.*, **32:** 487–492.

KEYES, D. C. & COMPERE, E. L. (1932). "The normal and pathological physiology of the nucleus pulposus of the intervertebral disc: an anatomical, clinical and experimental study." *J. Bone Joint Surg.*, **14:** 897–938.

MIKI, I. & MORISAKI, N. (1954). "Pathological physiology in low back pain." *J. Bone Joint Surg.*, **36A:** 195–196.

NAYLOR, A. (1962). "The biophysical and biochemical aspects of intervertebral disc herniation and degeneration." *Ann. Roy. Coll. Surg. Engl.*, **31:** 91–114.

NAYLOR, A. (1971). "The biochemical changes in the human intervertebral disc in degeneration and nuclear prolapse." *Orthop. Clin. Nth. Amer.*, **2:** 343–358.

OSTERHOLM, J. L. (1974). "The pathophysiological response to spinal cord injury. The current status of related research." *J. Neurosurg.*, **40:** 5–33.

PENNING, L. & ZWAGG, P. VAN DER. (1966). "Biochemical aspects of spondylotic myelopathy." *Acta Radiol. Diagn.*, **5:** 1090–1103.

ROTHMAN, R. H. (1973). "The pathophysiology of disc degeneration." *Clin. Neurosurg.*, **20:** 174–182.

SOKOLOFF, L. (1975). "Biochemical and physiological aspects of degenerative joint diseases with special reference to hemophilic arthropathy." *Ann. N.Y. Acad. Sci.*, **340:** 285–290.

STARÝ, O., DRECHSLER, B., HLADKA, V. & NEVISMAL, O. (1955). "Pathophysiology of paravertebral tissues in acute discogenic syndrome." *Cas. Lek. Česk.*, **13:** 339–346.

TUCKER, D. H. & SIEKER, H. O. (1960). "The effect of change in body position on lung volumes and intrapulmonary gas mixing in patients with obesity, heart failure and emphysema." *Amer. Rev. Resp. Dis.*, **82:** 787–791.

WIZE, J. (1975). "Hydroxyproline levels and collagenolytic activity in synovial fluids of patients with rheumatic diseases." *Scand. J. Rheumatol.*, **4:** 65–72.

WYKE, B. D. (1974). "Clinical physiology of peripheral nerve injuries." In *Scientific Foundations of Surgery*. 2nd Ed. pp. 242–253. Ed. by C. Wells, J. Kyle and J. E. Dunphy. London; Heinemann.

WYKE, B. D. (1976). "Neurological Aspects of Low Back Pain." Chap. 10 in *The Lumbar Spine and Back Pain*, pp. 189–256. Ed. M. I. V. Jayson. London; Sector Publishing Co.

## (d) Chemical Pathology

AKIL, H. & MAYER, D. J. (1972). "Antagonism of stimulation produced analgesia by p-CPA and serotonin synthesis inhibitor." *Brain Res.*, **44:** 692–697.

ARMSTRONG, D., JEPSON, J. B., KEELE, C. A. & STEWART, J. W. (1957). "Pain producing substances in human inflammatory exudates and plasma." *J. Physiol.*, **135:** 350.

BENJAMIN, F. B. (1968). "Release of intracellular potassium as a factor in pain production." In *The Skin Senses*. pp. 466–478. Ed. by D. R. Kenshalo. Springfield, Illinois; Thomas.

BRENDSTRUP, P., JESPERSEN, K. & ASBOE-HANSEN, G. (1957). "Morphological and chemical tissue changes in fibrositic muscles." *Ann. Rheum. Dis.*, **16:** 438–440.

GOLDSMITH, N. F. (1973). "Bone mineral in the radius and vertebral osteoporosis in an insured population. A correlative study using 125-I photon absorption and miniature roentgenography." *J. Bone Joint Surg.*, **55A:** 1276–1293.

GOLDSMITH, N. F. & JOHNSTON, J. O. (1973). "Mineralization of the bone in an insured population: correlation with reported fractures and other measures of osteoporosis." *Int. J. Epid.*, **2:** 211–327.

MARSHALL, L. L. & TRETHEWI, E. R. (1973). "Chemical irritation of nerve root in disc prolapse." *Lancet*, **2:** 320.

MICHELI, A. (1975). "Frequency of the atypical gene El-a of serum cholinesterase among patients with ankylosing spondylitis." *Ann. Rheum. Dis.*, **34:** 198.

MILICIC, M. & JOWSEY, J. (1968). "Effect of fluoride on diffuse osteoporosis in the cat." *J. Bone Joint Surg.*, **50A:** 701–708.

# 5

# BIOMECHANICS AND ERGONOMICS

## (a) General

ALVIK, I. (1969). "Biomechanics of the back." *T. Norske Laegeforen*, **89**: 1340.

BERGER, N., FISHMAN, S. & BENNETT, L. (1971). "Studies of spinal orthoses and below knee prostheses." *Report from the Department of Prosthetics and Orthotics, New York University Postgraduate Medical School.*

BREIG, A. (1964). *Biomechanics of the Central Nervous System: Some Basic Normal and Pathologic Phenomena.* Stockholm; Almqvist and Wiksel.

CASHMAN, P. M. M. (1974). "A semi-automatic system for the analysis of 24 hour ECR recordings from ambulant subjects." *Biomed. Eng.*: 54–74.

CHAFFIN, D. B. (1969). "A computerized biomechanical model: Development of and use in studying gross body actions." *J. Biomech.*, **2**: 429–441.

DATTA, S. R., CHATTERJEE, B. B. & ROY, B. N. (1974). "An improved simple exercise test for evaluation of physical fitness." *Ergonomics*, **17**: 105–112.

DAVIES, C. T. M. & SERGEANT, A. J. (1975). "Circadian variation in physiological responses to exercise on a stationary bicycle ergometer." *Br. J. Indust. Med.*, **32**: 110–114.

DAVIS, P. R. & TROUP, J. D. G. (1966). "Human thoracic diameters at rest and during activity." *J. Anat.*, **100**: 397–410.

DREYFUSS, H. (1959). *The Measure of Man.* New York: Whitney Publications Inc.

EVANS, F. G. (Ed.). (1961). *Biomechanical Studies of the Musculoskeletal System.* Springfield, Illinois; Thomas.

EVANS, G. F. (1970). "Some basic aspects of biomechanics of the spine." *Archiv. Phys. Med. Rehab.*, **51**: 214–226.

EVANS, J. H. (1966). "Biomechanical study of human ligamentum flavum." *J. Anat.*, **105**: 188–189.

GALABOV, G. & WASSILEV, W. (1965). "Studies on the biomechanics of the lumbar vertebral column." *Bull. Inst. Morph., Sofia*, **11:** 79–103.

GALLOIS, M. & JAPIOT, M. (1925). "Internal architecture of the vertebrae: statics and physiology of the vertebral column." *Rev. Chir.*, **63:** 688–708.

GAMBURGEV, V. A. (1956). "The dynamics of the development of the curvatures of the vertebral column in relation with the position of the pelvis and the determination of the posture of the human body." *Arkh. Anat. Gistol. Embriol.*, **33:** 75–89.

GOLDTHWAIT, J. E., BROWN, L. T., SWAIM, L. T. & KUHNS, J. G. (1952). *Essentials of Body Mechanics.* 5th Ed. Philadelphia: Lippincott.

HAGELSTAM, L. (1949). "Retroposition of lumbar vertebrae." *Acta Chir. Scand., Suppl.*, **134:** 1.

HUIZINGA, J. VAN, HEIDEN, J. A. & VINKEN, P. J. J. G. (1952). "The human lumbar vertebral canal: a biometric study." *Proc. Section of Science, Konink. Ned. Akad. van Wetenschappen. Series C.* **55:** 22–23.

JACKSON, J. K. (1968). "Biomechanical hazards in the dockworker." *Ann. Occup. Hyg.*, **11:** 147–157.

JONCK, L. M. (1961). "The mechanical disturbance resulting from lumbar disc space narrowing." *J. Bone Joint Surg.*, **43B:** 362–375.

JOSEPH, J., NIGHTINGALE, A. & WILLIAMS, P. L. (1954). "A detailed study of the electric potentials recorded over some postural muscles while relaxed and standing." *J. Physiol.*, **127:** 617–625.

KESTER, N. C. (1968). "Low back pain: Patho-mechanics and a regimen of treatment." *Arch. Phys. Med. Rehab.*, **49:** 396–402.

KETTLEWELL, P. J. (1974). "Biochemical engineering—an annotated guide to sources of information." *Biomed. Eng.*, 209–213.

McKAY, R. S. (1964). "The application of physical transducers to intracavity pressure measurement with special reference to tonometry." *Med. Electronics Biol. Eng.*, **2:** 3–19.

McPHERSON, A. & JUHASZ, L. (1965). *The Haemodynamics of Bone: Biochemics and Related Engineering Topics.* Oxford; Pergamon Press.

MORRIS, J. M. (1973). "Biomechanics of the spine." *Arch. Surg.*, **107:** 418–423.

NACHEMSON, A. (1962). "Some mechanical properties of the lumbar intervertebral discs." *Bull. Hosp. J. Dis.*, **23:** 130–143.

NACHEMSON, A. L. & EVANS, J. H. (1968). "Some mechanical

properties of the third human lumbar interlaminar ligament (ligamentum flavum)." *J. Biomechanics*, **1:** 211–220.

RIDGE, M. D. & WRIGHT, V. (1966). "Rheological analysis of connective tissue—a bio-engineering analysis of the skin." *Ann. Rheum. Dis.*, **25:** 509–515.

ROAF, R. (1960). "A study of the mechanics of spinal injuries." *J. Bone Joint Surg.*, **42B:** 810–823.

ROBERTS, V. L., NOYES, F. R., HUBBARD, R. P. & MCCABE, J. (1971). "Biomechanics of snowmobile spine injuries." *J. Biomechanics*, **4:** 569–577.

SMITH, F. P. (1969). "Experimental biomechanics of intervertebral disc rupture through a vertebral body." *J. Neurosurg.*, **30:** 134–139.

SOKAL, R. R. & ROHLF, J. F. (1969). *Biometry*. San Francisco and London; Freeman.

SWANSON, S. A. V. & FREEMAN, M. A. R. (1966). "Is bone hydraulically strengthened?" *Med. Biol. Eng.*, **4:** 433–438.

### (b) Statics (including Posture)

AGAN, T., ANDERSON, E., REES, I. L. & CARSON, A. M. (1965). "A method of measuring postural attitudes". *Ergonomics*, **8:** 207–211.

AHLMANN, K. L., ERANO, E. D. & VIRTAMA, P. (1955). "Alterations of the lumbar curve and intervertebral spaces related to lying." *Ann. Chir. Cyn.* **44:** 291–299.

AKERBOLM, B. (1948). *Standing and Sitting Posture*. Stockholm: Nordiska Bokhandeln (trans. by Ann Synge).

ANDERSSON, B. J. G. (1974). "Myoelectric back muscle activity during sitting." *Scand. J. Rehab. Med., Suppl.* **3:** 73–90.

ANDERSSON, B. J. G. (1975). "The sitting posture: an electromyographic and discometric study." *Orthop. Clin. Nth. Amer.*, **6:** 105–120.

ANDERSSON, B. J. G., JOHNSSON, B. & ORTENGREN, B. (1974). "Myoelectric activity in individual lumbar erector spinae muscles in sitting. A study with surface and wire electrodes." *Scand. J. Rehab. Med.* (Suppl. 3): 91–108.

ANDERSSON, B. J. G. & ORTENGREN, R. (1964). "Lumbar disc

pressure and myoelectric back muscle activity during sitting. II. Studies on an office chair." *Scand. J. Rehab. Med.*, **6**: 115–121.

ANDERSSON, B. J. G. & ORTENGREN, R. (1974). "Lumbar disc pressure and myoelectric back muscle activity during sitting. III. Studies on a wheelchair." *Scand. J. Rehab. Med.*, **6**: 122–127.

ANDERSSON, B. J. G., ORTENGREN, R., NACHEMSON, A. & ELFSTROM, G. (1974). "Lumbar disc pressure and myoelectric back muscle activity during sitting. IV. Studies in a car driver's seat." *Scand. J. Rehab. Med.*, **6**: 128–133.

ANDERSSON, B. J. G., ORTENGREN, R., NACHEMSON, A. & ELFSTROM, G. (1974). "Lumbar disc pressure and myoelectric back muscle activity during sitting. Studies on an experimental chair." *Scand. J. Rehab. Med.*, **6**: 104–114.

ARKIN, A. M. (1950). "The mechanism of rotation in combination with lateral deviation in the normal spine." *J. Bone Joint Surg.*, **32A:** 180–188.

ASMUSSEN, E. & HEEBOLL-NEILSEN, K. (1959). "Posture, mobility and strength of the back in boys 7—16 years old." *Acta. Orthop. Scand.*, **28:** 174–189.

ASMUSSEN, E. & KLAUSEN, K. (1962). "Form and function of the erect human spine. *Clin. Orthop.*, **25:** 55–63.

ASMUSSEN, E. & POULSEN, E. (1968). "On the role of intra-abdominal pressure in relieving the back muscles while holding weights in a forward inclined position." *Dan. Nat. Ass. Infantile Paralysis*, Comm. No. **28:** 1.

ATTINGER, E. O., HERSCHFUL, J. A. & SEGAL, M. S. (1956). "Mechanics of breathing in different body positions." *J. Clin. Invest.*, **35:** 904–911.

BARACH, A. L. & BECK, G. L. (1954). "Ventilatory effects of head-down position in pulmonary emphysema." *Amer. J. Med.* **16:** 55–60.

BARKLA, D. (1961). "The estimation of body measurement of British population in relation to seat design." *Ergonomics*, **4:** 123–132.

BURANDT, U. (1969). "Radiological studies of the posture of the pelvis and vertebral column while sitting on a flat surface." *Ergonomics*, **12:** 356–364.

BURANDT, U. & GRANDJEAN, E. (1963). "Sitting habits of office employees." *Ergometrics*, **6:** 217–228.

CALDWELL, L. S. (1964). "The load-endurance relationship for a static manual response." *Human Factors*, pp. 71–79.

CALDWELL, L. S. (1964). "Measurement of static muscle endurance." *Engineering Psychol.*, **3**: 16–22.

COTTON, F. S. (1934). "Centre of gravity in man." *Amer. J. Phys. Anthrop.*, **18**: 401–405.

CRAIG, A. B. (1960). "Effects of position on expiratory reserve volume of the lungs." *J. Appl. Physiol.*, **15**: 59–61.

CURETON, T. K. & WICKENS, J. S. (1935). "The centre of gravity of the human body in the antero-posterior plane and its relation to posture, physical fitness and athletic ability." *Res. Quart.*, (Suppl.) **6**: 93–105.

DAVIS, P. R. (1961). "Human lower lumbar vertebrae: some mechanical and osteological considerations." *J. Anat.*, **95**: 337–344.

DELMAS, A. (1950). "Sacro-iliac joint and body statics." *Rev. Rheum.*, **17**: 1.

DENNY-BROWN, D. B. (1929). "On the nature of postural reflexes." *Proc. Roy. Soc.*, **104B**: 252–301.

DHESI, J. K. & FIREBAUGH, F. M. (1973). "The effects of stages of chappati-making and angles of body position on heart rate." *Ergonomics*, **16**: 811–815.

ELDRED, E. (1960). "Posture and locomotion." In *Handbook of Physiology*, Sect. I. Vol. 2: pp. 1067–1088. Ed. J. Field, H. W. Magoun and V. E. Hill. Washington; Amer. Physiol. Soc.

ELDRED, E. (1965). "Reflex plasticity in relation to posture." *Arch. Phys. Med.*, **46**: 10–25.

ERANKO, O. & VIRTAMA, P. (1955). "X-Ray anatomical observations on alternatives in the intervertebral spaces and curvature of the lumbar spine related to posture." *Duodeim (Helsinki)*, **71**: 261–268.

EVANS, F. G. (1962). "Stress and strain on posture expressed in the construction of man's weight-bearing skeletal structures." *Clin. Orthop.*, **25**: 42–54.

FARFAN, H. F. (1975). "Comment on the sitting posture and electro-myographic and diometric study." *Orthop. Clin. Nth. Amer.*, **6**: p. 120.

FEISS, H. O. (1907). "The mechanics of lateral curvature." *Amer. J. Orthop. Surg.*, **5**: 152–177.

FINEMAN, S., BORRELLI, F. J., RUBINSTEIN, H. & JACKSON, S. G.

(1963). "The cervical spine: transformation of the normal lordotic pattern into a linear pattern in the neutral posture." *J. Bone Joint Surg.*, **45A:** 1179.

FLINT, M. M. (1963). "Lumbar posture: a study of roentgenographic measurement and the influence of flexibility and strength." *Res. Quart.*, **34:** 15–20.

FLOYD, W. F. (1949). "E.M.G. study of standing man." *J. Physiol.*, **110:** 5P.

FLOYD, W. F. & SILVER, P. H. S. (1950). "Electromyographic studies of posture in man." *Abstr. of Communications, 18th International Physiological Congress, Copenhagen*, pp. 203–204. Copenhagen: Bianco Lunos.

FLOYD, W. F. & SILVER, P. H. S. (1950). "E.M.G. study of standing in man." *J. Physiol.*, **111:** 5P.

FLOYD, W. F. & SILVER, P. H. S. (1955). "The function of the erector spinae muscles in certain movements and postures in man." *J. Physiol.*, **129:** 184–203.

FLOYD, W. F. & WARD, J. (1967). "Posture in industry." *Int. Prod. Res.*, **5:** 213–224.

FOX, M. G. & YOUNG, O. G. (1964). "Placement of the gravitational line in anteroposterior standing position." *Res. Quart.*, **25:** 277–285.

FRADD, N. W. (1923). "A new method of recording posture." *J. Bone Joint Surg.*, **5A:** 757–758.

GEORGE, C. O'C. (1970). "Effects of the asymmetrical tonic neck posture upon grip strength of normal children." *Res. Quart.*, **41:** 361–364.

GEORGE, C. O'C. (1975). "Influence of tonic neck posture on grip strength of institutionalised mental retardates." *Res. Quart. Amer. Ass. Health Phys. Educ.*, **46:** 17–22.

GOFF, C. W. (1951). "Mean posture patterns with new postural values." *Amer. J. Phys. Anthrop.*, **9:** 335–346.

GOFF, C. W. (1952). "Orthograms of posture." *J. Bone Joint Surg.*, **34A:** 116–122.

GOFF, C. W. (1955). "Postural evolution related to backache." *Clin. Orthop.*, **5:** 8–16.

GOTZE, H.-G. (1973). "The rotation index in idiopathic thoracic scoliosis." *Zeit. Orthop.*, **111:** 737–743.

GRANDJEAN, E., HUNTING, W., WOTSKA, G. & SCHARER, R. (1973).

"An ergonomic investigation of multipurpose chairs." *Human Factors*, **15**: 247–255.

GROH, H., THOS, F. R. & BAUMANN, W. (1967). "The static load on the vertebral column during sagittal bending." *Int. Zeit. Angew. Physiol.*, **24**: 129–159.

GUTMAN, G. (1970). "Clinical-radiological studies of the statics of the vertebral column." In *Manuelle Medizin und Ihre Wissenschaftlichen Grundlagen.* pp. 109–127. Ed. H.-D. Wolf. Heidelberg; Verlag Phys. Med.

HALL, F. G. & SALZANO, J. (1959). "Maximal inspiratory and expiratory stroke volumes in human subjects as related to posture." *J. Aviation Med.*, **30**: 167–172.

HAMILTON, W. F. & MORGAN, A. B. (1932). "Mechanism of postural reduction in vital capacity in relation to orthopnea and storage of blood in the lungs." *Amer. J. Physiol.*, **99**: 526–532.

HANSEN, J. W. (1964). "Statometric studies on patients operated upon for slipped disc in the lumbar region." *Acta Orthop. Scand.*, **34**: 225–238.

HARRIS, R. (1955). "A single posture meter." *Ann. Rheum. Dis.*, **14**: 90–91.

HELLEBRANDT, F. A. (1938). "Standing as a geotropic reflex." *Amer. J. Physiol.*, **121**: 471–474.

HELLEBRANDT, F. A. (1943). "The eccentricity of standing and its causes." *Amer. J. Physiol.*, **140**: 205–211.

HELLEBRANDT, F. A., BROGDON, E. & TEPPER, R. H. (1940). "Posture and its cost." *Amer. J. Physiol.*, **129**: 773–781.

HELLEBRANDT, F. A. & FRANSEN, F. B. (1943). "Physiological study of the vertical stance of man." *Physiol. Rev.*, **23**: 220–255.

HELLEBRANDT, F. A., HOUTZ, S. H., PARTRIDGE, M. J. & WALTERS, C. E. (1956). "Tonic neck reflexes in exercises of stress in man." *Amer. J. Phys. Med.*, **35**: 144–159.

HELLEBRANDT, F. A., TEPPER, R. H., BRAUN, G. L. & ELLIOTT, M. C. (1938). "The location of the cardinal anatomical orientation planes passing through the center of weight in young adult women." *Amer. J. Physiol.*, **121**: 465–470.

HERTLE, F. & HETZEL, C. (1961). "The synchronised unloading frequency of motor activity in the erector spinae muscles in healthy men." *Arch. ges. Physiol.*, **273**: 235–236.

HEUER, F. (1929). "Forward and backward movement of the vertebral column." *Zeit. Orthop. Clin.* **52**: 374–387.

HINOJOSA, R. & BERGER, R. A. (1965). "Effects of variations in handgrip on recorded dynamometer back strength." *Res. Quart.*, **36**: 366–367.

HINRICSSON, H. & HJALMARS, K. (1964). "The biomechanism of the lumbar disc." *Tidskr. Milt. Halsor.*, **89**: 144–146.

HOLLAND, C. & WOLCK, H. (1967). "Upper thigh amputation and statics of the vertebral column." *Arch. Orthop. Unfall-Chir.*, **62**: 325–338.

HOLT, L. E., KAPLAN, H. M. & HOSHIKO, M. (1969). "The influence of antagonistic contraction and head position on the responses of agonistic muscles." *Arch. Phys. Med.*, **50**: 279–284.

HOUTZ, S. J., LEBOW, M. J. & BEYER, F. R. (1957). "Effect of posture on strength of the knee flexor and extensor muscles." *J. Appl. Physiol.*, **11**: 475–480.

HOWORTH, M. B. (1947). "Dynamic posture." *Hygeia*, **25**: 198–200.

HUGH-JONES, P. (1947). "The effect of limb position in seated subjects on their ability to utilize the maximum contractile force of the limb muscles." *J. Physiol.*, **105**: 332–344.

HUNTER, W. J. (1974). "Some aspects of occupational health." *Update*, 1283–1297.

HURTADO, A. & FRAY, W. W. (1933). "Studies of total pulmonary capacity and its subdivisions. III. Changes with body posture." *J. Clin. Invest.*, **12**: 825–832.

HUTCHINGS, G. L. (1965). "The relationship of selected strength and flexibility variables to the antero-posterior posture of college women." *Res. Quart.*, **36**: 353–369.

JANSEN, K. (1960). "Postural factors in paralytic scoliosis: a clinical, radiologic and electromyographic study." *Proc. 3rd Int. Cong. Phys. Med., Chicago.* pp. 665–670.

JIROUT, J. (1967). "Dynamics of the spinal dural sac under normal conditions." *Brit. J. Radiol.*, **40**: 209–213.

JONES, F. P. (1963). "The influence of postural set on pattern of movement in man." *Inter. J. Neurol.* **4**: 60–70.

JONES, F. P. & GILLEY, P. F. M (1960). "Head balance and sitting posture: an X-ray analysis. *J. Psych.*, **49**: 289–293.

JONES, F. P., GRAY, F. E., HANSON, J. A. & O'CONNELL, D. N. (1959). "An experimental study of the effect of head balance on patterns of posture and movement in man." *J. Psych.*, **47**: 247–258.

JONES, F. P., HANSON, J. A. & GRAY, P. E. (1961). "Head balance and sitting posture. II. The role of the sternomastoid muscle." *J. Psych.*, **52**: 363–367.

JONES, F. P. & O'CONNELL, D. N. (1958). "Posture as a function of time". *J. Psych.*, **46**: 287–294.

JOSEPH, J. (1960). *Man's Posture: Electromyographic Studies.* Springfield, Illinois; Thomas.

JOSEPH, J. (1964). "Electromyographic studies on muscle tone and the erect posture in man." *Brit. J. Surg.*, **51**: 616–622.

JOSEPH, J. & McCOLL, I. (1961). "Electromyography of muscles of posture: posterior vertebral muscles in males." *J. Physiol.*, **157**: 33–37.

JOSEPH, J. & NIGHTINGALE, A. (1952). "Electromyography of muscles of posture: leg muscles in males." *J. Physiol.*, **117**: 484–491.

JOSEPH J. & NIGHTINGALE, A. (1955). "Electromyography of muscles of posture: thigh muscles in males." *Arch. Phys. Med. Rehab.*, p. 116.

KAMON, E. (1966). "Electromyography of static and dynamic postures of the body supported on the arms." *J. Appl. Physiol.*, **21**: 1611–1618.

KAPLAN, B. H. (1974). "Method of determining spinal alignment and level of probable fracture during static elevation of ejection seats." *Aerosp. Med.*, **45**: 942–944.

KAPTEYN, T. S. (1972). "Data processing of posturographic curves." *Aggressologie*, **13B**: 29–34.

KARVONEN, M. J., KOSKALA, A. & NORO, L. (1962). "Preliminary report on the sitting postures of school children." *Ergometrics*, **5**: 471–477.

KEATS, S. & MORGESE, A. N. (1969). "Excessive lumbar lordosis in ambulatory spastic children with iliopsoas tenotomy." *Clin. Orthop.*, **65**: 130–137.

KEEGAN, T. J. (1953). "Alterations of lumbar curve related to posture and seating." *J. Bone Joint Surg.*, **35A**: 589–603.

KELTON, I. W. & WRIGHT, R. D. (1949). "The mechanisms of easy standing in man." *Aust. J. Exp. Biol. Med. Sci.*, **27**: 505–515.

KIERANDER, B. (1956). "Discussion on postural re-education – a critical examination of methods." *Proc. Roy. Soc. Med.*, **49**: 667–670.

KLAUSEN, K. (1965). "The form and function of the loaded human spine." *Acta Physiol. Scand.*, **65**: 176–190.

KLAUSEN, K. & RASMUSSEN, B. (1968). "On the location of the line of gravity in relation to L5 in standing." *Acta Physiol. Scand.*, **72:** 45–52.

KNUTSSON, B., LINDH, K. & TELHAG, H. (1966). "Sitting: an electromyographic and mechanical study." *Acta Orthop. Scand.*, **37:** 415–428.

KOTZ, Y. M. (1966). "Interaction of muscle antagonists of human trunk at rest and in postural activity." *Bull. Exp. Biol. Med.*, **62:** 7–11.

KRAUS, H. & WEBER, S. E. (1945). "Evaluation of posture based on structural and functional measurements." *Physiotherapy Rev.*, **25:** 267–271.

LAGNEAU, D., NAMUR, N. & PETIT, J. M. (1960). "Influence of body position on lung volume in the normal man." *Arch. Int. Physiol.*, **68:** 596–607.

LEGER, W. (1959). "The form of the vertebral column, with studies of its relation to the pelvis and upright posture, together with a study of the value of radiological examination of the vertebral column." *Beit. Zeit. Orthop.*, **91:** 1–108.

LEKSZAS, G. (1971). "A new measuring instrument for diagnostic study of the vertebral column." *Zeit. Ärztl. Fortbild.*, **64:** 602–608.

LEWIT, K. (1973). "X-ray criteria of spinal statics." *Agressologie*, **14B:** 41–48.

LIM, T. P. & LUFT, U. C. (1959). "Alterations in lung compliance and functional residual capacity with posture." *J. Appl. Physiol.*, **14:** 164–166.

LINDERHOLK, H. (1963). "Lung mechanics in sitting and horizontal postures studied by body plethysmographic methods." *Amer. J. Physiol.*, **204:** 85–90.

LIVINGSTONE, J. L. (1928). "Variations in the volume of the chest with changes in posture." *Lancet*, **1:** 754–755.

LOEBEL, W. Y. (1967). "Measurement of spinal posture and range of spinal movement." *Ann. Phys. Med.*, **9:** 103–110.

MACCONAILL, M. A. (1958). "Mechanical anatomy of motion and posture." In *Therapeutic Exercise*. Ed. S. Licht. New Haven, Connecticut; Licht.

MCMICHAEL, J. & MCGIBBON, J. D. (1939). "Postural changes in the lung volume." *Clin. Sci.*, **4:** 175–183.

MAGNUS, R. (1926). "Some results of studies in the physiology of posture." *Lancet*, **2:** 531–536; 585–588.

MANN, J. & KLEINSORG, H. (1956). "The influence of body posture on the lung volume of healthy subjects in different age groups." *Dtsch. Arch. Klin. Med.*, **203:** 234–240.

MARCELLE, R. & PETTIT, J. M. (1963). "Influence of body posture on pulmonary resistance." *Rev. Franc. d'Etud. Clin. Biol.*, **8:** 166.

MARTIN, J. P. (1967). *The Basal Ganglia and Posture.* London; Pitman.

MARTIN, J. V. & CHAFFIN, D. B. (1972). "Biomechanical computerized simulation of human strength in sagittal-plane activities." *Amer. Inst. Industr. Eng. Trans.*, **4:** 19–28.

MATSUO, S., YOCHIOKA, M., YANO, K. & HASHIBA, K. (1973). "Straight back syndrome: Clinical and haemodynamic study of 9 cases." *Amer. Heart J.*, **86:** 828–834.

MEYER, H. V. (1866). "The mechanics of scoliosis." *Virchows Arch.*, **35:** 225–253.

MIYAZAKI, A. (1968). "Posture and low back pain: electromyographic evaluation." *Electromyography*, **8:** 191–193.

MOHR, G. C., BRINKLEY, J. W., KAZARIAN, L. E. & MILLARD, W. W. (1969). "Variation of spinal alignment in egress systems and their effect." *Aerospace Med.*, **40:** 983–988.

MORENO, F. & LYONS, H. A. (1961). "Effect of body posture on lung volumes." *J. Appl. Physiol.*, **16:** 27–29.

MORIMOTO, S. (1973). "Effect of sitting posture on human body." *Bull. Tokyo Med. Dent. Univ.*, **20:** 19–34.

MORIOKA, M. (1965). "Some physiological responses to static muscular exercise." *Proc. 2nd Int. Erg. Cong., Dortmund, 1964*: 35–40.

MORRIS, J. M. & LUCAS, D. B. (1964). "Biomechanics of spinal bracing." *Arizona Medicine*, **21:** 170–176.

MUNRO, D. (1966). "The factors that govern the stability of the spine." *Paraplegia*, **3:** 219–228.

MURRAY, M. P. & PETERSON, R. M. (1973). "Weight distribution and weight shifting activity during normal standing posture." *Physical Therapy*, **53:** 741–748.

NACHEMSON, A. (1966). "Electromyographic studies on the vertebral portion of the psoas muscle, with special reference to the stabilizing function of the lumbar spine." *Acta Orthop. Scand.*, **37:** 177–190.

NACHEMSON, A. (1968). "The possible importance of the psoas

muscle for stabilization of the lumbar spine." *Acta Orthop. Scand.*, **39:** 47–57.

NAIMARK, A. & WASSERMAN, K. (1962). "The effect of posture on pulmonary capillary blood flow in man." *J. Clin. Invest.*, **41:** 949–954.

NEUGEBAUER, H. (1970). "A spinal measuring instrument for group studies." *Zeit. Orthop.*, **108:** 395–406.

NEUGEBAUER, H. (1973). "Kyphometric studies of 9,000 school children in Austria." *Zeit. Orthop.*, **111:** 633–639.

NEWMAN, P. H. (1952). "The erect posture." *Archiv. Middlesex Hosp.*, **2:** 118–128.

OKODA, M. (1972). "An electromyographic estimation of the relative muscular load in different human postures." *J. Hum. Ergon.* **1:** 75–93.

OKODA, M., KOGI, K. & ISHI, M. (1970). "Loading capacity of the erectors spinae muscles in static work." *J. Anthrop. Soc. Nippon*, **78:** 99–110.

OLSEN, G. A. & ALLAN, J. H. (1969). "The lateral stability of the spine." *Clin. Orthop.*, **65:** 143–156.

PAGE, R. L. (1974). "The position and dependence on weight and height of the centre of gravity of the young adult male." *Ergometrics*, **17:** 613–612.

PATTON, H. D. (1960). "Reflex regulation of movement and posture." In *Medical Physiology and Biophysics.* pp. 167–180. Ed. T. C. Ruch and J. F. Fulton: Philadelphia; Saunders.

PEARCE, D. J. (1957). "The role of posture in laminectomy." *Proc. Roy. Soc. Med.*, **50:** 109–112.

PHELPS, W. M., KIPHUTH, R. J. H. & GOFF, G. W. (1955). *The Diagnosis and Treatment of Postural Defects.* 2nd ed., Springfield, Illinois; Thomas.

RADEMAKER, G. G. J. (1931). *Standing Posture.* Berlin; Springer.

REYNOLDS, E. & LOVETT, R. W. (1909). "Method of determining the position of the centre of gravity in its relation to certain bony landmarks in the erect position." *Amer. J. Physiol.*, **24:** 286–293.

RILEY, R. L., PERMUTT, S., GODFREY, M., CHENG, T. O., HOWELL, J. B. AND SHEPARD, R. H. (1959). "Effect of posture on pulmonary dead space in man." *J. Appl. Physiol.*, **14:** 339–340.

ROAF, R. (1972). "Rib function as a means of maintaining spinal stability." *J. Bone Joint Surg.*, **54B:** 751–752.

ROBERTS, D. F. (1960). "Functional anthropometry of elderly women." *Ergometrics*, **3**: 321–327.

ROBERTS, J. B. & CURTISS, P. H. (1970). "Stability of the thoracic and lumbar spine in traumatic paraplegia following fracture or fracture-dislocation." *J. Bone Joint Surg.*, **52A**: 1115–1130.

ROBERTS, T. D. M. (1967). *Neurophysiology of Postural Mechanisms.* London; Butterworth.

ROCHE, A. F. & DAVILLA, G. H. (1974). "Differences between recumbent length and stature within individuals." *Growth*, **38**: 313–320.

ROSEMEYER, B. (1971). "Electromyographic studies of the shoulder musculature in relation to the posture of the motorist." *Arch. Orthop. Unfall-Chir.*, **69**: 59–7C.

ROSEMEYER, B. (1972). "A method of pelvic fixation in working seats." *Zeit. Orthop.*, **110**: 514–517.

ROSEMEYER, B. (1974). "The upright posture in man: a comparative study." *Zeit. Orthop.*, **112**: 151–159.

RUCH, T. C. (1960). "Pontobulbar control of posture and orientation in space." In *Medical Physiology and Biophysics.* pp. 206–219. Ed. T. C. Ruch and J. F. Fulton. Philadelphia; Saunders.

SANTSCHI, W. R., DUBOIS, J. & OTOTO, C. (1963). "Moments of inertia and centers of gravity of the living human body." *Tech. Docum. Rept.* No. AMRL-TNR: 36–63.

SCULTZ, A. H. (1942). "Conditions for balancing the head in primates." *Amer. J. Phys. Anthrop.*, **29**: 483.

SCHWARTZ, L., BRITTEN, R. H. & THOMPSON, L. R. (1928). "Studies in physical development and posture." *Publ. Hlth. Bull. No. 179.*

SEYSS, R. (1967). "On the biostatics of the spine." *Zeit. Orthop.*, **102**: 395–405.

SKOGLUND, S. (1960). "On the postnatal development of postural mechanisms as revealed by electromyography and myography in decerebrate kittens." *Acta Physiol. Scand.*, **49**: 299–317.

SLACK, C. C. (1966). "Sleeping with a painful neck." *Physiotherapy*, **5**: 248.

SMITH, J. W. (1953). "The act of standing." *Acta Orthop. Scand.*, **23**: 159–168.

SNIDJERS, C. J. (1972). "The form of the spine related to human posture." *Aggressologie*, **13B**: 5–14.

SNOOK, S. H., IRVIN, C. H. & BASS, S. F. (1970). "Maximum weights and work loads acceptable to male industrial workers: a study of lifting, pushing, pulling, carrying and walking tasks." *Amer. Industr. Hyg., Ass. J.*, **31**: 579–586.

SPLITHOFF, C. A. (1947). "Origin and development of the erect posture." *Surg. Gynec. Obstet.*, **84**: 943–949.

STRAUS, E. W. (1952). "The upright posture." *Psychiat. Quart.*, **26**: 529–561.

STRAUS, W. L. & CAVE, A. J. E. (1957). "Pathology and the posture of Neanderthal man." *Quart. Rev. Biol.*, **32**: 348–363.

STRONG, R., THOMAS, P. E. & EARL, W. D. (1967). "Patterns of muscle activity in leg, hip and torso during quiet standing." *J. Amer. Osteopath. Ass.*, **66**: 1035–1038.

SVANBERG, L. (1957). "Influence of posture on lung volumes, ventilation and circulation in normals: a spirometric-broncho-spirometric investigation." *Scand. J. Clin. Lab. Invest.*, **9** (Suppl. **25**): 1–195.

THOMAS, D. P. & WHITNEY, R. J. (1959). "Postural movements during normal standing in man." *J. Anat.*, **93**: 534–539.

TRIBE, D. H. (1954). "Posture". *J. Amer. Med. Sc.*, **1**: 206–211.

TROUP, J. D. G. & CHAPMAN, A. E. (1969). "The strength of the flexor and extensor muscles of the trunk." *J. Biomechanics*, **2**: 49–62.

TYLEMAN, D. (1973). "Rotation and torsion of the vertebrae in scoliosis." *Chir. Narz. Ruchu. Ortop. Pol.*, **38**: 151–158.

UCHINISHI, K. (1968). "Radiographic study of the weight-bearing line of human vertebrae." *J. Jap. Orthop. Ass.*, **42**: 951–964.

UMEZEWA, F. (1971). "The study of comfortable sitting postures." *J. Jap. Orthop. Ass.*, **45**: 1015–1022.

VERNON, H. M. (1924). "The effects of posture and rest in muscular work. Part B. The influence of rest pauses and changes of posture on the capacity for muscular work." *M.R.C. Indust. Fatigue Res. Bd. Rep.*, **No. 29**: 28–55.

VOLKERT, H. F. (1971). "An attempt at a demonstration of the most favourable conditions for sleep in painful vertebral conditions." *Manuelle Medizin*, **1**: 15–18.

VOS, H. W. (1973). "Physical workload in different body postures while working near to, or below ground level." *Ergonomics*, **16**: 817–828.

WADE, O. L. & GILSON, V. C. (1951). "Effect of posture on diaphragmatic movement and vital capacity in normal subjects, with a note on spirometry as an aid in determining radiologic chest volumes." *Thorax*, **6:** 103–126.

WELHAM, W. C. & BEHNKE, A. R. (1942). "The specific gravity of healthy men." *J. Amer. Med. Assoc.*, **118:** 498–501.

VON WENSOWETZ, K. (1952). "Biophysical basis for the selection of functional back braces." *Arch. Phys. Med.*, **33:** 676.

WHITNEY, R. J. (1962). "The stability provided by the feet during manoeuvres while standing." *J. Anat.*, **96:** 103–111.

WILES, P. (1937). "Postural deformities of the antero-posterior curves of the spine." *Lancet*, **1:** 911–919.

WILSON, W. H. (1927). "The influence of posture on the volume of the reserve air." *J. Physiol.*, **64:** 54–64.

YAMADA, K., IKATA, T., YAMAMOTO, H., NAKAGAWA, Y., TANAKA, H. & TEZUKA, A. (1969). "Equilibrium function in scoliosis and active corrective plaster jacket for treatment." *Tokushima J. Exp. Med.*, **16:** 1–7.

YOSHITAKE, J. (1963). "The postural influence on lung volumes of normal and obese subjects." *Kyushu J. Med. Sci.*, **14:** 305–315.

### (c) Dynamics (including Mobility)

ADRICHEM, J. A. M. VAN AND VAN DER KORST, J. K. (1973). "Assessment of the flexibility of the lumbar spine." *Scand. J. Rheumatol.* **2:** 87–91.

AHLBACK, S. O. & LINDAHL, O. (1964). "Sagittal mobility of the hip joint." *Acta Orth. Scand.*, **34:** 310–322.

AHO, A. & TAHTI, E. (1957). "Significance of functional radiography of the lumbar spine in forward and backward flexion." *Ann. Chir. Gyn. Fenn.*, **46:** 336–350.

AHO, A., VARTIAINEN, O. & SALO, O. (1955). "Segmentary mobility of the lumbar spine in antero-posterior flexion." *Ann. Med. Int. Fenn.*, **44:** 275–285.

AHO, A., VARTIAINEN, O. & SALO, O. (1955). "Segmentary antero-posterior mobility of the cervical spine." *Ann. Med. Int. Fenn.*, **44:** 287.

ALBERS, D. (1954). "Study of the function of the cervical vertebral column in dorsal and ventral flexion." *Fortschr. Roentgenol.*, **81:** 606–615.

ALLBROOK, D. B. (1954). "Characteristics of the East African vertebral column." *J. Anat.*, **88:** 599(P).

ALLBROOK, D. B. (1955). "The East African vertebral column." *Amer. J. Phys. Anthrop.*, **13:** 489–514.

ALLBROOK, D. B. (1957). "Movements of the lumbar spinal column." *J. Bone Joint Surg.*, **39B:** 339–345.

ALLEN, C. E. L. (1948). "Muscle action potentials used in the study of dynamic anatomy." *Brit. J. Phys. Med.*, **11:** 66–73.

ALSTON, W., CARLSON, K. E., FELDMAN, D. J., GRIMM, Z. & GERONTINOS, E. (1966). "A quantitative study of muscle factors in the chronic low back syndrome." *J. Amer. Geriat. Soc.*, **14:** 1041–1047.

ALVICK, I. (1949). "Tuberculosis of the spine. I. The mobility of the lumbar spine after tuberculous spondylitis." *Acta Chir. Scand.*, Suppl. **141:** p. 1.

ANDERSON, T. M. (1971). "Human kinetics and good movement." *Physiotherapy*, **57:** 169.

ANDERSSON, S. & ECKSTRÖM, T. (1941). "The mobility of the vertebral column." *Morph. Jahrb.*, **85:** 135–185.

ARJOUTS, M. M. (1971). "The biomechanics of pushing and pulling tasks." *U.S. Govt. Res. L. Dev. Report No. AD-729827.*

ARNOTT, P. & GRIEVE, G. (1960). "The relationship between torque and velocity of axial rotation of the human trunk during maximum effort." *J. Physiol.*, **201:** 87P-89P.

ASMUSSEN, E., HANSEN, O. & LAMMERT, O. (1965). "The relation between isometric and dynamic muscle strength in man." *Danish Nat. Ass. Infantile Paralysis Comm.*, **20.**

ASMUSSEN, E. & HEEBOLL-NIELSEN, K. (1958). "Posture, mobility and strength of the back in boys, 7–10." *Acta Orthop. Scand.*, **28:** 184–189.

BALL, J. & MEYERS, K. A. E. (1974). "On cervical mobility." *Ann. Rheum. Dis.*, **23:** 429–438.

BARNETT, C. H. & COBBOLD, A. F. (1969). "Muscle tension and joint mobility." *Ann. Rheum. Dis.*, **28:** 652–654.

BARRETT, T. E. & GRANT, J. H. (1968). "Distribution of lumbar motion in lumbar extension and flexion." *J. Amer. Osteopath. Ass.*, **67:** 1046–1047.

BATTYE, C. K. & JOSEPH, J. (1966). "An investigation by telemetering of the activity of some muscles in walking." *Med. Biol. Eng.*, **4:** 125–135.

BEEVOR, C. (1904). *Croonian Lectures on Muscular Movements.* London; Macmillan.

BENNETT, J. G., BERGMANIS, L. E., CARPENTER, J. E. & SKOWLUND, H. V. (1963). "Range of motion of the neck." *J. Amer. Phys. Ther. Assoc.*, **43**: 45–47.

BERNSTEIN, N. A. (1940). "Investigations on the biodynamics of walking, running and jumping: Part 2." *Moscow, Central Scientific Institute of Physical Culture.* p. 1.

BLOCKEY, N. J. & SCHORSTEIN, J. (1960). "The stiff back in children." *J. Bone Joint Surg.*, **42B**: 651.

BOCK, A. V., VANCAULAERT, C., DILL, D. B., FOLLING, A. & HURXTHAL, L. M. (1928). "Studies in muscular activity. III. Dynamic changes occurring in man at work." *J. Physiol.*, **66**: 136–161.

BOHM, K. (1959). "Description of an apparatus for measurement of the mobility of the lumbar vertebrae." *Zeit. Orthop.*, **92**: 125–217.

BORELL, U. & FERNSTROM, I. (1957). "The movements at the sacroiliac joints and their importance to changes in the pelvic dimensions during parturition." *Acta Obst. Gynec. Scand.*, **36**: 42–57.

BRADFORD, E. H. (1922). "Spinal flexibility." *Boston Med. Sci. J.*, **187**: 785–788.

BURANDT, U. & GRANDJEAN, E. (1969). "Studies of the sitting behaviour of office furniture and the influence of a good sitting profile." *Ergonomics*, **12**: 338–347.

BURKE, D. C. & BERRYMAN, D. (1971). "The place of closed manipulation in the management of flexion-rotation dislocations of the cervical spine." *J. Bone Joint Surg.*, **53B**: 165–182.

CALDWELL, L. S. (1964). "Body position and the strength and endurance of manual pull." *Human Factors*, **6**: 476–484.

CARTER, C. & SWEETNAM, R. (1958). "Familial joint laxity and recurrent dislocation of the patella." *J. Bone Joint Surg.*, **40B**: 126.

CARTER, C. & WILKINSON, J. (1954). "Persistent joint laxity and congenital dislocation of the hip." *J. Bone Joint Surg.*, **46B**: 40–45.

CLAYSON, S. J., NEWMAN, I. M., DEBEVEC, D. F., ANGER, R. W., SKOWLUND, H. V. & KOTTKE, F. (1962). "Evaluation of mobility of the hip and lumbar vertebrae of normal young women." *Arch. Phys. Med.*, **43**: 1–8.

COERMANN, R. R., ZIERGENRYRECKER, G. H., WITTWER, A. L. & VON GIERKE, H. E. (1960). "The passive dynamic mechanical properties of the lumbar-thorax-abdomen system and of the whole body system." *Aerospace Med.*, **31:** 443–455.

COLACHIS, S. C. & STROHM, B. R. (1965). "Radiographic studies of cervical spine motion in normal subjects: flexion and hyper-extension." *Arch. Phys. Med.*, **46:** 753–760.

COSSETTE, J. L., FARFAN, H. F., ROBERTSON, G. H. & WELLS, R. V. (1971). "The instantaneous centre of rotation of the third lumbar intervertebral joint." *J. Biomechanics*, **4:** 149–153.

COVENTRY, M. B. & TAPPER, E. M. (1972). "Pelvic instability." *J. Bone Joint Surg.*, **54A:** 83–101.

CROWDEN, G. D. (1928). "The physiological cost of the muscular movements involved in barrow work." *Industr. Fat. Res. Bd., Rep.* No. 50.

DAVIS, P. R. (1958). "The medical inclination of the thoracic inter-vertebral articular facets in relation to axial rotation." *J. Anat.*, **92:** 653.

DAVIS, P. R. (1959). "The medical inclination of the human thoracic intervertebral articular facets." *J. Anat.*, **93:** 68–74.

DAVIS, P. R. (1959). "Posture of the trunk during the lifting of weight." *Brit. Med. J.*, **1:** 64–68; 87–89.

DAVIS, P. R. (1967). "The mechanics and movements of the back in the working situation." *Physiotherapy*: **53:** 44–47.

DAVIS, P. R. (1969). "Trunk mechanics and intra-truncal pressures." *J. Anat.*, **105:** 185–186.

DAVIS, P. R. & TROUP, J. D. G. (1966). "Effects on the trunk of erecting pit props at different working heights." *Ergonomics*, **9:** 475–484.

DAVIS, P. R., TROUP, J. D. G. & BURNARD, J. H. (1965). "Movements of the thoracic lumbar spine when lifting: a chronocyclophoto-graphic study." *J. Anat.*, **99:** 13–26.

DELMAS, A. & RAOU, R. (1953). "Movements of the spinal column." *Compt. Rend. Ass. Anat.*, **39:** 784–787.

DELMAS, A. & RAOU, R. (1953). "Study of movements of the vertebrae in the lumbar region." *Sem. Hôp. Paris Arch. Anat.*, **29:** A8–10.

DEMPSTER, W. T. (1955). "The anthropometry of body action." *Ann. N.Y. Acad. Sc.*, **63:** 559–585.

ELDRED, E. (1960). "Posture and locomotion." In *Handbook of*

*Physiology*. Sect. 1. Vol. 2. pp. 1067–1088. Ed. J. Field, H. W. Magoun, and V. E. Holt. Washington; American Physiological Society.

ELFTMAN, H. (1939). "The function of muscles in locomotion." *Amer. J. Physiol.*, **125**: 357–366.

ELFTMAN, H. (1966). "Biomechanics of muscle: with particular application to studies of gait." *J. Bone Joint. Surg.*, **48A**: 363–377.

ELWARD, J. F. (1939). "Motion in the vertebral column." *Amer. J. Roentgenol.*, **42**: 91–99.

ERIKSON, G. E. (1963). "Brachiation in New World monkeys and in anthropoid apes." *Sym. Zool. Soc. Lond.*, **10**: 135–364.

FIELDING, J. W. (1964). "Normal and selected abnormal motion of cervical spine from C2-C7, based on cineroentgenography." *J. Bone Joint Surg.*, **46A**: 1779–1781.

FISHER, B. (1967). "A biomechanical model for the analysis of dynamic activities." Part II of "A biomechanical analysis of materials handling activities." *Report. Industr. Eng. Dept., Univ. Michigan*.

FITZGERALD, J. G. (1972). "The role of the intervertebral space in the prevention of ejection injury." *R.A.F. Inst. Aviation Med.*, I.A.M. Report No. 510.

FLINT, M. M. (1958). "Effect of increasing back and abdominal muscle strength on low back strain." *Res. Quart.*, **29**: 160–171.

FLINT, M. M. (1964). "Relationship of the gravity line test to posture, trunk strength and hip trunk flexibility of elementary schoolgirls." *Res. Quart.*, **35**: 141–146.

FLINT, M. M. & DIEHL, B. (1961). "Influence of abdominal strength, back extensor strength and trunk strength balance upon antero-posterior alignment of elementary schoolgirls." *Res. Quart.*, **32**: 490–498.

FLOYD, W. F. & SILVER, P. H. S. (1951). "Function of erectores spinae in flexion of the trunk." *Lancet*, **1**: 133–134.

FLOYD, W. F. & SILVER, P. H. S. (1951). "Further observations concerning erectores spinae function in trunk flexion." *J. Anat.*, **85**: 433.

FLOYD, W. F. & SILVER, P. H. S. (1952). "E.M.G. of the erectores spinae muscles in flexion of the lumbar vertebrae." *J. Anat.*, **86**: 484.

FRIEDEBOLD, G. (1958). "The normal activity of the spinal musculature in the electromyogram in different postural states: a study of skeletal muscle mechanics." *Zeit. Orthop.*, **90:** 1–18.

FRIGERIO, N. A., STOWE, R. R. & HOWE, J. W. (1974). "Movement of the sacroiliac joint." *Clin. Orthop.*, **100:** 370–377.

GIANTURCO, C. (1944). "A roentgen analysis of motion of lower lumbar vertebrae in normal individuals and in patients with low back pain." *Amer. J. Roentgenol.*, **52:** 261–268.

GLANVILLE, A. D. & KREEZER, G. (1937). "The maximum amplitude and velocity of joint movement in normal male human adults." *Hum. Biol.*, **9:** 197–211.

GLOVER, J. R. (1970). "Occupational health research and the problem of back pain." *Trans. Soc. Occup. Med.*, **21:** 2–12.

GREGERSEN, G. G. (1966). "An 'in vivo' study of axial rotation of the thoraco-lumbar spine." *J. Bone Joint Surg.*, **48A:** 1223 (P).

GREGERSEN, G. G. & LUCAS, D. B. (1967). "An 'in vivo' study of the axial rotation of the human thoraco-lumbar spine." *J. Bone Joint Surg.*, **49A:** 247–262.

GUERN, M. J. (1976). "Note on the movements of flexion and inclination of the vertebral column." *Bull. Acad. Med.*, **5:** 935–943.

HAFNER, R. H. V. (1952). "The relation of the hamstring muscles and movements of the spine." *Proc. Roy. Soc. Med.*, **45:** 139–142.

HALL, M. C. (1965). *The Locomotive System: Functional Anatomy.* Springfield, Illinois; Thomas.

HARDY, R. H. (1959). "A method of studying muscular activity during walking." *Med. Biol. Illust.*, **9:** 158–163.

HART, F. D., STRICKLAND, D. & CLIFFE, P. (1974). "Measurement of spinal mobility." *Ann. Rheum. Dis.*, 136–139.

HILL, A. V. (1922). "The maximum work and mechanical efficiency of human muscles and their most economical speed." *J. Physiol.*, **56:** 19–41.

HILL, A. V. (1951). "The mechanics of voluntary muscle." *Lancet*, **2:** 947–951.

HILTON, R. C. & BALL, J. (1975). "Mobility, end-plate defects and disc degeneration in the lower spine." *Ann. Rheum. Dis.*, **34:** 201.

HINCK, V. C., CLARK, W. M. & HOPKINS, C. E. (1966). "Normal interpediculate distances (minimum and maximum) in children and adults." *Amer. J. Roentgenol.*, **97:** 141–153.

HIRSCH, C. & LEWIN, T. (1968). "Lumbosacral synovial joints in flexion-extension." *Acta Orthop. Scand.*, **39**: 303–311.

HIRSCH, C. & NACHEMSON, A. (1954). "New observations on the mechanical behaviour of lumbar discs." *Acta Orthop. Scand.*, **23**: 254–283.

HIRSCH, C. & WHITE, A. A. (1971). "Characteristics in the thoracic spine motion: studies on autopsy specimens." *Clin. Orthop.*, **75**: 156–163.

HOAG, J. M., KOSOK, M. & MOSER, J. R. (1960). "Kinematic analysis and classification of vertebral motion." *J. Amer. Osteop. Assoc.*, **59**: 899–908.

HOHL, M. (1964). "Normal motions in the upper portion of the cervical spine." *J. Bone Joint Surg.*, **46A**: 1777–1779.

ISRAEL, M. (1969). "A quantitative method of estimating flexion and extension of the spine: a preliminary report." *Military Med.*, **124**: 181–186.

JAMIOLKOWSKA, K. (1973). "Planes and axes of rotation of the vertebral column in man." *Folia Morphol. (Warsz.)*, **32**: 371–379.

JEFFREYS, M., MILLARD, J. B., HYMAN, M. & WARREN, M. D. (1969). "A set of tests for measuring motor impairment in prevalence studies." *J. Chron. Dis.*, **22**: 303–319.

JIROUT, J. (1956). "Studies on the dynamics of the spine." *Acta Radiol.*, **46**: 55–60.

JIROUT, J. (1957). "The normal motility of the lumbosacral spine." *Acta Radiol.*, **47**: 345–348.

JIROUT, J. (1963). "Mobility of the thoracic spinal cord under normal conditions." *Acta Radiol.*, **54**: 729–735.

JIROUT, J. (1972). "The effect of mobilisation of the segmental blockade on the sagittal component of the reaction on lateroflexion of the cervical spine." *Neuroradiol.*, **3**: 210–215.

JIROUT, J. (1972). "Changes in the sagittal component of the reaction of the cervical spine to lateroflexion after manipulation of movement restriction." *Česk. Neurol.*, **35**: 175–180.

JIROUT, J. (1972). "Motility of the cervical vertebrae in lateral flexion of the head and neck." *Acta Radiol. (Diagn.)*, **13**: 919–927.

JIROUT, J. (1973). "Suprasegmental effect of ante- and retroflexion." *Česk. Neurol.*, **36**: 72–76.

JIROUT, J. (1974). "The dynamic dependence of the lower cervical vertebrae on the atlanto-occipital joints." *Neuroradiol.*, **7:** 249–252.

JIROUT, J., SIMON, J. & SINOMOVA, O. (1957). "Disturbances in the lumbosacral dynamics following poliomyelitis." *Acta Radiol.*, **48:** 361–365.

JONCK, L. M. & NIEKERK, J. M. VAN. (1961). "A roentgenological study of the motion of the lumbar spine of the Bantu." *Sth. Afr. J. Lab. Clin. Med.*, **7:** 67–71.

JONES, R. P., HANSON, J. A. & MILLER, J. F. (1963). "Quantitative analysis of abnormal movement. The sit-to-stand pattern." *Amer. J. Phys. Med.*, **42:** 208–218.

JOSEPH, J. (1968). "The pattern of activity of some muscles in women walking on high heels." *Ann. Phys. Med.*, **9:** 295–299.

JOSEPH, J. (1975). 'Movements at the hip joint." *Ann. Roy. Coll. Surg. Engl.*, **56:** 192–201.

KARPOVICH, P. V. (1937). "Physiological and psychological dynamogenic factors in exercise." *Arbeitsphysiol.*, **9:** 626–629.

KAZARIAN, L. (1972). "Dynamic response characteristics of the human vertebral column. An experimental study on human autopsy specimens." *Acta Orthop. Scand.* (Suppl.), 1–186.

KAZARIAN, L. E. (1975). "Creep characteristics of the human spinal column." *Orthop. Clin. Nth. Amer.*, **6:** 3–18.

KEENE, C. W. (1906). "Some experiments on the mechanical rotation of the normal spine." *Amer. J. Orthop. Surg.*, **4:** 69–79.

KELLER, H. (1924). "A clinical study of the mobility of the human spine: its extent and clinical importance." *Arch. Surg.*, **8:** 627–257.

KENDALL, H. O. & KENDALL, F. P. (1948). "Normal flexibility according to age groups." *J. Bone Joint. Surg.*, **30A:** 690–694.

KILSHAW, J. & OLLERENSHAW, R. (1954). "Assessment of spinal movement." *Med. Biol. Illustr.*, **4:** 166–177.

KINZEL, G. L., HILLBERRY, B. M. & HALL, A. S. (1972). "Measurement of the total motion between two body segments. 1. Analytical development." *J. Biomech.*, **5:** 93–105.

KIRK, J. A., ANSELL, B. M. & BYWATERS, E. G. L. (1967). "The hypermobility syndrome: musculo-skeletal complaints associated with generalised joint hypermobility." *Ann. Rheum. Dis.*, **26:** 419–425.

KNUTSSON, F. (1944). "The instability associated with disc degeneration in the lumbar spine." *Acta Radiol.*, **25:** 593–609.

KORR, I. M. & THOMAS, P. E. (1955). "Symposium on the functional implications of segmental facilitation." *J. Amer. Osteopath. Ass.*, **54:** 265–283.

KOTTKE, F. J. & LESTER, R. G. (1958). "Use of cinefluorography for evaluation of normal and abnormal motion in the neck." *Arch. Phys. Med.*, **39:** 229–231.

KOTTKE, F. J. & MUNDALE, M. O. (1959). "Range of mobility of the cervical spine." *Arch. Phys. Medicine*, **40:** 379–382.

KRAUSOVA, L. & LEWIT, K. (1965). "The mechanism and the measuring of the motility in the cranio-cervical joints during lateral inclination." *Acta Univ. Carol. Med., Suppl.* **21:** 123–126.

KULAK, R. F., SCHULTZ, A. B., BELYTSCHO, T. & GALANTE, J. (1975). "Biomechanical characteristics of vertebral motion segments and intervertebral discs." *Orthop. Clin. Nth. Amer.*, **6:** 121–123.

LANGE, W. & COERMANN, R. (1965). "Relative movements of adjacent vertebrae under an oscillating load." *Int. Zeit. Ang. Physiol. Arbeitsphysiol.*, **21:** 326–334.

LASSERRE, C. & WANGERMEZ, J. (1967). "A test of clinical assessment of the flexibility of the lumbar spine." *Ann. Méd. des Accidents et du Trafic*, **4:** 29–32.

LAUBACH, L. L. & MCCONVILLE, J. T. (1966). "Muscle strength, flexibility and body size of adult males." *Res. Quart.*, **37:** 384–392.

LAURU, L. (1957). "Physiological study of motions." *Advanced Management*, **22:** 17–24.

LEIGHTON, J. R. (1942). "A simple objective and reliable measure of flexibility." *Res. Quart.*, **13:** 205–216.

L'EPÉE, P. (1970). "Numerical assessment of lumbar spine flexibility." *Concours Médical*, **92:** 2953.

LEWIT, K. J. & KRAUSOVA, L. (1962). "A study of flexion of the cervical spine." *Fortschr. Röntgenstr.*, **97:** 38–44.

LEWIT, K. J. & KRAUSOVA, L. (1963). "Measurements of intervertebral and dorsal flexion of the cranio-cervical junction." *Česk. Neurol.*, **26:** 371–376.

LIBERSON, W. T. (1965). "Biomechanics of gait: a method of study." *Arch. Phys. Med.*, **46:** 37–48.

LINDAHL, O. (1966). "Determination of the sagittal mobility of the lumbar spine: a clinical method." *Acta Orthop. Scand.*, **37:** 241–254.

LOEBL, W. Y. (1967). "Measurement of spinal posture and range of spinal movement." *Ann. Phys. Med.*, **9**: 103–110.

LOVETT, R. W. (1900). "Movements of the normal spine in their relation to scoliosis." *J. Boston Soc. Med. Sci.*, **4**: 243.

LOVETT. R. W. (1905). "The mechanism of the normal spine and its relation to scoliosis." *Boston Med. Sci. J.*, **153**: 349–358.

LUCAS, D. B. (1970). "Mechanics of the spine." *Bull. Hosp. Joint Dis.*, **31**: 115–131.

LUCAS, D. B. & BRESLER, B. (1966). "Stability of the ligamentous spine." *Biomechanics Lab. Univ. California, Tech. Rep.*, **Ser. 11** No. 40.

LUMSDEN, R. M. & MORRIS, J. M. (1968). "An in vivo study of axial rotation and immobilization at the lumbosacral joint." *J. Bone Joint Surg.*, **50A**: 1591–1602.

MACRAE, I. F. & WRIGHT, V. (1969). "Measurement of back movement." *Ann. Rheum. Dis.*, **28**: 584–589.

McSWEENEY, T. (1971). "Stability of the cervical spine following injury accompanied by grave neurological damage." *Proc. Veterans Adm. Spinal Cord Inj. Conf.*, **18**: 61–65.

MATSUMOTO, Y. (1967). "Validity of the force/velocity relation for muscle control in the length region L10." *J. Gen. Physiol*, **50**: 1125–1137.

MEHTA, M. H. (1973). "Radiographic estimation of vertebral rotation in scoliosis." *J. Bone Joint Surg.*, **55B**: 513–520.

MENSOR, M. C. & DUVALL, G. (1959). "Absence of motion at the 4th and 5th lumbar interspaces in patients with and without low back pain." *J. Bone Joint Surg.*, **41A**: 1047–1054.

MILES, M. & SULLIVAN, W. E. (1961). "Lateral bending of the lumbar and lumbosacral joints." *Anat. Rec.*, **139**: 387–398.

MINNE, J., DEPREUX, R. & MESTDAGH, H. (1970). "The movements of rotation of the inferior cervical spine (from C3 to C7). *Compt. Rend. Assoc. Anat.*, **149**: 929–935.

MOFFATT, C. A., ADVANI, S. H. & LIN, C. J. (1971). "Analytical and experimental investigations of human spine flexure." *Amer. Soc. Mech. Eng.*, Publ. No. 71-WA/BHF-7.

MOLL, J. M. H. (1974). "Chest and spinal movement in ankylosing spondylitis." *Rheumatol. Rehab.*, **13**: 30–31.

MOLL, J. M. H., LIYANAGE, S. P. & WRIGHT, V. (1972). "An objective clinical method to measure spinal extension." *Rheumatol. Phys. Med.*, **11**: 225–239; 293–312.

MOLL, J. M. H. & WRIGHT, V. (1971). "Normal range of spinal mobility: an objective clinical study." *Ann. Rheum. Dis.*, **30:** 381–386.

MOLL, J. M. H. & WRIGHT, V. (1972). "An objective study of chest expansion." *Ann. Rheum. Dis.*, **31:** 1–8.

MOLL, J. M. H. & WRIGHT, V. (1973). "The pattern of chest and spinal mobility in ankylosing spondylitis: an objective clinical study of 106 patients." *Rheumatol. Rehab.*, **12:** 115–134.

MORRIS, J. R. W. (1973). "Accelerometry—a technique for the measurement of human body movements." *J. Biomechanics*, **6:** 729–736.

MORTON, D. J. (1952). *Human Locomotion and Body Form. A Study of Gravity and Man.* Baltimore; Williams and Wilkins.

MOULTON, A. & SILVER, J. R. (1970). "Chest movement in patients with traumatic injuries of the cervical cord." *Clin. Sci.*, **39:** 407–422.

MURDALE, M. O., HISLOP, H. J., RABIDEAU, R. J. & KOTTKE, F. S. (1956). "Evaluation of extension of limb." *Arch. Phys. Med.*, **37:** 75–80.

MURRAY, P. M., DROUGHT, A. B. & KORY, R. C. (1964). "Walking patterns of normal men." *J. Bone Joint Surg.*, **34A:** 647–650.

NAKAJIMA, H. (1969). "A study of the dynamic aspect of facet syndrome with considerations for therapy." *J. Jap. Orthop. Ass.*, **43:** 629–643.

NASH, C. L. & MOE, J. H. (1969). "A study of vertebral rotation." *J. Bone Joint Surg.*, **51A:** 223–229.

PATTERSON, F. P. (1973). "Instability of the upper cervical spine." *J. Bone Joint Surg.*, **55B:** 456–457.

RASCH, P. J. & BURKE, R. K. (1963). *Kinesiology and Applied Anatomy: The Science of Human Movement.* 2nd ed. Philadelphia: Lea and Febiger.

REICHMANN, S. (1971). "Motion of the lumbar articular processes in flexion-extension and lateral flexions of the spine." *Acta Morph. Néerl. Scand.*, **8:** 261–272.

REICHMANN, S., BERGLUND, E. & LUNDGREN, R. (1972). "The centre of movement in the lumbar spine in flexion and extension." *Zeit. Anat. Entwickl.*, **138:** 283–287.

REID, J. D. (1960). "Effects of flexion-extension movements of the head and spine upon the spinal cord and nerve roots." *J. Neurol. Neurosurg. Psychiat.*, **23:** 214.

REISS, J. H. O. (1921). "The changing forces during movement." *Archiv. ges. Physiol*, **191**: 234–259.

REYNOLDS, P. M. G. (1975). "Measurement of spinal mobility: a comparison of three methods." *Rheumatol. Rehab.*, **14**: 180–185.

ROLANDER, S. D. (1966). "Motion of the lumbar spine with special reference to the stabilizing effect of posterior fusion." *Acta Orthop. Scand.* (Suppl. **90**): 1.

ROSENBERG, P. (1955). "The R-Center method. A new method for analysing vertebral motion by X-Rays." *J. Amer. Orthop. Ass.*, **55**: 103–111.

ROSTOCK, P. (1938). "A study of the range of movement of the vertebral column." *Med. Klin.*, **34**: 1465–1467.

SCHALMITZEK, M. (1958). *Radiological Functional Studies of the Vertebral Column.* Aarhus; Universitäts Forlagd.

SCHENK, J. K. & FORWARD, E. M. (1965). "Quantitative strength changes with rest repetitions." *J. Amer. Phys. Therap. Ass.*, **45**: 562–569.

SCHOENING, H. A. & HANNAN, V. (1964). "Factors related to cervical mobility." Part 1. *Arch. Phys. Med. Rehab.*, **45**: 602–609.

SCHULTZ, A. B., BELYTSCHCKO, T. B. & ANDRIACCHI, T. P. (1973). "Analog studies of forces in the human spine: mechanical properties and motion segment behaviour." *J. Biomechanics*, **6**: 373–383.

SELECKI, B. R. (1969). "The effects of rotation of the atlas on the axis: experimental work." *Med. J. Aust.*, **1**: 1012–1015.

SEMLAK, K. & FERGUSON, A. B. (1970). "Joint stability maintained by atmospheric pressure." *Clin. Orthop.*, **68**: 294–300.

SHELDON, J. H. (1963). "The effect of age on the control of sway." *Geront. Clin. (Basel).*, **5**: 129–138.

SILVER, P. H. S. (1954). "Direct observations on changes in tension in the supraspinous and interspinous ligaments during flexion and extension of the vertebral column in man." *J. Anat.*, **88**: 550–551(P).

SOMERVILLE, E. W. (1952). "Rotational lordosis: development of the single curve." *J. Bone Joint Surg.*, **34B**: 421.

STEEN, B. (1966). "The function of certain neck muscles in different positions of the head with and without loading of the cervical spine." *Acta Morph. Néerl. Scand.*, **6**: 301–310.

STEINBECK, W. (1974). "Functional diagnosis during lumbar myelography." *Zeit. Orthop.*, **112**: 801–804.

STEINDLER, A. (1935). *Mechanics of Normal and Pathological Locomotion in Man*. London; Baillière, Tindall and Cox.

STEINDLER, A. (1953). "A historical review of the studies and investigations made in relation to human gait." *J. Bone Joint Surg.*, **35A**: 540–542.

STEINDLER, A. (1955). *Kinesiology of the Human Body Under Normal and Pathological Conditions*. Springfield, Illinois; Thomas.

STURROCK, R. D., WOJTULEWSKI, J. A. & HART, F. D. (1973). "Spondylometry in a normal population and in ankylosing spondylitis." *Rheumatol. Rehab.*, **12**: 135–142.

SWEETMAN, B. J., ANDERSON, J. A. D. & DALTON, E. R. (1974). "The relationships between little-finger mobility, lumbar mobility, straight-leg-raising and low back pain." *Rheumatol. Rehab.*, **13**: 161–166.

SWIDERSKI, G. (1968). "A radiological study of vertebral instability in overloaded lumbar spondylolisthesis." *Beitr. Orthop. Trauma*, **15**: 598–604.

TANZ, S. S. (1950). "To-and-fro motion range at the 4th and 5th lumbar interspaces." *J. Mt. Sinai Hosp.*, **16**: 303–307.

TANZ, S. S. (1953). "Motion of the lumbar spine: a roentgenographic study." *Amer. J. Roentgenol.*, **69**: 399–412.

THOMAS, G. (1967). "Studies of the mechanics of flattening of lordosis in the lumbar vertebral region." *Zeit. Orthop.*, **102**: 524–533.

TIMM, H. (1970). "A comparable representation of the shape and mobility of the vertebral column by means of a plastic curved ruler." *Manual Med.*, **6**: 140–150.

TOWNSEND, E. H. & ROWE, M. (1952). "Mobility of the upper cervical spine in health and disease." *Paediatrics*, **10**: 567–573.

TROUP, J. D. G., HOOD, C. A. & CHAPMAN, A. E. (1968). "Measurements of the sagittal mobility of the lumbar spine and hips." *Ann. Phys. Med.*, **9**: 308–321.

TYLMAN, D. (1973). "Rotation and torsion and the vertebrae in scoliosis." *Chir. Narz. Ruchu Orthop. Pol.*, **38**: 151–158.

UMEHARA, K. (1969). "Studies of spondylosis: mainly an unstable movement of the lumbar spine." *J. Osaka City Med. Center*, **18**: 457–469.

UNIVERSITY OF CALIFORNIA (1947). *Fundamental Studies of Human*

*Locomotion and Other Information Relating to Design of Artificial Limbs*. 2 vols. Berkeley, California.

VIRCHOW, H. (1911). "Individual studies of sagittal bending of the human vertebral column." *Anat. Anz. (Ergangsheft)*, **38:** 176–183.

VIRCHOW, H. (1928). "Sagittal flexion movements of the human cervical spine." *Arch. Orthop. Unfall-Chir.*, **26:** 1–42.

VRV, L. (1957). "Physiological study of motions." *Advanced Management*, **22:** 17–24.

VYHNANEK, L., SEMAN, M. & JANATA, M. (1972). "Functional examination during peridurography of the lumbar spine." *Česk. Radiol.*, **26:** 189–195.

WALLACE, N. W. (1941). "Stair climbing by postmen." *The Post*, **26:** 24–25.

WATERLAND, J. C. & MUNSON, N. (1964). "Reflex association of head and shoulder girdle in nonstressful movements of man." *Amer. J. Phys. Med.*, **43:** 98–108.

WATERS, R. L. & MORRIS, J. M. (1972). "Electrical activity of muscles of the trunk during walking." *J. Anat.*, **111:** 191–199.

WATERS, R. L., MORRIS, J. M. & PERRY, J. (1973). "Translational motion of the head and trunk during normal walking." *J. Biomechanics*, **6:** 167–172.

WERNE, S. (1959). "The possibilities of movement in the cranio-vertebral joints." *Acta Orthop. Scand.*, **28:** 165–173.

WHITE, A. A. (1971). "Kinematics of the normal spine as related to scoliosis." *J. Biomechanics*, **4:** 405–411.

WHITE, A. A. & HIRSCH, C. (1971). "The significance of the vertebral posterior elements in the mechanics of the thoracic spine." *Clin. Orthop.*, **81:** 2–14.

WILES, P. (1935). "Movements of the lumbar vertebrae during flexion and extension." *Proc. Roy. Soc. Med.*, **28:** 647–651.

WILKIE, D. R. (1950). "The relation between force and velocity in human muscle." *J. Physiol.*, **110:** 249–280.

WILLIAMS, M. & STUTZMAN, L. (1959). "Strength variations through the range of joint motion." *Phys. Therapy Rev.*, **39:** 145–152.

WILLIS, T. A. (1923). "The lumbosacral vertebral column in man: its stability of form and function." *Amer. J. Anat.*, **32:** 95–123.

WILLIS, T. A. (1963). "Lumbosacral retrodisplacement." *Amer. J. Roentgenol.*, **90:** 1263–1266.

WOLFF, H. D. (1972). "Painful fixation of the vertebral column; vertebral blocking and its manual therapy." *Verh. Dtsch. ges. Rheumatol.*, **2** (Suppl. **2**): 215–226.

WORTZMAN, G. & DEWAR, F. P. (1968). "Rotary fixation of the atlantoaxial joint." *Radiology*, **90**: 479–487.

WRIGHT, V. (1971). "The lubrication and stiffness of joints." *Mod. Trends Rheumatol.*, **2**: 30–45.

WRIGHT, V. (1972). "Joint mechanics." *Physiotherapy*, **58**: 367–370.

WRIGHT V. (1973). "Stiffness: a review of its measurement and physiological importance." *Physiotherapy*, **59**: 107.

WRIGHT, V. & JOHNS, R. J. (1960). "Physical factors concerned with the stiffness of normal and diseased joints." *Bull. Johns Hopkins Hosp.*, **106**: 215–231.

WRIGHT, V., LONGFIELD, M. D. & DOWSON, D. (1969). "Joint stiffness—its characterisation and significance." *Biomed. Eng.*, Jan.: 1–9.

WRIGHTS, J. (1944). "Mechanics in relation to derangement of the facet joints of the spine." *Arch. Phys. Ter.*, **25**: 201–206.

WYKE, B. D. (1972). "Arthrokinetic reflex contributions to motor control." *Proc. 2nd Int. Symp. (I.U.P.S.) on Motor Control, Varna, Bulgaria:* p. 109.

YAMAJI, K. (1968). "Kinesiologic study with electromyography of low back pain." *Electromyography*, **8**: 119.

## (d) Mechanical Analysis

ANDRIACCHI, T. (1974). "A model for studies of mechanical interactions between the human spine and rib cage." *J. Biomech.*, **1**: 497–507.

ASMUSSEN, E., POULSEN, E. & ASMUSSEN, B. (1965). "Quantitative evaluation of the activity of the back muscles in lifting." *Danish Nat. Ass. Infantile Paralysis, Communication No. 21.*

BATTYE, C. K. & JOSEPH, J. (1966). "An investigation by telemetering of the activity of some muscles in walking." *Med. Biol. Engin.*, **4**: 125–135.

BREKERMANS, W. A. M. (1972). "A new method to analyse the mechanical behaviour of skeletal parts." *Acta Orthop. Scand.*, **43**: 301–317.

BROWN, T., HANSEN, R. J. & YORRA, A. J. (1957). "Some mechanical tests on the lumbosacral spine with particular reference to the intervertebral discs: a preliminary report." *J. Bone Joint Surg.*, **39A:** 1135–1164.

CAMASSO, M. E. & MAROTTI, G. (1962). "The mechanical behaviour of articular cartilage under compressive stress." *J. Bone Joint Surg.*, **44A:** 699–709.

CAVE, E. F. & ROBERTS, S. M. (1936). "A method of measuring and recording joint function." *J. Bone Joint Surg.*, **34A:** 455–465.

DEMPSTER, W. T. (1965). "Mechanics of shoulder movement." *Arch. Phys. Med.*, **46:** 49–70.

DIERSSEN, G., LORENC, M. & SPITALERI, R. M. (1961). "A new method for graphic study of human movements." *Neurology*, **11:** 610–618.

DILL, D. B., TALBOTT, J. H. & EDWARDS, H. T. (1930). "Studies in muscular activity. VI. Response of several individuals to a fixed task." *J. Physiol.*, **69:** 267–305.

DINNAR, U. (1975). "Lubrication theory in synovial joints." *CRC Crit. Rev. Bioeng.*, **2:** 159–177.

DITTMAR, O. (1929). "Sagittal and lateral flexion movement of the human lumbar spine in radiographs." *Zeit. ges. Anat.*, **92:** 644–667.

DITTMAR, O. (1930). "Observations on joint behaviour in the lumbar region in sagittal and lateral flexion movements. The mechanics of the vertebral column: Part II." *Zeit. ges. Anat.*, **93:** 477–483.

DITTMAR, O. (1931). "Radiological studies of the mechanics of the vertebral column." *Zeit. Orthop. Chir.*, **55:** 321–351.

DRILLIS, R. J. (1959). "The use of gliding cyclograms in the biomechanical analysis of movements." *Human Factors*, **1:** 1–11.

DUCHENNE, G. B. (1867). *Physiology of Movements.* Trans. and ed. by E. M. Kaplan (1949). Philadelphia; Saunders.

DUNLAP, K., SHANDS, A. R., HOLLISTER, L. C., GAUL, J. S. & STREIT, H. A. (1953). "A new method for determination of torsion of the femur." *J. Bone Joint Surg.*, **35A:** 289–311.

EBERHART, H. D. & INMAN, V. T. (1951). "An evaluation of experimental procedures used in a fundamental study of human locomotion." *Ann. N.Y. Acad. Sci.*, **51:** 1213–1228.

FITZGERALD, E. R. & FREELAND, A. E. (1971). "Viscoelastic response of intervertebral discs at audiofrequencies." *Med. Biol. Eng.*, **9:** 459–478.

GAUGHRAN, G. R. L. & DEMPSTER, W. T. (1956). "Force analyses of horizontal 2-handed pushes and pulls in the sagittal plane." *Human Biology*, **28**: 67–92.

GRAY, J. (1944). "Studies in the mechanics of the tetrapod skeleton." *J. Exper. Biol.*, **20**: 88–116.

HARTMAN, W. F. (1974). "Deformation and failure of spinal materials. Human vertebrae and intervertebral discs are shown to have stress-strain relations and failure criteria that can be experimentally replicated." *Experimental Mechanics*, **14**: 98–103.

HIRSCH, C. _(1956). "The mechanical response in normal and degenerated lumbar discs." *J. Bone Joint Surg.*, **38A**: 242–243.

HIRSCH, C. & GALENTE, J. (1967). "Laboratory conditions for tensile tests in annulus fibrosus." *Acta Orthop. Scand.*, **38**: 148.

HUTTON, W. C. & DRABBLE, G. E. (1972). "New appliance. An apparatus to give the distribution of vertical load under the foot." *Rheum. Phys. Med.*, **11**: 313–317.

JOSEPH, J. (1962). "The analysing projector in investigating movements." *J. Anat.*, **96**: 413.

KING, A. I. & VULCAN, A. P. (1971). "Elastic deformation characteristics of the spine." *J. Biomechanics*, **4**: 413–429.

KRAUSE, H. (1963). "The vibratory mechanical behaviour of the spine." *Int. Zeit. Ang. Physiol.*, **20**: 125–255.

KUMAR, S. (1974). "A study of spinal motion during lifting." *Irish J. Med. Sci.*, **143**: 86–95.

INDAHL, O. & RAEDER, E. (1962). "Mechanical analysis of forces in idiopathic scoliosis." *Acta Orth. Scand.*, **32**: 27–38.

MAROTZKY, H. H. (1972). "Isometric force measurements in the head and neck system in young and old human subjects." *Arch. Orthop. Unfall.-Chir.*, **74**: 42–62.

MORRIS, J. M., LUCAS, D. B. & BRESLER, B. (1961). "Role of the trunk in stability of the spine." *J. Bone Joint Surg.*, **43A**: 327–351.

PALKA, M. (1975). "An evaluation of work load in paving plate production." *Ergonomics*, **18**: 271–278.

PANJABI, M. (1973). "Three-dimensional mathematical model of the human spine structure." *J. Biomech.*, **6**: 671–680.

PANJABI, M. & WHITE, A. A. (1971). "A mathematical approach for three-dimensional analysis of the mechanics of the spine." *J. Biomech.*, **4**: 203–211.

PEREY, O. (1957). "Fracture of the vertebral end plate in the lumbar spine: an experimental biomechanical investigation." *Acta Orthop. Scand.*, (Suppl. **25**): p. 101.

PLAUE, R. (1972). "Fracture characteristics of thoracic and lumbar vertebral bodies. Compression tests in fresh cadavers." *Zeit. Orthop.*, **110**: 357–362.

PLAUE, R. (1974). "Fracture characteristics of thoracic and lumbar vertebral bodies. Discussion of a theoretical fracture model." *Zeit. Orthop.*, **112**: 1071–1077.

PLAUE, R., GERNER, J. J. & PUHL, W. (1973). "Fracture characteristics of thoracic and lumbar vertebral bodies. Studies on the morphology of vertebral compression damage." *Zeit. Orthop.*, **111**: 139–146.

POULSEN, E. (1970). "Prediction of maximum loads in lifting from measurements of muscular strength." *Progr. Phys. Therapy*, **1**: 146–149.

ROAF, R. (1958). "Rotation movements of the spine with special reference to scoliosis." *J. Bone Joint Surg.*, **40B**: 312–332.

ROAF, R. (1972). "The significance of horizontal forces in the development and control of spinal deformities." *Paraplegia*, **9**: 183.

ROGERS, S. P. (1933). "Mechanics of scoliosis." *Arch. Surg.*, **26**: 962–980.

RUSSELL, M. R. (1970). "The mechanics of lifting and carrying by manual means." *J. Jenner Inst. Engineers*, **80**: 265–272.

SEIREG, A. (1975). "The prediction of muscular load sharing and joint forces in the lower extremities during walking." *J. Biomech.*, **8**: 89–102.

THORNTON BROWN, J., HANSEN, R. J. & YORRA, A. J. (1957). "Some mechanical tests on the lumbosacral spine with particular reference to the intervertebral discs. *J. Bone Joint Surg.*, **39A**: 1135–1164.

TICHAUER, E. R. (1971). "A pilot study of the biomechanics of lifting in simulated industrial work situations." *J. Safety Res.*, **3**: 98–115.

WEISS, M. & BENTKOWSKI, Z. (1974). "Biomechanical study in dynamic spondylodesis of the spine." *Clin. Orthop.*, **103**: 199–203.

WHITE, A. A. (1969). "Analysis of the mechanics of the thoracic spine in man." *Acta Orthop. Scand.*, (Suppl. **127**): 1.

WHITE, A. A. (1975). "Biomechanics analysis of the clinical stability in the cervical spine." *Clin. Orthop.*, **109**: 85–96.


### (e) Stress Measurement

ANDERSON, T. McL. (1960). *Manual of Lifting and Handling*. London; Industrial Welfare Society.

ARKIN, A. M. (1949). "Mechanism of the structural changes in scoliosis." *J. Bone Joint Surg.*, **31A**: 519–527.

ASMUSSEN, E. (1960). "The weight carrying function of the human spine." *Acta Orth. Scand.*, **29**: 276–290.

ASMUSSEN, E. & HEEBOLL-NIELSEN, K. (1961). "Isometric muscle strength of adult men and women." *Danish Nat. Assoc. Infantile Paralysis, Communication No. 11*.

ASMUSSEN, E., HEEBOLL-NIELSEN, K. & MOLBECH, S. (1959). "Methods for evaluation of muscle strength." *Danish Nat. Assoc. Infantile Paralysis, Communication No. 5*.

ASMUSSEN, E. & POULSEN, E. (1968). "On the role of intra-abdominal pressure in relieving the back muscles while holding weights in a forward inclined position." *Danish Nat. Assoc. Infantile Paralysis, Communication No. 28*.

ASMUSSEN, E., POULSEN, E. & RASMUSSEN, B. (1965). "Quantitative evaluation of the activity of the back muscles in lifting." *Danish Nat. Assoc. Infantile Paralysis Communication No. 21*.

BASMAJIAN, J. V. (1961). "Weightbearing by ligaments and muscles." *Canadian J. Surg.*, **4**: 166–170.

BEARN, J. G. (1961). "Function of certain shoulder muscles in posture and in holding weights." *Ann. Phys. Med.*, **6**: 100–104.

BEARN, J. G. (1961). "The significance of the abdominal muscles in weight lifting." *Acta Anat.*, **45**: 83–89.

BECKER, R. O. (1960). "The electrical response of human skeletal muscle to passive stretch." *J. Bone Joint Surg.*, **42A**: 1091–1103.

BEDALE, E. M. (1924). "Comparison of the energy expenditure of a woman, carrying loads in eight different positions." *M.R.C. Industr. Fatigue Res. Board, Rep.*, No. 29: 1–27.

BEDFORD, T. & WARNER, C. G. (1937). "Strength test: Observations on the effect of posture on strength of pull." *Lancet*, **2**: 1328–1329.

BELYTSCHKO, T. B., ANDRIACCHI, T. P., SCHULTZ, A. B. & TALANTE,

157

J. O. (1973). "Analog studies of forces in the human spine: computational techniques." *J. Biomechanics*, **6**: 361–371.

BELYTSCHKO, T. B., KULAK, R. F., SCHULTZ, A. B. & GALANTE, J. O. (1974). "Finite element stress analysis of an intervertebral disc." *J. Biomechanics*, **7**: 277–285.

BREIG, A. (1966). "Effects of mechanical stresses on the spinal cord in cervical spondylosis." *J. Neurosurg.*, **25**: 45.

BREIG, A., TURNBULL, I. & HASSLER, O. (1966). "Effects of mechanical stresses on the spinal cord in cervical spondylosis. A study on fresh cadaver material." *J. Neurosurg.*, **25**: 45–56.

CARLOCK, J., WEASNER, M. H. & STRAUSS, P. S. (1963). "Portability: A new look at an old problem." *Human Factors*, **5**: 577–581.

CARLSÖÖ, S. (1961). "The static muscle load in different work positions: an electromyographic study." *Ergonomics*, **4**: 193–211.

CARLSÖÖ, S. (1964). "Influence of frontal and dorsal loads on muscle activity and on the weight distribution in the feet." *Acta Orthop. Scand.*, **34**: 299–309.

CHAFFIN, D. B. (1974). "Human strength capability and low back pain." *J. Occup. Med.*, **16**: 248–254.

CHAFFIN, D. B. & MOULIS, E. J. (1969). "An empirical investigation of low back strains and vertebral geometry." *J. Biomechanics*, **2**: 89–96.

CLARKE, H. H. (1966). *Muscular Strength and Endurance in Man.* New Jersey; Prentice Hall.

COLLUMBINE, H., BIBILE, S. W., WIKRAMANAYAKE, T. W., & WATSON, R. S. (1950). "X says 60% for weight lifting." *J. Appl. Phys.*, **2**: 488–511.

DAS, R. (1951). "Energy expenditure in weight lifting by different methods." *Ph.D. Thesis, University of London.*

DAVIS, P. R. (1956). "Variations of the human intra-abdominal pressure during weight-lifting in different postures." *J. Anat.*, **90**: 601 (P).

DAVIS, P. R. (1963). "Some effects of lifting, pushing and pulling on the human trunk." *Ergonomics*, **6**: 303–304.

DAVIS, P. R. & TROUP, J. D. G. (1964). "Effects on the trunk of handling heavy loads in different postures." *Ergonomics*, **7**: 323–327.

DAVIS, P. R. & TROUP, J. D. G. (1964). "Pressure in the trunk cavities when pulling, pushing and lifting." *Ergonomics*, **7**: 465–474.

DEMPSTER, W. T. (1958). "Analysis of two-handed pulls using free body diagrams." *J. Appl. Physiol.*, **13:** 469–480.

DENSLOW, J. S. & CHACE, J. A. (1962). "Mechanical stresses in the human lumbar spine and pelvis." *J. Amer. Osteopath. Ass.*, **61:** 705–712.

DE VRIES, H. A. (1961). "Electromyographic observations of the effect of static stretching upon muscular distress." *Research Quart.*, **32:** 468–479.

DUPUIS, H. (1959). "Effect of tractor operation on human stresses." *Agric. Engineering*, **42:** 510–525.

DUPUIS, J. (1974). "Stress during mechanical vibration and possible injuries in the region of the vertebral column. 1. Vibratory stress and physiological reactions." *Fortschr. Med.*, **92:** 618–620.

DUQUETTE, R. (1963). "Allowances for weight pushing." *Time and Motion Study*, **12:** 36–39.

EIE, N. (1966). "Load capacity of the low back." *J. Oslo City Hosp.*, **16:** 73–98.

EIE, N. (1973). "Recent measurements of the intra-abdominal pressure." In *Perspectives in Biomedical Engineering.* pp. 121–122. Ed. Kenedi, R. M. London; Macmillan.

EIE, N. & WEHN, P. (1962). "Measurements of the intra-abdominal pressure in relation to weight bearing of the lumbo-sacral spine." *J. Oslo City Hosp.*, **12:** 205–217.

EVANS, F. G. & LISSNER, H. R. (1957). "Studies on the compressive strength of the lumbar discs and vertebrae." *Anat. Rec.*, **121:** 290.

FITZGERALD, J. G. (1972). "Changes in spinal stature following brief periods of static shoulder loading." *R.A.F. Inst. Aviation Med.*, I.A.M. Report No. 514.

FRANKE, J. & WOLF, H. (1970). "A temporary apparatus for preventing high vertebral column stresses during knee bending under heavy loads." *Medizin und Sport*, **10:** 365–369.

FRANKE, J. & WOLF, H. (1970). "Experiences with an orthopaedic-type temporary apparatus for relieving the vertebral column during bending under heavy loads in sport." *Beitr. Orthop.*, **17:** 712–714.

FUSE, K. (1969). "Study on tensile strength of the vertebral arch in the spinal supporting system, with special reference to the isolated arch of the vertebrae in spondylosis." *Jap. Nippon Ika, Daig. Z.*, **36:** 132–159.

GARRY, R. C. (1930). "The factors determining the most effective push or pull which can be exerted by a human being on a straight lever moving in a vertical plane." *Arbeitsphysiol.*, **3**: 330–346.

HANAOKA, H. (1967). "Experimental study on the effects of repeated mechanical strokes on the intervertebral disc in the lumbosacral region." *J. Jap. Orthop. Ass.*, **41**: 399–410.

HANSEN, A. T. (1949). "Pressure measurement in human organism." *Acta Physiol. Scand.*, **19** (Suppl. **68**): 1.

HELLEBRANDT, F. A., HOUTZ, S. J., PARTRIDGE, M. J. & WALTERS, C. E. (1956). "Tonic neck reflexes in exercises of stress in man." *Amer. J. Phys. Med.*, **35**: 144–159.

HIRSCH, C. (1955). "The reaction of intervertebral discs to compression forces." *J. Bone Joint Surg.*, **37A**: 1188–1196.

HISLOP, H. J. (1963). "Quantitative changes in human muscular strength during isometric exercise." *J. Amer. Phys. Therap. Assoc.*, **43**: 21–28.

HODGSON, V. R., LISSNER, H. R. & PATRICK, L. M. (1963). "The effects of jerk on the human spine." *Amer. Soc. Mech. Eng., Paper No. 63-WA-316.*

HODGSON, V. R., LISSNER, H. R. & PATRICK, L. M. (1963). "Response of the seated human cadaver to acceleration and jerk with and without seat cushions." *Human Factors*, **5**: 505–523.

HOUTZ, S. J. (1964). "Influence of gravitational forces on function of lower extremity muscles." *J. Appl., Physiol.*, **19**: 999–1004.

HUNT, T. A. (1974). "Tissue reactions to pressure stresses in miners." *Practitioner*, **213**: 189–194.

HURXTHAL, L. M. (1968). "Measurement of anterior vertebral compressions and biconcave vertebrae." *Amer. J. Roentgenol.*, **103**: 635–644.

ISHIGE, S. (1970). "Study of the strain on intervertebral discs." *Arch. Jap. Chir.*, **39**: 137–146.

IXAI, M. & STEINHAUS, A. H. (1961). "Some factors modifying the expression of human strength." *J. Appl. Physiol.*, **16**: 157–163.

JAYSON, M. I. V., HERBERT, C. M. & BARKS, J. S. (1973). "Intervertebral discs: nuclear morphology and bursting pressures." *Ann. Rheum. Dis.*, **32**: 308–315.

JOHNSON, J. W. (1964). "Sacro-iliac strain." *J. Amer. Osteopath. Ass.*, **63**: 1015–1029 and 1046–1132.

JONCK, L. M. (1964). "The influence of weight-bearing on the lumbar spine: a radiological study." *Sth. Afr. J. Radiol.*, **2**: 25–30.

KANEMATSU, H. (1970). "An experimental study of intradiscal pressure." *J. Jap. Orthop. Ass.*, **44**: 589–599.

KARVEN, M. J. & RONNHOLM, J. (1964). "E.M.G.s and energy expenditure studies of rhythmic and paced lifting work." *Ann. Acad. Sci. Tenn., A.V. Med., 106/19.*

KELLOGG, L. C. (1923). "Impossibility of moving vertebrae." *J. Amer. Med. Ass.*, **81**: 233.

KLAUSEN, K. (1965). "The form and function of the loaded human spine." *Acta Physiol. Scand.*, **65**: 176–190.

KONZ, S., DEY, S. & BENNETT, C. (1973). "Forces and torques in lifting." *Human Factors*, **15**: 237–245.

KROEMER, K. H. E. (1974). "Horizontal push and pull forces exerted when standing in working positions on various surfaces." *Applied Eng.*, **52**: 94–102.

KROEMER, K. H. E. & BERNARD, E. (1969). "Push forces exerted in 65 common working positions." *Aerospace Medical Res. Lab., Wright Patterson Report No. A.M.R.L.T.R.*, **68**: 143.

KRUTZ, R. W., ROSITANO, S. A. & MANCINI, R. E. (1975). "Comparison of techniques for measuring +G3 tolerance in man." *J. Appl. Physiol.*, **38**: 1143–1145.

KUMAR, S. & DAVIS, P. R. (1973). "Lumbar vertebral innervation and intra-abdominal pressure." *J. Anat.*, **114**: 47–53.

LANGMAACK, B. (1953). "Pressure and impact experiments on cadaveric lumbar spines." *Zeit. Anat. Entw.*, **118**: 20–27.

LANYON, L. E. (1971). "Strain in sheep lumbar vertebrae recorded during life." *Acta Orthop. Scand.*, **43**: 102–112.

LIETZKE, M. H. (1956). "Relation between weight-lifting totals and body weight." *Science*, **124**: 486–487.

LIU, Y. K. (1975). "The resistance of the lumbar spine to direct stress." *Orthop. Clin. Nth. Amer.*, **6**: 215–231.

MARKOLF, K. L. (1972). "Deformation of the thoracolumbar intervertebral joints in response to external loads. A biomechanical study using autopsy material." *J. Bone Joint Surg.*, **54A**: 511–533.

MARKOLF, K. L. & MORRIS, J. M. (1974). "The structural components of the intervertebral disc: a study of their contributions to the ability of the disc to withstand compressive forces." *J. Bone Joint Surg.*, **56A**: 675–687.

MERTON, P. A. (1954). "Voluntary strength and fatigue." *J. Physiol.*, **123**: 553–564.

MERTON, P. A. (1956). "Problems of muscular fatigue." *Brit. Med. Bull.*, **12**: 219–221.

MILLS, J. N. (1950). "The pressures developed in abdomen and thorax during the Flack tests." *J. Physiol.*, **111**: 368–375.

MOLBECH, S. (1963). "Average percentage force at repeated maximum isometric muscle contractions at different frequencies." *Danish Nat. Assoc. Infantile Paralysis Communication No. 16.*

MURPHY, D. R. & MENGERT, W. F. (1933). "Intra-abdominal pressures created by muscular effort." *Surg. Gynec. Obst.*, **57**: 487–493.

MYERS, S. J. & SULLIVAN, W. P. (1968). "Effect of circulatory occlusion on time of muscular fatigue." *J. Appl. Physiol.*, **24**: 54–59.

NACHEMSON, A. (1959). "Measurement of intradiscal pressure." *Acta Orthop. Scand.*, **28**: 269–289.

NACHEMSON, A. (1960). "Lumbar intradiscal pressure: experimental studies on postmortem material." *Acta Orthop. Scand.* (Suppl. **43**): 1.

NACHEMSON, A. (1963). "The influence of spinal movements on the lumbar intra-discal pressure and on the tensile stresses in the annulus fibrosus." *Acta Orthop. Scand.*, **33**: 183–207.

NACHEMSON, A. (1965). "The effect of forward leaning on lumbar intra-discal pressure." *Acta Orthop. Scand.*, **35**: 314–328.

NACHEMSON, A. (1965). "*In vivo* discometry in lumbar discs with irregular nucleograms." *Act. Orthop. Scand.*, **35**: 418–434.

NACHEMSON, A. (1966). "The load on lumbar discs in different positions of the body." *Clin. Orthop.*, **45**: 107–122.

NACHEMSON, A. (1966). "Mechanical stresses on lumbar discs." *Curr. Pract. Orthop. Surg.*, **3**: 208–224.

NACHEMSON, A. (1972). "The mechanical properties of the lumbar intervertebral discs and their clinical implications." *J. Bone Joint Surg.*, **54B**: 195.

NACHEMSON, A. & ELFSTROM, G. (1970). "Intravital dynamic pressure measurements in lumbar discs: a study of common movements, manoeuvres and exercises." *Scand. J. Rehab. Med.* (Suppl. **1**): 1.

NACHEMSON, A. & ELFSTROM, G. (1971). "Intravital wireless telemetry of axial forces in Harrington Distraction Rods in patients with idiopathic scoliosis." *J. Bone Joint Surg.*, **53A**: 445–465.

NACHEMSON, A. & ELFSTROM, G. (1973). "Intravital measurements of forces in the human spine: their clinical implications for low back pain and scoliosis." In *Perspectives in Biomedical Engineering*. pp. 111–119. Ed. Kenedi, R. M. London; Macmillan.

NACHEMSON, A. & LINDH, M. (1973). "Measurement of abdominal and back muscle strength with and without low back pain." *Scand. J. Rehab. Med.*, **1:** 60–65.

NACHEMSON, A. & MORRIS, J. M. (1963). "Lumbar discometry: lumbar intradiscal pressure measurements *in vivo*." *Lancet*, **1:** 1140–1142.

NACHEMSON, A. & MORRIS, J. M. (1964). "*In vivo* measurements of intradiscal pressure. Discometry, a method for the determination of pressure in the lower lumbar discs." *J. Bone Joint Surg.*, **46A:** 1077–1092.

NEWMAN, P. H. (1970). "Muscle action on the vertebral column." *Brit. J. Sports Med.*, **5:** 34–37.

ORNE, D. & LIU, Y. K. (1971). "A mathematical model of spinal response to impact." *J. Biomechanics*, **4:** 49–71.

PEDERSON, O. F. & STAFFELDT, E. S. (1972). "The relationship between four tests and back muscle strength in untrained subjects." *Scand. J. Rehab. Med.*, **4:** 175–181.

PFEIL, E. (1971). "Experimental studies on the problem of the origin of spondylosysis." *Zeit. Orthop.*, **109:** 231–238.

PLAUE, R. (1972). "The behaviour of fractures of the thoracic and lumbar vertebrae: compression experiments." *Zeit. Orthop.*, **110:** 159–166.

PLAUE, R. & ROESLER, H. (1972). "The behaviour of fractures of the thoracic and lumbar vertebrae: studies of the mechanical anisotropism of the vertebral marrow." *Zeit. Orthop.*, **110:** 582–586.

RENNIE, W. & MITCHELL, N. (1973). "Flexion distraction fractures of the thoracolumbar spine." *J. Bone Joint Surg.*, **55A:** 386–390.

ROAF, R. (1960). "A study of the mechanics of spinal injuries." *J. Bone Joint Surg.*, **42B:** 810–823.

ROCKOFF, S. D., STREET, E. & BLEUSTEIN, J. (1969). "The relative contribution of trabecular and cortical bone to the strength of the human lumbar vertebrae." *Calif. Tissue Res.*, **3:** 163–175.

RUSHMER, R. F. (1946). "Nature of intraperitoneal and intrarectal pressure." *Amer. J. Physiol.*, **147:** 242–247.

RUSHMER, R. F. (1947). "The change in pressure in the peritoneal cavity produced by sudden deceleration of experimental animals." *J. Aviation Med.*, **18**: 199–206.

PUSI-PUCE, S. & SASAKI, N. (1969). "Effect of weight lifting by push and pull on intrathoracic pressure." *J. Labour Science*, **45**: 410–421.

SCHERRER, J. & BOURGUIGNON, A. (1959). "Changes in the electromyogram produced by fatigue in man." *Amer. J. Phys. Med.*, **38**: 148–158.

SCHERRER, J., LEFEBRE, J. & BOURGUIGNON, A. (1957). "Electrical activity of skeletal striated muscle and fatigue." *Proc. 4th Int. Congr. Electroencephalograph Clin. Neurophysiol., Brussels*: pp. 99–112.

SCHERRER, J. & MONOD, H. (1960). "Local muscular work and fatigue in man." *J. Physiol., Paris*, **52**: 419–501.

SCHULTZ, A. B. (1974). "Force-deformation properties of human costo-sternal and costo-vertebral articulations." *J. Biomech.*, **7**: 311–318.

SHAH, J. S. (1975). "A preliminary investigation of stress distribution in lumbar vertebrae." *Ann. Rheum. Dis.*, **34**: 199.

SHAVER, L. G. (1975). "Crosstransfer effects of conditioning and deconditioning on muscular strength." *Ergonomics*, **18**: 9–16.

SMITH, R. N. & STEPHENS, D. B. (1968). "Deformation of canine intervertebral discs and vertebral bodies subjected to axial compression." *J. Anat.*, **103**: 196–197.

SNOOK, S. H. & IRVINE, C. H. (1967). "Maximum acceptable weight of lift." *Amer. Industr. Hyg. Assoc. J.*, **28**: 322–329.

SNOOK, S. H. & IRVINE, C. H. (1968). "Maximum frequency of lift acceptable to male industrial workers." *Amer. Industr. Hyg. Assoc. J.*, **53**: 1–536.

SODEN, P. D. & KERSHAW, I. (1974). "Tensile testing of connective tissues." *Med. Biol. Eng.*, **12**: 510–518.

SOECHTING, J. F. & PASLAY, P. R. (1973). "A model for the human spine during impact including musculature influence." *J. Biomechanics*, **6**: 195–203.

SONODA, T. (1962). "Studies on the strength for compression, tension and torsion of the human vertebral column." *J. Kyoto Pref. Med. Univ.*, **71**: 659–702.

SUGGE, C. W. (1969). "The effect of load on muscle output." *Human Factors*, **11**: 273–280.

TEMMING, H. & ROHMERT, W. (1972). "Investigations into the

physical stresses of miners in carrying and handling heavy loads in different mechanised collieries." *Arbeitmedizin, Sozialmedizin, Arbeitshygiene,* **No. 48:** 9–143.

THOMAS, D. D. (1959). "The effect of load carriage on normal standing in man." *J. Anat.,* **93:** 75–86.

THOMAS, G. (1967). "Studies of the mechanics of lordosis in the lumbar region of the vertebral column." *Zeit. Orthop.,* **102:** 524–533.

TORNVALL, G. (1963). "Assessment of physical capabilities with special reference to the evaluation of maximal voluntary isometric muscle strength and maximal working capacity: an experimental study on civilian and military subject groups." *Acta Physiol. Scand.,* (Suppl. **201**): p. 1.

TROUP, J. D. G. & CHAPMAN, A. E. (1972). "Changes in the waveform of the electromyogram during fatiguing activity in the muscles of the spine and hips: the analysis of postural stress." *Electromyography,* **12:** 347–365.

TROUP, J. D. G. & GRIEVE, D. W. (1970). "Methods of assessing physical stress at work." *Proc. Roy. Soc. Med.,* **63:** 199–200.

TUTTLE, W. W., JANNEY, C. D. & SALZANO, J. V. (1955). "Relation of maximum back and leg strength to back and leg strength endurance." *Res. Quarterly,* **26:** 96–106.

ULRICH, S. P. (1972). "The lordosis-kyphosis test in assessing an effective extension therapy for discogenic pain." *Praxis,* **61:** 546–1556.

VULCAN, A. P., KING, A. I. & NAKAMURA, G. S. (1970). "Effects of bending on the vertebral column during +G acceleration." *Aerospace Med.,* **41:** 294–300.

WEIS, E. B. (1975). "Stresses at the lumbosacral junction." *Orthop. Clin. Nth. Amer.,* **6:** 83–91.

WHITE, G. H., LANGE, K. O. & COERMANN, R. R. (1962). "The effects of simulated buffeting on the internal pressure of man." *Human Factors,* **4:** 275–290.

WHITNEY, R. J. (1958). "The strength of the lifting action of man." *Ergonomics,* **1:** 101–128.

WILLIAMS, J. F. (1975). "The effect of collision severity on the motion of the head and neck during 'whiplash'." *J. Biomech.,* **8:** 257–259.

WOOD, G. A. & HAYES, K. C. (1974). "A kinetic model of

intervertebral stress during lifting." *Brit. J. Sports Med.*, **8:** 74–79.

YOSHIZAWA, H. (1969). "Photoelastic study on the relation between lumbar lordosis and load." *J. Jap. Orthop. Ass.*, **43:** 645–662.

ZAJACZKOWSKA, A. (1962). "Constant velocity in lifting as a criterion of muscular skill." *Ergonomics*, **5:** 337–356.

## (f) Ergonomic Principles and Applications

AMERICAN INDUSTRIAL HYGIENE ASSOCIATION (1970). "Ergonomics guide to manual lifting." *Amer. Industr. Hyg. Ass. J.*, **31:** 511–516.

BERGSTRÖM, R. N. (1959). "The mechanical work produced by voluntarily controlled muscle action and the frequency of the motor discharge." *Acta Physiol. Scand.*, **47:** 191–198.

CHAPANIS, A. (1974). "National and alkinal variables in ergonomics." *Ergonomics*, **17:** 135–175.

CHRIST, W. (1974). "On the possibility of health injury arising from vertical vibration of the spine." *Fortschr. Med.*, **92:** 705–708.

CHYATTE, S. B. & BIRDSONG, J. H. (1972). "Methods time measurement in assessment of motor performance." *Arch. Phys. Med.*, **53:** 38–44.

DAVIES, B. T. (1972). "Moving loads manually." *Applied Ergonomics*, **3:** 190–194.

DEGREENE, K. B. (1974). "Models of man in systems in retrospect and prospect." *Ergonomics*, **17:** 437–446.

HALL, M. A. W. (1972). "Back pain and car seat comfort." *Applied Ergonomics*, **3:** 82–91.

KEENEY, C. E. (1955). "Relationships of bodyweight to strength-bodyweight ratio in championship weight lifters." *Res. Quart.*, **26:** 54–57.

KHALIL, T. M. (1974). "Dentistry: a growing domain for ergonomics." *Ergonomics*, **17:** 75–86.

KIERKE, H. E. (1971). "Biodynamic models and their applications." *J. Acoust. Soc. Amer.*, **50:** 1397–1413.

KINZEL, G. L., HALL, A. S. & HILLBERRY, B. M. (1972). "Measurement of the total motion between two body segments: 2. Description of application." *J. Biomechanics*, **5:** 283–293.

LIETZKE, M. H. (1956). "Relation between weight lifting totals and body weight." *Science*, **124**: 486–487.

MACCONAILL, M. A. & BASMAJIAN, J. V. (1969). *Muscles and Movements: A Basis for Human Kinesiology.* Baltimore; Williams and Wilkins.

METTLEWELL, P. J. (1974). "Biomedical engineering—an annotated guide to sources of information. Part 2." *Biomed. Eng.*, **9**: 252–255.

PAUL, J. P. (1974). "Techniques of gait analysis." *Proc. Roy. Soc. Med.*, **67**: 401–404.

PIERSON, W. R. & RASCH, P. J. (1964). "Effect of knowledge of results in isometric strength scores." *Research Quart.*, **35**: 313–315.

PLANGENHOEF, S. C. (1964). "Methods for obtaining kinetic data to analyse human motions." *Research Quart.*, **37**: 103–112.

PLAUE, R. (1974). "Fracture behaviour in thoracic and lumbar vertebrae: discussion of theoretical fracture models." *Zeit. Orthop.*, **112**: 1071–1077.

QUIRING, D. P. (1952). "Background for an understanding of spine and trunk function." *Arch. Phys. Med.*, **33**: 414–424.

RONNHOLM, N. (1962). "Physiological studies on the optimum rhythm of lifting work." *Ergonomics*, **5**: 51–52.

ROWLAND, G. E. & KULP, C. M. (1960). "A method of making dimensional measurements of complex motions." *Rowland & Company Report 60-1-2.* March 1960.

ROY, S. (1970). "Bio-engineering in relation to spinal mechanisms." *J. Industr. Med. Assoc.*, **54**: 566–568.

SALTER, N. (1955). "Methods of measurement of muscle and joint function." *J. Bone Joint Surg.*, **37B**: 474–491.

SCHULTZ, A. B. & GALANTE, J. O. (1970). "A mathematical model for the study of the mechanics of the human vertebral column." *J. Biochemics*, **3**: 405–416.

SNOOK, S. H. (1971). "The effects of age and physique on continuous work capacity." *Human Factors*, **13**: 467–479.

SNOOK, S. H. & CIRIELLO, V. M. (1974). "Maximum weights and work loads acceptable to female workers." *J. Occup. Med.*, **16**: 527–534.

SNOOK, S. H. & IRVINE, C. H. (1966). "The evaluation of physical tasks in industry." *Amer. Industr. Hyg. Assoc. J.*, **27**: 228–233.

STRASSER, H. (1913). *Textbook of Muscle and Joint Mechanics.* Berlin; Springer.

TICHAUER, E. R., MILLER, M. & NATHAN, I. M. (1973). "Lordosity: a new technique for the measurement of postural response to materials handling." *Amer. Industr. Hyg. Ass. J.*, **34:** 1–12.

WILLIAMS, B. (1974). "A demonstration analogue for ventricular and intraspinal dynamics." *J. Neurol. Sci.*, **23:** 445–461.

# 6

# NEUROLOGY

## (a) Morphology and Physiology

ALBE-FESSARD, D. & BOWSHER, D. (1965). "Responses of monkey thalamus to somatic stimuli under chloralose anaesthesia." *Electroenceph. Clin. Neurophysiol.*, **19**: 1–15.

ALBE-FESSARD, D. & KRAUTHAMER, G. (1964). "Inhibition of units of non-specific afferent system by stimulating the basal ganglia." *J. Physiol.*, **175**: 54–55P.

ALBE-FESSARD, D. & LIEBESKIND, J. (1966). "Origin of somatosensory impulses activating the cells of the motor cortex in the monkey." *Exper. Brain Res.*, **1**: 127–246.

ALIPERTA, K. (1970). "Disturbances of the autonomic nervous system in subjects with disk hernia." *Excerpta Medica*, **13**: 119.

ANDERSEN, P., BROOKS, C. McC., ECCLES, J. C. & SEARS, T. A. (1964). "The ventrobasal nucleus of the thalamus: potential fields, synaptic transmission and excitability of both presynaptic and postsynaptic components." *J. Physiol.*, **174**: 348–369.

ANDERSEN, P., ECCLES, J. C. & SEARS, J. C. (1964). "Cortically evoked depolarization of primary afferent fibers in the spinal cord." *J. Neurophysiol.*, **27**:63–77.

ANDERSEN, P., ECCLES, J. C. & SEARS, T. A. (1964). "The ventrobasal complex of the thalamus: types of cells, their responses and their functional organisation." *J. Physiol.*, **174**: 370–399.

ANDREW, B. L. (Ed.). (1966). *Control and Innervation of Skeletal Muscle*. Edinburgh; Livingstone.

BANERJEE, T. (1974). "Transcutaneous nerve stimulation for pain after spinal injury." *New Eng. J. Med.*, **291**: 796.

BARKER, D. (Ed.) (1926). *Symposium on Muscle Receptors*. Hong Kong: University Press.

BENJAMIN, R. M. (1970). "Single neurones in the rat medulla responsive to nociceptive stimulation." *Brain Res.*, **24**: 525–529.

BERNHAUT, M., GELLHORN, E. & RASMUSSEN, A. T. (1953). "Experimental contributions to the problem of consciousness." *J. Neurophysiol.*, **16**: 21–35.

169

BISHOP, G. H. (1946). "Neural mechanisms of cutaneous sense." *Physiol. Rev.*, **26**: 77–102.

BISHOP, G. H. (1959). "The relation between nerve fiber size and sensory modality: Phylogenetic implications of the afferent innervation of the cortex." *J. Nerv. Ment. Dis.*, **128**: 89–114.

BOURLAND, A. & WINKELMANN, R. K. (1966). "Study of cutaneous innervation in congenital anesthesia." *Arch. Neurol., Chicago*, **14**: 223–227.

BOWKER, J. H. & LEDBETTER, C. A. (1974). "Low back pain." *Amer. J. Physiol.* **10**: 179–190.

BOWSHER, D. (1961). "The termination of secondary somatosensory neurons within the thalamus of Macaca mulatta: an experimental degeneration study." *J. Comp. Neurol.*, **117**: 213–228.

BOYD, I. A. (1967). "The innervation of mammalian neuromuscular spindles." *J. Physiol.*, **140**: 14P.

BRADLEY, K. C. (1974). "The anatomy of backache." *Aust. N.Z. J. Surg.*, **44**: 227–232.

BRAZIER, M. A. B. (Ed.). (1970). *The Interneuron*. Berkeley, California; University of California Press.

BRIDGE, C. J. (1969). "Innervation of the spinal meninges and epidural structures." *Anat. Rec.*, **133**: 553–563.

BRIEF, A. (1960). *Biomechanics of The Central Nervous System: Some Basic Normal and Pathologic Phenomena*. Chicago; Year Book Publishers.

BROMAGE, P. R. (1973). "Nerve physiology and control of pain." *Orthop. Clin. Nth. Amer.*, **4**: 897–906.

BROWNE, E. Z. & SNYDER, C. C. (1971). "Intercosto-sacral neural anastomosis." *Surg. Forum*, **22**: 474–476.

BRUCKMOSER, P., HEPP-RAYMOND, M. C. & WIESENDANGER, M. (1970). "Cortical influence on single neurons of the lateral ventricular nucleus of the cat." *Exper. Neurol.*, **26**: 239–252.

BRUNSCHWIG, A. & JUNG, A. (1932). "The importance of peri-articular innervation in the pathological physiology of sprained joints." *J. Bone Joint Surg.*, **14B**: 273.

BURCHFIELD, J. L. & DUFFY, F. H. (1972). "Muscle afferent input to single cells in primate somatosensory cortex." *Brain Res.*, **45**: 241–246.

BURGESS, P. R. & PERL, E. R. (1967). "Myelinated afferent fibres responding specifically to noxious stimulation of the skin." *J. Physiol.*, **190**: 541–562.

170

CALMA, I. (1965). "The activity of the posterior group of thalamic nuclei in the cat." *J. Physiol.*, **180:** 350–370.

CAMPBELL, J. B. (1948). "Congenital anomalies of the neural axis." *Amer. J. Surg.*, **75:** 231–256.

CARPENTER, D., ENGBERG, L. & LUNDBERG, A. (1966). "Primary afferent depolarization evoked from the brainstem and the cerebellum." *Arch. Ital. Biol.*, **104:** 73–85.

CARPENTER, D., LUNDBERG, A. & NORSELL, U. (1963). "Primary afferent depolarization evoked from the sensorimotor cortex." *Acta Physiol. Scand.*, **59:** 126–142.

CASEY, K. L. (1966). "Unit analysis of nociceptive mechanisms in the thalamus of the awake squirrel monkey. *J. Neurophysiol.*, **29:** 727–750.

CHANG, L. W., GOWANS, J. D. GRANGER, C. V., *et al.* (1972). "Entrapment neuropathy of the posterior interosseous nerve." *Arth. Rheum.*, **15:** 350–353.

CHOW, K. L. & PRIBAM, K. H. (1956). "Cortical projection of the thalamic ventrolateral nuclear group in monkeys." *J. Comp. Neurol.*, **104:** 57–75.

CLARK, W. E. LE GROS (1936). "The thalamic connections of the temporal lobe of the brain in the monkey." *J. Anat.*, **70:** 447–464.

CLARK, W. E. LE GROS (1948). "The connections of the frontal lobes of the brain." *Lancet*, **254:** 353–356.

CLARK, W. E. LE GROS, BEATTIE, J., RIDDOCH, F. & DOTT, N. M. (1938). *The Hypothalamus. Morphological, Functional, Clinical and Surgical Aspects.* Edinburgh; Oliver and Boyd.

CLARK, W. E. LE GROS AND BOGGON, R. H. (1933). "On the connections of the anterior nucleus of the thalamus." *J. Anat.*, **67:** 215–116.

CLARK, W. E. LE GROS & BOGGON, R. H. (1935). "The thalamic connections of the parietal and frontal lobes of the brain in the monkey.' *Phil. Trans. Roy. Soc. Lond.*, **224B:** 313–359.

COOK, A. W. (1973). "Regeneration in the central nervous system." *Lancet*, **1:** 1442–1443.

COOTE, J. H. (1975). "Physiological significance of somatic afferent pathways from skeletal muscle and joints with reflex effects on the heart and circulation." *Brain Res.*, **87:** 139–144.

CURRY, M. J. (1972). "The exteroceptive properties of neurones in the somatic part of the posterior group." *Brain Res.*, **44:** 439–462.

DEE, R. (1969). "Structure and function of hip joint innervation." *Ann Roy. Coll. Surg. Engl.*, **45**: 357–374.

DEE, R. (1978). "The innervation of joints." In *The Joints and Synovial Fluid*. pp. 177–204. Ed. M. Sokoloff. New York; Academic Press.

DESIRAJU, T. & PURPURA, D. P. (1970). "Organisation of specific and non-specific thalamic internuclear synaptic pathways." *Brain Res.*, **21**: 169–181.

DOUGLAS, W. W. & RITCHIE, J. M. (1962). "Mammalian non-myelinated nerve fibres." *Physiol. Rev.*, **42**: 297–334.

EARLE, K. M. (1952). "The tract of Lissauer and its possible relation to the pain pathway." *J. Comp. Neurol.*, **96**: 93–111.

ECCLES, J. C. (1964). *The Physiology of Synapses*. Berlin; Springer.

EDGAR, M. A. & NUNDY, S. (1966). "Innervation of the spinal dura mater." *J. Neurol. Neurosurg. Psychiat.*, **29**: 530–534.

ETEMADI, A. A. (1963). "Observations on the musculature and innervation of the human back." *M. Sc. Thesis, Univ. London*.

FEINDEL, W., HINSHAW, J. R. & WEDDELL, G. (1952). "The pattern of motor innervation in mammalian striated muscle." *J. Anat.*, **86**: 35–48.

FERLIC, D. C. (1963). "The nerve supply of the cervical inter-vertebral disc in man." *Bull. John Hopkins Hosp.*, **113**: 347–351.

FOX, J. E. (1970). "Reticulospinal neurons in the rat." *Brain Res.*, **23**: 35–40.

FREEMAN, M. A. R. & WYKE, B. D. (1964). "The innervation of the cat's knee joint." *J. Anat.*, **98**: 299–300.

FREEMAN, M. A. R. & WYKE, B. D. (1967). "The innervation of the ankle joint: an anatomical and histological study in the cat." *Acta Anat., Basel.*, **68**: 321–333.

FREEMAN, M. A. R. & WYKE, B. D. (1967). "The innervation of the knee joint: an anatomical and histological study in the cat." *J. Anat.*, **101**: 505–532.

GARDNER, E. D. (1948). "The nerve supply of diarthordial joints." *Stanford Med. Bull.*, **6**: 367–373.

GARDNER, E. D. (1953). "Blood and nerve supply of joints." *Bull. Rheumat. Dis.*, **4**: 42–43.

GARDNER, E. D. (1954). "Physiology of the nerve supply of joints." *Bull. Hosp. Joint Dis.*, **15**: 35–44.

GARDNER, E. D. (1956). "Nerves and nerve endings in joints and associated structures of monkey (Macaca mulatta)." *Anat. Rec.*, **124**: 293.

GARDNER, E. D. (1960). "The nerve supply of muscles, joints and other deep structures." *Bull. Hosp. Joint. Dis.*, **21**: 153–161.

GARDNER, E. D. (1967). "Spinal cord and brain stem pathways for afferents from joints." In *Myotatic, Kinesthetic and Vestibular Mechanisms.* pp. 56–76. Ed A. V. S. de Reuck and J. Knight. London; Churchill.

GARDNER, E. D. (1969). "Pathways to the cerebral cortex for nerve impulses from joints." *Acta Anat., Basel.* **73** (Suppl. **56**): 203–216.

GARDNER, E. D. & NOER, R. (1952). "Projection of afferent fibres from muscles and joints to the cerebral cortex of the cat." *Am. J. Physiol.*, **168**: 437–441.

GARDNER, E., PEDERSEN, H. E. & BLUNCK, C. F. J. (1955). "The anatomy of the lumbosacral posterior primary divisions and sinuvertebral nerves, with an experimental study of their functions." *Anat. Rec.*, **121**: 297.

GERLACH, F. (1889). "Corpuscular endings of sensory nerves in joint capsules." *Jahresb. Anat. Physiol., Leipzig*, **18**: 381–383.

GERNANDT, B. E., KATSUKIY, I. & LIVINGSTON, R. B. (1957). "Functional organisation of descending vestibular influences." *J. Neurophysiol.*, **20**: 453–469.

GERNANDT, B. E. & MEGIRIAN, D. (1961). "Ascending propriospinal mechanisms." *J. Neurophysiol.*, **24**: 364–376.

GERNANDT, B. E. & SHIMAMURA, M. (1961). "Mechanisms of interlimb reflexes in cat." *J. Neurophysiol.*, **24**: 665–676.

GERNECK, I. (1930). "The nerves of the synovial membrane." *Archiv. Orthop.*, **28**: 599–604.

GERNECK, I. (1932). "The innervation of the synovial membrane in man." *Zeit. Anat. Entwickl.*, **97**: 515–534.

GODWIN-AUSTEN, R. B. (1969). "The mechanoreceptors of the costovertebral joints." *J. Physiol.*, **202**: 737–753.

GOLDBERG, J. M. & LAVINE, R. A. (1968). "Nervous system: afferent systems." *Ann. Rev. Physiol.*, **30**: 319–358.

GOLGI, C. (1878). "Investigation of the distribution and termination of the nerve endings in the tendons of man and other vertebrates." *Gazz. Med. Ital. Lombardia*, **38**: 221–224.

GRAHAME, R. (1974). "Musculo-skeletal pain." *Physiotherapy*, **60**: 99–100.

GRANIT, R. (1955). *Receptors and Sensory Perception*. New Haven; Yale University Press.

HAGBARTH, K. E. & KERR, D. I. B. (1954). "Central influences on spinal afferent conduction. *J. Neurophysiol.*, **17**: 295–307.

HANSEN, K. & SCHLIAK, H. (1962). *Segmental Innervation: Its Clinical and Therapeutic Significance*. Stuttgart; Thieme.

HARRIS, G. W., REED, M. & FAWCETT, C. P. (1966). "Hypothalamic releasing factors and the control of anterior pituitary function." *Brit. Med. Bull.*, **22**: 266–272.

HASSLER, R. (1972). "Afferent systems: the division of pain conduction into systems of pain sensation and pain awareness." In *Pain: Basic Principles, Pharmacology, Therapy*. pp. 98–112. Ed. R. Jansen, W. D. Keidel, A. Herz and C. Steichele. Stuttgart; Thieme.

HAUGEN, F. P. (1968). "The autonomic nervous system and pain." *Anesthiology*, **29**: 785–792.

HEINBECKER, P., BISHOP, G. H. & O'LEARY, J. L. (1933). "Pain and touch fibers in peripheral nerves." *Arch. Neurol. Psychiat.*, **29**: 771–789.

HELLEBRANDT, F. A. & BRAUN, G. L. (1939). "The influence of sex and age on postural sway of man." *Amer. J. Phys. Anthrop.*, **24**: 347–460.

HERNANDEZ-PEÓN, R. (1969). "A neurophysiological and evolutionary model of attention" In *Attention in Neurophysiology*, pp. 417–432. Ed. C. R. Evans and T. B. Mulholland, London; Butterworth.

HERNANDEZ-PEÓN, R. & HAGBARTH, K. E. (1955). "Interaction between afferent and cortically induced reticular responses." *J. Neurophysiol.*, **18**: 44–55.

HILLMAN, P. & WALL, P. D. (1969). "Inhibitory and excitatory factors influencing the receptive fields of lamina 5 spinal cord cells." *Exper. Brain Res.*, **9**: 284–306.

HIRSCH, C., INGELMARK, B. E. & MILLER, M. (1953). "The anatomical basis for low back pain: studies on the presence of sensory nerve endings in ligamentous, capsular and intervertebral disc structures in the human lumbar spine." *Acta Orthop. Scand.*, **33**: 1–17.

HODES, R. (1953). "The innervation of skeletal muscle." *Ann. Rev. Physiol.*, **15**: 139–164.

HOLMQVIST, B. (1961). "Crossed spinal reflex actions evoked by volleys in somatic afferents." *Acta Physiol. Scand.*, **52** (Suppl. 181): 1–66.

HOSOKAWA, O. (1964). "The histological study on the type and distribution of the sensory nerve endings in human hip joint capsule and ligament." *J. Jap. Orthop. Assoc.*, **38**: 887–901.

HROMADA, J. (1958). "Two observations concerning the innervation of the joint capsule." *Acta Chir. Orthop. Traumatol. Česk.*, **25**: 118–123.

HROMADA, J. (1961). "Anatomical studies on cases of denervation of the joints." *Zeit. Orthop.*, **94**: 419–428.

IGGO, A. (1952). "Non-myelinated visceral, muscular and cutaneous afferent fibres and pain." In *U.F.A.W. Symposium on Assessment of Pain in Man and Animals.* pp. 74–87. Ed. C. A. Keele and R. Smith. London; Livingstone.

IGGO, A. (1959). "A single unit analysis of cutaneous receptors with C afferent fibres. In *Pain and Itch.* pp. 41–56. Ed. G. E. W. Wolstenholme and M. O'Connor. London; Churchill.

IGGO, A. (1966). "Cutaneous receptors with a high sensitivity to mechanical displacement" In *Touch, Heat, Pain.* pp. 237–256. Ed. A. V. S. Reuck and J. Knight. London; Churchill.

IGGO, A. (1972). "The case for 'pain' receptors". In *Pain: Basic Principles, Pharmacology, Therapy.* pp. 60–67. Ed. R. Janzen, W. D. Keidel, A. Herz and C. Steichele. Stuttgart; Thieme.

INDRA, P. (1957). "Innervation of the shoulder joint in man." *Morph. Česk.*, **5**: 35–38.

IRIUCHIJIMA, J. & ZOTTERMAN, Y. (1960). "The specificity of afferent cutaneous C fibres in mammals." *Acta Physiol. Scand.*, **49**: 267–278.

ISHIJIMA, B. (1975). "Nociceptive neurons in the human thalamus." *Confin. Neurol.*, **37**: 99–106.

IWAMA, K. & YAMAMOTO, C. (1961). "Impulse transmission in thalamic somatosensory relay nuclei as modified by electrical stimulation of the cerebral cortex." *Jap. J. Physiol.*, **11**: 169–182.

JABBER, S. J., BAKER, M. A. & TOWE, A. L. (1972). "Wide-field neurons in thalamic nucleus ventralis posterolateralis of the cat." *Exper. Neurol.*, **36**: 213–238.

JACKSON, H. C., WINKELMANN, R. K. & BICKEL, W. H. (1966). "Nerve endings in the human lumbar spinal column and related structures." *J. Bone Joint Surg.*, **48B**: 1272–1281.

JUNG, A. & BRUNSCHWIG, A. (1932). "Histological studies on the innervation of the joints of the vertebral bodies." *Presse Méd.*, **40**: 316.

KAADA, B. (1960). "Cingulate, posterior orbital, anterior insular and temporal pole cortex." In *Handbook of Physiology. Sect. I: Neurophysiology Vol. II.* pp. 1345–1372. Ed. J. Field, H. W. Magoun and V. E. Hall. Washington; Amer. Physiol. Society.

KASPRZAK, H., MANN, M. D. & TAPPER, D. N. (1970). "Pyramidal modulation of responses of spinal neurones to natural stimulation of cutaneous receptors." *Brain Res.*, **24**: 121–124.

KEEGAN, J. J. & GARRETT, F. D. (1948). "The segmental distribution of the cutaneous nerves in the limbs of man." *Anat. Rec.*, **102**: 409–437.

KEITH, A. (1923). "The adaptation of the abdomen and of its viscera to the orthograde posture." *Brit. Med. J.*, **1**: 587–590.

KELLGREN, J. H. (1950). "The sensitivity and innervation of the articular capsule." *J. Bone Joint Surg.*, **32B**: 84.

KENSHALO, D. R. (Ed.) (1968). *The Skin Senses.* Springfield, Illinois; Thomas.

KERR, F. W. (1972). "Central relationships of trigeminal and cervical primary afferents in the spinal cord and medulla." *Brain Res.*, **43**: 561–572.

KNIGHTON, R. S. & DUMKE, P. R. (EDS.) (1966). *Pain: An International Symposium.* Boston; Little, Brown.

KORR, I. M. WRIGHT, H. M. & CHACE, J. A. (1964). "Cutaneous patterns of sympathetic activity in clinical abnormalities of the musculoskeletal system." *Acta Neurovegetativa*, **25**: 589–606.

KORR, I. M., WRIGHT, H. M. & THOMAS, P. E. (1962). "Effects of experimental myoficial insults on cutaneous patterns of sympathetic activity in man." *Acta Neurovegetativa*, **23**: 329–355.

KRAFT, G. H. (1972). "Axillary, musculocutaneous and suprascapular nerve latency studies." *Arch. Phys. Med. Rehabil.*, **53**: 383–387.

KUMAR, S. & DAVIS, P. R. (1973). "Lumbar vertebral innervation and intra-abdominal pressure." *J. Anat.*, **114**: 47–53.

LAROCHELLS, J. L. & JOBIN, P. (1949). "Anatomical research on the innervation of the hip joint." *Anat. Rec.*, **103**: 480–481.

LIBET, B., FEINSTEIN, B. L. & WRIGHT, E. W. (1959). "Tendon afferents in autogenetic inhibition in man." *Electroenceph. Clin. Neurophysiol.*, **11**: 128.

LIM, R. K. S. (1968). "Cutaneous and visceral pain and somesthetic chemoreceptors." In *The Skin Senses*. pp. 458–464. Ed. D. R. Kenshalo, Springfield, Illinois; Thomas.

LINDBLOM, U. F. & OTTOSSON, J. O. (1957). "Influence of pyramidal stimulation upon the relay of coarse cutaneous afferents in the dorsal horn." *Acta Physiol. Scand.*, **38**: 309–318.

LIPCOMB, P. R. & WINKELMANN, R. K. (1961). "A whole-mount cholinesterase technic for study of innervation of the deep structures of the limbs." *J. Invest. Derm.*, **37**: 481–483.

LIPPMAN, H. H. & KERR, F. W. L. (1972). "Light and electron microscopic study of crossed ascending pathways in the antero-lateral funiculus in monkey." *Brain Res.*, **40**: 496–499.

LUND, R. D. & WEBSTER, K. E. (1967). "Thalamic afferents from the spinal cord and trigeminal nuclei: an experimental anatomical study in the rat." *J. Comp. Neurol.*, **130**: 313–328.

LUNDBERG, A., NORSELL, U. & WOORHOEVE, P. (1962). "Pyramidal effects on lumbo-sacral interneurones activated by somatic afferents." *Acta Physiol. Scand.*, **56**: 220–229.

McCOUGH, G. P., DEERING, I. D. & LING, T. H. (1951). "Location of receptors for tonic neck reflexes." *J. Neurophysiol.*, **14**: 191–195.

MAGNI, F. & WILLIS, W. D. (1964). "Afferent connections to reticulospinal neurons." *Progr. Brain Res.*, **12**: 246–258.

MALINOVSKÝ, L. (1966). "Some problems connected with the evaluation of skin receptors and their classification." *Folia Morph., Prague.* **15**: 18–25.

MATTHEWS, P. B. C. (1972). *Mammalian Muscle Receptors and Their Central Action*. London; Arnold.

MONTAGNA, W. (Ed.). (1960). *Cutaneous Innervation*. Oxford; Pergamon Press.

MORIN, F., KENNEDY, D. T. & GARDENER, E. D. (1966). "Spinal afferents to the lateral reticular nucleus. I. A histological study." *J. Comp. Neurol.*, **126**: 511–522.

MORSE, R. W. & TOWE, A. L. (1964). "The dual nature of the lemniscocortical afferent system in the cat." *J. Physiol.*, **171**: 231–246.

MOUNTCASTLE, V. B. (1957). "Modality and topographic properties of single neurons of cat's somatic sensory cortex." *J. Neurophysiol.*, **20**: 408–434.

MOUNTCASTLE, V. B., COVIAN, M. R. & HARRISON, C. R. (1950).

"The central representation of some forms of deep sensibility." *Res. Pub. Assoc. Nerv. Ment. Dis.*, **30:** 339–370.

MOUNTCASTLE, V. B., POGGIO, G. F. & WERNER, G. (1963). "The relation of thalamic cell response to peripheral stimuli varied over an intensity continuum." *J. Neurophysiol.*, **26:** 807–834.

MOUNTCASTLE, V. B. & POWELL, T. P. S. (1959). "Central nervous mechanisms subserving position sense and kinesthesis." *Bull. Johns Hopkins Hosp.*, **105:** 173–200.

MOUNTCASTLE, V. B. & POWELL, T. P. S. (1959). "Neural mechanisms subserving cutaneous sensibility with special reference to the role of afferent inhibition in sensory perception and discrimination." *Bull. Johns Hopkins Hosp.*, **105:** 201–232.

MULLIGAN, J. H. (1957). "The innervation of the ligaments attached to the bodies of the vertebrae." *J. Anat.*, **91:** 455–463.

NAKAGWA, T. (1966). "A study of the distribution of nerve filaments over the ilio-sacral joint and its adjacent region." *J. Jap. Orth. Ass.*, 419–430.

NATHAN, P. B. (1953). "Nervous discharge from small painless lesions in skin and muscle." *J. Neurol. Neurosurg. Psychiat.*, **16:** 144–151.

NETSKY, M. G. (1949). "Studies on sweat secretion in man: innervation of sweat glands of upper extremity and newer methods of studying sweating." *Arch. Neurol. Psychiat.*, **60:** 279–287.

NOORDENBOS, W. (1972). "Remarks on afferent systems in the antero-lateral quadrant." In *Pain: Basic Principles, Pharmacology, Therapy.* pp. 112–115. Ed. by R. Janzen, W. D. Keidel, A. Herz and C. Steichele. Stuttgart; Thieme.

NOZAKI, K. (1955). "On the innervation, especially the sensory innervation, of the periosteum and the area surrounding it in the earlier stage of human embryo." *Arch. Histol. Jap.*, **9:** 269–281.

NYBERG-HANSEN, R. (1965). "Sites and mode of termination of reticulo-spinal fibers in the cat: an experimental study with silver impregnation methods." *J. Comp. Neurol.*, **124:** 71–100.

NYBERG-HANSEN, R. & BRODAL, A. (1963). "Sites of termination of corticospinal fibers in the cat.: an experimental study with silver impregnation methods." *J. Comp. Neurol.*, **120:** 369–391.

OSCARSSON, O. (1958). "Further observations on ascending spinal tracts activated from muscle, joint and skin nerves." *Arch. Ital. Biol.*, **96:** 199–215.

OSCARSSON, O. & ROSEN, I. (1963). "Cerebral projection of Group I afferents in forelimb muscle nerves of cat." *Experimentia, Basel*, **19:** 206–207.

OSCARSSON, O. & ROSEN, I. (1966). "Short latency projections to the cat's cerebral cortex from skin and muscle afferents in the contralateral forelimb." *J. Physiol.*, **182:** 164–184.

PAILLARD, J. (1959). "Functional organisation of afferent innervation studies in man by monosynaptic testing." *Amer. J. Phys. Med.*, **38:** 239–247.

PERL, E. R. (1968). "Myelinated afferents innervating the primate skin and their response to noxious stimuli." *J. Physiol.*, **197:** 593–615.

PETIT, D. & BURGESS, P. R. (1968). "Dorsal column projections of receptors in cat having skin supplied by myelinated fibres." *J. Neurophysiol.*, **31:** 849–855.

POLÁČEK, P. (1954). "The innervation of fat cells of the joint capsule and its environs." *Morphol. Česk.* **2:** 190–198; 315–316.

POLÁČEK, P. (1955). "Innervation of the periosteum, bone and bone marrow." *Acta Clin. Orthop. Traumatol. Česk.*, **22:** 201–204.

POLÁČEK, P. (1956). 'Morphological changes in the innervation of the joints in laboratory animals under experimental, functional and pathological conditions." *Acta Clin. Orthop. Traumatol. Česk.*, **23:** 286–292.

POLÁČEK, P. (1966). *Receptors of the Joints*. Brno; Univ. Bruneris.

POLLEY, E. H. (1955). "Innervation of blood vessels in striated muscle and skin." *J. Comp. Neurol.*, **103:** 253–267.

POMERANZ, B., WALL, P. D. & WEBER, E. V. (1968). "Cord cells responding to fine myelinated afferents from viscera, skin and muscle." *J. Physiol.*, **199:** 511–532.

POMPEIANO, O. & SWETT, J. E. (1962). "Identification of cutaneous and muscular afferent fibers producing E.E.G. synchronization or arousal in normal cats." *Archiv. Ital. Biol.*, **100:** 343–380.

POMPEIANO, O. & SWETT, J. E. (1963). "Actions of graded cutaneous and muscular afferent volleys on brain stem units in the decerebrate, cerebellectomized cat." *Archiv. Ital. Biol.*, **101:** 552–582.

QUILLIAM, T. A. & SATO, M. (1955). "The distribution of myelin on nerve fibres from Pacinian corpuscles." *J. Physiol.*, **129:** 167–176.

RALSTON, H. J., MILLER, M. R. & KASAHARA, M. (1960). "Nerve endings in the human fasciae, tendons, ligaments, periosteum and joint synovial membrance." *Anat. Rec.*, **136:** 137–148.

RÉGAUD, C. (1907). "Nerve terminations and sensory nerve organs in the locomotor apparatus." *Rev. Gen. Histol.*, **2:** 583–689.

RÉGAUD, C. & FAVRE, M. (1904). "Nerve terminations and sensory nerve organs in the locomotor apparatus. I. Nerve terminations and sensory nerve organs in the skeletal striated muscles." *Rev. Gen. Histol.*, **1:** 1–140.

ROOFE, P. G. (1940). "Innervation of annulus fibrosus and posterior longitudinal ligament." *Arch. Neurol. Psychiat.*, **44:** 100–103.

ROSÉN, I. & SCHEID, P. (1972). "Cutaneous afferent responses in neurones of the lateral reticular nucleus." *Brain Res.*, **43:** 259–263.

RÜDINGER, N. (1857). *The Articular Nerves of the Human Body.* Erlangen; Ferdinand Enke.

SCULMAN, L. & DORFMANN, H. D. (1970). "Nerve fibres in osteoid osteoma." *J. Bone Joint Surg.*, **52A:** 1351.

SEARS, T. A. (1964). "Efferent discharges in alpha and fusimotor fibres of intercostal nerves of the cat." *J. Physiol.*, **174:** 295–315.

SELZER, M. & SPENCER, W. A. (1969). "Convergence of visceral and cutaneous afferent pathways in the lumbar spinal cord." *Brain Res.*, **14:** 331–348.

SELZER, M. & SPENCER, W. A. (1969). "Interactions between visceral and cutaneous afferents in the spinal cord: reciprocal primary afferent fiber depolarization." *Brain Res.*, **14:** 349–366.

SFAMENI, A. (1900). "Contribution to the understanding of the nerve endings in adipose tissue, perichondrium and periosteum in some animals." *Giorn. Reale Acad. Med. Torino.*, (No. **5**): 362–364.

SFAMENI, A. (1902). "Anatomical studies on the presence of nerves and their mode of termination in adipose tissue, periosteum and perichondrium, and in the tissues that re-inforce the joints." *Archiv. Ital. Biol.*, **38:** 49–101.

STILWELL, D. L. (1957). "The innervation of tendons and aponeuroses." *Amer. J. Anat.*, **100:** 289–317.

STILWELL, E. (1957). "Regional variations in the innervation of deep fasciae and aponeuroses." *Anat. Rec.*, **127:** 635–653.

TAUB, A. (1964). "Local, segmental and supraspinal interaction with a dorsolateral spinal cutaneous afferent system." *Exper. Neurol.*, **10:** 357–374.

TROUP, J. D. G. (1968). "The function of the lumbar spine: a biomechanical and peripheral neurological study." *Ph.D. Thesis, Univ. London.*

VAN HEES, J. & GYBELS, J. M. (1972). "Pain related to simple afferent C fibers from human skin." *Brain Res.*, **48:** 397–400.

VRETTOS, X. C. & WYKE, B. D. (1974). "Articular reflexogenic systems in the costovertebral joints." *J. Bone Joint Surg.*, **56B:** 382.

WEDDELL, G. (1941). "The pattern of cutaneous innervation in relation to cutaneous sensibility." *J. Anat., Lond.*, **75:** 346–368.

WEDDELL, G., PALMER, E. & PALLIE, W. (1955). "Nerve endings in mammalian skin." *Biol. Rev.*, **30:** 159–195.

WEISS, R. A. & ROOT, W. S. (1959). "Innervation of the vessels of the marrow cavity of certain bones." *Amer. J. Physiol.*, **197:** 1255–1257.

WINKELEMANN, R. K. (1960). *Nerve Endings in Normal and Pathologic Skin: Contributions to Anatomy of Sensation.* Springfield, Illinois; Thomas.

WOOLSEY, C. N. (1947). "Patterns of sensory representation in the cerebral cortex." *Fed. Proc.*, **6:** 437–441.

WOOLSEY, C. N. (1964). "Cortical localization as defined by evoked potential and electrical stimulation studies. In *Cerebral Localization and Organization.* pp. 17–32. Ed. G. Schaltenbrand and C. N. Woolsey. Madison; University of Wisconsin Press.

WOOLSEY, C. N. & FAIRMAN, D. (1946). "Contralateral, ipsilateral and bilateral representation of cutaneous receptors in somatic areas I and II of the cerebral cortex of the pig, sheep and other mammals." *Surgery*, **19:** 684–702.

WRIGHT, H. M., KORR, I. M. & THOMAS, P. E. (1960). "Local and regional variations in cutaneous vasomotor tone of the human trunk." *Acta Neuroveg.*, **22:** 32–52.

WYKE, B. D. (1966). "The neurology of joints." *Ann. Roy. Coll. Surg. Engl.*, **41:** 25–50.

WYKE, B. D. (1969). *Principles of General Neurology: An Introduction to the Basic Principles of Medical and Surgical Neurology.* Amsterdam and London; Elsevier.

WYKE, B. D. (1970). "The neurological basis of thoracic spinal pain." *Rheumatol. Phys. Med.*, **10:** 356–367.

WYKE, B. D. (1972). "Articular neurology: a review." *Physiotherapy*, **58:** 94–99.

WYKE, B. D. (1975). "The neurological basis of movement: a

developmental review." In *Movement and Child Development*. pp. 19–33. Ed. K. S. Holt, London; Heinemann.

WYKE, B. D. (1975). "Morphological and functional features of the innervation of the costovertebral joints." *Folia Morphol., Prague*, **25:** 178–186.

WYKE, B. D. (1976). "Neurological aspects of low back pain." In *The Lumbar Spine and Back Pain*. pp. 189–256. Ed. M. I. V. Jayson. London; Sector Publishing Co.

WYKE, B. D. (1976). "Neurological mechanisms in spasticity." *Physiotherapy*, **62:** 316–319.

WYKE, B. D. (1977). "Neurological mechanisms of spinal pain." In *Patología de la Columna Vertebral*. pp. 45–56. Ed. S. Hernández Conesa and J. Sequier. Murcia; Ferrer Internacional.

WYKE, B. D. (1979). "Neurology of the cervical spinal joints." *Physiotherapy*, **65:** 72–76.

WYKE, B. D. & MOLINA, F. (1972). "Articular reflexology of the cervical spine." *Proc. 6th Int. Congr. Phys. Med., Barcelona*: p. 4.

WYKE, B. D. & POLÁČEK, P. (1973). "Structure and function of the joint receptor apparatus." *Acta Clin. Orthop. Traum. Česk.*, **40:** 489–497.

YAMAMOTO, S., MIYAJIMA, M. & URABE, M. (1960). "Respiratory neuronal activities in spinal afferents of cat." *Jap J. Physiol.*, **10:** 509–517.

### (b) Neuromuscular systems (including Electromyography)

ANDRADE, J. R. DE, GRANT, C. & DIXON, A. S. G. (1964). "Articular sensation and muscle response in joint disease." *J. Bone Joint Surg.*, **46A:** 1367.

ANGEL, R. W. & HOFMANN, W. W. (1963). "The H-reflex in normal, spastic and rigid subjects." *Arch. Neurol.*, **8:** 591–596.

APRESLE, J., FARBEAU, M. & SAID, G. (1973). "Muscular hypertrophy secondary to a peripheral nerve injury." *Rev. Neurol.*, **128:** 153–160.

BARBER, H. S. (1957). "Myalgic syndrome with constitutional effects: polymyalgia rheumatica." *Ann. Rheumat. Dis.*, **16:** 230–237.

BARKER, E. (Ed.). (1962). *Symposium on Muscle Receptors*. Hong Kong; University Press.

BASMAJIAN, J. (1974). *Muscles Alive. Their Functions Revealed by Electromyography*. 3rd ed. Baltimore; Williams and Wilkins.

BATTYE, C. K., & JOSEPH, J. (1966). "An investigation by telemetering of the activity of some muscles in walking. *Med. Biol. Eng.*, **4:** 125.

BEARN, J. G. (1961). "The significance of the abdominal muscles in weight lifting." *Acta Anat.*, **45:** 83.

BESSOU, P. & LAPORTE, Y. (1958). "Activation of unmyelinated afferent fibres of muscular origin." *Compt. Rend. Soc. Biol., Paris*, **152:** 1587–1590.

BLOM, S. & LEMPERG, R. (1967). "Electromyographic analysis of the lumbar musculature in patients operated on for lumbar rhizopathy." *J. Neurosurg.*, **26:** 25–30.

BOURNE, G. H. (Ed.). (1960). *The Structure and Function of Muscle*. 3 vols. New York; Academic Press.

BRODAL, A. (1969). *Neurological Anatomy in Relation to Clinical Medicine*. 2nd ed. London; Oxford University Press.

BUCHANEN, F. (1908). "The electrical response of muscle to voluntary, reflex, and artificial stimulation." *Quart. J. Exp. Physiol.*, **1:** 211–242.

BUCHTHAL, F., GULD, C. & ROSENFALCK, P. (1955). "Innervation zone and propagation velocity in human muscle." *Acta Physiol. Scand.*, **35:** 174–190.

BUCHTHAL, F., GULD, C. & ROSENFALCK, P. (1957). "Volume conduction of the spike of the motor unit potential investigated with a new type of multielectrode." *Acta Physiol. Scand.*, **38:** 331–354.

BUCHTHAL, F., GULD, C. & ROSENFALCK, P. (1957). "Multielectrode study of the territory of a motor unit." *Acta Physiol. Scand.*, **39:** 83–104.

CAMPBELL, E. D. R., & GREEN, B. A. (1965). "An attempt to measure spasticity objectively and the effect on these measurements of 'carisoprodol'." *Ann. Phys. Med.*, **8:** 4–11.

CAMPBELL, E. J. H., AGOSTONI, E. & NEWSOM DAVIS, J. (1970). *The Respiratory Muscles: Mechanics and Neural Control*. 2nd ed. London; Lloyd-Luke.

CARLÖÖ, S. (1961). "The static muscle load in different work positions: an electromyographic study." *Ergonomics*, **4:** 193.

CAVE, A. J. E. (1937). "The innervation and morphology of the cervical intertransverse muscles." *J. Anat.*, **71:** 497–515.

CHRISTENSEN, E. H. (1962). "Muscular work and fatigue." In *Muscle As A Tissue.* p. 176. Ed. K. Rodhal and S. M. Harvath. New York; McGraw-Hill.

COBB, C. R., DE VRIES, H. A., URBAN, R. T., LUEKENS, C. A. & BAGG, R. J. (1975). "Electrical activity in muscle pain." *Amer. J. Phys. Med.*, **54:** 80–87.

COHEN, L. A. (1961). "Role of the eye and neck proprioceptive mechanisms in body orientation and motor co-ordination." *J. Neurophysiol.*, **24:** 1–11.

DENSLOW, J. S. & CLOUGH, G. H. (1941). "Reflex activity in the spinal extensors." *J. Neurophysiol.*, **4:** 430–437.

DENSLOW, J. S. & GUTENSOHN, O. R. (1967). "Neuromuscular reflexes in response to gravity." *J. Appl. Physiol.*, **23:** 243–247.

DESCUNS, P., COLLET, M., RESCHE, F., LAJAT, Y., GUIHENEUC, P. & GINET, J. (1973). "Relevance of the Hoffmann reflex in examination of lumbosacral radicular lesions of discal origin." *Neurochirurgie*, **19:** 627–640.

DESPLAND, P. A. (1974). "Electromyographic study of 250 operated cases of lumbar radicular syndromes." *Arch. Suisse Neurol. Neurochir. Psychiat.*, **114:** 229–236.

DE VRIES, H. A. (1961). "Electromyographic observations of the effects of static stretching upon muscular distress." *Research Quart.*, **32:** 468–479.

DONISCH, E. W. & BASMAJIAN, J. V. (1972). "Electromyography of deep back muscles in man." *Amer. J. Anat.*, **133:** 25–36.

DRECHSLER, B., LASTOVKA, M. & KALVUDOVA, E. (1966). "Neurophysiological study of patients with herniated intervertebral discs." *Electroenceph. Clin. Neurophysiol.*, **22:** 287–288.

DUBOWITZ, V. (1973). "Rigid spine syndrome: a muscle syndrome in search of a name." *Proc. Roy. Soc. Med.*, **66:** 219–220.

EARL, W. D., STRONG, R. & THOMAS, P. E. (1967). "A qualitative analysis of the specificity of the surface electrode in detecting the electrical activity of muscular action." *J. Amer. Osteopath. Ass.*, **66:** 1030–1035.

EBLE, J. N. (1961). "Reflex relationships of paravertebral muscles." *Amer. J. Physiol.*, **200:** 939.

ECCLES, J. C. & O'CONNOR, W. (1939). "Responses which nerve

impulses evoke in mammalian striated muscles." *J. Physiol.*, **97:** 44–102.

ELDRED, E., GRANIT, R. & MERTON, P. (1953). "Supraspinal control of the muscle spindles and its significance." *J. Physiol.*, **122:** 498–523.

ELLIOTT, F. A. (1944). "Tender muscles in sciatica." *Lancet*, **1:** 47–49.

FARFAN, H. F. (1975). "Comment on the sitting posture: an electromyographic and discometric study." *Orthop. Clin. Nth. Amer.*, p. 120.

FEINSTEIN, B., LINDEGARD, B., EBERHARD, N. & WOHLFART, G. (1954). "Studies on action potentials in normal human muscles." *Acta Psychiat. Neurol. Scand.*, **29:** 189–195.

FERNAND, V. S. V. & YOUNG, J. Z. (1951). "The sizes of the nerve fibres of muscle nerves." *Proc. Roy. Soc. Lond.*, **139B:** 38–58.

FERRAZ DE CARVALHO, C. A., GARCIA, O. S., VITTI, M. & BERZIN, F. (1972). "Electromyographic study of the m. tensor fascia latae and m. sartorius." *Electroenceph. Clin. Neurophysiol.*, **12:** 387–400.

FIDEL-OSIPOVA, S. I. & GRISHKO, F. E. (1962). "Features specific to electromyograms taken during voluntary muscle contraction in old age." *Byull. Eksp. Biol. Med.*, **3:** 9–14.

FISCHER, F. J. & HOUTZ, S. J. (1968). "Evaluation of the function of the gluteus maximus muscle: an electromyographic study." *Amer. J. Phys. Med.*, **47:** 182–191.

FLINT, M. M. (1965). "An electromyographic comparison of the function of the iliacus and the rectus abdominis muscles: a preliminary report." *J. Amer. Phys. Therap. Ass.*, **45:** 248–253.

FLINT, M. M. & GUDGELL, J. (1965). "Electromyographic study of abdominal muscular activity during exercise." *Research Quart.*, **36:** 29–37.

FLOYD, W. F. (1949). "E.M.G. study of standing man." *J. Physiol.*, **110:** 5P.

FLOYD, W. F. (1952). "Electromyographic studies of muscle function in health and in certain disorders of the nervous system and musculature." *Ph. D. Thesis. Univ. London.*

FLOYD, W. F. & SILVER, P. H. S. (1950). "E.M.G. study of standing in man." *J. Physiol.*, **111:** 5P.

FLOYD, W. F. & SILVER, P. H. S. (1950). "Electromyographic study of patterns of activity of the anterior abdominal wall muscles in man." *J. Anat.*, **84**: 132–145.

FLOYD, W. F. & SILVER, P. H. S. (1952). "Electromyography of the erectores spinae muscles in flexion of the lumbar vertebrae." *J. Anat.*, **86**: 484.

FLOYD, W. F. & WALLS, E. W. (1953). "Electromyography of the sphincter ani externus in man." *J. Physiol.*, **122**: 599–609.

FRASER, E. J. (1967). "Extensor muscles of the low back: an electromyographic study." *Physical Therapy*, **47**: 200–207.

FREIBERG, J. A. (1938). "The scalenus anterior muscle in relation to shoulder and arm pain." *J. Bone Joint Surg.*, **20**: 860–869.

GARDNER-MEDWIN, D. & WALTON, J. N. (1969). "A classification of the neuromuscular disorders and a note on the clinical examination of the voluntary muscles." In *Disorders of Voluntary Muscle*. 2nd ed. pp. 411–453. Ed. J. N. Walton. London; Churchill.

GILSON, A. S. & MILLS, W. B. (1941). "Activities of single motor units in man during slight voluntary efforts." *Amer. J. Physiol.*, **133**: 658–669.

GOLDSTEIN, I. B. (1965). "The relationship of muscle tension and autonomic activity to psychiatric disorders." *Psychosomat. Med.*, **27**: 39–52.

GRACANIN, F. (1975). "Optimal stimulus parameters for minimum pain in the chronic stimulation of innervated muscle." *Arch. Phys. Med. Rehab.*, **56**: 243–249.

GRANIT, R. (Ed.). (1966). *Muscular Afferents and Motor Control*. Stockholm; Almqvist and Wiksell.

GRANIT, R. (1970). *The Basis of Motor Control*. New York; Academic Press.

GRONBAEK, P. & SKOUBY, A. P. (1960). "The activity pattern of the diaphragm and some muscles of the neck and trunk in chronic asthmatics and normal controls. A comparative electromyographic study." *Acta Med. Scand.*, **168**: 413–425.

GUTTMAN, L. & SILVER, J. R. (1965). "Electromyographic studies on reflex activity in the intercostal and abdominal muscles in cervical cord lesions." *Paraplegia*, **3**: 1–22.

HATAMI, T. (1961). "Electromyographic studies of influence of pregnancy on activity of the abdominal wall muscles." *Tohoku J. Exp. Med.*, **75**: 71–80; 81–88.

HINSON, M. M. (1969). "An electromyographic study of the push-up for women." *Research Quart.*, **40**: 305–311.

HNÍK, P. (1966). "Increased sensory outflow from atrophying muscles and muscles after functional activity." In *Muscular Afferents and Motor Control*. pp. 445–447. Ed. R. Granit. New York; Wiley.

HNÍK, P., HUDHČKÁ, O. & STULCOVÁ, B. (1964). "Afferent activity from striated muscles related to changes in intramuscular circulation." *J. Physiol., Paris*, **56**: 569.

HOLT, L. E., KAPLAN, H. M. & HOSHIKO, M. (1969). "The influence of antagonistic contraction and head position on the responses of agonistic muscles." *Arch. Phys. Med.*, **50**: 279–284.

HUNT, C. C. & PERL, E. R. (1960). "Spinal reflex mechanisms concerned with skeletal muscle." *Physiol. Rev.*, **40**: 538–579.

IGGO, A. (1966). "Muscle nociceptors with C fibres." In *Touch, Heat, Pain*. pp. 364–365. Ed. A. V. S. de Reuck and J. Knight. London; Churchill.

INMAN, V. T., RALSTON, H. T., SAUNDERS, J. B. DE C. M., FEINSTEIN, B. & WRIGHT, E. W. (1952). "Relation of human electromyogram to muscular tension." *Electroenceph. Clin. Neurophysiol.*, **4**: 187–194.

ITAMI, Y. & HASEGAWA, Y. (1968). "Electromyogram of the trunk muscles in view of its spine protections." *Electromyography*, **8**: 187.

JACOBS, A. & FELTON, G. S. (1969). "Visual feedback of myoelectric output to facilitate muscle relaxation in normal persons and patients with neck injury." *Arch. Phys. Med. Rehab.*, **50**: 34–39.

JONSSON, B. (1969). "Morphology, innervation and electromyographic study of the erector spinae." *Arch. Phys. Med. Rehab.*, **50**: 638–641.

JONSSON, B. (1970). "The functions of individual muscles in the lumbar part of the erector spinae muscle." *Electromyography*, **1**: 3–19.

JONSSON, B. (1970). "Topography of the lumbar part of the erector spinae muscle: an analysis of the morphologic conditions precedent for insertion of E.M.G. electrodes into individual muscles of the lumbar part of the erector spinae muscle." *Zeit. Anat. Entwickl. Gesch.*, **130**: 177–191.

JONSSON, B. & STEEN, B. (1963). "Function of hip and thigh muscles in Romberg's test and standing at rest. An E.M.G. study." *Acta Morph. Néerl-Scand.*, **5**: 269–276.

JOSEPH, J. (1960). *Man's Posture: Electromyographic Studies*. Springfield, Illinois; Thomas.

JOSEPH, J. (1964). "Electromyographic studies on muscle tone and the erect posture in man." *Brit. J. Surg.*, **51**: 616–622.

JOSEPH, J. & BATTYE, C. K. (1961). "A telemetering electromyograph for investigating muscles in walking." *J. Anat.*, **95**: 607.

JOSEPH, J. & McCOLL, I. (1961). "Electromyography of muscles of posture: posterior vertebral muscles in males." *J. Physiol.*, **157**: 33–37.

JOSEPH, J. & NIGHTINGALE, A. (1952). "Electromyography of muscles of posture: leg muscles in males." *J. Physiol.*, **117**: 484–491.

JOSEPH, J. & NIGHTINGALE, A. (1955). "Electromyography of muscles of posture: thigh muscles in males." *Arch. Phys. Med. Rehab.*, **36**: 116.

JOSEPH, J., NIGHTINGALE, A. & WILLIAMS, P. L. (1955). "A detailed study of the electric potentials recorded over some postural muscles while relaxed and standing." *J. Physiol.*, **127**: 617–625.

JOSEPH, J. & WATSON, R. (1967). "Telemetering electromyography of muscles used in walking up and down stairs." *J. Bone Joint Surg.*, **49B**: 774–780.

JOSEPH, J. & WILLIAMS, P. L. (1957). "Electromyography of certain hip muscles." *J. Anat.*, **91**: 286–299.

KAMON, G. (1966). "Electromyography of static and dynamic postures of the body supported on the arms." *J. Appl. Physiol.*, **21**: 1611–1618.

KARVONEN, M. J. & RONNHOLM, N. (1914). "E.M.G.s and energy expenditure studies of rhythmic and paced lifting work." *Ann. Acad. Sci. Fenn., A. V. Med.*, **106**: 19.

KEAGY, R. D., BRUMLIK, J. & BERGAN, J. J. (1966). "Direct electromyography of the psoas major muscle in man." *J. Bone Joint Surg.*, **48A**: 1377–1382.

KIRSCHNER, H. & KOSLOWSKI, S. (1966). "Evaluation of the dispersion of electrical activity in muscles during work of varying intensity." *Bull. Akad. Pol. Sci.*, **14**: 75–79.

KNUTSSON, B., LINDH, K., & TELHAG, H. (1966). "Sitting—an electromyographic and mechanical study." *Acta Orthop. Scand.*, **37**: 415–428.

KURODA, E., KLISSOURAS, V. & MULSUM, J. H. (1970). "Electrical and metabolic activities and fatigue in human isometric contraction." *J. Appl. Physiol.*, **29**: 358.

LABAN, N. M., RAITOU, A. D. & JOHNSON, E. W. (1965). "Electromyographic study of the function of the iliopsoas muscle." *Arch. Phys. Med.*, **46**: 676–679.

LANDGREN, S. & WOLSK, D. (1966). "A new cortical area receiving input from Group I muscle afferents." *Life Sciences*, **5**: 75–79.

LAPRESSE, J., FABEAU, M. & SAID, G. (1973). "True muscular hypertrophy secondary to a peripheral nerve lesion." *Rev. Neurol.*, **128**: 153–160.

LEFEBRE, J., TRIBOULET-CHASSEVANT, A. & MISSIRLIU, M. F. (1961). "Electromyographic data in idiopathic scoliosis." *Arch. Phys. Med.*, **42**: 710–711.

LENMAN, J. A. R. (1959). "Quantitative electromyographic changes associated with muscular weakness." *J. Neurol. Neurosurg. Psychiat.*, **22**: 306–310.

LIM, R. K. S., GUZMAN, F. & RODGERS, D. W. (1962). "Note on the muscle receptors concerned with pain." In *Symposium on Muscle Receptors*. p. 215. Ed. D. Barker. Hong Kong University Press.

LINDAHL, P. (1970). "Experimental muscle pain produced by chemical stimulus." *Acta Orthop. Scand.*, **40**: 741.

LINGE, B. VAN. (1963). "The behaviour of the quadriceps muscle during walking. An electromyographic investigation." *Acta Morph. Néerl-Scand.*, **5**: 293.

LUNDERVOLD, A. J. S. (1951). *Electromyographic Investigations of Position and Manner of Working in Typewriting*. Oslo; Brøggers.

MACCONAILL, M. A. & BASMAJIAN, J. V. (1969). *Muscles and Movements: A Basis for Human Kinesiology*. Baltimore; Williams and Wilkins.

MANNI, E. (1975). "Trigeminal influences on extensor muscles of the neck." *Exp. Neurol.*, **47**: 330–342.

MATTHEWS, P. B. C. (1964). "Muscle spindles and their motor control." *Physiol. Rev.*, **44**: 219–288.

MATTHEWS, P. B. C. (1972). *Mammalian Muscle Receptors and Their Central Actions*. London; Arnold.

MERTON, P. A. (1954). "Voluntary strength and fatigue." *J. Physiol.*, **123**: 553.

MIYAZAKI, A. (1968). "Posture and low back pain: electromyographic evaluation." *Electromyography*, **8**: 191–193.

MOLINA, F., RAMCHARAN, J. A. & WYKE, B. D. (1976). "Structure and function of articular receptor systems in the cervical spine." *J. Bone Joint Surg.*, **58B**: 255.

189

Moore, J. C. (1966). "Fabrication of suction cup electrodes for electromyography." *Electroenceph. Clin. Neurophysiol.*, **20:** 405–406.

Morinaga, H. (1973). "An electromyographic study on the function of the psoas major muscle." *J. Jap. Orthop. Ass.*, **47:** 351–365.

Morris, J. M., Benner, G. & Lucas, D. B. (1962). "An electromyographic study of the intrinsic muscles of the back in man." *J. Anat.*, **96:** 509–520.

Morris, J. M., Lucas, D. B. & Bresler, B. (1961). "Role of the trunk in stability of the spine." *J. Bone Joint Surg.*, **43A:** 327–351.

Morris, R. (1970). "Effects of spinal supports on the electrical activity of muscles of the trunk." *J. Bone Joint Surg.*, **52A:** 51–60.

Morrison, A. B. (1954). "The levatores costarum and their nerve supply." *J. Anat.*, **88:** 19–24.

Myers, S. J. & Sullivan, W. P. (1968). "Effects of circulation occlusion on time of muscular fatigue." *J. Appl. Physiol.*, **24:** 54.

Nastuk, W. L. & Hodgkin, A. L. (1950). "The electrical activity of single muscle fibres." *J. Cell Comp. Physiol.*, **35:** 39–73.

O'Connel, A. L. & Gardner, E. B. (1963). "The use of electromyography in kinesiological research." *Research Quart.*, **34:** 166–184.

Ono, M. (1963). "Electromyographic kinesiologic studies on weight-lifters." *Tairyoku-kagagu*, **12:** 1–29.

Ono, M. & Kubota, N. (1963). "An electromyographic study on weight-lifters." *Kijeikai Med. J.*, **10:** 124–144.

Partridge, L. D. & Huber, F. C. (1967). "Factors in the interpretation of the electromyogram based on muscle response to dynamic nerve signals. *Amer. J. Phys. Med.*, **46:** 1276–1289.

Partridge, M. H. & Walters, C. E. (1959). "Participation of the abdominal muscles in various movements of the trunk in man: an electromyographic study." *Phys. Therap. Rev.*, **39:** 791–800.

Pauly, J. E. (1966). "An electromyographic analysis of certain movements and postures. I. Some deep muscles of the back." *Anat. Rec.*, **155:** 223.

Pavelka, K. (1970). "Measurement of vertebral column rotation." *Zeit. Rheumatforsch.*, **29:** 366–370.

Portinoy, H. & Morin, F. (1956). "Electromyographic studies of postural muscles in various positions and movements." *Amer. J. Physiol.*, **186:** 122–126.

Price, J. P., Claire, M. H. & Ewerhardt, F. H. (1948). "Studies in low backache with persistent muscle spasm." *Arch. Phys. Med.*, **29**: 703–709.

REEDER, T. (1963). "Electromyographic study of the latissimus dorsi muscle." *J. Amer. Phys. Ther. Ass.*, **43**: 165–172.

SCHERRER, J. & MONOD, H. (1960). "Local muscular work and fatigue in man." *J. Physiol., Paris*, **52**: 419.

SHEFFIELD, J. F. (1962). "E.M.G. study of the abdominal muscles in walking and other movements." *Amer. J. Phys. Med.*, **41**: 142–147.

SILVER, P. H. S. (1952). "An anatomical study in co-ordinated muscle action and movement patterns, including electromyographic studies in man." *Ph. D. Thesis. Univ. London.*

SIMONS, D. G. (1976). "Muscle pain syndromes. Part II." *Amer. J. Phys. Med.*, **55**: 15.

SKOGLUND, S. (1960). "On the postnatal development of postural mechanisms as revealed by electromyography and myography in decerebrate kittens." *Acta Physiol. Scand.*, **49**: 299–317.

STEPANOV, A. D. (1959). "Electromyogram changes produced by training in weight lifting." *Sechenov J. Physiol.*, **45**: 115–121.

SULEMANA, C. A. & SUCHENWIRTH, R. (1972). "Regional differences in the histoenzyme composition of 5 skeletal muscles." *J. Neurol. Sci.*, **16**: 433–444.

TAKAHASHI, K. & KAMEYAMA, M. (1972). "Electromyography and histopathology of muscle and spinal cord: analysis of 105 skeletal muscles from 31 autopsy cases." *J. Neurol. Sci.*, **16**: 465–479.

TANIGUCHI, Y. (1970). "An electromyographic study of low back pain." *J. Jap. Orthop. Ass.*, **44**: 475–491.

TESHIMA, H. (1958). "Electromyographic study of patterns of activity of the abdominal wall muscles in man." *Tohoku. J. Exp. Med.*, **67**: 281–292.

THOMAS, G. (1969). "The function of the extensor muscles of the back." *German Med. Monthly*, **14**: 564–566.

THOMAS, G. & RAU, E. (1969). "Function of the back-stretching muscles." *Zeit. Orthop.*, **106**: 737–745.

TIEGS, O. W. (1953). "Innervation of voluntary muscle." *Physiol. Rev.*, **33**: 90–144.

TOKAROWSKI, A. (1965). "On the function of the deep muscles of the spine." *Chir. Narzad. Ruchm. Ortop. Pol.*, **30**: 525–526.

TOKIZANE, T., MURAO, M., OGATA, T. & KONDO, T. (1951).

"Electromyographic studies on tonic neck, lumbar and labyrinthine reflexes in normal persons." *Jap. J. Physiol.*, **2:** 130–146.

TOKIZANE, T. & SHIMAZU, H. (1964). *Functional Differentiation of Human Skeletal Muscle*. Tokyo; University of Tokyo Press.

TROUP, J. D. G. & CHAPMAN, A. E. (1972). "Changes in the waveform of the electromyogram during fatiguing activity in the muscles of the spine and hips: the analysis of postural stress." *Electromyography*, **12:** 347–365.

VRETTOS, X. C. & WYKE, B. D. (1974). "Articular reflexogenic systems in the costovertebral joints." *J. Bone Joint Surg.*, **56B:** 382.

WALTER, S. N. (Ed.). (1964). *Anatomy of the Motor Unit*. London; Churchill.

WALTERS, C. E. & PARTRIDGE, M. J. (1957). "Electromyographic study of the differential action of the abdominal muscles during exercise." *Amer. J. Phys. Med.*, **36:** 259–268.

WALTERS, R. L. & MORRIS, J. M. (1970). "Effect of spinal supports on the electrical activity of muscles of the trunk." *J. Bone Joint. Surg.*, **52A:** 51–60.

WALTERS, R. L. & MORRIS, J. M. (1972). "Electrical activity of muscles of the trunk during walking." *J. Anat.*, **111:** 101–109.

WALTON, J. N. (Ed.). (1969). *Disorders of Voluntary Muscle*. 2nd ed. London; Churchill.

WEDDELL, G., FEINSTEIN, B. & PATTLE, R. E. (1944). "The electrical activity of voluntary muscle in man under normal and pathological conditions." *Brain*, **67:** 178–257.

WEIDENBAUER, M. M. & MORTENSEN, O. A. (1952). "An electromyographic study of the trapezius muscle." *Amer. J. Phys. Med.*, **31:** 363–372.

WOHLFART, G. & HENRIKSSON, K. G. (1960). "Observations on the distribution of Golgi musculo-tendinous organs." *Acta Anat.*, **41:** 192–204.

WYKE, B. D. (1969). *Principles of General Neurology*. Amsterdam and London; Elsevier.

WYKE, B. D. (1972). "Arthrokinetic reflex contributions to motor control." *Proc. 2nd Ind. Symp. (I.U.P.S.) on Motor Control, Varna, Bulgaria, p. 109*.

WYKE, B. D. (1975). "Morphological and functional features of the innervation of the costovertebral joints." *Folia Morphol., Prague*. **25:** 178–186.

WYKE, B. D. (1975). "The neurological basis of movement: a developmental review." In *Movement and Child Development.* pp. 19–33. Ed. K. S. Holt, London; Heinemann.

WYKE, B. D. (1976). "Neurological mechanisms in spasticity." *Physiotherapy*, **62:** 316–319.

WYKE, B. D. (1976). "Neurological aspects of low back pain." In *The Lumbar Spine and Back Pain.* pp. 189–256. Ed. M. I. V. Jayson; London; Sector Publishing Co.

WYKE, B. D. (1979). "The neurology of the cervical spine." *Physiotherapy*, **65:** 72–76.

WYKE, B. D. (1979). "Cervical articular contributions to posture and gait: Their relation to senile disequilibrium." *Age and Ageing*, **8:** 251–258.

YAMAJI, K. & MISU, A. (1968). "Kinesiologic study with electromyography of low back pain." *Electromyography*, **8:** 189.

YAP, C. B. & HIROTA, T. (1967). "Sciatic nerve motor conduction velocity study." *J. Neurol. Neurosurg. Psychiat.*, **30:** 233–239.

YOSHIDA, T. (1966). "Electromyographic study of backache: especially on the function of erector trunci muscle." *J. Jap. Orthop. Ass.*, **40:** 147–173.

### (c) Spinal Cord and Nerve Roots: Spinal Tracts

ADAMS, C. B. T. & LOGUE, V. (1971). "Studies in cervical spondylitic myelopathy." *Brain*, **94:** 557–594.

ALBE-FESSARD, D. (1968). "Central nervous mechanisms involved in pain and analgesia." In *Pharmacology of Pain.* pp. 131–168. Ed. R. K. S. Lim, D. Armstrong and E. G. Pardo. Oxford; Pergamon Press.

ALLEN, K. (1952). "Neuropathies caused by bony spurs in the cervical spine with special reference to surgical treatment." *J. Neurol. Neurosurg. Psychiat.*, **15:** 20–36.

ARING, C. D. (1974). "Lesions about the junction of medulla and spinal cord." *J. Amer. Med. Ass.*, **229:** 1879.

ASCHER, P. W. (1969). "Intrathecal cortisone management of lumbar radiculopathy." *Zbl. Chir.*, **94:** 1678–1679.

BALAKRISHNAN, V., RICE, M. S. & SIMPSON, D. A. (1974). "Spinal neuroblastomas: diagnosis, treatment and prognosis." *J. Neurosurg.*, **40:** 631–638.

BARNETT, H. G. (1975). "Lumbosacral nerve root avulsion: report of a case and review of literature." *J. Trauma*, **15**: 532–535.

BERTRAND, G. (1975). "The 'battered root' problem." *Orthop. Clin. Nth. Amer.*, **6**: 305–310.

BHARUCHA, E. P. (1974). "Postconjunctival myeloradiculopathy." *Neurol. India*, **22**: 79–82.

BOLDREY, E. B. (1969). "Sensory levels associated with painful lesions affecting the spinal roots in man." *Trans. Amer. Neurol. Ass.*, **94**: 227–228.

BONICA, J. J. (Ed.). (1974). *International Symposium on Pain*. New York; Raven Press.

BONICA, J. J. & ALBE-FESSARD, D. (Eds.). (1976). *Advances in Pain Research and Therapy*. Vol. I. New York; Raven Press.

BONICA, J. J., LIEBESKIND, J. C. & ALBE-FESSARD, D. (Eds.). (1979). *Advances in Pain Research and Therapy*. Vol. III. New York; Raven Press.

BOWSHER, E. B. (1969). "The topographical projection of fibres from the antero-lateral quadrant of the spinal cord to the subdiencephalic brain stem in man." *Psychiat. Neurol., Basel*, **143**: 75–99.

BRENNER, L. (1973). "Subcutaneous lumbar 'rhizolysis'. Correspondence." *Med. J. Aus.*, **2**: 707–708.

BRIEG, A. (1966). "Effects of mechanical stresses on the spinal cord in cervical spondylosis." *J. Neurosurg.*, **25**: 45.

BRIEG, A. & MARIONS, O. (1963). "Biomechanics of the lumbosacral nerve roots." *Acta Radiol. (Diagn.)*, **1**: 1141–1160.

BRODAL, A. (1969). *Neurological Anatomy in Relation to Clinical Medicine*. 2nd ed. Oxford University Press.

BURKE, D. C. (1973). "Spinal cord injuries and seat belts." *Med. J. Aust.*, **2**: 801–806.

CARPENTER, M. B., STEIN, B. M. & SHRINER, J. E. (1968). "Central projections of spinal dorsal roots in the monkey. II." *Amer. J. Anat.*, **123**: 75.

CARTLIDGE, N. E. F., McCOLLUM, J. P. K. & AYYAR, R. D. A. (1972). "Spinal cord compression in Paget's disease." *J. Neurol. Neurosurg. Psychiatr.* **35**: 825–828.

CHAKRAVORTY, B. G. (1967). "Arterial supply of the cervical spinal cord and its relation to the cervical myelopathy in spondylosis." *Ann. Roy. Coll. Surg. Engl.*, **45**: 232.

CHESTERMAN, P. J. (1964). "Spastic paraplegia caused by seques-

194

trated thoracic intervertebral disc." *Proc. Roy. Soc. Med.*, **57:** 87–88.

CHIN, J. H. (1974). "Changes in the dorsal root potential with diazepam and with the analgesics aspirin, nitrous oxide, morphine and meperidine." *Neuropharmacology*, **13:** 303–315.

CHRISTENSEN, B. N. & PERL, E. R. (1970). "Spinal neurons specifically excited by noxious or thermal stimuli: marginal zone of the dorsal horn." *J. Neurophysiol.*, **33:** 293–307.

COOK, A. W. (1974). "Electrical stimulation of the spinal cord." *Lancet*, **1:** 869–870.

COOK, A. W. (1974). "Stimulation of the spinal cord in motoneurone disease." *Lancet*, **2:** 230–231.

COPPOLA, A. R. (1974). "Disease of the cervical spine and nerve root pain." *Virginia Med. Month.*, **101:** 199–201.

CORBIN, K. B. & GARDNER, E. D. (1937). "Decrease in number of myelinated fibres in human spinal roots with age." *Anat. Rec.*, **68:** 63.

CRACCO, J. B. (1975). "The spinal evoked response in infants and children." *Neurology*, **25:** 31–36.

CRAIG, H. & WALSH, H. N. (1941). "Neuroanatomical and physiological aspects and significance of sciatica." *J. Bone Joint Surg.*, **23A:** 417–434.

CREED, R. S., DENNY-BROWN, D., ECCLES, J. C., LIDDELL, E. G. T. & SHERRINGTON, C. S. (1932). *Reflex Activity of The Spinal Cord.* Oxford; Clarendon Press.

CROFT, T. J., BRODKEY, J. S., NULSEN, F. E. (1972). "Reversible spinal cord trauma: a model for electrical monitoring of spinal cord function." *J. Neurosurg.*, **36:** 402–406.

CURRY, M. J. & GORDON, G. (1972). "The spinal input to the posterior group in the cat: an electrophysiological investigation." *Brain Res.*, **44:** 417.

DANZIGER, J. (1973). "Arteriovenous malformation of the cervical cord." *Sth. Afr. Med. J.*, **47:** 1413–1416.

DECKER, K. (1965). "Neuroradiological study of the mobility of the spinal cord." *Verh. Anat. Ges.*, **115:** 35–47.

DEE, R. (1978). "The innervation of joints." In *The Joints and Synovial Fluid.* pp. 177–204. Ed. L. Sokoloff. New York; Academic Press.

DENNIS, S. G. & MELZACK, R. (1977). "Pain-signalling systems in the dorsal and ventral spinal cord." *Pain*, **4:** 97–132.

DETWILER, S. R. & HOLTSER, H. (1955). "The inductive and formative influence of the spinal cord upon the vertebral column." *Bull. Hosp. Joint Dis.*, **15**: 114.

EARLE, K. M. (1952). "The tract of Lissauer and its possible relation to the pain pathway." *J. Comp. Neurol.*, **96**: 93–111.

EPSTEIN, B. S., EPSTEIN, J. A. & LAVINE, L. (1964). "The effect of anatomic variations in the lumbar vertebrae and spinal canal on cauda equina and nerve root syndromes." *Amer. J. Roentgenol.*, **91**: 1055–1065.

EPSTEIN, B. S., EPSTEIN, J. A., LAVINE, L., CARRAS, R., ROSENTHAL, A. D. & SUMNER, P. (1973). "Lumbar nerve root compression at the intervertebral foramina caused by arthritis of the posterior facets." *J. Neurosurg.*, **39**: 363–369.

EPSTEIN, J. A. (1954). "The syndrome of herniation of the lower thoracic intervertebral discs with nerve root and spinal cord compression: a presentation of four cases with a review of the literature, methods of diagnosis and treatment." *J. Neurosurg.*, **11**: 525–538.

FETZ, E. E. (1968). "Pyramidal tract effects on the interneurons in the cat lumbar dorsal horn." *J. Neurophysiol.*, **31**: 69–80.

FIELDS, H. L. (1974). "The spinoreticular tract: an alternate pathway mediating pain." *Trans. Amer. Neurol. Ass.*, **99**: 211–213.

FOX, A. J. (1975). "Myelographic cervical nerve root deformities." *Radiology*, **116**: 355–361.

FRAHER, J. P. (1974). "A numerical study of cervical and thoracic ventral nerve roots." *J. Anat.*, **118**: 127–142.

FREIDBERG, S. R. (1973). "Cauda equina compression secondary to swollen nerve roots in narrow lumbar canal." *Lahey Clin. Fndtn. Bull.*, **22**: 65–67.

FRYKHOLM, R. (1951). "Lower cervical nerve roots and their investments." *Acta Chir. Scand.*, **101**: 457–471.

GARDNER, E. D. (1967). "Spinal cord and brain stem pathways for afferents from joints." In *Myotatic, Kinesthetic and Vestibular Mechanisms*. pp. 56–76. Ed. A. V. S. de Rueck and J. Knight. London; Churchill.

GARDNER, E. D. & CUNEO, H. M. (1945). "Lateral spinothalamic tract and associated tracts in man." *Arch. Neurol. Psychiat.*, **53**: 423–430.

GELFAN, F. & TARLOV, I. M. (1956). "Physiology of spinal cord, nerve root and peripheral nerve compression." *Amer. J. Physiol.*, **185**: 217–229.

GLEES, P. (1953). "The central pain tract." *Acta Neuroveg., Wien*, **7**: 160–174.

GRANGER, C. V. & FLANIGAN, S. (1968). "Nerve root conduction studies during lumbar disc surgery." *J. Neurosurg.*, **28**: 439–444.

GREGOR, M. & ZIMMERMANN, M. (1972). "Characteristics of spinal neurons responding to cutaneous myelinated and unmyelinated fibres." *J. Physiol.*, **221**: 555–556.

GUNTHER, L. & SAMPSON, J. J. (1929). "The radicular syndrome in hypertrophic osteoarthritis of the spine." *J. Amer. Med. Ass., 1929.* 514–517.

HAGBARTH, K. E. & FOX, J. (1959). "Centrifugal influences on single unit activity in spinal sensory paths." *J. Neurophysiol.*, **22**: 321–338.

HANAK, J. (1969). "Significance of the preoperative finding of denervation activity in discogenic radicular syndromes of the lumbosacral region." *Scripta Med.*, **8**: 385–387.

HANDWERKER, H. O., IGGO, A. & ZIMMERMANN, M. (1975). "Segmental and supraspinal actions on dorsal horn neurones responding to noxious and non-noxious skin stimulation." *Pain*, **1**: 147–165.

HARRIES, B. (1970). "Spinal cord compression." *Brit. Med. J.*, **1**: 611–614.

HASSLER, R. (1960). "The central system of pain." *Acta Neurochir., Wien*, **8**: 353–423.

HEIMER, L. & WALL, P. D. (1968). "The dorsal root distribution to the substantia gelatinosa of the rat with a note on the distribution in the cat." *Exper. Brain Res.*, **6**: 89–99.

HILLMAN, P. & WALL, P. D. (1969). "Inhibitory and excitatory factors influencing the receptive fields of lamina 5 spinal cord cells." *Exper. Brain Res.*, **9**: 284.

HOVELACQUE, A. (1925). "The sinu-vertebral nerve." *Ann. d'Anat. Pathol. Méd.- chir.*, **2**: 435.

JANZEN, R., KEIDEL, W. D., HERZ, A. & STEICHELE, C. (Eds.). (1972). *Pain: Basic Principles, Pharmacology, Therapy.* Stuttgart; Thieme.

KAPLAN, E. B. (1947). "Recurrent meningeal branch of the spinal nerves." *Bull. Hosp. Joint Dis.*, **8**: 108.

KEELE, K. D. (1957). *Anatomies of Pain.* Oxford; Blackwell.

KERR, F. W. L. (1975). "Neuroanatomical substrates of nociception in the spinal cord." *Pain*, **1**: 325–356.

KOBAYASHI, S. (1974). " 'Tract pain syndrome' associated with chronic herniation." *Hawaii Med. J.*, **33**: 376–381.

LIPPMAN, H. H., & KERR, F. W. L. (1972). "Light and electron microscopic study of crossed ascending pathways in the antero-lateral funiculus in monkey." *Brain*, **40**: 496.

LUNDBERG, A. & VOORHOEVE, P. (1962). "Effects from the pyramidal tract on spinal reflex arcs." *Acta Physiol Scand.*, **56**: 201–209.

LUSCHKA, H. VON (1850). *The Nerves of the Human Spinal Canal.* Tübingen; Laupp and Siebeck.

MATTHEWS, P. B. C. (1972). *Mammalian Muscle Receptors and Their Central Action.* London; Arnold.

MAYER, D. G. & PRICE, D. (1976). "Central nervous system mechanisms of analgesia." *Pain*, **2**: 379–404.

MORIN, F., SCHARTZ, H. G. & O'LEARY, J. L. (1951). "Experimental study of the spinothalamic and related tracts." *Acta Psychiat. Neurol. Scand.*, **26**: 371–396.

NADE, S., BELL, E. & WYKE, B. D. (1978). "Articular neurology of the feline lumbar spine." *Proc. Aust. N.Z. Orthop. Ass.*, Oct.: p. 6.

NATHAN, P. W. & SMITH, M. C. (1959). "Fasciculi proprii of the spinal cord: a review of present knowledge." *Brain*, **82**: 610–668.

PALLIE, W. (1959). "The intersegmental anastomoses of posterior spinal rootlets and their significance." *J. Neurosurg.*, **16**: 188.

PEDERSEN, H. S., BLUNCK, C. F. J. & GARDNER, E. D. (1956). "The anatomy of the lumbosacral posterior rami and meningeal branches of spinal nerves (sinu-vertebral nerves): with an experimental study of their functions." *J. Bone Joint Surg.*, **38A**: 377–391.

PRICE, D. D. & DUBNER, R. (1977). "Neurons that subserve the sensory-discriminative aspects of pain." *Pain*, **3**: 307–338.

PRICE, D. D. & MAYERS, D. J. (1975). "Neurophysiological characterization of the anterolateral quadrant neurons subserving pain in *M. mulatta.*" *Pain*, **1**: 59–72.

POGGIO, G. F. & MOUNTCASTLE, V. B. (1960). "A study of the functional contributions of the lemniscal and spinothalmic systems to somatic sensibility." *Bull. Johns Hopkins Hosp.*, **106**: 266–316.

RALSTON, H. J. (1965). "The organisation of the substantia gelatinosa Rolandi in the cat lumbosacral cord." *Zeit. Zellforsch.*, **67:** 1–23.

RALSTON, H. J. (1968). "Dorsal root projections to dorsal horn neurons in the cat spinal cord." *J. Comp. Neurol.*, **132:** 303–330.

SCHEIBEL, M. E. & SCHEIBEL, A. B. (1968). "Terminal axonal patterns in cat spinal cord. II. The dorsal horn." *Brain Res.*, **9:** 32–58.

SCHEIBEL, M. E. & SCHEIBEL, A. B. (1969). "Terminal patterns in cat spinal cord. III. Primary afferent collaterals." *Brain Res.*, **13:** 417–443.

SELZER, M. & SPENCER, W. A. (1969). "Convergence of visceral and cutaneous afferent pathways in the lumbar spinal cord." *Brain Res.*, **14:** 331–348.

SINDOU, M. (1974). "Fiber organization at the posterior spinal cord-rootlet junction in man." *J. Comp. Neurol.*, **153:** 15–26.

STEER, J. C. & HORNEY, F. D. (1968). "Evidence for passage of cerebrospinal fluid along spinal nerves." *Canad. Med. Ass. J.*, **98:** 71–74.

SWEET, W. H., WHITE, J. C., SELVERSTONE, B. & NILGES, R. (1950). "Sensory responses from anterior roots and from surface and interior of spinal cord in man." *Trans. Amer. Neurol. Ass.*, **75:** 165–169.

TOMLINSON, B. E. (1973). "Total numbers of limb motor neurones in the human lumbosacral cord and an analysis of the accuracy of various sampling procedures." *J. Neurol. Sci.*, **20:** 313–327.

TREVINO, D. L., MAUNZ, R. A., BRYAN, R. N. & WILLIS, W. D. (1972). "Location of cells of origin of the spinothalamic tract in the lumbar enlargement of the cat." *Exper. Neurol.*, **34:** 64–77.

VERHAART, W. J. C. (1954). "Fiber tracts and fiber patterns in the anterior and the lateral funiculus of the cord in *Macaca ira.*" *Acta Anat., Basel*, **20:** 330–373.

VRETTOS, X. C. & WYKE, B. D. (1974). "Articular reflexogenic systems in the costovertebral joints." *J. Bone Joint Surg.*, **56B:** 382.

WALKER, A. E. (1940). "The spinothalamic tract in man." *Arch. Neurol. Psychiat.*, **43:** 284–298.

WALL, P. D. (1960). "Cord cells responding to touch, damage and temperature of skin." *J. Physiol.*, **23:** 197–210.

WALL, P. D. (1964). "Presynaptic control of impulses at the first central synapse in the cutaneous pathway." *Progr. Brain Res.*, **12:** 92–118.

WALL, P. D. (1967). "The laminar organization of dorsal horn and effects of descending impulses." *J. Physiol.*, **188:** 403–423.

WALL, P. D. (1970). "The sensory and motor role of impulses travelling in the dorsal columns towards the cerebral cortex." *Brain*, **93:** 505–524.

WEAVER, T. A. & WALKER, A. E. (1941). "Topical arrangement within the spinothalmic tract of the monkey." *Archiv. Neurol. Psychiat.*, **46:** 877–883.

WHITLOCK, D. G. & PERL, E. R. (1961). "Thalamic projections of spinothalamic pathways in monkey." *Exp. Neurol.*, **3:** 240–255.

WIESENDANGER, M. (1969). "The pyramidal tract: recent investigations on its morphology and function." *Ergebn. Physiol.*, **61:** 72–136.

WYKE, B. D. (1967). "The neurology of joints." *Ann. Roy. Coll. Surg. Engl.*, **41:** 25–50.

WYKE, B. D. (1969). *Principles of General Neurology.* Amsterdam and London; Elsevier.

WYKE, B. D. (1970). "The neurological basis of thoracic spinal pain." *Rheumatol. Phys. Med.*, **10:** 356–367.

WYKE, B. D. (1975). "Morphological and functional features of the innervation of the costovertebral joints." *Folia Morphol., Prague*, **23:** 296–305.

WYKE, B. D. (1976). "Neurological aspects of low back pain." In *The Lumbar Spine and Back Pain.* pp. 189–256. Ed. M. I. V. Jayson. London: Sector Publishing Co.

WYKE, B. D. (1979). "Neurology of the cervical spinal joints." *Physiotherapy*, **65:** 72–76.

WYKE, B. D. (1979). "Neurological mechanisms in the experience of pain." *Acupuncture Electrotherap. Res. J.*, **4:** 27–35.

## (d) Mechanisms of Pain: Pain Threshold and Pain Tolerance

ALBE-FESSARD, D. (1968). "Central nervous mechanisms involved in pain and analgesia." In *Pharmacology of Pain*. pp. 131–168. Ed. R. K. S. Lim, D. Armstrong and E. G. Pardo. Oxford; Pergamon Press.

AMOLI, C. C. (1972). "Intravertebral pressures in patients with lumbar pain." *Acta Orthop. Scand.*, **43:** 109–117.

ANDREWS, F. M. (1973). "Bone pain." *Rev. Rheum. Dis.*, **54:** 245–246.

ARMSTRONG, D., JEPSON, J. B. L., KEELE, C. A. & STEWART, J. W. (1957). "Pain producing substances in human inflammatory exudates and plasma." *J. Physiol.*, **135:** 350.

ARNOLDI, C. C. (1972). "Intravertebral pressures in patients with lumbar pain; a preliminary communication." *Acta Orthop. Scand.*, **43:** 109–117.

ARONSON, P. R., MURRAY, D. G. & FITZSIMONS, R. M. (1971). "Myofascitis: a frequently overlooked cause of pain in cervical root distribution." *Nth. Carolina Med. J.*, **32:** 463–465.

BAILEY, R. R. (1974). "Acute arthralgia after high-dosage intravenous methylprednisolone." *Lancet*, **2:** 1014.

BARNES, C. G. (1971). "The differential diagnosis of backache." *Brit. J. Hosp. Med.*, 219–231.

BARR, J. S. (1937). "Sciatica caused by intervertebral disc lesions." *J. Bone Joint Surg.*, **19B:** 323–342.

BARR, J. S. (1947). "Ruptured intervertebral disc and sciatic pain." *J. Bone Joint Surg.*, **29B:** 429–437.

BARR, J. S. (1951). "Protruded discs and painful backs." *J. Bone Joint Surg.*, **33B:** 3–4.

BARR, J. S., HAMPTON, A. & MIXTER, W. J. (1937). "Pain low in the back and sciatica." *J. Amer. Med. Assoc.*, **109:** 1265–1270.

BARTLETT, J. (1970). "The problem of sciatica." *Practitioner*, **203:** 529–536.

BECKER, D. P., GLUCK, H., NULSEN, F. E. & JANE, J. A. (1969). "An inquiry into the neurophysiological basis for pain." *J. Neurosurg.*, **30:** 1–13, **31:** 1–3.

BEECHER, H. K. (1953). "A method for quantifying the intensity of pain." *Science*, **118**, 322–324.

BEECHER, H. K. (1956). "Relationship of significance of wound to the pain experienced." *J. Amer. Med. Assoc.*, **161:** 1609–1613.

BEECHER, H. K. (1956). "The subjective response and the reaction to sensation." *Amer. J. Med.*, **20**: 107–113.

BEECHER, H. K. (1957). "The measurement of pain." *Pharmacol. Rev.*, **9**: 59–209.

BEECHER, H. K. (1959). *The Measurement of Subjective Responses*. New York; Oxford University Press.

BEECHER, H. K. (1968). "The measurement of pain in man." In *Pain*, pp. 207–208. Ed. A. Soulairac, J. Cahn and J. Charpentier. New York; Academic Press.

BENJAMIN, F. B. (1968). "Release of intracellular potassium as a factor in pain production." In *The Skin Senses*. pp. 466–478. Ed. D. R. Kenshalo. Springfield, Illinois; Thomas.

BENJAMIN, R. M. (1970). "Single neurons in the rat medulla responsive to nociceptive stimulation." *Brain Res.*, **24**: 525.

BENNETT, M. H. (1973). "The pathophysiology of pain." *Curr. Probl. Surg.*, 6–15.

BERGSTRÖM, M. (1973). "Pain". *Ann. Clin. Gynaecol. Fenn.*, **62**: 63.

BERNSTEIN, S. A. (1975). "Acute cervical pain associated with soft-tissue calcium deposition anterior to the interspace of the first and second cervical vertebrae." *J. Bone Joint Surg.*, **57A**: 426–428.

BESSOU, P. & PERL, E. R. (1969). "Response of cutaneous sensory units with unmyelinated fibres to noxious stimuli." *J. Neurophysiol.*, **32**: 1025–1043.

BIANCO, A. J. (1968). "Low back pain and sciatica: diagnosis and indications for treatment." *J. Bone Joint Surg.*, **50A**: 170–181.

BIGELOW, N., HARRISON, O., GOODELL, H., WOLFF, H. G. (1945). "Studies on pain: quantitative measurements of two pain sensations in the skin, with reference to the nature of the hyperalgesia of peripheral neuritis." *J. Clin. Invest.*, **24**: 503–512.

BINKS, F. A. (1974). "Geriatric pain." *Physiotherapy*, **60**: 132–133.

BITTENBENDER, J. B. (1969). "Pain syndromes in the neck, shoulder and low back from a neurologic point of view." *Penn. Med.*, **72**: 91–93.

BLOEDEL, J. R. (1974). "The substrate for integration in the central pain pathways." *Clin. Neurosurg.*, **21**: 194–228.

BLUMENTHAL, L. S. (1974). "Injury to the cervical spine as a cause of headache." *Postgrad. Med.*, **56**: 147–153.

BOND, M. R. & PILOWSKY, I. (1966). "Subjective assessment of pain and its relationship to the administration of analgesics in patients with advanced cancer." *J. Psychosomatic Med.*, **10:** 203–208.

BOWSHER, D. (1957). "Termination of the central pain pathway in man: the conscious appreciation of pain." *Brain*, **80:** 606–622.

BOWSHER, D. (1976). "Role of the reticular system in response to noxious stimulation." *Pain*, **2:** 361–378.

BRADLEY, K. C. (1974). "The anatomy of backache." *Aust. N.Z. J. Surg.*, **44:** 227–232.

BRISH, A., LERNER, M. A. & BRAHAM, J. (1964). "Intermittent claudication from compression of cauda equina by a narrowed spinal canal." *J. Neurosurg.*, **21:** 207–211.

BUZZELLI, G., VOEGELIN, M. R., PROCACCI, P. & BOZZA, G. (1968). "Changes in the cutaneous pricking pain threshold during the menstrual cycle." *Archiv. Physiol.*, **66:** 97.

CASEY, K. L. (1973). "The neurophysiologic basis of pain." *Postgrad. Med.*, **53:** 58–63.

CASEY, K. L. (1973). "Pain: a current view of neural mechanisms." *Ann Sci.*, **61:** 194–200.

CHAPMAN, C. R. & FEATHER, B. W. (1973). "Effects of diazepam on human pain tolerance and pain sensitivity." *Psychosomat. Med.*, **35:** 330.

CHAPMAN, W. P. (1944). "Measurements of pain sensitivity in normal control subjects and in psychoneurotic subjects." *Psychosomat. Med.*, **6:** 252.

COLLINA, W. R., NULSEN, F. E. & RANDT, C. T. (1960). "Relation of peripheral nerve fibre size and sensation in man." *Archiv. Neurol.*, **3:** 381–385.

CRITCHLEY, M. (1956). "Congenital indifference to pain." *Ann. Intern. Med.*, **45:** 737–747.

CYRIAX, J. (1945). "Lumbago: mechanism of dural pain." *Lancet*, **2:** 427–429.

DALLENBACH, K. M. (1939). "Pain: history and present status." *Amer. J. Psychol.*, **52:** 331.

DE JONG, R. H. & CULLEN, S. C. (1963). "Theoretical aspects of pain." *Anesthesiology*, **24:** 628–635.

DELAFRESNAYE, J. F. (Ed.). (1954). *Brain Mechanisms and Consciousness*. Oxford; Blackwell.

DELGADO, J. M. R. (1955). "Cerebral structures involved in transmission and elaboration of noxious stimulation." *J. Neurophysiol.*, **18:** 261.

DENNIS, S. G. & MELZACK, R. (1977). "Pain-signalling systems in the dorsal and ventral spinal cord." *Pain*, **4:** 97–132.

DUTTON, C. B. & RILEY, L. H. JR. (1969). "Cervical migraine—not merely a pain in the neck." *Amer. J. Med.*, **47:** 141–148.

EDGAR, M. A. & PARK, W. M. (1974). "Induced pain patterns on passive straight-leg raising in lower lumbar disc protrusion. A prospective clinical, myelographic and operative study in fifty patients." *J. Bone Joint Surg.*, **56B:** 658–667.

FEINDEL, W. H., WEDDELL, G. & SINCLAIR, D. C. (1948). "Pain sensibility in deep somatic structures." *J. Neurol. Neurosurg. Psychiat.*, **11:** 113–116.

FELLNER, C. H. (1971). "Alterations in pain perception under conditions of multiple sensory modality stimulation." *Psychosomatics*, **12:** 313–315.

FRYKHOLM, R., HYDE, J., NORLEN, G. & SKOGLUND, C. R. (1953). "On pain sensations produced by stimulation of ventral roots in man." *Acta Physiol. Scand.*, **29** (Suppl. 106): 455–469.

GELFAND, S. (1964). "The relationship of experimental pain tolerance to pain threshold." *Canad. J. Psychol.*, **18:** 36–42.

GLOVER, J. R. (1960). "Back pain and hyperaesthesia." *Lancet*, **1:** 1165–1168.

GLYN, J. H. (1971). "Rheumatic pain: some concepts and hypotheses." *Proc. Roy. Soc. Med.*, **64:** 354–360.

GLYNN, C. J. & LLOYD, J. W. (1976). "The diurnal variation in perception of pain." *Proc. Roy. Soc. Lond.*, **69B:** 369.

GRACANIN, F. (1975). "Optimal stimulus parameters for minimum pain in the chronic stimulation of innervated muscle." *Arch. Phys. Med. Rehab.*, **56:** 243–249.

HAGBARTH, K. E. & FEX, J. (1959). "Centrifugal influences on single unit activity in spinal sensory paths." *J. Neurophysiol.*, **22:** 321–338.

HALLIDAY, A. M. & MINGAY, R. (1961). "Retroactive raising of a sensory threshold by a contralateral stimulus." *Quart. J. Exp. Psychol.*, **13:** 1–11.

HARDY, J. D. (1963). "Pain threshold and the nature of pain sensation." *Postgrad. Med.*, **34:** 579.

HARDY, J. D., WOLFF, H. G. & GOODELL, H. (1943). "The pain threshold in man." *Res. Pub. Assoc. Nerv. Ment. Dis.*, **23:** 1–15.

HARDY, J. D., WOLFF, H. G. & GOODELL, H. (1952). *Pain Sensations and Reactions*. Baltimore; Williams and Wilkins.

HART, F. D. (1969). "Polymalgia rheumatica." *Brit. Med. J.*, **2**: 99–100.

HART, F. D. (1974). "Pain in osteoarthrosis." *Practitioner*, **212**: 244–250.

HART, F. D. & HUSKISSON, E. C. (1972). "Pain patterns in the rheumatic disorders." *Brit. Med. J.*, **4**: 213–216.

HART, F. D., TAYLOR, R. T. & HUSKISSON, E. C. (1970). "Pain at night." *Lancet*, **1**: 881–884.

HASSLER, R. (1960). "The central system of pain." *Acta Neurochir., Wien*, **8**: 353–423.

HEWER, A. J. H. & KEELE, C. A. (1948). "A method of testing analgesics in man." *Lancet*, **2**: 683–686.

HIRSCH, C. (1951). "Studies on the mechanism of low back pain." *Acta Orthop. Scand.*, **20**: 261–274.

HOCKADAY, J. M. & WHITTY, C. W. M. (1967). "Patterns of referred pain in normal subjects." *Brain*, **90**: 481–496.

HOLDER, A. R. (1974). "Recent decisions on pain and suffering." *J. Amer. Med. Ass.*, **227**: 1204–1205.

HORLAND, A. A. & WOLFF, B. B. (1973). "Changes in descending pain threshold related to rate of noxious stimulation." *J. Abnormal Psychol.*, **81**: 39–45.

HUSKISSON, E. C. (1974). "Measurement of pain." *Lancet*, **2**: 1127–1131.

HUSKISSON, E. C. & HART, F. D. (1972). "Pain threshold and arthritis." *Brit. Med. J.*, **4**: 193–195.

HUSSAR, A. E. (1956). "Correlation of pain and roentgenographic findings of spondylosis of the cervical and lumbar spine." *Amer. J. Med. Sci.*, **232**: 518–527.

IKARI, C. (1954). "A study of the mechanism of low back pain: the neurohistological examination of the disease." *J. Bone Joint Surg.*, **36A**: 195.

INMAN, V. T. & SAUNDERS, J. B. D. (1944). "Patterns of referred pain from skeletal structures." *J. Nerv. Ment. Dis.*, **99**: 660.

JANZEN, R., KEIDEL, W. D., HERZ, A. & STEICHELE, C. (Eds.). (1972). *Pain: Basic Principles, Pharmacology, Therapy*. Stuttgart; Thieme.

JELSMA, F. & PLOETNER, E. J. (1953). "Painful spina bifida occulta: with review of literature." *J. Neurosurg.*, **10**: 19–27.

JEWSBURY, E. C. O. (1951). "Insensitivity to pain." *Brain*, **74:** 336–353.

JUDOVICH, B. & BATES, W. (1944). *Segmental Neuralgia in Painful Syndromes*. Philadelphia; Davis.

KEEGAN, J. J. (1943). "Dermatome hypalgesia associated with herniation of intervertebral disc." *Arch. Neurol. Psychiat.*, **50:** 67–83.

KEEGAN, J. J. (1944). "Neurosurgical interpretation of dermatome hypalgesia with herniation of the lumbar intervertebral disc." *J. Bone Joint Surg.*, **26A:** 238–248.

KEELE, C. A. (1967). "The chemistry of pain production." *Proc. Roy. Soc. Med.*, **60:** 419–422.

KEELE, C. A. & ARMSTRONG, D. (1964). *Substances Producing Pain and Itch*. London; Arnold.

KEELE, C. A. & ARMSTRONG, D. (1968). "Mediators of pain." In *Pharmacology of Pain*. pp. 3–24. Ed. R. K. S. Lim, D. Armstrong and E. G. Pardo. Oxford: Pergamon Press.

KEELE, C. A. & SMITH, R. (Eds.). (1961). *Assessment of Pain in Man and Animals*. Edinburgh; Livingstone.

KEELE, K. D. (1954). "Pain-sensitivity tests: the pressure algometer." *Lancet*, **1:** 636–639.

KEELE, K. D. (1957). *Anatomies of Pain*. Oxford; Blackwell.

KEELE, K. D. (1967). "Discussion on research into pain." *Practitioner*, **198:** 287–288.

KEELE, K. D. (1968). "Pain complaint threshold in relation to pain of cardiac infarction." *Brit. Med. J.*, **1:** 670–673.

KEIDEL, W. D. (1972). "Is pain measurable? The problem of 'subjective' and 'objective' quantification of pain." in *Pain: Basic Principles, Pharmacology, Therapy*. pp. 16–27. Ed. R. Janzen, W. D. Keidel, A. Herz and C. Steichele. Stuttgart; Thieme.

KELLGREN, J. H. (1939). "On the distribution of pain arising from deep structures, with charts of segmental pain areas." *Clin. Sci.*, **4:** 35–46.

KELLGREN, J. H., MCGOWAN, A. J. & HUGHES, E. S. R. (1949). "On deep hyperalgesia and cold pain." *Clin. Sci.*, **7:** 13–27.

KERR, F. W. L. (1975). "Neuroanatomical substrates of nociception in the spinal cord." *Pain*, **1:** 325–356.

KOSTERLITZ, H. W. (Ed.). (1976). *Opiates and Endogenous Opiate Peptides*. Amsterdam; North-Holland Press.

206

KNIGHTON, R. S. & DUMKE, P. R. (Ed.). (1966). *Pain—An International Symposium*. Boston; Little, Brown.

KRUGER, L. (1966). "The thalamic projection of pain." In *Pain: An International Symposium*. pp. 67–81. Ed. R. S. Knighton and P. R. Dumke.

KRYZHANOVSKII, G. N. (1975). "Investigation of a pain syndrome of spinal origin (on the concept of the generator mechanism of the pain syndrome)" *Bull. Exp. Biol. Med.*, **77**: 732–736.

KUNKLE, E. C. & CHAPMAN, W. P. (1943). "Insensitivity to pain in man." *Res. Pub. Assoc. Nerv. Ment. Dis.*, **23**: 100–109.

LEAVITT, F., GARRON, D. C., WHISTLER, W. W. & SHEINKOP, M. B. (1978). "Affective and sensory dimensions of back pain." *Pain*, **4**: 273–282.

LIU, H. M. (1972). "Alterations in pain sensibility during hypothermia." *Clin. J. Physiol.*, **21**: 113–116.

MANCIA, M., BROGGI, G. & MARGNELLI, M. (1971). "Brain stem reticular effects on intralaminar thalamic neurons in the cat." *Brain Res.*, **25**: 638.

MARSHALL, J. (1951). "Sensory disturbances in cortical wounds with special reference to pain." *J. Neurol. Neurosurg. Psychiat.*, **14**: 187–204.

MARSHALL, J. (1953). "The paraesthesiae induced by cold." *J. Neurol. Neurosurg. Psychiat.*, **16**: 19–24.

MAYER, D. J. & PRICE, D. (1976). "Central nervous system mechanisms of analgesia." *Pain*, **2**: 379–404.

MAYER, D. J., PRICE, D. & BECKER, D. P. (1975). "Neurophysiological characterization of the anterolateral spinal cord neurons contributing to pain perception in man." *Pain*, **1**: 51–58.

MEHLER, W. R. (1962). "The anatomy of the so-called 'pain tract' in man: an analysis of the course and distribution of the ascending fibres of the fasciculus anterolateralis." In *Basic Research in Paraplegia*. pp. 26–55. Ed. J. D. French and R. W. Porter. Springfield, Illinois; Thomas.

MEHLER, W. R. (1974). "Central pain and the spinothalamic tract." *Advan. Neurol.*, **4**: 127–146.

MELZACK, R. (1972). "Mechanisms of pathological pain." In *Scientific Foundations of Neurology*, pp. 153–165. Ed. M. Critchley, J. L. O'Leary and B. Jennett. London; Heinemann.

MELZACK, R. (1973). *The Puzzle of Pain*. New York; Basic Books.

MELZACK, R. & CASEY, K. L. (1968). "Sensory, motivational and central control determinants of pain: a new conceptual model." In *The Skin Senses*. pp. 423–439. Ed. D. R. Kenshalo. Springfield, Illinois; Thomas.

MELZACK, R., STOTLER, W. A. & LIVINGSTON, W. K. (1958). "Effects of discreet brainstem lesions in cats on perception of noxious stimulation." *J. Neurophysiol.*, **21**: 353–367.

MELZACK, R. & WALL, P. D. (1965). "Pain mechanisms: a new theory." *Science*, **150**: 971–979.

MELZACK, R. & WALL, P. D. (1968). "Gate control theory of pain." In *Pain*. pp. 11–31. Ed. A. Soulairac, J. Cahn and J. Charpentier. New York; Academic Press.

MENDEL, D. (1973). "Physiological basis of pain sensation." *J. Postgrad. Gen. Pract.*, **7**: 993–1002.

MERSKEY, H. (1973). "The perception and measurement of pain." *J. Psychosomatic Res.*, **17**: 251–255.

MERSKEY, H. (1974). "Assessment of pain." *Physiotherapy*, **60**: 96–98.

MESSING, R. B. & LYTLE, L. D. (1977). "Serotonin-containing neurons: their possible role in pain and analgesia." *Pain*, **4**: 1–21.

MONNIER, M. (1953). "The role of the thalamus in the organization of pain." *Acta Neuroveg., Wien.* **7**: 85–92.

MURPHEY, F. (1968). "Sources and patterns of pain in disc disease." *Clin. Neurosurg.*, **15**: 343–351.

NAKAHAMA, H. (1975). "Pain mechanism in the central nervous system." *Jap. Anesthesiol. Clin.*, **13**: 109–148.

NASHOLD, B. S. (1974). "Central pain: its origins and treatment." *Clin. Neurosurg.*, **21**: 311–322.

NATHAN, P. W. (1956). "Reference of sensation at the spinal level." *J. Neurol. Neurosurg. Psychiat.*, **19**: 88–100.

NATHAN, P. W. (1960). "Improvement in cutaneous sensibility associated with relief of pain." *J. Neurol. Neurosurg. Psychiat.*, **23**: 202–206.

NATHAN, P. W. (1962). "Pain traces left in the central nervous system." In *U.F.A.W. Symposium on Assessment of Pain in Man and Animals*. pp. 129–134. Ed. C. A. Keele and R. Smith, Edinburgh; Livingstone.

NATHAN, P. W. (1976). "The gate-control theory of pain: a critical review." *Brain*, **99**: 123–158.

NATHAN, P. W. & RUDGE, P. (1974). "Testing the gate-control

theory of pain in man." *J. Neurol. Neurosurg. Psychiat.*, **37**: 1366–1372.

NEMIAH, J. C. (1962). "The effect of leukotomy on pain." *Psychosomat. Med.*, **24**: 75.

NOORDENBOS, W. (1959). *Pain: Problems Pertaining to the Transmission of Nerve Impulses Which Give Rise to Pain.* Amsterdam; Elsevier.

O'DRISCOLL, S. L. (1975). "Pain threshold (PT) analysis in patients with osteoarthrosis of the hip." *Ann. Rheum. Dis.*, **34**: 195–196.

O'DRISCOLL, S. L. & JAYSON, M. I. V. (1974). "Pain threshold analysis in patients with osteoarthrosis of hip." *Brit. Med. J.*, **3**: 714–715.

OSUNTOKUN, B. O., OKEKU, E. L. & LUZZATO, L. (1968). "Congenital pain asymbolia and auditory imperception." *J. Neurol. Neurosurg. Psychiat.*, **31**: 291–296.

POGGIO, G. F. & MOUNTCASTLE, V. B. (1960). "A study of the functional contributions of the lemniscal and spinothalamic systems to somatic sensibility." *Bull. Johns Hopkins Hosp.*, **106**: 266–316.

POMERANZ, B. (1973). "Specific nociceptive fibres projecting from spinal cord neurons to the brain: a possible pathway for pain." *Brain Res.*, **50**: 447–451.

POMERANZ, B., WALL. P. D. & WEBER, W. V. (1968). "Cord cells responding to fine myelinated afferents from viscera, skin and muscle." *J. Physiol.*, **199**: 511–532.

PRICE, D. D. & DUBNER, R. (1977). "Neurons that subserve the sensory-discriminative aspects of pain." *Pain*, **3**: 307–338.

PRICE, D. D. & MAYER, D. J. (1974). "Physiological laminar organization of the dorsal horn of *M. mulatta.*" *Brain Res.*, **79**: 321–325.

PRICE, D. D. & MAYER, D. J. (1975). "Neurophysiological characterization of the anterolateral quadrant neurons subserving pain in *M. mulatta.*" *Pain*, **1**: 59–72.

PROCACCI, P. (1972). "Circadian and circatringintan changes in the cutaneous pricking pain theshold." In *Pain: Basic Principles, Pharmacology, Therapy.* pp. 45–47. Ed. R. Janzen, W. D. Keidel, A. Herz and C. Steichele. Stuttgart; Thieme.

RANDT, C. T. & COLLINS, W. F. (1959). "Effect of anesthetic agents on spinal cord of cat." *Amer. J. Physiol.*, **196**: 340–342.

REUCK, A. V. S. DE & KNIGHT, J. (Eds.). (1966). *Touch, Heat and Pain*. London; Churchill.

RICHARDS, D. E. (1972). "Frequency dependence in the 'pain system'." *Surg. Forum*, **23**: 421–423.

RUSSELL, W. J. (1973). "A critical assessment of pain threshold measurements by pressure." *Brit. J. Anaesth.*, **45**: 1234–1235.

RYAN, E. D. & KOVACIC, C. R. (1966). "Pain tolerance and athletic participation." *Percept. Motor Skills*, **22**: 383–390.

SICUTERI, F., FANCIULLACI, M., FRANCHI, G. & DEL BIANCHO, P. L. (1965). "Seratonin-bradykinin potentiation of the pain receptors in man." *Life Sci.*, **4**: 309.

SIMONS, D. G. (1976). "Muscle pain syndromes. II." *Amer. J. Phys. Med.*, **55**: 15.

SINCLAIR, D. C. & STOKES, B. A. R. (1964). "The production and characteristics of second pain." *Brain*, **87**: 609–618.

SATOH, M. & TAKAGI, H. (1971). "Enhancement by morphine of the central descending inhibitory influence on spinal sensory transmission." *Europ. J. Pharmacol.*, **14**: 60.

SELZER, M. & SPENCER, W. A. (1969). "Convergence of visceral and cutaneous afferent pathways in the lumbar spinal cord." *Brain Res.*, **14**: 331–348; 349–366.

STERNBACH, R. A., MURPHY, R. W., TIMMERMANS, G., GREENHOOT, J. H. & AKESON, W. H. (1974). "Measuring the severity of clinical pain." In *International Symposium on Pain*. pp. 281–288. Ed. J. J. Bonica. New York; Raven Press.

SWEET, W. H. (1959). "Pain" In *Handbook of Physiology. Section I. Neurophysiology*. Vol. I. pp. 459–506. Ed. F. Field, H. W. Magoun and V. E. Hall. Washington; American Physiological Society.

SWEET, W. H. & WEPSIC, J. G. (1974). "Stimulation of the posterior columns of the spinal cord for pain control: indications, techniques, and results." *Clin. Neurosurg.*, **21**: 278–310.

THOMAS, P. K. (1974). "The anatomical substratium of pain: evidence derived from morphometric studies on peripheral nerve." *Trans. Amer. Neurol. Ass.*, **99**: 67–70.

TROUP, J. D. G. (1962). "Pain pathways in orthopaedic practice." *Postgrad. Med. J.*, **38**: 157–161.

TROUP, J. D. G. (1970). "Some problems of measurement in clinical trials of physiotherapy with particular reference to the assessment of pain." *Physiotherapy*, **56**: 491.

TROUP, J. D. G. (1973). "The biology of back pain." *New Scientist*, 17–19.

TSUCHIHASHI, Z. (1972). "A clinical study on the mechanism of onset of pain in spondylolysis and spondylolisthesis." *J. Jap. Orthop. Ass.*, **46:** 387–403.

WALKER, A. E. (1943). "Central representation of pain." *Res. Pub. Ass. Nerv. Ment. Dis.*, **23:** 63–85.

WALL, P. D. (1978). "The gate control theory of pain mechanisms: a re-examination and restatement." *Brain*, **101:** 1–18.

WALL. P. D. & CRONLY-DILLON, J. R. (1960). "Pain, itch and vibration." *Arch. Neurol.*, **2:** 365–375.

WEDDELL, G. & HARPMAN, J. A. (1940). "Neurohistological basis for the sensation of pain provoked from deep fascia, tendon and periosteum." *J. Neurol. Psychiat.*, **3:** 319–328.

WERLE, E. (1972). "On endogenous pain-producing substances, with particular reference to plasmakinins." In *Pain: Basic Principles, Pharmacology, Therapy.* p. 86. Ed. R. Janzen, W. D. Keidel, A. Herz, and C. Steichele. Stuttgart; Thieme.

WHITE, J. C. & SWEET, W. H. (1955). *Pain: Its Mechanism and Neurosurgical Control.* Springfield, Illinois; Thomas.

WHITE, J. C. & SWEET, W. H. (1969). *Pain and the Neurosurgeon: A Forty Years' Experience.* Springfield, Illinois; Thomas.

WILSON, M. E. (1974). "The neurological mechanisms of pain: a review." *Anaesthesia*, **29:** 407–421.

WOLFF, B. B. & JARVIK, M. E. (1963). "Variations in cutaneous and deep somatic pain sensitivity." *Canad. J. Psychol.*, **17:** 37.

WOLFF, H. G. & GOODELL, H. (1943). "The relation of attitudes and suggestion to the perception of and reaction to pain." *Res. Pub. Assoc. Nerv. Ment. Dis.*, **23:** 434.

WOLFF, H. G. & HARDY, J. D. (1947). "On the nature of pain." *Physiol. Rev.*, **27:** 167–199.

WOLFF, H. G. & WOLF, S. (1948). *Pain.* Springfield, Illinois; Thomas.

WOLSTENHOLME, G. E. W. & O'CONNOR, M. (Eds.). (1959). *Pain and Itch: Nervous Mechanisms.* London; Churchill.

WOODROW, K. M., FRIEDMAN, G. D., SIEGELAUB, A. B. & COLLEN, M. F. (1972). "Pain tolerance: differences according to age, sex and race." *Psychosomat. Med.*, **34:** 548.

WYKE, B. D. (1947). "The pain pathway." *Bull. N.S.W. Postgrad. Comm. Med., Univ. Syd.*, **3:** 1–21.

WYKE, B. D. (1969). *Principles of General Neurology*. Amsterdam and London; Elsevier.

WYKE, B. D. (1970). "The neurological basis of thoracic spinal pain." *Rheumatol. Phys. Med.*, **10:** 356–367.

WYKE, B. D. (1976). "Neurological aspects of low back pain." In *The Lumbar Spine and Back Pain*. pp. 189–256. Ed. M. I. V. Jayson. London; Sector Publishing Co.

WYKE, B. D. (1977). "Neurological mechanisms of spinal pain." In *Patología de la Columna Vertebral*. pp. 45–56. Ed. S. Hernández Conesa and J. Sequier. Murcia; Ferrer Internacional.

WYKE, B. D. (1979). "Neurology of the cervical spinal joints." *Physiotherapy*, **65:** 72–76.

WYKE, B. D. (1979). "Neurological mechanisms in the experience of pain." *Acupuncture Electrotherap. Res. J.*, **4:** 27–35.

ZOTTERMAN, Y. (1939). "Touch, pain and tickling: an electrophysiological investigation on sensory nerves." *J. Physiol.*, **95:** 1–28.

ZOTTERMAN, Y. (1959). "The peripheral nervous mechanism of pain: a brief review." In *Pain and Itch: Nervous Mechanisms*. pp. 13–24. Ed. G. E. W. Wolstenholme and M. O'Connor. London; Churchill.

ZOTTERMAN, Y. (1972). "Pain and tickle: a brief review of electrophysiological studies of cutaneous nerves." In *Pain: Basic Principles, Pharmacology, Therapy*. pp. 4–15. Ed. R. Janzen, W. D. Keidel, A. Herz and C. Steichele. Stuttgart; Thieme.

# PATHOLOGY

## *(a) Congenital Malformations and Anomalies*

ALEXANDER, E. (1969). "Significance of the small lumbar spinal canal: cauda equina compression syndromes due to spondylosis." *J. Neurosurg.*, **31**: 513–519.

ALVIK, I. (1969). "Spondylolisthesis." *Tids. Norsk. Laegef.*, **89**: 1344.

AMINOFF, M. J. (1974). "Clinical features of spinal vascular malformations." *Brain*, **97**: 197–210.

AMINOFF, M. J. (1974). "The prognosis of patients with spinal vascular malformities." *Brain*, **97**: 211–218.

AMINOFF, M. J. (1974). "The pathophysiology of spinal vascular malformations." *J. Neurol. Sci.*, **23**: 255–263.

AMUSO, S. J. & MANKIN, H. J. (1967). "Hereditary spondylolisthesis and spina bifida." *J. Bone Joint Surg.*, **49A**: 507–513.

ARAI, M. (1971). "Aetiology of spondylolysis: question on the theory of hypoplasia of the neural arch." *Orthop. Surg. (Tokyo)*, **22**: 1–8.

AYLETT, M. J. (1973). "Spina bifida in general practice." *Practitioner*, **211**: 75–81.

AYLETT, M. J., ROBERTS, C. J. & LLOYD, S. (1974). "Neural tube defects in a country town: confirmation of clustering within a particularly small area. *Brit. J. Prev. Soc. Med.*, **28**: 177–179.

BAGCHI, A. K. (1973). "Cervical spondylosis as an ecological problem." *J. Ind. Med. Ass.*, **60**: 382–383.

BAKER, D. R. & McHOLLICK, W. (1956). "Spondyloschisis and spondylolisthesis in children." *J. Bone Joint Surg.*, **38A**: 933–934.

BALE, P. M. (1973). "A congenital intraspinal gastroenterogenous cyst in diastematomyelia." *J. Neurol. Neurosurg. Psychiat.*, **36**: 1011–1017.

BARDSLEY, J. L. & HANELIN, L. G. (1971). "The unilateral hypoplastic lumbar pedicle." *Radiology*, **101**: 315–317.

BELLAMY, R., LIEBER, A. & SMITH, S. D. (1974). "Congenital spondylolisthesis of the sixth cervical vertebra: case report and description of operative findings." *J. Bone Joint Surg.*, **56A:** 405–407.

BERQUET, K. H. (1965). "Concordant spondylolisthesis in identical twins." *Zeit. Orthop.*, **99:** 507–509.

BISTRÖM, O. (1954). "Congenital anomalies of the lumbar spine of persons with painless backs." *Ann. Chir. Gyn. Fenn.*, **43:** 102–115.

BLECK, E. E. (1974). "Spondylolisthesis: acquired, congenital or developmental." *Dev. Med. Child Neurol.*, **16:** 680–682.

BLOUNT, W. P. (1973). "Scoliosis treatment: skeletal maturity evaluation." *Minn. Med.*, **56:** 383–390.

BLUMEL, J., EVANS, E. B., HANDNOTT, J. L. & EGGERS, G. W. N. (1962). "Congenital skeletal anomalies of the spine: an analysis of the charts and roentgenograms of 264 patients." *Amer. Surg.*, **28:** 501–509.

BORKOW, S. E. & KLEIGER, B. (1971). "Spondylolisthesis in the newborn." *Clin. Orthop.*, **81:** 73–76.

BRILL, P. W., BAKER, D. H. & EWING, M. L. (1973). "Bone-within-bone in the neonatal spine: stress change or normal development." *Radiology*, **108:** 363–366.

BULL, J., ELGAMMAL, T. & POPHAM, M. (1969). "A possible genetic factor in cervical spondylosis." *Brit. J. Radiol.*, **42:** 4–16.

BULOS, S. (1974). "Dysphagia caused by cervical osteophyte. Report of a case." *J. Bone Joint Surg.*, **56B:** 148–152.

BURWELL, R. G. (1973). "The biological component of the orthopaedic troika with particular reference to scoliosis." *Acta Orthop. Belg.*, **39:** 444–459.

CABITZA, A. (1971). "Spondylolisthesis in the adult: review of cases treated with laminectomy followed by Bosworth's vertebral osteosynthesis." *Clin. Orthop.*, **23:** 170–175.

CAMPBELL, J. B. (1948). "Congenital anomalies of the neural axis." *Amer. J. Surg.*, **75:** 231–256.

CARLIOZ, H. & DUBOUSSET, J. (1973). "Instabilities between atlas and axis in the child." *Rev. Chir. Orthop.*, **59:** 291–307.

CARTER, C. & WILKINSON, J. (1954). "Persistent joint laxity and congenital dislocation of the hip." *J. Bone Joint Surg.*, **46B:** 40–45.

CAUTILLI, R. A., JOYCE, M. F. & LIN, P. M. (1972) "Congenital elongation of the pedicles of the sixth cervical vertebra in identical twins." *J. Bone Joint Surg.*, **54A:** 653–656.

CHANDLER, F. A. (1931). "Lesions of the 'isthmus' (pars interarticularis) of the laminae of the lower lumbar vertebrae and their relation to spondylolisthesis." *Surg. Gynec. Obst.*, **53:** 273–306.

CHRISTIAN, J. C. (1975). "A dominant syndrome of metacarpal and metatarsal assymetry with tarsal and carpal fusions, syndactyly, articular dysplasia and platyspondyly." *Clin. Genet.*, **8:** 75–80.

COHEN, M. M. (1971). "Variability versus incidental findings in the first and second branchial arch syndrome: unilateral variants with anophthalmia." *Birth Defects*, **7:** 103–108.

COLE, W. R. & LEVIN, S. (1951). "Cleidocranial dysostosis." *Brit. J. Radiol.*, **24:** 286.

COMPERE, E. L. (1932). "Excision of hemivertebrae for correction of congenital scoliosis." *J. Bone Joint Surg.*, **14A:** 555–562.

CONGDON, R. T. (1932). "Spondylolisthesis and vertebral anomalies in skeletons of American aborigines with clinical notes on spondylolisthesis." *J. Bone Joint Surg.*, **14A:** 511–524.

CRITCHLEY, M. (1956). "Congenital indifference to pain." *Ann. Intern. Med.*, **45:** 737–747.

CRUESS, R. L. & TURNER, N. S. (1970). "Paralysis of hip abductor muscles in spina bifida: results of treatment by the mustard procedure." *J. Bone Joint Surg.*, **52A:** 1364–1372.

DAHL, D. S. (1974). "Congenital root disease. Further evidence of innervational abnormalities as the basis for the clinicopathologic features." *J. Neurol. Sci.*, **23:** 371–385.

DANDY, D. J. & SHANNON, M. J. (1971). "Lumbo-sacral subluxation (Group 1 spondylolisthesis)." *J. Bone Joint Surg.*, **53B:** 578–595.

DANZIGER, J. (1975). "Congenital absence of a pedicle in a cervical vertebra." *Clin. Radiol.*, **26:** 53–56.

DAWLEY, J. A. (1971). "Spondylolisthesis of the cervical spine." *J. Neurosurg.*, **34:** 99–101.

DAWSON, R. H. (1956). "Spondylolisthesis with intact pedicles." *J. Bone Joint Surg.*, **38B:** 952.

DELAHAYE, R. P., MANGIN, H., GUEFFIER, G., COMBES, A., CREN, M. & METGES, P. J. (1970). "Systematic radiological examination of the spine in groups of navigating personnel at admission inspection: definition of normality and procedure to be followed in the presence of congenital anomalies." *Rev. Corps. Santé d'Armée*, **11:** 667–683.

DOSEN, M. & KRAJCINOVIC, J. (1971). "Lumbarization of the first sacral vertebra and osseous bridging between the transverse processes of the fourth and fifth lumbar vertebrae." *Rev. Chir. Orthop.*, **57:** 69–72.

DUBOWITZ, V. (1973). "Rigid spine syndrome: a muscle syndrome in search of a name." *Proc. Roy. Soc. Med.*, **66:** 219–220.

DUTTA, T. (1974). "Rare combination of duplication of genito-urinary tract, hindgut, vertebral column and other associated anomalies." *Brit. J. Urol.*, **46:** 577–582.

EDLICH, R. & SCHWERDTNER, H. P. (1974). "A rare combined atlas defect." *Arch. Orthop. Unfall-Chir.*, **78:** 12–20.

EKELUND, L. & CRONQUIST, S. (1973). "Roentgenological changes in spinal malformations and spinal tumours in children." *Radiologie*, **13:** 541–546.

EXARHOU, E. & PANTAZOPOULOS, T. (1973). "Spondylolytic spondylolisthesis." *Int. Surg.*, **58:** 446–450.

EYRING, E. J. & EISENBERG, E. (1968). "Congenital hypophosphatasia." *J. Bone Joint Surg.*, **50A:** 1099–1117.

FIELDEN, P. & RUSSELL, J. G. B. (1970). "Coronally cleft vertebra." *Clin. Radiol.*, **21:** 327–328.

FORESTIER, J. & BYWATERS, E. (1967). "Glossary of terminology of the spondylopathies." *Proc. IV. Congr. Europ. Rheum.*, pp. 463–480.

FULCHER, O. H. (1970). "Diastematomyelia in the adult." *Neurol. Neurocir. Psiquiatr.*, **11:** 31–39.

GEGINAT, G. (1970). "Two cases of interarticular spondylolysis with spondylolisthesis." *Med. Welt.*, **21:** 897–899.

GIANNESTRAS, N. J., MAYFIELD, F. H., PROVENCIO, F. P. & MAURER, J. (1964). "Congenital absence of the odontoid process." *J. Bone Joint Surg.*, **46A:** 839–843.

GRANT, D. N. (1972). "Spinal dysraphism." *Postgrad. Med. J.*, **48:** 493–495.

GRANTHAM, S. A. (1975). "Double-level spondylosis and transitional vertebrae." *J. Bone Joint Surg.*, **57A:** 713–714.

GREENFIELD, G., ROMANO, A., STEIN, R. & GOODMAN, R. M. (1973). "Blue sclerae and keratoconus; key features of a distinct heritable disorder of connective tissue." *Clin. Genet.*, **4:** 8–16.

GROS, S., DELLENBACK, P., VANDERVELLEN, R. & WALTER, J. P. (1967). "Sacroiliization of the fifth lumbar vertebra: obstretic incidence." *J. Radiol. Electrol. Med. Nucl.*, **49:** 856–857.

GUIRAUD, G. (1972). "Congenital straightness of the cervical spinal canal (diagnostic radiological approach.)." *Rheumatologie*, **24:** 221–225.

GÜNTZ, E. & SCHLÜTTER, K. (1956). "Dysplasia of the neural arch and its clinical manifestation (spondylolisthesis). *Clin. Orthop.*, **8:** 71–90.

GUTHKELCH, A. N. (1974). "Diastematomyelia with median septum." *Brain*, **97:** 729–742.

HAMMER, B. & TELLER, W. (1972). "Late spondyloepiphyseal dysplasia: report of two cases." *Fortschr. Geb. Röntgenstr.*, **116:** 477–486.

HANDELSMAN, J. D. (1971). "Lumbosacral agenesis." *J. Bone Joint Surg.*, **53:** 564.

HANNAPPEL, A. (1970). "The radiological appearance of developmental defects in the interarticular portion of the fourth or fifth lumbar vertebrae." *Arch. Orthop. Unfall-Chir.*, **69:** 35–38.

HANSON, R. (1926). "Some anomalies, deformities and diseased conditions of the vertebrae during their different stages of development, elucidated by anatomical and radiological findings." *Acta Chir. Scand.*, **60:** 309–368.

HARNACH, Z. G., GOTFRYD, O. & BAUDYSOVA, J. (1966). "Spondylolisthesis with hamstring spasticity." *J. Bone Joint Surg.*, **48A:** 879–882.

HARPER, P. S., JENKINS, P. & LAURENCE, K. M. (1973). "Spondyloepiphyseal dysplasia tarda: a report of four cases in two families." *Brit. J. Radiol.*, **46:** 676–684.

HARRINGTON, P. R. & TULLOS, H. S. (1969). "Reduction of severe spondylolisthesis in children." *Southern Med. J.*, **61:** 1–8.

HARRINGTON, P. R. & TULLOS, H. S. (1971). "Spondylolisthesis in children: observations and surgical treatment." *Clin. Orthop.*, **79:** 75–84.

HARRIS, R. I. (1951). "Spondylolisthesis." *Ann. Roy. Coll. Surg. Engl.*, **8:** 259–297.

HARRIS, R. I. (1956). "Spondylolisthesis." *J. Bone Joint Surg.*, **38B:** 601.

HARRIS, R. I. (1959). "Congenital anomalies." In *Modern Trends in Diseases of the Vertebral Column.* pp. 29–66. Ed. R. Nassim and H. J. Burrows. London; Butterworth.

HENRY, A. P. J. & MICKEL, R. E. (1974). "Spina bifida in African and Indian babies." *J. Bone Joint Surg.*, **56B:** 650–657.

HENSINGER, R. N., LANG, J. E. & MACEWEN, G. D. (1974). "Klippel-

Feil syndrome: a constellation of associated anomalies." *J. Bone Joint Surg.*, **56A:** 1246–1253.

HERMANN, G. & GOLDMANN, H. (1973). "Double urethra with vertebral anomaly." *Int. Surg.*, **58:** 574–575.

HERMANN, J. (1974). "The USR syndrome. Studies of malformation syndromes of man." *Birth Defects*, **10:** 227–239.

HEYER, H. V. (1866). "The mechanics of scoliosis." *Virchows Arch.*, **35:** 225–253.

HILAL, S. K., MARTON, D. & POLLACK, E. (1974). "Diastematomyelia in children: radiographic study of 34 cases." *Radiology*, **112:** 609–621.

HIRT, H. R., ZDROJEWSKI, B. & WEBER, G. (1972). "The manifestations and complications of intraspinal congenital dermal sinuses and dermoid cysts." *Neuropädiatrie*, **3:** 231–247.

HITCHCOCK, H. H. (1940). "Spondylolisthesis: observations on its development, progression and genesis." *J. Bone Joint Surg.*, **22A:** 1–16.

HOLMQUIST, B. (1959). "Spondylolisthesis with ischiitis." *Acta Orthop. Scand.*, **29:** 168.

HOLT, S. & YATES, P. O. (1966). "Cervical spondylosis and nerve root lesions." *J. Bone Joint Surg.*, **48B:** 407–423.

HUMPHRIES, S. V. (1975). "Spondylolisthesis." *Sth. Afr. Med. J.*, **49:** 271.

JAMES, C. C. M. & LASSMANN, L. P. (1962). "Spinal dysraphism: the diagnosis and treatment of progressive lesions in spina bifida occulta." *J. Bone Joint Surg.*, **44B:** 828–840.

JAMES, J. I. P. (1951). "Two curve patterns in idiopathic structural scoliosis." *J. Bone Joint Surg.*, **33B:** 399–406.

JAMES, J. I. P. (1954). "Idiopathic scoliosis." *J. Bone Joint Surg.*, **36B:** 36–49.

JAMES, J. I. P. (1967). *Scoliosis.* Edinburgh; Livingstone.

JAMES, J. I. P. (1970). "The etiology of scoliosis." *J. Bone Joint Surg.*, **52B:** 410–419.

JAMES, J. I. P., LLOYD-ROBERTS, G. C. & PILCHER, M. F. (1959). "Infantile structural scoliosis." *J. Bone Joint Surg.*, **41B:** 719–735.

JANSEN, K. (1960). "Postural factors in paralytic scoliosis: a clinical, radiologic and electromyographic study." *Proc. 3rd. Int. Cong. Phys. Med., Chicago.* pp. 665–670.

JANSSEN, F. (1974). "Spinal and costal abnormalities in congenital atresia of the esophagus." *Zeit. Kinderheilk.*, **117**: 275–280.

JELSMA, F. & PLOETNER, E. J. (1953). "Painful spina bifida occulta: with review of literature." *J. Neurosurg.*, **10**: 19–27.

JOOSTEN, E. (1974). "Hypertrophy of peripheral nerves in the syndrome of multiple mucosal neuromas, endocrine tumours and marfanoid habitus: autonomic disturbances and sural nerve findings." *Acta Neuropath.*, **30**: 251–261.

JUNGHANNS, J. (1933). "Anatomical peculiarities of the fifth lumbar vertebra and the last lumbar intervertebral disc." *Arch. Orthop. Unfall-Chir.*, **33**: 260–278.

KALBAK, K., ANDERSON, S. & WINCKLER, R. (1972). "Incidence of spondylolisthesis among natives of Greenland over the age of 40." *Ugeskr. Laeger*, **134**: 2532–2537.

KANSHEPOLSKY, J., AGNEW, D., ECHOLS, C. & HODAK, J. (1973). "The missing cervical spine pedicle." *Bull. Los Angeles Neurol. Soc.*, **38**: 85–90.

KAUFMAN, H. E. (1974). "Genetic inflammatory disease." *Invest. Ophthalmol.*, **13**: 555–556.

KAUFMAN, R. L. (1974). "Family studies in congenital heart disease. VI. The association of severe obstructive left heart lesions, vertebral and renal anomalies: a second family." *Birth Defects*, **10**: 93–104.

KAY, S. P. (1971). "A new conception and approach to the problem of scoliosis." *Clin. Orthop.*, **81**: 21–33.

KEIM, H. A. & GREENE, A. F. (1973). "Diastematomyelia and scoliosis." *J. Bone Joint Surg.*, **55A**: 1425–1435.

KEIM, H. A. & KEAGY, R. D. (1967). "Congenital absence of lumbar articular facets." *J. Bone Joint Surg.*, **49A**: 523–526.

KENEFICK, J. S. (1973). "Hereditary sacral agenesis associated with presacral tumours." *Brit. J. Surg.*, **60**: 271–279.

KETTELKAMP, D. B. & WRIGHT, D. G. (1971). "Spondylolysis in the Alaskan Eskimo." *J. Bone Joint Surg.*, **53A**: 563–566.

KING, J. D. & BOBECHKO, W. O. (1971). "Osteogenesis imperfecta." *J. Bone Joint Surg.*, **53B**: 72–89.

KIRKALDY-WILLIS, W. H., PAINE, K. W. E., CAUCHOIX, J. & McIVOT, G. (1974). "Lumbar spinal stenosis." *Clin. Orthop.*, **99**: 30–50.

KLEMS, H. & WEIGERT, M. (1973). "The syndrome of hip-lumbar-leg stiffness." *Arch. Orthop. Unfall-Chir.*, **76**: 225–231.

KLINGHOFFER, L., MURDOCH, M. G. & HERMEL, M. B. (1975).

"Congenital absence of lumbar articular facets." *Clin. Orthop.*, **106**: 151–154.

KNUTSSON, F. (1940). "The anterior vertebral body fissure." *Acta Radiol.*, **21**: 597–602.

KOKAN, P. J. (1974). "Factors associated with failure of lumbar spine fusion." *Canad. J. Surg.*, **17**: 294–300.

KOROBKIN, M., NOVICK, H. P. & PALUBINKAS, A. J. (1972). "Asymptomatic sacral agenesis with neurogenic bladder in a 42 years old man." *Amer. J. Roentgenol.*, **115**: 611–613.

KOZLOWSKI, K. S. (1974). "Humero-spinal dystostosis with congenital heart disease." *Amer. J. Dis. Child.*, **127**: 407–410.

KOZLOWSKI, K. S. & TROJANOWSKA, J. (1971). "Dominant spondyloepiphyseal dysplasia with particular involvement of the vertebral column." *Fortschr. Geb. Roentgenstr.*, **115**: 296–302.

KREYENBUHL, W. & HESSLER, C. (1973). "A variation of the sacrum on the lateral view." *Radiology*, **109**: 49–52.

KUDELKA, P. (1968). "Spondylolisthesis in childhood." *J. Bone Joint Surg.*, **50B**: 682.

LANCE, E. M. (1966). "Treatment of severe spondylolisthesis with neural involvement." *J. Bone Joint Surg.*, **48A**: 883–891.

LANE, W. A. (1884). "Three forms of spinal deformity." *Med. Chir. Trans.*, **67**: 233–247.

LANE, W. A. (1893). "Case of spondylolisthesis associated with progressive paraplegia." *Lancet*, **1**: 991–992.

LAURENT, L. E. (1958). "Spondylolisthesis." *Acta Orthop. Scand.* (Suppl. **35**): 1–45.

LAURENT, L. E. & OSTERMAN, K. (1969). "Spondylolisthesis in children and adolescents: a study of 173 cases." *Acta. Orthop. Belg.*, **35**: 717–727.

LE QUESNE, G. W. & KOZLOWSKI, K. (1973). "Spondylometaphyseal dysplasia." *Brit. J. Radiol.*, **46**: 685–691.

LERNER, H. L. & GAZIN, A. I. (1946). "Interarticular isthmus hiatus (spondylolysis)." *Radiology*, **46**: 573–578.

LESTER, C. W. & SHAPIRO, H. L. (1968). "Vertebral arch defects in the lumbar vertebrae of pre-historic American Eskimos." *Amer. J. Phys. Anthrop.*, **28**: 43–48.

LEVINE, R. A., ROSENBAUM, A. E., WALTZ, J. M. *et al.* (1970). "Cervical spondylosis and dyskinesias." *Neurology*, **20**: 1194–1199.

LINDGREN, E. (1941). "Myelographic changes in kyphosis dorsalis juvenalis." *Acta Radiol.*, **22**: 461–470.

LINDSTROM, J. A. (1971). "A diabetic embryopathy: the caudal regression syndrome." *Birth Defects*, **7**: 278–279.

LOGAN, W. W. & STUARD, I. D. (1973). "Absent posterior arch of the atlas." *Amer. J. Roentgenol.*, **118**: 431–434.

LOUIS, R. (1971). "Lumbosacral spondylolisthesis: anatomico-pathological basis." *Rev. Chir. Orthop.*, **57** (Suppl. 1): 99–105.

LOUYOT, P., MONTET, Y., HENLE, J. M. & DUVAL, J. M. (1969). "On spina bifida and malformation of the posterior arch of the vertebrae of the dorsolumbar joints." *J. Belge Rheum. Med. Phys.*, **24**: 233–254.

McINTYRE, J. M. (1957). "Spondylolisthesis in children." *J. Bone Joint Surg.*, **39B**: 797.

McKEE, B. W., ALEXANDER, W. J. & DUNBAR, J. S. (1971). "Spondylosis and spondylolisthesis in children: a review." *J. Canad. Assoc. Radiol.*, **22**: 100–109.

McLOUGHLIN, D. P. & WORTZMAN, G. (1972). "Congenital absence of a cervical vertebral pedicle." *J. Canad. Assoc. Radiol.*, **23**: 195–200.

MACNAB, I. (1950). "Spondylolisthesis with an intact neural arch: the so-called pseudospondylolisthesis." *J. Bone Joint Surg.*, **32B**: 325–333.

MACNAB, I. (1970). "Spondylolisthesis in childhood." *J. Bone Joint Surg.*, **52B**: 190.

MACNAB, I. (1975). "Cervical spondylosis." *Clin. Othop.*, **109**: 69–77.

MADIGAN, R. (1974). "Cervical cord compression in hereditary multiple exostosis." *J. Bone Joint Surg.*, **56A**: 401–404.

MARCH, H. O. & TEJANO, N. A. (1973). "Four cases of lumbosacral and sacral agenesis." *Clin. Orthop.*, **92**: 214–219.

MARDEAU, M., LACERT, P., GROSSIORD, A. & DUVAL-BEAUPÈRE, G. (1974). "Six cases of congenital kyphosis or kypho-scoliosis with neurological complications." *Ann. Med. Phys.*, **17**: 117–135.

MARFAN, A. B. (1896). "A case of congenital deformation of the four limbs, more pronounced at their extremities, characterized by elongation of the bones with some degree of thinning." *Bull. Med. Soc. Med. Sop. Paris*, **13** (3rd ser.): 220–226.

MARGO, E. (1960). "Spondylolisthesis and spondylolysis: a clinico-statistical report on 589 cases treated over a 13 year period (1945 through 1958)." *Southern Med. J.*, **53**: 1096–1100.

MARMOR, L. & BECHTOL, C. O. (1961). "Spondylolisthesis: complete slip following the McGill procedure." *J. Bone Joint Surg.*, **43A**: 1068–1071.

MASEL, J. P. (1966). "Neural arch lesions in young people." *Aust. Radiol.*, **10**: 360–364.

MASSARE, C. & BERNAGEAU, J. (1971). "Lumbosacral spondylolisthesis: radiological examination." *Rev. Chir. Orthop.*, **57** (Suppl. 1): 110–114.

MATTÄUS, H. (1974). "A study of the treatment of congenital lumbar kyphosis." *Zeit. Orthop.*, **112**: 1312–1314.

MELAMED, A. (1965). "Spondylolysis and spondylolisthesis are not congenital." *Wisconsin Med. J.*, **64**: 130–133.

MENSINK, H. J. (1974). "Congenital scoliosis." *Arch. Chir. Neurol.*, **26**: 109–129.

MEYER, H. (1931). "Spondylolisthesis and accidents." *Arch. Orthop. Unfall-Chir.*, **29**: 109–117.

MEYRDING, H. W. (1931). "Spondylolisthesis." *J. Bone Joint Surg.*, **13A**: 39–48.

MICHELI, L. J. & HALL, J. E. (1974). "The management of spine deformities in the myelomeningocele patient." *Med. Ann. Dis. Child.*, **43**: 21–24.

MONGEAU, M. & LECLAIRE, R. (1972). "Complete agenesis of the lumbo-sacral spine: a case report." *J. Bone Joint Surg.*, **54A**: 161–164.

MONTICELLI, G. (1975). "Spondylolysis and spondylolisthesis." *Acta Orthop. Scand.*, **46**: 498–506.

MORIN, M. E. & PALACIOS, E. (1974). "The aplastic hypoplastic lumbar pedicle." *Amer. J. Roentgenol.*, **122**: 639–642.

MUTCH, J. & WALMSLEY, R. (1956). "The aetiology of cleft vertebral arch in spondylolisthesis." *Lancet*, **1**: 74–77.

NADKARNI, A. S. (1974). "Lumbo-sacral agenesis. Review of the literature with a case report." *J. Postgrad. Med.*, **20**: 193–195.

NAKAGAWA, K. (1970). "Site of irritability in spondylolysis and spondylolisthesis." *J. Jap. Orthop. Ass.*, **44**: 99–116.

NASCA, R. J. (1975). "Progression of congenital scoliosis due to hemivertebrae and hemivertebrae with bars." *J. Bone Joint Surg.*, **57A**:

NATHAN, H. (1959). "Spondylolysis: its anatomy and mechanism of development." *J. Bone Joint Surg.*, **41A:** 303–320.

NATHAN, H. & ARENSBURGH, B. (1972). "An unusual variation in the fifth lumbar and sacral vertebrae: a possible cause of vertebral canal narrowing." *Anat. Anz.*, **132:** 137–148.

NEWMAN, P. H. (1974). "Spondylolisthesis." *Physiotherapy*, **60:** 14–16.

NEWTON, T. H. (1958). "Cervical intervertebral-disc calcification in children." *J. Bone Joint Surg.*, **40A:** 107–113.

NICOL, W. J. (1972). "Lumbosacral agenesis in a 60 year old man." *Brit. J. Surg.*, **59:** 577–579.

NORMAN, W. J. & JOHNSON, C. (1973). "Congenital absence of a pedicle of a lumbar vertebra." *Brit. J. Radiol.*, **46:** 631–633.

OESTREICH, A. E. & YOUNG, L. W. (1969). "The absent cervical pedicle syndrome: a case in childhood." *Amer. J. Roentgenol.*, **107:** 505–510.

OPPENHEIMER, A. (1942). "Supernumerary ossicle at isthmus of neural arch." *Radiology*, **39:** 98.

ORSO, C. A. (1970). "Syndrome of the telegraph key-shaped 5th lumbar vertebra: considerations on its surgical treatment." *Minerva Ortop.*, **21:** 114–121.

OSUNTOKUN, B. O., OKEKU, E. L. & LUZZATO, L. (1968). "Congenital pain asymbolia and auditory imperception." *J. Neurol. Neurosurg. Psychiat.*, **31:** 291–296.

OZER, F. L. (1974). "Achondroplasia with spinal neurologic complications in mother and son." *Birth Defects*, **10:** 351–355.

PAGE, R. E. (1974). "Intraspinal enterogenous cyst associated with spondylolisthesis and spina bifida occulta." *J. Bone Joint Surg.*, **56A:** 541–544.

PARISH, J. B. (1960). "Skeletal syndromes associated with arachnodactyly." *Proc. Roy. Soc. Med.*, **53:** 515–526.

PECKER, J., SIMON, J., BOU-SALAH, A & PIVAULT, C. (1974). "Gunbarrel fusion of the spinal roots: a diagnostic pitfall." *Nouv. Presses Méd.*, **3:** 1155–1156.

PENNAL, G. F. & SCHATZKER, J. (1971). "Stenosis of the lumbar spinal canal." *Clin. Neurosurg.*, **18:** 86–105.

PEROVIC, M. N., KOPITS, S. E. & THOMPSON, R. C. (1973). "Radiological evaluation of the spinal cord in congenital atlanto-axial dislocation." *Radiology*, **109:** 713–716.

PFEIL, E. (1970). "The therapy of spondylolysis and spondylolisthesis in early childhood." *Beitr. Orthop.*, **17:** 719–721.

PFEIL, E. (1971). "Spondylolysis and spondylolisthesis in children." *Zeit. Orthop.*, **109:** 17–33.

PHALEN, G. S. & DICKSON, J. A. (1961). "Spondylolisthesis and tight hamstrings." *J. Bone Joint Surg.*, **43A:** 505–512.

PIGGOTT, H. (1974). "Scoliosis in the young child." *Proc. Roy. Soc. Med.*, **67:** 205–206.

PITKIN, H. C. & PHEASANT, H. C. (1936). "Sacroarthrogenetic telalgia." *J. Bone Joint Surg.*, **18A:** 111–133; 365–374; 706–716; 1008–1017; **19A:** 169–184.

POLGA, J. P. & CRAMER, G. G. (1974). "Cleft anterior arch of atlas simulating odontoid fracture." *Radiology*, **113:** 341.

POU-SERRADELL, A. & CASADEMONT, M. (1972). "Cauda equina syndrome in the presence of vertebral apophyseal appendices, or accessory articular apophyses, in the lumbar region (concerning two cases)." *Rev. Neurol., Paris*, **126:** 435–440.

RAJU, G. C. (1975). "Congenital lesions of the craniospinal axis." *Indian J. Pediat.*, **42:** 112; 115.

RANEY, R. B. (1945). "Isthmus defects of the fifth lumbar vertebra." *Southern Med. J.*, **38:** 166–174.

RANIERI, L. & TRAINA, G. C. (1972). "Familial inheritance and spondylolysis." *Chir. Org. Mov.*, **50:** 453–461.

RAPPAPORT, I. (1973). "Congenital arteriovenous fistulas of the head and neck." *Arch. Otolaryngol.*, **97:** 350–353.

RAUSER, V., REHÁČEK, J. & PETRÁČEK, V. (1973). "Electrophysiological examination of paravertebral muscles in scoliosis." *Acta Chir. Orthop. Traumatol. Česk.*, **40:** 33–38.

RAVELLI, A. (1955). "Malformations of arch and joint processes of the lumbar vertebrae." *Fortschr. Roentgenol.*, **82:** 827.

REDMAN, J. F. (1973). "Congenital absence of the lumbosacral spine." *Southern Med. J.*, **66:** 770–771.

REICHMANN, S. & LEWIN, T. (1969). "Coronal cleft vertebrae in growing individuals: a preliminary report." *Acta Orthop. Scand.*, **40:** 3–22.

REICHMANN, S. & LEWIN, T. (1970). "Aplasia of lumbar intervertebral joints." *Acta Morph. Néerl.-Scand.*, **8:** 183–186.

REINHARDT, K. (1973). "A supplementary vertebral body between the 4th and 5th lumbar vertebrae." *Fortschr. Röntgentstr.*, **119:** 252–253.

REITH, P. (1960). "Pathologic and anatomic factors in back pain." *Arch. Phys. Med. Rehab.*, **41**: 256.

REMPE, W. (1955). "The condition of sagittal sacralization of the lower vertebrae and its significance for the development of spondylolysis and spondylolisthesis." *Zeit. Orthop.*, **85**: 237–247.

RIGGS, W. & SUMMITT, R. L. (1971). "Spondylometaphyseal dysplasia (Kozlowski): report of affected mother and son." *Radiology*, **101**: 375–381.

RISEBOROUGH, E. J. & WYNNE-DAVIES, R. (1973). "A genetic survey of idiopathic scoliosis in Boston, Massachusetts." *J. Bone Joint Surg.*, **55A**: 974–982.

RISSER, J. C. (1964). "Scoliosis: past and present." *J. Bone Joint Surg.*, **46A**: 167–199.

ROAF, R. (1956). "Paralytic scoliosis." *J. Bone Joint Surg.*, **38B**: 640–659.

ROAF, R. (1966). *Scoliosis.* Edinburgh and London; Livingstone.

ROBERSON, G. H., LLEWELLYN, H. J. & TAVERAS, J. M. (1973). "The narrow lumbar spinal canal syndrome." *Radiology*, **107**: 89–97.

ROBERTS, G. M. (1973). "The assessment of constitutional stenosis of the lumbar spinal canal." *Brit. J. Radiol.*, **46**: 735.

ROCHE, M. B. (1949). "The pathology of neural arch defects: a dissection study." *J. Bone Joint Surg.*, **31A**: 529–537.

ROCHE, M. B. & BRYAN, C. S. (1946). "Spondylolisthesis: additional variations in anomalies." *Arch. Surg.*, **53**: 675–682.

ROCHE, M. B. & ROWE, G. G. (1952). "Incidence of separate neural arch and coincident bone variations: summary." *J. Bone Joint Surg.*, **34A**: 491.

ROGERS, H. M., LONG, D. M., CHOU, S. N. & FRENCH, L. A. (1971). "Lipomas of the spinal cord and cauda equina." *J. Neurosurg.*, **34**: 349–354.

ROGERS, S. P. (1933). "Mechanics of scoliosis." *Arch. Surg.*, **26**: 962–980.

ROSE, H. (1971). "Defective articular process of L3 combined with true spondylolisthesis of L5–S1 as a secondary symptomless finding." *Fortschr. Roentgenstr.*, **114**: 424–426.

ROSS, O. A. & VYAS, U. S. (1972). "Thoracic outlet syndrome due to congenital anomalous joint of the first thoracic rib." *Canad. J. Surg.*, **15**: 186–190.

ROSSONI, L. (1973). "A case of sliding vertebra." *Minverva Orthop.*, **24**: 525–533.

Rowe, G. G. & Roche, M. B. (1953). "The etiology of separate neural arch." *J. Bone Joint Surg.*, **35A**: 102–110.

Russell, A. S. (1975). "Transplantation antigens in Crohn's disease: linkage of associated ankylosing spondylitis with HL-A W27." *Amer. J. Dig. Dis.*, **20**: 359–361.

Saguchi, T. (1972). "A study of separated laminae in patients with spondolysis, with special reference to morphological and histo-pathological observations." *J. Jap. Orthop. Assoc.*, **46**: 105–123.

Saha, M. M., Bhardwaj, O. P., Srivasta, G., Praminick, A. & Gupta, A. (1970). "Osteopetrosis with spondylolysis: four cases in one family." *Brit. J. Radiol.*, **43**: 738–740.

Schmorl, G. (1929). "On the pathological anatomy of the vertebral column." *Klin. Wschr.*, **8**: 1243–1249.

Scoville, W. B. & Corkill, G. (1974). "Lumbar spondylolisthesis and ruptured disc." *J. Neurosurg.*, **40**: 529–534.

Seegelken, K. & Schulte, G. A. (1972). "Late development of the vertebral column." *Fortschr. Röntgenstr.*, **116**: 473–477.

Sensenbrenner, J. A. (1974). "Achondroplasia with hypoplastic vertebral bodies secondary to surgical fusion." *Birth Defects*, **10**: 356–357.

Sever, L. E. (1974). "A case of meningomyelocele in a kindred with multiple cases of spondylolisthesis and spina bifida occulta." *J. Med. Genet.*, **11**: 94–96.

Seze, S. de, & Durieu, J. (1950). "Retrolisthesis: a clinical and radiological study of retrodisplaced vertebrae based on 50 personal observations." *Sem. Hôp., Paris*, **29**: 409–427.

Sherk, H. H., Shut, L. & Chung, S. (1974). "Iniencephalic deformity of the cervical spine with Klippel-Feil anomalies and congenital elevation of the scapula: report of three cases." *J. Bone Joint Surg.*, **56A**: 1254–1259.

Shore, L. R. (1930). "Abnormalities of the vertebral column in a series of skeletons of Bantu natives in South Africa." *J. Anat.*, **64**: 206–238.

Sim, G. P. G. (1973). "Vertebral contour in spondylolisthesis." *Brit. J. Radiol.*, **46**: 250–254.

Soren, A. (1974). "Spondylolisthesis and related conditions." *Acta Orthop. Belg.*, **40**: 294–307.

Spring, W. E. (1973). "Spondylolisthesis—a new clinical test." *J. Bone Joint Surg.*, **55B**: 229.

STARK, W. A. (1971). "Spina bifida occulta and engagement of the fifth lumbar spinous process." *Clin. Orthop.*, **81:** 71–76.

STERNBACH, R. A. (1963). "Congenital insensitivity to pain: a critique." *Psychol. Bull.*, **60:** 252–264.

STEVENSON, R. E. (1972). "Extra vertebrae associated with esophageal atresias and tracheo-esophageal fistulas." *J. Pediat.*, **81:** 1123–1129.

STURKIE, P. D. (1941). "Hypermobile joints in all descendants for two generations." *J. Hered.*, **32:** 232–234.

SUTRO, C. J. (1974). "Spondylolisthesis of the fifth lumbar vertebra (4th degree)—autogenous fusion." *Bull. Hosp. Joint Dis.*, **35:** 42–44.

SWISCHUK, L. E. (1970). "The beaked, notched or hooked vertebra: its significance in infants and young children." *Radiology*, **95:** 661–664.

TAILLARD, W. (1954). "Spondylolisthesis in the child and adolescent (a study of 50 cases)." *Acta Orthop. Scand.*, **24:** 115–144.

TAILLARD, W. (1971). "Microscopic anatomy of spondylolysis." *Rev. Chir. Orthop.*, **57** (Suppl. 1.): 106.

TALUKDER, B. C. (1974). "Congenital lumbar hernia." *J. Pediat. Surg.*, **9:** 419–420.

TCHANG, S. P. K. (1974). "The cervical spino-laminar line." *J. Canad. Assoc. Radiol.*, **25:** 224–226.

THOMALSKE, G. & MOHR, R. (1974). "Intradural segmentation of lumbar disk hernias with special reference to achondroplasia." *Nervenartzt.*, **45:** 376–379.

THOMPSON, I. M. (1974). "Sacral agenesis." *Pediatrics*, **54:** 236–238.

THOMPSON, W. (1974). "The association of spinal and genito-urinary abnormalities with low anorectal anomalies (imperfect anus) in female infants." *Radiology*, **113:** 693–698.

TOMSICK, T. A., LEBOWITZ, M. E. & CAMPBELL, F. (1974). "The congenital absence of pedicles in the thoracic spine." *Radiology*, **111:** 587–589.

TRAPNELL, D. H., GIBBERD, F. B., STARRER, G., FLETCHER, I., REDHEAD & VITALL, M. (1970). "Congenital absence of the lumbar spine." *Brit. J. Hosp. Med.*, (Dec.), 857–860.

TYLMAN, D. (1973). "Rotation and torsion of the vertebrae in scoliosis." *Chir. Narzad, Ruchu Ortop. Pol.*, **38:** 151–158.

VAN DER LINDEN, A. (1966). "Spondylolisthesis." *J. Bone Joint Surg.*, **48B:** 852.

VEBOSTAD, A. (1974). "Spondylolisthesis: a review of 71 patients." *Acta Orthop. Scand.*, **45:** 711–723.

VERHAAK, R. (1973). "Lumbar vertebral arch defect due to unilateral dyssegmentation." *Radiol. Clin. Biol.*, **42:** 117–125.

VERHAAK, R. (1974). "Congenital defect of a lumbar vertebral pedicle with dysplasia of the intervertebral joint." *Radiol. Clin. Biol.*, **43:** 127–137.

VIDAL, J., ALLIEU, Y., FASSIO, B., ADREY, J. & GOALARD, C. (1973). "Spondylolisthesis: reduction with Harrington's apparatus." *Rev. Chir. Orthop.*, **59:** 21–41.

WALSKI, A. (1972). "Congenital dysplasia of the isthmus in the arches of the lumbosacral spine in pre-school children." *Chir. Narzad. Ruchu Ortop., Pol.*, **37:** 345–351.

WANGERMEZ, J., ROQUES, J. C. & WANGERMEZ, A. (1969). "Inheritance of spondylolisthesis: its sexual variations and the associated modifications of the lumbo-pelvic skeleton." *J. Radiol. Electrol. Med. Nucl.*, **50:** 311–314.

WILLNER, S. (1974). "A study of growth in girls with adolescent idiopathic structural scoliosis." *Clin. Orthop.*, **101:** 129–135.

WILTSE, L. L. (1975). "Fatigue fracture: the basic lesion is isthmic spondylolisthesis." *J. Bone Joint Surg.*, **57A:** 17–22.

WINTER, R. B. (1973). "Congenital spine deformity." *J. Med. Sci.*, **9:** 719–727.

WINTER, R. B. (1975). "Scoliosis and other spinal deformities." *Acta Orthop. Scand.*, **46:** 400–424.

WINTER, R. B., MOE, J. H. & WANG, J. F. (1973). "Congenital kyphosis: its natural history and treatment as observed in a study of 130 patients." *J. Bone Joint Surg.*, **55A:** 223–256 and 274.

WINTER, R. B., HAVEN, J. J., MOE, J. H. & LAGAARD, S. M. (1974). "Diastematomyelia and congenital spine deformities." *J. Bone Joint Surg.*, **56A:** 27–39.

WYNNE-DAVIES, R. (1968). "Familial (idiopathic) scoliosis: a family survey." *J. Bone Joint Surg.*, **50B:** 24–30.

YAMADA, K., IKATA, T., YAMMAMOTO, H., NAKAGAWA, Y., TANAKA, H. & TEZUKA, A. (1969). "Equilibrium function in scoliosis and active corrective plaster jacket for the treatment." *Tokushima J. Exp. Med.*, **16:** 1–7.

ZUK, T. (1957). "Electrodiagnostic investigations in scoliosis." *Chir. Narzad. Ruchu Ortop. Pol.*, **22:** 131–138.

ZUK, T. (1962). "The role of spinal and abdominal muscles in the pathogenesis of scoliosis." *J. Bone Joint Surg.*, **44B:** 101–105.

ZUK, T., ZMYSLOWSKI, W. & CZAYKOWSKI, L. (1957). "Electrodiagnostic picture of scoliosis following operation." *Chir. Narzad. Ruchu Ortop. Pol.*, **22:** 297–303.

## (b) Acquired Deformities and Abnormalities

ABBOTT, K. E. & RETTER, R. H. (1956). "Protrusions of thoracic intervertebral disks." *Neurology*, **6:** 1–10.

ABDULLAH, A. F., DITTO, E. W., BYRD, E. B. & WILLIAMS, R. (1974). "Extreme lateral lumbar disc herniations: clinical syndrome and special problems of diagnosis." *J. Neurosurg.*, **41:** 229–234.

ALEXANDER, M. A. (1972). "Can experimental dorsal rhizotomy produce scoliosis?" *J. Bone Joint Surg.*, **54A:** 1509–1513.

ALVIK, I. (1969). "Scoliosis." *Tidj. Norske Laegef.*, **89:** 1361.

ANDERSON, C. E. (1956). "Spondyloschisis following spinal fusion." *J. Bone Joint Surg.*, **38A:** 1142–1146.

ANTIN, S. P. (1974). "The syndrome of lumbar spinal stenosis." *Mount Sinai J. Med., (N.Y.)*, **41:** 23–26.

APPLEBY, A. & STABLER, J. (1969). "A new sign of spondylolisthesis." *Clin. Radiol.*, **20:** 314–319.

ARCT, W. A. (1971). "Fatigue fracture of the lower segments of the lumbar vertebral column." *Hefte zur Unfallheilkunde*, **108:** 202–220.

ARKIN, A. M. (1952). "Prophylaxis of scoliosis." *J. Bone Joint Surg.*, **34A:** 47–54.

ARKIN, A. M., PACK, G. T., RANSOHOFF, N. S. & SIMON, N. (1950). "Radiation-induced scoliosis." *J. Bone Joint Surg.*, **32A:** 401–404.

ARKIN, A. M. & SIMON, N. (1950). "Radiation scoliosis." *J. Bone Joint Surg.*, **32A:** 396–401.

ARMSTRONG, J. R. (1964). "Lumbar disc lesion." *Physiotherapy*, **50:** 284.

ARMSTRONG, J. R. (1967). *Lumbar Disc Lesions*. 3rd ed. Edinburgh; Livingstone.

ARONSON, H. A. & DUNSMORE, R. H. (1963). "Herniated upper lumbar discs." *J. Bone Joint Surg.*, **45A:** 311–317.

BANNA, M., PEARCE, G. W. & ULDALL, R. (1971). "Scoliosis: a rare

manifestation of intrinsic tumours of the spinal cord in children."
*J. Neurol. Neurosurg., Psychiat.*, **34:** 637–641.

BARASH, H. L., GALANTE, J. O., LAMBERT, C. N. & RAY. R. D.
(1970). "Spondylolisthesis and tight hamstrings." *J. Bone Joint
Surg.*, **52A:** 1319–1328.

BAUZE, R. J. (1975). "The mechanisms of forward dislocation in
the human cervical spine." *J. Bone Joint Surg.*, **57B:** 253–254.

BEAL, M. C. (1950). "A review of the short leg problem." *J. Amer.
Osteopathic Assoc.*, **50:** 109–121.

BEELER, J. W. (1970). "Further evidence on the acquired nature of
spondylolisthesis." *Amer. J. Roentgenol.*, **108:** 796–798.

BERESFORD, O. D. (1952). "Osteophytosis of the lumbar spine:
comparison between the incidence in Saskatchewan, Canada and
Bristol, England." *Ann. Rheum. Dis.*, **2:** 289–291.

BERNELL, W. R., KEPES, J. J. & CLOUGH, C. A. (1973). "Subarachnoid hemorrhage from malignant schwannoma of cauda
equina." *Texas Med.*, **69:** 101–104.

BISGARD, J. D. & MUSSLEMAN, M. M. (1940). "Scoliosis. Its
experimental production and growth correction: growth and
fusion of vertebral bodies." *Surg. Gynec. Obst.*, **70:** 1029.

BLECK, E. E. (1974). "Spondylolisthesis: acquired, congenital or
developmental." *Dev. Med. Child Neurol.*, **16:** 680–682.

BØRGESSEN, S. E. & VANG, P. S. (1974). "Herniation of the lumbar
intervertebral disk in children and adolescents." *Acta Orthop.
Scand.*, **45:** 540–549.

BRAGDON, F. H. & SHAFTER, W. A. (1951). "Herniation of the
lumbar intervertebral disk. A ten-year follow-up study." *Penn.
Med. J.*, 350–351.

CARTER, T. (1972). "Camptocornia." *Bull. Menninger Clin.*, **36:**
555–561.

CLIFF, J. M. (1971). "Spinal bony ridging and carditis in Reiter's
disease." *Ann. Rheum. Dis.*, **30:** 171–179.

DIXON, A. S. & CAMPBELL-SMITH, S. (1969). "Long leg
arthropathy." *Ann. Rheum. Dis.*, **28:** 359.

FARKAS, A. (1941). "Physiological scoliosis." *J. Bone Joint Surg.*,
**23A:** 607–627.

FARKAS, A. (1954). "The pathogenesis of idiopathic scoliosis." *J.
Bone Joint Surg.*, **36A:** 617.

FARMER, H. L. (1936). "Accessory articular processes in lumbar
spine: review of 40 cases." *Amer. J. Roentgenol.*, **36:** 763–767.

FIELDING, J. W. & GRIFFIN, P. P. (1974). "Os odontoideum: an acquired lesion." *J. Bone Joint Surg.*, **56A:** 187–190.

FORESTIER, J. (1971). "Vertebral ankylosing hyperostosis." *Mod. Trends Rheumatol.*, **2:** 323–327.

FRANCOIS, R. J. (1969). "A microradiographic and histological study of vertebral osteophytes." *Pathol. Europaea*, **4:** 193.

FRANKS, A. S. (1968). "Cervical spondylosis presenting as the facial pain of temporomandibular joint disorder." *Ann. Phys. Med.*, **9:** 193.

FREJKA, B. (1932). "Kyphosis adolescentium." *J. Bone Joint Surg.*, **14A:** 545–554.

GOI, Y. (1968). "Acquired spondylosis in child and young adult." *J. Bone Joint Surg.*, **50A:** 1649–1656.

GRIFFITHS, E. R. (1974). "Growth problems in cervical injuries." *Paraplegia*, **11:** 277–289.

GRITZKA, T. L. & TAYLOR, T. K. F. (1970). "A ganglion arising from a lumbar articular facet associated with low back pain and sciatica." *J. Bone Joint Surg.*, **52B:** 528–531.

HAAS, H. (1974). "Postraumatic bony bar formation between two lumbar vertebral processes." *Fortschr. Röntgenstr.*, **120:** 497–498.

HADLEY, L. A. (1951). "Intervertebral joint subluxation, bony impingement and foramen encroachment with nerve root changes." *Amer. J. Roentgenol.*, **65:** 377–402.

HANNUKSELA, M. & KARAHARJUE, E. D. (1972). "Syphilis of the spine." *Brit. J. Vener. Dis.*, **48:** 397–399.

HARRIS, J., CARTER, A. R., GLICK, E. N. & STOREY, G. O. (1974). "Ankylosing hyperostosis. I. Clinical and radiological features." *Ann. Rheum. Dis.*, **33:** 210–215.

HARRIS, R. I. & WILEY, J. J. (1963). "Acquired spondylolysis as a sequel to spine fusion." *J. Bone Joint Surg.*, **45A:** 1159–1170.

HARTMAN, J. T. & DOHN, D. F. (1966). "Paget's disease of the spine with cord and nerve root compression." *J. Bone Joint Surg.*, **48A:** 1079–1084.

HIPPS, H. E. (1939). "Fissure formation in articular facets of lumbar spine." *J. Bone Joint Surg.*, **21A:** 289–303.

HORENSTEIN, S., HAMBROOK, G. & EYERMAN, E. (1971). "Spinal cord compression by vertebral acromegaly." *Trans. Amer. Neurol. Assoc.*, **96:** 254–256.

HUNTER, G. A. (1968). "Non-traumatic displacement of the atlanto-axial joint: report of 7 cases." *J. Bone Joint Surg.*, **50B:** 44–51.

JANETOS, G. P. (1966). "Paget's disease of the cervical spine." *Amer. J. Roentgenol.*, **97**: 655.

JOHNSON, C., PENRY, J. B. & BURWOOD, R. J. (1972). "An unusual presentation of cervical block vertebrae." *Australasian Radiol.*, **16**: 63–65.

JONCK, L. M. (1961). "The distribution of osteophytes in the lumbar spine of the Bantu." *Sth. Afric. J. Lab. Clin. Med.*, **7**: 71–77.

JONES, W. K. & SMITH, M. J. (1973). "Acquired spondylolysis and spondylolisthesis: case report." *Rocky Mt. Med. J.*, **70**: 40–41.

JULKUNEN, H. (1975). "The epidemiology of hyperostosis of the spine together with its symptoms and related mortality in a general population." *Scand. J. Rheumatol.*, **4**: 23–27.

JULKUNEN, H., HEINONEN, O. P. & PYORALA, K. (1971). "Hyperostosis of the spine in an adult population: its relation to hyperglycaemia and obesity." *Ann. Rheum. Dis.*, **30**: 605–612.

JULKUNEN, H., PYORALA, K. & LEHTOVIRTA, E. (1968). "Hyperostosis of the spine in relation to age and hyperglycaemia in men aged 30–69." *Ann. Med. Int. Fenn.*, **57**: 1–7.

KAISER, E., BIEDERMANN, F., LEHMANN, R. & SZUDUZY, D. (1972). "Lumbosacral vertebral displacement with resulting spondylolisthesis." *Fortschr. Röntgenstr.*, **117**: 223–225.

KIM, J. H. & SCHUCART, W. A. (1974). "Symptomatic arachnoid diverticula." *Arch. Neurol.*, **31**: 35–37.

KIM, Y. W. (1974). "Post-operative pseudodiverticula (spurious meningoceles) of the cervical subarachnoid space." *Acta Radiol. Diagn.*, **15**: 16–20.

KING, J. O. (1972). "Localized clubbing and hypertrophic osteoarthropathy due to infection in an aortic prosthesis." *Brit. Med. J.*, **4**: 404–405.

KLEINBERG, S. (1931). "Sciatic scoliosis." *Arch. Phys. Therap.*, **12**: 333–342.

KOBRINE, A. & BUCY, P. C. (1971). "Spondylolisthesis following lumbar disc surgery in a child." *J. Neurosurg.*, **34**: 563–568.

KOTANI, P. T., ICHIKAWA, N., WAKABAYASHI, W., YOSHII, T. & KOSHIMUNE, M. (1971). "Studies of spondylolysis found among weightlifters." *Brit. J. Spc ts Med.*, **6**: 4–8.

LANE, W. A. (1885). "Some of the changes which are produced by pressure in the lower part of the spinal column: spondylolisthesis, displacement backwards of the 5th lumbar vertebra, torticollis, etc." *Trans. Path. Soc.*, **3v**: 364–378.

LANGENSKIOLD, A. (1967). "The stages of development of the cartilaginous foci in dyschondroplasia (Ollier's disease)." *Acta Orthop. Scand.*, **38**: 174–180.

LANGENSKIOLD, A. (1967). "The development of multiple cartilaginous exostoses." *Acta Orthop. Scand.*, **38**: 259–266.

LAWRENCE, M. S., ROSSI, N. P. & TIDRICK, R. T. (1967). "Thoracic-outlet compression syndrome." *J. Iowa Med. Soc.*, **57**: 561–566.

LEFEBRE, J., TRIBOULET-CHASSEVANT, A. & MIDDIRLIU, M. F. (1961). "Electromyographic data in idiopathic scoliosis." *Arch. Phys. Med.*, **42**: 710–711.

LEHNER, M. & RICHTER, G. (1973). "Idiopathic calcification of the intervertebral disc and prevertebral ligament." *J. Pediatr. Surg.*, **8**: 979.

MELAMED, A. (1965). "Spondylolysis and spondylolisthesis are not congenital." *Wisconsin Med. J.*, **64**: 130–133.

MERKI, A. (1969). "Late post-traumatic spondylolysis of L4 with compression fractures of 11th and 12th thoracic vertebrae." *Zeit. Orthop.*, **105**: 433–435.

MEYERDING, H. W., BAKER, G. S., LOVE, J. G. & CAMERON, M. D. (1939). "Spondylolisthesis with protrusion of intervertebral disk and hypertrophied ligamentum flavum associated with multiple loose bodies (osteochondromatosis) of right shoulder joint." *Proc. Staff Meetings Mayo Clin.*, **14**: 801–806.

MILES, J. & BHANDARI, Y. S. (1971). "Ossifying spinal arachnoiditis." *Neurochirurgia*, **14**: 184–188.

NATHAN, H. (1962). "Osteophytes of the vertebral column: an anatomical study of their development according to age, race and sex with considerations as to their etiology and significance." *J. Bone Joint Surg.*, **44A**: 243–264.

NATHAN, H., ALKALAJ, I. & AVIAD, I. (1960). "Spondylosis in the aged." *Geriatrics*, **15**: 187–196.

NELSON, M. A. (1972). "Spinal stenosis in achondroplasia." *Proc. Roy. Soc. Med.*, **65**: 1028–1029.

NELSON, M. A. (1973). "Lumbar spinal stenosis." *J. Bone Joint Surg.*, **55B**: 506–512.

NEWMAN, A. J. (1973). "Vertebral compression in childhood leukemia." *Amer. J. Dis. Child*, **125**: 863–865.

NICOLA, G. C. & NIZZOLI, G. (1974). "Intermittent claudication in the lower limbs due to total stenosis of the lumbar canal." *Neurochir.*, **17**: 48–57.

ODOM, J. A. (1974). "Scoliosis in paraplegia." *Paraplegia*, **11:** 290–294.

OLSSON, S. S. & SODERMANN, B. (1974). "Spinal intermittent dysbasia." *Acta Orthop. Scand.*, **45:** 683–692.

OOL, Y., SUZUKI, Y., SUGAWARA, S., YAMAZAKI, N. & MORISAKI, N. (1968). "Acquired spondylolysis in child and young adult." *J. Bone Joint Surg.*, **50A:** 1649–1656.

OSBORNE, G. (1974). "Spinal stenosis." *Physiotherapy*, **60:** 7–9.

PAINE, K. W. & HAUNG, P. W. (1972). "Lumbar disc syndrome." *J. Neurosurg.*, **37:** 75–82.

PALLIS, C., JONES, A. M. & SPILLANE, J. D. (1954). "Cervical spondylosis: incidence and implications." *Brain*, **77:** 274–289.

PANI, K. C., MUDULI, H., CHANDER, K. & KAK, V. K. (1972). "Intrathecal disc prolapse associated with lumbar canal stenosis." *Neurol. India*, **20:** 64–69.

PETRAKIS, N. L. (1954). "Bone marrow pressure in leukemic and non-leukemic patients." *J. Clin. Invest.*, **33:** 27–34.

PHILLIPS, D. G. (1975). "Upper limb involvement in cervical spondylosis." *J. Neurol. Neurosurg. Psychiat.*, **38:** 386–390.

QUADERY, L. A. (1974). "Myelopathy in cervical spondylosis." *Lancet*, **2:** 1453.

QUESADA, R. S. (1975). "Widened interpedicular distance secondary to trauma." *J. Trauma*, **15:** 167–169.

QUINLAN, A. G. (1954). "Post-tetanic kyphosis." *J. Bone Joint Surg.*, **36B:** 80–83.

RABUSHKA, S. E., APFELBACH, H. & LOVE, L. (1973). "Spontaneous healing of spondylolysis of the fifth lumbar vertebra: case report." *Clin. Orthop.*, **93:** 256–259.

RAHBEK, K. S. & SNORRASON, E. (1973). "Lumbar spondylopathies in conscripts: report of hospital material from the years 1966–1971." *Ugeskr. Laeger.*, **135:** 1–3.

RAVAULT, P. P., MEUNIER, P., SAMBIN, P., CRET, R. & BIANCH, G. S. (1969). "An early sign of spinal osteoporosis: enlargement of lumbar disc spaces." *Rev. Lyon. Med.*, **18:** 603–613.

RAWKINS, M. D. (1954). "The diagnosis of herniation of intervertebral discs in the cervical spine." *Brit. J. Phys. Med.*, **17:** 219–223.

RESNICK, D. (1975). "Diffuse idiopathic skeletal hyperostosis: Forestier's disease with extraspinal manifestations." *Radiology*, **115:** 513–524.

RILEY, G. (1954). "Cervical spondylosis." *J. Bone Joint Surg.*, **36B:** 681.

SALERNO, N. R. & EDEIKEN, J. (1970). "Vertebral scalloping in neurofibromatosis." *Radiol.*, **97:** 509–510.

SCHECHTER, L. S. & PEARL, M. (1972). "Intervertebral disc calcification in childhood." *Amer. J. Dis. Child.*, **123:** 608–611.

SHORE, L. R. (1931). "A report on the nature of certain bony spurs arising from the dorsal arches of the thoracic vertebrae." *J. Anat.*, **65:** 379–387.

SIM, F. H., SVIEN, H. J., BICKEL, W. H. & JAMES, J. M. (1974). "Swan-neck deformity following extensive cervical laminectomy." *J. Bone Joint Surg.*, **56A:** 564–580.

SIMURDA, M. A. (1959). "Spontaneous healing of spondylosis." *J. Bone Joint Surg.*, **41B:** 879.

SONG, J. U. & RANSOHOFF, J. (1962). "Surgical lesions of spine and spinal cord simulating disc syndrome." *N.Y. State J. Med.*, **62:** 556–559.

SPILBERG, I. & LIEBERMAN, D. M. (1972). "Ankylosing hyperostosis of the cervical spine." *Arth. Rheum.*, **15:** 208–212.

STEWART, D. H. & RED, D. E. (1971). "Spinal arachnoid diverticula." *J. Neurosurg.*, **35:** 65–70.

STEWART, P. E., SILBIGER, M. L. & WOLFSON, S. L. (1974). "Intervertebral disc calcification in childhood." *Clin. Pediatr.*, **13:** 363–366.

STILWELL, D. L. (1962). "Structural deformities of vertebrae: bone adaptation and modelling in experimental scoliosis and kyphosis." *J. Bone Joint Surg.*, **44A:** 611–634.

SULLIVAN, C. R. & BICKELL, W. H. (1960). "The problem of traumatic spondylolysis: a report of three cases." *Amer. J. Surg.*, **100:** 698–708.

SULLIVAN, J. D. & FARFAN, H. F. (1975). "The crumpled neural arch." *Orthop. Clin. Nth. Amer.*, **6:** 199–214.

SWIDERSKI, G. (1968). "Progressive and dysplastic disorders of the lumbar neural arch." *Acta Chir. Orthop. Traum. Česk.*, **35:** 323–327.

TAILLARD, W. (1961). "Acquired spondylolises." *Revue de Clinique Orthopédique*, **16** (No. 5): 617–623.

THOMAS, G. E. (1947). "Idiopathic scoliosis." *J. Bone Joint Surg.*, **29A:** 907–917.

THOMPSON, W. A. L. & RALSTON, E. L. (1949). "Pseudoarthrosis following spine fusion." *J. Bone Joint Surg.*, **31A**: 400–405.

UNANDER-SCHARIN, L. (1950). "A case of spondylolisthesis lumbalis aquisita." *Acta Orthop. Scand.*, **19**: 536–544.

VAN DRIEST, J. J. & MAXWELL, H. R. (1952). "Central lumbar disk simulating cauda equina tumor occurring in a twelve year old boy with dyschondroplasia." *Wisconsin Med. J.*, 374–375.

VERBIEST, H. (1955). "Further experiences on the pathological influence of a developmental narrowness of the bony lumbar vertebral canal." *J. Bone Joint Surg.*, **37B**: 576–583.

VERBIEST, H. (1973). "Absolute and relative stenosis of the lumbar vertebral canal." *Clin. Neurosurg.*, **16**: 204–214.

VERBIEST, H. (1973). "Neurogenic intermittent claudication in cases with absolute and relative stenosis of the lumbar vertebral canal, in cases with narrow lumbar vertebral foramina and in cases with both entities." *Clin. Neurosurg.*, **20**: 204–214.

VERBIEST, H. (1973). "The management of cervical spondylosis." *Clin. Neurosurg.*, **20**: 262–294.

VERBIEST, H. (1975). "Pathomorphological aspects of developmental lumbar stenosis." *Orthop. Clin. Nth. Amer.*, **6**: 177–196.

VERCAUTEREN, M. (1972). "Etiopathogenic approach to idiopathic scoliosis." *Acta Orthop. Belg.*, **38**: 429.

VRETTOS, X. C. & WYKE, B. D. (1974). "Articular reflexogenic systems in the costovertebral joints and their possible relevance to the production of scoliosis." *J. Bone Joint Surg.*, **56B**: 382.

WAGENRECHT, L. V. & REME, H. (1973). "Solitary Schwannoma in the lumbosacral region (case report and review of literature.)" *Beitr. Klin. Chir.*, **220**: 334–340.

WALKER, C. S. (1954). "Calcification of intervertebral discs in children." *J. Bone Joint Surg.*, **36B**: 601–605.

WALTZ, T. A. (1967). "Physical factors in the production of the myelopathy of cervical spondylosis." *Brain*, **90**: 395–404.

WEBER, A. (1971). "Spinal stenosis." *J. Bone Joint Surg.*, **53B**: 564.

WEBER, F. A. & DE KLERK, D. J. J. (1973). "Spinal stenosis." *Sth. Afr. Med. J.*, **47**: 207–213.

WEEDEN BUTLER, R. (1971). "Spontaneous anterior fusion of vertebral bodies." *J. Bone Joint Surg.*, **53B**: 230–235.

WEIL, M. P. & TISCIER, A. (1953). "Painless large osteophytic deformations of vertebrae." *Rev. Rheum.*, **20**: 157–158.

WILKINSON, M. (1960). "The morbid anatomy of cervical spondylitis and myelopathy." *Brain*, **93**: 589.

WILKINSON, M. (1970). "Cervical spondylosis." *Practitioner*, **204**: 537–545.

WILSON, P. J. E. & CAST, I. P. (1972). "Lumbar stenosis revisited." *J. Neurol. Neurosurg. Psychiat.*, **12**: 35: 919–920.

WOLF, B. S., KHILNANI, M. & MATIS, L. I. (1956). "Sagittal diameter of bony cervical canal and its significance in cervical spondylosis." *J. Mt. Sinai Hosp.*, **23**: 283–292.

WOLMAN, L. (1949). "Cramp in cases of prolapsed intervertebral disc." *J. Neurol. Neurosurg. Psychiat.*, **12**: 251–257.

YADAY, S. S. (1973). "Traction spur." *J. Postgrad. Med.*, **19**: 136–138.

ZORAB, P. (1972). "Spinal deformity in neurofibromatosis." *Lancet*, **2**: 823.

## (c) Trauma

ABEL, M. S. & HARMON, P. H. (1960). "Oblique motion studies and other non-myelographic roentgenographic criteria for diagnosis of traumatised or degenerated lumbar intervertebal discs." *Amer. J. Surg.*, **99**: 717–726.

AMBRUS, L. & PAPATHEODOROU, C. (1973). "Trauma and lumbar disc herniation in childhood." *Calif. Med.*, **119**: 66–68.

ANDROP, S., MARGOLIN. S. E., MARSHALL, J. R. & RITTENHOUSE, M. (1941). "Vertebral compression fractures sustained during convulsions." *Arch. Surg.*, **42**: 550–556.

ARMSTRONG, K. (1975). "Nursing care study: spinal injury." *Nursing Times*, **71**: 1092–1094.

ARNDT, R. D. (1975). "Cervical-thoracic transverse process fracture: further observations on the seatbelt syndrome." *J. Trauma*, **15**: 600–602.

ARNOLD, J. S. (1973). "Amount and quality of trabecular bone in osteoporotic vertebral fractures." *Clin. Endocrinol. Metabol.* **2**: 221–238.

ATCHESON, S. G. (1975). "Ill effects of cardiac resuscitation: report of two unusual cases." *Chest*, **67**: 615–616.

BANERJEE, T. (1974). "Transcutaneous nerve stimulation for pain after spinal injury." *New Eng. J. Med.*, **291**: 796.

BARR, J. S. (1974). "Ruptured intervertebral disc and sciatic pain." *J. Bone Joint Surg.*, **29:** 429–437.

BATLEY, H. L. & KATO, F. (1972). "Paravertebral ossification of the cervical spine." *Southern Med. J.* **65:** 189–192.

BEALS, R. K. & HICKMAN, J. W. (1972). "Industrial injuries of the back and extremities. Comprehensive evaluation—an aid in prognosis and management: study of 180 patients." *J. Bone Joint Surg.*, **54A:** 1593–1611.

BEDBROOK, G. M. (1973). "Study of spinal deformity in traumatic spinal paralysis." *Paraplegia*, **10:** 321–335.

BEIGHTON, P. & CRAIG, C. (1973). "Atlanto-axial subluxation in the Morquio syndrome: report of a case." *J. Bone Joint Surg.*, **55B:** 478–481.

BOHLER, J. (1970). "Operative treatment of fractures of the dorsal and lumbar spine." *J. Trauma*, **10:** 1119–1122.

BOHLMAN, H. H. (1972). "Pathology and current treatment concepts of cervical spine injury." *A.A.O.S. Instructional Course Lectures*, **21:** 108–115.

BRUNSCHWIG, A. & JUNG, A. (1932). "The importance of peri-articular innervation in the pathological physiology of sprained joints." *J. Bone Joint Surg.*, **14B:** 273.

BUCKMAN, J. R. & DIJKSTRA, T. E. (1975). " 'Secondary' fractures in the region of the vertebral arch and projections in wedge fractures of the thoracic and lumbar spine." *Arch. Chir. Neurol.*, **25:** 95–105.

BURKE, D. C. (1971). "Hyperextension injuries of the spine." *J. Bone Joint Surg.*, **53B:** 3–12.

BURKE, D. C. (1975). "The management of thoracic and thoraco-lumbar injuries of spine with neurological involvement." *J. Bone Joint Surg.*, **57B:** 254.

BURMAN, M. (1952). "Tear of the sacrospinous and sacrotuberous ligaments." *J. Bone Joint Surg.*, **34A:** 331–339.

CLOWARD, R. B. (1975). "Multiple ruptured lumbar discs." *Ann. Surg.*, **142:** 190–195.

CORNISH, B. L. (1968). "Traumatic spondylolisthesis of the axis." *J. Bone Joint Surg.*, **50B:** 31–43.

DICKSON, J. H., HARRINGTON, P. R. & ERWIN, W. D. (1973). "Harrington instrumentation in the fractured, unstable thoracic and lumbar spine." *Texas Med.*, **69:** 91–98.

DUNN, E. J. (1974). "Fracture dislocation of the posterior elements of C7 associated with bilateral pedicle fractures of C7: a case report." *J. Trauma*, **14:** 527–536.

ECTORS, P. & BREMEN, J. (1971). "Management of cervical spine trauma—eleven years' experience. Review of literature." *Lyon Chir.*, **67:** 429–434.

FALCKE, H. S. (1973). "A case of lumbar disc prolapse." *Proc. Mine Med. Off. Assoc.*, **52:** 74.

FARHAT, S. M., SCHNEIDER, R. C. & GRAY, J. M. (1973). "Traumatic spinal extradural hematoma associated with cervical fractures in rheumatoid arthritis. *J. Trauma*, **13:** 591–599.

FORSYTH, H. F. (1964). "Extension injuries of cervical spine." *J. Bone Joint Surg.*, **46A:** 1792–1796.

FRIED, L. C. (1973). "Atlanto-axial fracture-dislocations: failure of posterior C1 to C2 fusion." *J. Bone Joint Surg.*, **55B:** 490–496.

FRIEDENBERG, Z. B. (1966). "Dislocation of the sacro-iliac joint." *Amer. J. Orthop.*, **8:** 90–95.

GABRIELSEN, T. O. & MAXWELL, J. A. (1966). "Traumatic atlanto-occipital dislocation." *Amer. J. Roentgenol.*, **97:** 624–629.

GALLAGHER, J. C. (1973). "The crush fracture syndrome in post-menopausal women." *Clin. Endocr. Metabol.*, **2:** 293–315.

GASS, H. (1972). "Supraclavicular cerebrospinal fluid effusion in brachial plexus avulsion injuries." *J. Bone Joint Surg.*, **54A:** 281.

GEDDES, E. W. (1970). "Complete subluxation of the fifth lumbar vertebra with cauda equina lesion." *Proc. Mine Med. Off. Assoc.*, **49:** 191–192.

GOLUB, B. S., ROVIT, R. L. & MANKIN, H. J. (1971). "Cervical and lumbar disc disease: a review." *Bull. Rheum. Dis.*, **21:** 635–642.

GOODMAN, J. H. (1974). "Edema formation and central hemorrhagic necrosis following impact injury to primate spinal cord." *Surg. Forum*, **24:** 440–442.

GRANT, F. C., AUSTIN, G., FRIEDENBERG, K. & HANSEN, A. (1948). "A correlation of neurologic, orthopedic and roentgenographic findings in displaced intervertebral disc." *Surg. Gynec. Obst.*, **87:** 561–568.

GRANT, F. C. & NULSEN, F. E. (1952). "Ruptured intervertebral disks." *Surg. Clin. Nth. Amer.*, **32:** 1777–1790.

GRIFFITH, H. B., GLEAVE, J. R. W. & TAYLOR, R. G. (1966). "Changing patterns of fracture in the dorsal and lumbar spine." *Brit. Med. J.*, **1:** 891–894.

GRIFFITHS, S. C. (1972). "Fracture of the odontoid process in children." *J. Pediatr. Surg.*, **1:** 680–683.

GUKELBERGER, M. (1972). "The uncomplicated post-traumatic cervical syndrome." *Scand. J. Rehab. Med.*, **4:** 150–153.

GURDJIAN, E. S., WEBSTER, J. E., OSTROWSKI, A. Z., HARDY, W. G., LINDER, G. & THOMAS, L. M. (1961). "Herniated lumbar intervertebral disc: an analysis of 1,176 operated cases." *J. Trauma*, **1:** 158–176.

HAASE, J., JEPSON, B. V., BECH, H. & LANGEBAEK, E. (1973). "Spinal fracture following radiculography using meglumine isthalamate (Conray)." *Neuroradiology*, **6:** 65–70.

HADLEY, L. A. (1936). "Apophyseal subluxation." *J. Bone Joint Surg.*, **18A:** 428–433.

HADLEY, L. A. (1951). "Intervertebral joint subluxation, bony impingement and foramen encroachment with nerve root changes." *Amer. J. Roentgenol.*, **65:** 377–402.

HARALSON, R. H. (1969). "Posterior dislocation of the atlas on the axis without fracture." *J. Bone Joint Surg.*, **51A:** 561–566.

HARRIS, W. R., RATHBUN, J. B., WORTZMAN, G. & HUMPHREY, J. G. (1973). "Avulsion of lumbar roots complicating fracture of the pelvis." *J. Bone Joint Surg.*, **55A:** 1436–1442.

HARRIS, W. R., WORTZMAN, G., RATHBUN, J. B. & HUMPHREY, J. G. (1973). "Lumbosacral nerve root avulsion." *J. Bone Joint Surg.*, **55B:** 662.

HASUE, M. (1974). "Cervical spine injuries in children." *Fukishima J. Med. Sci.*, **20:** 115–123.

HENDERSON, E. D., SANTOS, R. E., CHIROFF, R. T. & JOHNSON, E. W. (1973). "Traumatic spondylolisthesis." *Minnesota Med.*, **56:** 53–57.

HENTZER, L. & SCHALTMIZEK, M. (1971). "Fractures and subluxations of the atlas and axis." *Acta Orthop. Scand.*, **42:** 251–258.

HIRSCH, C. (1960). "Cervical disc rupture." *Acta Orthop. Scand.*, **30:** 172–186.

HOHL, M. (1974). "Soft tissue injuries of the neck in automobile accidents. Factors affecting prognosis." *J. Bone Joint Surg.*, **56A:** 1675–1682.

HOHL, M. (1975). "Soft tissue injuries of the neck." *Clin. Orthop.*, **109:** 42–49.

HOLDSWORTH, F. (1970). "Fractures, dislocations and fracture-dislocations of the spine." *J. Bone Joint Surg.*, **52A:** 1534–1551.

HOLSCHER, E. C. (1968). "Vascular and visceral injuries during lumbar disc surgery." *J. Bone Joint Surg.*, **50A:** 383–393.

HOOPER, J. (1973). "Low back pain and manipulation: paraparesis after treatment of low back pain by physical methods." *Med. J. Austr.*, **1:** 549–551.

HORLYCK, E. (1974). "Cervical spine injuries." *Acta Orthop. Scand.*, **45:** 845–853.

HUBBARD, D. D. (1974). "Injuries of the spine in children and adolescents." *Clin. Orthop.*, **100:** 56–65.

HUITTINEN, V. M. (1972). "Nerve injury in double vertical pelvic fractures." *Acta Chir. Scand.*, **138:** 571–575.

HUITTINEN, V. M. (1972). "Lumbosacral nerve injury in fracture of the pelvis: a postmortem radiographic and patho-anatomical study." *Acta Chir. Scand.*, (Suppl. **429**): 1.

HUMPHRIES, S. V. (1974). "A case of displaced disc." *Cent. Afr. J. Med.*, **20:** 263–264.

INMAN, V. T. & SAUNDERS, J. B. DE C. M. (1947). "Anatomicophysiological aspects of injuries to the intervertebral disc." *J. Bone Joint Surg.*, **29A:** 461–475.

ISDALE, I. C. & CONLON, P. W. (1971). "Atlanto-axial subluxation: a six year follow-up report." *Ann. Rheum. Dis.*, **30:** 387–389.

JACOBS, B. (1975). "Cervical fractures and dislocations (C3-7)." *Clin. Orthop.*, **109:** 18–32.

JANECKA, V. (1973). "Isolated dislocations of vertebral bodies L2/3 with breaking of joint processes without simultaneous serious damage of the spinal cord." *Česk. Radiol.*, **27:** 64–68.

JEFFERSON, G. (1928). "Discussion on spinal injuries." *Proc. Roy. Soc. Med.*, **21:** 625–637.

JONES, S. R. (1973). "Bacterial meningitis complicating cranial-spinal trauma." *J. Trauma*, **13:** 895–900.

KAUFER, H. & HAYES, J. T. (1966). "Lumbar fracture dislocation: a study of 21 cases." *J. Bone Joint Surg.*, **48A:** 712–730.

KEITH, W. S. (1974). "Traumatic infarction of the spinal cord." *Can. J. Neurol. Sci.*, **1:** 124–126.

KEMPF, I., BRIOT, B., FERNANDEZ, M., GROSSE, A. & REBARD, M. (1973). "Treatment of vertebro-medullary injuries." *Rev. Chir. Orthop.*, **59:** 377–389.

KENNEDY, A. (1960). "Spinal injury involving the jejunum." *Lancet*, **1:** 1025.

KESSLER, L. A. (1973). "Delayed traumatic dislocation of the cervical spine." *J. Amer. Med. Ass.*, **224:** 124–125.

KOCHER, T. (1896). "Injuries of the vertebral column, with a study of the physiology of the human spinal cord." *Grenz. Geb. Med. Chir.*, **1:** 420.

KOSOY, J. (1974). "Audiovestibular findings with cervical spine trauma." *Texas Med. J.*, **70:** 66–71.

KUNKLE, E. C., MULLER, J. C. & ODOM, G. L. (1952). "Traumatic brainstem thrombosis: report of case and analysis of mechanism of injury." *Ann. Int. Med.*, **36:** 1329–1335.

LANGLOH, N. D., JOHNSON, E. W. & JACKSON, C. B. (1972). "Traumatic sacro-iliac disruptions." *J. Trauma*, **12:** 931–935.

LAPEYRE, B., JOUVINROUX, P., BOUSQUET, G., ONIMUS, M. & MICHEL, C. R. (1971). "Treatment of unstable fractures of the dorso-lumbar spine (with and without neurological complications)." *Rev. Chir. Orthop.*, **57:** 567–571.

LAURITZEN, J. (1968). "Diagnostic difficulties in lower cervical spine dislocations." *Acta Orthop. Scand.*, **39:** 439–446.

LAVARDE, G. (1973). "Isolated fractures of the articular processes of the cervical spine." *J. Chir. (Paris)*, **105:** 241–248.

LEWIS, J. (1974). "The treatment of unstable fracture-dislocations of the thoraco-lumbar spine accompanied by paraplegia." *J. Bone Joint Surg.*, **56B:** 603–612.

LICHMBLAV, S. (1962). "Dislocation of the sacro-iliac joint." *J. Bone Joint Surg.*, **44A:** 192–198.

LOWREY, J. J. (1973). "Dislocated lumbar vertebral epiphysis in adolescent children." *J. Neurosurg.*, **38:** 232–234.

McCALL, I. W., PARK, W. M. & McSWEENEY, T. (1973). "The radiological demonstration of acute lower cervical injury." *Clin. Radiol.*, **24:** 235–240.

McCARTER, C. C., GRIFFIN, P. P. & BYRD, E. B. (1972). "Ruptured calcified thoracic disc in a child: report of a case." *J. Bone Joint Surg.*, **54A:** 1272–1278.

MARKS, R. L. (1973). "Non-penetrating injuries of the neck and cerebrovascular accident." *Arch. Neurol.*, **28:** 412–414.

MATTEI, F., MARSILL, G. C. & JULET, R. (1973). "Postraumatic subluxation of the thoracic vertebrae with major displacement." *Chirurgie*, **98:** 716–717.

MAURICE-WILLIAMS, R. S. (1972). "Survival after a 'hangman's fracture'." *Guy's Hosp. Rep.*, **121:** 327–331.

MEIJERS, K. A. (1973). "Treatment of dislocation in the cervical spine in rheumatoid arthritis and ankylosing spondylitis, complicated by signs of cord compression." *Ann. Rheum. Dis.*, **32:** 88–89.

MEIJERS, K. A. (1974). "Dislocation of the cervical spine with cord compression in rheumatoid arthritis." *J. Bone Joint Surg.*, **56B:** 668–680.

MELAMED, A. (1965). "Fracture of pars interarticularis of lumbar vertebra." *Amer. J. Roentgenol.*, **94:** 584–586.

MENSOR, M. C. (1937). "Injuries to the accessory processes of the spinal vertebrae." *J. Bone Joint Surg.*, **19A:** 381–388.

MILLER, R. F. (1970). "Subluxation of the sacro-iliac joint." *Lancet*, **1:** 193–194.

MIXTER, W. J. & BARR, J. S. (1934). "Rupture of the intervertebral disc with involvement of the spinal canal." *New Eng. Med. J.*, **211:** 210–214.

MOAZER, E. H. (1968). "A case of lumbo-dorsal hernia with some unusual features." *Med. J. Aust.*, **1:** 60.

MOSS, L. (1970). "Subluxation of the sacro-iliac joint." *Lancet*, **1:** 412–413.

MOULTON, A. & SILVER, J. R. (1970). "Chest movement in patients with traumatic injuries of the cervical cord." *Clin. Sci.*, **39:** 407–422.

MOURGES, G. DE, FISCHER, L., JARSAILLON, B. & MACHENAUD, A. (1973). "Fractures of the posterior arch of the axis." *Rev. Chir. Orthop.*, **59:** 549–564.

MUKHERJEE, S. K. (1974). "Fractured vertebra following tetanus." *Indian Med. Ass.*, **63:** 158–160.

NATHAN, F. F. & BICKEL, W. H. (1968). "Spontaneous axial subluxation in a child as the first sign of juvenile rheumatoid arthritis." *J. Bone Joint Surg.*, **50A:** 1675–1678.

NEWMAN, P. H. (1965). "A clinical syndrome associated with severe lumbosacral subluxation." *J. Bone Joint Surg.*, **47B:** 472–481.

NICOLL, E. A. (1949). "Fractures of the dorsolumbar spine." *J. Bone Joint Surg.*, **31B:** 376–394.

NIELSEN, P. B. (1965). "Asymptomatic vertical fracture of a cervical vertebra." *Acta Orthop. Scand.*, **36:** 250–256.

NIEMINEN, R. (1973). "Fractures of spinous processes of the lower cervical spine." *Ann. Chir. Gynaec. Fenn.*, **62:** 328–333.

NIEMINEN, R. (1974). "Fractures of the articular processes of the lower cervical spine." *Ann. Chir. Gynaec. Fenn.*, **63**: 204–211.

OSGOOD, C., (1975). "Multiple spine fractures in ankylosing spondylitis." *J. Trauma*, **15**: 163–166.

OSGOOD, C., MARTIN, L. G. & ACKERMAN, E. (1973). "Fracture-dislocation of the cervical spine with ankylosing spondylitis: report of 2 cases." *J. Neurosurg.*, **39**: 764–769.

PAGE, C. P., STORY, J. L., WISSINGER, J. P. & BRANCH, C. L. (1973). "Traumatic atlanto-occipital dislocation." *J. Neurosurg.*, **39**: 394–397.

PALMER, B. C. M. (1932). "A case of fracture of five lumbar transverse processes." *Guy's Hosp. Rep.* (4th series), **12**: 502–506.

PARK, W. M. & O'BRIEN, W. (1969). "Suddenly fatal neck lesions from arthritis." *Acta Radiol.*, **8**: 529.

PARKER, A. J. (1974). "Traumatic occlusion of segmental spinal veins." *J. Trauma*, **14**: 868–872.

PARKER, J. M. (1971). "Ureteral injury secondary to lumbar disc operation." *J. Urol.*, **105**: 85.

PATRICK, L. M. (1961). "Caudo-cephalad static and dynamic injuries to the vertebrae." *Proc. 5th Stapp Automotive Crash Conference, Univ. Minnesota*. pp. 171–181.

PATZAKIS, M. J., KNOPF, A., ELFERING, M., HOFFER, M. & HARVEY, J. P. (1974). "Posterior dislocation of the atlas on the axis: a case report." *J. Bone Joint Surg.*, **56A**: 1260–1262.

PEARSON, R. C. (1970). "Fracture of spine with neurological lesions." *Proc. Mine Med. Off. Assoc.*, **49**: 181–184.

PERVÈS, A. (1972). "Fractures of the dorsal and lumbar spine." *Bull. Mém. Soc. Chir. (Paris)*, **62**: 364–371.

PERVÈS, A. & PIDHORZ, L. (1973). "Fractures of the dorsal and lumbar spine." *Rev. Chir. Orthop.*, **59**: 491–512.

PETRIE, J. G. (1964). "Flexion injuries of cervical spine." *J. Bone Joint Surg.*, **46A**: 1800–1806.

PIERCE, D. S. (1972). "Long-term management of thoracolumbar fractures and fracture-dislocations." *A.A.O.S. Instructional Course Lectures*, **21**: 102–107.

PROLO, D. J., RUNNELS, J. B. & HAMESON, R. M. (1973). "The injured cervical spine: immediate and long-term immobilisation with the halo." *J. Amer. Med. Assoc.*, **224**: 591–594.

PURSER, D. W. (1969). "Displaced fracture of the sacrum." *J. Bone Joint Surg.*, **51B:** 346–347.

QUADERY, L. A. (1974). "Myelopathy in cervical spondylosis." *Lancet*, **2:** 1453.

RABUSHKA, E. S., APFELBACH, H. & LOVE, L. (1973). "Spontaneous healing of spondylolysis of the fifth lumbar vertebra: case report." *Clin. Orthop.*, **93:** 256–259.

RANA, N. A., HANCOCK, D. O., TAYLOR, A. R. & HILL, A. G. S. (1973). "Atlanto-axial subluxation in rheumatoid arthritis." *J. Bone Joint Surg.*, **55B:** 458–470.

RAPP, G. F. & KERNEK, C. B. (1974). "Spontaneous fracture of the lumbar spine with correction of deformity in ankylosing spondylitis." *J. Bone Joint Surg.*, **56A:** 1277–1278.

RENNIE, W. & MITCHELL, N. (1973). "Flexion distraction fractures of the thoracolumbar spine." *J. Bone Joint Surg.*, **55A:** 386–390.

RICH, W. V. (1974). "A case of subluxation in the dorsal region." *Med. J. Aust.*, **2:** 886–887.

RIGAMONTI, L., GHINDINI, O., MOLINARI-TOSATTI, P., SLAVI, S., DIMONDA, V., CERNIC, F. & RIGAMONTI, D. (1972). "Fractures and displacements of the cervical vertebrae." *Archiv. Scienze Med.*, **129:** 1–10.

RIJSBOSCH, J. K. (1971). "Fracture of the posterior arch of the atlas (combined with fracture of the spinous process of sixth and seventh cervical vertebrae)." *Arch. Chir. Néerl.*, **23:** 83–89.

ROAF, R. (1960). "A study of the mechanics of spinal injuries." *J. Bone Joint Surg.*, **42B:** 810–823.

ROAF, R. (1961). "Spinal injuries." *Lancet*, **1:** 99–101.

ROAF, R. (1972). "International classification of spinal injuries." *Paraplegia*, **10:** 78–84.

ROBERTSON, D. E. (1957). "Fracture-dislocation of the lumbar spine." *J. Bone Joint Surg.*, **39B:** 742–745.

ROBINSON, H. S. (1966). "Rheumatoid arthritis—atlanto-axial subluxation and its clinical presentation." *Can. Med. Ass. J.*, **94:** 470.

ROBINSON, P. N. & TIBBS, D. J. (1957). "Aneurysm complicating traumatic spondylolisthesis." *J. Bone Joint Surg.*, **39B:** 498–501.

ROBLES, J. (1968). "Brachial plexus avulsion." *J. Neurosurg.*, **28:** 434–438.

ROTHMAN, R. H. (1975). "The acute cervical disc." *Clin. Orthop.*, **109:** 59–68.

SCHATZKER, J., RORABECK, C. H. & WADDELL, J. P. (1971). "Fractures of the dens (odontoid process): an analysis of 37 cases." *J. Bone Joint Surg.*, **53B:** 393–405.

SCHNEIDER, D. (1973). "Traumatic cervical vertebral lesions, with particular reference to the bony lesions." *Arch. Orthop. Unfall-Chir.*, **75:** 113–120.

SCHNEIDER, R. C. (1949). "Acute traumatic posterior dislocation of an intervertebral disc with paralysis." *J. Bone Joint Surg.*, **31A:** 566–570.

SERRE, H. & SIMON, L. (1966). "Atlanto-axial dislocation in rheumatoid arthritis." *Rheumatism*, 53–58.

SHAPIRO, R. (1973). "The differential diagnosis of traumatic lesions of the occipito-atlanto-axial segment." *Radiol. Clin. Nth. Amer.*, **11:** 505–526.

SHERK, H. H. & NICHOLSON, J. T. (1970). "Fractures of the atlas." *J. Bone Joint Surg.*, **52A:** 1017–1024.

SHRAGO, G. G. (1973). "Cervical spine injuries: association with head trauma. A review of 50 patients." *Amer. J. Roentgenol.*, **118:** 670–673.

SMITH, (1962). "Transvertebral rupture of intervertebral disc." *J. Neurosurg.*, **19:** 594.

SPENCE, K. F., DECKER, S. & SELL, K. W. (1970). "Bursting atlantal fracture associated with rupture of the transverse ligament." *J. Bone Joint Surg.*, **52A:** 543–549.

SPURLING, R. G. & GRANTHAM, E. G. (1948). "Ruptured intervertebral discs in the lower lumbar regions." *Amer. J. Surg.*, **75:** 140.

STANGER, J. K. (1947). "Fracture dislocation of the thoracolumbar spine, with special reference to reduction by open and closed operations." *J. Bone Joint Surg.*, **29A:** 107–118.

STEIN, A. & KALIK, F. (1974). "Selective conservatism in the management of penetrating wound of the neck." *Sth. Afr. J. Surg.*, **12:** 31–40.

STEVENS, J. C., CARTLIDGE, N. E. F., SAUNDERS, M., *et al.* (1971). "Atlanto-axial subluxation and cervical myelopthy in rheumatoid arthritis." *Quart. J. Med.*, **40:** 391.

STUART, E. (1972). "Persistent dislocation of cervical vertebrae 5 and 6." *Nursing Times*, **68:** 1376–1378.

SUNDERLAND, S. (1974). "Mechanisms of cervical nerve root

246

avulsion in injuries of the neck and shoulder." *J. Neurosurg.*, **41:** 705–714.

SWINSON, D. R., HAMILTON, E. B. D., MATHEWS, J. A. & YATES, D. A. H. (1972). "Vertical subluxation of the axis in rheumatoid arthritis." *Ann. Rheum. Dis.*, **31:** 359–363.

TAKASE, B. (1969). "A clinical discourse on the electro-pathological findings in whiplash injury." *J. West. Pacif. Orthop. Ass.*, **6:** 199–204.

TERMANSESN, N. B. (1974). "Hangman's fracture." *Acta Orthop. Scand.*, **45:** 529–539.

THAMBYRAJAH, K. (1972). "Fractures of the cervical spine with minimal or no symptoms." *Med. J. Malaya*, **26:** 244–249.

THOMPSON, S. M. (1960). "Dislocation of the cervical spine." *J. Bone Joint Surg.*, **42B:** 858.

THORSON, J. (1972). "Neck injuries in road accidents: incidence of acute injuries and sequelae among in-patients." *Scand. J. Rehab. Med.*, **4:** 110–113.

TORRES, F. & SHAPIRO, S. K. (1961). "Electroencephalograms in whiplash injury." *Arch. Neurol.*, **5:** 28–35.

VASCONCELOS, D. (1973). "Compression fractures of the vertebrae during major epileptic seizures." *Epilepsia*, **14:** 323–328.

VERNON-ROBERTS, B. & PIRIE, C. J. (1973). "Healing trabecular microfractures in the bodies of lumbar vertebrae." *Ann. Rheum. Dis.*, **32:** 406–412.

VOGELSANG, H., ZEIDLER, H., WITTENBORG, A. & WEIDNER, A. (1973). "Rheumatoid cervical luxation with fatal neurological complications." *Neuroradiology*, **6:** 87–92.

WEINBERG, P. E. (1973). "Traumatic vertebral arteriovenous fistula." *Surg. Neurol.*, **1:** 162–167.

WEISS, M. H. & KAUFMANN, B. (1973). "Hangman's fracture in an infant." *Amer. J. Dis. Child.*, **126:** 268–269.

WERNE, S. (1955–6). "Spontaneous atlas dislocation." *Acta Orthop. Scand.*, **25:** 32–43.

WIGREN, A. & AMICI, F. (1973). "Traumatic atlanto-axial dislocation without neurological disorder." *J. Bone Joint Surg.*, **55A:** 642–644.

WILDE, C. S. (1963). "Persons injured while at work." *Ind. Med. Surg.*, **32:** 191–196.

WIRSCHING, M. (1972). "The relation between the form, severity and localisation of cervical vertebral lesions in injury mechanics." *Arch. Orthop. Unfall-Chir.*, **74:** 63–90.

WOODHALL, B. (1947). "Anatomicophysiological aspects of injuries to the intervertebral disc. A. Sensory patterns in the localization of disc lesions. B. Preliminary appraisal of Army results." *J. Bone Joint Surg.*, **29A:** 470–475.

YAU, A. C. (1974). "Stress fracture of the fused lumbo-sacral spine in ankylosing spondylitis." *J. Bone Joint Surg.*, **56B:** 681–687.

YOUNG, M. H. (1973). "Long-term consequences of stable fractures of the thoracic and lumbar vertebral bodies." *J. Bone Joint Surg.*, **55B:** 295–300.

ZARLING, M. E. (1966). "Vertebral column injuries." *Lancet*, **86:** 281–284.

## (d) Degenerative and Rheumatic Conditions

ABEL, M. S. & HARMON, P. H. (1960). "Oblique motion studies and other non-myelographic roentgenographic criteria for diagnosis of traumatised or degenerated lumbar intervertebral discs." *Amer. J. Surg.*, **99:** 717–726.

ABRAHAMSON, M. N. (1968). "Disseminated asymptomatic osteosclerosis with features resembling myelorheostosis, osteo-poikilosis and osteopathia striata." *J. Bone Joint Surg.*, **50A:** 991–996.

ADAMS, P., DAVIES, G. T. & SWEETNAM, P. (1970). "Osteoporosis and the effects of ageing on bone mass in elderly men and women." *Quart. J. Med.*, **39:** 601–615.

ALLBROOK, D. B. (1956). "Changes in lumbar vertebral body height with age." *Am. J. Phys. Anthrop.*, **14:** 35–37.

ALLEN, K. (1952). "Neuropathies caused by bony spurs in the cervical spine with special reference to surgical treatment." *J. Neurol. Neurosurg. Psychiat.*, **15:** 20–36.

ARNOLD, J. S., BARTLEY, M. H., TONT, S. A. & JENKINS, D. P. (1966). "Skeletal changes in ageing and disease." *Clin. Orthop.*, **49:** 17–38.

ATKINSON, P. J. & WOODHEAD, C. (1973). "The development of osteoporosis: a hypothesis based on a study of human bone structure." *Clinical Orthop.*, **90:** 217–228.

AUQUIER, L., HIRSCH, J. F., PAOLAGGI, J. B. & ROUQUES, C. (1972). "Stenosis of the lumbar spinal canal and sciatic claudication: a report of 29 cases, including 12 operated upon." *Rec. Rheum. Mal. Osteoartic.*, **39**: 429–437.

AUQUIER, L., HIRSCH, J. F., PAOLOGGI, J. B., ROUQUES, C. & GHOSLAN, R. (1970). "Stenosis of lumbar spinal canal and sciatic claudications: a study of 29 cases, 13 of which were operated upon." *Ann. Rheum. Dis.*, **29**: 691–692.

AUQUIER, L., PAOLAGGI, J. B., ROUQUES, C. & GHOSLAN, R. (1973). "Intermittent claudication due to irritation of the lumbosacral nerve roots: a report of 9 cases due to stenosis of the lumbar spinal canal confirmed at operation." *Ann. Méd. Int. (Paris)*, **124**: 265–277.

BARNETT, E. & NORDIN, B. E. C. (1960). "The radiological diagnosis of osteoporosis: a new approach." *Clin. Radiol.*, **11**: 166–174.

BEDFORD, P. D., BOSANQUET, F. D. & RUSSELL, W. R. (1952). "Degeneration of the spinal cord associated with cervical spondylosis." *Lancet*, **2**: 55–59.

BELL, G. H., DUNBAR, O., BECK, J. S. & GIBB, A. (1967). "Variations in strength of vertebrae with age and their relation to osteoporosis." *Calcif. Tissue Res.*, **1**: 75–86.

BOYLE, A. C. (1954). "Discussion on spondylosis (level of osteophyte frequencies.)" *Proc. Roy. Soc. Med.*, **47**: 49–56.

BRADFORD, F. K. & SPURLING, R. G. (1945). *The Intervertebral Disc*. Springfield, Illinois; Thomas.

BRADSHAW, P. (1957). "Some aspects of cervical spondylosis." *Quart. J. Med.*, **26**: 177–208.

BRAIN, R. (1954). "Spondylosis." *Lancet*, **1**: 687–693.

BRAIN, R. & WILKINSON, M. (Eds.) (1967). *Cervical Spondylosis and Other Disorders of the Cervical Spine*. London; Heinemann.

BRAIN, W. R. (1954). "Cervical spondylosis." *Ann. Int. Med.*, **41**: 439.

BRAIN, W. R. (1963). "Some unsolved problems of cervical spondylosis." *Brit. Med. J.*, **1**: 771.

BRAIN, W. R., NORTHFIELD, D. & WILKINSON, M. (1952). "The neurological manifestations of cervical spondylosis." *Brain*, **75**: 187–225.

BROOKER, A. E. W. (1965). "Cervical spondylosis." *Brain*, **88**: 925.

BULL, J., EL GAMMAL, T. & POPHAM, M. (1969). "A possible genetic factor in cervical spondylosis." *Brit. J. Radiol.*, **42**: 9–16.

BURKE, J. F. & MILLER, J. W. (1963). "Chronaxie determinations in intervertebral disc pathology." *J. Amer. Phys. Ther. Ass.*, **43:** 265–267.

CHACO, J. (1974). "Cervical spondylosis and pseudomyotonia." *Scand. J. Rehab. Med.*, **6:** 99–101.

CLEVELAND, M., BOSWORTH, D. M. & THOMPSON, F. R. (1948). "Pseudoarthrosis in the lumbosacral region." *J. Bone Joint Surg.*, **30A:** 302–311.

COLLINS, D. H. (1959). "Degenerative diseases." In *Modern Trends in Diseases of the Vertebral Column*, pp. 101–124. Ed. by R. Nassim and H. J. Burrows. London; Butterworth.

COSH, J. & KERSLEY, G. D. (1959). *The Degenerative Back*. Elsevier; Amsterdam.

COVENTRY, M. H. (1970). "Calcification in a cervical disc with anterior protrusion and dysphagia." *J. Bone Joint Surg.*, **52A:** 1463.

CRANDALL, P. H. & BATZDORF, U. (1966). "Cervical spondylotic myelopathy." *J. Neurosurg.*, **25:** 57–66.

DEHAIS, J. (1969). "Narrowing of the lumbar spinal canal." *Rheumatologie*, **21:** 387–393.

DE PALMA, A. F. & ROTHMAN, R. H. (1968). "The nature of pseudarthrosis." *Clin. Orthop.*, **59:** 113–118.

DE PALMA, A. F., ROTHMAN, R. H., LEVITT, R. L. & HAMMOND, N. L. (1972). "The natural history of severe disc degeneration." *Acta Orthop. Scand.*, **43:** 392–396.

DEQUEKER, J., FRANSSENS, R. & BORREMANS, A. (1971). "Relationship between peripheral and axial osteoporosis and osteoarthrosis." *Clin. Radiol.*, **22:** 74–77.

DIXON, A. ST. J. & LIENCE, E. (1961). "Sacro-iliac joint in adult rheumatoid arthritis and psoriatic arthropathy." *Ann. Rheum. Dis.*, **20:** 247–251.

ELLER, M. J. & SIEBERT, P. E. (1969). "Sclerotic vertebral bodies: an unusual manifestation of disseminated coccidio-idomycosis." *Radiology*, **93:** 1099–1100.

FENLIN, J. M. (1971). "Pathology of degenerative disease of the cervical spine." *Orthop. Clin. Nth. Amer.*, **2:** 371–387.

FERRY, A. M. (1956). "The degenerative disc syndrome of the low back." *Virginia Med. Monthly*, **83:** 146: 150.

FLEISCHLI, D. J. (1967). "Lytic lesion in a cervical vertebra." *J. Amer. Med. Ass.*, **201:** 192–193.

FLETCHER, G. H. (1947). "Backward displacement of the fifth

lumbar vertebra in degenerative disc disease." *J. Bone Joint Surg.*, **29A:** 1019–1026.

FORCIER, P. & HORSEY, W. J. (1970). "Calcification of the posterior longitudinal ligament at the thoracolumbar junction." *J. Neurosurg.*, **6:** 684–685.

FOX, J. L., BYRD, E. B. & McCULLOUGH, D. C. (1973). "Results of cervical laminectomy with dural graft for severe spondylosis with narrow canal." *Acta Neurol. Latinoamer*, **18:** 90–95.

FRIBERG, S. & HIRSCH, C. (1949). "Anatomical and clinical studies on lumbar disc degeneration." *Acta Orthop. Scand.*, **19:** 222–242.

FRIEDENBERG, Z. B. & MILLER, W. T. (1963). "Degenerative disease of the cervical spine." *J. Bone Joint Surg.*, **45A:** 1171–1178.

FUSE, K. (1969). "Study of tensile strength of the vertebral arch in the spinal supporting system, with special reference to the isolated arch of the vertebrae in spondylosis." *Nippon Ika Diag. Z.*, **36:** 132–159.

GENTENBERG, R. (1929). "The significance of deformed vertebral processes with particular reference to their incidence in the lumbar region." *Fortschr. Röntgenol.*, **39:** 650–656.

GARDNER, R. C. (1970). "The lumbar intervertebral disc: a clinicopathological correlation based on over 100 laminectomies." *Arch. Surg.*, **100:** 101–104.

GARGANO, F. P., MEYER, J. D. & SHELDON, J. J. (1974). "Transfemoral ascending lumbar catheterization of the epidural vein in lumbar disc disease." *Radiology*, **3:** 329–336.

GARTNER, J. (1968). "Photoelastic and ultrasonic studies on the structure and senile changes of the intervertebral disc and of the vitreous body." *Mod. Probl. Ophthal.*, **8:** 136–148.

GOLDING, D. N. (1975). "The musculoskeletal features of Wilson's disease: a clinical, radiological and serological survey." *Ann. Rheum. Dis.*, **32:** 201.

GOLUB, B. S., ROVIT, R. L. & MANKIN, H. J. (1971). "Cervical and lumbar disc disease: a review." *Bull. Rheum. Dis.*, **21:** 635–642.

GOOD, A. E. (1967). "Non-traumatic fracture of the thoracic spine in ankylosing spondylitis." *Arth. Rheum.*, **10:** 467.

GRONERT, H. J. (1973). "The differential diagnosis of iliosacral ankylosis." *Arch. Orthop. Unfallchir.*, **77:** 55–63.

GUPTA, B. D. (1973). "Cervical spondylosis: a correlative clinico-radiological study." *J. Ind. Med. Ass.*, **60:** 364–371.

HADLEY, L. A. (1963). "Stress fracture with spondylolysis." *Amer. J. Roentgenol.*, **90**: 1258–1262.

HARRIS, J., CARTER, A. R., GLICK, E. J. & STOREY, G. O. (1974). "Ankylosing hyperostosis. Clinical and radiological features." *Ann. Rheum Dis.*, **33**: 210–215.

HART, F. D. (1974). "Pain in osteoarthrosis." *Practitioner*, **212**: 244–250.

HASNER, E., JACOBSEN, H. H., SCHALIMTZEK, M., SKATUN, J. & SNORRASON, E. (1952). "Degeneration of lumbar intervertebral discs." *Amer. J. Phys. Med.*, **31**: 441–449.

HAVERBUSH, T. J., WILDE, A. H., HAWK, W. A. & SCHERBEL, A. L. (1974). "Osteolysis of the ribs and cervical spine in progressive systemic sclerosis (scleroderma): a case report." *J. Bone Joint Surg.*, **56A**: 637–640.

HAWK, W. A. (1936). "Spinal compression caused by ecchondrosis of the intervertebral fibrocartilage: with a review of the recent literature." *Brain*, **59**: 204–224.

HENDERSON, R. S. (1952). "The treatment of lumbar intervertebral disc protrusion: an assessment of conservative measures." *Brit. Med. J.* **2**: 597–598.

HENTZER, L. A. (1973). "Conservative and operative treatment of disc prolapse." *Ugeskr. Laeg.*, **135**: 2258–2262.

HILEL, N. (1968). "Compression of the sympathetic trunk by osteophytes of the vertebral column in the abdomen: an anatomical study with pathological and clinical considerations." *Surgery*, **63**: 609–625.

HILTON, R. C. & BALL, J. (1975). "Mobility, end-plate defects, and disc degeneration in the lower spine." *Ann. Rheum. Dis.*, **34**: 201.

HOHMANN, P. & GASTEIGER, W. (1973). "A radiological study of the costotransverse joints." *Röntgenpraxis*, **26**: 173–179.

HYNDMAN, O. R. (1946). "Pathologic intervertebral disc and its consequences." *Arch. Surg.*, **53**: 247–297.

IVES, D. R. (1973). "Urticaria pigmentosa with spinal osteoporosis." *Proc. Roy. Soc. Med.*, **66**: 175–176.

JACKSON, D. W. (1975). "Unilateral osseous bridging of the lumbar transverse processes following trauma." *J. Bone Joint Surg.*, **57A**: 125–126.

JESPERSON, N. B., LUND, H. T. & EGEBALD, M. (1973). "Intervertebral disc calcification in childhood." *Acta Paediat. Scand.*, **62**: 437–439.

KARAHARJU, E. O., ALHO, A. & LAASONEN, E. (1974). "Herniated lumbar disc: postoperative condition and correlation with pre-operative and operative findings." *Ann. Chir. Gynaec.*, **63**: 53–56.

KELLGREN, J. H. & LAWRENCE, J. S. (1958). "Osteoarthrosis and disc degeneration in an urban population." *Ann. Rheum. Dis.*, **17**: 388–397.

KELLY, M. (1958). "Physical changes in the prolapsed disc." *Lancet*, **2**: 584.

KIRKALDY-WILLIS, W. H., PAINE, K. W. E., CAUCHOIX, J. & McIVOR, G. (1974). "Lumbar spinal stenosis." *Clin. Orthop.*, **99**: 30–50.

KNUTSSON, F. (1942). "The vacuum phenomenon in the inter-vertebral discs." *Acta Radiol.*, **23**: 173–179.

KNUTSSON, F. (1944). "The instability associated with disc degener-ation in the lumbar spine." *Acta Radiol.*, **25**: 593–609.

KOBAYASHI, H. (1973). "Studies on symptomatology and radiology of cervical spondylotic myelopathy." *J. Jap. Orthop. Ass.*, **47**: 495–514.

KOBAYASHI, H. (1974). "Tract pain syndrome associated with chronic cervical disc herniation." *Hawaii Med. J.*, **33**: 376–381.

KOCZOCIK-PRZEDPELSKA, J., SWIDERSKI, G., WALSKI, A., GRUSZ-CZYNSKI, W. & KOWALSKA, H. (1973). "Electromyographic and thermometric studies and assessment of motor and sensory excitability in patients with low back pains." *Pol. Tyg. Lek.*, **28**: 315–317.

KRENZ, J. & TROUP, J. D. G. (1973). "The structure of the pars inter-articilaris of the lower lumbar vertebrae and its relation to the etiology of spondylosis: with a report of a healing fracture in the neural arch of a fourth lumbar vertebra." *J. Bone Joint Surg.*, **55B**: 735–741.

LAGIER, R. & SIT'AJ, S. (1974). "Vertebral changes in ochronosis: anatomical and radiological study of one case." *Ann. Rheum. Dis.*, **33**: 86–92.

LASKAR, F. H. & SARGISON, K. D. (1970). "Ochronotic arthropathy; a review with four case reports." *J. Bone Joint Surg.*, **52B**: 653–666.

LAWRENCE, J. S. (1969). "Disc degeneration: its frequency and relationship to symptoms." *Ann. Rheum. Dis.*, **28**: 121–138.

LAWRENCE, J. S. (1969). "Generalized osteoarthrosis in a population sample." *Amer. J. Epidem.*, **90:** 381–389.

LAWRENCE, J. S., BREMNER, J. M. & BIER, F. (1966). "Osteoarthrosis: prevalence in the population and the relationship between symptoms and X-ray changes." *Ann. Rheum. Dis.*, **25:** 1–24.

LECHOWSKI, S. & LORENS, M. (1973). "Unilateral multilevel protrusion of nucleus pulposus in the lumbar area." *Neurol. Neurochir. Pol.*, **7:** 429–433.

LeVINE, M. E. & DOBBINS, W. O. (1973). "Joint changes in Whipple's disease." *Semin. Arthritis Rheum.*, **3:** 79–93.

LINDBLOM, K. (1944). "Protrusions of discs and nerve compression in the lumbar region." *Acta Radiol.*, **25:** 195–212.

LINDBLOM, K. (1957). "Intervertebral disc degeneration considered as a pressure atrophy." *J. Bone Joint Surg.*, **39A:** 933–945.

LINDBLOM, K. & REXED, B. (1948). "Spinal nerve injury in dorsolateral protrusions of the lumbar discs." *J. Neurosurg.*, **5:** 413–432.

LOGUE, V. (1952). "Thoracic intervertebral disc prolapse with spinal cord compression." *J. Neurol. Neurosurg. Psychiat.*, **15:** 227–241.

LORINCZ, G., TRAUB, N. E., CHUKE, P. O. & HUSSAIN, S. F. (1974). "African haemosiderosis associated with osteoporosis and vertebral collapse." *East Afr. Med. J.*, **51:** 488–495.

LOURIE, H., SHENDE, M. C. & STEWART, D. H. (1973). "The syndrome of central cervical soft disc herniation." *J. Amer. Med. Ass.*, **266:** 302–305.

McCARTY, D. J. & GATTER, R. A. (1964). "Pseudogant syndrome (articular chondrocalcinosis)." *Bull. Rheum. Dis.*, **14:** 331–334.

McCONKEY, B., FRASER, G. M. & BLIGH, A. S. (1965). "Transparent skin and osteoporosis—a study in patients with rheumatoid disease." *Ann. Rheum. Dis.*, **24:** 219–223.

McDOUGALL, A. & ROBERTSON, J. M. (1960). "Prolapsed intervertebral disc in the adolescent." *J. Bone Joint Surg.*, **42B:** 651.

MACNAB, I. (1969). "Pain and disability in degenerative disc disease." *Texas Med.*, **65:** 56.

MACNAB, I. (1973). "Pain and disability in degenerative disc disease." *Clin. Neurosurg.*, **20:** 193–196.

McRAIE, D. L. (1956). "Asymptomatic intervertebral disc protrusion." *Acta Radiol.*, **46:** 9–27.

254

MAGILL, C. G. (1974). "Soft cervical disc herniation." *J. Amer. Med. Ass.*, **227**: 560.

MAINZER, F. (1973). "Herniation of the nucleus pulposus: a rare complication of intervertebral disc calcification in children." *Radiology*, **107**: 167–170.

MARIN, G. A. (1974). "Lumbar disc protrusion: evaluation and study of 600 diskectomies with one to ten years follow-up." *Int. Surg.*, **59**: 154–155.

MARSDEN, C. D. (1973). "Myopathy associated with anti-convulsant osteomalacia." *Brit. Med. J.*, **4**: 526–527.

MARVEL, J. P. (1971). "The clinical syndrome of cervical disease." *Orthop. Clin. Nth. Amer.*, **2**: 419–433.

MASSE, G., DI TARANTO, G. & MOHOVICH, F. (1973). "Lumbosciatic pain due to root compression." *Minerva Ortop.*, **24**: 500–516.

MEEKS, L. W. & RENSHAW, T. S. (1973). "Vertebral osteophytosis and dysphagia: two case reports of the syndrome recently termed ankylosing hyperostosis." *J. Bone Joint Surg.*, **55A**: 197–201.

MEYERDING, H. W., BAKER, G. S., LOVE, J. G. & CAMERON, M. D. (1939). "Spondylolisthesis with protrusion of intervertebral disk and hypertrophied ligamentum flavum associated with multiple loose bodies (osteochondromatosis) of right shoulder joint." *Proc. Staff Meet. Mayo Clin.*, **14**: 801–806.

MONCUR, J. A. (1965). "Scheuermann's disease in students of physical education." *Bull. Brit. Assn. Sports Med.*, **2**: 14–18.

MOOSA, A. (1973). "Spinal muscular atrophy in childhood." *Arch. Dis. Child.*, **48**: 386–388.

MORGAN, B. (1973). "Ageing and osteoporosis: in particular, spinal osteoporosis." *Clin. Endocr. Metabol.*, **2**: 187–201.

MULLER, R. (1951). "Protrusion of thoracic intervertebral disks with compression of the spinal cord." *Acta Med. Scand.*, **139**: 99–104.

MUNRO, D. (1956). "Lumbar and sacral compression radiculitis (herniated lumbar disk syndrome)." *New Eng. J. Med.*, **254**: 243–252.

NACHEMSON, A. (1959). "Physical changes in the prolapsed disc." *Lancet*, **1**: 1150.

NAKANISHI, T. (1974). "Symptomatic ossification of the posterior longitudinal ligament of the cervical spine." *Neurology*, **24**: 1139–1143.

NAKANISHI, T., MANNEN, T. & TOYOKURA, Y. (1973). "Asymptomatic ossification of the posterior longitudinal ligament of the cervical spine: incidence and roentgenological findings." *J. Neurol. Sci.*, **19:** 375–381.

NAMBA, T., ABERFELD, D. C. & GROB, D. (1970). "Chronic proximal spinal muscular atrophy." *J. Neurol. Sci.*, **11:** 401–423.

NASSIM, R. (1959). "Osteoporosis." In *Modern Trends in Diseases of the Vertebral Column.* pp. 125–141. Ed by R. Nassim and H. J. Burrows, London; Butterworth.

NELSON, C. L., JANECKI, C. J., GILDENBERG, P. H. & SAVA, G. (1972). "Disk protrusions in the young." *Clin. Orthop.*, **88:** 142–150.

NEWMAN, P. H. (1975). "Degenerative spondylolisthesis." *Orthop. Clin. Nth. Amer.*, **6:** 197–198.

NEWMAN, P. H. & FITZGERALD, J. A. W. (1972). "Degenerative spondylolisthesis." *J. Bone Joint Surg.*, **54B:** 174.

NURICK, S. (1972). "The natural history and the results of surgical treatment of the spinal cord disorder associated with cervical spondylosis." *Brain*, **95:** 101–108.

O'CONNELL, J. E. A. (1951). "Protrusions of the lumbar intervertebral discs." *J. Bone Joint Surg.*, **33B:** 8–30.

O'CONNELL, J. E. A. (1955). "Involvement of the spinal cord by intervertebral disc protrusions." *Brit. J. Surg.*, **63:** 225–247.

O'CONNELL, J. E. A. (1956). "Contribution to a discussion on cervical spondylosis." *Proc. Roy. Soc. Med.*, **49:** 202–208.

O'CONNELL, J. E. A. (1959). "Intervertebral disc protrusions in childhood and adolescence." *Brit. J. Surg.*, **47:** 611–616.

OROFINO, C., SHERMAN, M. S. & SCHECHTER, D. (1960). "Luschka's joint – a degenerative phenomenon." *J. Bone Joint Surg.*, **42A:** 853–858.

PARRELLA, G. S. & ZOVICKIAN, A. (1950). "The ruptured intervertebral disc problem in the veteran." *Surgery*, **27:** 762–769.

PATERSON, J. E. & GRAY, W. (1951–52). "Herniated nucleus pulposus: the free fragment." *Brit. J. Surg.*, **39:** 509–513.

PECK, F. C. (1957). "A calcified thoracic intervertebral disk with herniation and spinal cord compression in a child." *J. Neurosurg.*, **14:** 105–109.

PENNYBACKER, J. (1968). "Lumbar disc protrusions." *Hosp. Med.*, (June): 1088–1095.

POHL, W. & KRANZLEIN, H. G. (1973). "Benign sclerosing spondylitis." *Fortschr. Röntgenstr.*, **119:** 352–357.

PRIDIE, K. H. (1949). "Prolapse of the intervertebral disc." *J. Bone Joint Surg.*, **31B**: 142.

RANIERI, L. & TRAINA, G. C. (1970). "Lumbar pain in the young: aetiopathological considerations." *Chir. Org. Mov.*, **59**: 121–131.

RANIERI, L. & TRAINA, G. C. (1972). "Correlation between metaphyseal chondropathy and growth: Scheuermann's disease and epiphysolysis." *Chir. Org. Mov.*, **60**: 203–219.

REEVES, D. L. & BROWN, H. A. (1968). "Thoracic intervertebral disc protrusion with spinal cord compression." *J. Neurosurg.*, **28**: 242.

RENGACHARY, S. S., MURPHY, D. & KEPES, M. (1973). "Spondylitic cord compression with focal destructive vertebral lesions." *J. Kansas Med. Soc.*, **74**: 82–84.

ROBINSON, R. G. (1965). "Massive protrusions of lumbar disks." *Brit. J. Surg.*, **52**: 858–865.

ROSENBERG, J. N. (1975). "Degenerative spondylolisthesis: predisposing factors." *J. Bone Joint Surg.*, **57A**: 467–474.

ROTHMAN, R. H. (1973). "The pathophysiology of disc degeneration." *Clin. Neurosurg.*, **20**: 174–182.

ROVIG, G. (1949–50). "Rupture of lumbar discs with intraspinal protrusions of the nucleus pulposus." *Acta Chir., Scand.*, **99**: (Suppl. 144): 175–180.

RUGTVEIT, A. (1966). "Juvenile lumbar disc herniations." *Acta Orthop. Scand.*, **37**: 348–358.

RYALL, R. G. (1964). "Multiple lumbar disc protrusions." *Proc. Roy. Soc. Med.*, **57**: 329.

SASHIN, D. (1931). "Intervertebral disk extensions into the vertebral bodies and the spinal canal." *Arch. Surg.*, **22**: 527–547.

SCHUMACHER, G. H., WETSTEIN, V. & FANGHABEL, J. (1971). "The anatomy of ageing of the vertebral bodies. I. Spondylitis deformans, costovertebral hyperostosis." *Zeit. Ärzt. Fortbild.*, **65**: 278–284.

SCOVILLE, W. B. & CORKILL, G. (1974). "Lumbar spondylolisthesis and ruptured disc." *J. Neurosurg.*, **40**: 529–534.

SCUDERI, C. (1956). "Herniated lumbar intervertebral disks: an 8-year survey." *Amer. J. Surg.*, **91**: 481–483.

SEBO, M., SMAJ, S. & SCHULTZ, P. (1974). "Osteoarthrosis and degeneration of discs in our rural population." *Fysiatr. Rheumatol.*, **52**: 65–75.

SEMMES, R. E. & MURPHEY, F. (1941). "The syndrome of unilateral rupture of the 6th cervical intervertebral disc with compression of the 7th cervical nerve root. Report of 4 cases simulating coronary disease." *J. Amer. Med. Ass.*, **121**:1209–1214.

SEMMES, R. E. & MURPHEY, F. (1954). "Ruptured intervertebral disks: cervical, thoracic and lumbar, lateral and central." *Surg. Clin. Nth. Amer.*, **34**: 1095–1111.

SEVERIN, E. (1943). "Degeneration of the intervertebral disks in the lumbar region: a clinicoroentgenologic study." *Acta Chir. Scand.*, **89**: 353–378.

SHARR, M. M., GARFIELD, J. S. & JENKINS, J. D. (1973). "The association of bladder dysfunction with degenerative lumbar spondylosis." *Brit. J. Urol.*, **45**: 616–620.

SILBERSTEIN, C. E. (1965). "The evolution of degenerative changes in the cervical spine and an investigation into the joints of Luschka." *Clin. Orthop.*, **40**: 184–204.

SIMMONS, E. H. (1975). "Discography: localisation of symptomatic levels." *J. Bone Joint Surg.*, **57B**: 261.

SKALPE, I. O. (1972). "Disturbances of bladder function in lumbar disc syndromes." *J. Oslo City Hospital*, **22**: 135–140.

SLATER, R. A. & PORTER, R. W. (1965). "Intradural herniation of lumbar intervertebral discs." *Arch. Surg.*, **90**: 266–269.

SODERBERG, L. & ANDREN, L. (1955–56). "Disc degeneration and lumbago-sciatica." *Acta Orthop. Scand.*, **25**: 137–148.

SPARUP, K. H. (1960). "Late prognosis in lumbar disc herniation: an investigation of the clinical importance of the degenerative disc on the basis of 1,026 patients having the lumbago-sciatica syndrome." *Acta Rheum. Scand.*, (Suppl. 3): 1.

SPURLING, R. G. & BRADFORD, F. (1939). "Neurologic aspects of herniated nucleus pulposus at fourth and fifth lumbar interspaces." *J. Amer. Med. Assoc.*, **113**: 2019–2022.

SPURLING, R. G. & GRANTHAM, E. D. (1940). "Neurologic pictures of herniations of the nucleus pulposus in the lower part of the lumbar region." *Arch. Surg.*, **40**: 375–388.

SUTRO, C. J. (1970). "Posterior paravertebral ossification in the cervical region in a Caucasian patient." *Bull. Hosp. Joint Dis.*, **31**: 111–113.

SUTTON, T. J. & TURCOTTE, B. (1973). "Posterior herniation of calcified intervertebral discs in children." *J. Canad. Ass. Radiol.*, **24**: 131–136.

TAYLOR, T. K. F. (1971). "Intervertebral disc prolapse in children and adolescents." *J. Bone Joint Surg.*, **53B:** 357.

TENG, P. & PAPATHEODOROU, C. (1963). "Lumbar spondylosis with compression of cauda equina." *Arch. Neurol.*, **8:** 221–229.

TENG, P. & PAPATHEODOROU, C. (1963). "Myelographic findings in spondylosis of the lumbar spine." *Brit. J. Radiol.*, **36:** 122–128.

TÖNNIS, D. (1970). "Degenerative changes in the iliosacral joints: their symptomatology and treatment." *Beitr. Orthop. Traumat.*, **17:** 680–682.

TOVI, D. & STRANG, R. R. (1960). "Thoracic intervertebral disk protrusions." *Acta Clin. Scand. Suppl.* **267:** p. 1.

TREVOR-JONES, R. (1970). "Spondylosis of the cervical spine." *Sth. Afr. Med. J.*, **44:** 752–756.

VERNON-ROBERTS, B., PIRIE, C. J. & TRENWITH, V. (1974). "Pathology of the thoracic spine in ankylosing hyperostosis." *Ann. Rheum. Dis.*, **33:** 281–288.

WARIS, W. (1948). "Lumbar disc herniation: clinical studies and late results of 374 cases of sciatica operated on the diagnosis of suspicion of lumbar disc hernia." *Acta Chir. Scand., Suppl.* **140:** p. 1.

WILLIAMS, R. (1954). "Complete protrusion of a calcified nucleus pulposus in the thoracic spine." *J. Bone Joint Surg.*, **36B:** 597–600.

WILSON, J. C. (1960). "Degenerative arthritis of lumbar intervertebral joints." *Ann. Surg.*, **100:** 313–322.

WILSON, J. N. (1949). "Prolapsed intervertebral disk after lumbar puncture." *Brit. Med. J.*, **2:** 1334–1335.

WILTSE, L. L. (1971). "The effect of the common anomalies of the lumbar spine upon disc degeneration and low back pain." *Orthop. Clinics.* **2:** 569–582.

WOLSON, A. H. (1975). "Upper lobe fibrosis in ankylosing spondylitis." *Amer. J. Roentgenol.*, **124:** 466–471.

ZARSKI, S. & DZIFUDZKO, J. (1972). "The value of vibration sense testing in the diagnosis and localisation of nucleus pulposus protrusion." *Neurol. Neurochir. Pol.*, **6:** 453–460.

ZARSKI, S. & DZIDUSZKO, J. (1972). "The mechanism of disturbances of vibratory sensation in nucleus pulposus protrusion." *Neurol. Neurochir. Pol.*, **6:** 595–600.

ZARSKI, S., DZIDUSZKO, J., ZBRODOWSKI, A. & LEO, W. (1972).

"Studies on radiculo-discal metameric relations in the lumbar spine." *Neurol. Neurochir. Pol.*, **6:** 589–593.

ZIMMERMAN, H. B. & FARRELL, W. J. (1970). "Cervical vertebral erosion caused by vertebral artery tortuosity." *Amer. J. Roentgenol.*, **108:** 767–770.


## *(e) Infection and Inflammation (Suppurative and Non-suppurative)*

AILSBY, R. L. (1974). "Pyogenic infections of the sacroiliac joint in children: radioisotope bone scanning as a diagnostic tool." *Clin. Orthop.*, **100:** 96–100.

ALEXANDER, C. J. (1970). "The aetiology of juvenile spondyloarthritis (discitis)." *Clin. Radiol.*, **21:** 178–187.

ALVIK, I. (1949). "Tuberculosis of the spine. I. and II. The mobility of the lumbar spine after tuberculous spondylitis." *Acta Chir. Scand.* (Suppl. **41**): 1.

ANDERSON, I. F. (1974). "Trial of a new antirheumatic agent." *Sth. Afr. Med. J.*, **48:** 899–903.

ANDERSON, I. F., CORRIGAN, A. B. & CHAMPION, G. D. (1972). "Rib erosions in rheumatoid arthritis." *Ann. Rheum. Dis.*, **31:** 16–21.

ANDERSON, J. A. D., DUTHIE, J. J. R. & MOODY, B. P. (1972). "Rheumatic diseases affecting men registered as disabled." *Ann. Rheum. Dis.*, **22:** 188–193.

ARCT, W. A. (1974). "Intraspinal tuberculous abscess imitating disc prolapse with compression of L5 and S1 nerve roots." *Arch. Orthop. Unfall-Chir.*, **80:** 13–19.

AUTIO, E., SUOLANEN, J., NORBACK, S. & SLATIS, P. (1972). "Adhesive arachnoiditis after lumbar myelography with meglumine iothalamate (Conray)." *Acta Radiol. (Diagn.)*, **12:** 17–24.

BAILEY, H. L., GABRIEL, M., HODGSON, A. R. & SHIN, J. S. (1972). "Tuberculosis of the spine in children." *J. Bone Joint Surg.*, **54A:** 1633–1657.

BAKALIM, G. (1966). "Results of radical evacuation and arthrodesis in sacro-iliac tuberculosis." *Acta Orth. Scand.*, **37:** 375–386.

BALASUBRAMIAM, P. (1973). "Case of cryptococcus of the spine." *Brit. Med. J.*, **2:** 27–28.

BALDWIN, D. M. (1974). "Vertebral sarcoidosis." *J. Bone Joint Surg.*, **56A:** 629–632.

BALL, J. (1970). "Rheumatoid and ankylosing spondylitis." *Ann. Rheum. Dis.*, **30:** 213–223.

BARRINGTON, T. W. (1973). "Cervical disc space infection." *J. Bone Joint Surg.*, **55B:** 232.

BELL, D. & COCKSHOTT, W. P. (1972). "Tuberculosis of the vertebral pedicles." *Radiol.*, **99:** 43–48.

BHALLA, S. K. (1970). "Metastatic disease of the spine." *Clin. Orthop.*, **73:** 52–60.

BLEASEL, K. (1973). "Cervical spondylitic myelopathy." *Proc. Aust. Ass. Neurol.*, **9:** 213–218.

BLÉCOURT, J. J. DE (1973). "533 patients with ankylosing spondylitis seen and followed in the period 1948–1971." *Ann Rheum. Dis.*, **32:** 383–385.

BOYLE, A. C. (1971). "The rheumatoid neck." *Proc. Roy. Soc. Med.*, **64:** 1161–1165.

BRYAN, G., FRANKS, L. & TORRES, H. (1973). "*Pseudomonas aeruginosa* cervical diskitis with chondro-osteomyelitis in an intravenous drug abuser." *Surg. Neurol.*, **1:** 142–144.

BUNCH, T. W. (1973). "Ankylosing spondylitis and primary hyperparathyroidism." *J. Amer. Med. Ass.*, **225:** 1108–1109.

BUTLER, R. W. (1955). "Nature and significance of vertebral osteochondritis." *Proc. Roy. Soc. Med.*, **48:** 895–902.

CAVE, A. J. E., GRIFFITHS, J. D. & WHITELEY, M. M. (1955). "Osteoarthritis deformans of the Luschka joints." *Lancet*, **2:** 176–179.

CHUNG, S. M. K. & BORNS, P. (1973). "Acute osteomyelitis adjacent to the sacroiliac joint in children: report of 2 cases." *J. Bone Joint Surg.*, **55A:** 630–634.

CLINICOPATHOLOGICAL CONFERENCE (1968). "A case of early ankylosing spondylitis with fatal secondary amyloidosis." *Brit. Med. J.*, **2:** 412–416.

COCKERELL, A. (1972). "Brucella infection of the spine." *J. Bone Joint Surg.*, **54B:** 558.

COSH, J. A. (1973). "Cardiac lesions of Reiter's syndrome and ankylosing spondylitis." *Brit. Heart J.*, **35:** 553.

COSH, J. A. (1975). "Cardiac lesions in Reiter's syndrome and ankylosing spondylitis." *Ann. Rheum. Dis.*, **34:** 195.

CROMPTON, G. K. (1974). "Pulmonary fibrosis, pulmonary tuberculosis and ankylosing spondylitis." *Brit. J. Dis. Chest*, **68:** 51–56.

DAVIES, D. (1972). "Ankylosing spondylitis and lung fibrosis." *Quart. J. Med.*, **41**: 395–417.

DAVIS, P. (1974). "Tuberculous arthropathy." *Proc. Roy. Soc. Med.*, **67**: 217–218.

DJUPESLAND, G. (1973). "Hearing and middle-ear function in patients with inflammatory rheumatoid joint diseases." *Scand. J. Rheumatol.*, **2**: 153–156.

DUKE, R. J. & HASHIMOTO, S. A. (1974). "Familial spinal arachnoiditis." *Arch. Neurol.*, **30**: 300–303.

DUNHAM, W. F. (1949). "Ankylosing spondylitis—measurement of hip and spine movements." *Brit. J. Phys. Med.*, 126–129.

EDGAR, M. A. (1973). "Post-radiation sarcoma in ankylosing spondylitis." *J. Bone Joint Surg.*, **55B**: 183–188.

EDGAR, M. A. (1974). "Nervous system involvement in ankylosing spondylitis." *Brit. Med. J.*, **1**: 394.

FALLET, G. H., MEYER, G., OTT, H. & RADI, I. (1970). "Familial co-existence of chronic rheumatismal inflammatory psycarthropathies with involvement of the sacro-iliac joints." *Rev. Rheum.*, **37**: 213–224.

FEASBY, T. E. (1975). "Isolated spinal cord arteritis." *Can. J. Neurol. Sci.*, **2**: 143–146.

FERRANNINI, E. (1975). "Suppurative spondylitis with pelvic abscess: localisation by 67-gallium scanning." *J. Nucl. Biol. Med.*, **19**: 39–44.

FITZPATRICK, S. C. (1965). "Hydatid disease of the lumbar vertebrae." *J. Bone Joint Surg.*, **47B**: 286–291.

FRASER, R. A. R., RATZAN, K., WOLPERT, S. M. & WEINSTEIN, L. (1973). "Spinal subdural empyema.' *Arch. Neurol.*, **28**: 235–238.

GACAD, G. (1974). "Pulmonary fibrosis and group IV mycobacteria infection of the lungs in ankylosing spondylitis." *Ann. Rev. Resp. Dis.*, **110**: 274–278.

GACAD, G. & HAMOSH, P. (1973). "The lung in ankylosing spondylitis." *Ann. Rev. Resp. Dis.*, **109**: 286–289.

GHOSE, T. (1975). "Immunopathological changes in rheumatoid arthritis and other joint diseases." *J. Clin. Path.*, **28**: 109–117.

GIESE, R. (1951). "Clinical study of ileosacral tuberculosis." *Zentralbl. für Chirurg.*, **76**: 1105–1115.

GINSBERG, S., GROSS, E. & FEIRING, E. H. (1967). "The neurological complications of tuberculous spondylitis." *Arch. Neurol.*, **16**: 265.

GOFTON, J. P., BENNETT, P. H., SMYTHE, H. A. & DECKER, J. L. (1972). "Sacro-iliitis and ankylosing spondylitis in North American Indians." *Ann. Rheum. Dis.*, **31**: 474–481.

GOFTON, J. P., LAWRENCE, J. S., BENNETT, P. H. & BURCH, T. (1966). "Sacro-iliitis in eight populations." *Ann. Rheum. Dis.*, **25**: 528–533.

GOLDBERG, D. (1974). "Cervical radiculitis." *J. Amer. Med. Ass.*, **230**: 374.

GOLDIE, I. & RYBA, W. (1971). "Non-specific spondylitis in children." *Clin. Orthop.*, **79**: 89–95.

GOLDING, D. N. (1973). "Haematology and biochemistry of ankylosing spondylitis." *Brit. Med. J.*, **2**: 663.

GOLDMAN, A. L. (1975). "Anterior cervical infections: Complications of transtracheal aspirations." *Ann. Rev. Respir. Dis.*, **111**: 707–708.

GOOD, A. E. (1967). "Non-traumatic fracture of the thoracic spine in ankylosing spondylitis." *Arth. Rheum.*, **10**: 467–469.

GORDON, A. L. & YUDELL, A. (1973). "Cauda equina lesion associated with rheumatoid spondylitis." *Ann. Intern. Med.*, **78**: 555–557.

GORDON, D. A. (1973). "Ankylosing spondylitis." *Ann. Intern. Med.*, **79**: 139–140.

GRAHAM, A. R. & DEWEY, P. (1972). "Osteomyelitis of the spinous process." *Med. J. Aust.*, **1**: 816–817.

GRAVES, V. B. & SCHREIBER, M. H. (1973). "Tuberculous psoas muscle abscess." *J. Ass. Canad. Radiol.*, **24**: 268–271.

GREEN, W. T. & BANKS, H. H. (1973). "Osteochondritis dissecans in children." *J. Bone Joint Surg.*, **35A**: 26–47.

GRIBBLE, L. D. (1972). "Syphilitic spinal pachymeningitis." *Sth. Afr. Med. J.*, **46**: 1326–1328.

GRIECO, M. H. (1972). "Pseudomonas arthritis and osteomyelitis." *J. Bone Joint Surg.*, **54A**: 1693–1704.

GRIFFITHS, H. E. D. & JONES, D. M. (1971). "Pyogenic infection of the spine: a review of 23 cases." *J. Bone Joint Surg.*, **53B**: 383–391.

GROLLMUS, J., PERKINS, R. K. & RUSSELL, W. (1974). "Erythrocyte sedimentation rate as a possible indicator of early disc space infection." *Neurochirurgia*, **17**: 30–35.

GROSSMAN, M. (1975). "Aspergillosis of bone." *Brit. J. Radiol.*, **48**: 57–59.

GUMPEL, J. M. (1974). "Ankylosing spondylitis." *Nurs. Times*, **70:** 1308–1310.

GUNTHER, L. & SAMPSON, J. J. (1929). "The radicular syndrome in hypertrophic osteoarthritis of the spine." *J. Amer. Med. Ass.*, **17:** 514–517.

GURI, J. P. (1946). "Pyogenic osteomyelitis of the spine." *J. Bone Joint Surg.*, **28A:** 29–30.

HAGADORN, B., SMITH, H. W. & ROSNAGLE, R. S. (1972). "Cervical spine osteomyelitis secondary to a foreign body in the hypopharynx." *Arch. Otolaryngol.*, **95:** 578–580.

HALE, J. E. (1974). "Vertebral osteomyelitis: a complication of urological surgery." *Brit. J. Surg.*, **61:** 867–872.

HANNUKSELA, M. & KARAHARJU, E. O. (1972). "Syphilis of the spine." *Brit. J, Vener. Dis.*, **48:** 397–399.

HARRIS, J. (1973). "Hand measurements in ankylosing spondylitis." *Ann. Rheum. Dis.*, **32:** 140–142.

HARRISON, M. H. M., SCHAJOWITZ, F. & TRUETA, J. (1953). "Osteoarthritis of the hip: a study of the nature and evolution of the disease." *J. Bone Joint Surg.*, **35B:** 598–626.

HART, F. D. (1955). "Ankylosing spondylitis—a review of 184 cases." *Ann. Rheum. Dis.*, **14:** 77–82.

HART, F. D. (1968). "Ankylosing spondylitis." *Lancet*, **2:** 1340–1344.

HART, G. M. (1958). "Circumscribed serous spinal arachnoiditis simulating protruded lumbar intervertebral disc." *Ann. Surg.*, **148:** 266–270.

HASLOCK, I. (1973). "Arthritis and Crohn's disease: a family study." *Ann. Rheum. Dis.*, **32:** 479.

HAUGE, B. N. (1973). "Diaphragmatic movement and spirometric volume in patients with ankylosing spondylitis." *Scand. J. Resp. Dis.*, **54:** 38–44.

HAVELKA, S., BARTUNKOVA, V., STREDA, A. & KUBANKOVA, V. (1973). "Bone indexes and cortical thickness in assessing osteoporosis in rheumatic patients." *Scand. J. Rheumatol.*, **2:** 57–60.

HEALD, C. B. (1951). "The nature and treatment of fibrositis: intensive study of 200 cases." *Trans. Med. Soc., Lond.*, **67:** 175–193.

HEINDEL, C. C., FERGUSON, J. P. I. & KUMARASAMY, T. (1974). "Spinal subdural empyema complicating pregnancy: case report." *J. Neurosurg.*, **40:** 654–656.

HENRY, M. O. (1972). "Tuberculosis of the fifth lumbar vertebra with spina bifida occulta: spinal fusion and cure." *J. Bone Joint Surg.*, **14A:** 690–692.

HICKLIN, J. A. (1968). "Erosive vertebral disease in ankylosing spondylitis." *Ann. Phys. Med.*, **9:** 206.

HIRSON, C. (1965). "Spinal subdural abscess." *Lancet,* **2:** 1215–1217.

HIRT, H. R., ZDROJEWSKI, B. & WEBER, G. (1972). "The manifestations and complications of intra-spinal congenital dermal sinuses and dermoid cysts." *Neuropädiatrie,* **3:** 231–247.

HOMBAL, J. (1971). "Osteomyelitis of the spine." *J. Bone Joint Surg.*, **53B:** 557.

HOPKYNS, J. C. W. (1948). "Unusual trophic ulcer." *Brit. Med. J.*, 905.

HORNINGE, H. (1972). "Discitis in children." *Arch. Chir. Neurol.*, **24:** 215–221.

HUGHES, G. R. V. & WHALEY, K. (1972). "Sjögren's syndrome." *Brit. Med. J.*, **4:** 533–536.

IRSTAM, L. (1974). "Lumbar myelography and adhesive arachnoiditis." *Acta Radiol.*, **15:** 356–368.

JENNY, A. B., LEHMAN, R. A. W. & SCHWARTZ, H. G. (1973). "Tuberculous infection of the cervical spine: case report." *J. Neurosurg.*, **38:** 362–365.

JOHNS, D. L. (1970). "Syphilitic disorders of the spine: report of two cases." *J. Bone Joint Surg.*, **52B:** 724–731.

JONES, S. R. (1973). Bacterial meningitis complicating cranial-spinal trauma." *J. Trauma*, **13:** 895–900.

JUNGE, H. (1973). "Spondylitis infectiosa artificialis." *Arch. Orthop. Unfall-Chir.*, **75:** 187–201.

KADRI, N. (1973). "Cervical spondylitis." *Paediatr. Indones.*, **13:** 135–144.

KARAHARJU, E. O. & HANNUKSELA, M. (1973). "Possible syphilitic spondylitis." *Acta Orthop. Scand.*, **44:** 289–295.

KAUFMAN, H. E. (1974). "Genetic inflammatory disease." *Invest. Ophthalmol.* **13:** 555–556.

KEENAN, J. D. & MET, C. W. (1972). "Brucella spondylitis: a brief review and case report." *Clin. Orthop.*, **82:** 87–91.

KELLGREN, J. H. & LAWRENCE, J. S. (1956). "Rheumatoid arthritis in a population sample." *Ann. Rheum Dis.*, **15:** 2a–11.

265

KEMP, G. B. S., JACKSON, J. W., JEREMIAH, J. D. & HALL, A. J. (1973). "Pyogenic infections occurring primarily in intervertebral discs." *J. Bone Joint Surg.*, **55B:** 698–714.

KEMP, G. B. S. & WORLAND, J. (1974). "Infections of the spine." *Physiotherapy*, **60:** 2–6.

KEMP, H. (1976). "Tuberculosis of the spine." *Brit. J. Hosp. Med.*, **15:** 39–48.

KENDALL, M. J. (1973). "Serum immunoglobulins in ankylosing spondylitis." *Brit. Med. J.*, **3:** 172.

KENDALL, M. J. (1973). "Synovial fluid in ankylosing spondylitis." *Ann. Rheum. Dis.*, **32:** 487–492.

KENDALL, M. J., LAWRENCE, D. S., SHUTTLEWORTH, G. R. & WHITFIELD, A. G. W. (1973). "Haematology and biochemistry of ankylosing spondylitis." *Brit. Med. J.*, **2:** 235–237.

KENNEDY, W. P. (1972). "Two unusual organisms, Aspergillus terrens and Metschnikowia pulchemina associated with the lung disease of ankylosing spondylitis." *Thorax*, **27:** 604–610.

KEON-COHEN, B. T. (1968). "Epidural abscess simulating disc hernia." *J. Bone Joint Surg.*, **50B:** 128–130.

KHOO, B. H. (1975). "Cervical lymphadenitis due to Candida albicans infection 920c." *J. Pediatr.*, **86:** 812–813.

KILLEBREW, K. (1973). "Psoriatic spondylitis." *Radiology*, **108:** 9–16.

KING, D. M. & MAYO, K. M. (1973). "Infective lesions of the vertebral column." *Clin. Orthop.*, **96:** 248–253.

KOLCZUN, M., WILDE, A. H. & GILDENBERG, P. (1973). "Tuberculosis of the first cervical vertebra." *Clin. Orthop.*, **90:** 116–118.

KROGHDAHL, T. & TORGERSON, O. (1940). "Arthritis deformans of the intervertebral joints in the cervical spine." *Acta Radiol.*, **21:** 231–262.

LADD, J. R., CASSIDY, J. T. & MARTEL, W. (1971). "Juvenile ankylosing spondylitis." *Arthritis Rheum.*, **14:** 579–590.

LAMB, T. W. (1954). "Localised osteochondritis of the lumbar spine." *J. Bone Joint Surg.*, **36B:** 591–596.

LANCET (Editorial) (1959). "Sacro-iliac arthritis." *Lancet*, **2:** 1073.

LANCET (Editorial) (1973). "Cervical spine involvement in rheumatoid arthritis." *Lancet*, **1:** 586–587.

LANCET (Editorial) (1973). "Ankylosing spondylitis and the HL-A antigen, W. 27." *Lancet*, **1:** 921–922.

LANE, W. A. (1886). "The causation and pathology of the so-called disease rheumatoid arthritis and of senile changes." *Trans. Path. Soc. Lond.*, **37**: 387–447.

LANGLAND, N. & ROAAS, A. (1971). "Spondylitis psoriatica." *Acta Orthop. Scand.*, **42**: 391–396.

LAWRENCE, J. S. (1974). "Family survey of Reiter's disease." *Brit. J. Vener. Dis.*, **50**: 140–145.

LAWRENCE, J. S., SHARP, J., BAU, J. & BIER, F. (1964). "Rheumatoid arthritis of the lumbar spine." *Ann. Rheum. Dis.*, **23**: 205–217.

LEWIN, T. (1964). "Osteoarthritis in lumbar synovial joints." *Acta Orthop. Scand.*, (Suppl. **73**): 1.

LEWIS, R., GORBACH, S. & ALTNER, P. (1972). "Spinal pseudomonas chondro-osteomyelitis in heroin users." *New Engl. J. Med.*, **286**: 1303.

LEACH, R. E. (1967). "Osteomyelitis of the odontoid process." *J. Bone Joint Surg.*, **49A**: 369–371.

LIPSON, R. L. & SLOCUMB, C. H. (1965). "The progressive nature of gout with inadequate therapy." *Arthr. Rheumat.*, **8**: 80–87.

LITTLE, H., UROWITZ, M. B., SMYTHE, H. A. & ROSEN, P. S. (1974). "Asymptomatic spondylitis—an unusual feature of ankylosing spondylitis." *Arthr. Rheumat.*, **17**: 487–493.

McBRYDE, A. M. & McCOLLUM, D. E. (1973). "Ankylosing spondylitis in women: the disease and its prognosis." *North Carolina Med. J.*, **34**: 34–37.

McCONKEY, B., FRASER, G. M. & BLIGHT, A. S. (1962). "Osteoporosis and purpura in rheumatoid disease: Prevalence and relation to treatment with corticosteroids." *Quart. J. Med.*, **31**: 419–427.

McEWEN, C., DiTATA, D., LINGG, G., PORINI, A., GOOD, A., & RANKIN, T. (1972). "Ankylosing spondylitis and spondylitis accompanying ulcerative colitis, regional enteritis, psoriasis and Reiter's disease." *Arth. Rheumat.*, **14**: 291–318.

MACRAE, I. F. & WRIGHT, V. (1970). "Ulcerative colitis and sacroiliitis: a family study." *Ann. Rheum. Dis.*, **29**: 559–560.

MACRAE, I. F. & WRIGHT, V. (1973). "A family study of ulcerative colitis, with particular reference to ankylosing spondylitis and sacroiliitis." *Ann. Rheum. Dis.*, **32**: 16–20.

MAIYA, M., PATIL, C. K. & VIRUPANNAVAR, C. M. (1972). "A case of disseminated primary tuberculosis: case report." *J. Assoc. Phys. India*, **20**: 723–725.

MALAWSKI, S. (1973). "Septic spondylitis." *Chir. Narzad. Ruchu. Ortop. Pol.* **38:** 701–709.

MALAWISTA, S. E., SEEGMILLER, J. E., HATHAWAY, B. E. & SOKOLOFF, L. (1965). "Sacro-iliac gout." *J. Amer. Med. Ass.*, **194:** 954–956.

MANTLE, J. A. (1959). "Non-tuberculous infections of the spine." In *Modern Trends in Diseases of the Vertebral Column*, pp. 142–154. Ed. by R. Nassim and H. J. Burrows. London, Butterworth.

MARTIN, N. S. (1970). "Tuberculosis of the spine." *J. Bone Joint Surg.*, **52B:** 613–628.

MASON, R. M., MURRAY, R. S., OATES, J. K. & YOUNG, A. C. (1958). "Prostatitis and ankylosing spondylitis." *Brit. Med. J.*, **1:** 748–751.

MATHEWS, J. A. (1974). "Atlanto-axial subluxation in rheumatoid arthritis: a 5 year follow-up study." *Ann. Rheum. Dis.*, **33:** 526–531.

MATTHEWS, W. B. (1974). "Cauda equina syndrome in ankylosing spondylitis." *Brit. Med. J.*, **1:** 517.

MEDSGER, T. A. (1974). "HL-A antigen 27 and psoriatic spondylitis." *Arthr. Rheumat.*, **17:** 323.

MEIKLE, J. A. & WILKINSON, M. (1971). "Rheumatoid involvement of the cervical spine. Radiological assessment." *Ann. Rheum. Dis.*, **30:** 154–161.

MENDELSON, J. (1974). "Meningococcal meningitis: an atypical case." *Can. Med. Ass. J.*, **111:** 549–550.

MENELAUS, M. B. (1964). "Discitis—an inflammation affecting the intervertebral discs in children." *J. Bone Joint Surg.*, **46B:** 16–23.

MILES, J. & BHANDARI, Y. S. (1971). "Ossifying spinal arachnoiditis." *Neurochirurgica*, **14:** 184–188.

MILLS, D. M. (1975). "HL-A antigens and sacroiliitis." *J. Amer. Med. Ass.*, **231:** 268–270.

MOFFAT, N. A. (1973). "Spondylitis following urinary tract instrumentation." *J. Urol.*, **110:** 339.

MOLL, J. M. (1973). "Ankylosing spondylitis." *Nurs. Times*, **69:** 985–988.

MOLL, J. M. (1974). "Psoriatic spondylitis: clinical radiological and familial aspects." *Proc. Roy. Soc. Med.*, **67:** 47–50.

MONTORSI, W., MORISI, M. & TERRAGNI, R. (1974). "Intervertebral meniscitis complicating laminectomy for lumbar disc herniation." *Minverva Chir.*, **29:** 201–207.

MUELLER, C. E., SEEGER, J. F. & MARTEL, W. (1974). "Ankylosing spondylitis and regional enteritis." *Radiology*, **112**: 579–581.

NAGRATH, S. P. (1974). "Tuberculosis of the spine: a diagnostic conundrum." *J. Assoc. Physicians India*, **22**: 405–407.

NATVIG, J. B. (1974). "Studies on the immunopathology of rheumatoid inflammatory joint tissue." *Acta. Pathol. Microbiol. Scand.*, (Suppl. **248**): 145–151.

NEUMANN, J. L. (1974). "Retropharyngeal abscess as the presenting feature of tuberculosis of the cervical spine." *Ann. Rev. Respir. Dis.*, **110**: 508–511.

NYUL-TOTH, P. & JOOS, M. (1974). "The vertebral manifestations of fibrous dysplasia." *Fortschr. Röntgenstr.*, **120**: 744–747.

OATES, J. K. (1958). "Sacro-iliitis in Reiter's disease." *Brit. J. Vener. Dis.*, **34**: 177–180.

OATES, J. K. & YOUNG, A. C. (1959). "Sacro-iliitis in Reiter's disease." *Brit. Med. J.*, 1013.

O'CONNELL, C. J. (1973). "Osteomyelitis of the cervical spine: candida guilliermondii." *Ann. Intern. Med.*, **79**: 748.

OSGOOD, C. P. (1975). "Multiple spine fractures in ankylosing spondylitis." *J. Trauma*, **15**: 163–166.

OSGOOD, C. P., MARTIN, L. G. & ACKERMAN, E. (1973). "Fracture dislocation of the cervical spine with ankylosing spondylitis: report of 2 cases." *J. Neurosurg.*, **39**: 764–769.

PAPATHANASSIOU, B. T., PAPACHRISTOU, G. & HARTOFILAKIDIS-GAROFILIDIS, G. (1972). "Brucellar spondylitis: report of 6 cases." *Acta Orthop. Scand.*, **43**: 384–391.

PARONEN, I. (1948). "Reiter's disease: a study of 344 cases in Finland." *Acta. Med. Scand.*, **131** (Suppl. **212**): 1.

PARTRIDGE, R. E. H. & KNOX, J. D. E. (1969). "Rheumatic complaints in general practice." *J. Roy. Coll. Gen. Pract.*, **17**: 144–154.

PAUS, B. (1973). "Tumour, tuberculosis and osteomyelitis of the spine: differential diagnostic aspects." *Acta. Orthop. Scand.*, **44**: 372–382.

PEARSON, C. M. (1969). "Polymyositis and related disorders." In *Disorders of Voluntary Muscle*, 2nd Ed. pp. 501–539. Ed. by J. N. Walton, London; Churchill.

PEARSON, C. M. & ROSE, A. S. (1961). "Myositis: the inflammatory disorders of muscle." *Res. Pub. Assoc. Nerv. Ment. Dis.*, **38**: 422–478.

PEPPER, H. W. (1973). "Extrapleural mass with neurologic signs." *Chest*, **64**: 345–346.

PILGAARD, S. (1973). "Discitis after lumbar disc prolapse surgery (closed space infection)." *Ugeskr. Laeger*, **135**: 1529–1530.

PILGAARD, S. & AARHUS, N. (1969). "Discitis (closed space infection) following removal of lumbar intervertebral disc." *J. Bone Joint Surg.*, **51A**: 713–716.

POHL, W. & KRANZLEIN, H. G. (1973). "Benign sclerosing spondylitis." *Fortschr. Röntgenstr.*, **119**: 352–357.

RANA, N. A., HANCOCK, D. O., TAYLOR, A. R. & HILL, A. G. S. (1973). "Upward translocation of the dens in rheumatoid arthritis." *J. Bone Joint Surg.*, **55B**: 471–477.

RANAWAT, N. S. & RIVELIS, M. (1972). "Strontium 85 scintimetry in ankylosing spondylitis." *J. Amer. Med. Ass.*, **222**: 553–558.

RANSFORD, A. O. & HARRIES, B. J. (1972). "Localised arachnoiditis complicating lumbar disc lesions." *J. Bone Joint Surg.*, **54B**: 656–665.

RAPP, G. F. & KERNEK, C. B. (1974). "Spontaneous fracture of the lumbar spine with correction of deformity in ankylosing spondylitis." *J. Bone Joint Surg.*, **56A**: 1277–1278.

REDISCH, W., MESSINA, E. J., HUGHES, G. & McEWEN, C. (1970). "Capillaroscopic observations in rheumatic diseases." *Ann. Rheum. Dis.*, **29**: 244–253.

RENGACHARY, S. S., MURPHY, D. & KEPES, M. (1973). "Spondylitic cord compression with focal destructive vertebral lesions." *J. Kansas Med. Soc.*, **74**: 82–84.

RESNICK, D. (1974). "Temporomandibular joint involvement in ankylosing spondylitis; comparison with rheumatoid arthritis and psoriasis." *Radiology*, **112**: 587–591.

REYNOLDS, M. D. (1974). "Diagnosis of 'rheumatoid variants': ankylosing spondylitis, the arthritides of gastrointestinal diseases and psoriasis, and Reiter's syndrome." *West. J. Med.*, **120**: 441–447.

RICE, D. H. (1975). "Sclerosing cervicitis: homologue of sclerosing retroperitonitis and mediastinitis." *Arch. Surg.*, **110**: 120–122.

RICHARDS, A. J. (1974). "Ankylosing spondylitis and pulmonary apical fibrosis." *Proc. Roy. Soc. Med.*, **67**: 45–46.

RICHARDS, A. J. (1975). "Osteitis condensans ilii." *Lancet*, **1**: 812:

RIFFAT, G., DOMENACH, M., FAYARD, J. & PICANO, C. (1970).

"Infectious spondylitis: a series of 12 cases." *J. Méd. Lyon*, **51:** 1779–1797.

RILEY, M. J., ANSELL, B. M. & BYWATERS, E. G. (1971). "Radiological manifestations of ankylosing spondylitis." *Ann. Rheum. Dis.*, **30:** 138–148.

ROBERTS, W. C. (1974). "Combined mitral and aortic regurgitation in ankylosing spondylitis; angiography and anatomical features." *Amer. J. Med.*, **56:** 237–243.

ROCCO, H. D. & EYRING, E. J. (1972). "Intervertebral disk infections in children." *Amer. J. Dis. Child.*, **123:** 448–451.

RONDIER, J., CAYLA, J., BOK, B., & BOUCHAREB, A. (1974). "Value of osseus scintillography with Strontium 87m in the diagnosis of infectious spondylodiscitis (or spondylitis)." *Rev. Rheum.*, **41:** 427–439.

RONDIER, J., DELRIEU, F., EVRARD, J., CAYLA, J., MENKS, C. J., AMOR, B. & DELBARRE, F. (1974). "Infectious sacro-iliitis with common organisms: a report of 12 cases." *Rev. Rhum.*, **41:** 11–24.

ROSENKRANZ, H. (1971). "Ankylosing spondylitis: cauda equina syndrome with multiple spinal arachnoid cysts." *J. Neurosurg.*, **34:** 241–243.

ROUX, H., SERRATRICE, G. & MAESTRACCI, D. (1975). "Muscular lesions in rheumatic pelvic spondylitis." *Rev. Rheumat.*, **42:** 231–238.

ROY, D. C. (1974). "Tubercular paravertebral abscess presenting as superior mediastinal compression syndrome." *J. Indian Med. Ass.*, **63:** 64–65.

RUSSELL, A. S. (1974). "HL-A (transplantation) antigens in ankylosing spondylitis and Crohn's disease." *J. Rheumatol.*, **1:** 203–209.

RUSSELL, A. S. (1974). "Deforming arthropathy in systemic lupus erythematosus." *Ann. Rheum. Dis.*, **32:** 204–209.

RUSSELL, M. L., GORDON, D. A., ORGYZLO, M. A. & PCPHERDRAN, R. S. (1973). "The cauda equina syndrome of ankylosing spondylitis." *Ann. Intern. Med.*, **78:** 551–554.

RUSSELL, N., VAUGHAN, R. & MORLEY, T. P. (1973). "Spinal epidural infection." *Trans. Amer. Neurol. Ass.*, **98:** 105–107.

SACHS, J. A. (1975). "Ankylosing spondylitis and the major histocompatibility system." *Tissue Antigens*, **5:** 120–127.

SAIRANEN, E., PARONEN, I. & MAHONEN, H. (1969). "Reiter's syndrome: a follow-up study." *Acta Med. Scand.*, **185:** 57–63.

SALAHUDDIN, N. I., MADHAVAN, T., FISHER, E. J., COX, F., QUINN, E. L. & EYLER, W. R. (1973). "Pseudomonas osteomyelitis: radiologic features." *Radiology*, **109:** 41–47.

SANTOS, G. H. (1972). "Vertebral coccidioidomycosis: unusual polymorphic disease." *N.Y. State J. Med.*, **72:** 2784–2785.

SAVAGE, T. R. (1950). "Chronic adhesive spinal meningitis associated with lumbar naevus and dimple." *Brit. Med. J.*, **2:** 709.

SCALABRINO, R. (1970). "The sacro-iliac joints in ulcerative colitis and in certain rheumatic diseases." *Rev. Rheumat.*, **37:** 151–154.

SCHARFETTER, F. & MULLER, G. (1971). "Postoperative lumbar intervertebral discitis." *Schweiz. Arch. Neurol. Neurochir. Psychiatr.*, **108:** 99–111.

SCHMID, F. R. & TESAR, J. T. (1972). "Chronic synarthritis in rheumatoid arthritis." *J. Chron. Dis.*, **25:** 483–489.

SCHONBERGER, M. VON & HELLMICH, K. (1974). "Sacroiliac shift and fibrositis." *Z. Allgemeinmed.*, **50:** 1097–1098.

SCHUMACHER, H. R. (1973). "Arthropathy in sickle-cell disease." *Ann. Intern. Med.*, **78:** 203–211.

SCULCO, T. P., WAXMAN, J. & LIEBOLT, F. L. (1974). "Cytomegalovirus infection after lumbosacral fusion (case report)." *Clin. Orthop.*, **100:** 109–110.

SELBY, R. C. (1972). "Osteomyelitis and disc infection secondary to Pseudomonas aeruginosa in heroin addiction." *J. Neurosurg.*, **37:** 463–466.

SERRE, H. & SIMON, L. (1964). "Rheumatoid spondylitis and ulcerative colitis." *Rheumatism*, **20:** 13–16.

SHIPP, F. L. & HAGGART, G. E. (1950). "Further experience in the management of osteitis condensans ilii." *J. Bone Joint Surg.*, **32A:** 841–847.

SHORBE, H. B. (1939). "Chronic myositis of lumbar region." *Arch. Phys. Therap.*, **20:** 102–106.

SHORE, L. (1935). "On osteoarthritis in the dorsal intervertebral joints: a study in morbid anatomy." *Brit. J. Surg.*, **22:** 833–849.

SHORE, L. (1935). "Polyspondylitis marginalis osteophytica." *Brit. J. Surg.*, **22:** 850–863.

SMITH, M. G. H. (1972). "Lumbar spondylarthritis in young children." *J. Pediatr. Surg.*, **7:** 684–690.

SMITH, R. F. & TAYLOR, T. K. F. (1967). "Inflammatory lesions of intervertebral discs in children." *J. Bone Joint Surg.*, **49A:** 1508–1520.

SMITH, R. W. & LOESER, J. D. (1972). "A myelographic variant in lumbar arachnoiditis." *J. Neurosurg.*, **36:** 441–446.

SMOLIK, E. A. & NASH, F. P. (1951). "Arachnoiditis: a complication of the intervertebral disc operation." *Ann. Surg.*, **133:** 490–495.

SMYTH, C. J. (1960). "Rheumatism and arthritis: review of American and English literature of recent years (13th rheumatism review)." *Ann. Intern. Med.*, **53** (Suppl.): 1.

SOLOMON, L. (1975). "Rheumatic disorders in the South African Negro, I: Rheumatoid arthritis and ankylosing spondylitis." *Sth. Afr. Med. J.*, **49:** 1292–1296.

SOTER, N. A. (1974). "Urticaria and arthralgias as manifestations of necrotizing angiitis (vasculitis)." *J. Invest. Derm.*, **63:** 485–490.

SPIEGEL, P. G., KENGLA, K. W., ISAACSON, A. S. & WILSON, J. C. (1972). "Intervertebral disc-space inflammation in children." *J. Bone Joint Surg.*, **54A:** 284–296.

STAHELI, L. T., NELP, W. B. & MARTY, R. (1973). "Strontium 87m scanning: early diagnosis of bone and joint infections in children." *J. Amer. Med. Assoc.*, **221:**1159–1160.

STEINBERG, V. L. & STOREY, G. (1957). "Ankylosing spondylitis and chronic inflammatory lesions of the intestine." *Brit. Med. J.*, **2:** 1157–1159.

STEINBROCKER, O. (1941). *Arthritis in Modern Practice*. Philadelphia; Saunders.

STERN, W. E. (1972). "Neurosurgical aspects of injuries of the thoracic spine." *Surg. Clin. Nth. Amer.*, **52:** 769–781.

STOCKMAN, R. (1920). *Rheumatism and Arthritis*. Edinburgh; Green.

STRANGE, F. G. ST. C. (1963). "Prognosis in sacro-iliac tuberculosis." *Brit. J. Surg.*, **50:** 561–571.

STROSBERG, J. M. (1975). "Ankylosing spondylitis in a large kindred: clinical and genetic studies." *Tissue Antigens*, **5:** 205–212.

STURROCK, R. D. (1975). "Raised levels of complement inactivation products in ankylosing spondylitis." *Ann. Rheum. Dis.*, **34:** 202–203.

SULLIVAN, C. R. (1961). "Diagnosis and treatment of pyogenic infections of the intervertebral disk." *Surg. Clin. Nth. Amer.*, **41:** 1077–1086.

SULLIVAN, C. R. & McCASLIN, F. E. (1960). "Further studies on experimental spondylitis and intercorporeal fusion of the spine." *J. Bone Joint Surg.*, **42A:** 1339–1348.

SYMMERS, W. S. (1973). "Fungal infections of the spine." *Brit. Med. J.*, **2**: 423.

TARZY, B. J., GARCIA, C. R., WALLACH, E. E., ZWEIMAN, B. & MYERS, A. R. (1972). "Rheumatic disease, abnormal serology and oral contraceptives." *Lancet*, **2**: 501–503.

TENG, P. (1972). "Post-operative lumbar diskitis." *Bull. Los Angeles Neurol. Soc.*, **37**: 114–123.

THIBODEAU, A. A. (1968). "Closed space infection following removal of lumbar intervertebral disc." *J. Bone Joint Surg.*, **50A**: 400–410.

THOMAS, D. J. (1974). "Nervous system involvement in ankylosing spondylitis." *Brit. Med. J.*, **1**: 148–150.

THOMPSON, M. (1953). "Osteitis condensans ilii and its differentiation from ankylosing spondylitis." *Ann. Rheum. Dis.*, **13**: 147.

TORRES, A. (1974). "Tuberculosis of the spine and sarcoidosis." *Indian J. Chest Dis.*, **16**: 191–194.

TRACH, S. (1970). "Gouty arthritis of the spine." *Clin. Orthop.*, **71**: 81–86.

TUCKER, A. L. (1974). "Retropharyngeal infection with disc space involvement and osteomyelitis following a pharyngeal flap operation." *Plastic Reconst. Surg.*, **53**: 477–478.

TULI, S. M. (1974). "Tuberculosis of the craniovertebral region." *Clin. Orthop.*, **104**: 209–212.

VALDIESERRI, L. (1974). "Malignant brucellar epiduritis with lumbosciatic pain." *Chir. Org. Mov.*, **61**: 601–607.

VAN DER MEER, P. (1965). "Rheumatoid arthritis and the cervical spine." *Acta Rheum. Scand.*, **11**: 81.

VAN KERCKOVE, H. (1970). "Involvement of the lateral atlanto-axial joints as first and late symptoms of rheumatoid arthritis." *Acta Rheum. Scand.*, **16**: 197.

VAUGHAN, B. (1968). "Lateral tomography of atlanto-axial joint in rheumatoid disease." *Austr. Radiol.*, **12**: 58–60.

VERBRUGGHEN, A. (1974). "Intervertebral infections following surgery." *Surg. Neurol.*, **2**: 426–429.

VERDIER, J. M., COMMANDRE, F., RIVOLLIER, P. & ZEIGLER, G. (1974). "Triple association of pelvic spondylitis, Paget's disease and myeloma." *Rev. Rhum.*, **41**: 353–356.

VEYS, E. M. (1973). "Serum IgM and IgA levels in ankylosing spondylitis." *Ann. Rheum. Dis.*, **32**: 493–496.

VEYS, E. M. (1974). "Hl-A and infective sacroileitis." *Lancet*, **2**: 349.

VOBECKY, J. (1974). "Rheumatoid arthritis and ankylosing spondylitis in an ethnically homogenous population: familial distribution of complaints." *J. Chronic Dis.*, **27**: 413–415.

VOGELSANG, H. (1973). "Cervical intervertebral discitis following discography." *Neurochirurg.*, **16**: 80–83.

WADIA, N. H., IRANI, P. F. & KATRAK, S. M. (1973). "Lumbosacral radiculomyelitis associated with pandemic acute haemorrhagic conjunctivitis." *Lancet*, **1**: 350–352.

WATANAKUNAKORN, C. (1973). "Vertebral osteomyelitis due to Mycobacterium kansaii." *Ann. Rev. Respir. Dis.*, **107**: 846–850.

WATANAKUNAKORN, C. (1975). "Vertebral osteomyelitis as a complication of pseudomonas aeruginosa pneumonia." *South. Med. J.*, **68**: 173–176.

WATT, I. (1971). "Septic abortion and sacro-iliitis." *Proc. Roy. Soc. Med.*, **64**: 55–56.

WEEDEN BUTLER, R. (1955). "The nature and significance of vertebral osteochondritis." *Proc. Roy. Soc. Med.*, **48**: 895–902.

WELLER, R. O., BRUCKNER, F. E. & CHAMBERLAIN, M. A. (1970). "Rheumatoid neuropathy: a histological and electro-physiological study." *J. Neurol. Neurosurg. Psychiat.*, **33**: 592–604.

WETTSTEIN, P. & CURATI, W. (1973). "Acute spondylitis and spondylodiscitis due to common organisms." *Radiol. Clin. Biol.*, **42**: 353–365.

WHALEY, K. & DICK, W. C. (1968). "Fatal subaxial dislocation of cervical spine in rheumatoid arthritis." *Brit. Med. J.*, **2**: 31.

WIESSMAN, J. G., WOOD, V. E. & KROLL, L. L. (1973). "Pseudomonas vertebral osteomyelitis in heroin addicts." *J. Bone Joint Surg.*, **55A**: 1416–1424.

WILEY, A. M. & TRUETA, J. (1959). "The vascular anatomy of the spine and its relationship to pyogenic vertebral osteomyelitis." *J. Bone Joint Surg.*, **41B**: 796–809.

WILKINSON, I. M. (1972). "Arteries of the head and neck in giant cell arteritis: a pathological study to show the pattern of arterial involvement." *Arch. Neurol.*, **27**: 378–391.

WILLIAMS, J. L., MOLLER, G. A. & O'ROURKE, T. L. (1968). "Pseudo-infections of the intervertebral disk and adjacent vertebrae." *Amer. J. Roentgenol.*, **103**: 611–615.

WILLIAMS, M. H., SHELDON, P. J., TORRIGANI, G. & EISEN, (1971).

"Palindromic rheumatism: clinical and immunological studies." *Ann. Rheum. Dis.*, **30:** 375–380.

WILLIAMS, M. S. (1975). "Leucocyte migration test in Crohn's disease, ulcerative colitis and ankylosing spondylitis using Crohn's colon homogenate, mitochondrial and microsomal fractions." *Amer. J. Dig. Dis.*, **20:** 425–429.

WOJTULEWSKI, J. A. (1973). "Cricoarytenoid arthritis in ankylosing spondylitis." *Brit. Med. J.*, **3:** 145–146.

WOLSON, A. H. (1975). "Upper lobe fibrosis in ankylosing spondylitis." *Amer. J. Roentgenol.*, **124:** 466–471.

WONG, M. L. (1974). "Cervical mycobacterial disease." *Trans. Amer. Acad. Ophth. Otolar.*, **78:** 175–187.

WOOD, P. H. N. (1970). "Rheumatic complaints." *Brit. Med. Bull.*, **27:** 82–88.

WRIGHT, R., LUMSDEN, K. & LUNTZ, M. H. (1965). "Abnormalities of the sacroiliac joints and uveitis in ulcerative colitis." *Quart. J. Med.*, **34:** 229–236.

WRIGHT, V. & WATKINSON, G. (1965). "Sacroiliitis and ulcerative colitis." *Brit. Med. J.*, **2:** 675–680.

YEOMAN, W. (1928). "The relation of arthritis of the sacro-iliac joint to sciatica, with an analysis of 100 cases." *Lancet*, **2:** 1119–1122.

YU, D. T. (1974). "Cellular immunological aspects of rheumatoid arthritis." *Semin. Arth. Rheum.*, **4:** 25–52.

ZEITER, W. J. & HOUSE, F. B. (1946). "Cervical periarthritis: diagnosis and treatment." *Arch. Phys. Med.*, **27:** 162–165.

ZILKHA, A. & NICOLETTI, J. M. (1974). "Acute spinal subdural hematoma: case report." *J. Neurosurg.*, **41:** 627–630.

ZUCKER, M. (1974). "Osteomyelitis of the vertebral column in heroin users." *Md. State Med. J.*, **23:** 77–79.

### (f) Neoplasms (Primary and Secondary)

ARLECCHINI, S. & FEDERSONI, F. (1974). "Fluid-filled pseudocysts." *Chir. Org. Mov.*, **61:** 443–451.

BAKER, H. W. & COLEY, B. L. (1953). "Chordoma of lumbar vertebrae." *J. Bone Joint Surg.*, **35A:** 403–408.

BALAKRISHNAN, V., RICE, M. S. & SIMPSON, D. A. (1974). "Spinal neuroblastomas: diagnosis, treatment and prognosis." *J. Neurosurg.*, **40:** 631–638.

BANNA, M. & GRYSPEERDT, G. L. (1971). "Intraspinal tumours in children (excluding dysraphism)." *Clin. Radiol.*, **22:** 17–32.

BANNA, M., PEARCE, G. W. & ULDALL, R. (1971). "Scoliosis: a rare manifestation of intrinsic tumours of the spinal cord in children." *J. Neurol. Neurosurg. Psychiat.*, **34:** 637–641.

BARUFFALDI, O., OERO, G. & SERRA, E. (1972). "Two cases of eosinophilic granuloma." *Minerva Ortop.*, **23:** 446–453.

BENDER, J. L., LANDINGHAM, J. H. VAN, & MANNO, N. J. (1974). "Epidural lipoma producing spinal cord compression: report of 2 cases." *J. Neurosurg.*, **41:** 100–103.

BENNETT, G. E. (1927). "Tumors of cauda equina and spinal cord: report of four cases in which marked spasm of erector spinae and hamstring muscle was outstanding sign." *J. Amer. Med. Ass.*, **89:** 1480–1483.

BERNELL, W. R., KEPES, J. J. & CLOUGH, C. A. (1973). "Subarachnoid hemorrhage from malignant Schwannoma of cauda equina." *Texas Med.*, **69:** 101–104.

BHALLA, S. K. (1970). "Metastatic disease of the spine." *Clin. Orthop.*, **73:** 52–60.

BILBAO, J. M. (1975). "Compression of the cauda equina due to a necrobiotic granuloma of ligamentum flavum." *Canad. J. Neurol. Sci.*, **2:** 135–138.

BLOCKEY, N. J. & SCHORSTEIN, J. (1961). "Intraspinal epidermoid tumours in the lumbar region in children." *J. Bone Joint Surg.*, **43B:** 556–562.

BLOOM, H. J. G., ELLIS, H. & JENNETT, W. B. (1955). "The early diagnosis of spinal tumours." *Brit. Med. J.*, **1:** 10–16.

BORGHI, G. (1973). "Extradural spinal meningiomas." *Acta Neurochir.*, **29:** 195–202.

BRISH, A. & PAYAN, H. M. (1972). "Lumbar intraspinal extradural ganglion cyst." *J. Neurol. Neurosurg. Psychiat.*, **35:** 771–775.

BURKE, W. J. (1973). "A case of cauda equina tumour presenting with stupor and papilloedema." *Proc. Austr. Assoc. Neurol.*, **9:** 95–97.

CERUTTI, P. & SANTOIANNI, P. (1973). "A relatively benign reticulosis: Crosti's 'reticulohistiocytoma of the back'." *Int. J. Dermatol.*, **12:** 35–40.

CHOPRA, J. S. (1972). "Solitary plexiform neurofibroma at an

277

unusual site. Report of a case in the lumbar region." *Neurol. India*, **20:** 104–105.

CHOREMIS, C., ECONOMOS, D., PAPADATOS, C. & GARBOULAS, A. (1956). "Intraspinal epidermoid tumours (cholesteatomas) in patients treated for tuberculous meningitis." *Lancet*, **2:** 437–439.

CITRIN, D. L., BESSENT, R. G. & TUOHY, J. B. (1974). "Bone scanning in malignant disease." *Brit. J. Hosp. Med.*, 424–430.

DICKSON, J. H., WALTZ, T. A. & FECHNER, R. E. (1971)."Intraosseous neurilemmoma of the third lumbar vertebra." *J. Bone Joint Surg.*, **53A:** 349–355.

EARLY, C. B. & SAYERS, M. P. (1966). "Spinal epidural meningioma." *J. Neurosurg.*, **25:** 571–573.

EDGAR, M. A. (1973). "Post-radiation sarcoma in ankylosing spondylitis." *J. Bone Joint Surg.*, **55B:** 183–188.

EGGLESTON, J. C. & HARTMAN, W. H. (1968). "Hodgkin's disease involving the spinal epidural space." *Johns Hopkins Hosp. Med. J.*, **123:** 265–270.

EKELUND, L. & CRONQUIST, S. (1973). "Roentgenological changes in spinal malformations and spinal tumours in children." *Radiologie*, **13:** 541–546.

FERRIS, R. A., PETTRONE, F. A., McELVIE, A. M., TWIGG, H. L. & CHUN, B. K. (1974). "Eosinophilic granuloma of the spine: an unusual radiographic presentation." *Clin. Orthop.* **99:** 57–63.

FIELDING, J. W. & RATZAN, S. (1973). "Osteochondroma of the cervical spine." *J. Bone Joint Surg.*, **55A:** 640–641.

FIELDS, W. S., ZULCH, K. J. & MASLENIKOV, V. (1972). "High cervical neurinoma: special neurologic and radiologic features." *Zbl. Neurochir.*, **33:** 90–102.

FORS, B. & STENKVIST, B. (1966). "Giant-cell tumour of thoracic vertebra." *Acta Orthop. Scand.*, **37:** 191–196.

GELBERMAN, R. H. & OLSON, C. O. (1974). "Benign osteoblastoma of the atlas: a case report." *J. Bone Joint Surg.*, **56A:** 808–810.

GLASAUER, F. E. (1966). "Lumbar extradural cyst." *J. Neurosurg.*, **25:** 567–570.

GLENN, J. J., RECKLING, R. W. & MANTZ, F. A. (1974). "Malignant hemangio-endothelioma in a lumbar vertebra: a rare tumour in an unusual location." *J. Bone Joint Surg.*, **56A:** 1279–1282.

GOLDENBERG, M. (1970). "Glioma of spinal cord demonstrated by angiography." *J. Canad. Ass. Radiol.*, **21:** 113–115.

GÖRDES, W. & FISCHER, V. (1973). "Intraspinal neuroblastomas in childhood." *Arch. Orthop. Unfall-Chir.*, **77:** 236–242.

GRAY, E. D. (1942). "Calcification and ossification of spinal tumours." *Brit. J. Radiol.*, **15:** 365–369.

GRNJA, V., ALLEN, W. E., OSBORN, D. J. & KIER, E. L. (1974). "Sacral neurofibrosarcoma: an angiographic evaluation: case report." *J. Neurosurg.*, **40:** 767–771.

GRUSZIEWICZ, J., DORON, Y. & GELLEI, B. (1969). "Plexiform neurofibroma of the lumbar region." *J. Neurosurg.*, **30:** 69–70.

HALLGRIMSSON, J., BJORNSSON, A. & GUDMUNDSSON, G. (1970). "Meningioma of the neck: case report." *J. Neurosurg.*, **23:** 695–699.

HAMILTON, E. B. (1972). "Hyperparathyroidism with chondrocalcinosis and periarticular calcification." *Proc. Roy. Soc. Med.*, **65:** 1013.

HARRY, R. D. (1973). "Elastofibroma dorsi: an unusual soft tissue tumor simulating sarcoma." *Amer. J. Surg.*, **125:** 713–714.

HEMMER, R. & PICK, S. (1971). "Laminectomy in metastases of the vertebral spine." *Arztliche Forschung*, **25:** 1.

HERDT, J. R., SHIMKIN, P. M., OMMAYA, A. D. & CHIRO, G. DI. (1972). "Angiography of vascular spinal tumours." *Amer. J. Roentgenol.*, **115:** 165–170.

HERNDON, J. H. & COHEN, J. (1970). "Chondroma of a lumbar vertebral body in a child: an unusual tumour resembling a chordoma." *J. Bone Joint Surg.*, **52A:** 1241–1247.

HUBBARD, D. D. (1972). "Secondary carcinoma of the spine with destruction of the intervertebral disk." *Clin. Orthop.*, **88:** 86–88.

IMMEMKAMP, M. (1971). "Benign osteoblastoma of the fourth lumbar vertebra with lumbosacral stiffness." *Z. Orthop.*, **109:** 616–625.

JACKSON, B. T. & KINMOTH, J. B. (1974). "The diagnosis of lumbar lymph node metastases by lymphography." *Clin. Radiol.*, **25:** 195–201.

JANECKI, C. J., NELSON, C. L. & DOHN, D. F. (1972). "Intrasacral cyst: report of a case and review of the literature." *J. Bone Joint Surg.*, **54A:** 423–428.

JELLINGER, K., MINAUF, M. & SALZER-KINTSCHIK, K. (1969). "Oligodendroglioma with extraneural metastases." *J. Neurol. Neurosurg. Psychiat.*, **32:** 249–253.

JEWELL, J. H. & BUSH, L. F. (1964). " 'Benign' giant-cell tumour of bone with a solitary pulmonary metastasis." *J. Bone Joint Surg.*, **46A:** 848–852.

JOHNSON, D. A. & HUGHES, R. L. (1974). "Extradural cyst." *Radiol.*, **112:** 93–94.

JOOSTEN, E. (1974). "Hypertrophy of peripheral nerves in the syndrome of multiple mucosal neuromas, endocrine tumours and Marfanoid habitus: autonomic disturbances and sural nerve findings." *Acta Neuropath.*, **30:** 251–261.

KAO, C. C., WINKLER, S. S. & TURNER, J. H. (1974). "Synovial cyst of spinal facet." *J. Neurosurg.*, **41:** 372–376.

KENEFICK, J. S. (1973). "Hereditary sacral agenesis associated with presacral tumours." *Brit. J. Surg.*, **60:** 271–279.

KUS, W. M. & KOKOSZCZYNSKA-LESZET, I. (1973). "Histiocytosis of the tenth thoracic vertebra." *Chir. Narzad. Ruchu Ortop. Pol.*, **38:** 361–364.

LICHTENSTEIN, L. (1964). "Histiocytosis X (Eosinophilic granuloma of bone, Letterer-Siewe disease and Schüller-Christian disease)." *J. Bone Joint Surg.*, **46A:** 76–90.

LIN, T. H. & COOK, A. W. (1966). "Primary melanoma within spinal canal." *N.Y. J. Med.*, **66:** 1914–1916.

MCALLISTER, V. L. (1975). "Symptomatic vertebral haemangiomas." *Brain*, **98:** 71–80.

MCDONALD, P. (1973). "Malignant sacrococcygeal teratoma." *Amer. J. Roentgenol.*, **118:** 444–449.

MCEVOY, B. F. & GATZEK, H. (1969). "Multiple neuroid basal cell carcinoma syndrome: radiological manifestation." *Brit. J. Radiol.*, **42:** 24–28.

MACLELLAN, D. I. & WILSON, F. C. (1967). "Osteoid osteoma of the spine." *J. Bone Joint Surg.*, **49A:** 111–121.

MARINONI, R. (1974). "A case of plasmocytoma." *Minerva Ortop.*, **25:** 5–31.

MARSH, H. O. & CHOON-BONG CHOI. (1970). "Primary osteogenic sarcoma of the cervical spine originally mistaken for benign osteoblastoma." *J. Bone Joint Surg.*, **52A:** 1467–1471.

NASH, C. L., KAUFMAN, B. & FRANKEL, V. (1971). "Postsurgical meningeal pseudocysts of the lumbar spine." *Clin. Orthop.*, **75:** 167–178.

PAAVOLAINEN, P. & SUNDELL, B. (1973). "Sacrococcygeal chereloma." *Duodecim.*, **89:** 1329–1336.

PAGE, R. E. (1974). "Intraspinal enterogenous cyst associated with spondylolisthesis and spina bifida occulta." *J. Bone Joint Surg.*, **56B:** 541–544.

PALMER, J. J. (1974). "Spinal arachnoid cysts: report of six cases." *J. Neurosurg.*, **41:** 728–735.

PAUS, B. (1973). "Tumour, tuberculosis and osteomyelitis of the spine: differential diagnostic aspects." *Acta Orthop. Scand.*, **44:** 372–382.

PEAR, B. L. & BOID, H. R. (1974). "Roentgenographically visible calcifications in spinal mengioma." *Amer. J. Roentgenol.*, **120:** 32–45.

PORTMANN, J. (1973). "Chordoma of the lumbar vertebral column." *Zeit. Orthop.*, **111:** 755–763.

POULSEN, J. O. (1975). "Ewing's sarcoma simulating vertebra plana." *Acta Orthop. Scand.*, **46:** 211–215.

RENGACHARY, S. S. & KEPES, J. J. (1969). "Spinal epidural metastatic 'mesenchymal chondrosarcoma'." *J. Neurosurg.*, **30:** 71–73.

REXED, B. & WENNSTROM, K. G. (1959). "Arachnoidal proliferation and cystic formation in the spinal nerve root pouches of man." *J. Neurosurg.*, **16:** 73–84.

RICHARDS, A. T., STICKE, L. & SPITZ, L. (1973). "Sacro-coccygeal chordomas in children." *J. Pediat. Surg.*, **8:** 911–914.

RINALDI, I. & HODGES, T. O. (1970). "Iatrogenic lumbar meningocele." *J. Neurol. Neurosurg. Psychiat.*, **33:** 484–492.

RINALDI, I. & PEACH, W. F. (1969). "Postoperative lumbar meningocele: report of 2 cases." *J. Neurosurg.*, **30:** 504–507.

ROGERS, H. M., LONG, D. M., CHOU, S. N. & FRENCH, L. A. (1971). "Lipomas of the spinal cord and cauda equina." *J. Neurosurg.*, **34:** 349–354.

ROSENKRANZ, W. (1971). "Ankylosing spondylitis: cauda equina syndrome with multiple spinal arachnoid cysts." *J. Neurosurg.*, **34:** 241–243.

ROTHMAN, R. H., JACOBS, S. R. & APPLEMAN, W. (1970). "Spinal epidural cysts: a report of 5 cases." *Clin. Orthop.*, **71:** 186–192.

SCALISE, L., STANCATI, G. & VENA, P. (1973). "Two cases of intradural meningioma." *Clin. Orthop.*, **24:** 187–193.

SCHULMAN, L. & DORFMANN, H. D. (1970). "Nerve fibres in osteoid osteoma." *J. Bone Joint Surg.*, **52A:** 1351–1356.

SISSONS, H. A. (1959). "Tumours of the vertebral column." In *Modern Trends in Diseases of the Vertebral Column.* pp. 192–209. Ed. by R. Nassim and H. J. Burrows. London; Butterworth.

SLOWICJ, F. A., CAMPBELL, C. J. & KETTELKAMP, D. B. (1968). "Aneurysmal bone cyst: an analysis of 13 cases." *J. Bone Joint Surg.*, **50A**: 1142–1151.

STENER, B. & JOHNSEN, O. E. (1971). "Complete removal of three vertebrae for giant-cell tumour." *J. Bone Joint Surg.*, **53B**: 278–287.

STJERNALL, L. (1970). "Vertebral angiosarcoma." *Acta Orthop. Scand.*, **41**: 165–168.

SUZUKI, R., KOYAMA, K., FUNAYAMA, M. & ITO, R. (1970). "Two cases of spinal extradural cysts." *J. Jap. Orthop. Ass.*, **45**: 1043–1049.

TACHDJIAN, M. O. & MATSON, D. D. (1965). "Orthopaedic aspects of intraspinal tumours in infants and children." *J. Bone Joint Surg.*, **47A**: 223–248.

TARLOV, I. M. (1970). "Spinal perineurial and meningeal cysts." *J. Neurol. Neurosurg. Psychiat.*, **33**: 833–843.

TRUMPY, J. H., BANERJI, A. K. & PRAKASH, B. (1973). "Congenital spinal extradural cysts, anterior meningocele and intraspinal root cysts: different manifestations of the same condition?" *Acta Neurochir.*, **29**: 177–193.

VALDERRAMA, J. A. F. & BULLOUGH, P. G. (1968). "Solitary myeloma of the spine." *J. Bone Joint Surg.*, **50B**: 82.

VALDISERRI, L. (1974). "Epidural brucellar neoplasm with lumbosacral pain." *Chir. Org. Mov.*, **61**: 601–607.

VERBIEST, H. (1965). "Giant-cell tumours and aneurysmal bone cysts of the spine: with special reference to the problems related to the removal of a vertebral body." *J. Bone Joint Surg.*, **47B**: 699–713.

VYHNANEK, K., ZEMAN, M. & TRIVEDI, R. M. (1972). "Radicular and subdural cysts in peridurography." *Fortschr. Röntgenstr.*, **116**: 160–163.

WIGHT, D. G. D., HOLLEY K. J. & FINBOW, J. A. H. (1973). "Metastasizing ependymoma of the cauda equina." *J. Clin. Pathol.*, **26**: 929–935.

WILKINSON, H. A. (1971). "Nerve-root entrapment in 'traumatic' extradural arachnoid cyst." *J. Bone Joint Surg.*, **53A**: 163–166.

WILLIAMS, D. C. (1971). "Some problems in cancer research." *Physiotherapy*, **57**: 102–108.

WISNIEWSKI, M., TOKER, C., ANDERSON, P. J., HUANG, Y. P. &

MALIS, L. I. (1973). "Chondroblastoma of the cervical spine: a case report." *J. Neurosurg.*, **38**: 763–766.

WOOD, W. G., ROTHMANN, L. M. & NUSSBAUM, B. E. (1975). "Intramedullary neurilemmoma of the cervical spinal cord." *J. Neurosurg.*, **42**: 465–468.

YOUNG, J. M. & FUNK, F. J. (1953). "Incidence of tumor metastasis to the lumbar spine." *J. Bone Joint Surg.*, **35A**: 55–64.

ZILKHA, A. & NICOLETTI, J. M. (1974). "Acute spinal subdural hematoma: case report." *J. Neurosurg.*, **41**: 627–630.

ZMOLEK, E. J. (1973). "Chordoma: case report." *Wisconsin Med. J.*, **72**: 246–247.

*(g) Neuropathology*

APPENZELLER, O. (1974). "Myelinated fibres in human paravertebral sympathetic chain: White rami communicantes in alcoholic and diabetic patients." *J. Neurol. Neurosurg. Psychiat.*, **37**: 1155–1161.

ARNOLD, N. & HARRIMAN, D. G. F. (1970). "The incidence of abnormality in control human peripheral nerves studied by simple axon dissection." *J. Neurol. Neurosurg. Psychiat.*, **33**: 55–61.

ASCHER, P. W. (1969). "Intrathecal cortisone management of lumbar radiculopathy." *Zentralbl. Chir.*, **94**: 1678–1679.

BOGORODINSKI, D. K. (1974). "Neurological complications of osteochondrosis of the lower lumbar intervertebral disks." *Sov. Med.*, (August): 5–9.

CHADDUCK, W. M. (1973). "Experimental spondylitic myelopathy." *Surg. Forum*, **24**: 438–440.

CHADDUCK, W. M., SEMINS, H. & NUGENT, G. R. (1973). "An experimental model for the study of spondylitic myelopathy." *Amer. J. Surg.*, **125**: 328–330.

CRANDALL, P. H. & BATZDORF, U. (1966). "Cervical spondylitic myelopathy." *J. Neurosurg.*, **25**: 57–66.

CURRAN, J. E. (1975). "Neurological sequelae of Paget's disease of the vertebral column and skull base." *Australasian Radiol.*, **19**: 15–19.

DEGENHARDT, D. P. & GOODWIN, M. A. (1960). "Neuropathic joints in diabetes." *J. Bone Joint Surg.*, **42B**: 769–771.

DELAGI, E. F. (1968). "Non-articular rheumatic pain syndromes: an introduction." *Arch. Phys. Med.*, **49**: 367–370.

DEVERELL, W. R. & FERGUSON, J. H. (1968). "An unusual case of sciatic nerve paralysis." *J. Amer. Med. Ass.*, **205**: 699–700.

DUYFJES, F. (1972). "Occipitocervical spondylodesis for atlanto-axial instability with neurological changes in rheumatoid conditions." *Acta Orthop. Belg.*, **38**: 40–46.

EDGAR, M. A. (1974). "Nervous system involvement in ankylosing spondylitis." *Brit. Med. J.*, **1**: 394.

EHNI, G. (1975). "Effects of certain degenerative diseases of the spine, especially spondylosis and disk protrusion, on the neural contents, particularly in the lumbar region. Historical account." *Mayo Clin. Proc.*, **50**: 327–338.

ELOESSER, L. (1917). "On the nature of neuropathic affections of the joints." *Ann. Surg.*, **66**: 201–207.

EVANS, J. A. (1946). "Reflex sympathetic dystrophy." *Surg. Gynec. Obstet.*, **82**: 36–43.

FELDMAN, F. (1974). "Acute axial neuroarthropathy." *Radiology*, **111**: 1–16.

FELDMAN, F. & SEAMAN, W. B. (1969). "The neurological complications of Paget's disease in the cervical spine." *Amer. J. Roentgenol.*, **105**: 375–382.

FETTERMAN, J. L. (1940). "Vertebral neuroses." *Psychosomatic Medicine*, **2**: 265–275.

FREWIN, D. B. (1973). "Neuropathic arthropathy." *Aust. N.Z. J. Med.*, **3**: 587–592.

GARCEAU, G. J. (1953). "The filum terminale syndrome (the cord-traction syndrome)." *J. Bone Joint Surg.*, **35A**: 711–716.

GINSBERG, S., GROSS, E. & FEIRING, E. H. (1967). "The neurological complications of tuberculous spondylitis." *Arch. Neurol., Chicago*, **16**: 265.

GRANT, F. C., AUSTIN, G., FRIEDENBERG, Z. B. & HANSEN, A. (1948). "A correlation of neurologic, orthopaedic and roentgenographic findings in displaced intervertebral disc." *Surg. Gynec. Obst.*, **87**: 561–568.

GRUSZIEWICZ, J., DORON, Y. & BELLEI, B. (1969). "Plexiform neurofibroma of the lumbar region." *J. Neurosurg.*, **30**: 69.

HAIMOVICI, H. (1972). "Peroneal sensory neuropathy: entrapment syndrome." *Arch. Surg.*, **105**: 586–590.

HARRIS, W. R., RATHBUN, J. B., WORTZMAN, G. & HUMPHREY, J. G.

(1973). "Avulsion of lumbar roots complicating fracture of the pelvis." *J. Bone Joint Surg.*, **55A:** 1436–1442.

HARTMAN, J. T. & DOHN, D. R. (1969). "Paget's disease of the spine with cord or nerve-root compression." *J. Bone Joint Surg.*, **48A:** 1079–1084.

HEATHFIELD, K. (1973). "Neurological complications of the rheumatic diseases." *Rheumatol. Rehab.*, **12:** 2–21.

HERMAN, R. M. (1964). "Reflex activity in spinal cord lesions." *Ann. Phys. Med.*, **43:** 252–259.

HILEL, N. (1968). "Compression of the sympathetic trunk by osteophytes of the vertebral column in the abdomen: an anatomical study with pathological and clinical considerations." *Surgery*, **63:** 609–625.

HILTZ, D. L. (1974). "Radicular femoral neuropathy." *Phys. Therap.*, **54:** 966–967.

HITSELBERGER, W. E. & WITTEN, R. M. (1968). "Abnormal myelograms in asymptomatic patients." *J. Neurosurg.*, **28:** 204–206.

HITSELBERGER, W. E. & WITTEN, R. M. (1969–70). "Asymptomatic positive myelograms." *Ann. Phys, Med.*, **10:** 154.

ILTCHEWSKI, S., KASSOROV, J. & WLACHKINOV, A. (1970). "Intraspinal applications of hydrocortisone in radiculitis due to protrusion of intervertebral disk." *Therap. Hung.*, **18:** 68–71.

JOOSTEN, E. (1974). "Hypertrophy of peripheral nerves in the syndrome of multiple mucosal neuromas, endocrine tumours and Marfanoid habitus: autonomic disturbances and sural nerve findings." *Acta Neuropath.*, **30:** 251–261.

KNUTSSON, B. (1962). "How often do the neurological signs disappear after the operation of a herniated disc." *Acta Orthop. Scand.*, **32:** 352–356.

LUNDBORG, G. (1970). "Ischemic nerve injury: experimental studies on intraneural microvascular pathophysiology and nerve function in a limb subjected to temporary circulatory arrest." *Scand. J. Reconstr. Surg.*, Suppl. **6:** 1.

McLENNAN, J. E. (1974). "Neuropathological correlation in Sjögren-Larsson syndrome: oligophrenia, ichthyosis and spasticity." *Brain*: **97:** 693–708.

McQUARRIE, H. G., HARRIS, J. W., ELLSWORTH, H. S., STONE, R. A. & ANDERSON, A. E. (1972). "Sciatic neuropathy complicating vaginal hysterectomy." *Amer. J. Obst. Gynecol.*, **113:** 223–232.

McSWEENEY, T. (1971). "Stability of the cervical spine following injury accompanied by grave neurological damage." *Proc. Veterans Adm. Spinal Cord Inj. Conf.*, **18**: 61–65.

MATSUYAMA, H. & HAYMAKER, W. (1967). "Distribution of lesions in the Landry-Guillain-Barré syndrome." *Acta Neuropath.*, **8**: 230.

MATTHEWS, W. T. (1968). "The neurological complications of ankylosing spondylitis." *J. Neurol. Sci.*, **6**: 561–573.

MICHIE, I. & CLARK, M. (1968). "Neurological syndromes associated with cervical and craniocervical anomalies." *Arch. Neurol., Chicago*, **18**: 241–247.

MINAGI, H. & GRONNER, A. T. (1969). "Calcification of the posterior longitudinal ligament: cause of cervical myelopathy." *Amer. J. Roentgenol.*, **105**: 365–369.

MONEY, R. A. (1968). "Some neurological aspects of vertigo." *Med. J. Aust.*, **I**: 1040–1043.

PEARSON, R. C. (1970). "Fracture of spine with neurological lesions." *Proc. Mine Med. Off. Ass.*, **49**: 181–184.

PEPPER, H. W. (1973). "Extrapleural mass with neurologic signs." *Chest*, **64**: 345–346.

SADAR, E. S., WALTON, R. J. & GOSSMAN, H. H. (1972). "Neurological dysfunction in Paget's disease of the vertebral column." *J. Neurosurg.*, **37**: 661–665.

SALERNO, N. R., & EDEIKEN, J. (1970). "Vertebral scalloping in neurofibromatosis." *Radiol.*, **97**: 509–510.

SATOYOSHI, E., DOI, Y. & KINOSHITA, M. (1972). "Pseudomyotonia in cervical root lesions with myelopathy." *Arch. Neurol., Chicago.*, **27**: 307–313.

SCHAJOWICZ, F. & SLULLITEL, J. (1973). "Eosinophilic granuloma of bone and its relationship to Hans-Schüller-Christian and Letterer-Siwe syndromes." *J. Bone Joint Surg.*, **55B**: 545–565.

SCHEIN, A. J. (1968). "Back and neck pain and associated nerve root irritation in the New York City Fire Department." *Clin. Orthop.*, **59**: 119–124.

SHEA, J. D., GIOFFRE, R., CARRION, H. & SMALL, M. P. (1973). "Autonomic hyperreflexia in spinal cord injury." *Southern Med. J.*, **66**: 869–872.

SHROYER, R. N., FORTSON, C. H. & THEODOTOU, C. B. (1960). "Delayed neurological sequelae of a retained foreign body (lead bullet) in the intervertebral disc space." *J. Bone Joint Surg.*, **42A**: 595–599.

SIMEONE, F. A. (1972). "Acute and delayed traumatic peripheral entrapment neuropathies." *Surg. Clin. Nth. Amer.*, **52**: 1329–1336.

SIMEONE, F. A. (1975). "Neurological complications of closed shoulder injuries." *Orthop. Clin. Nth. Amer.*, **6**: 499–506.

SMITH, R. W. & LOESER, J. D. (1972). "A myelographic variant in lumbar arachnoidities." *J. Neurosurg.*, **36**: 441–446.

SODERBERG, L. (1959). "Neurological complications following myelography." *Acta Orthop. Scand.*, **29**: 170.

SOGANI, K. C. (1972). "Paravertebral lumbar meningomyelocele: Report of 2 cases." *J. Neurosurg.*, **37**: 746–748.

SPURLING, R. G. & BRADFORD, F. (1939). "Neurologic aspects of herniated nucleus pulposus at fourth and fifth lumbar interspace." *J. Amer. Med. Ass.*, **113**: 2019–2022.

SPURLING, R. G. & GRANTHAM, E. G. (1940). "Neurological pictures of herniations of the nucleus pulposus in the lower part of the lumbar region." *Arch. Surg.*, **40**: 375–388.

STEWART, D. Y. (1962). "Current concepts of the 'Barré syndrome' in the postcervical sympathetic syndrome." *Clin. Orthop.*, **24**: 40–48.

SUKOFF, M. H., KADIN, M. M. & MORAN, T. (1972). "Transoral decompression for myelopathy caused by rheumatoid arthritis of the cervical spine." *J. Neurosurg.*, **37**: 493–497.

SUNDERLAND, S. (1974). "Mechanisms of cervical nerve root avulsions in injuries of the neck and shoulder." *J. Neurosurg.*, **41**: 705–714.

TENG, P. (1972). "Meralgia paresthetica." *Bull. Los Angeles Neurol. Soc.*, **37**: 75–83.

THAGE, O. (1965). "The 'quadriceps syndrome': an electromyographic and histological evaluation." *Acta Neurol. Scand.*, **41** (Suppl. 13): 245–249.

UIHLEIN, A. & HOLMAN, C. B. (1968). "Neurologic changes, surgical treatment and postoperative evaluation." *J. Bone Joint Surg.*, **50A**: 182–188.

VERITY, A. & WALTER, R. D. (Eds.). (1974). "Neuroclinical-pathology conference: NPC-1-74 (A-6523). Ptosis, upper thoracic radiculopathy and paraplegia." *Bull. Los Angeles Neurol. Soc.*, **39**: 158–164.

WAYLONIS, G. W. (1968). "Electromyographic findings in chronic cervical radicular syndromes." *Arch. Phys. Med. Rehab.*, **49:** 407–412.

WILKINSON, H. A. (1971). "Nerve-root entrapment in 'traumatic' extradural arachnoid cyst." *J. Bone Joint Surg.*, **53A:** 163–166.

WILKINSON, M. (1960). "The morbid anatomy of cervical spondylitis and myelopathy." *Brain*, **93:** 589.

WILKINSON, M. (1975). "Symposium on lumbar intervertebral disc lesions. 2. A neurological perspective." *Rheumatol. Rehab.*, **14:** 162–163.

WILLIAMS, B. (1971). "Sciatica caused by sacral-nerve-root cysts." *Lancet*, **1:** 137.

WILLIS, T. A. (1941). "Anatomical variations and roentgenographic appearance of low back pain in relation to sciatic pain." *J. Bone Joint Surg.*, **23A:** 410–416.

WILSON, P. J. E. (1967). "Painful sensory disturbance in cervical dermatomes after head injury." *Lancet*, **2:** 1391.

WINNIE, A. P., HARTMAN, J. T., MEYERS, H. L., RAMAMURTHY, S. & BARANGAN, V. (1972). "Pain clinic II: intradural and extradural corticosteroids for sciatica." *Anesth. Analg.*, **51:** 990–1003.

WOHLFAHRT, G. & SWANK, R. L. (1941). "Pathology of amyotrophic lateral sclerosis: fiber analysis of ventral roots and pyramidal tracts of spinal cord." *Arch. Neurol. Psychiat.*, **46:** 783–799.

YEOMAN, W. (1928). "The relation of arthritis of the sacroiliac joint to sciatica, with an analysis of 100 cases." *Lancet*, **2:** 1119–1122.

YUTAKA ONJI (1967). "Posterior paravertebral ossification causing cervical myelopathy." *J. Bone Joint Surg.*, **49A:** 1314.

ZARSKI, S. & DZIDUSZKO, J. (1972). "The mechanism of disturbances of vibratory sensation in nucleus pulposus protrusion." *Neurol. Neurochir. Pol.*, **6:** 595–600.

ZARSKI, S., DZIDUSZKO, J., ZBRODOWSKI, A. & LEO, W. (1972). "Studies on radiculo-discal metameric relation in lumbar spine." *Neurol. Neurochir. Pol.*, **6:** 589–593.

ZEINER-HENRIKSEN, T. (1966). "Sickness among male sciatica patients." *J. Oslo City Hosp.*, **16:** 153–172.

## (h) Histopathology and Chemical Pathology

CRISSEY, R. E. & DAY, A. J. (1950). "Ochronosis." *J. Bone Joint Surg.*, **32A**: 688–690.

DAVIDSON, E. A. & WOODALL, B. (1959). "Biochemical alterations in herniated intervertebral discs." *J. Biol. Chem.*, **234**: 2951.

HALL, D. A. (1973). "Protein-polysaccharide relationships in tissues subjected to repeated stress throughout life. II. The intervertebral disc." *Age and Ageing*, **2**: 218–224.

HANSEN, H. J. & ULLBERG, S. (1960). "Uptake of S35 in the intervertebral discs after injection of S35 sulphat." *Arch. Phys. Med. Rehab.*, **42**: 378.

HARRIS, E. D. & KRANE, S. M. (1974). "Collagenases." *New Engl. J. Med.*, **291**: 557.

HERBERT, C. M., LINDBERG, K. A., JAYSON, M. I. V. & BAILEY, A. J. (1975). "Changes in the collagen of human intervertebral discs during ageing and degenerative disc disease." *J. Mol. Med.*, **1**: 79.

LAPIERE, C. M., LENEARS, A. & KOHN, L. D. (1971). "Procollagen peptidase." *Proc. U.S. Nat. Acad. Sci.*, **68**: 3054.

MALLEN, A. (1962). "The collagen and ground substance of human intervertebral discs at different ages." *Acta Chem. Scand.*, **16**: 705.

NAYLOR, A. (1962). "The biophysical and biochemical aspects of intervertebral disc herniation and degeneration." *Ann. Roy. Coll. Surg. Engl.*, **31**: 91.

PASION, E. G. (1975). "Pre-ankylosing spondylitis; histopathological report." *Ann. Rheum. Dis.*, **34**: 92–97.

SAGUCHI, T. (1972). "A study of separated laminae in patients with spondylosis, with special reference to morphological and histo-pathological observations." *J. Jap. Orthop. Ass.*, **46**: 105–123.

SHINOHARA, H. (1970). "A study of lumbar disc lesion: significance of histology of free nerve endings in lumbar discs." *J. Jap. Orthop. Ass.*, **44**: 553–570.

TAILLARD, W. (1971). "Microscopic anatomy of spondylolysis." *Rev. Chir. Orthop.*, **57** (Suppl. 1): 106.

TAKAHASHI, K. & KAMEYAMA, M. (1972). "Electromyography and histopathology of muscle and spinal cord: analysis of 105 skeletal muscles from 31 autopsy cases." *J. Neurol. Sci.*, **16**: 465–479.

THOMAS, D. J. (1974). "Nervous system involvement in ankylosing spondylitis." *Brit. Med. J.*, **1:** 148–150.

TRAUB, W. W. & PIEZ, K. A. (1971). "The chemistry and structure of collagen." *Adv. Protein Chem.*, **25:** 243.

WADIA, N. H. (1967). "Myelopathy complicating congenital atlanto-axial dislocation." *Brain*, **90:** 449–472.

WIERNIK, P. H. (1972). "Amyloid joint disease." *Medicine*, **51:** 465–479.

*Section Two*

# CLINICAL ASPECTS

# 1

# DIAGNOSTIC FEATURES AND PROCEDURES

## (a) General

ARCHIBALD, K. C. & WIECHEC, F. (1970). "A reappraisal of Hoover's test." *Arch. Phys. Med.*, **51**: 234–238.

ARIEFF, A. J., TIGAY, E. L., LARMON, W. A. & JURTZ, J. F. (1961). "The Hoover sign: an objective sign of pain and/or weakness in the back or lower extremities." *Arch. Neurol.*, **5**: 673–678.

BAILY, N. A., TIGAY, E. L., & LASSER, E. C. (1972). "Holographic imaging of the vertebral column." *Radiol.*, **103**: 197–198.

BLOOM, H. J. G., ELLIS, H. & JENNETT, W. B. (1955). "The early diagnosis of spinal tumours." *Brit. Med. J.*, **1**: 10–16.

BLUMENTHAL, J. H. (1975). "Pitfalls in diagnosis." *J. Amer. Med. Assoc.*, **231**: 344.

BOOTH, R. E. (1975). "Differential diagnosis of shoulder pain." *Orthop. Clin. Nth. Amer.*, **6**: 353–379.

BROWN, M. D. (1975). "Diagnosis of pain syndromes of the spine." *Orthop. Clin. Nth. Amer.*, **6**: 233–248.

BUFALINI, C. (1968). "Differential diagnosis of lumbosciatalgia due to disc hernia: the psoas sign." *Arch. Putti. Chir. Org. Mov.*, **23**: 292–295.

CAILLIET, P. (1968). "Diagnosis of low back pain." *Lawyer's Med. J.*, **4**: 199–228.

CRAIG, F. S. (1956). "Vertebral body biopsy." *J. Bone Joint Surg.*, **38A**: 93–102.

DIVELEY, R. L. (1960). "The diagnosis and treatment of the painful back." *J. Bone Joint Surg.*, **42B**: 859–860.

FERRANNINI, E. (1975). "Suppurative spondylitis with pelvic abscess: localization by 67-gallium scanning." *J. Nucl. Biol. Med.*, **19**: 39–44.

FILTZER, D. L. & BAHNSON, H. T. (1959). "Low back pain due to arterial obstruction." *J. Bone Joint Surg.*, **41B**: 244–247.

FRIBERG, S. (1969). "Diagnosis of lumbar disc lesions." *J. Bone Joint Surg.*, **51B**: 391.

GIBBENS, M. E. (1968). "Diagnosis and treatment of low back pain." *Amer. J. Orthop. Surg.*, **10**: 218–221.

GOLDENBERG, R. R. (1953). "Diagnostic problems in herniated intervertebral disc." *J. Joint Dis.*, **14**: 86–100.

GOLDING, D. N. (1975). "The musculoskeletal features of Wilson's disease: a clinical, radiological and serological survey." *Ann. Rheum Dis.*, **34**: 201.

GOLDNER, J. L. (1956). "Lesions in the back and lower extremities which may simulate a ruptured intervertebral disk." *North Carolina Med. J.*, (June): 260–267.

HAKELIUS, A. & HINDMARSH, J. (1972). "The comparative reliability of pre-operative diagnostic methods in lumbar disc surgery." *Acta Orthop. Scand.*, **43**: 234–238.

HARMON, P. H. (1961). "Practical application of non-myelographic methods of screening, diagnosis and localization of lumbar disc degenerations: with special reference to injection of saline into the disc at operation." *Trans. Coll. Phys. Surg. Gynec. (S.A.)*, **5**: 29–42.

HEYMAN, W. C. (1968). "Considerations of a diagnostic test for sacroiliac lesions. *J. Amer. Osteopath. Ass.*, **67**: 1013–1017.

HIRSCH, C. (1966). "Diagnosis of cervical disc syndrome." *J. Bone Joint Surg.*, **48**: 392–401.

HODGES, C. V. & BARRY, J. M. (1975). "Non-urologic flank pain: a diagnostic approach." *J. Urol.*, **113**: 644–649.

HORROCKS, J. C., McCANN, A. P., STANILAND, J. R., LEAPER, D. J. & DE DOMBAL, F. T. (1972). "Computer-aided diagnosis." *Brit. Med. J.*, **1**: 5–9.

JACOBSON, B. & LINDBERG, B. (1960). "FM receiving system for endoradiosonde techniques." *IRE Trans. Med. Electron.*, **7**: 334–339.

JACOBSON, D. P. & WILSON, W. W. (1972). "Closed biopsy in diagnosis of lesions of the vertebral bodies." *Rocky Mountain Med. J.*, **69**: 56–59.

KARPMAN, H. L., SEMAL, C. J. & COOPER, J. (1970). "Clinical studies in thermography." *Arch. Environ. Hlth.*, **20**: 412–417.

KATZ, G. A. (1973). "The shoulder-pad sign—a diagnostic feature of amyloid arthropathy." *New Eng. J. Med.*, **288**: 354–355.

KESTER, N. C. (1969). "Evaluation and medical management of low back pain." *Med. Clin. Nth. Amer.*, **53**: 525–540.

KONDO, S., ANDO, T., IKEURA, T., TAMAI, H. & MARUMO, M. (1969).

"A statistical study of the diagnosis of lumbar intervertebral disc herniation." *Bull. Osaka Med. Sch.*, **15**: 38–45.

LAURITZEN, J. (1968). "Diagnostic difficulties in lower cervical spine dislocations." *Acta Orthop. Scand.*, **39**: 439–446.

LEBROWSKI, J., POLOCKI, B., BORUCKI, Z., DUDEK, H., SZPAKOWICZ, P. & TOMCZYK, H. (1973). "Determination of the level of prolapsed intervertebral disk in ischialgia by means of an electric thermometer." *Pol. Tyg. Lek.*, **28**: 907–908.

LEEDY, R. F. (1973). "Defining the origin of low-back pain: an injection technique." *J. Amer. Osteopath. Ass.*, **73**: 237–238.

McFARLAND, H. R. (1963). "Differential diagnosis of sacroiliac joint disease." *Journal–Lancet*, **83**: 316–319.

MACKAY, R. S. (1961). "Radio telemetering from within the body." *Science*, **134**: 1196–1202.

MACKAY, R. S. (1964). "Radio telemetry from inside the body." *New Scientist*, **19**: 650–673.

MACKAY, R. S. & JACOBSON, B. (1957). "Endoradiosonde." *Nature*, **179**: 1239–1240.

McMASTERS, R. E. (1974). "A clinical approach to pain." *South Med. J.*, **67**: 173–176.

MacNAB, I. (1973). "Management of low back pain." In *Current Practice in Orthopaedic Surgery*, **5**: 241–278. Saint Louis; Mosby Company.

MONTREUIL, B., RAMPTON, S., BUSSIERE, J.-L., VENT, E., DOLY, J. & FLORI, B. (1972). "Diagnostic and operative problems in thoracic disc herniation." *Rheumatologie*, **24**: 239–245.

NAGRATH, S. P. (1974). "Tuberculous spine: a diagnostic conundrum." *J. Ass. Phys. India*, **22**: 405–407.

POLICOFF, L. (1960). "Diagnostic challenge of back pain." *Arch. Phys. Med. Rehab.*, **41**: 441–445.

RAWKINS, J. (1954). "The diagnosis of herniation of intervertebral discs in the cervical spine." *Brit. J. Phys. Med.*, **17**: 219.

REYNOLDS, M. D. (1974). "Diagnosis of 'rheumatoid variants': ankylosing spondylitis, the arthritides of gastrointestinal diseases and psoriasis, and Reiter's syndrome." *West. J. Med.*, **120**: 441–447.

ROOS, B. O. (1974). "Dual photon absorptiometry in lumbar vertebrae: I. Therapy and method." *Acta Radiol. (Ther.)*, **13**: 266–280.

ROWBOTHAM, G. F. (1955). "Early diagnosis of compression of the spinal cord by neoplasms." *Lancet*, **2:** 1220–1222.

RYMER, M. M. & KAO, C. C. (1974). "Pitfalls in the diagnosis of low back and leg pain." *Postgrad. Med.*, **56:** 76–80.

SINGH, M., RIGGS, B. L., BEABOUT, J. W. & JOWSEY, J. (1972). "Femoral trabecular-pattern index for evaluation of spinal osteoporosis." *Ann. Intern. Med.*, **77:** 63–67.

SPILLANE, J. D. & LLOYD, G. H. T. (1952). "The diagnosis of lesions of the spinal cord in association with osteoarthritic disease of the cervical spine." *Brain*, **75:** 177–186.

STUCKY, E. K. (1944). "Diagnosis and treatment of low back pain." *Arch. Phys. Ther.*, **25:** 34–40.

SULLIVAN, C. R. (1961). "Diagnosis and treatment of pyogenic infections of the intervertebral disk." *Surg. Clin. Nth. Amer.*, **41:** 1077–1086.

THOMPSON, M. (1953). "Osteitis condensans ilii and its differentiation from ankylosing spondylitis." *Ann. Rheum. Dis.*, **13:** 147.

TUCKER, R. F. & SCOTT, R. N. (1968). "Development of a surgically implanted myo-telemetry control system." *J. Bone Joint Surg.*, **50B:** 771–779.

WALTER, W. G. (1969). "Telemetering of biological data in man and animals." *Proc. Roy. Soc. Med.*, **62:** 449–450.

WATSON, B. W., ROSS, B. & KAY, A. W. (1962). "Telemetering from within the body using a pressure-sensitive radio pill." *J. Brit. Soc. Gastroent.*, **3:** 181–186.

WEBB, J., COLLINS, L. T., SOUTHWELL, P. B. & DICK-SMITH, J. B. (1971). "Fluorine-18 isotope scan in the early diagnosis of sacroiliitis." *Med. J. Austr.*, **2:** 1270–1274.

ZEITER, W. J. & HOUSE, F. B. (1946). "Cervical periarthritis: diagnosis and treatment." *Arch. Phys. Med.*, **27:** 162–165.

### (b) Clinical History, Examination and Differential Diagnosis

ALLEN, M. L. & LINDEN, M. C. (1950). "Significant roentgen findings in routine pre-employment examination of the lumbosacral spine." *Amer. J. Surg.*, **80:** 762–766.

ANDERSSON, G. (1972). "Hip assessment: a comparison of nine different methods." *J. Bone Joint Surg.*, **54B:** 621–625.

BALAU, J. & HUPFAUER, W. (1974). "The differential diagnosis of injuries of the atlanto-axial region in childhood." *Arch. Orthop. Unfall-Chir.*, **78**: 343–355.

BARNES, C. D. (1971). "The differential diagnosis of backache." *Brit. J. Hosp. Med.*, 219–231.

BERGSMAN, A., VON REIS, G. & SAHLGREN, E. (1952). "Diagnosis and treatment of sciatica based on a follow-up study." *Acta Med. Scand.*, **144**: 71–73.

BIANCO, A. J. (1968). "Low back pain and sciatica: diagnosis and indications for treatment." *J. Bone Joint Surg.*, **50A:** 170–181.

CAILLIET, R. (1968). "The diagnosis of neck and arm pain by examination." *Illinois Med. J.*, **133:** 277.

CAILLIET, R. (1969). "Low back pain: diagnosis by history and examination." *Southern Med. J.*, **62:** 1459–1462.

CHURCHER, M. D. (1973). "Pain clinic cases." *Practitioner*, **210:** 243–246.

COLLETTE, J. & LUDWIG, E. G. (1968). "Low back disorders: an examination of a stereotype." *Indust. Med. Surg.*, **37:** 685–687.

CYRIAX, J. (1970). "Examination of the spinal column." *Physiotherapy*, **56:** 2.

DIVELEY, R. L. & OGELVIE, R. R. (1956). "Pre-employment examinations of the low back." *J. Amer. Ass.*, **160:** 856–858.

ELLIOTT, F. A. & SCHUTTA, H. S. (1971). "The differential diagnosis of sciatica." *Orthop. Clin. Nth. Amer.*, **2:** 477–484.

FRIBERG, S. (1939). "Studies on spondylolisthesis." *Acta Chir. Scand.*, Suppl. **55:** 1.

GARDNER, R. C. (1971). "New test for intervertebral disc disease." *Ann. Intern. Med.*, **75:** 450–481.

GARDNER-MEDWIN, D. & WALTON, J. N. (1969). "A classification of the neuro-muscular disorders and a note on the clinical examination of the voluntary muscles." In *Disorders of Voluntary Muscle*, 2nd ed. pp. 411–453. Ed. by J. N. Walton. London; Churchill.

GERBERSHAGEN, H. U. (1975). "The pain clinic: an interdisciplinary team approach to the problem of pain." *Brit. J. Anaesth.*, **47:** 526–529.

GOB, A. & STOTZ, S. (1974). "The differential diagnosis of lumbago and its operative treatment." *Munich Med. Wochenschr.*, **116:** 273–280.

GOFTON, P. (1968). "Differential diagnosis of ankylosing spondylitis and rheumatoid arthritis." *Med. Clin. Nth. Amer.*, **52:** 517.

GORDON, E. J. (1968). "Diagnosis and treatment of acute low back disorders." *Industr. Med. Surg.*, **37**: 756–761.

GRONERT, H.-J. (1973). "The differential diagnosis of ankylosis of the sacro-iliac joints. *Arch. Orthop. Unfall-Chir.*, **77**: 55–63.

HAINS, J. D. (1973). "Fibreoptic laryngoscopy in ankylosing spondylitis." *J. Laryngol. Otol.*, **87**: 699–703.

HAKELIUS, A. (1970). "Prognosis in sciatica: a clinical follow-up of surgical and non-surgical treatment." *Acta Orthop. Scand.* Suppl. **129**: 1–76.

HAMMOND, W. (1969). "Clinical examination and the physiotherapist." *Aust. J. Physiotherapy*, **June: 47.**

HART, D. (1968). "The stiff aching back: the differential diagnosis of ankylosing spondylitis." *Lancet*, **1**: 740.

HIRSCH, C. (1958). "The clinical evaluation of sciatica." *Acta Orthop. Scand.*, **27**: 210–218.

HIRSCH, C. & NACHEMSON, A. (1961). "Clinical observations on the spine in ejected pilots." *Acta Orthop. Scand.*, **31**: 135–145.

HIRSCH, C. & NACHEMSON, A. (1963). "Clinical observations on the spines of ejected pilots. *Industr. Med. and Surg.*, **16**: 28–29.

HORAL, J., NACHEMSON, A. & SCHELLER, S. (1972). "Clinical and radiological long term follow-up of vertebral fractures in children." *Acta Orthop. Scand.*, **43**: 491–503.

HOWORTH, A. (1962). *Examination and Diagnosis of the Spine and Extremities*. Springfield, Illinois; Thomas.

ILLOUZ, G. & COSTE, F. (1964). "The 'tripod sign' in clinical examination of the sacro-iliac joints." *Presse Méd.*, **72**: 1979–1980.

INGHAM, J. G. (1969). "Quantitative evaluation of subjective symptoms." *Proc. Roy. Soc. Med.*, **62**: 492–494.

JAMES, J. J. (1975). "Expanded role for the physical therapist. Screening musculoskeletal disorders." *Phys. Ther.*, **55**: 121–131.

KAISER, G. (1974). "Orthopaedic backache and its differential diagnosis." *Beitr. Orthop. Traumatol.*, **21**: 121–128.

KEEGAN, J. J. (1958). "Variation of symptoms with herniation of intervertebral discs." *Nebraska State Med. J.*, **43**: 191–194.

LINDAHL, O. (1966). "Determination of the sagittal mobility of the lumbar spine: a clinical method." *Acta Orthop. Scand.*, **37**: 241–254.

McBRIDE, E. D. (1967). "Evaluation of disability of the back." *J. Okla. Med. Ass.*, **60**: 660–663.

MAGNUSON, H. J. (1969). "A periodic examination program for occupational health." *J. Occup. Med.*, **11**: 349–354.

MAGORA, A. (1974). "Investigation of the relation between low back pain and occupation: 6. Medical history and symptoms." *Scand. J. Rehab. Med.*, **6**: 81–88.

MAITLAND, G. D. (1971). "Examination of the lumbar spine." *Aust. J. Physiother.*, **17**: 5–11.

MILLARD, L. (1975). "Clinical evaluation of low back pain." *J. Arkansas Med. Soc.*, **71**: 309–311.

MILLER, D. S. (1973). "Low back pain: differential diagnosis determines treatment." *Med. Trials Tech. Clinics.*, **20**: 1–41.

MILWEE, R. H. (1939). "Impressions gained in analysing 10,000 lumbar spines." *Texas State J. Med.*, **34**: 691.

MOLEN, H. R. VAN DER, & CONINX, S. H. A. (1971). "A new symptom aiding the differential diagnosis between vascular and radicular pain in the lower limb." *Phlebologie*, **24**: 364–368.

MOLL, J. M. H. & WRIGHT, V. (1973). "New York clinical criteria for ankylosing spondylitis: a statistical evaluation." *Ann. Rheum. Dis.*, **32**: 354–363.

NACHLAS, I. W. (1936). "The knee flexion test for pathology in the lumbosacral and sacroiliac joints." *J. Bone Joint Surg.*, **18**: 724–725.

NATHAN, F. F. & BICKEL, W. H. (1968). "Spontaneous axial subluxation in a child as the first sign of juvenile rheumatoid arthritis." *J. Bone Joint Surg.*, **50A**: 1675–1678.

NÖLLER, H. G. (1960). "Clinical applications of telemetering techniques." *Proc. 3rd Int. Cong. Med. Electronics.*" **1**: 111–114.

O'CONNELL, J. E. A. (1946). "Clinical diagnosis of lumbar intervertebral disk protrusions with indications for their operative removal." *Brit. Med. J.*, **1**: 122–124.

OLINGER, C. P. (1973). "A wide-angle needle endoscope." *Trans. Amer. Neurol. Assoc.*, **98**: 38–42.

PITKIN, H. C. & PHEASANT, H. C. (1936). "Sacrarthrogenetic telalgia." *J. Bone Joint Surg.*, **18**: "Studies on referred pain." 111–133; "Sacroiliac mobility": 365–374; "Alternating scoliosis:" 706–716; "Differential diagnosis:" 1008–1017; "Treatment:" **19**: 169–184.

RISSER, J. C., AGUSTINI, S., SAMPAIO, J. R. DE A. & GARIBALDI,

C. A. H. (1973). "The sitting-standing height ratio as a method of evaluating early spine fusion in the growing child." *Clin. Orthopedica*, **24**: 7–14.

RUBACKY, G. E. (1970). "Claw toes: an early sign of lumbar diskogenic disease." *J. Amer. Med. Assoc.*, **214**: 375.

RUBIN, L. (1948). "Linea scleroderma: association with abnormalities of the spine and nervous system." *Archiv. Dermatol. Syph.*, **58**: 1–18.

SCHAM, S. M. & TAYLOR, T. K. F. (1971). "Tension signs in lumbar disc prolapse." *Clin. Orthop.*, **75**: 195–204.

SEGIL, C. M. (1973). "The localisation of symptomatic levels in discogenic disease of the spine." *J. Bone Joint Surg.*, **55B**: 665.

SHAPIRO, R. (1973). "The differential diagnosis of traumatic lesions of the occipito-atlanto-axial segment." *Radiol. Clin. Nth. Amer.*, **11**: 505–526.

SHARP, J. (1966). "The differential diagnosis of ankylosing spondylitis." *Proc. Roy. Soc. Med.*, **59**: 453–455.

SMITH, F. P. (1958). "Confirmation test of reaction to straight leg raising." *Surg. Forum*, **9**: 696–697.

SPRANGFORT, E. V. (1971). "Lasègue's sign in patients with lumbar disc herniation." *Acta Orthop. Scand.*, **42**: 459–460.

SPRANGFORT, E. V. (1972). "The lumbar disc herniation: a computeraided analysis of 2,504 operations." *Acta Orthop. Scand.*, Suppl. **142**: 1.

STEWART, S. F. (1947). "Pre-employment examination of the back." *J. Bone Joint Surg.*, **29**: 215–221, 236.

SWEETMAN, B. J., ANDERSON, J. A. D. & DALTON, E. R. (1974). "The relationships between little-finger mobility, lumbar mobility, straight-leg-raising and low back pain." *Rheumatol. Rehab.*, **13**: 161–166.

SWERDLOW, M. (1972). "The pain clinic." *Brit. J. Clin. Pract.*, **26**: 403–407.

TAYLOR, T. K. F. & WIENIR, M. (1969). "Great toe reflexes in the diagnosis of lumbar disc disorder." *Brit. Med. J.*, **2**: 487–489.

TEPPER, F. R. (1974). "Acute nontraumatic back pain: differential diagnosis in the emergency room." *J. Amer. Osteopath. Assoc.*, **73**: 398–401.

THOMPSON, M. (1957). "Discussion on the clinical and radiological aspects of sacroiliac disease." *Proc. Roy. Soc. Med.*, **50**: 847–858.

WEBB, K. J. (1974). "Early assessment of orthopedic injuries." *Amer. J. Nurs.*, **74:** 1048–1052.

WILKINS, R. H. & BRODY, I. A. (1969). "Lasèque's sign." *Arch. Neurol.*, **21:** 219–221.

WOODHALL, B. & HAYES, G. J. (1950). "The well-leg-raising test of Fajerstajn in the diagnosis of ruptured lumbar intervertebral disc." *J. Bone Joint Surg.*, **32A:** 786–792.

YAMADA, K., IKATA, T., YAMAMOTO, H., NAKAGAWA, Y., TANAKA, H. & TEZUKA, A. (1969). "Equilibrium function in scoliosis and active corrective plaster jacket for the treatment." *Tokushima J. Exp. Med.*, **16:** 1–7.

YERGASSON, P. (1932). "A diagnostic sign in examination of affections of the sacroiliac joint: chair test." *J. Bone Joint Surg.*, **14:** 116–117.

ZINOVIEFF, A. & HARBOROW, P. R. H. (1975). "Inclinometer for measuring straight-leg raising." *Rheumatol. Rehab.*, **14:** 115.

### *(c) Goniometry and other Measuring Procedures*

BECK, A. & KILLUS, J. (1973). "Normal posture of the spine determined by mathematical and statistical methods." *Aerospace Med.*, **44:** 1277–1281.

BENNET, J. G., BERGMANIS, L. E., CARPENTER, J. E. & SKOWLUND, H. V. (1963). "Range of motion of the neck." *J. Amer. Phys. Ther. Ass.*, **43:** 45–47.

BURROWS, E. H. (1963). "Sagittal diameter of the spinal canal in cervical spondylosis." *Clin. Radiol.*, **14:** 77–86.

CURETON, T. K. (1931). "The validity of anteroposterior spinal measurements." *Research Quart.*, **2:** 101–113.

DEANE, G. & DUTHIE, R. B. (1973). "A new projectional look at articulated scoliotic spines." *Acta Orthop. Scand.*, **44:** 351–365.

DELMAS, A. & PINEAU, H. (1970). "Relations between the diameters and superior and inferior surfaces of the fifth lumbar vertebra." *Arch. Anat. Path. (Sem. Hôp. Paris)*, **18:** 293–296.

DELMAS, A. & PINEAU, H. (1970). "Surface of the lumbosacral articular apophyses." *Compt. Rend. Assoc. Anat.*, **148:** 353–356.

DUTHIE, R. B. (1975). "The projectional aspects of scoliosis." *J. Bone Joint Surg.*, **57B:** 246.

FARFAN, H. F., HEUBERDEAU, R. M. & DUBOW, H. I. (1972).

"Lumbar intervertebral disc degeneration. The influence of geometrical features on the pattern of disc degeneration—a post mortem study." *J. Bone Joint Surg.*, **54A:** 492–510.

GÖTZE, H. G. (1973). "The rotation index in idiopathic thoracic scoliosis." *Zeit. Orthop.*, **111:** 737–743.

HELLEMS, H. K. & KEATS, T. E. (1971). "Measurement of the normal lumbosacral angle." *Amer. J. Roentgenol.*, **113:** 642–645.

HIGASHI, H. (1974). "Studies on pathogenesis of cervical spondylotic myelopathy: sagittal diameter of the spinal canal and cerebrospinal fluid characteristics in cervical spondylosis." *Folia Psychiatr. Neurol. Jap.*, **28:** 35–44.

HILLEM, H. K. & KEATS, T. (1971). "Measurement of the normal lumbosacral angle." *Amer. J. Roentgenol.*, **113:** 642–646.

HINCK, V. C., HOPKINS, C. E. & CLARK, W. M. (1965). "Sagittal diameter of the lumbar spinal canal in children and adults." *Radiol.*, **85:** 929–937.

KARPOVICH, P. V., HERDEN, E. L. & ASA, M. M. (1960). "Electrogoniometric study of joints." *U.S. Armed Forces M. J.*, **11:** 424–450.

LEDENT, R. (1908). "Measuring apparatus in physiotherapy: the goniometer." *Ann. Med. Phys., Anvers.*, **4:** 141–147.

LINDAHL, O. & MOVIN, A. (1968). "Measurement of the deformity in scoliosis." *Acta Orthop. Scand.*, **39:** 291–302.

LUKAS, R. (1959). "Contribution on the determination of degree of rotation of vertebral bodies by angle measurement." *Zeit. Orthop.*, **91:** 286–296.

MERLINO, A. F. (1973). "A protractor for measuring scoliosis by the Cobb technique." *J. Bone Joint Surg.*, **53A:** 1098–1099.

MILCH, M. (1942). "The pelvifemoral angle-determination of hip-flexion deformity." *J. Bone Joint Surg.*, **24:** 148–153.

MITCHELSON, D. L. (1973). "An opto-electronic technique for analysis of angular movements." *Biomechanics*, **3:** 181–184.

MURONE, I. (1974). "The importance of the sagittal diameters of the cervical spinal canal in relation to spondylosis and myelopathy." *J. Bone Joint Surg.*, **56B:** 30–36.

NEUGEBAUER, H. (1972). "Cobb or Ferguson: an analysis of the two commonly used radiographic measuring methods in scoliosis." *Zeit. Orthop.*, **110:** 342–356.

NEUKOMM, P. A. (1974). "The rubber band goniometer: a telemetric method for the measurement of angle, angular velocity, displacement and velocity." *Biotelemetry J.*, **2**: 12–20.

REED, D. J. & REYNOLDS, P. J. (1969). "A joint angle detector." *J. Appl. Physiol.*, **27**: 745–748.

SCHULTZ, A. B., LAROCCA, H. GALANTE, J. O. & ANDRIACCHI, T. (1972). "A study of geometrical relationships in scoliotic spines." *J. Biomechanics*, **5**: 409–420.

STURROCK, R. D., WOJTULEWSKI, J. A. & HART, F. D. (1973). "Spondylometry in a normal population and in ankylosing spondylitis." *Rheumatol. Rehab.*, **12**: 135–142.

SWIDERSKI, G. (1973). "Spondylogoniometer." *Beit. Orthop. Traum.*, **20**: 593–600.

THIJN, C. J. (1975). "Measurements in the normal spinal column and their use in the diagnosis of platyspondylosis." *Radiol. Clin., Basel*, **44**: 45–59.

WIESS, M. (1964). "A multiple purpose goniometer." *Arch. Phys. Med. Rehab.*, **45**: 197–198.

WIECHEC, F. J. & KRUSEN, F. H. (1939). "A new method of joint measurement and a new review of the literature." *Amer. J. Surg.*, **43**: 659–668.

WISELL, R. A. & O'CONNELL, E. R. (1973). "Measurement of trunk lateral flexion: a clinical note." *J. Amer. Correct. Ther.*, **27**: 5–8.

WOLF, B. S., KHILNANI, M. & MATIS, L. I. (1956). "Sagittal diameter of bony cervical canal and its significance in cervical spondylosis." *J. Mt. Sinai Hosp.*, **23**: 283–292.

## (d) Neurology

ABDULLAH, A. F., DITTO, E. W., BYRD, E. B. & WILLIAMS, R. (1974). "Extreme-lateral lumbar disc herniations: clinical syndrome and special problems of diagnosis." *J. Neurosurg.*, **41**: 229–234.

AHLGREN, E. W., STEPHEN, C. R., LLOYD, E. A. C. & McCOLLUM, D. E. (1966). "Diagnosis of pain with a graduated spinal block technique." *J. Amer. Med. Ass.*, **195**: 813–816.

AIRD, R. B. & NAFFZIGER, H. C. (1940). "Prolonged jugular compression: a new diagnostic test of neurological value." *Trans. Amer. Neurol. Ass.*: 45–49.

BECHAR, M., BEKS, J. W. F. & PENNING, L. (1972). "Intradural arachnoid cysts with scalloping of vertebrae in the lumbosacral region: a case report and review of the literature." *Acta Neurochir.*, **26**: 275–283.

BORGESEN, S. E. & VANG, P. S. (1973). "Extradural pseudocysts: a cause of pain after lumbar disc operation." *Acta Orthop. Scand.*, **44**: 12–20.

BRIDENBAUGH, P. O., TUCKER, G. T., MOORE, D. C., BRIDENBAUGH, L. D. & THOMPSON, G. E. (1973). "Etidocaine: clinical evaluation for intercostal nerve block and lumbar epidural block." *Anesth. Analg.*, **52**: 407–413.

BURKE, J. F. (1965). "Correlation of chronaxy and motor nerve conduction velocity." *J. Amer. Phys. Ther. Ass.*, **45**: 955–961.

BURKE, J. F. & MILLER, J. W. (1963). "Chronaxic determinations in intervertebral disc pathology." *J. Amer. Phys. Ther. Ass.*, **43**: 265–267.

COLLINS, J. D. (1975). "Percutaneous spinal biopsy." *J. Natl. Med. Ass.*, **67**: 220–234.

CRANE, P. (1968). "Significance of polyphasic potentials in the diagnosis of cervical root involvement." *Arch. Phys. Med. Rehab.*, **49**: 403.

DEBELLE, M. (1973). "Electrocutaneous reflex as a tool for objective studies of pain sensitivity in man." *J. Belge Rhumatol. Med. Phys.*, **28**: 141–152.

EHNI, G. & McNEEL, D. (1970). "The spinal manometric examination (Quckenstedt's test): the effects of certain factors as seen in a hydraulic model." *J. Neurosurg.*, **33**: 654–661.

ELSBERG, G. A. & DYKE, C. G. (1934). "Diagnosis and localization of tumours of the spinal cord by means of measurements made on X-ray films of vertebrae, and the correlation with clinical findings." *Bull. Neurol. Inst., New York*, **3**: 359–394.

FAHRNI, W. H. (1966). "Observations on straight leg-raising with special reference to nerve root adhesions." *Canad. J. Surg.*, **9**: 44–48.

FALCONER, M. A., McGEORGE, M. & BEGG, A. C. (1948). "Observations of the cause and mechanism of symptom production in sciatica and low back pain." *J. Neurol. Neurosurg. Psychiat.*, **11**: 13–26.

FERGUSON, J. F. & KIRSCH, W. M. (1974). "Epidural empyema following thoracic epidural block. Case report." *J. Neurosurg.*, **41**: 762–764.

FIELDS, W. S., *et al.* (1972). "High cervical neurinoma: special neurologic and radiologic features." *Zentralbl. Neurochir.*, **33:** 90–102.

GODDARD, M. D. & REID, J. D. (1965). "Movements induced by straight leg raising in the lumbosacral roots, nerves and plexus, and in the intrapelvic section of the sciatic nerve." *J. Neurol. Neurosurg. Psychiat.*, **28:** 12–18.

GRANT, W. T. & CONE, W. V. (1934). "Graduated jugular compression in the lumbar manometric test for spinal subarachnoid block." *Arch. Neurol.*, **32:** 1194–1201.

GREITZ, T. & LINDBLOM, U. (1966). "Selective nerve root blocking with phenol under myelographic control." *Investigative Radiol.*, **1:** 257–261.

HAKELIUS, A. (1970). "Prognosis in sciatica: a clinical follow-up of surgical and non-surgical treatment." *Acta Orthop. Scand.*, Suppl. **129:** 1–76.

HAKELIUS, A. & HINDWARSH, J. (1972). "The significance of neurological signs and myelographic findings in the diagnosis of lumbar root compression." *Acta Orthop. Scand.*, **43:** 239–246.

HIGASHI, H. (1974). "Studies on pathogenesis of cervical spondylotic myelopathy: sagittal diameter of the spinal canal and cerebrospinal fluid characteristics in cervical spondylosis." *Folia Psychiat. Neurol. Jap.*, **28:** 35–44.

HOOPER, J. (1973). "Low back pain and manipulation: paraparesis after treatment of low back pain by physical methods." *Med. J. Austr.*, **1:** 549–551.

JAMES, C. C. M. & LASSMAN, L. P. (1962). "Spinal dysraphism: the diagnosis and treatment of progressive lesions in spina bifida occulta." *J. Bone Joint Surg.*, **44B:** 828–840.

JELASIC, F. (1974). "Functional restitution after cervical avulsion injury with typical myelographic findings." *Folia Haematol.*, **101:** 158–163.

JOHNSON, E. R., POWELL, J., CALDWELL, J. & CRANE, F. (1974). "Intercostal nerve conduction and posterior rhizotomy in the diagnosis and treatment of thoracic radiculopathy." *J. Neurol. Neurosurg. Psychiatr.*, **37:** 330–332.

KEEGAN, J. (1944). "Diagnosis of herniation of lumbar intervertebral disks by neurological signs." *J. Amer. Med. Ass.*, **126:** 868–873.

KENDALL, P. H. (1960). "New inventions—a trephine needle for vertebral body biopsy." *Lancet*, **1:** 474.

KEWALRAMANI, L. S. (1975). "Brachial plexus root avulsion. Role of myelography—review of diagnostic procedures." *J. Trauma*, **15**: 603–608.

KRUITSSON, B. (1961). "Comparative value of electromyographic, myelographic and clinical-neurological examinations in diagnostic lumbar root compression syndrome." *Acta Orth. Scand.* Suppl. **49**: 1.

KREMPEN, J. F. (1975). "Selective nerve root infiltration for the evaluation of sciatica." *Orthop. Clin. Nth. Amer.*, **6**: 311–315.

KREMPEN, J. F. & SMITH, B. S. (1974). "Nerve-root injection: a method for evaluating the etiology of sciatica." *J. Bone Joint Surg.*, **56A**: 1435–1444.

LADER, M. H. & MONTAGU, J. D. (1962). "The psycho-galvanic reflex: a pharmacological study of the peripheral mechanism." *J. Neurol. Neurosurg. Psychiat.*, **25**: 126–133.

LAKE, M. (1972). "Combined abdominal and jugular compression: a test for spinal subarachnoid obstruction." *Neurochir.*, **15**: 95–98.

LANSCHE, W. E. & FORD, L. T. (1960). "Correlation of the myelogram with clinical and operative findings in lumbar disc lesions." *J. Bone Joint Surg.*, **42A**: 193–206.

LECHOWSKI, S. & LORENS, M. (1973). "Unilateral multilevel protrusion of nucleus pulposus in the lumbar region." *Neurol. Neurochir. Pol.*, **7**: 429–433.

LIEBERMAN, L. M., TOURTELOTTE, W. W. & NEWKIRK, T. A. (1971). "Prolonged post-lumbar puncture cerebrospinal fluid leakage from lumbar subarachnoid space demonstrated by radioisotope myelography." *Neurology*, **21**: 925–929.

LIVESON, J. A. & ZIMMER, A. E. (1972). "A localizing symptom in thoracic myelopathy: a variation of Lhermitte's sign." *Ann. Intern. Med.*, **76**: 769–771.

MICHELE, A. A. (1958). "The flip sign in sciatic nerve function." *Surg.*, **44**: 940–942.

MICHELE, A. A. (1959). "The buckling sign—a determinative in sciatic nerve tension." *N.Y. State J. Med.*, **59**: 2173–2175.

NORDQVIST, L. (1961). "The sagittal diameter of the spinal cord and subarachnoid space in different age groups: a roentgenographic postmortem study." *Acta Radiol.*, Suppl. **227**: 1.

NORLEN, G. (1944). "On the value of the neurological symptoms in sciatica for the localization of a lumbar disc herniation." *Acta Chir. Scand.*, Suppl. **95**: 1.

PSAKI, R. C. & KUITERT, J. H. (1952). "Diagnosis of injury to the roots and branches of the lumbar plexus." *Arch. Phys. Med.*, **33**: 10–14.

ROBERSON, G. H., LLEWELLYN, H. J. & TAVERAL, J. M. (1973). "The narrow lumbar spinal canal syndrome." *Radiology*, **107**: 89–97.

ROGOFF, E. E., DECK, M. D. F. & D'ANGIO, G. (1974). "The second sac: a complicating factor in regimens based on intrathecal medications." *Amer. J. Roentgenol.*, **120**: 568–572.

ROSOMOFF, H. L., JOHNSTON, J. D. H., GALLO, A. E., LUDMER, M., GIVENS, F. T., CARNEY, F. R. & CUEHN, C. A. (1963). "Cystometry in the evaluation of nerve root compression in the lumbar spine." *Surg. Gynec. Obst.*, **117**: 263–270.

ROSOMOFF, H. L., JOHNSTON, J. D. G., GALLO, A. E., LUDMER, M., GIVENS, F. T., CARNEY, F. T. & CUEHN, C. A. (1970). "Cystometry as an adjunct in the evaluation of lumbar disc syndromes." *J. Neurosurg.*, **33**: 67–74.

RUSSELL, M. L., GORDON, D. A., ORGYZLO, M. A. & MCPHEDRAN, R. S. (1973). "The cauda equina syndrome of ankylosing spondylitis." *Ann. Int. Med.*, **78**: 551–554.

SARNOFF, S. J. & ARROWOOD, J. G. (1946). "Differential spinal block: a preliminary report." *Surg.*, **20**: 150–159.

SARNOFF, S. J. & ARROWOOD, J. G. (1947). "Differential spinal block: II. The reaction of sudomotor and vasomotor fibres." *J. Clin. Invest.*, **26**: 203–216.

SARNOFF, S. J. & ARROWOOD, J. G. (1947). "Differential spinal block: III. The block of cutaneous and stretch reflexes in the presence of unimpaired position sense." *J. Neurophysiol.*, **10**: 205–210.

SCHUTZ, H., LOUGHEED, W. M., WORTZMAN, G. & AWERBUCH, B. G. (1973). "Intervertebral nerve-root block in the investigation of chronic lumbar disc disease." *Canad. J. Surg.*, **16**: 217–221.

SHEALY, C. N. (1966). "Dangers of spinal injections without proper diagnosis." *J. Amer. Med. Ass.*, **197**: 1104–1106.

SICARD, A. & LAVARDE, G. (1969). "Radiculography in the diagnosis of lumbosciatica." *Acta Orthop. Belg.*, **35**: 631–635.

SINCLAIR, D. J. & RITCHIE, G. W. (1972). "Morbidity in post-myelogram patients: a survey of 100 patients." *J. Canad. Ass. Radiol.*, **23**: 278–283.

SKALPE, I. O. (1975). "Lumbar radiculography with metrizamide." *Radiology*, **115:** 91–95.

SKALPE, I. O. & TALLE, K. (1973). "Lumbar radiculography with meglumine iocarmate (Dimer-X): a clinical report with reference to the adverse effects." *J. Oslo City Hosp.*, **23:** 121–127.

SODERBERG, L. (1959). "Neurological complications following myelography." *Acta Orthop. Scand.*, **29:** 170.

SPRANGFORT, E. V. (1972). "The lumbar disc herniation: a computer-aided analysis of 2,504 operations." *Acta Orthop. Scand.*, Suppl. **142:** 1.

STEINESS, I. (1958). "Biothesiometry in the diagnosis of lumbar disk protrusion." *Neurology*, **8:** 793–795.

TENG, P. & PAPATHEODOROU, C. (1963). "Myelographic findings in spondylosis of the lumbar spine." *Brit. J. Radiol.*, **36:** 122–128.

TENG, P. & PAPATHEODOROU, C. (1966). "Spinal arachnoid diverticula." *Brit. J. Radiol.*, **39:** 249–254.

THOMSON, J. L. G. (1966). "Myelography in dorsal disc protrusion." *Acta Radiol.*, **5:** 1140–1146.

WALK, L. (1953). "Diagnostic lumbar disk puncture." *Arch. Surg.*, **66:** 232–243.

WINNIE, A. P. & COLLINS, V. J. (1968). "The pain clinic. I: Differential neural blockade in pain syndromes of questionable etiology." *Med. Clin. Nth. Amer.*, **52:** 123–129.

WOOLSEY, R. D. (1954). "The mechanism of neurological symptoms and signs in spondylolisthesis at the fifth lumbar, first sacral level." *J. Neurosurg.*, **11:** 67–76.

WRIGHT, F. W., SANDERS, R. C., STEEL, W. M., & O'CONNOR B. T. (1971). "Some observations on the value and techniques of myelography in lumbar disc lesions: results over a five-year period at the Nuffield Orthopaedic Centre." *Clin. Radiol.*, **22:** 33–43.

WYKE, B. D. (1967). "The neurology of joints." *Ann. Roy. Coll. Surg. Engl.*, **41:** 25–50.

WYKE, B. D. (1970). "The neurological basis of thoracic spinal pain." *Rheumatol. Phys. Med.*, **10:** 356–362.

WYKE, B. D. (1976). "Neurological aspects of low back pain." In *The Lumbar Spine and Back Pain.* pp. 189–256. Ed. by M. I. V. Jayson. London; Sector Publishing.

WYKE, B. D. (1977). "Neurological mechanisms of spinal pain." In

*Patología de la Columna Vertebral.* pp. 45–56. Ed. by S. Hernández Conesa and J. Seiguer. Murcia; Ferrer Internacional.

WYKE, B. D. (1979). "Neurology of the cervical spinal joints." *Physiotherapy*, **65**: 72–76.

### (e) Radiography

ABEL, M. S. & HARMON, P. H. (1960). "Oblique motion studies and other non-myelographic roentgenographic criteria for diagnosis of traumatised or degenerated lumbar intervertebral discs." *Amer. J. Surg.*, **99**: 717–726.

ADLER, E. & LAVIS, S. (1956). "Clinical evaluation of X-ray findings in the cervical spine." *Acta Med. Orient. (Tel Aviv)*, **15**: 129–136.

AGNOLI, A. L. (1974). "Studies with a water-soluble contrast medium without anaesthesia in the diagnosis of disease processes in the lumbosacral region." *Fortschr. Röntgenstr.*, **120**: 608–616.

ALARCÓN-SEGOVIA, D., CETINA, J. A. & DÍAZ-JOUANEN, E. (1973). "Sacro-iliac joint in primary gout: clinical and roentgenographic study of 143 patients." *Amer. J. Roentgenol.*, **118**: 438–443.

ALLEN, M. L. & LINDEM, M. C. (1950). "Significant roentgen findings in routine pre-employment examination of the lumbo-sacral spine." *Amer. J. Surg.*, **80**: 762–766.

ALLEN, R. J. (1974). "Aid to lumbar puncture in myelography and encephalography." *Australas. Radiol.*, **18**: 229.

ANDERSON, R. K. (1951). "Diodrast studies of the vertebral and cranial venous systems to show their probable role in cerebral metastases." *J. Neurosurg.*, **8**: 411–422.

ARBUCKLE, R. K., SHELDON, R. K. & PUDENZ, R. H. (1945). "Pantopaque myelography: correlation of roentgenologic and neurologic findings." *Radiology*, **45**: 356.

BABIN, E. (1974). "The value of frontal zonographic sections in sacro-radiculography." *Neuroradiol.*, **7**: 161–166.

BAKKE, S. N. (1931). "Radiological observations on movements of the spine." *Acta Radiol.*, Suppl. **13**: 1.

BARNETT, E. & NORDIN, B. E. C. (1960). "The radiological diagnosis of osteoporosis: a new approach." *Clin. Radiol.*, **11**: 166–174.

BARNHARD, H. J. & DODD, D. (1973). "Radiographic anatomy of the lumbar vertebrae." *Med. Radiog. Photog.*, **49**: 7–20.

BARTON, P. N. & BIRAM, J. H. (1946). "Preplacement X-ray examination of the lower back." *Indust. Med.*, **15:** 319–322.

BAUER, G. C. H. (1968). "The use of radionucleides in orthopaedics. Part IV: Radionucleide scintimetry of the skeleton." *J. Bone Joint Surg.*, **50A:** 1681–1709.

BEGG, A. C. & FALCONER, M. A. (1949). "Plain radiography in intraspinal protrusion of lumbar intervertebral disks: correlation with operative findings." *Brit. J. Surg.*, **36:** 225–239.

BEGG, A. C., FALCONER, M. A. & McGEORGE, M. (1946). "Myelography in lumbar intervertebral disk lesions: a correlation with operative findings." *Brit. J. Surg.*, **34:** 141–157.

BERMAN, T. (1974). "X-ray conference: spine changes in a 20-year-old black male." *Minn. Med.*, **57:** 725–727.

BERNAGEAU, J. & GOUTALLIER, D. (1973). "Value of discography in the pre-operative assessment of chronic lumbago." *Rev. Rhum.*, **40:** 760–763.

BLAND, D. (1965). "Study of roentgenologic criteria for rheumatoid arthritis of the cervical spine." *Amer. J. Roentgenol.*, **95:** 949.

BLUMEL, J., EVANS, E. B., HADNOTT, J. L. & EGGERS, G. W. N. (1962). "Congenital skeletal anomalies of the spine: an analysis of the charts and roentgenograms of 261 patients." *Amer. Surg.*, **28:** 501–509.

BOHATIRCHUK, F. (1955). "The ageing vertebral column (macro- and historadiographical study)." *Brit. J. Radiol.*, **28:** 389–404.

BOND, M. B. (1964). "Low-back X-rays: criteria for their use in placement examination in industry." *J. Occup. Med.*, **6:** 373–380.

BROCHER, J. E. (1970). "Vertebral column disorders and their differential diagnosis." *Arch. Norm. Path. Anat. Roentgenbild.*, **68:** 1–881.

BROMER, R. S. (1939). "Significant skeletal changes in low back and sciatic pain: roentgenologic observations." *Radiology*, **33:** 688–694.

BUMSTEAD, P. (1955). "Routine examinations of the cervical spine." *X-ray Techn.*, **27:** 247.

BURN, J. M., GUYER, P. B. & LANGDON, L. (1973). "The spread of solutions injected into the epidural space: a study using epidurograms in patients with the lumbosciatic syndrome." *Brit. J. Anaesth.*, **45:** 338–345.

BURWOOD, R. J. & WATT, I. (1974). "Assimilation of the atlas and basilar impression: review of 1,500 skull and cervical spine radiographs." *Clin. Radiol.*, **25:** 327–333.

CASEY, B. M., EATON, S. B., DUBOIS, J. J., TREMAINE, M. D. & MANI, C. L. (1973). "Thoracolumbar neural arch fractures: evaluation by hyposcycloidal tomography." *J. Amer. Med. Ass.*, **224:** 1263–1265.

CASUCCIO, C. & SCAPINELLI, R. (1961). "Clinical and anatomico-radiological studies of pathological changes in the vertebral spinous processes and adjacent soft tissues." *J. Bone Joint Surg.*, **44B:** 218–219.

CEVANSIR, B. & BASERER, J. (1972). "Cervical osteophytes: clinical and radiological findings." *J. Otolaryng. Soc. Austr.*, **3:** 359–361.

CHYNN, K. Y. (1973). "Painless myelography: introduction of a new aspiration cannula and review of 541 consecutive studies." *Radiology*, **109:** 361–367.

CIARPAGLINI, L. & FUSI, G. (1955). "Histochemical and radiographic studies of the vertebrae in old subjects." *Sperimentale*, **105:** 129–131.

CITRIN, D. L., BESSENT, R. G. & TUOHY, J. B. (1974). "Bone scanning in malignant disease." *Brit. J. Hosp. Med.*, **13:** 424–436.

CLARKE, G. R. (1972). "Unequal leg length: an accurate method of detection and some clinical results." *Rheum Phys. Med.*, **11:** 385–390.

CLOWARD, R. B. (1959). "Cervical diskography." *Ann. Sur.*, **150:** 1052.

CLOWARD, R. B. & BUZAID, L. L. (1952). "Discography: technique, indications and evaluation of the normal and abnormal intervertebral disc." *Amer. J. Roentgenol.*, **68:** 552–564.

COCKSHOTT, W. P. (1958). "Anatomical anomalies observed in radiographs of Nigerians." *West Afr. Med. J.*, **7:** 179–184.

COHEN, A. S., MCNEILL, J. M., CALKINS, E., SHARP., J. T. & SCHUBART, A. (1967). "The normal sacroiliac joint: analysis of 88 sacroiliac roentgenograms." *Amer. J. Roentgenol.*, **100:** 559–563.

COHEN, J. & ABRAHAM, E. (1973). "The calcified intervertebral disc: a non-specific roentgenologic sign." *J. Med. Soc. New Jersey*, **70:** 459–460.

COLCHER, A. E. & HURSH, A. M. W. (1952). "Pre-employment low back X-ray survey: review of 1,500 cases." *Indust. Med.*, **21:** 319–321.

COLE, T. B. (1973). "Radiographic evaluation of the prevertebral space." *Laryngoscope*, **83**: 721–732.

COLLINS, H. R. (1975). "An evaluation of cervical and lumbar discography." *Clin. Orthop.*, **107**: 133–138.

CORRIGAN, J. (1969). "Radiological changes in rheumatoid cervical spines." *Aust. Radiol.*, **13**: 370–375.

CURRAN, J. T. (1975). "New approach to positioning for lumbosacral junction in lateral projection." *Radiol Technol.*, **46**: 294–297.

DANZIGER, J. (1972). "The use of Dimer-X in lumbar radiculography." *Sth. Afr. Med. J.*, **46**: 1967–1969.

DANZIGER, J. & BLOCH, (1973). "A clinical evaluation of Dimer-X in lumbar radiculography." *Clin. Radiol.*, **24**: 231–234.

DAVATCHI, F., BENOIST, M., MASSARE, C., HELENON, C. & BLOCH-MICHEL, H. (1969). "Contribution to the study of narrow canals in the lumbar region: radiological techniques and normal values." *Sem. Hôp., Paris*, **45**: 2008–2012.

DAVATCHI, F., BENOIST, M., MASSARE, C., HELENON, C. & BLOCH-MICHEL, H. (1969). "Study of the lumbar bony canal in common vertebral sciatica." *Sem. Hôp., Paris*, **45**: 2013–2016.

DEBAENE, A., ACQUAVIVA, P., DUFOUR, M. & LEGRÉ, J. (1973). "Hyperconcavity (scalloping) of the lumbar vertebrae in von Recklinghausen's disease." *J. Radiol. Electrol.*, **54**: 149–151.

DECKER, K. (1965). "Neuroradiological studies of movements of the spinal cord." *Verh. Anat. Ges.*, **115**: 35–47.

DELAYAYE, R. P., MANGIN, H., GUEFFIER, G., COMBES, A., CREN, M. & METGES, P. J. (1970). "Systematic radiological examination of the spine at the admission inspection of sea-faring personnel: definition of normality and procedure to be followed in the presence of congenital anomalies." *Rev. Corps Santé Armées*, **11**: 667–683.

DEQUEKER, J. (1974). "Femoral trabecular patterns in asymptomatic spinal osteoporosis and femoral neck fracture." *Clin. Radiol.*, **25**: 243–246.

D'ESHOUGUES, J. R., DELCAMBRE, B., ASCHER, J. & WAGHEMACKER, R. (1974). "Introduction to the radiological diagnosis and surgical treatment of lumbago." *Sem. Hôp., Paris*, **50**: 615–625.

DE VILLIERS, P. D. (1973). "Large-dose Dimer-X radiology and thoracic myelography." *Sth. Afr. Med. J.*, **47**: 2461–2465.

DE VILLIERS, P. D. (1974). "Dimer-X myelography, including the neck." *Sth. Afr. Med. J.*, **48**: 2629–2633.

DI CHIRO, G. & TIMINS, E. L. (1974). "Supine myelography and the septum posticum." *Radiol.*, **111**: 319–327.

DIHLMANN, W. (1962). "Radiological diagnostic studies of the sacro-iliac joints." *Fortschr. Roentgenstr.*, **96**: 812–822.

DIHLMANN, W. (1967). "Radiological diagnosis of the sacro-iliac joints." *Fortschr. Roentgenstr.*, Suppl. **97**: 1.

DITTRICH, R. J. (1938). "Roentgenologic aspects of spina bifida occulta." *Amer. J. Roentgenol.*, **39**: 937.

EDEIKEN, J., & PITT, M. J. (1971). "The radiologic diagnosis of disc disease." *Orthop. Clin. Nth. Amer.*, **2**: 405–417.

EICKHOFF, U. & VOIGT, K. (1973). "Functional diagnosis of chronic cervical vertebrogenic myelopathy." *Fortschr. Roentgenstr.*, **119**: 230–234.

ELIES, W. & TODOROW, S. (1974). "Studies on the resorption routes of an oily contrast medium (Durioliopaque) after spinal myelography." *Fortschr. Roentgenstr.*, **120**: 603–608.

EPSTEIN, B. S. (1964). "The evacuation of pantopaque from the lumbar spinal canal by siphon action." *Radiology*, **83**: 472.

EPSTEIN, B. S. (1964). "The myelographic demonstration of the anterior spinal and radicular arteries." *Amer. J. Roentgenol.*, **91**: 427.

EPSTEIN, B. S. (1966). "Anatomic, myelographic and cinemyelographic study of the dentate ligaments." *Amer. J. Roentgenol.*, **98**: 704–712.

EPSTEIN, B. S. & DAVIDOFF, L. M. (1943). "The roentgenologic diagnosis of dilation of the spinal cord veins." *Amer. J. Roentgenol.*, **49**: 476.

EPSTEIN, B. S. & EPSTEIN, J. A. (1966). "Syphonage technic for removal of pantopaque." *Acta Radiol.*, **5**: 1007.

EPSTEIN, J. A., EPSTEIN, B. S., LAVINE, L. S., CARRAS, R., ROSENTHAL, A. D. & SUMNER, P. (1973). "Lumbar nerve root compression at the intervertebral foramina caused by arthritis of the posterior facets." *J. Neurosurg.*, **39**: 362–369.

ERLACHER, P. R. (1952). "Nucleography." *J. Bone Joint Surg.*, **34B**: 204–210.

FAHRNI, W. H. & TRUEMAN, G. E. (1965). "Comparative radiological study of the spine of a primitive population with North Americans and Northern Europeans." *J. Bone Joint Surg.*, **47B**: 552–555.

FALLET, G. H., WETTSTEIN, P., OTT, H., RADI, I. & MOSIMANN, U.

(1972). "Radiological study of the sacro-iliac joints in sero-negative rheumatoid arthritis." *Schweiz. Med. Wochenschr.*, **100:** 1610–1616.

FERGUSON, A. B. (1934). "The clinical and roentgenographic interpretation of lumbosacral anomalies." *Radiology*, **22:** 548–558.

FERNSTROM, U. (1963). "Will plain film examination of the lumbar spine be a reliable method to exclude or disclose ruptured discs?" *Acta Orthop. Scand.*, **33:** 105–115.

FERRIS, R. A., PETTRONE, F. A., McKELVIE, A. M., TWIGG, H. L. & CHUN, B. K. (1974). "Eosinophilic granuloma of the spine: an unusual radiographic presentation." *Clin. Orthop.*, **99:** 57–63.

FIELDING, J. W. (1957). "Cineradiography of the normal cervical spine." *J. Bone Joint Surg.*, **39B:** 585.

FIELDING, J. W. (1957). "Cineroentgenography of the normal cervical spine." *J. Bone Joint Surg.*, **39A:** 1280.

FIELDS, W. S. (1972). "High cervical neurinoma: special neurologic and radiologic features." *Zbl. Neurochir.*, **33:** 90–102.

FISCHER, F. J., FRIEDMAN, M. M. & DENMARK, R. E. VAN. (1958). "Roentgenographic abnormalities in soldiers with low back pain: a comparative study." *Amer. J. Roentgenol.*, **79:** 673–676.

FORD, L. T. & GOODMAN, F. G. (1966). "X-ray studies of the lumbosacral spine." *Southern Med. J.*, **59:** 1123–1128.

FORD, L. T. & KEY, J. A. (1950). "An evaluation of myelography in the diagnosis of intervertebral disc lesions in the back." *J. Bone Joint Surg.*, **32A:** 257–266.

FORD, L. T., RAMSEY, R. H., HOLT, E. P. & KEY, J. A. (1952). "An analysis of one hundred consecutive lumbar myelograms followed by disc operations for relief of low back pain and sciatica." *Surgery*, **32:** 961–966.

FOX, J. L. (1973). "Identification of radiologic co-ordinates for the posterior articular nerve of Luschka in the lumbar spine." *Surg. Neurol.*, **1:** 343–346.

FOX, L. (1966). "Lumbar discography. A myelographic correlation." *Acta Neurol. Latino-amer.*, **12:** 114–124.

FRANÇOIS, R. J. (1974). "Microradiographic study of the normal human vertebral body." *Acta Anat.*, **89:** 251–265.

FREYDSCHMIDT, J., RITTMEIYER, K. & KAISER, G. (1973). "Comparing thermographic and myelographic studies in lumbosacral disc prolapse." *Forts. Geb. Roentgenst. Nuklearmed.*, (Suppl.): 336–337.

FRIEDMAN, M. M., FISCHER, F. J. & DENMARK, R. E. VAN (1946). "Lumbosacral roentgenograms of 100 soldiers: a control study." *Amer. J. Roentgenol.*, **55**: 292–298.

FULLENLOVE, T. M. & WILLIAMS, A. J. (1957). "Comparative roentgen findings in symptomatic and asymptomatic backs." *Radiology*, **68**: 572–574.

GANZ, R. (1972). "The odontoid bone." *Zeit. Unfallmed. Berufskr.*, **65**: 28–34.

GARGANIO, F. P., MEYER, J., HOUDEK, P. V. & CHARYULU, K. K. N. (1974). "Transverse axial tomography of the cervical spine." *Radiology*, **113**: 363–367.

GARNERI, L. & LAGNA-FIETTA, E. (1972). "Indications for contrast radiography of the roots in the syndrome of lumbar root compression." *Minerva Ortop.*, **23**: 122–126.

GAUCHER, A. & PONCIN, B. (1973). "Medico-legal value of radiological examination in lumbar injuries at work: importance of the anterior view." *Rev. Rhum.*, **40**: 727–732.

GIANTURCO, C. (1944). "Roentgen analysis of motion of lower lumbar vertebrae in normal individuals and in patients with low back pain." *Amer. J. Roentgenol.*, **52**: 261–268.

GIMLETT, D. M. (1972). "The back X-ray controversy." *J. Occup. Med.*, **14**: 785–786.

GOLD, L. H., LEACH, C. G., KIEFFER, S. A., CHOU, S. N. & PETERSON, H. O. (1970). "Large volume myelography: an aid in the evaluation of curvature of the spine." *Radiology*, **97**: 531–536.

GOLDMAN, S. M. (1974). "Xeroradiography: nonmammographic applications." *South. Med. J.*, **67**: 813–817.

GOLDSMITH, N. F. (1973). "Bone mineral in the radius and vertebral osteoporosis in an insured population. A correlative study using 125-I photon absorption and miniature roentgenography." *J. Bone Joint Surg.*, 1276–1293.

GOLDSMITH, N. F., JOHNSTON, J. O., GARCIA, C. & PICETTI, G. (1973). "Use of miniature roentgenograms of the abdomen to detect aortic calcification, osteoporosis and other radiological abnormalities in an insured population." *Int. J. Epidem.*, **2**: 303–310.

GOUTALLIER, D. & DEBEYRE, J. (1973). "Arthrodesis and discography in the surgical treatment of lumbago." *Rev. Rheum.*, **40:** 763–765.

GRAHAM, C. E. (1966). "Symposium on lumbar disc surgery: lumbar discography." *J. Bone Joint Surg.*, **48B:** 595.

GRAINGER, R. G., GUMPERT, J., SHARPE, D. M. & CARSON, J. (1971). "Water-soluble lumbar radiculography: a clinical trial of Dimer-X—a new contrast medium." *Clin. Radiol.*, **22:** 57–62.

GRAY, F. J. & HOSKING, H. J. (1963). "A radiological assessment of the effect of body weight traction on the lumbar disc spaces." *Med. J. Aust.*, **2:** 953–954.

GREENE, L. B. & ARMSTRONG, W. E. (1967). "Radiographic measurement of the lumbo-sacral angle." *Arch. Phys. Med.*, **48:** 240–243.

GRESHAM, J. L. & MILLER, R. (1969). "Evaluation of the lumbar spine by diskography and its use in selection of proper treatment of herniated disk syndrome." *Clin. Orthop.*, **67:** 29–41.

GRUSS, P., NADJMI, M., AUER-DOINET, G. & RICKER, H. (1973). "Myelography of the lumbosacral region with a water-soluble contrast medium in lesions of the intervertebral discs." *Münch. Med. Wschr.*, **115:** 498–503.

GUIRAUD, G. (1972). "Congenital straight cervical canal (diagnostic radiological approach)." *Rheumatologie*, **24:** 221–225.

GUPTA, B. D. (1973). "Cervical spondylosis: a correlative clinico-radiological study." *J. Indian Med. Ass.*, **60:** 364–371.

GUTMANN, G. (1970). "Clinical radiological studies on the statics of the vertebral column." In *Manuelle Medizin und Ihre Wissenschaftlichen Grundlagen*, pp. 109–127. Ed. by H. D. Wolf. Heidelberg; Verlag Phys. Med.

HAASE, J., JEPSON, B. V., BECH, H. & LANGEBAEK, E. (1973). "Spinal fracture following radiculography using meglumine isthalamate (Conray)." *Neuroradiol.*, **6:** 65–70.

HADLEY, L. A. (1961). "Anatomico-roentgenographic studies of the posterior spinal articulations." *Amer. J. Roentgenol.*, **86:** 270.

HAGEN, D. P. (1964). "A continuing roentgenographic study of rural school children over a 15 year period." *J. Amer. Osteopath. Assoc.*, **63:** 546–556.

HAGEN, D. P. (1965). "A roentgenographic evaluation of the lumbar spine and pelvis: the lateral projection." *J. Amer. Osteopath. Assoc.*, **64:** 1030–1037.

HALABURT, H. (1973). "Leptomeningeal changes following lumbar myelography with water-soluble contrast media (meglumine iothalamate and methiodal sodium)." *Neuroradiol.*, **5:** 70–76.

HAMMER, B. (1971). "Delayed resorption of contrast media and radio-elements in cases of lumbosacral malformations." *Neuroradiol.*, **3:** 97–101.

HANNAPEL, A. (1970). "The radiological appearance of the space in the interarticular region between the 4th and 5th lumbar vertebrae." *Arch. Orthop. Unfallchir.*, **69:** 35–38.

HARMON, P. H. (1962). "Saline injection test applied to lower lumbar disc degeneration: comparative myelography." *Ann. Surg.*, **156:** 767–775.

HARTMAN, J. T., KENDRICK, J. I. & LORMAN, P. (1971). "Discography as an aid to evaluation for lumbar and lumbosacral fusion." *Clin. Orthop.*, **81:** 77–81.

HARVIAINEN, S., LAHTI, P. & DAVIDSSON, L. (1971). "On cervical injuries: a radiographic analysis." *Acta Chir. Scand.*, **138:** 349–356.

HERDER, B. A. DEN (1972). "Modifications of the axial projection of the true pelvis." *Radiol. Clin. Biol.*, **41:** 347–349.

HILAL, S. K., MARTON, D. & POLLACK, E. (1974). "Diastematomyelia in children: radiographic study of 34 cases." *Radiol.*, **112:** 609–621.

HIRSCH, C., ROSENCRANTZ, M. & WICKBOM, I. (1969). "Lumbar myelography with water-soluble contrast media: with special reference to the appearances of root pockets." *Acta Radiol.*, **8:** 54–64.

HODGES, F. J. & PECK, W. S. (1937). "Clinical and roentgenological study of low back pain with sciatic radiation. B. Roentgenological aspects." *Amer. J. Roentgenol.*, **37:** 461–468.

HOLT, E. P. (1968). "The question of lumbar discography." *J. Bone Joint Surg.*, **50A:** 720–726.

HOLT, E. P. (1970). "The status of lumbar discography." *Lawyer's Med. J.*, **6:** 219–232.

HOLT, E. P. (1975). "Further reflections on cervical discography." *J. Amer. Med. Ass.*, **231:** 613–614.

HOWLAND, W. J. & CURRY, J. L. (1966). "Experimental studies of pantopaque arachnoiditis." *Radiology*, **87:** 253–261.

HUSSAR, A. E. & GULLER, E. J. (1956). "Correlation of pain and roentgenographic findings of spondylosis of the cervical and lumbar spine." *Amer. J. Med. Sci.*, **232:** 518–527.

317

IRSTAM, L. (1973). "Side-effects of water-soluble contrast media in lumbar myelography." *Acta Radiol.*, **14**: 647–656.

IRSTAM, L. (1974). "Lumbar myelography and adhesive arachnoiditis." *Acta Radiol.*, **15**: 356–368.

IRSTAM, L. & ROSENCRANTZ, M. (1972). "Water-soluble contrast media and adhesive arachnoiditis." *Diag. Radiol.*, **11**: 126.

IRSTAM, L. & ROSENCRANTZ, M. (1973). "Water-soluble contrast media and adhesive arachnoiditis: 1. Reinvestigation of non-operated cases." *Acta Radiol.*, **14**: 497–506.

IRSTAM, L. & ROSENCRANTZ, M. (1974). "Water-soluble contrast media and adhesive arachnoiditis: II. Reinvestigation of operated cases." *Acta Radiol.*, **15**: 1–15.

IRSTAM, L., SUNDSTRÖM, R. & SIGSTEDT, B. (1974). "Lumbar myelography and adhesive arachnoiditis." *Acta Radiol.*, **15**: 356–368.

JACOBS, G. B. (1975). "Lumbar discography in the diagnosis of herniated disks." *Int. Surg.*, **60**: 6–9.

JACOBSON, R. E., GARGANO, F. P. & ROSOMOFF, H. L. (1975). "Transverse axial tomography of the spine. Part 1: axial anatomy of the normal lumbar spine. Part 2. The stenotic spinal canal." *J. Neurosurg.*, **42**: 406–419.

JAJIC, I. (1968). "Radiological changes in the sacroiliac joints and spine of patients with arthritis and psoriasis." *Ann. Rheum. Dis.*, **27**: 1–6.

JEANMART, L. (1973). "Low back pain of occupational origins." *J. Belge Radiol.*, **56**: 1–9.

JELBERT, M. (1970). "A pilot study of the incidence and distribution of certain skeletal and soft tissue abnormalities: discovered by mass miniature radiography in a group of indigenous Rhodesian Africans." *Centr. Afr. J. Med.*, **16**: 37–40.

JIROUT, J. (1969). "Pneumographic examination of lumbar disc lesions: a new method." *Acta Radiol.*, **9**: 727–732.

JOHANNSEN, A. (1974). "Radiological and scintigraphical examination of the sacroiliac joints in the diagnosis of sacroiliitis." *Dan. Med. Bull.*, **21**: 246–250.

JONES, A. (1967). "Cineradiographic studies of abnormalities of the high cervical spine." *Arch. Surg.*, **94**: 206.

JONES, F. P. & GILLEY, P. F. M. (1960). "Head balance and sitting posture: an X-ray analysis." *J. Psych.*, **49**: 289–293.

JONSSON, B. & REICHMANN, S. (1970). "Radiographic control in the insertion of EMG electrodes in the lumbar part of the erector spinae muscle." *Z. Anat. Entwickl. -Gesch.*, **130:** 192–206.

JUNGHANNS, H. (1931). "The intervertebral discs in X-ray pictures." *Fortschr. Röntgenol.*, **43:** 275–305.

KELLGREN, J. H. (1963). *Atlas of Standard Radiographs of Arthritis.* Oxford; Blackwell.

KELLGREN, J. H. & LAWRENCE, J. S. (1952). "Rheumatism in miners. Part II: X-ray study." *Brit. J. Industr. Med.*, **9:** 197–207.

KELLY, F. J. (1974). "Preemployment back X-rays." *J. Occup. Med.*, **16:** 442.

KEMP, H. B. S., JOHNS, D. L., McALISTER, J. & GODLER, J. N. (1973). "The role of Fluorine-18 and Strontium-87m scintigraphy in the management of infective spondylitis." *J. Bone Joint Surg.*, **55B:** 301–311.

KEOGH, A. J. (1974). "Meningeal reactions seen with myodil myelography." *Clin. Radiol.*, **25:** 361–365.

KIM, Y. W. (1975). "Evaluation of cervical spondylosis by gas myelography." *Wis. Med. J.*, **74:** 564–568.

KOBAYASHI, H. (1973). "Studies on symptomatology and radiology of cervical spondylotic myelopathy." *J. Jap. Orthop. Ass.*, **47:** 495–514.

KONO, R. (1974). "Clinical significance of the sagittal air myelography in the cervical spinal region: especially clinical studies on cervical spondylotic myelopathy." *J. Jap. Orthop. Ass.*, **48:** 581–602.

KOSARY, I. Z., TADMORE, R., QUAKNINE, G. & BRAHAM, J. (1973). "Lumbo-sacral myelography with Dimer-X: report of 100 cases." *J. Neurosurg.*, **39:** 359–361.

KOTTKE, F. J. & LESTER, R. G. (1958). "Use of cinefluorography for evaluation of normal and abnormal motion of the neck." *Arch. Phys. Med.*, **39:** 229–231.

KUNDEL, H. L. & REVESZ, G. (1974). "The evaluation of radiographic techniques in observer tests: problems, pitfalls and procedures." *Investigative Radiol.*, **9:** 166–173.

LACSAY, A. (1973). "Degenerative disorders of the costotransverse and costovertebral joints." *Fortschr. Röntgenstr.*, **119:** 108–111.

LANDRY, W. J., BRIERRE, J. T. & HUNT, N. S. (1956). "Radiological evaluation of low back pain." *J. Amer. Med. Assoc.*, **160:** 606.

LANE, B. & KRICHEFF, I. I. (1974). "Cerebrospinal fluid pulsations at myelography: a videodensitometric study." *Radiology*, **110:** 579–587.

LA ROCCA, H. & MACNAB, I. (1969). "Value of pre-employment radiographic assessment of the lumbar spine." *Canad. Med. Ass. J.*, **101:** 383–388.

LAUX, G., GUERRIER, Y., PALEIRAC, R. & COLIN, R. (1954). "Tomographic documentation of the cranio-spinal articulation." *Compt. Rend. Acad. Sci., Paris*, **40:** 291–292.

LAVARDE, G. (1973). "Isolated fractures of the articular apophyses of the cervical spine." *J. Chir., Paris*, **105:** 241–248.

LEE, S. H. (1974). "Radiologic evaluation of dorsal column stimulators." *J. Can. Assoc. Radiol.*, **25:** 196–201.

LEGGO, F. & MATHIASEN, H. (1973). "Preliminary results of a pre-employment back X-ray programme for state traffic officers." *J. Occup. Med.*, **15:** 973–974.

LE GO, P. & WELFLING, J. (1968). "Data obtained from systematic radiological examination of the lumbopelvic skeleton in the applicants for employment in the S.N.C.F." *Presse Méd.*, **76:** 901–902.

LEGRÉ, J., DUFOUR, M., DEBAENE, A., DALMAS, P. & BURROU, A. (1971). "Lumbar discography: value and indications on the bases of 300 examinations." *Neurochirurgie*, **17:** 559–578.

LEHTINEN, E. & SEPPÄNEN, S. (1972). "Side effects of Conray Meglumin 282 and Dimer-X in lumbar myelography." *Acta Radiol.*, **12:** 12–16.

LETHE, P. (1962). "Radiological study of the normal pelvis: some unrecognised aspects." *J. Belg. Radiol.*, **45:** 659–681.

LEVERETT, J. K. (1966). "X-rays of the low back in pre-employment physical examinations." *Texas Med.*, **62:** 83–84.

LIEBEN, J. (1974). "Pre-employment back X-rays." *J. Occup. Med.*, **16:** 278–279.

LILIEQUIST, B. & LINDSTROM, B. (1974). "Lumbar myelography and arachnoiditis." *Neuroradiol.*, **7:** 91–94.

LIN, P. M. & CLARKE, J. (1974). "Spinal fluid-venous fistula: a mechanism for intravascular Pantopaque infusion during myelography: report of two cases." *J. Neurosurg.*, **41:** 773–776.

LINDBLOM, K. (1948). "Diagnostic puncture of intervertebral discs in sciatica." *Acta Orthop. Scand.*, **17:** 231.

LINDBLOM, K. (1951). "Technique and results of diagnostic puncture and injection (Discography) in lumbar region." *Acta Orthop. Scand.*, **20**: 315–326.

LINDGREN, E. (1941). "Myelographic changes in kyphosis dorsalis juvenalis." *Acta Radiol.*, **22**: 461–470.

LOBO, M. (1974). "A modified oblique view of the cervical spine." *Radiography*, **40**: 113–114.

LOUYOT, P., POUREL, J., TAMISTER, J.-M., FAURE, G., LARDE, D. & NETTER, P. (1973). "Radiological study of the posterior arch in lumbago." *Rev. Rheum.*, **40**: 699–709.

LUYENDIJK, W. (1963). "Canalography: roentgenological examination of the peridural space in the lumbosacral part of the vertebral canal." *J. Belg. Radiol.*, **46**: 236–252.

LUYENDIJK, W. & VOORTHUISEN, A. E. VAN. (1966). "Contrast examination of the spinal epidural space." *Acta Radiol.*, **5**: 1051–1066.

MCCALL, I. W., PARK, W. M. & MCSWEENEY, T. (1973). "The radiological demonstration of acute lower cervical injury." *Clin. Radiol.*, **24**: 235–240.

MCCLOY, C. H. (1938). "X-ray studies of innate differences in straight and curved spines." *Res. Quart.*, **9**: 50–57.

MACRAE, I. F., HASLOCK, D. I. & WRIGHT, V. (1971). "Grading of films for sacroiliitis in population studies." *Ann. Rheum. Dis.*, **30**: 58–66.

MALCOLMSON, P. H. (1935). "Radiologic study of the development of the spine and pathologic changes of the intervertebral disc." *Radiol.*, **25**: 98–104.

MANTEL, J. (1974). "Xeroradiography in transverse axial tomography for radiation therapy treatment planning." *Radiology*, **113**: 732–733.

MASSARE, C., BARD, M. & TRIISTANT, H. (1974). "Cervical discography: considerations regarding the technique and indications based on our experience." *J. Radiol. Electrol.*, **55**: 395–399.

MASSARE, C., BENOIST, M. & CAUCHOIX, J. (1973). "The diagnosis of lumbar and lumbo-sacral disc herniation: relevance of discography." *Rev. Chir. Orthop.*, **59**: 61–67.

MASSARE, C. & BERNAGEAU, J. (1971). "Lumbosacral spondylolisthesis: radiological examination." *Rev. Chir. Orthop.*, **57** (Suppl. 1): 110–114.

MASSARE, C. & BERNAGEAU, J. (1972). "Indications for discography:

assessment based on 1200 discographies." *J. Radiol. Electrol.*, **53:** 229–231.

MESCHAM, I. (1945). "Spondylolisthesis: a commentary on etiology and an improved method of roentgenographic mensuration and detection of instability." *Amer. J. Roentgenol.*, **53:** 230–243.

METZGER, J., LAVARDE, G. & FISCHOLD, H. (1969). "Tomography with gas myelography: vertebral trauma and intraspinal lesions." *Med. Leg. Dommage Corp.*, **2:** 58–61.

MILLER, S. W., CASTRONOVO, F. P., PENDERGRASS, H. P. & POTSAID, M. S. (1974). "Technetium 99M labelled disphosphonate bone scanning in Paget's disease." *Amer. J. Roentgenol.*, **121:** 310–316.

MITCHIE, I. (1972). "Radiological changes and their significance in aged men." *Gerent. Clin.*, **14:** 310–316.

MORETON, R. D. (1974). "The role of preplacement roentgen examination of the spine in evaluation of low back pain." *South. Med. J.*, **67:** 1105–1110.

MORETON, R. D., WINSTON, J. R. & BIBBY, D. E. (1958). "Value of preplacement examination of the lumbar spine." *Radiology*, **70:** 661–665.

MOVIN, A. (1967). "Myelographic appearances of disk protrusions in different positions." *Acta Radiol.*, **6:** 524–528.

MURPHEY, F. (1973). "Myelographic demonstration of avulsing injuries of the nerve roots of the brachial plexus—a method of determining the point of injury and the possibility of repair." *Clin. Neurosurg.*, **20:** 18–28.

NACHEMSON, A. (1965). "In vivo discometry in lumbar discs with irregular nucleograms." *Acta Orthop. Scand.*, **36:** 418–434.

NATHAN, M. H. & BLUM, L. (1960). "Evaluation of vertebral venography." *Amer. J. Roentgenol.*, **83:** 1027–1033.

NICHOLS, B. H. (1941). "Some roentgen findings which may be responsible for low back pain." *Arch. Phys. Therap.*, **22:** 600–606.

NIEMER, P. (1963). "Functional roentgenographic examination in a case of cervical spondylolisthesis." *J. Bone Joint Surg.*, **45A:** 1671.

NORDIN, B. E., YOUNG, M. M., BENTLEY, B., ORMONDROYD, P. & SYKES, J. (1968). "Lumbar spine densitometry: methodology and results in relation to the menopause." *Clin. Radiol.*, **19:** 459–464.

OBERSON, R., FOROGLOU, G. & ZANDER, E. (1972). "Myelography and vertebral angiography in traumatic lesions of the cervical spine." *Zeit. Unfallmed. Berufskr.*, **65:** 31–40.

O'BRIEN, J. P. (1975). "Discography in paralytic scoliosis." *Acta Orthop. Scand.*, **46:** 216–220.

OCCLESHAW, J. V. & HOLYLAND, J. N. (1972). "Comparative study of Conray 280 and Dimer-X in lumbar radiculography." *Brit. J. Radiol.*, **44:** 946–948.

OESTREICH, A. E. (1974). "Hip pain and its variants: radiological aspects." *J. Natl. Med. Assoc.*, **66:** 208–210.

OKUBO, J. (1973). "Study of the upper cervical spine by means of panoramic tomography." *Bull. Tokyo Med. Dent. Univ.*, **20:** 105–119.

ORTNER, W. D., KUBIN, H. & KOLLAR, W. A. F. (1972). "Functional lumbar myelography with a water-soluble contrast medium in discopathies." *Die Radiologie*, **12:** 69–73.

PAGE, K. M. (1972). "Water-soluble lumbar radiculography." *Radiography*, **38:** 193–196.

PATRICK, B. S. (1973). "Lumbar discography: a five year study." *Surg. Neurol.*, **1:** 267–273.

PATTON, J. T. (1973). "Recent advances in the diagnosis of inter-vertebral disc disease." *Radiography*, **39:** 62–68.

PEREY, O. (1951). "Contrast medium examination of intervertebral discs of lower lumbar spine." *Acta Orthop. Scand.*, **20:** 327–334.

PEROVIC, M. N., KOPITS, S. E. & THOMPSON, R. C. (1973). "Radio-logical evaluation of the spinal cord in congenital atlanto-axial dislocation." *Radiology*, **109:** 713–716.

PETERSON, H. O. & KIEFFER, S. A. (1972). "Radiology of inter-vertebral disk disease." *Seminars in Roentgenology*, **7:** 260–276.

PRAESTHOLM, J. & LESTER, J. (1970). "Water soluble contrast lumbar myelography with meglumine iothalamate (Conray)." *Brit. J. Radiol.*, **43:** 303–308.

PRAESTHOLM, J. & OLGAARD, K. (1972). "Comparative histological investigation of the sequelae of experimental myelography using sodium methiodal and meglumine iothalamate." *Neuroradiol.*, **4:** 14–19.

PRENTICE, W. B., KIEFFER, S. A., GOLD, L. H. A. & BJORNSON, R. G. (1973). "Myelographic characteristics of metastasis to the spinal cord and cauda equina." *Amer. J. Roentgenol.*, **118:** 681–689.

PRESENT, A. J. (1974). "Radiography of the lower back in pre-employment physical examinations." *Radiology*, **112:** 229–230.

RADBERG, C. & WENNBERG, E. (1973). "Late sequelae following

myelography with water-soluble contrast media." *Acta Radiol.*, **14:** 507–512.

RAL, J., NACHEMSON, A. & SCHELLER, S. (1972). "Clinical and radiological long term follow-up of vertebral fractures in children." *Acta Orthop. Scand.*, **43:** 491–503.

RANAWAT, N. S. & RIVELIS, M. (1972). "Strontium 85 scintimetry in ankylosing spondylitis." *J. Amer. Med. Assoc.*, **222:** 553–558.

RAVAULT, P. P., MEUNIER, P., SAMBIN, P., CRET, R. & BIANCHI, G. S. (1969). "An early sign of spinal osteoporosis: enlargement of lumbar disc spaces." *Rev. Lyon. Méd.*, **18:** 603–613.

REDFIELD, J. T. (1971). "The low back X-ray as a pre-employment screening tool in the forest products industry." *J. Occup. Med.*, **13:** 219–226.

REICHMANN, S. (1972). "Tomography of the lumbar intervertebral joints." *Acta Radiol.*, **12:** 641–659.

REICHMANN, S. (1973). "Radiography of the lumbar intervertebral joints." *Acta Radiol.*, **14:** 161–170.

RIENHARDT, K. (1974). "Puncture and contrast medium demonstration of osteomyelitis of the lumbar vertebrae and of paravertebral abscesses." *Röntgen-Blätter*, **27:** 45–50.

RETIF, J., JEANMART, L. & BRIHAYE, J. (1969). "Myelographic differential diagnosis between disc herniation and tumour of the cauda equina." *Acta Orthop. Belge.*, **35:** 665–678.

REYMOND, R. D., WHEELER, P. S., PEROVIC, M. & BLOCK, B. (1972). "The lucent cleft, a new radiographic sign of cervical disc injury or disease." *Clin. Radiol.*, **23:** 188–192.

RILEY, J. (1971). "Radiological manifestations of ankylosing spondylitis." *Ann. Rheum. Dis.*, **30:** 138.

ROBERTS, A., LOUPE, J., GOLDSMITH, J., COMEAUX, L. & WICKSTROM, J. (1972). "Lumbar diskography using a posterolateral approach with a guide." *South. Med. J.*, **65:** 358–360.

ROCCA, H. L. (1969). "Value of pre-employment radiographical assessment of the lumbar spine." *Can. Med. Assoc. J.*, **101:** 383–388.

ROCKOFF, S. D. (1967). "Radiographic trabecular quantitation of human lumbar vertebrae in situ. I: Theory and method for study of osteoporosis." *Invest. Radiol.*, **2:** 272–289.

ROGERS, L. F. (1971). "The roentgenographic appearance of transverse or chance fractures of the spine: the seat-belt fracture." *Amer. J. Roentgenol.*, **111:** 844–849.

ROGOFF, E. E., DECK, M. D. F. & D'ANGIO, G. (1974). "The second sac: a complicating factor in regimens based on intrathecal medications." *Amer. J. Roentgenol.*, **120**: 568–572.

ROMANINI, L. & URSO, S. (1969). "Aspects of diagnostic radiculography in lumbago and lumbo-sciatica." *Acta Orthop. Belg.*, **35**: 636–664.

RONDIER, J., CAYLA, J., BOK, B. & BOUCHAREB, A. (1974). "Value of bone scintigraphy with Strontium 87M in the diagnosis of infectious spondylodiscitis (or spondylitis)." *Rev. Rheum.*, **41**: 427–439.

ROOSEN, K., RÖMER, F. & SCHULTZ, S. (1973). "Myeloscintography and pantopaque myelography in traumatic cervical dislocations." *Acta Orthop. Belg.*, **35**: 636–664.

ROSENBERG, P. (1955). "The R-center method. A new method for analysing vertebral motion by X-rays." *J. Amer. Orthop. Assoc.*, **55**: 103–111.

ROSS, E. (1966). "Results of an X-ray check of the spine in 5,000 young men." *Fortschr. Röntgenol.*, **97**: 734–751.

ROTH, M. (1963). "Gas myelography by the lumbar route." *Acta Radiol.*, **1**: 53.

ROTHMAN, R. H., CAMPBELL, R. E. & MENKOWITZ, E. (1974). "Myelographic patterns in lumbar disk degeneration." *Clin. Orthop.*, **99**: 18–29.

RUNGE, C. L. (1954). "Roentgenographic examination of the lumbosacral spine in routine pre-employment examination." *J. Bone Joint Surg.*, **36A**: 75–84.

SALAHUDDIN, N. I., MADHAVAN, T., FISHER, E. J., COX, F., QUINN, E. L. & EYLER, W. R. (1973). "Pseudomonas osteomyelitis: radiologic features." *Radiology*, **109**: 41–47.

SARATCHEV, T. M. (1965). "Discarthrosis and interapophyseal arthrosis: a clinico-statistical study in dockers and railway workers." *Rev. Rhum.*, **32**: 663–669.

SCHAERER, J. P. (1971). "A choice of contrast studies in the diagnosis of lumbar disc problems." *Schweiz. Arch. Neurol. Neurochir. Psychiat.*, **108**: 87–89.

SCHALIMTZEK, M. (1954). "Functional roentgen examination of degenerated and normal intervertebral discs of the lumbar spine." *Acta Radiol.*, Suppl. **116**: 300–306.

SCHOBINGER, R. A. & KRUEGER, E. G. (1963). "Intraosseous

epidural venography in the diagnosis of surgical diseases of the lumbar spine." *Acta Radiol.*, **1**: 763–776.

SCHOBINGER, R. A., KRUEGER, E. G. & SOBEL, G. L. (1961). "Comparison of intraosseous vertebral venography and pantopaque myelography in the diagnosis of surgical conditions of the lumbar spine and nerve roots." *Radiology*, **77**: 376.

SCOTT, J. W. (1963). "Dorsal facet study of body section radiography." *J. Amer. Orthop. Assoc.*, **62**: 735–738.

SEIDLITZ, L. (1974). "Doses to the vertebral marrow during common X-ray examinations in clinical situations." *Invest. Radiol.*, **9**: 419–424.

SEUR, N. H. (1972). "Subtraction in cervical pneumomyelography and an application of RISA myelography." *Radiol. Clin. Biol.*, **41**: 387–396.

SEVERIN, E. (1943). "Degeneration of the intervertebral disks in the lumbar region: a clinicoroentgenologic study." *Acta Chir. Scand.*, **89**: 353–378.

SEZE, S. DE & DURIEU, J. (1950). "Retrolisthesis: a clinical and radiological study of backward displacement of the vertebrae, based on 50 personal observations." *Sem. Hôp., Paris*, **26**: 409–427.

SHORT, D. B. (1975). "Radioisotope myelography in detection of spinal fluid leaks due to dorsal column stimulator implantation." *J. Nucl. Med.*, **16**: 616–618.

SIBTHROPE, E. M. (1958). "A radiological survey in the measurement of specimens of the female pelvis in Uganda." *J. Obst. Gynec. Brit. Emp.*, **64**: 600–605.

SIGNORINI, E., GUATTRINI, A., GENTILE, E. & CHIURULLA, C. (1973). "The problem of total block in radiculography." *Clin. Ortopedica*, **24**: 53–62.

SIMMONS, E. H. & SEGIL, C. H. (1975). "An evaluation of discography in the localization of symptomatic levels in discogenic disease of the spine." *Clin. Orthop.*, **108**: 57–69.

SKALPE, I. O., TORBERGSEN, T., AMUNDSEN, P. & PRESTHUS, J. (1973). "Lumbar myelography with metrizamide." *Acta Radiol.*, Suppl. **335**: 367–379.

SOMOGYI, B. (1963). "A functional roentgen study of the vertebral arches." *Radiologica Diagnostica*, **4**: 227–248.

SONCINI, G. & UGOLOTTI, G. (1968). "Direct radiographic examination in the diagnosis of disc hernia." *Ann. Radiol. Diag., Bologna*, **41**: 275–283.

Soo, Y. S. & ANG, A. H. (1973). "The value of the lateral cervical myelogram in the evaluation of cervical spondylosis." *Austral. Radiol.*, **17**: 371–374.

Soo, Y. S. & SACHDEV, A. S. (1972). "The value of pantopaque (Iodophendylate) myelography in cervical spondylosis." *J. Western Pacific Orthop. Assoc.*, **22**: 32–39.

SPINELLI, R. (1974). "Value of scintigraphy of the vertebral column in assessing the age of fractures." *Minerva Ortop.*, **25**: 1–3.

STEIN, H. (1953). "Rotation of the vertebrae: a clinical, radiological and anatomical study." *Medizinische, No.* **5**: 154–161.

STEINBECK, W. (1974). "Functional diagnosis in lumbar myelography." *Zeit. Orthop.*, **112**: 801–804.

STENSTRÖM, R. & LINDFORS, M. (1971). "Lumbar myelography with water-soluble contrast medium in children." *Acta Radiol.*, **11**: 243–249.

STUCK, R. M. (1972). "Myelography and discography help pinpoint ruptured cervical discs." *Med. Times*, **100**: 100–101.

SUH, C. H. (1974). "The fundamentals of computer-aided X-ray analysis of the spine." *J. Biochem.*, **7**: 161–169.

SUZUKI, T. (1972). "Cervical air myelography and its significance in cervical spondylosis." *J. Jap. Orthop. Ass.*, **46**: 125–138.

SWEZEY, R. & SILVERMAN, T. R. (1971). "Radiographic demonstration of induced vertebral facet displacements." *Arch. Phys. Med. Rehab.*, **52**: 244–249.

SWIDERSKI, G. (1968). "Roentgen study of vertebral instability in overloaded lumbar spondylolisthesis." *Beitr. Orthop. Trauma*, **15**: 598–604.

TANAKA, Y. (1975). "A radiographic analysis of human vertebrae in the aged." *Virchows Arch. (Pathol. Anat.)*, **366**: 187–201.

TANZ, S. S. (1953). "Motion of the lumbar spine: a roentgenographic study." *Amer. J. Roentgenol.*, **69**: 399–412.

THOMPSON, M. (1957). "Discussion on the clinical and radiological aspects of sacro-iliac disease." *Proc. Roy. Soc. Med.*, **50**: 847–858.

THUN, R. & FRIEDMAN, G. (1973). "The significance of tomography in differential diagnosis of the lumbar syndrome without disc disease." *Röntgen-Blätter*, **26**: 171–176.

TROWBRIDGE, W. V. & FRENCH, J. D. (1954). "The false positive lumbar myelogram." *Neurology*, **4**: 339–344.

UCHINISHI, K. (1968). "Radiographic study of the weight-bearing line of human vertebrae." *J Jap. Orthop. Ass.*, **42**: 954–964.

VAUGHAN, G. (1968). "Lateral tomography of atlanto-axial joint in rheumatoid disease." *Austr. Radiol.*, **12**: 58.

VIGNAUD, J., MORET, J., FAURES, B. & CHAOUAT, Y. (1974). "Lumbar spinal phlebography: its application in lumbo-radicular pathology." *Rev. Rhum.*, **41**: 441–447.

VINES, F. S. (1974). "Integrated isocentric diagnostic system for neuroradiology." *Amer. J. Roentgenol.*, **122**: 648–657.

VOGELSANG, H. (1973). "Cervical intervertebral discitis and discography." *Neurochirur.*, **(Stuttgart), 16:** 80–83.

VYHNANEK, L. & ZEMAN, M. (1972). "Peridurography in post-operative conditions of the spine." *Sborn. Lek.*, **74**: 313–316.

VYHNANEK, L., ZEMAN, M. & JANATA, M. (1972). "Functional examination during peridurography of the lumbar spine." *Česk. Radiology*, **26**: 189–195.

VYHNENEK, L., ZEMAN, M. & TRIVEDI, R. M. (1972). "Radicular and subdural cysts in peridurographic films." *Fortschr. Röntgenstr.*, **116**: 160–163.

WALDRON, R. L. & WOOD, E. H. (1973). "Cervical myelography." *Clin. Orthop.*, **97**: 74–89.

WALK, L. (1962). "Lumbar diskography and its clinical evaluation." *Bibliotheca Radiologica*, **3**: 1–135.

WEIGERT, M., GRONERT, H. J. & KEMES, H. (1975). "Experiences with Dimer-X in lumbosacral myelography." *Arch. Orthop. Unfall-Chir.*, **81**: 155–162.

WEIR, D. C. (1975). "Roentgenographic signs of cervical injury." *Clin. Orthop.*, **109**: 9–17.

WILKINSON, J. (1969). "Roentgenographic correlations in cervical spondylosis." *Amer. J. Roentgenol.*, **105**: 370.

WILKINSON, M. & MEIKLE, J. A. K. (1966). "Tomography of the sacroiliac joints." *Ann. Rheum Dis.*, **25**: 433–440.

WILLIS, T. A. (1941). "Anatomical variations and roentgenographic appearances of low back pain in relation to sciatic pain." *J. Bone Joint Surg.*, **23**: 410–416.

WOESNER, M. E. & MITTS, M. G. (1972). "The evaluation of cervical spine motion below C2: a comparison of cineroentgenographic and conventional roentgenographic methods." *Amer. J. Roentgenol.*, **115**: 148–154.

WOLBRINK, A. J. (1974). "Occult roentgenographic changes in the cervical spine." *Mayo Clin. Proc.*, **49**: 879–883.

WOOD, P. H. N. (1967). "Radiology in the diagnosis of arthritis and rheumatism." *Trans. Soc. Occup. Med.*, **22**: 69–73.

YATES, D. A. H. (1965). "Epidural myelography with water soluble contrast material (Urografin)." *Ann. Phys. Med.*, **8**: 81–85.

YOUNG, D. A. & BURNEY, R. E. (1971). "Complication of myelography: transection and withdrawal of a nerve filament by the needle." *New Eng. J. Med.*, **285**: 156–157.

ZINGESSER, L. H. (1973). "Radiological aspects of anomalies of the upper cervical spine and craniocervical junction." *Clin. Neurosurg.*, **20**: 220–231.

## (f) Electromyography

AGOSTONI, E., SANT'AMBROGIO, G. & CARRASCO, H. DEL P. (1960). "Electromyography of the diaphragm and transdiaphragmatic pressure during coughing, sneezing and laughing." *Atti. Acad. Nazion. Lincei*, **28**: 493–496.

ANDERSSON, B. J. G. (1974). "Myoelectric back muscle activity during sitting." *Scand. J. Rehab. Med.*, Suppl. **3**: 73–90.

ANDERSSON, B. J. G. (1974). "Myoelectric activity in individual erector spinae muscles in sitting. A study with surface and wire electrodes." *Scand. J. Rehab. Med.* Suppl. **3**: 91–108.

ANDERSSON, B. J. G. (1975). "The sitting posture: an electromyographic and discometric study." *Orthop. Clin. Nth. Amer.*, **6**: 105–120.

ANDERSSON, B. J. G. & ÖRTENGREN, R. (1974). "Lumbar disc pressure and myoelectric back muscle activity during sitting. II: Studies on an office chair." *Scand. J. Rehab. Med.*, **6**: 115–121.

ANDERSSON, B. J. G. & ÖRTENGREN, R. (1974). "Lumbar disc pressure and myoelectric back muscle activity during sitting. III: Studies on a wheelchair." *Scand. J. Rehab. Med.*, **6**: 122–127.

ANDERSSON, B. J. G., ÖRTENGREN, R., NACHEMSON, A. & ELFSTRÖM, G. (1974). "Lumbar disc pressure and myoelectric back muscle activity during sitting. I: Studies on an experimental chair." *Scand. J. Rehab. Med.*, **6**: 104–114.

ANDERSSON, B. J. G., ÖRTENGREN, R., NACHEMSON, A. & ELFSTRÖM, G. (1974). "Lumbar disc pressure and myoelectric back muscle activity during sitting. IV: Studies on a car driver's seat." *Scand. J. Rehab. Med.*, **6:** 128–133.

APPEL, L., CLAES, C., JACOBS, J. & SELOSSE, P. (1969). "Comparison of myelographic, electromyographic and operative observations in sciatic pain." *Acta Orthop. Belg.*, **35:** 687–692.

BASMAJIAN, J. V. (1958). "Electromyography of iliopsoas." *Anat. Rec.*, **132:** 127–132.

BASMAJIAN, J. V. (1960). "Electromyography of postural muscles." *Anat. Rec.*, **136:** 160.

BASMAJIAN, J. V. (1974). *Muscles Alive. Their Functions Revealed by Electromyography.* 3rd ed. Baltimore; Williams and Wilkins.

BASMAJIAN, J. V. & STECKO, G. (1962). "A new bipolar electrode for electromyography." *J. Appl. Physiol.*, **17:** 849.

BEARN, J. G. (1961). "An electromyographic study of the trapezius, deltoid, pectoralis major, biceps and triceps muscles, during static loading of the upper limb." *Anat. Rec.*, **140:** 103–107.

BECKER, R. O. (1960). "The electrical response of human skeletal muscle to passive stretch." *J. Bone Joint Surg.*, **42A:** 1091–1103.

BERATO, J. & ALBATRO, J. (1971). "Electromyography and lumbo-sciatic pain: based on 200 observations." *Rhumatol.*, **23:** 47–60.

BERGER, H. (1965). "Electromyographic studies in sciatica." *Roczn. Acad. Med., Marchlewski*, **11:** 119–135.

BERGSTROM, R. M. (1959). "The relation between the number of impulses and the integrated electrical activity in electromyograms." *Acta Physiol. Scand.*, **45:** 97.

BLOM, S. & LEMPERG, R. (1967). "Electromyographic analysis of the lumbar musculature in patients operated on for lumbar rhizopathy." *J. Neurosurg.*, **26:** 25–30.

BONNER, F. J. & SCHMIDT, W. H. (1957). "Electromyography in disc disease." *Arch. Phys. Med.*, **38:** 689–691.

BRADDOM, R. I. & JOHNSON, E. W. (1974). "Standardisation of H-reflex and diagnostic use in S1 radiculopathy." *Arch. Phys. Med. Rehab.*, **55:** 161–166.

BROWN, B. J. (1968). "Wave form analysis of surface electrode E.M.G.s used to give independent control signals from adjacent muscles." *Med. Biol. Eng.*, **6:** 653–658.

CARLSON, K. E., ALSTON, W. & FELDMAN, D. J. (1964). "Electromyographic study of ageing in skeletal muscle." *Amer. J. Phys. Med.*, **43**: 141–145.

CARLSÖÖ, S. (1961). "The static muscle load in different work positions: an electromyographic study." *Ergonomics*, **4**: 193–211.

CARUSO, I. (1967). "Electromyographic study of the normal activity of erector spine muscle in symmetrical gymnastic exercises." *Orizz. Ortop. Ordierna. Riab.*, **12**: 31–41.

CHAPMAN, A. E. & TROUP, J. D. G. (1969). "The effect of increased maximal strength on the integrated electrical activity of lumbar erectores spinae." *Electromyography*, **9**: 263–280.

CHAPMAN, A. E. & TROUP, J. D. G. (1969). "Electromyographic study of the effect of training on the lumbar erectores spinae." *J. Anat.*, **105**: 286.

CHAPMAN, A. E. & TROUP, J. D. G. (1970). "Prolonged activity of lumbar erectores spinae: an electromyographic dynamometric study of the effect of training." *Ann. Phys. Med.*, **10**: 263–269.

CRUE, B. L., PUDENZ, R. H. & SHELDEN, C. H. (1957). "Observations on the value of clinical electromyography." *J. Bone Joint Surg.*, **39A**: 492–500.

CURRY, M. J. & GORDON, G. (1972). "The spinal input to the posterior group in the cat: an electrophysiological investigation." *Brain Res.*, **44**: 417–437.

DAKATA, T. (1966). "Electromyographic studies of lumbago." *Jikei Med. J.*, **13**: 113–114.

DAVID, H., HAMLEY, E. J. & SAUNDERS, G. R. (1968). "Electromyographic and cinematographic analysis of spinal extension under stress." *J. Physiol.*, **200**: 4–6.

DENISCHI, A. & PANAIT, G. (1969). "Electromyography in the determination of certain aetiopathogenic aspects of scoliosis." *Electroenceph. Clin. Neurophysiol.*, **27**: 636.

DE VRIES, H. A. (1968). "EMG fatigue curves in postural muscles: a possible etiology for idiopathic low back pain." *Amer. J. Phys. Med.*, **47**: 175–181.

DRECHSLER, B. (1970). "Spinal muscle control and root compression." In *Manuelle Medizin und Ihre Wissenschaftlichen Grundlagen.*" pp. 92–105. Ed. by H. D. Wolff. Heidelberg; Verlag Phys. Med.

DRECHSLER, B., LASTOVKA, M. & KALVODOVA, E. (1966). "Electrophysiological study of patients with herniated intervertebral discs." *Electromyography*, **6**: 187–204.

EASON, R. G. (1960). "Electromyographic study of local and generalized muscular impairment." *J. Appl. Physiol.*, **15:** 479–482.

ECHTERNACH, J. L. (1967). "Chronaximetry and strength-duration curve testing for intervertebral disc pathology." *J. Amer. Phys. Ther. Ass.*, **47:** 709–712.

EISEN, A. A. (1973). "Electromyography and nerve conduction as a diagnostic aid." *Arth. Clin. Nth. Amer.*, **4:** 885–895.

ENGLAND, R. W. W. & DEIBERT, P. W. (1972). "Electromyographic studies: Part 1—Consideration in the evaluation of osteopathic therapy." *J. Amer. Osteopath. Ass.*, **72:** 221–223.

FLAX, H. J., BERRIOS, R. & RIVERA, D. (1964). "Electromyography in the diagnosis of herniated lumbar disc." *Arch. Phys. Med. Rehab.*, **45:** 520–524.

FLAX, H. J., BERRIOS, R. & RIVERAL, D. (1965). "Electromyographic diagnosis of herniated lumbar disc." *Bol. Ass. Med. Puerto Rico*, **57:** 1–7.

GIOVINE, G. P. (1958). "Electromyographic diagnosis of the localization of herniated discs." *Osped. Maggiore*, **46:** 58–62.

GOUGH, J. G. & KOEPKE, G. H. (1966). "Electromyographic determination of motor root levels in erector spinae muscles." *Arch. Phys. Med.*, **47:** 9–11.

GULD, C., ROSENFALCK, A. & WILLISON, R. G. (1970). "Technical contributions: Report of the committee on EMG instrumentation. Technical factors in recording electrical activity of muscle and nerve in man." *Electroenceph. Clin. Neurophysiol.*, **28:** 399–413.

HANAK, L., MORAVEK, V. & SCHRODER, R. (1970). "Electromyography in the preoperative diagnosis of lumbar root discopathies: a comparative clinical and electromyographic study." *Česk. Neurol.*, **33:** 6–11.

HARDING, R. H. & SEN, R. N. (1969). "A single method of quantifying the electromyogram to evaluate total muscular activity." *J. Physiol.*, **204:** 66–68P.

HOEFER, P. F. A. & GUTMAN, S. A. (1944). "Electromyography as a method for determination of level of lesions in the spinal cord." *Arch Neurol.*, **51:** 415–422.

HOOVER, B. B., CALDWELL, J. W., KRUSEN, E. M. & MUCKELROY, R. N. (1970). "Value of polyphasic potentials in diagnosis of lumbar root lesions." *Arch. Phys. Med.*, **51:** 546–548.

HORN, C. V. (1969). "Electromyographic investigation of muscle imbalance in patients with paralytic scoliosis." *Electromyography*, **4**: 447–456.

HOWARD, F. M. (1972). "Electromyography and conduction studies in peripheral nerve injuries." *Surg. Clin. Nth. Amer.*, **52**: 1343–1352.

JANSEN, K. (1960). "Postural factors in paralytic scoliosis: a clinical, radiologic and electromyographic study." *Proc. 3rd Int. Cong. Phys. Med.*, pp. 668–670. Chicago; Westlake Press.

JEBSON, R. H. & LONG, E. (1973). "Radiculopathy and the electromyogram in disability applicants." *Arch. Phys. Med. Rehab.*, **54**: 471–474.

JOHNSON, E. W., & MELVIN, J. L. (1971). "Value of electromyography in lumbar radiculopathy." *Arch. Phys. Med. Rehab.*, **52**: 239–243.

JOHNSON, E. W. & MELVIN, J. L. (1972). "Electromyography in postlaminectomy patients." *Arch. Phys. Med. Rehab.*, **53**: 407–409.

JONSSON, B. & REICHMANN, S. (1970). "Radiographic control in the insertion of EMG electrodes in the lumbar part of the erector spinae muscle." *Zeit. Anat. Entwickl.-Gesch.*, **130**: 192–206.

KAESER, H. E. (1965). "Electromyographic studies in lumbar disc herniation." *Deutsche Zeit. Nervenheilk.*, **187**: 285–299.

KINALSKI, R. (1975). "Accuracy of electromyographic examination in pre-operative diagnosis of patients with sciatica." *Chir. Narzadow Ruchu. Ortop. Pol.*, **40**: 65–69.

KIWERSKI, J. (1970). "Functional trunk muscle disorders in so-called disk disease." *Pol. Tyg. Lek.*, **25**: 2027–2029.

KNUTSSON, B. (1961). "Comparative value of electromyographic, myelographic and clinical neurological examination in diagnosis of lumbar root compression syndrome." *Acta Orthop. Scand.*, Suppl. **49**: 1.

KNUTSSON, B., LINDH, K. & TELHAG, H. (1966). "Sitting: an electromyographic and mechanical study." *Acta Orthop. Scand.*, **37**: 415–428.

KOCZOCIK-PRZEDLEPSKA, J., SWIDERSKI, G., WALSKI, A., GRUSZ-CZUNSKI, W. & KOWALSKA, H. (1973). "Electromyographic and thermometric studies and assessment of motor and sensory excitability in patients with low back pains." *Pol. Tyg. Led.*, **28**: 315–317.

KROTT, H. M. (1968). "Electromyography of the lumbar muscula-ture in radicular syndromes." *Deutsch. Zeit. Nervenheilk.*, **194:** 280–295.

KROTT, H. M., BUSSE, M. J., POREMBA, M. B. & JACOBI, H. M. (1969). "Electromyographic and myelographic studies in lumbar disc surgery." *Deutsch. Zeit. Nervenheilk.*, **196:** 300–295.

LABAN, M. M., DWORKIN, H. J. & SCHEVITZ, H. (1972). "Metastatic disease of the spine: electromyography and bone scan in early detection." *Arch. Phys. Med. Rehab.*, **53:** 232–235.

LABAN, M. M. & GRANT, A. E. (1971). "Occult spinal metastases: early electromyographic manifestation." *Arch. Phys. Med. Rehab.*, **52:** 223–226.

LENMAN, J. A. R. (1969). "Integration and analysis of the electro-myogram and related techniques." In *Disorders of Voluntary Muscle, 2nd ed.* pp. 843–876. Ed. by J. N. Walton. London; Churchill.

LIPPOLD, O. C. T., REDFEARN, J. W. J. & VUCO, J. (1960). "The electromyography of fatigue." *Ergonomics*, **3:** 121–131.

LUNDERVOLD, A. J. S. (1951). *Electromyographic Investigations of Position and Manner of Working in Typewriting*. Oslo; Brøggers.

McBRYDE, A. M., URBANIAK, J. R., CLIPPINGER, F. W. & BUGG, E. (1972). "Electromyography as a diagnostic aid in lumbosacral nerve root irritation." *J. South Carolina Med. Ass.*, **68:** 144–148.

MACK, E. W. (1951). "Electromyographic observations on the postoperative disc patient." *J. Neurosurg.*, **8:** 469–472.

MAGILL, C. D. (1969). "The aggravated EMG: a new sign in lumbar disk lesions." *Rocky Mt. Med. J.*, **66:** 32–34.

MAGORA, F. (1974). "An electromyographic investigation of the neck muscles in headache." *Electromyography Clin. Neurophy-siol.*, **14:** 453–462.

MARGUTH, F., ORBACH, H. & VETTER, K. (1955). "The electro-myogram in the diagnosis of spinal nerve root compression." *Nervenarzt.*, **20:** 137–139.

MARINACCI, A. A. (1955). *Clinical Electromyography*. Los Angeles; San Lucas Press.

MARINACCI, A. A. (1965). "Electromyogram in the evaluation of lumbar herniated disc." *Bull. Los Angeles Neurol. Soc.*, **30:** 47–62.

MARINACCI, A. A. (1966). "Electromyogram in the evaluation of lumbar herniated disc." *Electromyography*, **6:** 25–43.

MARINACCI, A. A. & LINDHEIMER, J. (1961). "Muscle spasms as a neurological symptom: their evaluation by electromyography." *Bull. Los Angeles Neurol. Soc.*, **26**: 186–197.

MASTERSON, J. H. & WHITE, A. E. (1966). "Electromyographic validation of pain relief: a pilot study in orthopedic patients." *Amer. J. Orthop.*, **8**: 36–40.

MAURY, M., FRANÇOIS, N. & SKODA, A. (1973). "About the neurological sequelae of herniated intervertebral disc." *Paraplegia*, **11**: 221–227.

MORTIER, G. & MOOR, L. DE (1969). "The nerve root innervation of the muscles of the lower limb: an electromyographic investigation." *Electromyography*, **9**: 181–184.

OP DE COUL, A. A. W. & LIE, T. A. (1970). "A comparative electromyographic study before and after operations for protruded lumbar disc." *Electromyography*, **10**: 193–200.

PANAYIOTOPOULOS, C. P. (1975). "Electrophysiological estimation of motor units in limb-girdle muscular dystrophy and chronic spinal muscular atrophy." *J. Neurol. Sci.*, **24**: 95–107.

PAULY, J. E. (1966). "An electromyographic analysis of certain movements and exercises: I. Some deep muscles of the back." *Anat. Rec.*, **155**: 223–234.

PAULY, J. E. & STEELE, R. W. (1966). "Electromyographic analysis of back exercises for paraplegic patients." *Arch. Phys. Med. Rehab.*, **47**: 730–736.

PORTNOY, H. D. & AHMAD, M. (1972). "Value of the neurological examination, electromyography and myelography in herniated lumbar disc." *Michigan Med.*, **71**: 429–434.

RAU, E. (1969). "Electromyography as a clinical and diagnostic method in intervertebral disk prolapse." *Zeit. Orthop.*, **107**: 46–52.

RAUSER, V., REHACEK, J. & PETRACEK, V. (1973). "Electrophysiological examination of paravertebral muscles in scoliosis." *Acta Chir. Orthop. Traumatol. Česk.*, **40**: 33–38.

RECORDIER, A. M., SERRATRICE, G., BISSCHOP, G. DE ACQUAVIVA, P. & ROUX, H. (1971). "Electromyographic survey of lumbo-sciatica." *Marseilles Méd.*, **108**: 823–835.

RIDDLE, H. F. V. & ROAF, R. (1955). "Muscle imbalance in the causation of scoliosis." *Lancet*, **1**: 1245–1247.

ROSEMEYER, B. (1971). "Electromyographic studies of the spinal

335

and shoulder musculature in standing and sitting." *Arch. Orthop. Unfall-Chir.*, **69**: 59–70.

SCHENKER, A. W. (1961). "The accurate measurement of neuromuscular and musculoskeletal disabilities." *Milit. Med.*, **126**: 207–213.

SEZE, S. DE, MARCHAND, J. H., DJIAN, A. & FARGEOT, R. (1957). "Electrodiagnosis of sciatica: personal experience with 50 cases." *Rev. Rhum.*, **24**: 607–616.

SHEA, P. A. & WOODS, W. W. (1956). "The diagnostic value of the electromyograph." *Brit. J. Phys. Med.*, **19**: 36–43.

SHEA, P. A., WOODS, W. W. & WERDEN, D. H. (1950). "Electromyography in diagnosis of nerve root compression syndrome." *Arch. Neurol.*, **64**: 94–104.

SHIZAWA, R. & MAVOR, H. (1969). "In vivo human sural nerve action potentials." *J. Appl. Physiol.*, **26**: 623–629.

SIEHL, D., OSLON, D. R., ROSS, H. E. & ROCKWOOD, E. E. (1971). "Manipulation of the lumbar spine with the patient under general anaesthesia: evaluation by electromyography and clinico-neurologic examination of its use for lumbar root compression syndrome." *J. Amer. Osteopath. Ass.*, **70**: 433–440.

STRONG, R. & THOMAS, P. E. (1969). "Patterns of muscle activity in the leg, hip and torso associated with anomalous fifth lumbar conditions." *J. Amer. Osteopath. Ass.*, **67**: 1039–1041.

STRONG, R., THOMAS, P. E. & EARL, W. D. (1967). "Patterns of muscle activity in leg, hip and torso during quiet standing." *J. Amer. Osteopath. Ass.*, **66**: 1035–1038.

TORRES, P. & SHAPIRO, A. (1961). "Electroencephalograms in whiplash injury." *Arch. Neurol.*, **5**: 40.

VISSER, S. L. (1965). "The significance of the Hoffman reflex in the electromyographic examination of patients with herniation of the nucleus pulposus." *Psychiat. Neurol. Neurochir.*, **68**: 300–305.

WATSON, R. (1975). "Paraspinal electromyographic abnormalities as a predictor of occult metastatic carcinoma." *Arch. Phys. Med. Rehab.*, **56**: 216–218.

WAYLONIS, G. W. (1968). "Electromyographic findings in chronic cervical radicular syndromes." *Arch. Phys. Med. Rehab.*, **49**: 407–412.

WEISS, M., MILKOWSKA, A. & KOZINSKA, M. (1957). "Conservative treatment based on electromyographic studies." *Chir. Narzad. Ruchu Ortop. Pol.*, **22:** 197–209.

WILLIAMS, N. E. & YATES, D. A. H. (1973). "Electrodiagnosis and electromyography." *Physiotherapy*, **59:** 288–291.

WINTER, D. A. & QUANBURU, A. O. (1975). "Special report. Multichannel biotelemetry systems for use in EMG studies, particularly in locomotion." *Amer. J. Phys. Med.*, **54:** 142–147.

WISE, C. S. & ARDISSONE, J. (1954). "Electromyography in intervertebral disc protrusions." *Arch. Phys. Med. Rehab.*, **35:** 442–446.

WOOLF, A. L. (1962). "The theoretical basis of clinical electromyography." *Ann. Phys. Med.*, **6:** 189–241.

YATES, D. A. H. (1964). "Unilateral lumbosacral root compression." *Ann. Phys. Med.*, **7:** 169–179.

ZALIS, P. (1970). "Electrophysiologic diagnosis of cervical nerve root avulsion." *Arch. Phys. Med. Rehab.*, **51:** 708.

ZUK, T. (1957). "Electrodiagnostic investigations in scoliosis." *Chir. Narzad. Ruchu Ortop. Pol.*, **22:** 131–138.

ZUK, T. (1962). "The role of spinal and abdominal muscles in the pathogenesis of scoliosis." *J. Bone Joint Surg.*, **44B:** 102–105.

ZUK, T., SYMYSLOWSKI, W. & CZAYKOWSKI, L. (1957). "Electrodiagnostic picture of scoliosis following operation." *Chir. Narzad. Ruchu Ortop. Pol.*, **22:** 297–303.

### (g) Dermography

AGARWAL, A., LLOYD, K. N. & DOVEY, P. (1970). "Thermography of the spine and sacroiliac joints in spondylitis." *Rheum. Phys. Med.*, **10:** 349–355.

ALBERT, S. M., GLICKMAN, M. & KALLISH, M. (1964). "Thermography in orthopedics." *Ann. New York Acad. Sci.*, **121:** 157–170.

COLLINS, A. J., RING, E. F. J., COSH, J. A. & BACON, P. A. (1974). "Quantitation of thermography in arthritis using multiisothermal analysis: 1. The "thermographic index." *Ann. Rheum. Dis.*, **33:** 113–115.

COSH, J. A. & RING, E. F. J. (1969/70). "Thermography and rheumatology." *Ann. Phys. Med.*, **10:** 342–348.

DARROW, C. W. (1934). "The significance of skin resistance in the

337

light of its relation to the amount of perspiration." *J. Gen. Physiol.*, **11:** 451–452.

DICK, J. C. (1951). "The tension and resistance to stretching from human skin and other membrances, with results from a series of normal and oedematous cases." *J. Physiol.*, **112:** 102–113.

DUENSING, F., BECKER, P. & RITTMEYER, K. (1973). "Thermographic findings in prolapse of lumbar intervertebral discs." *Arch. Psychiat. Nervenkr.*, **217:** 52–70.

DYLEWSKA, D. (1965). "Skin temperature as a sign of vasomotor disturbances in sciatica." *Pol. Tyg. Lek.*, **20:** 1390–1392.

FLOYD, W. F. (1936). "A modification of the apparatus for recording electrical phenomena from the skin." *J. Physiol.*, **87:** 24P–25P.

FORBES, T. W. (1964). "Problems in measurement of electrodermal phenomena—choice of method and phenomena—potential, impedance, resistance." *Psychophysiol.*, **1:** 26–30.

FREYSCHMIDT, J., RITTMEIYER, K. & KAISER, G. (1973). "Comparative thermographic and myelographic studies in lumbosacral disc prolapse." *Fortschr. Geb. Roetgenst. Nuklearmed.*, (Suppl.): 366–367.

FUHRER, M. J. (1968). "Electrodermal study of patients with spinal-cord injuries." *Arch. Phys. Med. Rehab.*, **49:** 728–734.

GEDDES, L. A., BOURLAND, J. D., SMALLING, R. W. & STEINBERG, R. B. (1975). "The use of the same pair of dry electrodes to record skin resistance and beat-by-beat heart rate." *Med. Biol. Eng.*, **(Jan.):** 89–96.

GOLDBERG, H. I., HEINZ, E. R. & TAVERAS, J. M. (1966). "Thermography in neurological patients: preliminary experiences." *Acta Radiol.*, **5:** 786–795.

GRAHAME, R. (1970). "A method for measuring human skin elasticity *in vivo*, with observations on the effects of age, sex and pregnancy." *Clinical Sci.*, **39:** 223–238.

GREGER, E. (1938). "Investigations on the skin temperature in patients with diseases of the joints." *Acta Orthop. Scand.*, **9:** 72–87.

JASPER, H. (1945). "An improved clinical dermometer." *J. Neurosurg.*, **2:** 257–260.

KAMAJIAN, G. K. (1975). "Thermography of the back in asymptomatic subjects." *J. Am. Osteopath. Ass.*, **74:** 429–431.

KORR, I. M., THOMAS, P. E. & WRIGHT, H. M. (1958). "Patterns of electrical skin resistance in man." *Acta Neuroveg.*, **17:** 77–96.

LEBROWSKI, J., POLOCKI, B., BORVCKI, Z., DUDEK, H., SZPAKOWICZ, P. & TOMCYZYK, H. (1973). "Determination of the level of prolapsed intervertebral disc in sciatica by means of an electric thermometer." *Pol. Tyg. Led.*, **28**: 907–908.

LYKKEN, D. T. (1959). "Properties of electrodes used in electrodermal measurement." *J. Comp. Physiol. Psychol.*, **52**: 629–634.

MILOSEVIČ, S. (1975). "Changes in detection measures and skin resistance during an auditory vigilance task." *Ergonomics*, **18**: 1–8.

NEUMANN, E. & BLANTON, R. (1970). "The early history of electrodermal research." *Psychophysiol.*, **6**: 453–475.

RICHTER, C. P. (1946). "Instructions for using the cutaneous resistance recorder, or "Dermometer", on peripheral nerve injuries, sympathectomies and paravertebral blocks." *J. Neurosurg.*, **3**: 181–191.

RICHTER, C. P. & WOODRUFF, J. (1945). "Lumbar sympathetic dermatomes in man determined by the electrical skin resistance method." *J. Neurophysiol.*, **8**: 325–338.

RING, E. F. J. & COLLINS, A. J. (1960). "Quantitative thermography." *Ann. Phys. Med.*, **10**: 337–341.

SARNOFF, S. J. & ARROWOOD, J. G. (1947). "Differential spinal block: II. The reaction of sudomotor and vasomotor fibers." *J. Clin. Invest.*, **26**: 203–216.

STERNBACH, R. A. & TURSKY, B. (1964). "Ethnic differences among housewives in psychophysiological and skin potential responses to electric shock." *Psychophys.* **1**: 241–246.

THIELE, F. A. J. & SENDEN, K. G. VAN (1966). "Relationship between skin temperature and the insensible perspiration of the human skin." *J. Invest. Derm.*, **47**: 307–312.

THOMAS, P. E. & KAWAHATA, A. (1962). "Neural factors underlying variations in electrical resistance of apparently non-sweating skin." *J. Appl. Physiol.*, **17**: 999–1002.

THOMAS, P. E. & KORR, I. M. (1957). "Relationship between sweat gland activity and electrical resistance of the skin." *J. Appl. Physiol.*, **10**: 505–510.

THOMAS, P. E., KORR, I. M. & WRIGHT, H. M. (1958). "A mobile instrument for recording electrical skin resistance patterns of the human trunk." *Acta Neuroveg.*, **17**: 97–106.

THOMPSON, H. B. & GELLHORN, E. (1945). "Influence of muscle

pain on electrical resistance of the human skin." *Proc. Soc. Exp. Biol.*, **58**: 146–149.

TROTT, P. H., MAITLAND, G. D. & GERRARD, B. (1972). "The neurocalometer: a survey to assess its value as a diagnostic instrument." *Med. J. Austr.*, **1**: 464–467.

WAGNER, H. N. (1952). "Electrical skin resistance studies in two persons with congenital absence of sweat glands." *Arch. Dermat. Syph.*, **65**: 543–548.

WHELAN, F. G. (1950). "An instrument for measuring electrical resistance to the skin." *Science*, **111**: 496–497.

WILCOTT, R. C. (1964). "The partial independence of skin potential and skin resistance from sweating." *Psychophysiol.*, **1**: 55–56.

WRIGHT, H. M. & KORR, I. M. (1965). "Neural and spinal components of disease: progress in the application of thermography." *J. Amer. Osteopath. Ass.*, **64**: 918–921.

WRIGHT, H. M. & WILLIAMS, P. M. (1966). "Thermography: a new diagnostic procedure." *J. Amer. Osteopath. Ass.*, **65**: 1085–1091.

# 2

# AETIOLOGY AND PATHOGENESIS

## (a) Congenital Malformations and Anomalies

BATTS, M. (1939). "The etiology of spondylolisthesis." *J. Bone Joint Surg.*, **21**: 879–884.

CARMEL, W. & KRAMER, F. J. (1968). "Cervical cord compression due to exostosis in a patient with hereditary multiple exostoses." *J. Neurosurg.*, **28**: 500–503.

CHATTERJEE, P. (1968). "Clinical significance of neural arch defects in the lumbar region." *Indian J. Radiol.*, **22**: 35.

COWELL, H. R., HALL, J. N. & MACEWEN, G. D. (1972). "Genetic aspects of idiopathic scoliosis." *Clinical Orthop.*, **86**: 121–131.

DICK, H. M. (1974). "Inheritance of ankylosing spondylitis and HL-A antigen W27." *Lancet*, **2**: 24–25.

FARCAS, A. (1954). "The pathogenesis of idiopathic scoliosis." *J. Bone Joint Surg.*, **36A**: 617.

HAGELSTAM, L. (1949). "Retroposition of lumbar vertebrae." *Acta Chir. Scand., Suppl.* **143**: 1.

HARMON, P. H. (1966). "Congenital and acquired anatomic variations including degenerative changes of the lower lumbar spine: role in production of painful back and lower extremity syndromes." *Clin. Orthop.*, **44**: 171–186.

JAMES, J. I. P. (1970). "The aetiology of scoliosis." *J. Bone Joint Surg.*, **52B**: 410–419.

JOFFE, R., APPLEBY, A. & ARJONA, V. (1966). " 'Intermittent ischaemia' of the cauda equina due to stenosis of the lumbar canal." *J. Neurol. Neurosurg. Psychiat.*, **29**: 315–318.

LEHNER, K. & RICHTER, G. (1973). "Idiopathic calcification of the intervertebral disc and prevertebral ligament." *J. Pediatr. Surg.*, **8**: 979.

LINDERMANN, P. (1955). "Pathogenesis of juvenile spine curvatures." *Zeit. Orthop.*, **86**: 540.

MESCHAM, I. (1945). "Spondylolisthesis: a commentary on aetiology, and an improved method of roentgenographic mensuration and detection of instability." *Amer. J. Roentgenol.*, **53**: 230–243.

MEYERDING, H. W. (1938). "Spondylolisthesis as an aetiologic factor in backache." *J. Amer. Med. Ass.*, **111:** 1971.

MEYERDING, H. W. (1941). "Low backache and sciatic pain associated with spondylolisthesis and protruded intervertebral disc: incidence and treatment." *J. Bone Joint. Surg.*, **23:** 461–470.

MOIEL, R. & EHNI, G. (1968). "Cauda equina compression due to spondylolisthesis with intact neural arch: report of two cases." *J. Neurosurg.*, **28:** 262–265.

NASCA, R. J. (1975). "Progression of congenital scoliosis due to hemi-vertebrae and hemivertebrae with bars." *J. Bone Joint Surg.*, **57A:** 456–466.

NEWMAN, P. H. (1955). "Spondylolisthesis: its cause and effect." *Ann. Roy. Coll. Surg. Engl.*, **16:** 305–323.

NEWMAN, P. H. (1963). "The aetiology of spondylolisthesis." *J. Bone Joint Surg.*, **45B:** 39–59.

NICHOLS, B. H. (1941). "Some roentgen findings which may be responsible for low back pain." *Arch. Phys. Ther.*, **22:** 600–606.

NORDWALL, A. (1973). "Studies in idiopathic scoliosis relevant to etiology, conservative and operative treatment." *Acta Orthop. Scand., Suppl.* **150:** 1.

PIONNIER, R. & DEPRAZ, A. (1956). "Costal anomalies of congenital origin." *Radiol. Clin., Basel*, **25:** 170–186.

REDLER, I. (1952). "Clinical significance of minor inequalities in leg length." *New Orleans Med. Surg. J.*, **104:** 308–312.

ROUSSEAU, J. (1969). "Radiological and clinical study of 16 cases with congenital malformation of the cervico-occipital joint." *Ann. Radiol.*, **12:** 499–521.

ROWE, G. G. & ROCHE, M. B. (1953). "The etiology of separate neural arch." *J. Bone Joint Surg.*, **35A:** 102–110.

SARPEYNER, M. A. (1945). "Congenital stricture of the spinal canal." *J. Bone Joint Surg.*, **27:** 70–79.

SARPEYNER, M. A. (1947). "Spina bifida aperta and congenital stricture of the spinal canal." *J. Bone Joint Surg.*, **29:** 817–821.

SAY, B. (1975). "Hereditary defect of the sacrum." *Humangenetik*, **27:** 231–234.

STEWART, T. D. (1953). "The age incidence of neural arch defects in Alaskan natives, considered from the standpoint of etiology." *J. Bone Joint Surg.*, **35A:** 937–950.

STONE, K. H. (1963). "The etiology of spondylolisthesis." *J. Bone Joint Surg.*, **45B:** 39–59.

TAILLARD, W. (1971). "Aetiology of spondylolisthesis." *Rev. Chir. Orthop.*, **57** (Suppl. 1): 90–98.

TOJNER, H. (1963). "Olisthetic scoliosis." *Acta Orthop. Scand.*, **33**: 291–300.

TURNEY, J. P. (1952). "A cauda equina lesion due to spondylolisthesis." *Brit. Med. J.*, **2**: 1028–1029.

WADIA, N. H. (1967). "Myelopathy complicating congenital atlanto-axial dislocation." *Brain*, **90**: 449–472.

WILTSE, L. L. (1962). "The etiology of spondylolisthesis." *J. Bone Joint Surg.*, **44A**: 539–560.

WYNNE-DAVIES, R. (1975). "Infantile idiopathic scoliosis. Causative factors, particularly in the first six months of life." *J. Bone Joint Surg.*, **57B**: 138–141.

### (b) Trauma (Injury, Fractures, Dislocations)

AHLGREN, P. & FOG, J. (1968). "Atlanto-epistrophical subluxation in rheumatoid arthritis." *Acta Rheum.* **14**: 210–221.

AHMANN, P. A. (1975). "Spinal cord infarction due to minor trauma in children." *Neurology*, **25**: 301–307.

AMBRUS, L. & PAPATHEODOROU, C. (1973). "Trauma and lumbar disc herniation in childhood." *Calif. Med.*, **119**: 66–68.

AUFDERMAUER, M. (1974). "Spinal injuries in juveniles: necropsy findings in twelve cases." *J. Bone Joint Surg.*, **56B**: 513–519.

BABCOCK, J. L. (1975). "Spinal injuries in children." *Pediat. Clin. Nth. Amer.*, **22**: 487–500.

BAILEY, I. C. (1975). "Fracture dislocation of the cervical spine with gross displacement." *J. Neurosurg.*, **42**: 209–211.

BAILEY, R. W. (1963). "Observations on cervical intervertebral disc lesions in fractures and dislocations." *J. Bone Joint Surg.*, **45A**: 461–466.

BALAU, J. & HUPFAUER, W. (1974). "The differential diagnosis of injuries of the atlanto-axial region in children." *Arch. Orthop. Unfall-Chir.*, **78**: 343–355.

BANNISTER, J. (1975). "Seat belt fractures of the spine." *J. Bone Joint Surg.*, **57B**: 252.

BARRIE, H. J. & HODSON-WALKER, N. (1970). "Incidence and pathogenesis of fractures of the lumbar transverse processes in air crashes." *Aerospace Med.*, **41**: 805–808.

BARWOOD, A. J. (1975). "Sources of ejection injury." *Proc. Roy. Soc. Med.*, **68:** 721–722.

BEROVIC, Z., LOPICIC, L., KICEVAC-MILJKOVIC, A. & BIDUMIR, M. (1974). "Spinal injury and disc disease." *Medicinski Archiv.*, **28:** 33–36.

BHATTACHARYA, S. K. (1974). "Fracture and displacement of the odontoid process in a child." *J. Bone Joint Surg.*, **56A:** 1071–1072.

BIRKELAND, I. W. & TAYLOR, T. K. F. (1969). "Major vascular injuries in lumbar disc surgery." *J. Bone Joint Surg.*, **51B:** 4–19.

BLOW, R. J. & JACKSON, J. M. (1971). 'An analysis of back injuries in registered dock workers." *Proc. Roy. Soc. Med.*, **64:** 1–4.

BLUMENTHAL, L. S. (1974). "Injury to the cervical spine as a cause of headache." *Postgrad. Med.*, **56:** 147–153.

BOONZAIER, A. C. (1973). "Fracture dislocation of the cervical spine." *Proc. Mine Med. Off. Ass.*, **52:** 57–58.

BOUKHRIS, R. & BECKER, K. L. (1973). "The inter-relationship between vertebral fractures and osteoporosis." *Clin. Orthop.*, **90:** 209–216.

BRAAKMAN, R. (1973). "Mechanisms of injury to the cervical cord." *Paraplegia*, **10:** 314–320.

BRAFF, M. M. (1975). "Trauma of cervical spine as cause of chronic headache." *J. Trauma*, **15:** 441–446.

BREITENFELDER, J. (1972). "Contribution to the problem of the treatment of fractured vertebral bodies without neurological symptoms." *Zeit. Orthop.*, **110:** 116–120.

BROWN, H. A. (1937). "Low back pain, with special reference to dislocation of intervertebral disc and hypertrophy of ligamentum flavum." *West. J. Surg.*, **45:** 527.

BUCK, J. E. (1970). "Direct repair to stress fractures in the lumbar spine." *Brit. J. Sports Med.*, **5:** 50–54.

BURKE, D. C. (1973). "Spinal cord injuries and seat belts." *Med. J. Austr.*, **2:** 801–806.

CANCEIMO, J. J. (1972). "Clay shoveler's fracture: a helpful diagnostic sign." *Amer. J. Roentgenol.*, **115:** 540–543.

CAPENER, N. (1960). "The origins of spondylolisthesis." *Bull. Hosp. Jt. Dis.*, **21:** 111–128.

CASEY, B. M., EATON, S. B., DU BOIS, J. J., TREMAINE, M. D. & MANI, C. J. (1973). "Thoracolumbar neural arch fractures: evaluation by hypocycloidal tomography." *J. Amer. Med. Ass.*, **224:** 1263–1265.

CHARI, P. R., CHOUDARY, H. R. & RAO, A. S. (1973). "A unique case of fracture dislocation of the spine." *Austr. N.Z. J. Surg.*, **42**: 289–291.

CICCONE, R. & RACHMANN, R. M. (1948). "The mechanism of injury and the distribution of three thousand fractures and dislocations caused by parachute jumping." *J. Bone Joint Surg.*, **30A**: 77–97.

CODE, C. F., WILLIAMS, M. D., BALDES, E. J. & GHORMLEY, R. K. (1947). "Are the intervertebral discs displaced during positive acceleration?" *J. Aviat. Med.*, **18**: 231–236; 296.

COHEN DE LARA, A., WEIL, E., AUQUIER, L. & GUIOT, G. (1974). "Sciatica of the S1 type due to herniation of the T12—L1 disc." *Rev. Rhum.*, **41**: 349–352.

COLLINS, S. D., PHILLIPS, F. R. & OLIVER, D. S. (1953). "Accident frequency by specific cause and by nature and site of injury as recorded in a general morbidity survey." *U.S. Treas. Dept. Public Health Monograph, No.* **1**: 3–22.

COOK, P. (1972). "Treatment of whiplash injuries by nerve block." *South. Med. J.*, **65**: 572–574.

COPPOLA, F. (1968). "Neck injury: a reappraisal." *Internat. Surg.*, **50**: 510–515.

COSTE, F., PIGUET, B. & CAROW, A. (1955). "Fractures and abnormalities of the lumbar articular apophyses." *Rev. Rhum.*, **22**: 824–826.

COX, H. H. (1927). "Sacroiliac subluxation as a cause of backache." *Surg. Gynec. Obst.*, **45**: 637–649.

CRELLIN, P. (1970). "Severe subluxation of the cervical spine in rheumatoid arthritis." *J. Bone Joint Surg.*, **52B**: 244.

CRISCI, V. & ORSO, C. A. (1968). "Lumbar spondylolisis and spondylolisthesis and trauma: medico-legal problems." *Minerva Ortop.*, **19**: 287–293.

CROOKS, L. M. (1970). "Long term effects of ejecting from aircraft." *Aerospace Med.*, **41**: 803–804.

DAVIS, P. R. & ROWLAND, H. A. K. (1965). "Vertebral fractures in West Indians suffering from tetanus." *J. Bone Joint Surg.*, **47B**: 61–71.

DEHNER, J. R. (1971). "Seat belt injuries of the spine and abdomen." *Amer. J. Roentgenol.*, **111**: 833–843.

DELAHAYE, R. P., FABRE, J., MAGIN, H. & GALBAN, P. (1964).

"Statistical studies of ejections observed in the French Army (1951–1963)." *Rev. Méd. Aeronaut.*, **3**: 27–37.

DEVADIGA, K. V. & GASS, H. H. (1973). "Chronic lumbar extradural haematoma simulating disc syndrome." *J. Neurol. Neurosurg. Psychiatr.*, **36**: 255–259.

DOURY, P., MILNE, J., DELAHAYE, P. R., PATTIN, S., BOCQUET, A., BAZIN, J. P. & ALLARD, P. (1974). "Spinal fractures in ankylosing spondyloarthritis: observations on two cases." *Rev. Rhum.*, **41**: 421–425.

ELLIS, J. D. (Ed.). (1940). *The Injured Back and Its Treatment.* Springfield, Ill.; Thomas.

EVERETT, W. G. (1973). "Traumatic lumbar hernia." *Injury*, **4**: 354–356.

EWING, C. L. (1971). "Non-fatal ejection vertebral fracture." *Aerospace Med.*, **42**: 1226–1228.

FARHAT, S. M., SCHNEIDER, F. R. & GRAY, J. M. (1973). "Traumatic spinal extradural hematoma associated with cervical fractures in rheumatoid arthritis." *J. Trauma*, **13**: 591–599.

FIELDING, J. W. (1974). "Tears of the transverse ligament of the atlas: a clinical and biomechanical study." *Brit. J. Radiol.*, **47**: 1683–1691.

FITZGERALD, J. G. (1972). "The role of the intervertebral space in the prevention of ejection injury." *R.A.F. Inst. Aviation Med., Report No.* **510**: 1.

FOURRIER, P. & BERT, G. (1972). "Evaluation of spinal adjustment after traumatic vertebral collapse." *Rev. Chir. Orthop.*, **58**: 131–136.

FRANKEL, V. H. (1970). "Temporomandibular joint pain syndrome following deceleration injury to the cervical spine." *J. Bone Joint Surg.*, **52A**: 825.

FRIED, L. C. (1974). "Cervical spinal cord injury during skeletal traction." *J. Amer. Med. Ass.*, **229**: 181–183.

FULLENLOVE, T. M. & WILSON, J. G. (1974). "Traumatic defects of the pars interarticularis of the lumbar vertebrae." *Amer. J. Roentgenol.*, **122**: 634–638.

GOFF, C. W., ALDES, J. H. & ALDEN, J. O. (1964). *Traumatic Cervical Syndrome and Whiplash.* Philadelphia; Lippincott.

GOLDIE, I. (1957). "Intervertebral disc changes after discography." *Acta Chir. Scand.*, **113**: 438–439.

GOLDSMITH, N. F. & JOHNSTON, J. O. (1973). "Mineralization of bone in an insured population: correlation with reported fractures and other measures of osteoporosis." *Int. J. Epid.*, **2:** 311–327.

GORMAN, W. (1974). "Whiplash—a neuropsychiatric injury." *Arizona Med.*, **31:** 414–416.

GREEN, P. & JOYNT, M. (1959). "Vascular accidents to the brain stem associated with neck manipulation." *J. Amer. Med. Ass.*, **170:** 522.

GRIEVE, D. W. & ARNOTT, A. W. (1970). "The production of torque during axial rotation of the trunk." *J. Anat.*, **107:** 147–164.

GRIFFIN, C. R. (1975). "Spinal ejection injuries." *Proc. Roy. Soc. Med.*, **68:** 722–723.

GRIFFITHS, R. W. (1975). "Acute vertebral collapse and cauda equina compression in tertiary syphilis." *J. Neurol. Neurosurg. Psychiat.*" **38:** 558–560.

GRISOLA, M. (1967). "Fractures and dislocations of the spine complicating ankylosing spondylitis." *J. Bone Joint Surg.*, **49A:** 339.

HADLEY, L. A. (1963). "Stress fracture with spondylolysis." *Amer. J. Roentgenol.*, **90:** 1258–1262.

HOOPER, J. (1973). "Low back pain and manipulation paraparesis after treatment of low back pain by physical methods." *Med. J. Aust.*, **1:** 549–551.

HORNER, D. B. (1964). "Lumbar back pain arising from stress fractures of the lower ribs. *J. Bone Joint Surg.*, **46A:** 1553–1556.

HUELKE, D. F. (1975). "Vertebral column injuries and seat belts." *J. Trauma*, **15:** 304–318.

HUITTINEN, V. M. (1972). "Lumbosacral nerve injury in fracture of the pelvis: a postmortem radiographic and patho-anatomical study." *Acta Chir. Scand., Suppl.* **429:** 1.

HUITTINEN, V. M. (1972). "Nerve injury in double vertical pelvic fractures resulting from shock therapy." *Amer. J. Roentgenol.*, **68:** 247.

IRARD, H. J. (1952). "A roentgenological evaluation of vertebral fractures resulting from convulsive shock therapy." *Amer. J. Roentgenol.*, **68:** 247.

JACKSON, D. W. (1975). "Unilateral osseous bridging of the lumbar transverse processes following trauma." *J. Bone Joint Surg.*, **57A:** 125–126.

KELLER, R. H. (1974). "Traumatic displacement of the cartilaginous vertebral rim: a sign of intervertebral disc prolapse." *Radiology*, **110**: 21–24.

KEWAIRAMANI, L. S. (1975). "Injuries to the cervical spine from diving accidents." *J. Trauma*, **15**: 130–143.

KIRBY, N. G. (1974). "Parachuting injuries." *Proc. Roy. Soc. Med.*, **67**: 17–21.

KIWERSKI, J., CHROSTOWSKA, T. & KAMOWSKI, J. (1974). "On the reasons and the mechanism of trauma to the cervical spine." *Chir. Narzod. Ruchu. Ortop. Pol.*, **39**: 1–6.

KLEIMAN, S. G., STEVENS, J., KOLB, L. & PANKOVICH, A. (1971). "Late sciatic-nerve palsy following posterior fracture-dislocation of the hip." *J. Bone Joint Surg.*, **53A**: 781–782.

KULOWSKI, J. (1972). "Spontaneous anterior dislocation of the atlas." *Missouri Med.*, **69**: 805–808; 812.

LANCE, P. (1971). "Relations of spondylolisis and spondylolisthesis to trauma." *Rev. Chir. Orthop., Suppl.* **1**: 107–109.

LAURELL, L. & NACHEMSON, A. (1963). "Some factors influencing spinal injuries in seat-ejected pilots." *Indust. Med. Surg.*, **16**: 27–28.

LEVY, P. M. (1964). "Ejection seat design and vertebral fractures." *Aerospace Med.*, **35**: 545–549.

LIVINGSTON, P. (1971). "Spinal manipulation causing injury." *Clin. Orthop.*, **81**: 82–86.

McLENNAN, J. A., McLAUGHLIN, W. T. & SKILLICORN, S. A. (1973). "Traumatic lumbar nerve root meningocele: case report." *J. Neurosurg.*, **39**: 532–538.

McSWEENEY, T. (1971). "Stability of the cervical spine following injury accompanied by grave neurological damage." *Proc. Veterans Adm. Spinal Cord Inj. Conf.*, **18**: 61–65.

MALLORY, T. H. (1973). "Posterior buttock pain following total hip replacement." *Clin. Orthop.*, **90**: 104–106.

MARAR, B. C. (1974). "Hyperextension injuries of the cervical spine." *Brit. J. Radiol.*, **47**: 1655–1662.

MEHALIC, T. (1974). "Vertebral artery injury from chiropractic manipulation of the neck." *Surg. Neurol.*, **2**: 125–129.

MILLER, P. R. (1974). "Stroke following chiropractic manipulation of the spine." *J. Amer. Med. Assoc.*, **229**: 189–190.

MOCK, H. E. (1941). "Low back pain and trauma." *Arch. Phys. Med.*, **22**: 430.

Mock, H. E. (1941). "Low back pain and trauma." *Amer. J. Surg.*, **51**: 779–802.

Newman, P. H. (1952). "Sprungback." *J. Bone Joint Surg.*, **34B**: 30–37.

Northrop, C. H. (1975). "Vertical fracture of the sacral ala." *Amer. J. Roentgenol.*, **124**: 102–106.

Ondruf, W. & Wolf, B. (1968). "Studies of sports injuries of the vertebral column in figure skating." *Beitr. Orthop. Traum.*, **15**: 233–238.

Rao, S. B. & Dinakar, I. (1970). "Spinal compression (analysis of 200 cases.)" *J. Assoc. Physicians India*, **18**: 1009–1013.

Richard, P. (1967). "Disk rupture with cauda equina syndrome after chiropractic adjustment." *N.Y. State J. Med.*, **67**: 2496.

Roberts, G. B. & Curtiss, P. H. (1970). "Stability of the thoracic and lumbar spine in traumatic paraplegia following fracture or fracture-dislocation." *J. Bone Joint Surg.*, **52A**: 115.

Roche, M. B. (1948). "Bilateral fracture of the pars interarticularis of a lumbar neural arch." *J. Bone Joint Surg.*, **30A**: 1005–1008.

Rogers, L. F. (1971). "The roentgenographic appearance of transverse or chance fractures of the spine: the seat-belt fracture." *Amer. J. Roentgenol.*, **111**: 844–849.

Rossier, A. B., Werner, A., Wildi, E. & Berni, J. (1968). "Contribution to the study of late cervical syringomyelic syndromes after dorsal or lumbar traumatic paraplegia." *J. Neurol. Neurosurg. Psychiat.*, **31**: 99–105.

Rotondo, G. (1975). "Spinal injury after ejection in jet pilots: mechanism, diagnosis, sequelae and prevention." *Aviat. Space Environ. Med.*, **46**: 842–848.

Russell, W. J. & Nakata, H. (1972). "Spondylolysis following trauma: a case report." *Radiology*, **91**: 973–974.

Sassard, W. R., Heinig, C. F. & Pitts, W. R. (1974). "Posterior atlanto-axial dislocation without fracture." *J. Bone Joint Surg.*, **56A**: 625–628.

Schneider, C. C. (1970). "Vascular insufficiency and differential distortion of brain and cord caused by cervicomedullary football injuries." *J. Neurosurg.*, **23**: 363–376.

Schreiber, A. (1974). "Spondylolisthesis and trauma." *Zeit. Orthop.*, **112**: 165–168.

Schultz, M. (1972). "Low back pain due to osteoporosis and fracture." *Proc. Mine Med. Off. Assoc.*, **52**: 53.

SCHUTT, J. (1968). "Neck injury to women in automobile accidents." *J. Amer. Med. Ass.*, **206:** 2688–2692.

SELETZ, M. (1958). "Whiplash injuries." *J. Amer. Med. Ass.*, **168:** 1750.

SHEA, J. D., GIOFFRE, R., CARRION, H. & SMALL, M.P. (1973). "Autonomic hyperreflexia in spinal cord injury." *Southern. Med. J.*, **66:** 869–872.

SHENNAN, J. (1973). "The seat belt syndrome." *Brit. J. Hosp. Med.*, **10:** 199.

SHEPHARD, R. H. (1959). "Diagnosis and prognosis of cauda equina syndrome produced by protrusion of the lumbar disc." *Brit. Med. J.*, **2:** 1434–1439.

SHROYER, R. N., FORTSON, C. H. & THEODOTOU, C. B. (1960). "Delayed neurological sequelae of a retained foreign body (lead bullet) in the intervertebral disc space." *J. Bone Joint Surg.*, **42A:** 595–599.

SIM, F. H., SVIEN, H. J., BICKEL, W. H. & JANES, J. M. (1974). "Swan-neck deformity following extensive cervical laminectomy." *J. Bone Joint Surg.*, **56A:** 564–580.

SIMEONE, F. A. (1972). "Acute and delayed traumatic peripheral entrapment neuropathies." *Surg. Clin. Nth. Amer.*, **52:** 1329–1336.

SMEULERS, J. (1975). "Cervical arthrosis in a young man subjected to electric shock during imprisonment." *Lancet*, **1:** 1249–1250.

SMITH, R. W. & ESTRIDGE, D. (1962). "Neurologic complications of head and neck manipulations." *J. Amer. Med. Ass.*, **182:** 528.

SMITH, R. W. & TAFT, P. M. (1967). "Relationship of vertebral size to fracture in osteoporotic spines." *Henry Ford Hosp. Med. J.*, **15:** 101–106.

SMITH, W. S. & KAUFFER, H. (1969). "Patterns and mechanisms of lumbar injuries associated with lap seat belts." *J. Bone Joint Surg.*, **51A:** 239–254.

SPURLING, R. G. & SCOVILLE, W. B. (1944). "Lateral rupture of the cervical intervertebral discs: a common cause of shoulder and arm pain." *Surg. Gynec. Obst.*, **78:** 350–358.

STECKLER, K. (1969). "Seat belt trauma to the lumbar spine: an unusual manifestation of the seat belt syndrome." *J. Trauma*, **9:** 508.

SULLIVAN, C. R. & BICKELL, W. H. (1960). "The problem of

traumatic spondylolysis: a report of 3 cases." *Amer. J. Surg.*, **100**: 698–708.

SYPERT, G. W., LEECH, R. W. & HARRIS, A. B. (1973). "Post-traumatic lumbar epidural true synovial cyst: a case report." *J. Neurosurg.*, **39**: 246–248.

TAILLARD, W. (1969). "Trauma and spondylolisthesis." *Acta Orthop. Belg.*, **35**: 703–716.

THROWER, W. R. (1972). "Injuries after small falls." *Lancet*, **1**: 1230.

TOGLIA, P. (1972). "Vestibular and medico-legal aspects of closed cranio-cervical trauma." *Scand. J. Rheum. Med.*, **4**: 126–132.

VENABLE, J. R., FLAKE, R. E. & KILIAN, D. J. (1964). "Stress fracture of the spinous process." *J. Amer. Med. Ass.*, **190**: 881–885.

WILSON, P. J. E. (1967). "Painful sensory disturbance in cervical dermatomes after head injury." *Lancet*, **2**: 1391.

WORTZMAN, G. (1974). "Spontaneous incarcerated herniation of the spinal cord into a vertebral body: a living case of paraplegia." *J. Neurosurg.*, **41**: 631–635.

## *(c) Intervertebral Disc Degeneration and Prolapse*

ANDREW, J. (1955). "Sacralization: an aetiological factor in lumbar intervertebral disc lesions, and a cause of misleading focal signs." *Brit. J. Surg.*, **42**: 304–311.

BACHYNSKI, M. (1970). "An expanding lesion of the intervertebral disc in a case of ankylosing spondylitis." *J. Ass. Canad. Radiol.*, **21**: 100.

BALAPARAMESWARA, R. A. (1970). "Lumbar disc prolapse, a study of 251 operated cases." *Neurology*, **18**: 120–125.

BEGG, A. C. (1954). "Nuclear herniations of the intervertebral disc." *J. Bone Joint Surg.*, **36B**: 180.

BEGG, A. C. & FALCONER, M. A. (1949). "Plain radiography in intraspinal protrusion of lumbar intervertebral disks: a correlation with operative findings." *Brit. J. Surg.*, **36**: 225–239.

BEGG, A. C., FALCONER, M. A. & McGEORGE, M. (1946). "Myelography in lumbar intervertebral disk lesions: correlation with operative findings." *Brit. J. Surg.*, **34**: 141–157.

BLAU, J. N. & LOGUE, V. (1961). "Intermittent claudication of the cauda equina: an unusual syndrome from central protrusion of a lumbar intervertebral disc." *Lancet*, **1:** 1081–1086.

BLAU, L, & KENT, L. (1974). "Conservative and surgical aspects of disc lesion management: follow-up of 244 cases." *Western J. Med.*, **120:** 353–357.

BOGORDINSKI, D. K. (1974). "Neurological complications of osteochondrosis of the lower lumbar intervertebral disk." *Sov. Med.*, **Aug:** 5–9.

BONNER, F. J. & SCHMIDT, W. H. (1957). "Electromyography in disc disease." *Arch. Phys. Med.*, **38:** 689–691.

BORGESEN, S. E. (1974). "Herniation of the lumbar intervertebral disk in children and adolescents." *Acta Orthop. Scand.*, **45:** 540–550.

BOUKHRIS, R. & BECKER, K. L. (1974). "Schmorl's nodes and osteoporosis." *Clin. Orthop.*, **104:** 275–280.

BOYD-WILSON, J. S. (1961). "Observations on the diagnosis of lumbar disc degeneration." *N.Z. Med. J.*, **60:** 202–205.

BRADFORD, D. S. & GARCIA, A. (1971). "Lumbar intervertebral disk herniations in children and adolescents." *Orthop. Clin. Nth. Amer.*, **2:** 583–592.

BRADFORD, F. K. & SPURLING, R. G. (1945). *The Intervertebral Disc.* Springfield, Ill.; Thomas.

BUKRA, K. (1969). "Intradural herniated lumbar disc." *J. Neurosurg.*, **31:** 676.

BULOS, S. (1973). "Herniated intervertebral lumbar disc in the teenager." *J. Bone Joint Surg.*, **55B:** 273–278.

CARSON, J., GUMPERT, J. & JEFFERSON, A. (1971). "Diagnosis and treatment of thoracic intervertebral disc protrusion." *J. Neurol. Neurosurg. Psychiat.*, **34:** 68–77.

CHAPCAL, G., FRIES, G., GAUMANN, J. U. & MULLER, E. (1966). "Discopathia lumbalis: degeneration of lumbar discs and their operative treatment." *Acta Orthop. Scand.*, **37:** 255–266.

CHARNLEY, J. (1951). "Orthopaedic signs in the diagnosis of disc protrusion with special reference to the straight leg raising test." *Lancet*, **1:** 186–192.

CHARNLEY, J. (1958). "Physical changes in the prolapsed disc." *Lancet*, **1:** 1277.

CHESTERMAN, P. J. (1964). "Spastic paraplegia caused by sequestrated thoracic intervertebral disc." *Proc. Roy. Soc. Med.*, **57:** 87–88.

CLARKE, H. A. & FLEMING, I. D. (1973). "Disk disease and occult malignancies." *Southern Med. J.*, **66:** 449–454.

CLOWARD, R. B. (1960). "The clinical significance of the sinu-vertebral nerve in relation to the cervical disc syndrome." *J. Neurol. Neurosurg. Psychiat.*, **23:** 321–326.

COHEN, J. & ABRAHAM, E. (1973). "The calcified intervertebral disc: a non-specific roentgenologic sign." *J. Med. Soc. New Jersey*, **70:** 459–460.

COHEN, J., CURRCRINO, G. & NEUHAUSER, E. B. D. (1956). "A significant variant in the ossification centers of the vertebral bodies." *Amer. J. Roentgenol.*, **76:** 469–475.

COLLIS, J. S. & GARDNER, W. J. (1961). "Lumbar discography: analysis of 600 degenerated discs and diagnosis of degenerated disc disease." *J. Amer. Med. Assoc.*, **178:** 67–70.

COLLIS, J. S. & GARDNER, W. J. (1962). "Lumbar discography: an analysis of 1,000 cases." *J. Neurosurg.*, **19:** 452–461.

COPPOLA, A. R. (1973). "Disc 'simulators'." *Virginia Med. Monthly*, **100:** 344–351.

COPPOLA, A. R. (1973). "Dilemma of herniated lumbar disc: experience with over 1,200 surgical cases." *Virginia Med. Monthly*, **100:** 1043–1049.

CRAFOORD, C., HIERTONN, T., LINDBLOM, K. & OLSSON, S. E. (1958). "Spinal cord compression caused by a protruded thoracic disc." *Acta Orthop. Scand.*, **28:** 103–107.

CRISP, E. J. (1945). "Damaged intervertebral disc. Early diagnosis and treatment." *Lancet*, **2:** 422–424.

CRISP, E. J. (1946). "Damaged intervertebral disc: early diagnosis and treatment." *Arch. Phys. Med.*, **27:** 181.

CROCK, H. V. (1970). "A reappraisal of intervertebral disc lesions." *Med. J. Aust.*, **1:** 983–989.

DAVIS, L., MARTIN, J. & GOLDSTEIN, S. L. (1952). "Sensory changes with herniated nucleus pulposus." *J. Neurosurg.*, **9:** 133–138.

DINAKAR, I. (1971). "Intradural rupture of lumbar intervertebral disc." *Ind. J. Med. Sci.*, **25:** 251.

DINAKAR, I. & BALAPARAMESWARARAO, S. (1972). "Lumbar disk prolapse: study of 300 surgical cases." *Int. Surg.*, **57:** 299–302.

DUNCAN, W. & HOEN, T. I. (1942). "A new approach to the diagnosis of herniation of the intervertebral disc." *Surg. Gynec. Obstet.*, **75:** 257–267.

EDEIKEN, J. & PITT, M. J. (1971). "The radiologic diagnosis of disc disease." *Orthop. Clin. Nth. Amer.*, **2:** 405–417.

EDGAR, M. A. & PARK, W. M. (1974). "Induced pain patterns on passive straight leg raising in lower lumbar disc protrusion. A prospective clinical, myelographic and operative study in fifty patients." *J. Bone Joint Surg.*, **56B:** 658–667.

EDGREN, W., KARAHARJU, E. O. & SNELLMAN, O. (1973). "Intervertebral disc calcification with complete protrusion intra-spongially." *Acta Orthop. Scand.*, **44:** 663–667.

EHNI, G. (1975). "Effects of certain degenerative diseases of the spine, especially spondylosis and disk protrusion, on the neural contents, particularly in the lumbar region. Historical account." *Mayo Clin. Proc.*, **50:** 327–338.

ELIES, W. *et al.* (1974). "Spontaneous repositioning of a severe medio-lateral lumbar disk prolapse." *Fortschr. Geb. Roentgenstr. Nuklear Med.*, **121:** 661–662.

ELVIDGE, A. R. & LI, C. L. (1950). "Central protrusion of cervical intervertebral disc involving descending trigeminal tract: report of a case." *Arch. Neurol. Psychiat.*, **63:** 455–466.

EPSTEIN, J. A. (1954). "The syndrome of herniation of the lower thoracic intervertebral discs with nerve root and spinal cord compression: presentation of 4 cases with literature review, methods of diagnosis and treatment." *J. Neurosurg.*, **11:** 525–538.

EPSTEIN, J. A. (1969). "Herniated discs of lumbar spine." *Lawyer's Med. J.* **5:** 129–150.

EPSTEIN, J. A. (1970). "Common errors in the diagnosis of herniation of the intervertebral disk." *Indust. Med. Surg.*, **39:** 47.

FALCONER, M. A., GLASGOW, G. L. & COLE, D. S. (1947). "Sensory disturbances occurring in sciatica due to intervertebral disc protrusions." *J. Neurol. Neurosurg. Psychiat.*, **10:** 72–84.

FALKE, H. (1972). "Low back pain due to disc prolapse." *Proc. Mine Med. Off. Assoc.*, **52:** 45.

FARFAN, H. F., HEUBERDEAU, R. M. & DUBOW, H. I. (1972). "Lumbar intervertebral disc degeneration. The influence of geometrical features on the pattern of disc degeneration. A post mortem study." *J. Bone Joint Surg.*, **54A:** 492–510.

FARFAN, H. F. & SULLIVAN, J. D. (1967). "The relation of facet orientation to intervertebral disc failure." *Canad. J. Surg.*, **10:** 179–185.

FERNSTROM, U. (1956). "Protruded lumbar intervertebral disc in children." *Acta Chir. Scand.*, **111:** 71–79.

FERNSTROM, U. (1957). "Lumbar intervertebral disc degeneration with abdominal pain." *Acta Chir. Scand.*, **113:** 436–437.

FERNSTROM U. (1960). "A discographic study of ruptured lumbar intervertebral discs. An investigation based on anatomical, pathological, surgical and clinical studies and on experiments in provocation of pain with special reference to simple ruptured lumbar discs and to discogenic pain." *Acta Chir. Scand., Suppl.* **258:** 1.

FERNSTROM, U. (1963). "Will plain film examination of lumbar spine be a reliable method to exclude or disclose ruptured discs?" *Acta Orthop. Scand.*, **33:** 105–115.

FIEFFER, S. A. (1969). "Discographic anatomical correlation of developmental changes with age in the intervertebral disc." *Acta Radiol.*, **9:** 733–739.

FINESCHI, G. (1971). "L1 and L2 radicular syndromes with discal herniation: a preliminary anatomico-clinical and diagnostic contribution." *Chir. Org. Mov.*, **60:** 15–26.

FRIBERG, S. (1941). "Low back and sciatic pain caused by intervertebral disc herniation." *Acta Chir. Scand., Suppl.* **85:** 64.

FRIBERG, S. (1954). "Lumbar disc degeneration in the problem of lumbago-sciatica." *Bull. Hosp. Joint Dis.*, **15:** 1–20.

FRIBERG, S. & HIRSCH, C. (1949). "Anatomical and clinical studies on lumbar disc degeneration." *Acta Orthop. Scand.*, **19:** 222–242.

FRYKHOLM, R. (1951). "Cervical nerve root compression resulting from disc degeneration and root sleeve fibrosis." *Acta Chir. Scand. Suppl.* **160:** 1.

GAINER, J. V. & NUGENT, G. R. (1974). "The herniated lumbar disk." *Amer. Family Phys.*, **10:** 127–131.

GARDNER, R. C. (1970). "The lumbar intervertebral disc: a clinico-pathological correlation based on over 100 laminectomies." *Arch. Surg.*, **100:** 101–104.

GASPARDY, G., BALINI, G., MITUSOVA, M. & LORINCZ, G. (1971). "Treatment of sciatica due to intervertebral disc herniation with 'chymoral' tablets." *Rheum. Phys. Med.*, **11:** 14–19.

GILLIAN, L. A. (1970). "Veins of the spinal cord—cord compression by disc herniation." *Neurology*, **20:** 860–868.

GREGG, G. (1974). "The commonest lumbar disc—L3." *Brit. J. Sports Med.*, **8:** 69–73.

GUTTERMAN, P. & SHENKIN, H. A. (1973). "Syndromes associated with protrusion of upper lumbar intervertebral discs." *J. Neurosurg.*, **38:** 499–503.

HABERMANN, H. (1949). "Prolapse of the nucleus pulposus in the lumbar region and its significance for the spinal column and the spinal root syndrome." *Nervenarzt*, **20:** 289–303.

HALEY, J. C. & PERRY, J. H. (1950). "Protrusions of intervertebral discs: study of their distribution, characteristics and effects on the nervous system." *Amer. J. Surg.*, **80:** 394–404.

HAWK, W. A. (1936). "Spinal compression caused by ecchondrosis of the intervertebral fibrocartilage, with review of literature." *Brain*, **59:** 204–224.

HUGHES, R. R. (1945). "Retropulsed intervertebral disk producing Froin's syndrome." *Lancet*, **2:** 401.

ILTCHEWSKI, S., KASSAROV, J. & WLACHKINOV, A. (1970). "Intraspinal application of hydrocortisone in radiculitis due to protrusion of intervertebral disc." *Plovdiv. Therhung.*, **18:** 68–71.

JENNET, W. B. (1956). "Study of 25 cases of compression of the cauda equina by prolapsed intervertebral discs." *J. Neurol. Neurosurg. Psychiat.*, **19:** 109–116.

JONES, D. L. & MOORE, T. (1973). "The types of neuropathic bladder dysfunction associated with prolapsed intervertebral discs." *Brit. J. Urol.*, **45:** 39–43.

JUDOVICH, B. & NOBEL, H. (1955). "Herniated cervical disk and atypical facial neuralgia." *Lancet*, **75:** 453–460.

KUGELBERG, E. & PETERSON, I. (1950). "Muscle weakness and wasting in sciatica due to lumbar disc herniations." *J. Neurosurg.*, **7:** 270–277.

LEVINE, M. E. (1971). "Depression, back pain and disc protrusion: relationships and proposed psychophysiological mechanisms." *Dis. Nerv. Syst.*, **32:** 41–45.

LOMBARDI, V. (1973). "Lumbar spinal block by posterior rotation of annulus fibrosus: case report." *J. Neurosurg.*, **39:** 642–644.

LOVE, J. G. (1939). "Protruded intervertebral discs, with a note regarding hypertrophy of the ligamenta flava." *J. Amer. Med. Assoc.*, **113:** 2029.

LOVE, J. G. (1947). "The disc factor in low back pain with or without sciatica." *J. Bone Joint Surg.*, **29:** 438–447.

LOVE, J. G. & KIEFER, E. J. (1950). "Root pain and paraplegia due to protrusions of thoracic intervertebral disks." *J. Neurosurg.*, **7:** 62–69.

LOVE, J. G. & RIVERS, M. H. (1961). "Protruded cervical disk simulating spinal-cord tumor." *Staff Meet. Mayo Clinic*: 344–346.

LOVE, J. G. & SCHORN, V. G. (1965). "Thoracic-disk protrusions." *J. Amer. Med. Assoc.*, **191:** 627–631.

LOVE, J. G. & SCHORN, V. G. (1967). "Thoracic disk protrusion." *Rheumatism*, **23:** 2.

MACNAB, I. (1971). "The whiplash syndrome." *Orthop. Clin. Nth. Amer.*, **2:** 389–403.

MALCAPI, C. (1967). "Statistical data and differential criteria for posterolateral and foraminal herniation in lumbosciatica." *Minerva Ortop.* **18:** 738–742.

MALCAPI, C. & GIANNANGELI, F. (1973). "Foraminal herniation in lumbosciatica." *Minerva Ortop.*, **24:** 69–75.

MALCAPI, C. & ZACCARELLO, L. (1969). "Lumbo-crural-sciatica and foraminal disc herniation. *Minerva Ortop.* **20:** 99–104.

MEYERDING, H. W. (1941). "Low backache and sciatic pain associated with spondylolisthesis and protruded intervertebral disc: incidence, significance and treatment." *J. Bone Joint Surg.*, **23:** 461–470.

MILES, W. A. (1974). "Discogenic and osteoarthritic disease of the cervical spine." *J. Nat. Med. Assoc.*, **66:** 300–304.

MILLER, D. (1962). "Sciatica due to intervertebral disc lesions." *Med. J. Aust.*, **1:** 621–624.

OPPENHEIMER, A. (1937). "Diseases affecting the intervertebral foramina." *Radiology*, **28:** 582–592.

PAILLAS, J. E., WINNINGER, J. & LOUIS, R. (1969). "Role of lumbosacral malformations in sciatica and lumbar pain. Study of 1,500 radio-clinical records including 500 proved disk herniae." *Presse Med.*, **77:** 853–855.

PALACIOS, E., BRACKETT, C. E. & LEARY, D. J. (1971). "Ossification of the posterior longitudinal ligament associated with a herniated intervertebral disk." *Radiology*, **100:** 313–314.

PANI, K. C., MUDULI, H., CHANDER, K. & KAK, V. K. (1972). "Intrathecal disc prolapse associated with lumbar canal stenosis." *Neurol. India*, **20:** 64–69.

RANIERI, L. & TRAINA, G. C. (1970). "Lumbago in children.: aetiopathogenetic considerations." *Chir. Org. Mov.*, **59:** 121–131.

ROSE, G. K. (1964). "Backache and the disc." *Lancet*, **1:** 1143–1149.

Ross, J. C. & Jameson, R. M. (1971). "Vesical dysfunction due to prolapsed disc." *Brit. Med. J.*, **3**: 752–754.

Rothman, R. H. (1971). "The clinical syndrome of lumbar disc disease." *Orthop. Clin. Nth. Amer.*, **2**: 463–475.

Rowbotham, G. F. & Whalley, N. (1948). "Low backache, sciatic pain and the herniated pulposus." *Practitioner*, **160**: 212–220.

Schein, A. J. (1968). "Evolution and pathogenesis of discogenic spine pain and associated radiculitis as seen in the New York City Fire Department." *J. Mt. Sinai Hosp.*, **35**: 371–389.

Schlesinger, E. B. & Taveras, J. M. (1953). "Factors in the production of cauda equina syndromes in lumbar discs." *Trans. Amer. Neurol. Assoc.*, **78**: 263–265.

Segil, C. M. (1973). "The localisation of symptomatic levels in discogenic disease of the spine." *J. Bone Joint Surg.*, **55B**: 665.

Selecki, B. R., Ness, T. D., Limbers, P., Blum, P. & Stening, W. R. (1973). "Low back pain: a joint neurosurgical and orthopaedic project." *Med. J. Austr.*, **2**: 889–893.

Spanos, N. C. & Andrews, J. (1966). "Intermittent claudication and lateral lumbar disc protrusion." *J. Neurol. Neurosurg. Psychiat.*, **29**: 273–277.

Steindler, A. (1947). "An analysis and differentiation of low-back pain in relation to the disc factor." *J. Bone Joint Surg.*, **29A**: 455–460.

Stookey, B. (1940). "Compression of spinal cord and nerve roots by herniation of the nucleus pulposus in the cervical region." *Arch. Surg.*, **40**: 417–432.

Tandon, R. (1967). "Cauda equina syndrome due to lumbar disc prolapse." *Indian J. Orthop.* **1**: 112–119.

Turbacci, P. (1970). "Lumbosciatic pain due to protrusion of a lumbar disc in a 12 year old girl." *Clinica Ortop.* **22**: 259–262.

Uttl, K. (1966). "On the incidence of discogenic disease (vertebrogenic disorders) with regard to work capacity." *Rev. Česk. Med.*, **12**: 116–122.

Wilson, P. D. (1960). "Low back pain and sciatica due to lesions of the lumbar discs." *Rhode Island Med. J.*, **43**: 167–176.

Wilson, P. J. E. (1962). "Cauda equina compression due to intrathecal herniation of an intervertebral disk." *Brit. J. Surg.*, **49**: 423–426.

Wolman, L. (1949). "Cramp in cases of prolapsed intervertebral disc." *J. Neurol. Neurosurg. Psychiat.*, **12**: 251–257.

## (d) Mechanical Stress (Fatigue, Posture, Deformity, Loading Instability).

AMOLDY, C. C. (1972). "Intravertebral pressures in patients with lumbar pain." *Acta Orthop. Scand.*, **43**: 109–117.

BILLENKAMP, G. (1972). "Body loading and spondylosis deformans." *Fortschr. Roentgenstr.*, **116**: 211–216.

BREIG, G. (1970). "Overstretching of a circumscribed pathological tension in the spinal cord—a basic cause of symptoms in cord disorders." *J. Biomechanics*, **3**: 7–9.

BRODY, I. A. & ILKINS, R. H. (1969). "The signs of Kernig and Brudzinski." *Arch. Neurol.*, **21**: 215–218.

CHATER, E. H., COLBERT, D. S., CONLON, G. & APPAJI, J. (1974). "Constructive spinal disease—another cause of back pain." *Brit. Med. J.*, **67**: 93–96.

CHRIST, W. (1974). "On the possibility of health injury arising from vertical vibration of the spine." *Fortschr. Med.*, **92**: 705–708.

CHRIST, W. & DUPUIS, H. (1963). "The influence of vertical oscillation on the spine and stomach (a cineradiographic study)." *Zeit. Arbeitsmed. Arbeitschutz*, **13**: 3–9.

CRIST, W. & DUPUIS, H. (1968). "Studies on the possibility of physical damage to the spinal area in tractor operators. II. Report on the second mass examination of 137 young farmers." *Med. Welt.*, **37**: 1967–1972.

CHRISTENSEN, E. H. (1962). "Muscular work and fatigue." In *Muscle as a Tissue*. pp. 176–189. Ed. by K. Rodahl and S. M. Horvath. New York; McGraw-Hill.

CYRIAX, J. (1965). "Lumbar spine disorders and lifting." *Lancet*, **2**: 80.

DAIL, C. W. & AFFELDT, J. E. (1957). "Effect of body position and respiratory muscle function." *Arch. Phys. Med. Rehab.*, **38**: 427–443.

DAVIS, P. R. (1959). "The causation of herniae by weight-lifting." *Lancet*, **2**: 155–157.

DORAN, P. (1969). "Mechanical and postural causes of chest pain." *Proc. Roy. Soc. Med.*, **62**: 876.

EMERSON, H. (1911). "Intra-abdominal pressures." *Arch. Int. Med.*, **7**: 754.

EVANS, F. G., LISSNER, H. R. & PATRICK, L. M. (1962). "Acceleration induced strains in the intact vertebral column." *J. Appl. Physiol.*, **17**: 405–409.

FARFAN, H. F. (1968). "Mechanical failure of the intervertebral joints." *J. Bone Joint Surg.*, **50B**: 435.

FARFAN, H. R. (1969). "Effects of torsion on the intervertebral joints." *Canad. J. Surg.*, **12**: 336–341.

FARFAN, H. F. (1970). "The role of torsion in the production of disc degeneration." *J. Bone Joint Surg.*, **52A**: 468–497.

FARFAN, H. F. (1970). "Mechanical instability of the lumbar spine in torsion." *J. Bone Joint Surg.*, **52B**: 784–785.

FARFAN, H. F. (1973). *Mechanical Disorders of the Low Back.* Philadelphia; Lea and Febiger.

FARFAN, H. F. (1975). "Muscular mechanism of the lumbar spine and the position of power and efficiency." *Orthop. Clin. Nth. Amer.*, **6**: 135–144.

FARFAN, H. F., COSSETTE, J. W., ROBERTSON, G. H., WELLS, R. V. & KRAUSE, H. (1970). "The effects of torsion on the lumbar intervertebral joints: the role of torsion in the production of disc degeneration." *J. Bone Joint Surg.*, **52A**: 468–497.

FLOYD, W. F., GOLDING, J. S. R. & STEVER, P. H. S. (1952). "Clinical applications of the functional anatomy of the lower back." *Proc. Roy. Soc. Med.*, **45**: 894.

GILLIAT, P. (1970). "Wasting of the hand associated with a cervical rib or band." *J. Neurol. Neurosurg. Psychiat.*, **33**: 615–624.

GRACZYK, M. (1973). "Lesions in the osseous-articular system of the upper extremities and cervical spine caused by mechanical vibration." *Bull. Inst. Mar. Med., Gdansk*, **24**: 63–72.

HABER, L. D. (1974). "Disabling effects of chronic disease and impairment." *J. Chron. Dis.*, **24**: 469–487.

HABER, L. D. (1976). "Disabling effects of chronic disease and impairment. 2: functional capacity limitations." *J. Chron. Dis.*, **26**: 127–151.

HADLEY, L. A. (1963). "Stress fracture with spondylolysis." *Amer. J. Roentgenol.*, **90**: 1258–1262.

HAMILTON, W. (1944). "Arterial, cerebrospinal and venous pressures in man during cough and strain." *Amer. J. Physiol.*, **141**: 42–50.

HARRIS, J. L. & CUNNINGHAM, E. B. (1965). "Stress fractures of the lumbar vertebrae." *J. Occup. Med.*, **7**: 255–256.

HENZEL, J. H., BRINKLEY, J. W. & MOHR, G. C. (1966). "Acceler-

ation profile associated with thoracic vertebral compression."
*J. Trauma*, **6**: 756–766.

HOWES, R. G. & ISDALE, I. C. (1971). "The loose back: an unrecognised syndrome." *Rheum. Phys. Med.*, **11**: 72–77.

IKATA, T. (1965). "Statistical and dynamic studies of lesions due to overloading on the spine." *Shikoku Acta Med.*, **21**: 262–286.

INGELMARK, B. E. & ECKHOMN, R. (1952). "The compressibility of the intervertebral discs." *Acta Soc. Med. (Ufas).* **57**: 202–212.

KAY, S. P. (1971). "A new conception and approach to the problem of scoliosis." *Clin. Orthop.*, **81**: 21–33.

KENDALL, H. O., KENDALL, F. P. & BOYNTON, D. A. (1952). *Posture and Pain*. London; Baillière, Tindall & Cox.

KENDALL, P. H. (1967). "Car seats and backache." *Proc. Roy. Soc. Med.*, **60**: 958–959.

KING, A. I., PRASAD, P. & EWING, C. L. (1975). "Mechanism of spinal injury due to caudocephalad acceleration." *Orthop. Clin. Nth. Amer.*, **6**: 19–31.

KING, A. I. & VULCAN, A. P. (1970). "Experimental studies on stresses in the lumbar vertebrae caused by caudocephalad acceleration." In *Neckache and Backache*. Ed. by E. Gurdjian and L. M. Thomas. Springfield, Ill.; Thomas.

KOTTKE, F. J. (1961). "Evaluation and treatment of low back pain due to mechanical causes." *Arch. Phys. Med. Rehab.*, **42**: 426–440.

KUHNS, J. G., KLEIN, A., REGAN, E., WILLIAMS, P. C. & CROWE, H. E. (1947). "Posture and relationship to orthopedic disabilities." *Report of the Posture Committee, Amer. Acad. Orthop. Surg.*, Chicago.

LAMY, C. (1975). "The strength of the neural arch and the etiology of spondylolysis." *Orthop. Clin. Nth. Amer.*, **6**: 215–231.

LANE, W. A. (1885). "Some of the changes which are produced by pressure in the lower part of the spinal column—spondylolisthesis, displacement backwards of the fifth lumbar vertebra, torticollis etc." *Trans. Path. Soc. Lond.*, **36**: 364–378.

LANE, W. A. (1885). "Extreme dorsal excurvation produced by a stooping occupation in a growing youth." *Trans. Path. Soc. Lond.*, **36**: 378–380.

LETTIN, A. W. F. (1967). "Diagnosis and treatment of lumbar instability." *J. Bone Joint Surg.*, **49B**: 520–529.

LIVINGSTONE, W. K. (1941). "Back disabilities due to multifidus strain." *West.J. Surg.*, **49**: 259.

McMILLAN, W. (1973). "Driving for backache." *Lancet*, **1**: 202.

MAROUN, F. B. & JACOB, J. C. (1970). "Uncommon causes of sciatica." *Canad. Med. Assoc. J.*, **103**: 1292–1295.

MEAD, C. A. (1967). "Adult postural back pain." *J. Florida Med. Ass.*, **54**: 956–957.

MENSOR, M. C. & FENDER, F. A. (1941). "The ligamentum flavum: its relationship to low back pain." *Surg. Gynec. Obst.*, **73**: 822–827.

MOHTASHAMI, M. (1973). "The lateral relationship of lumbar disc prolapse in static and idiopathic scoliosis." *Zeit. Orthop.*, **111**: 560–564.

MORGAN, F. P. & KING, T. (1957). "Primary instability of lumbar vertebrae as a common cause of low back pain." *J. Bone Joint Surg.*, **39B**: 6–22.

MURRAY, R. O. & COLWILL, M. R. (1968). "Stress fractures of the pars interarticularis." *Proc. Roy. Soc. Med.*, **61**: 555–557.

NACHEMSON, A. L. (1965). "Lumbar spine disorders and lifting." *Lancet*, **1**: 1401.

NACHEMSON, A. & ELFSTRÖM, G. (1973). "Intravital measurements of forces in the human spine: their clinical implications for low back pain and scoliosis." In *Perspectives in Biomedical Engineering*. pp. 111–119. Ed. by R. M. Kenedi. London; Macmillan.

O'CONNELL, J. E. A. (1960). "Lumbar disc protrusions in pregnancy." *J. Neurol. Neurosurg. Psychiat.*, **23**: 138–141.

OVERHOLT, R. H. (1931). "The intraperitoneal pressure." *Arch. Surg.*, **22**: 691–703.

POILLEUX, F. (1949). "Lumbar backache due to tilted sacrum." *Presse Méd. (Suppl. 57)*: 470c–478d.

REDDY, D. R. (1972). "Lesions of the vertebral column in relation to spinal compression." *Neurol. India*, **20**: 49–54.

RIDDLE, H. V. F. & ROAF, R. (1955). "Muscle imbalance in the causation of scoliosis." *Lancet*, **1**: 1245–1247.

ROBERTS, R. A. (1947). *Chronic Structural Low Backache Due to Low-Back Structural Derangement*. London; Lewis.

ROTH, M. (1968). "Idiopathic scoliosis caused by a short spinal cord." *Acta Radiol.*, **7**: 256.

SCHATZKER, J. & PENNAL, G. F. (1968). "Spinal stenosis, a cause of cauda equina compression." *J. Bone Joint Surg.*, **50B:** 606–618.

SCHLESINGER, P. T. (1955). "Incarceration of the first sacral nerve in the lateral bony recess of the spinal canal as a cause of sciatica." *J. Bone Joint Surg.*, **37A:** 115.

SCHLEZINGER, P. T. (1957). "Low lumbar nerve-root compression and adequate operative exposure." *J. Bone Joint Surg.*, **39A:** 541–553.

SMIBERT, J. (1971). "Does lifting cause prolapse?" *Aust. N.Z.J. Obstet. Gynaecol.*, **11:** 180–182.

STYCZYNSKI, T., ZARSKI, S. & KOZINA, W. (1972). "The vertebro-radicular conflict in lumbar spine and the blood flow to lower extremities in the light of an observed case." *Reumatologia*, **10:** 81–85.

SUTRO, C. J. (1947). "Hypermobility of bones due to 'overlengthened' capsular and ligamentous tissues. A cause for interarticular effusions." *Surgery*, **21:** 67–76.

SWIDERSKI, P. (1968). "X-ray examination of vertebral instability in lumbar spondylolisthesis due to excessive weight bearing." *Beitr. Orthop. Traum.*, **15:** 598–604.

TAILLARD, W. (1969). "The lumbar spine and inequality of the legs." *Acta Orthop. Belg.*, **35:** 601–613.

TAKAHASHI, K. (1968). "Headache caused by cervical spondylosis." *Clin. Neurol.*, **11:** 643.

TEWNE, E. B. & REICHERT, F. L. (1931). "Compression of lumbosacral nerve roots of spinal cord by thickened ligamenta flava." *Ann. Surg.*, **94:** 327–336.

THIEME, F. P. (1950). "Lumbar breakdown caused by erect posture in man, with emphasis on spondylolisthesis and herniated intervertebral discs." *Anthrop. Papers, No. 4, Museum of Anthropology*. Univ. Michigan: Ann Arbor.

TILLEY, P. (1970). "Is sacralization a significant factor in lumbar pain?" *J. Amer. Osteopath. Ass.*, **70:** 238–241.

TRIAS, A. (1961). "Effects of persistent pressure on the articular cartilage." *J. Bone Joint Surg.*, **43B:** 376–386.

TROISI, F. M. (1969). "Lumbago with changes of the spinal column caused by defective posture in sedentary work." *Med. Lavoro*, **60:** 21–27.

TSIV'YAN, Y. L. (1972). "Results of the clinical study of pressure within intervertebral lumbar discs." *Ortop. Traumatol. Protey*, **33**: 31–35.

TULSI, R. S. (1974). "Sacral arch defect and low backache." *Australasian Radiol.*, **18**: 43–50.

VALTONEN, P. (1968). "The tension neck syndrome: its etiology, clinical features and results of physical treatment." *Ann. Med. Int. Fenn.*, **57**: 139.

VELENEAU, C. (1975). "Morphofunctional peculiarities of the transverse processes of the axis: considerations of their pathogenetic significance." *Acta Anat.*, **92**: 301–309.

WALDE, J. (1962). "Obstetrical and gynaecological back and pelvic pains, especially those contracted during pregnancy." *Acta Obst. Gynec. Scand., Suppl.* **2**: 11–53.

WALTZ, J. (1967). "Physical factors in the production of the myelopathy of cervical spondylosis." *Brain*, **90**: 395.

WILSON, C. B. (1969). "Significance of the small lumbar spinal canal: cauda equina compression syndromes due to spondylosis. Part 3: Intermittent claudication." *J. Neurosurg.*, **31**: 499–506.

WILTSE, L. L. (1971). "The effect of the common anomalies of the lumbar spine upon disc degeneration and low back pain." *Orthop. Clin. Nth. Amer.*, **2**: 569–582.

WILTSE, L. L. (1975). "Fatigue fracture: the basic lesion in isthmic spondylolisthesis." *J. Bone Joint Surg.*, **57A**: 17–22.

YAMADA, H., OHYA, M., OKADA, T. & SCHIOZAWA, Z. (1972). "Intermittent cauda equina compression due to narrow spinal canal." *J. Neurosurg.*, **37**: 83–88.

YOUNG, J. (1940). "Relaxation of the pelvic joints in pregnancy." *J. Obst. Gynec. Brit. Emp.*, **47**: 493.

### (e) Obesity and Habitus

DISTEFANO, V. J., KLEIN, K. S., NIXON, J. E. & ANDREWS, E. T. (1974). "Intra-operative analysis of the effects of position and body habitus on surgery of the low back." *Clin. Orthop.*, **99**: 51–56.

GITELSON, S. & MANN, K. J. (1959). "The influence of body build and posture on the expiratory reserve volume." *Israel Med. J.*, **18**: 71–81.

HAMER, M. C. & DENNISTON, H. D. (1933). "Dysmenorrhea and its relation to abdominal strength as tested by the Wisconsin method." *Research Quart.*, **4**: 229–237.

JULKUNEN, H., NEINONEN, O. P. & PYRÄLÄ, K. (1971). "Hyperostosis of the spine in an adult population: its relation to hyperglycaemia and obesity." *Ann. Rheum Dis.*, **30**: 605–612.

LAUBACH, L. L. & McCONVILLE, J. T. (1966). "Muscle strength, flexibility and body size of adult males." *Res. Quart.*, **37**: 384–392.

MIR-MADJLESSI, S. H. (1974). "Articular complications in obese patients after jejunocolic bypass." *Cleveland Clin. Quart.*, **41**: 119–133.

STEWART, T. D. (1956). "Examination of the possibility that certain skeletal characters predispose to defects in the lumbar arches." *Clin. Orthop.*, **8**: 44–59.

STRUTHERS, J. (1863). "On the relative weight of the viscera on the two sides of the body, and on the consequent position of the centre of gravity to the right side." *Edinburgh Med. J.*, **8**: 1086–1104.

## *(f) Degenerative Conditions (Other than Discs)*

BOUKHRIS, R. & BECKER, K. L. (1973). "The inter-relationship between vertebral fractures and osteoporosis." *Clin. Orthop.* **90**: 209–216.

BOUKHRIS, R. & BECKER, K. L. (1974). "Schmorl's nodes and osteoporosis." *Clin. Orthop.*, **104**: 275–280.

BREMNER, J. M., LAWRENCE, J. S. & MIALL, W. E. (1968). "Degenerative joint disease in a Jamaican rural population." *Ann. Rheum. Dis.*, **27**: 326–332.

CAPLAN, P. S. (1962). "Degenerative joint disease of the lumbar spine in coal miners—a clinical and X-ray study." *Arth. Rheum.*, **5**: 288.

CAPLAN, P. S., FREEDMAN, L. M. J. & CONNELLY, T. P. (1966). "Degenerative joint disease of the lumbar spine in coal miners: clinical and X-ray study." *Arth. Rheum.*, **9**: 693–702.

CARLSON, M. H. (1974). "Ankylosing vertebral hyperostosis causing dysphagia." *Arch. Surg.*, **109**: 567–570.

CHATER, E. H., CONLON, G., COLBERT, D. S. & APPAJ, I. J. (1974). "Constrictive spinal disease: another cause of back pain." *J. Irish Med. Ass.*, **67**: 93–96.

CASUCCIO, C. & SCAPINELLI, R. (1962). "Clinical and anatomico-radiological studies of pathological changes in the vertebral spinous processes and adjacent soft tissues." *J. Bone Joint Surg.*, **44B**: 218–219.

CURREY, H. L. F., KEY, K. J., MASON, R. M. & SWEETENHAM, K. V. (1966). "Significance of radiological calcification of joint carti-lage." *Ann. Rheum. Dis.*, **25**: 295.

DEQUECKER, J. (1974). "Femoral trabecular patterns in asympto-matic spinal osteoporosis and femoral neck fracture." *Clin. Radiol.*, **25**: 243–246.

DEVLIN, H. B. & GOLDMAN, M. (1966). "Backache due to osteo-porosis in an industrial population: surgery of 481 patients." *Irish J. Med. Sci.*, **6**: 141–148.

EPSTEIN, J. A., EPSTEIN, B. S. & LAVINE, L. (1962). "Nerve root compression associated with narrowing of the lumbar spinal canal." *J. Neurol. Neurosurg. Psychiat.*, **25**: 165–176.

FARKAS, M. (1950). "Low back pain syndrome and osteoporosis of the spine." *Rheumatol.*, **6**: 157.

GOLDSMITH, N. F. & JOHNSTON, J. O. (1973). "Mineralization of the bone in an insured population: correlation with reported fractures and other measures of osteoporosis." *Int. J. Epidem.*, **2**: 311–327.

GOLDSMITH, N. F., JOHNSTON, J. O., GARCIA, C. & PICETTI, G. (1973). "Use of miniature roentgenograms of the abdomen to detect aortic calcification, osteoporosis and other radiological abnormalities in an insured population." *Int. J. Epidem.*, **2**: 303–310.

GOODING, M. R. (1974). "Pathogenesis of myelopathy in cervical spondylosis." *Lancet*, **2**: 1180–1181.

HARMON, P. H. (1966). "Congenital and acquired anatomic varia-tions including degenerative changes of the lower lumbar spine: role in production of painful back and lower extremity syn-dromes." *Clin. Orthop.*, **44**: 171–186.

HAWKINS, J. C. (1975). "Pathogenesis of myelopathy in cervical spondylosis." *Lancet*, **1**: 1194–1195.

HODESS, A. B. (1974). "Leber's optic atrophy associated with spondylo-epiphyseal dysplasia." *Neurology*, **11**: 1082–1085.

JONCK, L. M. (1961). "The mechanical disturbance resulting from lumbar disc space narrowing." *J. Bone Joint Surg.*, **43B**: 362–375.

LITVAK, J. & BRINEY, W. (1973). "Extradural spinal deposition of urates producing paraplegia: case report." *J. Neurosurg.*, **39**: 656–658.

McEwan, P. (1967). "Role of cervical spondylosis in aetiology of cerebral embolism." *Brit. J. Clin. Pract.*, **21**: 465.

Nathan, H. (1962). "Osteophytes of the vertebral column—a study of their development according to age, race and sex, with consideration as to their etiology and significance." *J. Bone Joint Surg.*, **44A**: 243–264.

Onji, Y. (1968). "Posterior paravertebral ossification causing cervical myelopathy." *J. Bone Joint Surg.*, **49A**: 1314.

Oppenheimer, A. (1937). "Disease affecting the intervertebral foramina." *Radiology*, **28**: 582–592.

Ramani, P. S. & Sengupta, R. P. (1973). "Cauda equina compression due to tabetic arthropathy of the spine." *J. Neurol. Neurosurg. Psychiat.*, **36**: 260–264.

## (g) Nutritional, Hormonal and Metabolic Influences

Boles, G. G., Friedlaender, M. H. & Smith, C. K. (1969). "Rheumatic symptoms and serological abnormalities induced by oral contraceptives." *Lancet*, **1**: 323–326.

Bregon, C., Chevalier, J., Bigorgne, H.-C. & Renier, J.-C. (1973). "Ankylosing vertebral hyperostosis: aetiological investigations and studies of hypersecretion of somatotrophin." *Rev. Rhum. Mal. Osteoartic.*, **40**: 319–327.

Bunch, T. W. (1973). "Ankylosing spondylitis and primary hyperparathyroidism." *J. Amer. Med. Assoc.*, **225**: 1108–1109.

Bywaters, E. G. L., Dixon, A. St. J. & Scott, J. T. (1963). "Joint lesions of hyperparathyroidism." *Ann. Rheum. Dis.*, **22**: 171–187.

Bywaters, E. G. L., Hamilton, E. B. D. & Williams, R. (1971). "The spine in idiopathic haemochromatosis." *Ann. Rheum Dis.*, **30**: 453–465.

Cesar, E. V., Kahn, M. F., Ryckewaert, A. & Séze, S. de (1966). "Comparative frequency of lumbar osteophytosis, calcification of the costal cartilages and calcification of the abdominal aorta in subjects with osteoporosis or osteomalacia." *Sem. Hôp. Paris*, **42**: 2513–2517.

Charnley, J. (1952). "The imbibition of fluid as a cause of herniation of the nucleus pulposus." *Lancet*, **1**: 124–127.

CHAYKIN, P. (1969). "Spondylitis: a clue to hypoparathyroidism." *Ann. Int. Med.*, **70:** 995.

DE SÉZE, S. (1972). "Joint and bone disorders and hypoparathyroidism in hemochromatosis." *Seminar. Arthr. Rheum.*, **2:** 71–94.

DICK, W. C., JASANI, M. K. & BOYLE, J. A. (1968). "Study of capillary resistance in rheumatoid arthritis with special reference to the effects of long-term low-dosage oral corticosteroid therapy." *Acta Med. Scand.*, **14:** 265.

DIHLMANN, W. & MULLER, G. (1972). "Pseudo-Bechterew syndrome: findings in hyperparathyroidism with real osteopathy." *Zeit. Rheumaforsch.*, **31:** 401–408.

DIHLMANN, W. & MULLER, G. (1973). "Sacro-iliac findings in hyperparathyroidism." *Radiologie*, **13:** 160–163.

FIELDMAN, F. & SEAMAN, P. (1969). "The neurologic complications of Paget's disease in the cervical spine." *Amer. J. Roentgenol.* **105:** 375–382.

FORREST, J. S. & BROOKS, D. L. (1972). "Cyclic sciatica of endometriosis." *J. Amer. Med. Assoc.*, **222:** 1177–1178.

FROST, H. M. (1972). "Managing the skeletal pain and disability of osteoporosis." *Orthop. Clin. Nth. Amer.*, **3:** 561–570.

FROST, H. M. (1973). "The spinal osteoporoses. Mechanisms of pathogenesis and pathophysiology." *Clin. Endocrinol. Metab.*, **2:** 257–275.

GILL, D. (1968). "Rheumatic complaints of women using anti-ovulatory drugs." *J. Chron. Dis.*, **21:** 235–244.

GOLDBERG, M. A. (1973). "Sickle cell anemia with joint effusion." *South Med. J.*, **66:** 956–958.

GOLDSMITH, N. F. (1973). "Bone mineral in the radius and vertebral osteoporosis in an insured population. A correlative study using 125-I photon absorption and miniature roentgenography." *J. Bone Joint Surg.*, **55A:** 1276–1293.

GREENWOOD, B. M. (1966). "Capillary resistance and skin-fold thickness in patients with rheumatoid arthritis—effect of corticosteroid therapy." *Ann. Rheum. Dis.*, **25:** 272–277.

HAMILTON, E. B. (1972). "Hyperparathyroidism with chondrocalcinosis and periarticular calcification." *Proc. Roy. Soc. Med.*, **65:** 1013.

HEBERDEN, S. (1959). "Crush fractures of vertebrae on steroid therapy." *Lancet*, **2:** 679.

HORENSTEIN, S., HAMBROOK, G. & EYERMAN, E. (1971). "Spinal

cord compression by vertebral acromegaly." *Trans. Amer. Neurol. Assoc.*, **96**: 254–256.

JULKUNEN, H., NEINONEN, O. P. & PYORÄLÄ, K. (1971). "Hyperostosis of the spine in an adult population: its relation to hyperglycaemia and obesity." *Ann. Rheum. Dis.*, **30**: 605–612.

JULKUNUN H., PYORÄLÄ, K. & LEHTOVIRTA, E. (1968). "Hyperostosis of the spine in relation to age and hyperglycaemia in men aged 30–69." *Ann. Med. Int. Fenn.*, **57**: 1–7.

KENNEDY, P. (1973). "Cervical cord compression in mucopolysaccharidosis." *Dev. Med. Child. Neurol.*, **15**: 194–199.

LASKAR, F. H. & SARGISON, K. D. (1970). "Ochronotic arthropathy: a review with four case reports." *J. Bone Joint Surg.*, **52B**: 653–666.

LORINCZ, G., TRAUB, N. E., CHUKE, P. O. & HUSSAIN, S. F. (1974). "African haemosiderosis associated with osteoporosis and vertebral collapse." *East Afr. Med. J.*, **51**: 488–495.

McCOLLUM, D. E. & ODOM, G. L. (1965). "Alkaptonuria, ochronosis and low back pain." *J. Bone Joint Surg.*, **47A**: 1389–1392.

McCONKEY, B., FRASER, G. M. & BLIGH, A. S. (1962). "Osteoporosis and purpura in rheumatoid disease: prevalence and relation to treatment with corticosteroids." *Quart. J. Med.*, **31**: 419–427.

MACNAB, I. (1955). "Low back pain. The hypertension syndrome." *Can. Med. Assoc. J.*, **73**: 448–454.

MILLER, S. W., CASTRONOVO, F. P., PENDERGRASS, H. P. & POTSAID, M. S. (1974). "Technitium 99m labelled diphosphonate bone scanning in Paget's disease." *Amer. J. Roentgenol.*, **121**: 177–183.

NAYLOR, A. (1970). "Pathogenesis of disc prolapse and degeneration." *Orthopaedics (Oxford)*, **3**: 23–44.

NEUMANN, H. W., ARNOLD, W. D. & HEIN, W. (1972). "The incidence of diabetes mellitus in 201 patients with fracture of the femoral neck and vertebral compression fractures." *Zentralbl. Chir.*, **97**: 831–836.

NEWMAN, A. J. (1973). "Vertebral compression in childhood leukemia." *Amer. J. Dis., Child.*, **125**: 863–865.

NORDIN, B. E. C. (1973). *Metabolic Bone and Stone Disease.* Edinburgh and London; Churchill Livingstone.

PETERSEN, A. (1960). "Arthropathia diabetica." *Acta Orthop. Scand.*, **30**: 217–225.

RABINOWITZ, J. G. & SACHER, M. (1974). "Gangliosidosis (G.M.):

a re-evaluation of the vertebral deformity." *Amer. J. Roentgenol.*, **121:** 155–158.

RICHARDS, P., CHAMBERLAIN, M. J. & WRONG, O. M. (1972). "Treatment of osteomalacia of renal tubular acidosis by sodium bicarbonate alone." *Lancet*, **2:** 993–997.

RUSSELL, J. G. B. (1965). "Gas in the sacro-iliac joint in pregnancy." *J. Obstet. Gyn. Brit. Comm.*, **72:** 797–798.

SADAR, E. S., WALTON, R. J. & GOSSMAN, H. H. (1972). "Neurological dysfunction in Paget's disease of the vertebral column." *J. Neurosurg.*, **37:** 661–665.

SAVILLE, P. D. (1973). "The syndrome of spinal osteoporosis." *Clin. Endocrinol. Metab.*, **2:** 117–185.

SCHAJOWICZ, F. & SLULLITEL, J. (1973). "Eosinophilic granuloma of bone and its relationship to Hand-Schüller-Christian and Letterer-Siwe Syndromes." *J. Bone Joint Surg.*, **55B:** 545–565.

SCHULTZ, M. (1972). "Low back pain due to osteoporosis and fracture." *Proc. Mine Med. Off. Assoc.*, **52:** 53.

SILBERBERG, R. (1973). "Vertebral aging in hypopituitary dwarf mice." *Gerontologia*, **19:** 281–294.

SILBERBERG, R. (1974). "Response of vertebral cartilage and bone to hormonal imbalances produced by anterior hypophyseal hormones and hypothyroidism." "*Pathol. Microbiol.*, **41:** 11–25.

SISSONS, H. A. (1970). "Osteoporosis and backache." In *Neckache and Backache*. pp. 61–68. Ed. by E. S. Gurdjian and L. M. Thomas. Springfield, Ill.; Thomas.

SOKOLOVA, N. F. (1974). "Role of antibiotics in intervertebral osteochondrosis." *Zhurnal Neurapatologii*, **74:** 1624–1626.

SPIERA, H. & PLOTZ, C. M. (1969). "Rheumatic symptoms and oral contraceptives." *Lancet*, **1:** 571–572.

STÖVER, B., BALL, F. & WALTHER, A. (1974). "Idiopathic juvenile osteoporosis." *Fortschr. Rontgenstr.*, **121:** 435–444.

TARZY, B. J., GARCIA, C.-R., WALLACH, E. E., ZWEIMAN, B. & MYERS, A. R. (1972). "Rheumatic disease, abnormal serology and oral contraceptives." *Lancet*, **2:** 501–503.

TAYLOR, T. K. F. & AKESON, W. H. (1971). "Intervertebral disc prolapse: a review of morphologic and biochemic knowledge concerning the nature of prolapse." *Clin. Orthop.*, **76:** 54–79.

VERDIER, J.-M., COMMANDRE, F., RIVOLLIER, P. & ZIEGLER, G. (1974). "Triple association of pelvispondylitis, Paget's disease and myeloma." *Rev. Rhum.*, **41:** 353–356.

VERNON-ROBERTS, B. & PIRIE, C. J. (1973). "Healing trabecular micro-fractures in the bodies of lumbar vertebrae." *Ann. Rheum. Dis.*, **32:** 406–412.

WALDE, J. (1962). "Obstetrical and gynaecological back and pelvic pains, especially those contracted during pregnancy." *Acta Obst. Gyn. Scand., Suppl.* **2:** 11–53.

WESTERMAN, M. P. (1974). " 'Fish-vertebrae,' homocystinuria and sickle cell anemia." *J. Amer. Med. Assoc.*, **230:** 261–262.

WOOD, A. E. (1973). "Dietary osteomalacia and bone pain in the elderly." *J. Amer. Med. Assoc.*, **66:** 241–243.

## (h) Infections and Inflammation (Local; Systemic—Including Rheumatic Diseases)

ABRAHAM, G. A., AWAD, E. A. & KOTTKE, F. J. (1974). "Interstitial myofibrositis. Serum and muscle enzymes and lactate dehydro-genase-isoenzymes." *Arch. Phys. Med. Rehab.*, **55:** 23–28.

AHLBACK, K. & COLLERT, P. (1970). "Destruction of the odontoid process due to atlanto-axial pyogenic spondylitis." *Acta Radiol.*, **14:** 419.

ALARCON-SEGOVIA, D., CETINA, J. A. & DIAZ-JOUANEN, E. (1973). "Sacroiliac joints in primary gout: clinical and roentgenographic study of 143 patients." *Amer. J. Roentgenol.*, **118:** 433–443.

ALLANDER, E. (1974). "Prevalence, incidence and remission rates of some common rheumatic diseases or syndromes." *Scand. J. Rheumatol.*, **3:** 145–153.

ANDERSON, J. A. D. (1971). "Rheumatism in industry: a review." *Brit. J. Indust. Med.*, **28:** 103–121.

ANDERSON, J. A. D. & DUTHIE, J. J. R. (1963). "Rheumatic complaints in dockyard workers." *Ann. Rheum Dis.*, **22:** 401–409.

ANDERSON, J. A. D., DUTHIE, J. J. R. & MOODY, B. P. (1962). "Social and economic effects of rheumatic diseases in a mining population." *Ann. Rheum. Dis.*, **21:** 342–351.

BAGGENSTOSS, A. H., BICKEL, W. H. & WARD, L. E. (1952). "Rheumatoid granulomatous nodules as destructive lesions of vertebrae." *J. Bone Joint Surg.*, **34A:** 601–609.

BALL, J. (1971). "Enthesopathy of rheumatoid and ankylosing spondylitis." *Ann. Rheum. Dis.*, **30:** 213–223.

BARDFELD, M. & STREDA, A. (1973). "Ankylosing spondyloarthritis of the cervical vertebrae in juvenile primary chronic polyarthritis —the significance of time factors." *Radiol. Diagn., Berlin,* **14:** 81–87.

BAUM, P. & ZIFF, M. (1971). "The rarity of ankylosing spondylitis in the black race." *Arth. Rheum.,* **14:** 12.

BEESON, P. B. & SCOTT, T. F. M. N. (1941). "Viral back pain." *Ann. Rheum. Dis.,* **2:** 247.

BERANT, M. (1974). "Vertebral osteomyelitis in a young infant." *Clin. Pediatr.,* **13:** 677–679.

BHARUCHA, E. P. (1974). "Postconjunctival myeloradiculopathy." *Neurol. India,* **22:** 79–82.

BIRKBECH, M. Q., BUCKLER, W. ST. J. & MASON, R. M. (1951). "Ileitis as the presenting symptom in ankylosing spondylitis." *Lancet,* **2:** 802.

BONFIGLIO, M., LANGE, T. A. & KIM, Y. M. (1973). "Pyogenic vertebral osteomyelitis: disk space infections." *Clin. Orthop.,* **96:** 234–247.

BROMLEY, L. L., CRAIG, J. D. & LIPMANN KESSEL, A. W. (1949). "Infected intervertebral disk after lumbar puncture." *Brit. Med. J.,* **1:** 132–133.

BYWATERS, E. G. L. (1974). "Rheumatoid discitis in the thoracic region due to spread from costovertebral joints." *Ann. Rheum. Dis.,* **33:** 408–409.

BYWATERS, E. G. L. & DIXON, A. ST. J. (1965). "Paravertebral ossification in psoriatic arthritis." *Ann. Rheum. Dis.,* **24:** 313.

CARTER, M. E. (1962). "Sacro-iliitis in Still's disease." *Ann. Rheum. Dis.,* **21:** 105–120.

CASHION, E. L. (1971). "Cervical intervertebral disc space infection following cerebral angiography." *Neuroradiology,* **2:** 176–178.

CAUGHEY, D. E. (1975). "Ankylosing spondylitis in Polynesian races." *N.Z. Med. J.,* **81:** 268.

CAVEN, W. R. (1948). "Backache and fibrositis." *Arch. Phys. Med.,* **29:** 56.

CAWLEY, M. I. D., CHALMERS, T. M., KELLGREN, J. H. & BALL, J. (1972). "Destructive lesions of vertebral bodies in ankylosing spondylitis." *Ann. Rheum. Dis.,* **31:** 345–358.

CHADDUCK, W. M. (1972). "Intraspinal tuberculous abscess simulating lumbar disc disease." *Virginia Med. Monthly,* **99:** 968–971.

CHALLENOR, Y. B., RICHTER, R. W., BRUUN, B. & PEARSON, J.

(1973). "Nontraumatic plexitis and heroin addiction." *J. Amer. Med. Assoc.*, **225**: 958–961.

CHAND, K. (1972). "Cervical spine and rheumatoid arthritis." *Internat. Surg.*, **57**: 721–726.

CLIFF, J. M. (1971). "Spinal bony ridging and carditis in Reiter's disease." *Ann. Rheum. Dis.*, **30**: 171–179.

COPEMAN, W. C. S. (1943). "Aetiology of the fibrositic nodule: a clinical contribution." *Brit. Med. J.*, **2**: 263–264.

COPEMAN, W. S. C. & ACKERMAN, W. L. (1944). " 'Fibrositis' of the back." *Quar. J. Med.*, **13**: 37–51.

COWAN, G. A. (1973). "Ankylosing spondylitis and auto-immunity." *Postgrad. Med. J.*, **49**: 667–668.

CRELLIN, B. (1970). "Severe subluxation of the cervical spine in rheumatoid arthritis." *J. Bone Joint Surg.*, **52B**: 244.

CUKIER, J., ALNOT, J.-Y. & BENHAMOU, G. (1972). "Bilateral peri-ureteritis secondary to infectious spondylodiscitis." *J. Urol. Nephrol., Paris*, **78**: 403–408.

DAVIDSON, R. I. (1974). "Bulbar symptoms and episodic aphonia associated with atlanto-occipital subluxation in ankylosing spondylitis." *J. Neurol. Neurosurg. Psychiat.*, **37**: 691–695.

DAVIS, P. R. & ROWLAND, H. A. K. (1965). "Vertebebral fractures in West Africans suffering from tetanus: clinical and osteological study." *J. Bone Joint Surg.*, **47B**: 61–71.

DERESINKI, S. C. (1974). "Anterior cervical infections: complications of transtracheal aspirations." *Amer. Rev. Respir. Dis.*, **110**: 354–356.

DHALIWAL, G. S. (1974). "Spinal myoclonus in association with herpes zoster infection." *Can. J. Neurol. Sci.*, **1**: 239–241.

DIXON, A. ST. J., BEARDWELL, C., KAY, A., WANKA, J. & WONG, Y. T. (1966). "Polymyalgia rheumatica and temporal arteritis." *Ann. Rheumat. Dis.*, **25**: 203–208.

DONALD, K. M. (1972). "Low back pain due to arachnoiditis of the lumbarsacral region." *Proc. Mine Med. Off. Assoc.*, **52**: 53–55.

FARHAT, S. M., SCHNEIDER, R. C. & GRAY, J. M. (1973). "Traumatic spinal extradural hematoma associated with cervical fractures in rheumatoid arthritis." *J. Trauma*, **13**: 591–599.

FEIGENBAUM, J. A. (1974). "Infections of cervical disc space after dental extractions." *J. Neurol Neurosurg. Psychiat.*, **37**: 1361–1365.

FISHBACH, R. S., ROSENBLATT, J. E. & DAHLREN, J. G. (1973).

"Pyogenic vertebral osteomyelitis in heroin addicts." *Calif. Med.*, **119**: 1–4.

FRIEDMAN, J. (1970). "Intraspinal rheumatoid nodule causing nerve root compression." *J. Neurosurg.*, **32**: 689.

GACAD, G. (1974). "Pulmonary fibrosis and Group IV mycobacteria infection of the lungs in ankylosing spondylitis." *Amer. Rev. Resp. Dis.*, **109**: 274–278.

GRIFFITHS, R. W. (1975). "Acute vertebral collapse and cauda equina compression in tertiary syphilis." *J. Neurol. Neurosurg. Psychiat.*, **38**: 558–560.

HANSON, T. A., KRAFT, J. P. & ADCOCK, D. W. (1973). "Subluxation of the cervical vertebrae due to pharyngitis." *Southern Med. J.*, **66**: 427–429.

HAZLETT, J. W. (1975). "Low back pain with femoral neuritis." *Clin. Orthop.*, **108**: 19–26.

HEKSTER, P. J. (1972). "The combination of occipitalization of the atlas with atlanto-axial dislocation due to an extravertebral (inflammatory) process in the head-neck region." *Phys. Neurol. Neurochir.*, **75**: 85–93.

HOLZMANN, H. (1974). "Joint involvement in psoriasis." *Arch. Dermatol. Fortsch.*, **250**: 95–107.

JAYSON, M. I. V. & BOUCHIER, I. A. D. (1968). "Ulcerative colitis with ankylosing spondylitis." *Ann. Rheum Dis.*, **27**: 219.

JAYSON, M. I. V., SALMON, P. R. & HARRISON, W. J. (1970). "Inflammatory bowel disease in ankylosing spondylitis." *Gut*, **11**: 506.

JIROUT, J., SIMON, J. & SIMONOVA, O. (1957). "Disturbances in the lumbosacral dynamics following poliomyelitis." *Acta Radiol.*, **48**: 361–365.

KEMP, H. B. S., JACKSON, J. W. & SHAW, N. C. (1974). "Laminectomy in paraplegia due to infective spondylosis." *Brit. J. Surg.*, **61**: 66–72.

KING, J. D. (1972). "Localized clubbing and hypertrophic osteoarthropathy due to infection in an aortic prosthesis." *Brit. Med. J.*, **4**: 404–405.

LIGHT, R. W. & DUNHAM, T. R. (1974). "Vertebral osteomyelitis due to pseudomonas in the occasional heroin user." *J. Amer. Med. Assoc.*, **228**: 1272.

LIPPMANN, R. K. (1953). "Arthropathy due to adjacent inflammation." *J. Bone Joint Surg.*, **35A**: 967–979.

LOCKSHIN, M. D. (1975). "Ankylosing spondylitis and HL-A. A genetic disease plus?" *Amer. J. Med.*, **58**: 695–703.

LOWMAN, E. W. (1951). "Muscle, nerve and synovial changes in lupus erythematosus." *Ann. Rheum. Dis.*, **10**: 16–21.

MACRAE, I. F. & WRIGHT, V. (1970). "Ulcerative colitis and sacroileitis." *Ann. Rheum. Dis.*, **29**: 559.

MARAR, B. C. & BALACHANDRANDRAN, N. (1973). "Non-traumatic atlanto-axial dislocation in children." *Clin. Orthop.*, **92**: 220–226.

MEIJERS, K. A. (1973). "Treatment of dislocations in the cervical spine in rheumatoid arthritis and ankylosing spondylitis, complicated by signs of cord compression." *Ann. Rheum. Dis.*, **32**: 88–89.

MEIJERS, K. A. (1974). "Dislocation of the cervical spine with cord compression in rheumatoid arthritis." *J. Bone Joint Surg.*, **56B**: 668–680.

MILES, W. A. (1974). "Discogenic osteoarthritic disease of the cervical spine." *J. Nat. Med. Assoc.*, **66**: 300–304.

MUKHERJEE, S. K. (1974). "Fractured vertebra following tetanus." *J. Indian Med. Assoc.*, **63**: 158–160.

NORMAN, G. F. (1968). "Sacroiliac disease and its relationship to lower abdominal pain." *Amer. J. Surg.*, **116**: 54–56.

OATES, J. K. (1958). "Sacro-iliitis in Reiter's disease." *Brit. J. Ven. Dis.*, **34**: 177–180.

OATES, J. K. & YOUNG, A. C. (1959). "Sacro-iliitis in Reiter's disease." *Br. Med. J.*, **2**: 1013.

OLL, J. M. H., HASLOCK, I., MACRAE, I. F. & WRIGHT, V. (1974). "Associations between ankylosing spondylitis, psoriatic arthritis, Reiter's disease, the intestinal arthropathies and Bechet's syndrome." *Medicine*, **53**: 343–364.

ORNILLA, E., ANSELL, B. M. & SWANNELL, A. J. (1972). "Cervical spine involvement in patients with chronic arthritis undergoing orthopaedic surgery." *Ann. Rheum. Dis.*, **31**: 364–368.

PALUMBO, P. J. (1973). "Musculoskeletal manifestations of inflammatory bowel disease." *Proc. Mayo Clinic*, **48**: 411–416.

RIFFAT, G., DOMENACH, M., VIGNON, H. & DORCHE, G. (1974). "Spondylodiscitis complicating septicaemia due to Candida albicans." *Rev. Rhum.*, **41**: 208–210.

ROBERTS, M., RINAUDO, P. A., VILINSKAS, J. & OWENS, G. (1974). "Solitary sclerosing plasma-cell myeloma of the spine: case report." *J. Neurosurg.*, **40**: 125–129.

ROBINSON, M. (1966). "Rheumatoid arthritis—atlanto-axial sub-luxation and its clinical presentation." *Canad. Med. Ass. J.*, **94:** 470.

RUSSELL, A. S. (1974). "Deforming arthropathy in systemic lupus erythematosus." *Ann. Rheum. Dis.*, **32:** 203–209.

SCHUMACHER, H. R. (1973). "Arthropathy in sickle-cell disease." *Ann. Intern. Med.*, **78:** 203–211.

SELBY, R. C. (1972). "Osteomyelitis and disc infection secondary to pseudomonas aeruginosa in heroin addiction." *J. Neurosurg.*, **37:** 463–466.

SERRE, H., BLOTMAN, F., SANDY, J. & SIMON, L. (1973). "Infectious spondylodiscitis: symptomatic aspects and course." *Rev. Rhum. Mal. Osteoartic.*, **40:** 243–253.

SERRE, H. & SIMON, L. (1964). "Rheumatoid spondylitis and ulcerative colitis." *Rheumatism*, **20:** 13–16.

SMITH, P. H. (1973). "Natural history of rheumatoid cervical luxations." *Ann. Rheum. Dis.*, **31:** 431–439.

SOTER, N. A. (1974). "Urticaria and arthralgias as manifestations of necrotizing angiitis (vasculitis)." *J. Invest. Derm.*, **63:** 485–490.

STEINBERG, V. L. & STOREY, G. (1957). "Ankylosing spondylitis and chronic inflammatory lesions of the intestines." *Brit. Med. J.*, **2:** 1157–1159.

STEVENS, P. (1971). "Atlanto-axial subluxation and cervical myelopathy in rheumatoid arthritis." *Quart. J. Med.*, **40:** 391.

SUKOFF, M. H. (1972). "Transoral decompression for myelopathy caused by rheumatoid arthritis of the cervical spine." *J. Neurosurg.*, **37:** 493–497.

SWINSON, D. R., HAMILTON, E. B. D., MATHEWS, J. A. & YATES, D. A. H. (1972). "Vertical subluxation of the axis in rheumatoid arthritis." *Ann. Rheum. Dis.*, **31:** 359–363.

VOGELSANG, H., ZEIDLER, H., WITTENBORG, A. & WEIDNER, A. (1973). "Rheumatoid cervical luxations with fatal neurological complications." *Neuroradiology*, **6:** 87–92.

WADIA, N. H., IRANI, P. R. & KATRAK, S. M. (1973). "Lumbosacral radiculomyelitis associated with pandemic acute haemorrhagic conjunctivitis." *Lancet*, **1:** 350–352.

WATANAKUNAKORN, F. (1973). "Vertebral osteomyelitis due to mycobacterium kansaii." *Amer. Rev. Resp. Dis.*, **107:** 846–850.

WEINBERG, H., NATHAN, H., MAGORA, F., ROBIN, G. C. T. & AVIAD,

I. (1972). "Arthritis of the first costovertebral joint as a cause of thoracic outlet syndrome." *Clin. Orthop.*, **86:** 159–163.

WHALEY, K. (1968). "Fatal sub-axial dislocation of cervical spine in rheumatoid arthritis." *Brit. Med. J.*, **2:** 31.

WHALEY, K., BLAIR, S., LOW, P. S., CHISHOLM, D. M., DICK, W. C. & BUCHANAN, W. W. (1972). "Sialographic abnormalities in Sjögren's syndrome, rheumatoid arthritis and other arthritides and connective tissue diseases: a clinical and radiological investigation using hydrostatic sialography." *Clin. Radiol.*, **23:** 474–482.

YAU, A. C. (1974). "Stress fracture of the fused lumbodorsal spine in ankylosing spondylitis." *J. Bone Joint Surg.*, **56B:** 681–687.

## (i) Neoplastic (Primary and Secondary)

BATSON, O. V. (1940). "The function of the vertebral veins and their role in the spread of metastases." *Ann. Surg.*, **112:** 138–149.

BOND, J. V. (1972). "Unusual presenting symptoms in neuroblastoma." *Brit. Med. J.*, **1:** 327–328.

BOND, M. R. & PILOWSKY, I. (1966). "Subjective assessment of pain and its relationship to the administration of analgesics in patients with advanced cancer." *J. Psychosomat. Med.*, **10:** 203–208.

BRISH, A. & PAYAN, H. M. (1972). "Lumbar intraspinal extradural ganglion cyst." *J. Neurol. Neurosurg. Psychiat.*, **35:** 771–775.

CHADDUCK, W. M. (1971). "Intraspinal neurilemmomas simulating lumbar disc disease." *Virginia Med. Monthly*, **98:** 25–30.

CHADDUCK, W. M. (1972). "Intraspinal meningiomas simulating disc disease." *Virginia Med. Monthly*, **99:** 627–631.

CHADDUCK, W. M. (1974). "Epidermoid tumor simulating lumbar disc disease." *Virginia Med. Monthly*, **101:** 196–198.

CHOREMIS, C., ECONOMOS, D., PAPADATOS, C. & GARGOULAS, A. (1956). "Intraspinal epidermoid tumours (cholesteatomas) in patients treated for tuberculous meningitis." *Lancet*, **2:** 437–439.

CHOUAT, Y., DESHAYES, P., CAUVIN, M. & SIMONIN, J.-L. (1973). "Localized lumbar pain due to intraspinal lesions." *Rev. Rhum.*, **40:** 741–744.

CITRIN, VESSENT & TUOSY. (1974). "Bone scanning in malignant disease." *Brit. J. Hosp. Med.*, **March:** 424–430.

CLARKE, H. A. & FLEMING, I. D. (1973). "Disk disease and occult malignancies." *Southern Med. J.*, **66:** 449–454.

CREASMAN, W. T. (1967). "Back and hip pain in pregnancy due to chordoma." *Amer. J. Obstet. Gynec.*, **99:** 1165–1166.

CRELLIN, R. Q. & JONES, E. R. (1973). "Sacral extradural cysts: a rare cause of low back ache and sciatica." *J. Bone Joint Surg.*, **55B:** 20–31.

DEBAENE, A., ACQUAVIVA, P., DUFOUR, M. & LEGRÉ, J. (1973). "Hyperconcavity (scalloping) of lumbar vertebrae in von Recklinghausen's disease." *J. Radiol. Electrol.*, **54:** 149–151.

DINAKAR, I. (1974). "Chronic nonspecific epidural granuloma simulating a lumbar disc prolapse." *Neurol. India*, **22:** 100–102.

DUBOVSKY, D. (1975). "Vertebral rarefaction in acute lymphoblastic leukaemia." *Sth. Afr. Med. J.*, **49:** 241–242.

DUNCAN, A. W. (1973). "Calcification of the anterior longitudinal vertebral ligaments in Hodgkin's disease." *Clinc. Radiol.*, **24:** 394–396.

ELSBERG, C. A. (1931). "The extradural ventral chondromas (ecchondroses), their favourite sites, the spinal cord and root. Symptoms they produce and their surgical treatment." *Bull. Neurol. Inst. N.Y.*, **1:** 350–388.

ELSBERG, C. A. & DYKE, C. G. (1934). "Diagnosis and localization of tumours of the spinal cord by means of measurements made on X-ray films of vertebrae, and the correlation with clinical findings." *Bull. Neurol. Inst. N.Y.*, **3:** 359–394.

FLOWERS, J. K. (1968). "Meralgia paresthetica: a clue to retroperitoneal malignant tumour." *Amer. J. Surg.*, **116:** 89–92.

FROMM, H. & WILD, K. VON (1974). "Clinical aspects, operative treatment and rehabilitation of paraplegia caused by lipomas of the spinal cord—with particular emphasis on the 'intramedullary' lipomas." *Paraplegia*, **12:** 15–20.

FUSTE, M. (1968). "Vertebral hemangioma with compression of the cord and Wallerian degeneration." *Southern Med. J.*, **61:** 32.

GELMAN, M. I. (1974). "Cauda equina compression in acromegaly." *Radiol.*, **112:** 357–360.

GOLDENBERG, J. (1968). "Osteochondroma with spinal cord compression." *J. Canad. Med. Assoc.*, **19:** 192.

GOLDING, P. (1969). "Cervical and occipital pain as presenting symptoms of intra-cranial tumour." *Ann. Phys. Med.*, **10:** 1.

GRANIERI, M. & SELOSSE, P. (1968). "Pure lumbosciatalgia due to neurinoma of the cauda equina." *Acta Neurol. Belg.*, **68:** 345–355.

GRIFFITHS, D. L. (1966). "Orthopaedic aspects of myelomatoses." *J. Bone Joint Surg.*, **48B:** 703–728.

HAASE, J. (1972). "Extradural cyst of ligamentum flavum of L4: a case." *Acta Orthop. Scand.*, **43:** 32–38.

HALL, A. J. & MACKAY, N. N. S. (1973). "The results of laminectomy for compression of the cord or cauda equina by extradural malignant tumour." *J. Bone Joint Surg.*, **55B:** 497–505.

HALL, J. H. & FLEMING, J. F. R. (1970). "The 'lumbar disc syndrome' produced by sacral metastases." *Canad. J. Surg.*, **13:** 149–156.

HASUE, M. & ITO, R. (1972). "Sacral nerve root cyst as a cause of low back pain and sciatica: report of six cases." *J. Jap. Orthop. Assoc.*, **46:** 451–459.

KEIM, H. A. (1975). "Osteoid-osteoma as a cause of scoliosis." *J. Bone Joint Surg.*, **57A:** 159–163.

LaFIA, D. J. (1955). "Ruptured lumbar intervertebral disk syndrome caused by metastatic disease." *Rhode Island Med. J.*, **4:** 212–213.

LAKE, P. A., MINCKLER, J. & SCAHLAN, R. L. (1974). "Spinal epidural cyst: theories of pathogenesis." *J. Neurosurg.*, **40:** 774–778.

LIEBESKIND, A., JACOBSON, R., ANDERSON, R. & SCHECHTER, M. M. (1973). "Unusual neurologic and roentgenographic manifestations of eosinophilic granuloma." *Arch. Neurol.*, **28:** 131–133.

LIEVRE, J.-A. & METZGER, J. (1974). "Intrasacral cysts." *Rev. Rhum.*, **41:** 483–489.

McNEUR, J. C. (1953). "Tumours of the proximal limb bones and hip simulating intervertebral disc lesions." *Proc. Roy. Soc. Med.*, **46:** 351–352.

PINER, J. (1972). "A rare cause of sciatic pain: pheochromocytoma of the sacral concavity eroding the sacrum and the iliac bone." *J. Radiol. Elect.*, **53:** 851–855.

ROWBOTHAM, G. F. (1955). "Early diagnosis of compression of the spinal cord by neoplasms." *Lancet*, **2:** 1220–1222.

SCHIRMER, M. (1974). "Sciatica with vertebral chondroma." *Münch. Med. Wschr.*, **116:** 105–106.

SCOTT, M. (1956). "Lower extremity pain simulating sciatica.

Tumors of the high thoracic and cervical cord as causes." *J. Amer. Med. Assoc.*, **160**: 528–534.

STOOKEY, B. (1928). "Compression of the spinal cord due to ventral extradural cervical chondromas." *Arch. Neurol. Psychiat.*, **20**: 275–291.

SYPERT, G. W., LEECH, R. W. & HARRIS, A. B. (1973). "Post-traumatic lumbar epidural true synovial cyst: case report." *J. Neurosurg.*, **39**: 246–248.

TARLOV, I. M. (1953). *Sacral Nerve-root Cysts: Another Cause of the Sciatic or Cauda Equina Syndrome.* Springfield, Ill.; Thomas.

TOUMEY, J. W., POPPEN, J. L. & HURLEY, M. T. (1950). "Cauda equina tumors as a cause of the low-back syndrome." *J. Bone Joint Surg.*, **32A**: 249–256.

WAGENRECHT, L. V. & REME, H. (1973). "Solitary Schwannoma in the lumbo-sacral region." *Beitr. Klin. Chir.*, **220**: 334–340.

WETZEL, N., ARIEFF, A. & TUNCBAY, E. (1963). "Retroperitoneal, lumbar and pelvic malignancies simulating the 'disc syndrome'." *Arch. Surg.*, **86**: 211–213.

WILLIAMS, J. (1971). "Sciatica caused by sacral nerve-root-cyst." *Lancet*, **1**: 137.

### (j) Neurological and Psychological

ALLEN, K. (1952). "Neuropathies caused by bony spurs in the cervical spine with special reference to surgical treatment." *J. Neurol. Neurosurg. Psychiat.*, **15**: 20–36.

ASHBY, J. G. (1975). "Pathogenesis of myelopathy in cervical spondylosis." *Lancet*, **1**: 980–981.

BADGLEY, C. A. (1937). "Clinical and roentgenological study of low back pain with sciatic radiation." *Amer. J. Roentgenol.*, **37**: 454–468.

BARBER, H. S. (1957). "Myalgic syndrome with constitutional effects: polymyalgia rheumatica." *Ann. Rheum. Dis.*, **16**: 230.

BECKER, D. P., GLUCK, H., NILLSEN, F. E. & JANE, J. A. (1969/70). "An inquiry into the neurophysiological basis for pain." *J. Neurosurg.*, **30**: 1–13; and **31**: 1–3.

BEECHER, H. K. (1968). "The measurement of pain in man." In *Pain.* pp. 207. Ed. by A. Soulairac, J. Cahn and J. Charpentier. New York; Academic Press.

BIEDMOND, A. & DEJONG, J. M. B. V. (1969). "On cervical nystagmus and related disorders." *Brain*, **92**: 437–458.

BLACK, P. (1970). *Physiological Correlates of Emotion*. New York; Academic Press.

BLAU, J. N. & LOGUE, V. (1961). "Intermittent claudication of the cauda equina." *Lancet*, **1**: 1018.

BOGORDINSKI, D. K. (1974). "Neurological complications of osteochondrosis of the lower lumbar intervertebral disks." *Sov. Med.*, **Aug.**: 5–9.

BONICA, J. J. (Ed.). (1974). *International Symposium on Pain*. New York; Raven Press.

BONICA, J. J. & ALBE-FESSARD, D. (Eds.). (1976). *Advances in Pain Research and Therapy*. New York; Raven Press.

BRADFORD, F. K. & GARCIA, H. (1969). "Neurological complications in Scheurmann's disease." *J. Bone and Joint Surg.*, **51A**: 567.

BRAIN, W. R., NORTHFIELD, D. & WILKINSON, M. (1952). "The neurological manifestations of cervical spondylosis." *Brain*, **75**: 187–224.

BRODSKY, A. E. (1975). "Low back pain syndromes due to spinal stenosis and posterior cauda equina compression." *Bull. Hosp. Joint Dis.*, **36**: 66.

BURKE, G. (1966). "The etiology and pathogenesis of pain of spinal origin." *App. Therap.*, **8**: 863–867.

CASAGRANDE, P. A. & DANAHY, P. R. (1971). "Delayed sciatic-nerve entrapment following the use of self-curing acrylic." *J. Bone Joint Surg.*, **53A**: 167–169.

CAUSEY, G. (1948). "The effect of pressure on nerve fibres." *J. Anat.*, **82**: 262–270.

CAUSEY, G. (1950). "The effect of pressure on conduction and nerve fibre size." *J. Anat.*, **84**: 65 (P).

CHAQUAT, Y., KANOVITCH, B., FAURES, B., GINET, C., PATECKI, A. & VIGNAUD, R. (1974). "Lumbar radiculalgia due to large canals. A variety of spino-radiculo-meningo-vertebral disharmony of duramatral origin." *Rev. Rheum. Mal. Osteoartic.*, **41**: 491–499.

CHEEK, W. R., ANCMONDO, H., RASO, E. & SCOTT, B. (1973). "Neurogenic bladder and the lumbar spine." *Urology*, **2**: 30–33.

CLOWARD, R. B. (1960). "The clinical significance of the sinu-vertebral nerve in relation to the cervical disc syndrome." *J. Neurol. Neurosurg. Psychiat.*, **23**: 321–326.

COGGESHAL, R. E. (1975). "Unmyelinated axons in human ventral roots, a possible explanation for the failure of dorsal rhizotomy to relieve pain." *Brain*, **98:** 157–166.

COLLETTE, J. & LUDWIG, E. G. (1968). "Low back disorders: an examination of the stereotype." *Indust. Med. Surg.*, **37:** 685.

COPE, S. & RYAN, G. M. S. (1959). "Cervical and otolith vertigo." *J. Laryngol. Otol.*, **63:** 113–120.

COPEMAN, W. S. C. (Ed.) (1964). *Textbook of the Rheumatic Diseases*. 3rd ed. Edinburgh; Livingstone.

CROWN, S. (1978). "Psychological aspects of low back pain." *Rheumat. Rehab.*, **17:** 114.

CULLING, J. (1974). "Charcot's disease of the spine." *Proc. Roy. Soc. Med.*, **67:** 1026–1027.

CURRAN, J. E. (1975). "Neurological sequelae of Paget's disease of the vertebral column and skull base." *Australas. Radiol.*, **19:** 15–19.

CYRIAX, J. (1970). *Textbook of Orthopaedic Medicine*. London; Baillière Tindall.

DAHL, D. S. (1974). "Congenital root disease. Further evidence of innervational abnormalities as the basis for the clinicopathologic features." *J. Neurol. Sci.*, **23:** 371–385.

DAVIES, F. L. (1956). "Effect of unabsorbed radiographic contrast media on the central nervous system." *Lancet*, **2:** 747–748.

DAVIS, L., MARTIN, J. & GOLDSTEIN, S. L. (1952). "Sensory changes with herniated nucleus pulposus." *J. Neurosurg.*, **9:** 133–138.

DELCHEF, J. (1949). "Nerve-root pain of vertebral origin not dependent on disc prolapse." *J. Bone Joint Surg.*, **31B:** 479.

DENNY-BROWN, D. & BRENNER, C. (1944). "The effect of percussion of nerve." *J. Neurol. Neurosurg. Psychiat.*, **7:** 76–95.

DENNY-BROWN, D. & BRENNER, C. (1944). "Paralysis of nerve induced by direct pressure and by tourniquet." *Arch. Neurol. Psychiat.*, **51:** 1–26.

DENNY-BROWN, D. & DOHERTY, M. M. (1945). "Effects of transient stretching of peripheral nerve." *Arch. Neurol. Psychiat.*, **54:** 116–129.

DENSLOW, J. S. (1944). "An analysis of the variability of spinal reflex threshold." *J. Neurophysiol.*, **7:** 207–215.

DENSLOW, J. S. & HASSETT, C. C. (1942). "The central excitatory state associated with postural abnormalities." *J. Neurophysiol.*, **5:** 393–402.

DIONNE, J. (1974). "Neck torsion nystagmus." *Canad. J. Oto-laryngol.*, **3**: 37–41.

EMMETT, J. L. & LOVE, J. G. (1971). "Vesical dysfunction caused by protruded lumbar disk." *J. Urol.*, **105**: 86–91.

EPSTEIN, J. A. & DAVIDOFF, L. M. (1953). "Recognition and management of spinal cord and nerve root compression caused by osteophytes." *Bull. Rheum. Dis.*, **3**: 29.

EPSTEIN, J. A., EPSTEIN, B. S. & LAVINE, L. S. (1962). "Nerve root compression associated with narrowing of the lumbar spinal canal." *J. Neurol. Neurosurg. Psychiat.*, **25**: 165–176.

EPSTEIN, J. A., EPSTEIN, B. S., LAVINE, L. S., CARRAS, R., ROSEN-THAL, A. D. & SUMNER, P. (1973). "Lumbar nerve root compression at the intervertebral foramina caused by arthritis of the posterior facets." *J. Neurosurg.*, **39**: 362–369.

EPSTEIN, J. A., EPSTEIN, B. S., ROSENTHAL, A. D., CARRAS, R. & LAVINE, L. S. (1972). "Sciatica caused by nerve root entrapment in the lateral recess: the superior facet syndrome." *J. Neurosurg.*, **36**: 584–589.

EVANS, J. G. (1964). "Neurogenic intermittent claudication." *Brit. Med. J.* **2**: 985–987.

FALCONER, M. A., GLASGOW, G. L. & COLE, D. S. (1947). "Sensory disturbances occurring in sciatica due to intervertebral disc protrusions." *J. Neurol. Neurosurg. Psychiat.*, **10**: 72–84.

FORREST, A. J. & WOLKIND, S. N. (1974). "Masked depression in men with low back pain." *Rheumat. Rehab.*, **13**: 148.

FRYKHOLM, R. (1951). "Cervical nerve root compression resulting from disc degeneration and root sleeve fibrosis." *Acta Chir. Scand., Suppl.* **160**: 1.

GAUTIER-SMITH, P. (1967). "Clinical aspects of spinal neurofibro-matosis." *Brain*, **90**: 359.

GILCHRIST, I. C. (1976). "Psychiatric and social factors related to low-back pain in general practice." *Rheumat. Rehab.*, **15**: 101.

GLYNN, C. J. & LLOYD, J. W. (1976). "The diurnal variation in the perception of pain." *Proc. Roy. Soc. Lond.*, **69B**: 369.

GOLDSTEIN, I. B. (1965). "The relationship of muscle tension and autonomic activity to psychiatric disorders." *Psychosomat. Med.*, **27**: 39–52.

GOODING, M. R. (1974). "Pathogenesis of myelopathy in cervical spondylosis." *Lancet*, **2**: 1180–1181.

Gu, J. (1973). "Abdominal and low-back pain associated with dysphagia." *N.Y. State J. Med.*, **73**: 992–995.

Guerrier, Y. & Colin, R. (1954). "Occipital pains: the role of the second cervical nerve and the dentate ligament." *Montpellier Méd.*, **46**: 151–153.

Gulati, D. R. & Rout, D. (1973). "Myelographic block caused by redundant lumbar nerve root: case report." *J. Neurosurgery*, **38**: 504–505.

Guttmann, L. (1940). "Topographic studies of disturbances of sweat secretion after complete lesions of peripheral nerves." *J. Neurol. Neurosurg. Psychiat.*, **3**: 197–210.

Hasue, M. & Ito, R. (1972). "Sacral nerve root cyst as a cause of low back pain and sciatica: report of 6 cases." *J. Jap. Orthop. Assoc.*, **46**: 451–459.

Heathfield, K. (1973). "Neurological complications of the rheumatic diseases." *Rheum. and Rehab.*, **12**: 2–21.

Hirsch, C. (1966). "Etiology and pathogenesis of low back pain." *Israel J. Med. Sci.*, **2**: 362.

Inman, V. T. & Saunders, J. B. D. (1944). "Referred pain from skeletal structures." *J. Nerv. Ment. Dis.*, **99**: 660.

Joffe, R., Appleby, A. & Arjona, V. (1966). "Intermittent ischaemia of the cauda equina due to stenosis of the lumbar canal." *J. Neurol. Neurosurg. Psychiat.*, **29**: 315.

Jones, D. L. & Moore, T. (1973). "The types of neuropathic bladder dysfunction associated with prolapsed intervertebral discs." *Brit. J. Urol.*, **45**: 39–63.

Judovich, B. & Bates, W. (1944). *Segmental Neuralgia in Painful Syndromes*. Philadelphia; Davis.

Karpovich, P. V. (1957). "Physiological and psychological dynamogenic factors in exercise." *Arbeitsphysiol.*, **9**: 626–629.

Kellgren, J. H. & Lewis, T. (1939). "Observations relating to referred pain, visceromotor reflexes and other associated phenomena." *Clin. Sci.*, **4**: 46–71.

Kelly, M. (1958). "Is pain due to pressure on nerves? Spinal tumours and intervertebral discs." *Lancet*, **2**: 584.

Konitturi, M. (1968). "Investigations into bladder dysfunction in prolapse of lumbar intervertebral disc." *Ann. Chir. Gynaec. Fenn., Suppl.* **57**: 162.

Kososy, J. (1974). "Audiovestibular findings with cervical spine trauma." *Texas Med. J.*, **70**: 66–71.

LEAVITT, F., GARRON, D. C., WHISLER, W. W. & SHEINKOP, M. B. (1978). "Affective and sensory dimensions of back pain." *Pain*, **4**: 273.

LEVINE, M. E. (1971). "Depression, back pain and disc protrusion: relationships and psychophysiological mechanisms." *Dis. Nerv. Syst.*, **32**: 41–45.

LI, C. L. (1973). "Neurological basis of pain and its possible relationship to acupuncture-analgesia." *Amer. J. Chir. Med.*, **1**: 61–74.

MAGORA, A. (1973). "Investigation of the relationship between low back pain and occupation. V. Psychological aspects." *Scand. J. Rehab. Med.*, **5**: 191–196.

MALCOLM, D. S. (1951). "A method of measuring reflex times applied to sciatica and other conditions due to nerve root compression." *J. Neurol. Neurosurg. Psychiat.*, **14**: 15–24.

MARAR, B. C. (1974). "The pattern of neurological damage as an aid to the diagnosis of the mechanism in cervical spine injuries." *Brit. J. Radiol.*, **47**: 1648–1654.

MASTROVITO, R. C. (1974). "Pain and suffering: psychogenic pain." *Amer. J. Nurs.*, **74**: 514–519.

MELZACK, R. (1973). *The Puzzle of Pain*. New York; Basic Books.

MELZACK, R. & CHAPMAN, P. (1973). "Psychologic aspects of pain." *Postgrad. Med.*, **53**: 69–75.

MELZACK, R. & SCOTT, T. H. (1957). "The effect of early experience on the response to pain." *J. Comp. Physiol. Psychol.*, **50**: 155–161.

MERSKEY H. & SPEAR, F. G. (1967). *Pain: Psychological and Psychiatric Aspects*. London; Baillière, Tindall.

MERUTA, T., SWANSON, D. W. & SWANSON, W. M. (1976). "Pain as a psychiatric symptom; comparison between low back pain and depression." *Psychosomatics*, **17**: 123.

MICHELSEN, J. J. (1943). "Subjective disturbances of the sense of pain from lesions of the cerebral cortex." *Res. Pub. Assoc. Nerv. Ment. Dis.*, **23**: 86–99.

MORGAN, H. C. (1968). "Neural complications of disc surgery." *J. Bone Joint Surg.*, **50A**: 411–417.

NURICK, S. (1972). "The pathogenesis of the spinal cord disorder associated with cervical spondylosis." *Brain*, **95**: 87–100.

PACE, J. B. (1974). "Psychogenic backache." *J. Fam. Pract.*, **1**: 2.

PETRIE, A. (1967). *Individuality in Pain and Suffering*. University of Chicago Press.

PLEWES, J. L. & JACOBSON, I. (1970). "Sciatica caused by sacral nerve root cysts." *Lancet*, **2:** 799–802.

POS, R. (1974). "Psychological assessment of factors affecting pain." *Can. Med. Assoc. J.*, **11:** 1213–1215.

RANSFORD, A. O. & HARRIES, B. J. (1972). "Localised arachnoiditis complicating disc lesions." *J. Bone Joint Surg.*, **54B:** 656–665.

REIS, G. VON (1945). "Pain in the distribution area of the 4th lumbar root: a study of pain interpreted as referred pain and as caused by direct irritation of the nerve root." *Acta Psych. Neurol., Suppl.* **36:** 1.

RENTON, A. (1971). "The psychogenesis of low back pain." *J. Bone Joint Surg.*, **53:** 771.

SCOTT, P. J. (1965). "Bladder paralysis in cauda equina lesions from disc prolapse." *J. Bone Joint Surg.*, **47B:** 224–235.

SELECKI, B. R., NESS, T. D., LIMBERS, P., BLUM, P. & STENING, W. R. (1973). "Low back pain: a joint neurosurgical and orthopaedic project." *Med. J. Austr.*, **2:** 889–893.

SHAHRESTANI, E. & CLOWARD, R. B. (1972). "Treatment of cervical disc pains without nerve root involvement." *J. Western Pacific Orthop. Assoc.*, **9:** 40–48.

SHARR, M. M., GARFIELD, J. S. & JENKINS, J. D. (1973). "The association of bladder dysfunction with degenerative lumbar spondylosis." *Brit. J. Urol.*, **45:** 616–620.

SIMONS, D. G. (1976). "Muscle pain syndromes." *Amer. J. Phys. Med.*, **55:** 15.

SKALPE, I. O. (1972). "Disturbances of bladder function in lumbar disc syndromes." *J. Oslo City Hosp.*, **22:** 135–140.

STERNBACH, R. A. (1974). *Pain Patients: Traits and Treatment*. New York; Academic Press.

TARLOV, I. M. (1953). *Sacral Nerve-root Cysts: Another Cause of the Sciatic or Cauda Equina Syndrome*. Springfield, Ill.; Thomas.

THOMAS, P. K. (1974). "Neurological aspects of pain." *Physiotherapy*, **60:** 101–103.

WATKINS, P. (1970). "Spinal ileus." *Brit. J. Surg.*, **57:** 142.

WEISS, E. (1947). "Psychogenic rheumatism." *Ann. Intern. Med.*, **26:** 890–900.

WILTSE, L. L. (1975). "Preoperative psychological tests as predictors of success of chemonucleosis in the treatment of the low-back syndrome." *J. Bone Joint Surg.*, **57A:** 478–483.

WILTSE, L. L. (1975). "Psychological testing in predicting the success of low back surgery." *Orthop. Clin. Nth. Amer.*, **6:** 317–318.

WOLKIND, S. N. (1976). "Psychogenic low back pain." *Brit. J. Hosp. Med.*, **15:** 17–24.

WOLKIND, S. N. & FORREST, A. J. (1972). "Low back pain: a psychiatric investigation." *Postgrad. Med. J.*, **48:** 76.

WOODROW, K. M., FRIEDMAN, G. D., SIGELAUB, A. B. & COLLEN, M. F. (1972). "Pain tolerance: differences according to age, sex and race." *Psychosomat. Med.*, **34:** 548.

WOOLARD, H. H., WEDDELL, G. & HARPMAN, J. A. (1940). "Observations on the neurohistological basis of cutaneous pain." *J. Anat.*, **74:** 413–440.

WYKE, B. D. (1970). "The neurological basis of thoracic spinal pain." *Rheumatol. Phys. Med.*, **10:** 356.

WYKE, B. D. (1976). "Neurological aspects of low back pain." In *The Lumbar Spine and Back Pain.* pp. 189–256. Ed. by M. I. V. Jayson. London; Sector Publishing.

WYKE, B. D. (1977). "Neurological mechanisms of spinal pain." In *Patología de la Columna Vertebral.* p. 45. Ed. by S. Hernández Conesa and J. Seiguer. Murcia, Spain: Ferrer.

ZORAB, P. (1972). "Spinal deformity in neurofibromatosis." *Lancet*, **2:** 823.

## *(k) Immunological*

AMOR, B. (1974). "HL-A antigen W27—a genetic link between ankylosing spondylitis and Reiter's syndrome?" *New Eng. J. Med.*, **290:** 572.

BREWERTON, D. A. (1975). "HL-A 27 and disease." *J. Bone Joint Surg.*, **57B:** 247.

BREWERTON, D. A. (1975). "HL-A 27 in Reiter's disease and psoriatic arthropathy." *Int. J. Dermatol.*, **14:** 39–40.

BREWERTON, D. A., CAFFREY, M., HART, F. D., JAMES, D. C. O., NICHOLLS, A. & STURROCK, R. D. (1973). "Ankylosing spondylitis and HL-A 27." *Lancet*, **1:** 904–907.

BREWERTON, D. A., CAFFREY, M. & NICHOLLS, A. (1973). "Acute anterior uveitis and HL-A 27." *Lancet*, **2**: 994.

BREWERTON, D. A., CAFFREY, M. & NICHOLLS, A. (1973). "Reiter's disease and HL-A 27." *Lancet*, **2**: 996.

BREWERTON, D. A., CAFFREY, M. & NICHOLLS, A. (1974). "HL-A 27 and arthropathies associated with ulcerative colitis and psoriasis." *Lancet*, **1**: 956–958.

BREWERTON, D. A. & JAMES, D. C. (1975). "The histocompatibility antigen (HL-A 27) and disease." *Seminars Arthritis Rheumatism*, **4**: 191–207.

CAFFREY, M. F. (1973). "Human lymphocyte antigen association in ankylosing spondylitis." *Nature*, **242**: 121.

CAFFREY, M. F. (1973). "Human lymphocyte antigens as a possible diagnostic aid in ankylosing spondylitis." *J. Clin. Path.*, **26**: 387.

CAIN, K. K. (1974). "Sciatica and herpes simplex." *J. Neurosurg.*, **41**: 518.

CALIN, A. (1974). "Ankylosing rheumatoid arthritis: ankylosing spondylitis and HL-A antigens." *Lancet*, **1**: 874.

DANIEREVICIUS, Z. (1973). "Role of the virus in collagen diseases." *J. Amer. Med. Assoc.*, **177**: 223.

DE DEUXCHAISNES, C., (1974). "Ankylosing spondylitis, sacroiliitis, regional enteritis and HL-A 27." *Lancet*, **1**: 1238–1239.

DICK, H. M. (1974). "Inheritance of ankylosing spondylitis and HL-A antigen W27." *Lancet*, **2**: 24–25.

DICK, H. M. (1975). "The association between HL-A antigens, ankylosing spondylitis and sacro-iliitis." *Tissue Antigens*, **5**: 26–32.

EVERALL, P. H. (1974). "Antibodies to candida albicans in hospital patients with and without spinal injury and in normal man and woman." *J. Clin. Path.*, **27**: 722–728.

FRANCK, W. A. (1974). "HL-A antigens and inflammatory bowel disease." *Lancet*, **1**: 817.

GERTZBEIN, S. D. (1975). "Autoimmunity in degenerative disc disease of the lumbar spine." *Orthop. Clin. Nth. Amer.*, **6**: 67–73.

GOWAN, G. A. (1973). "Ankylosing spondylitis and auto-immunity." *Postgrad. Med. J.*, **49**: 667–668.

GRAHAME, R., KENNEDY, L. & WOOD, P. H. N. (1975). "HL-A 27 and the diagnosis of back problems." *Rheumat. Rehab.*, **14**: 168–172.

GRANCK, W. A. (1974). "HL-A antigens and inflammatory bowel disease." *Lancet*, **1**: 817.

HERD, J. K. (1974). "HL-A W27, spondylitis and enteritis." *New Eng. J. Med.*, **291**: 680–681.

HOWELL, D. (1972). "IgG antiglobulin levels in patients with psoriatic arthropathy, ankylosing spondylitis and gout." *Ann. Rheumat. Dis.*, **31**: 129.

JAIN, K. K. (1974). "Sciatica and herpes simplex." *J. Neurosurg.*, **41**: 518.

JEZIERSKA, K. (1972). "Investigations of the role of immunological mechanisms in spinal muscular atrophy." *Polish Med. J.*, **11**: 1319–1325.

MASSELL, D. E. & SOLOMAN, R. (1935). "Viral back pain." *New Eng. J. Med.*, **123**: 399.

MEDSGER, T. A. (1964). "HL-A antigen 27 and psoriatic spondylitis." *Arth. Rheumat.*, **17**: 323.

MILLS, D. M. (1975). "HL-A antigens and sacroiliitis." *J. Amer. Med. Assoc.*, **231**: 268–270.

MORRIS, H. H. & PETERS, B. H. (1974). "Recurrent sciatica associated with herpes simplex." *J. Neurosurg.*, **41**: 97–99.

MORRIS, R. I., METZGER, A. L., BLUESTONE, R. & TERASAKI, P. I. (1974). "HL-A W27—a useful discrimination in the arthopathies of inflammatory bowel disease." *New Eng. J. Med.*, **290**: 1117–1119.

MYERS, B. W. (1975). "Ankylosing spondylitis in a black woman. Association with HL-A W27." *J. Amer. Med. Assoc.*, **231**: 278–279.

NATVIG, J. B. (1974). "Studies on the immunopathology of rheumatoid inflammatory joint tissue." *Acta Path. Microbiol. Scand.*, *Suppl.* **248**: 145–151.

RUSSELL, A. S. (1974). "HL-A (transplantation) antigens in ankylosing spondylitis and Crohn's disease." *J. Rheumatol.*, **1**: 203–209.

RUSSELL, A. S. (1975). "Transplantation antigens in Crohn's disease: linkage of associated ankylosing spondylitis with HL-A W27." *Amer. J. Digest. Dis.*, **20**: 359–361.

SACHS, J. A. (1975). "Ankylosing spondylitis and the major histocompatibility system." *Tissue Antigens*, **5**: 120–127.

SCHLOSSTEIN, L., TERASKI, P. I., BLUESTONE, R. & PEARSON, C. M.

(1975). "High association of an HL-A antigen W27." *New Eng. J. Med.*, **288**: 704–706.

SEIGNALET, J. (1974). "HL-A antigens and arthropathies in psoriasis." *Lancet*, **1**: 1350.

SHERR, C. J. & GOLDBERG, B. (1973). "Antibodies to a precursor of human collagen." *Science*, **180**: 1190–1191.

SMITH, C. (1974). "Some implications of HL-A and disease associations." *Lancet*, **1**: 450.

STURROCK, R. D. (1975). "Raised levels of complement inactivation products in ankylosing spondylitis." *Ann. Rheumat. Dis.*, **34**: 202–203.

VAN DER LINDEN, J. M. (1975). "HL-A 27 and ankylosing spondylitis." *Lancet*, **1**: 520.

VEYS, E. M. (1974). "HL-A and infective sacroiliitis." *Lancet*, **2**: 349.

WILSON, D. (1946). "Viral back pain." *Ann. Rheumat. Dis.*, **5**: 211.

YU, D. T. (1974). "Cellular immunological aspects of rheumatoid arthritis." *Arth. Rheumat.*, **4**: 25–52.

# 3

# PSYCHOLOGICAL AND PSYCHIATRIC ASPECTS

## (a) General

CARTER, A. B. (1972). "A physician's view of hysteria." *Lancet*, **2:** 1241–1243.

DIXON, A. ST. J. (1976). "Diagnosis of low back pain—sorting the complainers." In *The Lumbar Spine and Back Pain*. pp. 77–92. Ed. by M. I. V. Jayson. London; Sector Publishing.

FORREST, A. J. & WOLKIND, S. N. (1974). "Masked depression in men with low back pain." *Rheumat. Rehab.*, **13:** 148–153.

GENTRY, W. D., SHOWS, W. D. & THOMAS, M. (1974). "Chronic low back pain: a psychological profile." *Psychosomatics*, **15:** 174–177.

KOLB, L. C. (1952). "Pain as a psychiatric problem." *Lancet*, **72:**50–54.

LASCELLES, B. T. (1974). "Plasma control in psychiatric and neurologic patients with pain." *Brain*, **97:** 533–538.

LEVINE, M. E. (1971). "Depression, back pain and disc protrusions: relationships and psychophysiological mechanisms." *Dis. Nerv. Syst.*, **32:** 41–45.

LEVIT, H. I. (1973). "Depression, back pain and hypnotherapy." *Amer. J. Clin. Hypn.*, **15:** 266–269.

MARUTA, T., SWANSON, D. & SWANSON, W. M. (1976). "Low back pain patients in the psychiatric population." *Mayo Clin. Proc.*, **51:** 57–71.

MEDSGER, A. R. & ROBINSON, H. (1972). "A comparative study of divorce in rheumatoid arthritis and other rheumatic diseases." *J. Chron. Dis.*, **25:** 269–275.

MELZACK, R. & WALL, P. D. (1970). "Psychophysiology of pain." *Internat. Anesthesiol.*, **8:** 3–34.

MERSKEY, H. (1965). "The characteristics of persistent pain in psychological illness." *J. Psychosom. Res.*, **9:** 291–298.

MERSKEY, H. (1968). "Psychological aspects of pain." *Postgrad. Med. J.*, **44:** 297–306.

MERSKEY, H. (1974). "Psychological aspects of pain." *Curr. Med. Res. Opin.*, **2:** 515–520.

MERSKEY, H. & SPEAR, F. G. (1967). *Pain: Psychological and Psychiatric Aspects.* London; Baillière, Tindall and Cassell.

METCALFE, M. & GOLDMAN, C. (1965). "Validation of an inventory for measuring depression." *Brit. J. Psychiat.*, **111:** 240–247.

MINC, S. (1968). "Psychological aspects of backache." *Med. J. Aust.*, **1:** 964–965.

NAGI, S. Z., RILEY, L. E. & NEWBY, L. G. (1973). "A social epidemiology of back pain in the general population." *J. Chron. Dis.*, **26:** 769–779.

PHILIPS, E. L. (1974). "Some psychological problems associated with orthopaedic complaints." *Curr. Pract. Orthop. Surg.*, **2:** 165–176.

TIBBETTS, R. W. & DONOVAN, W. M. (1974). "The orthopaedic surgeon and the psychiatrist." *J. Bone Joint Surg.*, **56:** 200.

VIOLON, A. (1973). "Pain as a disease: psychological investigation." *Headache*, **13:** 25–28.

WHITE, A. W. M. (1966). "The compensation back." *Appl. Therap.*, **8:** 871–874.

WILFLING, F. J., KLONOFF, H. & KOKAN, P. (1973). "Psychological, demographic and orthopaedic factors associated with prediction of outcome of spinal fusion." *Clin. Orthop.*, **90:** 153–160.

WILTSE, L. L. & ROCCHIO, P. D. (1975). "Pre-operative psychological tests as predictors of success of chemonucleolysis in the treatment of the low back syndrome." *J. Bone Joint Surg.*, **57A:** 478–483.

WOLKIND, S. N. (1972). "Low back pain: a psychiatric investigation." *Postgrad. Med. J.*, **48:** 76–79.

WOLKIND, S. N. (1974). "Psychiatric aspects of low back pain." *Physiotherapy*, **60:** 75–77.

WYKE, B. D. (1960). *Neurological Aspects of Hypnosis.* London; Dental and Medical Society for the Study of Hypnosis.

WYKE, B. D. (1972). "Pain and hypnosis." *New Scientist*, **56:** 585–586.

## (b) Personality Correlates

BLACK, P. (1970). *Physiological Correlates of Emotion*. New York; Academic Press.

CARR, J. E., BROWNSBERGER, C. M. & RUTHERFORD, R. S. (1966). "Characteristics of symptom matched psychogenic and real pain patients in the MMPI." *Proc. 74th Annual Convention Amer. Psychol. Assoc.*: 215–216.

DEVINE, R. & MERSKEY, H. (1966). "The description of pain in psychiatric and general medical patients." *J. Psychosomat. Res.*, **9:** 311–316.

ELLISON, K. (1975). "Pain tolerance, arousal and personality relationships of athletes and nonathletes." *Res. Quart. Amer. Assoc. Health Phys. Educ.*, **45:** 250–255.

FREEMAN, C., CALYSON, D. & LOUKS, J. (1976). "The use of the MMPI with chronic low back pain patients with a mixed diagnosis." *J. Clin. Psychol.*, **32:** 532–536.

GANT, W. H. (1973). "Pain, conditioning and schizokinesis." *Cond. Reflex.*, **8:** 63–66.

GREGORY, R. L. (1974). "Behaviourism and pain." *Perception*, **3:** 121.

HALLAUER, D. S. (1972). "Illness behaviour—an experimental investigation." *J. Chron. Dis.*, **25:** 599–610.

HANVICK, L. J. (1951). "MMPI profiles in patients with low-back pain." *J. Consult. Clin. Psychol.*, **5:** 350–353.

LINDFORD, R. (1970). "Attitudes and emotional reactions to physical illness." *St. Barts. Hosp. J.*, **74:** 259–263.

MUMFORD, J. M. (1973). "Personality, pain perception and pain tolerance." *Brit. J. Psychol.*, **64:** 105–107.

PETRIE, A. (1967). *Individuality in Pain and Suffering*. Chicago: University of Chicago Press.

PICHOT, P., PERSE, J. & LEKOUS, M. O. (1972). "The personality of subjects presenting with functional back pain: the value of the MMPI inventory." *Rev. Psychol. Appliqué*, **22:** 145–172.

ROSILLO, R. H. & FOGEL, M. L. (1973). "Pain: effects and progress in physical rehabilitation." *J. Psychosomat. Res.*, **17:** 21–28.

SCHILD, R. (1973). "Medico-psychological studies of patients with rheumatic diseases." *Psyche*, **27:** 50–68.

SHAFFER, J. W., NUSSBAUM, K. & LITTLE, J. M. (1972). "Profiles of disability insurance claimants." *Amer. J. Psychiat.*, **129:** 403–407.

SINGH, S. P. (1975). "Sex and self: the spinal cord-injured." *Rehab. Lit.*, **36:** 2–10.

STERNBACH, R. A. (1973). "Traits of pain patients: the low-back 'loser'." *Psychosomatics*, **14:** 226–229.

STERNBACH, R. A. (1974). *Pain patients: Traits and Treatment.* New York; Academic Press.

STERNBACH, R. A., MURPHY, R. W., AKESON, W. H. & WOLF, S. R. (1973). "Chronic low back pain—the 'low back loser'." *Postgrad. Med.*, **53:** 135–138.

STERNBACH, R. A., WOLF, S. R., MURPHY, R. W. & AKESON, W. H. (1974). "Aspects of chronic low back pain." *Psychosomatics*, **14:** 52–56.

TAYLOR, P. J. (1968). "Personal factors associated with sickness absence." *Brit. J. Indust. Med.*, **25:** 106–118.

VON KNORRING, L. (1974). "Average evoked responses, pain measures and personality variables in patients with depressive disorders." *Acta Psychiat. Scand., Suppl.* **255:** 99–108.

WALTERS, A. (1966). "Emotion and low back pain." *Appl. Therap.* **8:** 868–871.

WEISENBERG, M. (1975). "Pain: anxiety and attitudes in black, white and Puerto Rican patients." *Psychosomat. Med.*, **37:** 123–135.

WESTRIN, C. G. (1974). "The reliability of auto-anamesis. A study of statements regarding low back trouble." *Scand. J. Soc. Med.*, **2:** 23–35.

WESTRIN, C. G., HIRSCH, C. & LINDEGARD, B. (1972). "The personality of the back patient." *Clin. Orthop.*, **87:** 209–216.

WILFLING, F. J., KLONOFF, H. & KAKAN, P. (1973). "Psychological, demographic and orthopaedic factors associated with prediction of outcome of spinal fusion." *Clin. Orthop.*, **90:** 153–160.

WILSON, P. & NASHOLD, J. (1970). "Pain and emotion." *Postgrad. Med.*, **47:** 183.

### (c) Psychosomatic Aspects

AITKEN, R. C. B. (1972). "Methodology of research in psychosomatic medicine." *Brit. Med. J.*, **4:** 285–287.

BAILEY, C. A. & DAVIDSON, P. O. (1976). "The language of pain: intensity." *Pain*, **2:** 319.

BEALS, R. K. & HICKMAN, N. W. (1972). "Industrial injuries of the back and extremities." *J. Bone Joint Surg.*, **54**: 1593–1611.

BOND, M. R. (1972). "Psychological aspects of pain." In *Scientific Foundations of Neurology*. Ed. by M. Critchley, J. L. O'Leary and B. Jennett. London; Heinemann. pp. 165–169.

CARTER, A. B. (1972). "A physician's view of hysteria." *Lancet*, **2**: 1241–1243.

COLLETTE, J. & LUDWIG, E. G. (1968). "Low back disorders: an examination of the stereotype." *Indust. Med. Surg.*, **37**: 685.

DELIUS, L. (1972). "Psychosomatic aspects of treating pain: the internist's view point." In *Pain: Basic Principles, Pharmacology, Therapy*. pp. 161–164. Ed. by R. Janzen, W. D. Keidel, A. Herz and C. Steichele. Stuttgart; Thieme.

DEVINE, R. & MERSKEY, H. (1965). "The description of pain in psychiatric and general medical patients." *J. Psychosomat. Res.*, **9**: 311.

DRASPA, L. J. (1961). "A behavioural investigation into muscular pain." *Psych. Neurol., Basel*, **141**: 367–380.

DRASPA, L. J. (1970). "The treatment of muscular pain resulting from covert behaviour." *Physiotherapy*, **56**: 548.

DUPERTIUS, C. W. & TANNER, J. M. (1950). "The pose of the subject for photogrammetric anthropometry with especial reference to somato-typing." *Amer. J. Phys. Anthrop.*, **8**: 27–48.

EASTWOOD, D. (1974). "Physiotherapy and psychotherapy." *Lancet*, **1**: 94.

ELITHORN, A., PIERCY, M. F. & CROSSKEY, M. A. (1955). "Prefrontal leucotomy and the anticipation of pain." *J. Neurol. Neurosurg. Psychiat.*, **18**: 34–43.

FORDYCE, W. E. (1968). "Some implications of learning in problems of chronic pain." *J. Chron. Dis.*, **21**: 179–190.

FORDYCE, W. E. (1973). "An operant conditioning method for managing chronic pain." *Postgrad. Med.*, **53**: 123–128.

FORDYCE, W. E., FOWLER, R. S., LEHMANN, J. F., DELATOUR, B. J., SAND, P. L. & TREISCHMANN, R. B. (1973). "Operant conditioning in the treatment of chronic pain." *Arch. Phys. Med. Rehab.*, **54**: 399–408.

FORREST, A. J. & WOLKIND, S. N. (1974). "Masked depression in men with low back pain." *Rheumatol. Rehabil.*, **13**: 148–153.

GAEBELEIN, J. (1974). "Effects of an external cue on psychophysiological reactions to a noxious event." *Psychophysiology*, **11**: 315–320.

GORMAN, W. (1974). "Whiplash—a neuropsychiatric injury." *Ariz. Med.*, **31**: 414–416.

HAMMER, H. M. (1973). "Psychogenic pain." *J. Med. Soc. New Jersey*, **70**: 757–759.

HARDY, J. D., WOLFF, H. G. & GOODELL, H. (1952). *Pain Sensations and Reactions*. Baltimore; Williams and Wilkins.

HILGARD, E. R. (1975). "The alleviation of pain by hypnosis." *Pain*, **1**: 213.

HILGARD, E. R. & HILGARD, J. R. (1975). *Hypnosis in the Relief of Pain*. Los Altos, California; Kaufmann.

HORDER, J. (1974). "Psychosomatic pain." *Physiotherapy*, **60**: 137–140.

JACOBS, S. (Ed.). (1973). "Backache: a multidisciplinary approach to its treatment." *Psychiatry in Medicine*, **4**: 221–230.

JOHNSON, E. W. & STEINHILBER, R. M. (1972). "Hysterical backache." *Amer. Assoc. Orthop. Surg., Instruct. Course Lectures*, **21**: 98–101.

KATZ, J. L., WEINER, H. & YU, T. F. (1975). "Psychobiological variables in the onset and recurrence of gouty arthritis." *J. Chron. Dis.*, **28**: 51–62.

KELLGREN, J. H. (1940). "Somatic simulating visceral pain." *Clinical Science*, **4**: 303.

KELMAN, H. C. (1975). "Was deception justified—and was it necessary? Comments on 'self-control techniques as an alternative to pain medication'." *J. Abnorm. Psychol.*, **84**: 172–174.

KOLB, L. C. (1952). "Pain as a psychiatric problem." *Lancet*, **2**: 50.

LADER, M. H. & WING, L. (1966). "Physiological measures, sedative drugs and morbid anxiety." *Institute of Psychiatry, Maudesley Monographs*, **No. 14**: 49–54.

LANGEN, D. (1972). "Psychosomatic aspects in the treatment of pain." In *Pain: Basic Principles, Pharmacology, Therapy*. pp. 164–168. Ed. by R. Janzen, W. D. Keidel, A. Herz and C. Steichele. Stuttgart; Thieme.

LANGEN, E. & SPOERRI, T. (Eds.). (1968). *Hypnosis and Pain*. Basel; Karger.

LASSNER, J. (Ed.). (1967). *Hypnosis and Psychosomatic Medicine*. Berlin; Springer Verlag.

Luck, J. V. (1964). "Psychosomatic problems in military ortho-paedic surgery." *J. Bone Joint Surg.*, **28**: 213–228.

Meruta, T., Swanson, D. W. & Swanson, W. M. (1976). "Pain as a psychiatric symptom: comparison between low back pain and depression." *Psychosomatics*, **17**: 123.

Paul, L. (1950). "Psychosomatic aspects of low back pain." *Psychosomatic Med.*, **12**: 116–123.

Rosenbaum, A. H. & Steinhilber, R. M. (1973). "Psychosomatic disorders: combined therapeutic approach." *Minn. Med.*, **56**: 677–679.

Rubin, D. (1970). "The 'No!'—or the 'Yes' and the 'How'—of sex for patients with neck, back and radicular syndromes." *California Med.*, **113**: 12–15.

Rudd, J. L. & Margolin, R. J. (1966). "A study of back cases in an out-patient clinic." *J. Assoc. Phys. Med. Rehab.*, **20**: 20.

Sargant, W. (1957). *Battle for the Mind*. London; Heinemann.

Sargent, M. M. (1946). "Psychosomatic backache." *New Eng. J. Med.*, **234**: 427–430.

Sarno, J. E. (1974). "Psychogenic backache: the missing dimen-sion." *J. Fam. Pract.*, **1**: 8–12.

Schild, R. (1971). "Medico-psychological criteria in rheumatol-ogy." *Zeit. Rheumaforsch.*, **30**: 129.

Schild, R. (1972). "Medico-psychological studies of patients with rheumatic diseases." *Psyche*, **26**: 929–938.

Spilken, A. Z. & Jacobs, M. A. (1971). "Prediction of illness behaviour from measures of life crisis, manifest distress and maladaptive coping." *Psychosomat. Med.*, **33**: 251–264.

Sternbach, R. A., Wolf, S. R., Murphy, R. W. & Akerson, W. M. (1973). "Aspects of chronic low back pain." *Psychoso-matics*, **14**: 52–56.

Sternbach, R. A., Wolf, S. R., Murphy, R. W. & Akerson, W. M. (1973). "Traits of pain patients: the low back 'loser'." *Psychosomatics*, **14**: 226–229.

Wolkind, S. N. & Forrest, A. J. (1972). "Low back pain: a psychiatric investigation." *Postgrad. Med. J.*, **48**: 76–79.

## (d) Pain Thresholds and Pain Tolerance

ANDY, O. J. (1975). "Development of pain appreciation after thalamotomy." *Confin. Neurol.*, **37**: 100–112.

BARBER, T. X. (1963). "The effects of 'hypnosis' on pain." *Psychosomat. Med.*, **25**: 303–333.

BEECHER, H. K. (1953). "A method for quantifying the intensity of pain." *Science*, **118**: 322.

BEECHER, H. K. (1959). *The Measurement of Subjective Responses: Quantitative Effects of Drugs*. New York; Oxford University Press.

BEECHER, H. K. (1968). "The measurement of pain in man." In *Pain*. p. 207. Ed. by A. Soulairac, J. Cahn and N. Charpentier. New York; Academic Press.

BENSON, T. B. & COPP, E. P. (1974). "The effects of therapeutic forms of heat and ice on the pain threshold of the normal shoulder." *Rheumatol. Rehab.*, **13**: 101–104.

BONICA, J. J. (Ed.). (1974). *International Symposium on Pain*. New York; Raven Press.

BONICA, J. J. & ALBE-FESSARD, D. (Eds.). (1976). *Advances in Pain Research and Therapy*. New York; Raven Press.

BUZZELLI, G., VOEGELIN, M. R., PROCACCI, P. & BOZZA, G. (1968). "Modification of the cutaneous pain threshold during the menstrual cycle." *Bull. Soc. Ital. Biol. Sper.*, **44**: 235.

CHAPMAN, C. R. & FEATHER, B. W. (1973). "Effects of diazepam on human pain tolerance and pain sensitivity." *Psychosomat. Med.*, **35**: 330.

CHAPMAN, W. P. (1944). "Measurements of pain sensitivity in normal control subjects and in psychoneurotic patients." *Psychosomat. Med.*, **6**: 252–257.

CLARKE, W. C. (1974). "Effects of suggestion on d' and Cx for pain detection and pain tolerance." *J. Abnorm. Psychol.*, **83**: 364–372.

CLARKE, W. C. (1974). "Pain sensitivity and the report of pain: an introduction to sensory decision theory." *Anesthesiol.*, **40**: 272–287.

EDELSTEIN, E. L. (1974). "Experience and mastery of pain." *Israel Ann. Psychiat.*, **12**: 216–226.

ENGEL, B. J. (1959). "Some physiological correlates of hunger and pain." *J. Exp. Psychol.*, **57**: 389–396.

GAMMON, G. D. & STAFF, I. (1941). "Studies on relief of pain by counter-irritation." *J. Clin. Invest.*, **20**: 13.

GANTT, W. H. (1973). "Pain, conditioning and schizokinesis." *Cond. Reflex.*, **8**: 63–66.

GANTT, W. H. (1973). "Objectivity and subjectivity: pain." *Cond. Reflex.*, **8**: 187–192.

GELFAND, S. (1964). "The relationship of experimental pain tolerance to pain threshold." *Canad. J. Psychol.*, **18**: 36.

GLOVER, J. R. (1960). "Back pain and hyperaesthesia." *Lancet*, **1**: 1165.

GLYNN, C. J. & LLOYD, J. W. (1976). "The diurnal variation in perception of pain." *Proc. Roy. Soc. Lond.*, **69B**: 369.

HARDY, J. D., WOLFF, H. G. & GOODELL, H. (1943). "The pain threshold in man." *Res. Pub. Assoc. Nerv. Ment. Dis.*, **23**: 1–15.

HARDY, J. D., WOLFF, H. G. & GOODELL, H. (1952). *Pain Sensations and Reactions*. Baltimore; Williams and Wilkins.

HILGARD, E. R. (1975). "Pain and dissociation in the cold pressor test: a study of hypnotic analgesia with 'hidden reports' through automatic key pressing and automatic talking." *J. Abnorm. Psych.*, **84**: 280–289.

HOLLANDER, E. M. D. (1939). "A clinical gauge for sensitivity to pain." *J. Lab. Med.*, **24**: 537–538.

LEAVITT, F., GARRON, D. C., WHISLER, W. W. & SHEINKOP, M. B. (1978). "Affective and sensory dimensions of back pain." *Pain*, **4**: 273.

LIBMAN, E. (1934). "Observations on individual sensitiveness to pain with special reference to abdominal disorders." *J. Amer. Med. Assoc.*, **102**: 335–341.

MELZACK, R. (1973). *The Puzzle of Pain*. New York; Basic Books.

MELZACK, R. & SCOTT, T. H. (1957). "The effect of early experience on the response to pain." *J. Comp. Physiol. Psychol.*, **50**: 155.

MICHELSEN, J. J. (1943). "Subjective disturbances of the sense of pain from lesions of the cerebral cortex." *Res. Pub. Assoc. Nerv. Ment. Dis.*, **23**: 86–89.

SHERMAN, E. D. (1943). "Sensitivity to pain (with an analysis of 450 cases)." *Canad. Med. Assoc. J.*, **48**: 437–441.

SIMMEL, N. L. (1959). "Phantoms, phantom pain and 'denial'." *Amer. J. Psychotherap.*, **13**: 603–613.

STEINDLER, A. (1959). *Lectures on the Interpretation of Pain in Orthopaedic Practice*. Springfield, Illinois; Thomas.

STERNBACH, R. A. (1963). "Congenital insensitivity to pain: a critique." *Psychol. Bull.*, **60**: 252–264.

STERNBACH, R. A. (1968). *Pain: A Psychophysiological Analysis*. New York: Academic Press.

STERNBACH, R. A. (1974). "Psychological aspects of pain and the selection of patients." *Clin. Neurosurg.*, **21**: 323–333.

STERNBACH, R. A. & TURSKY, B. (1964). "Ethnic differences among housewives in psychophysical and skin potential responses to electric shock." *Psychophysiology*, **1**: 241–246.

VON KNORRING, L. (1974). "An intraindividual comparison of pain measures—average evoked responses and clinical ratings during depression and after recovery." *Acta Psychiat. Scand., Suppl.* **225**: 109–120.

VON KNORRING, L. (1974). "Experimentally induced pain in patients with depressive disorders." *Acta Psychiat. Scand., Suppl.* **255**: 121–133.

WEST, L. J., NIELL, K. S. & HARDY, J. D. (1952). "Effects of hypnotic suggestion on pain perception and galvanic skin response." *Arch. Neurol. Psychiat.*, **68**: 549–560.

WOLFF, B. B. & JARVIC, M. E. (1963). "Variations in cutaneous and deep somatic pain sensitivity." *Canad. J. Psychol.*, **17**: 37–44.

WOLFF, H. G. & GOODELL, H. (1943). "The relation of attitude and suggestion to the perception of and reaction to pain." *Res. Pub. Assoc. Nerv. Ment. Dis.*, **23**: 434–448.

WOLFF, H. G. & WOLF, S. (1948). *Pain*. Springfield, Ill.; Thomas.

WOODROW, K. M., FRIEDMAN, G. D., SIEGELAUB, A. B. & COLLEN, M. F. (1972). "Pain tolerance: differences according to age, sex and race." *Psychosomat. Med.*, **34**: 548.

WYKE, B. D. (1972). "Pain and hypnosis." *New Scientist*, **56**: 585.

# 4
## SOCIOLOGICAL, ERGONOMIC AND MEDICO-LEGAL ASPECTS

*(a) General*

BENN, R. T. & WOOD, P. H. N. (1975). "Pain in the back: an attempt to estimate the size of the problem." *Rheumatol. Rehab.*, **14**: 121–128.

BROOKS, R. G. & BUCHANAN, W. W. (1970). "Economic aspects of arthritis and rheumatism." *Health Bull.*, **28**: 42–43.

DEPARTMENT OF HEALTH AND SOCIAL SECURITY (1979). *Report of the Working Group on Back Pain.* London; Her Majesty's Stationery Office.

DUTHIE, F. F. R. & ANDERSON, J. A. D. (1962). "Social and economic effects of rheumatic disease." *Arch. Environ. Hlth.*, **5**: 511–518.

DUTHIE, J. J. R., THOMPSON, M., WEIR, M. M. & FLETCHER, W. B. (1955). "Medical and social aspects of the treatment of rheumatic arthritis—with special reference to factors affecting prognosis." *Ann. Rheum. Dis.*, **14**: 133–148.

HOOK, E. K. (1972). "Criteria for return to work—low back pain." *Indust. Med.*, **41**: 32–34.

ISHERWOOD, P. (1970). "Ergonomics and the disabled." *Int. Rehab. Rev.*, **21**: 9–11.

KAHN, M. F. (1973). "Medicological aspects of backache." *Rev. Rheum. Mal. Osteo.*, **Dec.**: 733–739.

L'EPEE, J. (1969). "Medico-legal interest in tests of lumbar spine mobility." *Soc. Legal Med.*, **2**: 68–69.

NOTKIN, K. (1951). "Vocational rehabilitation and public health." *Amer. J. Pub. Hlth.*, **41**: 1096–1100.

PARSONS, T. (1951). *The Social System.* Glencoe, Illinois; Free Press.

SPARUP, K. H. (1969). "A sociomedical evaluation of back insufficiency." *Scand. J. Rehab. Med.*, **1**: 74–79.

STEVENSON, M. (1970). "Back injury and depression—a medico-legal problem." *Med. J. Aust.*, **1**: 1300.

## (b) Relations to Social Class and Occupation

ABERG, U. (1962). "Force-time relationship with some types of manual work." *Ergonomics*, **5**: 71–73.

ALLEN, M. L. & LINDEN, M. C. (1950). "Significant roentgen findings in routine pre-employment examination of the lumbosacral spine." *Amer. J. Surg.*, **80**: 762–766.

ANDERSON, J. A. D. (1976). "Back pain in industry." In *The Lumbar Spine and Back Pain*. pp. 29–46. Ed. by M. I. V. Jayson. London; Sector Publishing.

ANDERSON, J. A. D. & DUTHIE, J. J. R. (1963). "Rheumatic complaints in dockyard workers." *Ann. Rheum. Dis.*, **22**: 401–409.

ANDERSON, J. A. D., DUTHIE, J. J. R. & MOODY, B. P. (1962). "Social and economic effects of rheumatic diseases in a mining population." *Ann. Rheum. Dis.*, **21**: 342–351.

ARCHER, I. A., MOLL, P. & WRIGHT, V. (1974). "Chest and spinal mobility in physiotherapists: an objective clinical study." *Physiotherapy*, **60**: 37–39.

ARMY DIRECTORATE BULLETIN (1959). "The soldier's back." *2nd Series, No. 10. War Office A.M.D. 7. W.O. Code No. 12389.*

ARNDT, R. D. (1975). "Cervical thoracic transverse process fracture: further observations on the seatbelt syndrome." *J. Trauma*, **15**: 600–602.

AYOUB, M. M. (1973). "Workplace design and posture." *Human Factors*, **15**: 265–268.

BAGCHI, A. K. (1973). "Cervical spondylosis as an ecological problem." *J. Indian Med. Assoc.*, **60**: 382–383.

BARKER, M. E. (1977). "Pain in the back and leg: a general practice survey." *Rheumat. Rehab.*, **16**: 37–45.

BILLENKAMP, G. (1972). "Body loading and spondylosis deformans." *Forschr. Roentgenol.*, **116**: 211–216.

BOCK, A. V., VANCAULERT, C., DILL, D. B., FÖLLING, A. & HURXTHAL, L. M. (1928). "Studies in muscular activity. III. Dynamic changes occurring in man at work." *J. Physiol.*, **66**: 136–161.

BROOKE, J. D. (1967). "Extraversion, physical performances and pain perception in physical education students." *Research in Physical Education*, **1**: 23–30.

BROWN, J. R. (1973). "Lifting as an industrial hazard." *Amer. Industr. Hyg. Assoc. J.*, **34**: 292–297.

BROWN, J. R. (1975). "Factors contributing to the development of low back pain in industrial workers." *Amer. Industr. Hyg. Assoc. J.*, **36**: 26–31.

BURANDT, U., & GRANDJEAN, E. (1963). "Sitting habits of office employees." *Ergonomics*, **6**: 217–228.

BURANDT, U. & GRANDJEAN, E. (1969). "Studies on the sitting habits of office workers and on the influence of various sitting profiles." *Ergonomics*, **12**: 338–347.

BURY, M. R. & WOOD, P. H. N. (1978). "Sociological perspectives in research on disablement." *Int. Rehab. Med.*, **1**: 24–32.

CANCELMO, J. J. (1972). "Clay-shoveler's fracture: a helpful diagnostic sign." *Amer. J. Roentgenol.*, **115**: 540–543.

CAPLAN, P. S. (1962). "Degenerative joint disease of the lumbar spine in coal miners; a clinical and X-ray study." *Arth. Rheum.*, **5**: 288.

CAPLAN, P. S., FREEDMAN, L. M. J. & CONNELLY, T. P. (1966). "Degenerative joint disease of the lumbar spine in coal miners: a clinical and X-ray study." *Arth. Rheum.*, **9**: 693–702.

CATHCART, C. P. (1935). "The physique of man in industry." *M.R.C. Industrial Health Research Board, Report No.* **71**: 1.

CATHCART, E. P., BEDALE, E. M., BLAIR, C., MACLEOD, K. & WEATHERHEAD, E. (1927). "The physique of women in industry: a contribution towards the determination of the optimum load." *Industrial Fatigue Research Board, Report No.* **44**: 1–14.

CECCHETTI, E. (1963). "Lumbar pain in a group of professional drivers." *Difesa Sociale*, **24**: 82–94.

CHAFFIN, D. B. (1974). "Human strength capability and low-back pain." *J. Occup. Med.*, **16**: 248–254.

CHAFFIN, D. B. & PARK, K. Y. (1973). "A longitudinal study of low-back pain as associated with occupational weight lifting factors." *Amer. Industr. Hyg. Assoc. J.*, **34**: 513–525.

CHOOK, E. K. (1972). "Criteria for return to work—low back pain." *Ind. Med. Surg. J.*, **41**: 32–34.

CHRIST, W. & DUPUIS, H. (1968). "Studies on the possibility of physical damage to the spinal area in tractor operators. Report on the second mass examination of 137 young farmers." *Med. Welt.*, **37**: 1967–1972.

CHUBB, R. M., DETRICK, W. R. & SHANNON, R. H. (1965).

"Compression fractures of the spine during U.S.A.F. ejections." *Rep. Life Sciences Division, Norton A.F.B., California.* p. 1.

CICCONE, R. & RACHMANN, R. M. (1948). "The mechanism of injury and the distribution of three thousand fractures and dislocations caused by parachute jumping." *J. Bone Joint Surg.*, **30A:** 77–97.

CROWDEN, G. P. (1928). "The physiological cost of the muscular movements involved in barrow work." *Industrial Fatigue Research Board Report No.* **50:** 1.

CUST, G., PEARSON, J. C. G. & MAIR, A. (1972). "The prevalence of low back pain in nurses." *Int. Nursing Rev.*, **19:** 169–179.

DAVIS, P. R. & TROUP, J. D. G. (1966). "Effects on the trunk of erecting pit props at different working heights." *Ergonomics*, **9:** 475–484.

DEMPSTER, W. T. (1955). "Space requirements of the seated operator." *W.A.D.C. Technical Report*, pp. 55–159.

DEMPSTER, W. T. (1959). "The anthropometry of the manual work space of the seated subject." *Amer. J. Phys. Anthrop.*, **17:** 289–317.

DEPARTMENT OF EMPLOYMENT (1971). "Research on absenteeism." *Dept. Employment Gazette*, **July,** 611–612.

DUNCAN, J. & FERGUSON, D. (1974). "Keyboard operating posture and symptoms in operating." *Ergonomics*, **17:** 651–662.

FANGER, P. O. (1974). "Physical parameters of living and working quarters of man." *Progr. Biometeorol.*, **1:** 129–137; 619–620.

FERGUSON, D. (1970). "Strain injuries in hospital employees." *Med. J. Aust.*, **1:** 376.

FERGUSON, D. (1971). "An Australian study of telegraphist's cramp." *Brit. J. Industr. Med.*, **28:** 280–285.

FERGUSON, R. J. (1974). "Low back pain in college football linemen." *J. Bone Joint Surg.*, **56A:** 1300.

FLAX, H. J. (1970). "The chronic low back syndrome." *Boletin Associación Medica de Puerto Rico*, **62:** 117–119.

FREDERIK, W. S. (1959). "Human energy in manual lifting." *Modern Materials Handling*, **14:** 74–76.

FRENKIL, J. (1959). "Some considerations in the employment of arthritics in industry." *Arch. Industr. Hlth.*, **20:** 359.

GISSANE, W. (1973). "Traveller's ankle and traveller's back." *Brit. Med. J.*, **4:** 551–552.

GLOVER, J. R. & DAVIES, B. T. (1961). "Manual handling and lifting: an introduction into a 6,000 employee works." *J. Indust. Nurses*, **13:** 289–300.

GOODSELL, J. O. (1967). "Correlation of ruptured lumbar disk with occupation." *Clin. Orthop.*, **50:** 225–229.

GRIEVE, G. P. (1958). "Manual lifting and handling." *Physiotherapy*, **44:** 341–344.

HALL, M. A. W. (1972). "Back pain and car seat comfort." *Appl. Ergon.*, **3:** 82–91.

HARLEY, W. J. (1972). "Lost time back injuries: their relationship to heavy work and preplacement injuries." *J. Occup. Med.*, **14:** 611–614.

HIMBURY, S. (1962). "Industry gets lessons in lifting methods." *Austr. Fact.*, **16:** 33–38.

HOME OFFICE. (1937). *"Weight Lifting by Industrial Workers. Home Office Safety Pamphlet, Number* **16:** London; Her Majesty's Stationery Office.

HUNTER, G. M. (1973). "Medical and social problems of two elderly women." *Brit. Med. J.*, **4:** 224–225.

JOKL, E. (1912). "Weight lifting records." *Amer. Correct. Ther. J.*, **26:** 112.

JONES, D. F. (1971). "Back strains: the state of the art." *J. Safety Res.*, **3:** 28–34.

JONES, D. F. (1972). "Back injury research: a common thread." *Amer. Industr. Hyg. Assoc. J.*, **33:** 596–602.

JØRGENSEN, K. (1970). "Back muscle strength and body weight as limiting factors for working in the standing slightly-stooped position." *Scand. J. Rehab. Med.*, **2:** 149–153.

JØRGENSEN, K. & POULSEN, E. (1974). "Physiological problems in repetitive lifting with special reference to tolerance limits to maximum lifting frequency." *Ergonomics*, **17:** 31–39.

KARVONEN, M. J. & RONNHOLM, N. (1941). "E.M.G.s and energy expenditure studies of rhythmic and paced lifting work." *Ann. Acad. Sci. Fenn. A. V. Med.*, **106:** 19.

KELSEY, J. L. (1975). "An epidemiological study of the relationship between occupations and acute herniated lumbar intervertebral discs." *J. Epidemiology*. **4:** 197–205.

KIDOKORO, Y. (1968). "Study on changes in shape of the lower lumbar intervertebral foramina in loading and unloading conditions." *J. Jap Orthop. Assoc.*, **42:** 217–231.

KRAUS, H. & WEBER, S. (1962). "Back pain and tension syndromes in a sedentary profession." *Arch. Environ. Hlth.*, **4**: 38–44.

KROEMER, K. H. & EBERHARD, J. (1969). "Push forces exerted in 65 common working positions." *Aerospace Med. Res. Lab., Wright Patterson, AFB. Rep. No. AMRL. TR.* **143**: 1.

KROEMER, K. H. & EBERHARD, J. (1973). "Horizontal push and pull forces exerted when standing in working positions on various surfaces." *Appl. Ergonom.*, **74**: 94–102.

KROEMER, K. H. & ROBERTSON, D. E. (1971). "Horizontal static forces exerted by men standing in common working conditions." *Aerospace Med. Res. Lab., Wright Patterson, AFB. Ohio. Rep. No. AMRL. TR.* **70.114**: 1.

KUNZ, F. & MEYER, H. R. (1969). "Backache and findings in the vertebral column in men operating heavy building machinery." *Zeit. Unfallmed. Berufskr.*, **62**: 178–189.

LEGGO, C. & MATHIASEN, H. (1973). "Preliminary results of a pre-employment back X-ray program for state traffic officers." *J. Occup. Med.*, **15**: 973–974.

LEGGO, P. & WELFLING, J. (1968). "Data obtained from systematic radiological examination of the lumbopelvic region in the applicants for employment in the S.N.C.F." *Presse Méd.*, **76**: 901–902.

LEVENS, E. (1971). "Worker safety: a function of the acceptability of risk." *J. Occup. Med.*, **13**: 342–347.

LEYSHON, G. E. & FRANCIS, H. W. S. (1975). "Lifting injuries in ambulance crews." *Public Hlth., Lond.*, **89**: 71–75.

LUNDERVOLD, A. J. S. (1951). *Electromyographic Investigations of Position and Manner of Working in Typewriting.* Oslo; Brøggers.

McGREGOR, D. (1960). "Sickness absence among forestry workers in the North of Scotland, 1958." *Brit. J. Industr. Med.*, **17**: 310–317.

MAGORA, A. (1973). "Investigation of the relation between low back pain and occupation: 5 psychological aspects." *Scand. J. Rehab. Med.*, **5**: 191–196.

MAGORA, A. (1974). "Investigation of the relation between low back pain and occupation: 6 medical history symptoms." *Scand. J. Rehab. Med.*, **6**: 81–88.

MARSK, A. (1958). "Studies on weight distribution upon the lower extremities in individuals working in a standing position." *Acta Orthop. Scand., Suppl.* **31**: 1.

MATTINGLEY, S. (1971). "Rehabilitation of registered dock workers at Garston Manor." *Proc. Soc. Med.*, **64:** 757–760.

MINISTRY OF LABOUR (1958). *Lifting and Carrying.* London; Her Majesty's Stationery Office.

ONISHI, N. & NOMURA, H. (1973). "Low back pain in relation to physical work capacity and local tenderness." *J. Human Ergon., Tokyo*, **2:** 119–132.

OSTEUND, E. W., LINDHOLM, A., SANDBERG, E. & LINDBERG, B. (1965). "Medical and ergonomic aspects of backache among certain groups of Swedish postal workers." *Proc. 2nd Int. Cong. Ergonomics, Dortmund*, (1964): 329–335.

ROHMERT, W. & LAURIG, W. (1971). "Work measurement. Psychological and physiological techniques for assessing operator and work load." *Int. J. Prod. Res.*, **9:** 157–168.

RONNHOLM, N. (1962). "Physiological studies on the optimum rhythm of lifting work." *Ergonomics*, **5:** 51–52.

RONNHOLM, N., KARVONEN, M. J. & LAPINLEIMU, V. D. (1962). "Mechanical efficiency of rhythmic and paced work." *J. Appl. Physiol.*, **17:** 765–770.

ROSEGGER, R. & ROSEGGER, S. (1960). "Industrial medical diagnosis in tractor workers." *Arch. Landtech.*, **2:** 3–66.

ROSEGGER, R. & ROSEGGER, S. (1960). "Health effects of tractor driving." *J. Agric. Eng. Res.*, **5:** 241–275.

ROWE, M. L. (1971). "Low back pain in industry—updated position." *J. Occup. Med.*, **13:** 476–478.

RUMIANTSEN, G. I. & CHUMAK, K. I. (1966). "Osseous changes in the spinal column of concrete placers subjected to the effect of total high-frequency vibration." *Gig. Truda Prof. Zabol.*, **4:** 619.

TEMMING, J. & ROMMERT, W. (1972). "Investigations into the physical strains of miners in carrying and handling heavy loads in different mechanical colliers." *Arbeitsmed.Sozialmed. Arbeitshyg.*, **48:** 9–143.

TOPLIS, J. W. (1970). "Studying people at work." *Occupat. Psychol.*, **44:** 95–114.

TROUP, J. D. G. (1965). "Relation of lumbar spine disorders to heavy manual work and lifting." *Lancet*, **1:** 857–861.

TROUP, J. D. G. & GRIEVE, D. W. (1970). "Load carrying and static effort." *Proc. Roy. Soc. Med.*, **63:** 199–200.

VENABLE, J. R., FLAKE, R. E. & KILIAN, D. J. (1964). "Stress fracture of the spinous process." *J. Amer. Med. Assoc.*, **190:** 881–885.

WALLACE, N. W. (1941). "Stair climbing by postmen." *The Post*, **July:** 24–25.

WELLS, R. L. (1969). "The hard life of people who must work for a living." *J. Occup. Med.*, **11:** 439–442.

ZINOVIEFF, A. (1966). "The effect of spinal injury on employment in heavy industry." *Proc. Roy. Soc. Med.*, **59:** 845–847.


*(c) Relations to Recreational Activity (Exercise and Sport)*

BILLINGS, R. A., BURRY, H. C. & JONES, R. (1977). "Low back injury in sport." *Rheumat. Rehab.*, **16:** 236–240.

CARUSO, I. (1967). "Electromyographic study of the normal activity of erector spinae muscles in symmetrical gymnastic exercises." *Ori. Ortop. Odierna. Riab.*, **12:** 31–41.

CHAPMAN, A. E. & TROUP, J. D. G. (1969). "Electromyographic study of the effect of training on the lumbar erectores spinae." *J. Anat.*, **105:** 186–187.

CHAPMAN, A. E. & TROUP, J. D. G. (1970). "Prolonged activity of lumbar erectores spinae: an electromyographic and dynamometric study of the effect of training." *Ann. Phys. Med.*, **10:** 263–269.

CHEAH, J. S. & TAN, B. Y. (1970). "The effect of exercise on the Achilles tendon reflex time." *Med. J. Austr.*, **1:** 1050–1051.

DARCUS, H. D. & SALTER, N. (1955). "The effect of repeated muscular exertion on muscle strength." *J. Physiol.*, **129:** 325–336.

DELHEZ, L. (1961). "Efficacy of certain abdominal exercises in adolescents." *Rev. Educ. Physique.*, **195:** 161.

EDHOLM, O. G. (1960). "Some effects of fatigue, temperature and training on muscular contraction in man." In *Structure and Function of Muscle*, Vol. II. pp. 449–453. Ed. by G. H. Bourne, New York: Academic Press.

EDWARDS, R. G. & LIPPOLD, O. C. J. (1956). "The relation between force and integrated electrical activity in fatigued muscle." *J. Phyiol.*, **132:** 677–681.

ELLISON, K. (1975). "Pain tolerance arousal and personality relationships of athletes and nonathletes." *Res. Quart. Amer. Assoc. Health Phys. Ed.*, **46:** 250–255.

FLEISHMAN, E. A., KREMER, E. J. & SHOUP, G. W. (1961). "The dimensions of physical fitness—factor analysis of strength tests." *Indust. Admin. and Psychol. Depts., Tech. Rep. No 2.* New Haven; Yale University.

FLINT, M. M. (1965). "Abdominal muscle involvement during the performance of various forms of sit-up exercise." *Amer. J. Phys. Med.*, **44:** 224–234.

FUNK, F. F. (1975). "Injuries of the cervical spine in football." *Clin. Orthop.*, **109:** 50–58.

GALLAGHER, J. R. & DELORME, T. L. (1949). "The use of the technique of progressive-resistance exercise in adolescence." *J. Bone Joint Surg.*, **31A:** 847–858.

GRANTHAM, V. A. (1977). "Backache in boys—a new problem?" *Practitioner*, **218:** 226–229.

HARRIS, H. A. (1939). "Anatomical and physiological basis for physical training." *Brit. Med. J.*, **2:** 939–943.

HELLEBRANDT, F. A., HOUTZ, S. J., PARTRIDGE, M. J. & WALTERS, C. E. (1956). "Tonic neck reflexes in exercises of stress in man." *Amer. J. Phys. Med.*, **35:** 144–159.

HINSON, M. M. (1969). "An electromyographic study of the push-up for women." *Res. Quart.*, **40:** 305–311.

HISLOP, H. J. (1963). "Quantitative changes in human muscular strength during isometric exercise." *J. Amer. Phys. Ther. Assoc.*, **43:** 21–28.

KARPOVICH, P. V. (1937). "Physiological and psychological dynamogenic factors in exercise." *Arbeitsphysiol.*, **9:** 626–629.

KARPOVICH, P. V. (1951). "Incidence of injuries in weight-lifting." *J. Phys. Ed.*, **48:** 81–84.

KEENEY, C. E. (1955). "Relationship of bodyweight to strength—bodyweight ratio in championship weight-lifters." *Res. Quar. (AAHPER)*, **26:** 54–57.

KENDALL, P. H. & JENKINS, J. M. (1968). "Lumbar isometric flexion exercises." *Physiotherapy*, **54:** 158–165.

KOTANI, P. T., ICHIKAWA, N., WAKABAYSHI, W., YOSHII, T. & KOSHIMUNE, M. (1971). "Studies of spondylolysis found among weight lifters." *Brit. J. Sports Med.*, **6:** 4–8.

LEADHORT, J. D. (1973). "Spinal injuries in athletes." *Orthop. Clin. Nth. Amer.*, **4:** 691–707.

LEITZIG, H. (1971). "Notalgia—degeneration of intervertebral discs and exercise tolerance." *Med. Welt*, **46:** 1815–1823.

Moe, J. H. (1968). "Back problems in the young athlete." *J. Amer. Coll. Health Assoc.*, **17:** 126–130.

Moncur, J. A. (1965). "Scheuermann's disease in students of physical education." *Bull. Brit. Assoc. Sports Med.*, **2:** 44–48.

Moody, D. M. (1974). "Large subdural collections of air following reverse somersault." *Radiology*, **111:** 721–723.

Morioka, M. (1965). "Some physiological responses to static muscular exercise." *Proc. 2nd Int. Ergonomics Congr., Dortmund* (1964), 35–40.

Murray-Leslie, C. F., Lintott, D. J. & Wright, V. (1977). "The spine in sport and veteran military parachutists." *Ann. Rheumat. Dis.*, **36:** 332–342.

Noro, L. (1967). "The medical aspects of weight carrying." *Indust. Med. Surg.*, **36:** 192–195.

Ondruf, W. & Wolf, B. (1968). "Studies of sports injuries of the vertebrae in ice skaters." *Beitr. Orthop. Traum.*, **15:** 233–238.

Ono, M. (1963). "E.M.G.'s, kinesiologic studies on weight-lifters." *Tairyoku-kagagu*, **12:** 1–29.

Ono, M. & Kubota, M. (1963). "An E.M.G. study on weightlifters." *Tikeikai Med. J.*, **10:** 124–144.

Pauly, J. E. & Steele, R. W. (1966). "Electromyographic analysis of back exercises for paraplegic patients." *Arch. Phys. Med. Rehab.*, **47:** 730–736.

Refior, H. J. (1972). "The vertebrae of gymnasts—developmental observations in children and young people." *Zeit. Orthop.*, **110:** 741–744.

Roberts, V. L., Noyes, F. R., Hubbard, R. P. & McCabe, J. (1971). "Biomechanics of snowmobile spine injuries." *J. Biomechanics*, **4:** 569–577.

Ross, H. A. (1974). "Swimmer's neck." *J. Amer. Osteopath. Assoc.*, **73:** 765–766.

Ryan, E. D. & Kovacic, C. R. (1966). "Pain tolerance and athletic participation." *Percept. Motor Skills*, **22:** 383–390.

Schmidt, H. (1970). "Spondylolisthesis and sport." *Beitr. Orthop.*, **17:** 717–719.

Schwerdtner, H. P. & Schoberth, H. (1973). "Spondylolysis in high-wire sport on gymnastic apparatus." *Zeit. Orthop.*, **111:** 934–940.

Stepanov, A. S. (1959). "Electromyographic changes produced by training in weight lifting." *Sechenov J. Physiol.*, **45:** 115–121.

STERN, P. H., McDOWELL, F., MILLER, J. M. & ROBINSON, M. (1970). "Effects of facilitation exercise techniques in stroke rehabilitation." *Arch. Phys. Med.*, **51**: 526–531.

TROUP, J. D. G. (1970). "The risks of weight training and lifting in young people: functional anatomy of the spine." *Brit. J. Sports Med.*, **5**: 27–33.

WALTERS, C. E. & PARTRIDGE, M. J. (1957). "Electromyographic study of the differential action of the abdominal muscles during exercise." *Amer. J. Phys. Med.*, **36**: 259–268.

WILMORE, J. H. (1974). "Alterations in strength, body composition and anthropometric measurement consequent to a 10-week weight training program." *Med. Sci. Sports*, **6**: 133–138.

WRIGHT, V. & PLUNKETT, T. G. (1968). "Scientific assessment of the results of physical treatment—measurement of stiffness." *Ann. Phys. Med.*, **8**: 280–291.

### (d) Prevention (Advice; Training; Design Criteria)

AYOUB, M. M. (1973). "Workplace design and posture." *Human Factors*, **15**: 265–268.

BARKLA, D. (1961). "The estimation of body measurements of a British population in relation to seat design." *Ergonomics*, **4**: 123–132.

BECKER, W. F. (1961). "Prevention of low back disability." *J. Occup. Med.*, **3**: 325–329.

BRITISH STANDARDS INSTITUTION (1958). "Anatomical, physiological and anthropometric principles in the design of office chairs and tables." **B.S. 3044**.

BRITISH STANDARDS INSTITUTION (1959). "Anthropometric recommendations for dimensions of nonadjustable office chairs, desks and tables." **B.S. 3079**.

BRITISH STANDARDS INSTITUTION (1961). "Anthropometric recommendations for dimensions of office machine operators' chairs and desks." **B.S. 3404**.

BURT, H. (1944). "Low back pain: its prevention and treatment." *Arch. Phys. Med.*, **25**: 432.

DARCUS, H., MERRICK, M. J. & BARKLA, D. (1960). "Anthropometric data for chair designers." *Furniture Development Council Research Report No. 8*.

DARCUS, H. D. & WEDDELL, A. G. M. (1947). "Some anatomical and physiological principles concerned in the design of seats of naval war weapons." *Brit. Med. Bull.*, **5**: 31–37.

DAVIS, B. T. (1969). "Preventing manual handling and lifting injuries in industry." *Arch. Gen. Health*, **19**: 593–594.

DUGGAR, B. C. & SWENGROSS, G. V. (1969). "The design of activity programs for industry." *J. Occup. Med.*, **11**: 322.

FEATHERSTONE, D. F. (1966). "Industry and the disc lesion." In *Backache and the Slipped Disc.* pp. 89–109. Thorsons Publications.

FITZGERALD, J. G. (1972). "The role of the intervertebral space in the prevention of ejection injury." *R.A.F. Inst. Aviation Med., I.A.M. Report No. 510.*

FLOYD, W. F. (1967). "Postural and safety factors in motor car design." *Proc. Roy. Soc. Med.*, **60**: 953.

FLOYD, W. F. & ROBERTS, D. F. (1959). "Anatomical and physiological principles in chair and table design." *Ergonomics*, **2**: 1–16.

GLOVER, J. R. (1976). "Prevention of back pain." In *The Lumbar Spine and Back Pain.* pp. 47–54. Ed. M. I. V. Jayson. London; Sector Publishing Co.

GRANDJEAN, E., HUNTING, W., WOTZKA, G. & SCHARER, R. (1973). "An ergonomic investigation of multipurpose chairs." *Human Factors*, **15**: 247–255.

HAWKINS, F. (1974). "Ergonomic aspects of crew seats in transport aircraft." *Aerospace Med.*, **45**: 196–203.

HEINRICH, H. W. (1959). *Industrial Accident Prevention.* 4th ed. New York; McGraw-Hill.

INTERNATIONAL LABOUR ORGANISATION (1964). "Maximum permissible weight to be carried by one worker." *Occup. Safety and Health Series, No. 5.* I.L.O. Geneva.

INTERNATIONAL LABOUR ORGANISATION (1966). *Report on Conference on Maximum Weight.* I.L.O.: Geneva.

KEEGAN, J. J. (1962). "Evaluation and improvement of seats." *Indust. Med. and Surg.*, **31**: 137–348.

KENDALL, P. H. (1967). "Car seats and backache." *Proc. Roy. Soc. Med.*, **60**: 9581959.

KOSIAK, M., AURELIUS, J. R. & HARTFIEL, W. F. (1968). "The low back problem: an evaluation." *J. Occup. Med.*, **10**: 588–593.

KRAUS, P. (1967). "Prevention of low back pain." *J. Occup. Med.*, 9: 555.

LEVY, P. M. (1964). "Ejection seat design and vertebral fractures." *Aerospace Med.*, 35: 545–549.

LEWITT, K. (1971). "The cause of impaired function of the spinal column and possible prevention." *Proc. 5th Sci. Mtg. Fac. Hyg. Charles Univ., Prague.*

MCMULLAN, J. J. (1969). "The prevention and management of disability in general practice." *J. Roy. Coll. Gen. Pract.*, 17: 80–90.

MATTHEWS, J. (1964). "Ride comfort for tractor operators. 1: Review of existing information." *J. Agric. Eng. Res.*, 9: 3–31.

MATTHEWS, J. (1964). "Ride comfort for tractor operators. 2: Analysis of ride vibrations on pneumatic-tyred tractors." *J. Agric. Eng. Res.*, 9: 147–158.

MORRISON, C. S. & HARRINGTON, R. E. (1962). "Tractor seating for operator comfort." *Agric. Eng.*, 43: 632–635; 650–652.

ROBERTS, C. D. (1974). "Automobile head restraints." *Amer. J. Pub. Health*, 64: 1100–1101.

VAN WELY, P. (1970). "Design and disease." *Appl. Ergonomics*, 1: 262–269.

WITTIG, W. (1962). "Problems of seat design in vehicles." *Verkehrsmed.*, 9: 229–249.

## (e) Certification and Compensation

ANDERSON, J. A. D., DUTHIE, J. J. R. & MOODY, B. P. (1962). "Rheumatic diseases affecting men registered disabled." *Ann. Rheum. Dis.*, 22: 188–193.

CHOOK, E. K. (1972). "Criteria for return to work—low back pain." *Indust. Med.*, 41: 32–34.

CRISCI, V. & ORSO, C. A. (1968). "Lumbar spondylolysis and spondylolisthesis and trauma: medico-legal problems." *Minerva Ort.*, 19: 287–293.

JOHNSTON, J. L. (1957). "Compensable low back disabilities." *J. Bone Joint Surg.*, 39B: 4.

LEE, K. (1968). "Assessment of the ability to work of the 'unfit'." *Trans. Soc. Occup. Med.*, 18: 61–66.

LEVERETT, J. K. (1966). "X-rays of the low back in pre-employment physical examinations." *Texas Med.*, **62:** 83–84.

LIEBEN, J. (1974). "Pre-employment back X-rays." *J. Occup. Med.*, **16:** 278–279.

McKENDRICK, A. (1916). *Back Injuries and Their Significance Under the Workmen's Compensation and Other Acts*. Edinburgh; Livingstone.

RUSSEK, A. S. (1955). "Medical and economic factors relating to the compensable back injury." *Arch. Phys. Med. Rehab.*, **36:** 316–322.

SEMMENCE, A. (1971). "Rising sickness absence in Great Britain— a general practitioner's view." *J. Roy. Coll. Gen. Pract.*, **21:** 25–146.

WESTRIN, C.-G. (1970). "Low back sick-listing: a nosological and medical insurance investigation." *Acta Socio-Med. Scand.*, **2–3:** 127–134.

WESTRIN, C.-G. (1973). "Low back sick-listing: a nosological and medical insurance investigation." *Scand. J. Soc. Med.*, *Suppl.* **7:** 1–116.

WHITE, A. W. M. (1966). "The compensation back." *Appl. Therap.* **8:** 857–874.

WHITE, A. W. M. (1966). "Low back pain in men receiving workmen's compensation." *Canad. Med. Assoc. J.*, **95:** 50–56.

WHITE, A. W. M. (1969). "Low back pain in men receiving workmen's compensation: a follow-up study." *Canad. Med. Assoc. J.*, **101:** 61–67.

WILDER, C. S. (1963). "Persons injured while at work." *Industr. Med. Surg.*, **32:** 191–196.

WILSON, A. K. (1969). "The lumbosacral angle: criterion for employability." *Rocky Mount. Med. J.*, **66:** 38–62.

WOOD, P. H. N. (1970). "Statistical appendix—digest of data on the rheumatic diseases. 2: Recent trends in sickness absence and mortality." *Ann. Rheumat. Dis.*, **29:** 324.

# 5

# EPIDEMIOLOGY AND STATISTICS

## (a) Relations to Age, Sex, Social Class and Race

ADAMS, P., DAVIES, G. T. & SWEETMAN, P. (1970). "Osteoporosis and the effects of ageing on bone mass in elderly men and women." *Quart. J. Med.*, **39**: 601–615.

ADRICHEM, J. A. M. VAN & VAN DER KORST, J. K. (1973). "Assessment of the flexibility of the lumbar spine: a pilot study in children and adolescents." *Scand. J. Rheumatol.*, **2**: 87–91.

ALBERT, J. (1950). "Intervertebral disc lesions in children and adolescents." *J. Bone Joint Surg.*, **32A**: 97–102.

ALLANDER, E. (1974). "Prevalence, incidence and remission rates of some common rheumatic diseases or syndromes." *Scand. J. Rheumatol.*, **3**: 145–153.

AMBRUS, L. & PAPATHEODOROU, C. (1973). "Trauma and lumbar disc herniation in childhood." *Calif. Med.*, **119**: 66–68.

ANDERSON, W. F. (1964). "Cervical spine studies in older people." *Rheumatism*, **20**: 7–12.

ARNOLD, J. S., BARTLEY, M. H., TONT, S. A. & JENKINS, D. P. (1966). "Skeletal changes in ageing and disease." *Clin. Orthop.*, **49**: 17–38.

ARTHRITIS AND RHEUMATISM COUNCIL (1972). *Symposium: The Painful Back from Youth to Age.* London; A.R.C.

ASMUSSEN, E. & HEERØLL-NIELSEN, K. (1958). "Posture, mobility and strength of the back in boys, 7–10." *Acta Orthop. Scand.*, **28**: 184–189.

ASMUSSEN, E. & HEERØLL-NEILSEN, K. (1959). "Posture, mobility and strength of the back in 7 to 16 year old boys." *Acta Orthop. Scand.*, **29**: 174–189.

ASTRAD, P. O. (1956). "Human physical fitness with special reference to sex and age." *Physiol. Rev.*, **36**: 307.

AUFERMAUR, M. (1974). "Spinal injuries in juveniles: necropsy findings in 12 cases." *J. Bone Joint Surg.*, **56B**: 513–519.

AYLETT, M. J., ROBERTS, J. C. & LLOYD, S. (1974). "Neural tube defects in a country town: confirmation of clustering within a particularly small area." *Brit. J. Prev. Soc. Med.*, **28:** 117–179.

BABCOCK, J. L. (1975). "Spinal injuries in children." *Pediat. Clin. Nth. Amer.*, **22:** 487–500.

BAILEY, N. J. (1952). "The normal cervical spine in infants and children." *Radiology*, **39:** 712.

BAILEY, N. J. & SCHORSTEIN, J. (1960). "The stiff back in children." *J. Bone Joint Surg.*, **42B:** 651.

BAKER, D. R. & McHOLLICK, W. (1956). "Spondyloschisis and spondylolisthesis in children." *J. Bone Joint Surg.*, **38A:** 933–934.

BANNA, M. & GRYSPEERDT, G. L. (1971). "Intraspinal tumours in children (excluding dysraphism)." *Clin Radiol.*, **22:** 17–32.

BARDFELD, K. & STREDA, A. (1973). "Ankylosing spondyloarthritis of the cervical spine in juvenile primary chronic polyarthritis (the influence of time factors). *Radiol. Diagn., Berlin*, **14:** 81–87.

BAUM, K. & ZIFF, M. (1971). "The rarity of ankylosing spondylitis in the black race." *Arthritis Rheumat.*, **14:** 12.

BEDALE, E. M. (1924). "Comparison of the energy expenditure of a woman, carrying loads in eight different positions." *M.R.C. Indust. Fatigue Res. Board Rep.*, **29:** 1–27.

BELBIN, R. M. (1955). "Older people and heavy work." *Brit. J. Indust. Med.*, **12:** 309–319.

BELL, G. H., DUNBAR, O., BECK, J. S. & GIBB, A. (1967). "Variation in strength of vertebrae with age and their relation to osteoporosis." *Calcif. Tissue Res.*, **1:** 75–86.

BENN, R. T. & WOOD, P. H. N. (1975). "Pain in the back: an attempt to estimate the size of the problem." *Rheumatol. Rehab.*, **14:** 121–128.

BENNETT, P. H. & WOOD, P. H. N. (Eds.). (1968). *Population Studies of the Rheumatic Diseases*. Amsterdam; Excerpta Medica.

BERESFORD, O. D. (1952). "Osteophytosis of the lumbar spine; a comparison between the incidence in Saskatchewan, Canada and Bristol, England." *Ann. Rheum Dis.*, **2:** 289–291.

BHATTACHARYYA, S. K. (1974). "Fracture and displacement of the odontoid process in a child." *J. Bone Joint Surg.*, **56A:** 1071–1072.

BINKS, F. A. (1974). "Geriatric pain." *Physiotherapy*, **60:** 132–133.

BLOCKLEY, N. J. & SCHORSTEIN, J. (1960). "The stiff back in children." *J. Bone Joint Surg.*, **42B:** 651.

BLOCKLEY, N. J. & SCHORSTEIN, J. (1961). "Intraspinal epidermoid tumours in the lumbar region in children." *J. Bone Joint Surg.*, **43B:** 556–562.

BOMEN, K. & JALAVISTO, E. (1953). "Standing steadiness in old and young persons." *Ann. Med. Exp. Biol. Fenn.*, **31:** 447–455.

BORGESEN, S. E. & VANG, P. S. (1974). "Herniation of the lumbar intervertebral disk in children and adolescents." *Acta Orthop. Scand.*, **45:** 540–549.

BRADFORD, D. S. & GARCIA, A. (1971). "Lumbar intervertebral disk herniations in children and adolescents." *Orthop. Clin. Nth. Amer.*, **2:** 583–592.

BREIDAHL, P. (1969). "Ossification of the posterior longitudinal ligament in the cervical spine: The Japanese Disease occurring in patients of British descent." *Australas. Radiol.*, **13:** 311–313.

BREMNER, J. M., LAWRENCE, J. S. & MIALL, W. E. (1968). "Degenerative joint disease in a Jamaican rural population." *Ann. Rheumat. Dis.*, **27:** 326–332.

BREWERTON, D. A. & BROWN, D. (1968). "Statistics in a physiotherapy department." *Ann. Phys. Med.*, **9:** 217–222.

BROTHWELL, D. R. (1967). "The Amerindians of Guyana." *Eugenics Rev.*, **59:** 22–45.

BULOS, S. (1973). "Herniated intervertebral lumbar disc in the teenager." *J. Bone Joint Surg.*, **55B:** 273–278.

BURWELL, R. G. (1973). "The biological component of the orthopaedic troika with particular reference to scoliosis." *Acta Orthop. Belg.*, **39:** 444–459.

CAILLIET, R. (1975). "Lumbar discogenic disease: why the elderly are more vulnerable." *Geriatrics*, **30:** 73–76.

CARLIOZ, H. & DUBOUSSET, J. (1973). "Instability between atlas and axis in the infant." *Rev. Chir. Orthop.*, **59:** 291–307.

CARTER, M. E. (1962). "Sacro-iliitis in Still's disease." *Ann. Rheumat. Dis.*, **21:** 105–120.

CARTER, M. E. & LOEWI, G. (1962). "Anatomical changes in normal sacroiliac joints during childhood and comparison with the changes in Still's disease." *Ann. Rheumat. Dis.*, **21:** 121–134.

CATTLE, H. S. & FILTZER, D. L. (1965). "Pseudosubluxation and other normal variations in the cervical spine in children: study of 160 children." *J. Bone Joint Surg.*, **47A:** 1295–1309.

CAUGHEY, D. E. (1975). "Ankylosing spondylitis in the Polynesian race." *N.Z. Med. J.*, **81:** 268.

CHAPANIS, A. (1974). "National and cultural variables in ergonomics." *Ergonomics*, **17**: 153–175.

CHEN, H.-T. (1969). "Tuberculosis of the spine in children." *J. West. Pacific Orthop. Assoc.*, **6**: 47–60.

CHUNG, S. M. K. & BORNS, P. (1973). "Acute osteomyelitis adjacent to the sacroiliac joint in children: report of two cases." *J. Bone Joint Surg.*, **55A**: 630–634.

COCKSHOTT, W. P. (1958). "Anatomical anomalies observed in radiographs of Nigerians." *West Afr. Med. J.*, **7**: 179–184.

CONGDON, R. T. (1932). "Spondylolisthesis and vertebral anomalies in skeletons of American aborigines with clinical notes on spondylolisthesis." *J. Bone Joint Surg.*, **14**: 511–524.

CRACCO, J. B. (1975). "The spinal evoked response in infants and children." *Neurology*, **25**: 31–36.

CULLUMBINE, P. (1950). "Influence of age, sex, physique and muscular development on physical fitness." *J. Appl. Physiol.*, **2**: 488–511.

DAVIS, P. R. (1960). "Observations on vertebrae in different races." *Actes du VI Congrès International des Sciences Anthropologiques et Ethnologiques, Paris*, **1**: 443–453.

DAVIS, P. R. (1961). "The thoraco-lumbar mortice joint in West Africans." *J. Anat.*, **95**: 589–593.

DAVIS, P. R. & ROWLAND, H. A. K. (1965). "Vertebral fractures in West Africans suffering from tetanus: a clinical and osteological study." *J. Bone Joint Surg.*, **47B**: 61–71.

DE MOULIN, D. (1970). "A historical phenomenological study of bodily pain in Western man." *Bull. Hist. Med.*, **48**: 540–570.

EKELUND, L. & CRONQUIST, S. (1973). "Roentgenological changes in spinal malformations and spinal tumours in children." *Radiologie*, **13**: 541–546.

ELANDT-JOHNSON, R. C. (1973). "Age at onset distribution in chronic diseases." *J. Chron. Dis.*, **26**: 529–545.

FAHRINI, W. H. & TRUEMAN, G. E. (1965). "Comparative radiological study of the spines of a primitive population with North Americans and Northern Europeans." *J. Bone Joint Surg.*, **47B**: 552–555.

FERNSTROM, U. (1956). "Protruded lumbar intervertebral disc in children." *Acta Clin. Scand.*, **111**: 71–79.

FIELDING, J. W. (1973). "Selected observations on the cervical spine in the child." *Current Practice in Orthopaedic Surgery*, **5:** 31–55.

FRANCIS, C. C. (1956). "Certain changes in the aged male white cervical spine." *Anat. Rec.*, **125:** 783–787.

FISK, J. W. (1970). "Backache in general practice." *J. Roy. Coll. Gen. Prac.*, **119:** 92.

GALLAGHER, J. C. (1973). "The crush fracture syndrome in post-menopausal women." *Clin. Endocr. Metab.*, **2:** 293–315.

GARRARD, J. & BENNETT, A. E. (1971). "A validated interview schedule for use in population surveys of chronic disease and disability." *Brit. J. Prev. Soc. Med.*, **25:** 97–104.

GAUFIN, L. M. (1975). "Cervical spine injuries in infants. Problems in management." *J. Neurosurg.*, **42:** 179–184.

GEUBELLE, F. & GOFFIN, C. (1962). "Respiratory studies in children. IV. Lung volumes and body positions in children." *Acta Paediat.*, **51:** 255–260.

GILCHRIST, I. C. (1976). "Psychiatric and social factors related to low-back pain in general practice." *Rheumatol. Rehab.*, **15:** 101.

GILL, D. (1968). "Rheumatic complaints of women using anti-ovulatory drugs." *J. Chron. Dis.*, **21:** 235–244.

GOFTON, J. P., BENNETT, P. H., SMYTHE, H. A. & DECKER, J. L. (1972). "Sacroiliitis and ankylosing spondylitis in North American Indians." *Ann. Rheumat. Dis.*, **31:** 474–481.

GOFTON, J. P., LAWRENCE, J. S., BENNETT, P. H. & BURCH, T. (1966). "Sacroiliitis in eight populations." *Ann. Rheumat. Dis.*, **25:** 528–533.

GOFTON, J. P., ROBINSON, H. S. & TRUEMAN, G. E. (1966). "Ankylosing spondylitis in a Canadian Indian population." *Ann. Rheumat. Dis.*, **25:** 525–527.

GORDES, W. & FISCHER, V. (1973). "Intraspinal neuroblastomas in childhood." *Arch. Orthop. Unfall-Chir.*, **77:** 236–242.

GOI, Y. (1968). "Acquired spondylosis in child and young adult." *J. Bone Joint Surg.*, **50A:** 1649–1656.

GOLDIE, I. & RYBA, W. (1971). "Non-specific spondylitis in children." *Clin. Orthop.*, **79:** 89–95.

GRAHAME, R. (1970). "A method for measuring human skin elasticity *in vivo* with observations on the effects of age, sex and pregnancy." *Clin. Sci.*, **39:** 223–238.

GRANTHAM, V. A. (1977). "Backache in boys—a new problem?" *Practitioner*, **218:** 226–229.

GREEN, W. T. & BANKS, H. H. (1953). "Osteochondritis dissecans in children." *J. Bone Joint Surg.*, **35A**: 26–47.

GRIFFITHS, S. C. (1972). "Fracture of odontoid process in children." *J. Pediat. Surg.*, **7**: 680–683.

GYNTELBERG, F. (1974). "One year incidence of low back pain among male residents of Copenhagen aged 40–59." *Danish Bull. Med.*, **21**: 30–36.

HAGEN, D. P. (1964). "A continuing roentgenographic study of rural school children over a 15 year period." *J. Amer. Osteopath. Assoc.*, **63**: 546–557.

HAMM, J. & KLEINSORG, H. (1956). "The influence of body posture on healthy lung volume in different age groups." *Dtsch. Arch. Klin. Med.*, **203**: 234–240.

HARRINGTON, P. R. & TULLOS, H. S. (1971). "Spondylolisthesis in children: observations and surgical treatment." *Clin. Orthop.*, **79**: 75–84.

HASEBE, K. (1913). "The vertebrae of the Japanese." *Zeit. Morphol. Anthrop.*, **15**: 259–280.

HASUE, M. (1974). "Cervical spine injuries in children." *Fukishima J. Med. Sci.*, **20**: 115–123.

HEERØLL-NIELSEN, K. (1964). "Muscular asymmetry in normal young men." *Danish Nat. Assoc. Infantile Paralysis Comm.*, **78**.

HELLEBRANDT, F. A. & BRAUN, G. L. (1939). "The influence of sex and age on postural sway of man." *Amer. J. Phys. Anthrop.*, **24**: 347–360.

HELLEBRANDT, F. A., TEPPER, R. H., BRAUN, G. L. & ELLIOTT, M. C. (1938). "The location of the cardinal anatomical orientation planes passing through the center of weight in young adult women." *Amer. J. Physiol.*, **121**: 465–470.

HENRY, A. P. J. & MICKEL, R. E. (1974). "Spina bifida in African and Indian babies." *J. Bone Joint Surg.*, **56B**: 650–657.

HINCK, V. C., CLARK, W. M. & HOPKINS, C. E. (1966). "Normal inter-pediculate distances (minimum and maximum) in children and adults." *Amer. J. Roentgenol.*, **97**: 141–153.

HINCK, V. C., HOPKINS, C. E. & CLARK, W. M. (1965). "Sagittal diameter of the lumbar spinal canal in children and adults." *Radiology*, **85**: 929–937.

HIRSCH, C., JONSSON, B. & LEWIN, T. (1969). "Low-back symptoms in a Swedish female population." *Clin. Orthop.*, **63**: 171–176.

HORAL, J. (1969). "The clinical appearance of low back disorders in the city of Gothenburg, Sweden." *Acta Orthop. Scand., Suppl.* **118:** 1.

HORAL, J., NACHEMSON, A. & SCHELLER, S. (1972). "Clinical and radiological long term follow-up of vertebral fractures in children." *Acta Orthop. Scand.,* **43:** 491–503.

HORNINGE, H. (1972). "Discitis in children." *Arch. Clin. Néerl.,* **24:** 215–221.

HRUBEC, Z. & NASHOLD, B. S. (1975). "Epidemiology of lumbar disc lesions in the military in World War II." *Amer. J. Epidemiol.,* **102:** 366–376.

HUBBARD, D. D. (1974). "Injuries of the spine in children and adolescents." *Clin. Orthop.,* **100:** 56–65.

HUTCHINS, G. L. (1965). "The relationship of selected strength and flexibility variables to the antero-posterior posture of college women." *Res. Quart.,* **36:** 253–269.

JACOBS, P. (1974). "Some lesions of the spine in immigrants." *Proc. Roy. Soc. Med.,* **67:** 862–866.

JASTER, D. (1974). "Low back pain in youngsters." *Beitr. Orthop. Traum.,* **21:** 389–393.

JELBERT, M. (1970). "A pilot study of the incidence and distribution of certain skeletal and soft tissue abnormalities: discovered by mass miniature radiography in a group of indigenous Rhodesian Africans." *Central Afr. Med. J.,* **16:** 37–40.

JESPERSON, N. B., LUND, H. T. & EGEBLAD, M. (1973). "Intervertebral disc calcification in childhood." *Acta Paediat. Scand.,* **62:** 437–439.

JONCK, L. M. (1961). "The distribution of osteophytes in the lumbar spine of the Bantu." *Sth. Afr. J. Lab. Clin. Med.,* **7:** 71–77.

JONCK, L. M. (1961). "A roentgenological study of the motion of the lumbar spine of the Bantu." *Sth. Afr. J. Lab. Clin. Med.,* **7:** 67–71.

JULKUNEN, H. (1975). "The epidemiology of hyperostosis of the spine together with its symptoms and related mortality in a general population." *Scand. J. Rheumatol.,* **4:** 23–27.

JULKUNEN H., PYORALA, K. & LEHTOVIRTA, E. (1968). "Hyperostosis of the spine in relation to age and hyperglycaemia in men aged 30–69." *Ann. Med. Int. Fenn.,* **57:** 1–7.

KALBAK, K., ANDERSON, S. & WINCKLER, F. (1972). "Incidence of spondylolisthesis among natives of Greenland over the age of 40." *Ugeskr. Laeger,* **134:** 2532–2537.

KARVONEN, M. J., KOSKELLA, A. & NORO, L. (1962). "Preliminary report on the sitting postures of school-children." *Ergonomics*, **5:** 471–477.

KATZ, S., FORD, A. B., MOSKOWITZ, R. W., JACKSON, B. A. & JAFFE, M. W. (1963). "Studies of illness in the aged." *J. Amer. Med. Assoc.*, **185:** 914–919.

KAUFMAN, H. (1965). "Statistical contribution to dorsal displacement of vertebral bodies." *Zeit. Orthop.*, **99:** 417–425.

KEATS, S. & MORGESE, A. N. (1969). "Excessive lumbar lordosis in ambulatory spastic children: iliopsoas tenotomy." *Clin. Orthop.*, **65:** 130–137.

KEITH, R. M. (1974). "Pain in childhood." *Physiotherapy*, **60:** 130–131.

KELLGREN, J. H. (1964). "The epidemiology of rheumatic diseases." *Ann. Rheum. Dis.*, **23:** 109–122.

KELLGREN, J. H. & LAWRENCE, J. S. (1956). "Rheumatoid arthritis in a population sample." *Ann. Rheumat. Dis.*, **15:** 2–11.

KELLGREN, J. H. & LAWRENCE, J. S. (1958). "Osteoarthrosis and disc degeneration in an urban population." *Ann. Rheumat. Dis.*, **17:** 388–397.

KELLGREN, J. H., LAWRENCE, J. S. & AITKEN-SWAN, J. (1953). "Rheumatic complaints in an urban population." *Ann. Rheumat. Dis.*, **12:** 5–15.

KELSEY, J. L. (1975). "An epidemiological study of acute herniated lumbar intervertebral discs." *Rheumatol. Rehab.*, **14:** 144–159.

KEMSLEY, W. F. P. (1952). "Body weight of different ages and heights." *Ann. Eugenics*, **16:** 316–334.

KENDALL, H. O. & KENDALL, F. P. (1948). "Normal flexibility according to age groups." *J. Bone Joint Surg.*, **30A:** 690–694.

KETTLEKAMP, D. B. & WRIGHT, D. G. (1971). "Spondylolysis in the Alaskan Eskimo." *J. Bone Joint Surg.*, **53A:** 563–566.

KLEIN, K. K. (1973). "Progression of pelvic tilt in adolescent boys from elementary through high school." *Arch. Phys. Med. Rehab.*, **54:** 57–59.

KONDO, S., ANDO, T., IKEURA, T., TAMAI, H. & MARUMO, M. (1969). "A statistical study on the diagnosis of lumbar intervertebral disc herniation." *Bull. Osaka Med. Sch.*, **15:** 38–45.

LADD, J. R., CASSIDY, J. T. & MARTEL, W. (1971). "Juvenile ankylosing spondylitis." *Arthritis Rheumat.*, **14:** 579–590.

LANIER, R. R. (1939). "The presacral vertebrae of American white and negro males." *Amer. J. Phys. Anthrop.*, **25**: 341–420.

LANNIN, D. R. (1954). "Intervertebral disc lesions in the teenage group." *Minn. Med.*, **37**: 136–137.

LAWRENCE, J. S. (1963). "The prevalence of arthritis." *Brit. J. Clin. Pract.* **17**: 699.

LAWRENCE, J. S. (1969). "Generalized osteoarthrosis in a population sample." *Amer. J. Epidemiol.*, **90**: 381–389.

LAWRENCE, J. S., BREMNER, J. M. & BIER, F. (1966). "Osteoarthrosis: prevalence in the population and the relationship between symptoms and X-ray changes." *Ann. Rheum. Dis.*, **25**: 1–24.

LEBLANC, H. J. (1974). "Spinal cord injuries in children." *Surg. Neurol.*, **2**: 411–414.

LESTER, C. W. & SHAPIRO, H. L. (1968). "Vertebral arch defects in the lumbar vertebrae of pre-historic American Eskimos." *Amer. J. Phys. Anthrop.*, **28**: 43–48.

LEVY, L. F. (1967). "Lumbar intervertebral disc disease in Africans." *J. Neurosurg.*, **26**: 31–34.

LOWREY, J. J. (1973). "Dislocated lumbar vertebral epiphysis in adolescent children." *J. Neurosurg.*, **38**: 232–234.

McBRYDE, A. M. & McCOLLUM, D. E. (1973). "Ankylosing spondylitis in women: the disease and its prognosis." *Nth. Carolina Med. J.*, **34**: 34–37.

MacCARTEE, C. C., GRIFFIN, P. P. & BYRD, E. B. (1972). "Ruptured calcified thoracic disc in a child: report of a case." *J. Bone Joint. Surg.*, **54A**: 1272–1278.

McDOUGALL, A. & ROBERTSON, J. M. (1960). "Prolapsed intervertebral disc in the adolescent." *J. Bone Joint Surg.*, **42B**: 651.

McINTYRE, J. M. (1957). "Spondylolisthesis in children." *J. Bone Joint Surg.*, **39B**: 797.

McKEE, B. W., ALEXANDER, W. J. & DUNBAR, J. S. (1971). "Spondylolysis and spondylolisthesis in children: a review." *J. Canad. Assoc. Radiol.*, **22**: 100–109.

McKERN, T. W. & STEWART, T. D. (1957). "Skeletal age changes in young American males, analysed from the standpoint of identification." *HQM Res. and Dev. Command, Tech. Rep. EP-45, Natick, Mass.*

MacNAB, I. (1970). "Spondylolisthesis in childhood." *J. Bone Joint Surg.*, **52B**: 190.

MAINZER, F. (1973). "Herniation of the nucleus pulposus: a rare complication of intervertebral disk calcification in children." *Radiology*, **107**: 167–170.

MANDELL, A. J. (1960). "Lumbosacral intervertebral disc disease in children." *Calif. Med.*, **93**: 307–308.

MARAR, B. C. & BALACHANDRANDRAN, N. (1973). "Non-traumatic atlanto-axial dislocation in children." *Clin. Orthop.*, **92**: 220–226.

MARGO, E. (1960). "Spondylolisthesis and spondylolysis: a clinico-statistical report on 589 cases treated over a 13 year period." *Southern Med. J.*, **53**: 1096–1100.

MASAL, K. (1966). "Neural arch lesions in young people." *Aust. Radiol.*, **10**: 360.

MATHESON, A. T. (1966). "The rarity of lumbar disc protrusion in the Rhodesian Bantu." *J. Bone Joint Surg.*, **48B**: 398.

MENELAUS, M. B. (1964). "Discitis—an inflammation affecting the intervertebral disc in children." *J. Bone Joint Surg.*, **46B**: 16–23.

MIKKELSEN, L. & DODGE, J. (1970). "Age, sex specific prevalence of radiographic abnormalities of the joints of the hands, wrists and cervical spine of adult residents of the Tecumseh, Michigan Community Health Study Area, 1962–1965." *J. Chron. Dis.*, **23**: 151–153.

MITCHIE, I. (1972). "Radiological changes and their significance in aged men." *Geront. Clin.*, **14**: 310–316.

MOLL, J. M. H. & WRIGHT, V. (1973). "New York clinical criteria for ankylosing spondylitis: a statistical evaluation." *Ann. Rheum. Dis.*, **32**: 354–363.

MOOSA, A. (1973). "Spinal muscular atrophy in childhood." *Arch. Dis. Child.*, **48**: 386–388.

NAGI, S. Z., RILEY, L. R. & NEWBY, L. G. (1973). "A social epidemiology of back pain in a general population." *J. Chron. Dis.*, **26**: 769–779.

NAKANISHI, T., MANNEN, T. & TOYOKURA, Y. (1973). "Asymptomatic ossification of the posterior longitudinal ligament of the cervical spine: incidence and roentgenological findings." *J. Neurol. Sci.*, **19**: 375–381.

NATHAN, H. (1962). "Osteophytes of the vertebral column: an anatomical study of their development according to age, race and sex, with considerations as to their etiology and significance." *J. Bone Joint Surg.*, **44A**: 243–264.

NATVIG, H. (1970). "Sociomedical aspects of low back pain causing prolonged sick leave: a retrospective study." *Acta Sociomed. Scand.*, **2**: 117–126.

NELSON, C. J., JANECKI, C. J., GILDENBERG, P. H. & SAVA, G. (1972). "Disk protrusions in the young." *Clin. Orthop.*, **88**: 142–150.

NEUGEBAUER, H. (1973). "Kyphometric studies of 9,000 pupils in Austria." *Zeit. Orthop.*, **111**: 633–639.

NEWMAN, A. J. (1973). "Vertebral compression in childhood leukemia." *Amer. J. Dis. Childhood*, **125**: 863–865.

NEWTON, P. (1958). "Cervical intervertebral disc calcification in children." *J. Bone Joint Surg.*, **40A**: 107.

NORDGREN, B. (1972). "Anthropometric measures and muscle strength in young women." *Scand. J. Rehab. Med.*, **4**: 165–169.

NORDIN, B. E., YOUNG, M. M., BENTLEY, B., ORMONROYD, P. & SYKES, J. (1968). "Lumbar spine densitometry: methodology and results in relation to the menopause." *Clin. Radiol.*, **19**: 459–464.

NORDQVIST, L. (1964). "The sagittal diameter of the spinal cord and subarachnoid space in different age groups: a roentgenographic postmortem study." *Acta Radiol.*, *Suppl.* **227**: 1.

OARRELLA, G. S. & ZOVICKIAN, A. (1950). "The ruptured intervertebral disc problem in the veteran." *Surgery*, **27**: 762–769.

O'CONNELL, J. (1960). "Intervertebral disc protrusions in childhood and adolescence." *Brit. J. Surg.*, **47**: 611–616.

ONKELINX, A. (1974). "Benign backache in the young adult." *Rev. Med. Liège*, **29**: 140–143.

PAAT, M. (1972). "Anthropometric and somatometric picture of spine in children and adolescents." *Fol. Morph., Prague*, **20**: 277–279.

PECK, F. C. (1957). "A calcified thoracic intervertebral disk with herniation and spinal cord compression in a child." *J. Neurosurg.*, **14**: 105–109.

PFEIL, E. (1970). "Therapy of premature childhood spondylolysis and spondylolisthesis." *Beitr. Orthop.*, **17**: 719–721.

PFEIL, E. (1971). "Spondylolysis and spondylolisthesis in children." *Zeit. Orthop.*, **109**: 17–33.

PIGGOTT, H. (1974). "Scoliosis in the young child." *Proc. Roy. Soc. Med.*, **67**: 205–206.

RAHBEK, K. S. & SNORRASON, E. (1973). "Lumbar spondylopathies in conscripts: report of hospital material from the years 1966–71." *Ugeskr. Laeger.*, **135**: 1–3.

REFIOR, H. J. (1972). "The vertebral columns in gymnasts: developmental observations in children and young people." *Zeit. Orthop.*, **110**: 741–744.

RICHARDS, A. T., STRICKE, L. & SPITZ, L. (1973). "Sacrococcygeal chordomas in children." *J. Pediatr. Surg.*, **8**: 911–914.

ROBERTS, D. F. (1960). "Functional anthropometry of elderly women." *Ergonomics*, **3**: 321–327.

ROCCO, H. D. & EYRING, E. J. (1972). "Intervertebral disk infections in children." *Amer. J. Dis Child.*, **123**: 448–451.

ROCHE, M. B. & ROWE, G. G. (1951). "The incidence of separate neural arch and coincident bone variations: a survey of 4,200 skeletons." *Anat. Rec.*, **109**: 233–252.

ROGERS, M. H. & CLEAVES, E. N. (1935). "The adolescent sacroiliac joint syndrome." *J. Bone Joint Surg.*, **17A**: 759–768.

ROWE, M. L. (1963). "Preliminary statistical study of low back pain." *J. Occup. Med.*, **5**: 336–341.

RUDD, J. L. & MARGOLIN, R. J. (1966). "A study of back cases in an out-patient clinic. *J. Assoc. Phys. Ment. Rehab.*, **20**: 20.

RUGTVEIT, A. (1966). "Juvenile lumbar disc herniations." *Acta Orthop. Scand.*, **37**: 348–358.

RUSSELL, A. S. (1975). "Prevalence of ankylosing spondylitis." *New Eng. J. Med.*, **292**: 1352.

RUSSIN, L. A. (1971). "Lumbar disc surgery in geriatric patients." *J. Bone Joint Surg.*, **53A**: 564.

SACCO, G., BUCHTHAL, F. & ROSENFALCK, P. (1962). "Motor unit potentials at different ages." *Arch. Neurol., Chicago*, **6**: 366–375.

SCHUTT, M. (1968). "Neck injury to women in automobile accidents." *J. Amer. Med. Assoc.*, **206**: 2688–2692.

SCOTT, P. (1974). "Spinal osteoporosis in the aged." *Aust. Fam. Phys.*, **3**: 281–283.

SEBO, M., SITAU, S. & SCHULTZ, P. (1974). "Osteoarthrosis and degeneration of discs in our rural population." *Fysiatr. Rheumatol. Vestn.*, **52**: 65–75.

SHELDON, J. H. (1963). "The effect of age on the control of sway." *Geront. Clin., Basel*, **5**: 129–138.

SHORE, L. R. (1930). "Abnormalities of the vertebral column in a series of skeletons of Bantu natives in South Africa." *J. Anat.*, **64:** 206–238.

SIBTHORPE, E. M. (1958). "A radiological survey on the measurements of specimens of the female pelvis in Uganda." *J. Obst. Gynaec. Brit. Emp.*, **64:** 600–605.

SMITH, M. G. H. (1972). "Lumbar spondyloarthritis in young children." *J. Pediat. Surg.*, **7:** 684–690.

SMITH, R. F. & TAYLOR, T. K. F. (1967). "Inflammatory lesions of intervertebral discs in children." *J. Bone Joint Surg.*, **49A:** 1508–1520.

SNOOK, S. H. (1971). "The effects of age and physique on continuous work capacity." *Human Factors*, **13:** 467–477.

SNOOK, S. H. & CIREILLO, V. M. (1974). "Maximum weights and work loads acceptable to female workers." *J. Occup. Med.*, **16:** 527–534.

SNOOK, S. H., IRVIN, C. H. & BASS, S. F. (1970). "Maximum weights and work loads acceptable to male industrial workers: a study of lifting, pushing, pulling, carrying and walking tasks." *Amer. Industr. Hyg. Assoc.*, **31:** 579–586.

SOLOMON, L. (1975). "Rheumatic disorders in the South African Negro. I. Rheumatoid arthritis and ankylosing spondylitis." *Sth. Afr. Med. J.*, **49:** 1292–1296.

SPIEGEL, P. G., KENGLA, K. W., ISAACSON, A. S. & WILSON, J. C. (1972). "Intervertebral disc space inflammation in children." *J. Bone Joint Surg.*, **54A:** 284–296.

STAHELI, L. &., NELP, W. B. & MARTY, R. (1973). "Strontium 87$^m$ scanning: early diagnosis of bone and joint infections in children." *J. Amer. Med. Assoc.*, **221:** 1159–1160.

STAINIER, L. & GEVEBELLE, F. (1963). "The time factor and the influence of body position and blood flow on the lung volumes of healthy children." *Ann. Pediat.*, **201:** 389–398.

STAINIER, L. & GEVEBELLE, F. (1963). "Effects of body position and venous blood flow on the lung volume in children." *Ann. Pediat.*, **201:** 489–497.

STENSTROM, R. & LINDFORS, M. (1971). "Lumbar myelography with water soluble contrast medium in children." *Acta Radiol.*, **11:** 243–249.

STERNBACH, R. & TURKSKY, B. (1964). "Ethnic differences among housewives in psychophysical and skin potential responses to electric shock." *Psychophysiology*, **1:** 241–246.

STEWART, P. E., SILBIGER, M. L. & WOLFSON, S. L. (1974). "Intervertebral disc calcification in childhood." *Clin. Pediatr.*, **13**: 363–366.

STEWART, T. D. (1932). "The vertebral column of the Eskimo." *Amer. J. Phys. Anthrop.*, **17**: 123–136.

STEWART, T. D. (1953). "The age incidence of neural arch defects in Alaskan natives, considered from the standpoint of etiology." *J. Bone Joint Surg.*, **35A**: 937–950.

STOVER, B., BALL, F. & WALTHER, A. (1974). "Idiopathic juvenile osteoporosis." *Fortschr. Röntgenstr.*, **121**: 435–444.

STRAUS, W. L. & CAVE, A. J. E. (1957). "Pathology and the posture of Neanderthal man." *Quart. Rev. Biol.*, **32**: 348–363.

TACHDJIAN, M. O. & MATSON, D. D. (1965). "Orthopaedic aspects of intraspinal tumours in infants and children." *J. Bone Joint Surg.*, **47A**: 223–248.

TAILLARD, W. (1954). "Spondylolisthesis in the infant and adolescent (study of 50 cases)." *Acta Orthop. Scand.*, **24**: 115–144.

TANAKA, Y. (1975). "A radiographic analysis of human lumbar vertebrae in the aged." *Virchows Arch. (Path. Anat.)*, **366**: 187–201.

TAYLOR, P. J. & FAIRRIE, A. J. (1968). "Chronic disability of men of middle age." *Brit. J. Prev. Soc. Med.*, **22**: 183–192.

TAYLOR, T. K. F. (1971). "Intervertebral disc prolapse in children and adolescents." *J. Bone Joint Surg.*, **53B**: 357.

THOMPSON, W. (1974). "The association of spinal and genitourinary abnormalities (imperforate anus) in female infants." *Radiology*, **113**: 693–698.

TROTTER, M. (1964). "Accessory sacroiliac articulations in East African skeletons." *Amer. J. Phys. Anthrop.*, **22**: 137–142.

TULSI, R. S. (1971). "Growth of the human vertebral column: an osteological study." *Acta Anat.* **79**: 570–580.

TULSI, R. S. (1972). "Vertebral column of the Australian aborigine: selected morphological and metrical features." *Zeit. Morph. Anthrop.*, **64**: 117–144.

TURNER, R. H. (1970). "Spondylolysis and spondylolisthesis in children and teenagers." *J. Bone Joint Surg.*, **52A**: 830.

TURNER, R. H. & BIANCO, A. J. (1971). "Spondylolysis and spondylolisthesis in children and teenagers." *J. Bone Joint Surg.*, **53A**: 1298–1306.

ULRICH, S. P. (1971). "Incidence of spinal pain in school children." *Schweiz. Rundschau Med.*, **60**: 208–211.

VOBECKY, J. (1974). "Rheumatoid arthritis and ankylosing spondylitis in an ethnically homogenous population: familial distribution of complaints." *J. Chronic Dis.*, **27**: 413–415.

WALFORD, P. A. (1962). "Diseases of bones and organs of movement." In *Morbidity Statistics from General Practice. Vol. III. Diseases in General Practice. General Register Office, Studies in Medical and Population Subjects.* pp. 77–87. London; HMSO.

WALKER, C. S. (1954). "Calcification of intervertebral discs in children." *J. Bone Joint Surg.*, **36B**: 601–605.

WALSKI, A. (1972). "Investigations on the anatomy of the isthmus of the neural arch in lumbar vertebrae of pre-school children." *Chir. Narz. Ruchu. Ortop. Pol.*, **37**: 25–33.

WALSKI, A. (1972). "Congenital dysplasia of the isthmus in the arches of the lumbosacral spine in pre-school children." *Chir. Narz. Ruchu. Ortop. Pol.*, **37**: 345–351.

WANGERMEZ, J., ROQUES, J. C. & WANGERMEZ, A. (1969). "Inheritance of spondylolisthesis: its sexual variations and the associated modifications of the lumbo-pelvic skeleton." *J. Radiol. Electrol. Med. Nucl.*, **50**: 311–314.

WARD, T., KNOWELDEN, J. & SHARRARD, W. J. W. (1968). "Low back pain: an epidemiological survey of low back pain in a rural practice." *J. Roy. Coll. Gen. Pract.*, **15**: 128–136.

WEISENBERG, M. (1975). "Pain: anxiety and attitudes in black, white and Puerto Rican patients." *Psychomatic Med.*, **37**: 123–135.

WEISS, P. & RASKINS, J. (1968). "The teenage lumbar disk syndrome." *Internat. Surg.*, **49**: 528.

WILFLING, F. J., KLONOFF, H. & KOKAN, P. (1973). "Psychological, demographic and orthopaedic factors associated with prediction of outcome of spinal fusion." *Clin. Orthop.*, **90**: 153–160.

WOOD, A. E. (1973). "Dietary osteomalacia and bone pain in the elderly." *J. Amer. Med. Assoc.*, **66**: 241–243.

WOOD, P. H. N. (1970). "Recent trends in sickness absence and mortality." *Ann. Rheum. Dis.*, **29**: 324–329.

WOOD, P. H. N. (1970). "Statistical appendix-digest of data on the rheumatic diseases. 2: Recent trends in sickness absence and mortality." *Ann. Rheum Dis.*, **29**: 19.

WOOD, P. H. N. (1972). "Epidemiology of back pain." In *The*

*Lumbar Spine and Back Pain*, pp. 13–27. Ed. by M. I. V. Jayson. London: Sector Publishing.

WOODROW, K. M., FRIEDMAN, G. D., SIEGELAUB, A. B. & COLLEN, M. F. (1972). "Pain tolerance: differences according to age, sex and race." *Psychosomatic Med.*, **34:** 548–556.

ZEINER-HENRICKSON, T. (1966). "Sickness among male sciatica patients." *J. Oslo City Hosp.*, **16:** 153–172.

ZIPPEL. H. & LORENZ, G. (1973). "Histological findings in vertebral displacements in childhood." *Beitr. Orthop. Traum.* **20:** 289–303.

### *(b) Occupational Correlations*

ANDERSON, J. A. D. (1971). "Rheumatism in industry: a review." *Brit. J. Indust. Med.*, **28:** 103–121.

ANDERSON, J. A. D. & DUTHIE, J. J. R. (1963). "Rheumatic complaints in dockyard workers." *Ann. Rheumat. Dis.*, **22:** 401–409.

ARMY MEDICAL DIRECTORATE (1959). "The soldier's back." *Bulletin (2nd Ser.) No. 10. War Office (AMD7). (WO Code No. 12389).*

AYER, H. E. & LUNCH, J. R. (1969). "Association of disability and selected occupational hazards." *Abstract on Hygiene. No.* **2359:** 685–686.

BEALS, R. K. & HICKMAN, N. W. (1972). "Industrial injuries of the back and extremities. Comprehensive evaluation—an aid in prognosis and management: a study of one hundred and eighty patients." *J. Bone Joint Surg.*, **54A:** 1593–1611.

BLOW, J. (1971). "Rehabilitation of registered dock workers." *Proc. Roy. Soc. Med.*, **64:** 753–757.

BLOW, R. J. & HACKSON, J. M. (1971). "An analysis of back injuries in registered dock workers." *Proc. Roy. Soc. Med.*, **64:** 1–4.

BOND, M. B. (1964). "Low back X-rays: criteria for their use in placement examinations in industry." *J. Occup. Med.*, **6:** 373–380.

BOND, M. B. (1969). "Low back injuries in industry." *National Safety Congress*: 68–72.

BOND, M. B. (1970). "Low back injuries in industry." *Indust. Med. Surg.*, **39:** 204–208.

BROWN, J. R. (1975). "Factors contributing to the development of low back pain in industrial workers." *Ann. Indust. Hyg. Assoc.*, **36:** 26–31.

CHRIST, W. (1974). "On the possibility of health injury arising from vertical vibration of the spine." *Fortschr. Med.*, **92:** 705–708.

CROOKSHANK, J. W. & WARSHAW, L. M. (1961). "The lumbar spine in the workman." *J. Southern Med. Assoc.*, **54:** 636–638.

CUST, G., PEARSON, J. C. G. & MAIR, A. (1972). "The prevalence of low back pain in nurses." *Int. Nurs. Rev.*, **19:** 169–179.

DELAHAYE, R. P., FABRE, J., MANGIN, H. & GALBAN, P. (1964). "Statistical study of ejections: studies in the French Army (1951 to 1963 inclusive)." *Rev. Méd., Aeronaut.*, **3:** 27–37.

DEVLIN, H. B. & GOLDMAN, M. (1966). "Backache due to osteoporosis in an industrial population: a survey of 481 patients." *Irish J. Med. Sci.*, **6:** 141–148.

EKRATH, F. A. & STRAUCH, W. (1968). "Lumbago and diminishing efficiency in female employees." *Deutsch. Gesundh.*, **23:** 1125–1129.

EWING, C. L. (1971). "Non-fatal ejection vertebral fracture, U.S. Navy fiscal years 1959 through 1965: costs." *Aerospace Med.*, **42:** 1226–1228.

FERGUSON, D. (1970). *The Work Causes of Back Injuries. Back Injuries at Work.* Wellington; N.Z. Institute of Industrial Safety.

FERGUSON, D. (1972). "Some characteristics of repeated sickness absence." *Brit. J. Indust. Med.*, **29:** 420–431.

FISCHER, F. J., FRIEDMAN, M. M. & DENMARK, R. E. VAN. (1958). "Roentgenographic abnormalities in soldiers with low back pain: comparative study." *Amer. J. Roentgenol.*, **79:** 673–676.

FISK, G. R. (1973). "Industrial injuries." *Practitioner*, **210:** 467–475.

FITZGERALD, J. G. (1968). "An approach to the problem of backache in aircrew." *RAF Institute of Aviation Medicine Report.*

FITZGERALD, J. G. & CROTTY, J. (1972). "The incidence of backache among aircrew and groundcrew of the Royal Air Force." *London Ministry of Defence, Flying Personnel Research Committee, FPRC/1313.*

FRIEDMAN, M. M., FISCHER, F. J. & DENMARK, R. E. VAN. (1946). "Lumbosacral roentgenograms of 100 soldiers: a control study." *Amer. J. Roentgenol.*, **55:** 292–298.

FROGGATT, J. (1970). "Short term absence from industry." *Brit. J. Indust. Med.*, **27:** 199; 211; 297.

GERBER, A. (1972). "The osteopathic orthopaedic surgeon and industrial back problems." *J. Occup. Med.*, **14**: 851–853.

GLOVER, J. R. (1970). "Occupational health research and the problems of back pain." *Trans. Soc. Occup. Med.*, **21**: 2–12.

GOODSELL, J. O. (1967). "Correlation of ruptured lumbar disk with occupation: a statistical analysis of 402 consecutive operations." *Clin. Orthop.*, **50**:

GURIN, J. (1971). "Analysis of the work of miners regarding its effect on the locomotor system." *Egyptian Orthop. J.*, **6**: 147–154.

HAKKAL, H. G. (1973). "Clay-shoveler's fracture." *Ann. Fenn. Phys. Med.*, **8**: 104–106.

HARLEY, W. J. (1969). "The physician's headaches: syndromes of the back, neck and shoulder. The industrial physician." *Penn. Med.*, **72**: 85–88.

HEALD, C. B. (1952). "Fibrositis in industry and the Laughton-Scott technique." *Trans. Assoc. Industr. Med. Off.*, **2**: 106.

HOCK, H. J. B. (1972). "Occupational low back pain injury." *Occupational Society of Health*, **50/10**: 354–364.

HOOVER, S. A. (1973). "Job-related back injury in hospital." *Amer. J. Nurs.*, **73**: 2078–2079.

HRUBEC, Z. & NASHOLD, B. S. (1975). "Epidemiology of lumbar disc lesions in the military in World War II." *Amer. J. Epidemiol.*, **102**: 366–376.

HUNT, T. A. (1974). "Tissue reactions to pressure stresses in miners." *Practitioner*, **213**: 189–194.

JACKSON, J. M. (1968). "Biomechanical hazards in the dockworker." *Ann. Occup. Hyg.*, **11**: 147–157.

JEANMART, L. (1973). "Dorso-lumbar pain of occupational origin." *J. Belge Radiol.*, **56**: 1–9.

KELLGREN, J. H. & LAWRENCE, J. S. (1952). "Rheumatism in miners. Part II. X-ray study." *Brit. J. Industr. Med.*, **9**: 197–207.

KELSEY, J. L. (1975). "An epidemiological study of the relationship between occupations and acute herniated lumbar intervertebral discs." *Int. J. Epidemiol.*, **4**: 197–205.

KELSEY, J. L. & HARDY, R. J. (1975). "Driving of motor vehicles as a risk factor for acute herniated lumbar intervertebral disc." *Amer. J. Epidemiol.*, **102**: 63–73.

KOSIAK, M., AURELIUS, J. R. & HARTFIEL, W. F. (1966). "Backache in industry." *J. Occup. Med.*, **8**: 51–58.

LAWRENCE, J. S. (1955). "Rheumatism in coal miners. Part III: a1 Occupational factors." *Brit. J. Industr. Med.*, **12**: 249–261.

LAWRENCE, J. S. (1961). "Rheumatism in cotton operatives." *Brit. J. Industr. Med.*, **18**: 270–276.

LAWRENCE, J. S. & AITKEN-SWAN, J. (1952). "Rheumatism in miners. Part II: Rheumatic complaints." *Brit. J. Industr. Med.*, **9**: 1–18.

LAWRENCE, J. S., MOLYNEUX, M. K. & DINGWALL-FORDYCE, I. (1966). "Rheumatism in foundry workers." *Brit. J. Industr. Med.*, **23**: 42–52.

LAWRENCE, J. S. & ROWE, M. L. (1971). "Low back disability in industry: updated position." *J. Occup. Med.*, **13**: 476–478.

LEAVITT, S. S., BEYER, R. D. & JOHNSTON, T. L. (1972). "Monitoring the recovery process: pilot results of a systematic approach to case management." *Industr. Med. Surg.*, **41**: 25–30.

LEAVITT, S. S., JOHNSTON, T. L. & BEYER, R. D. (1971). "The process of recovery: patterns in industrial back injury." *Industr. Med. Surg.*, **40**: 7–14.

LEITZ, G. (1971). "On backache, disc degeneration and working capacity in industry." *Med. Welt.*, **46**: 1815–1823.

LEVY, M. (1968). "Porter's neck." *Brit. Med. J.*, **2**: 16.

LINDEN, V. (1969). "Absence from work and physical fitness." *Brit. J. Indust. Med.*, **26**: 47–53.

LOCKSHIN, M. D., HIGGINS, I. T. T., HIGGINS, M. W., DODGE, H. & CANALE, N. (1969). "Rheumatism in mining communities in Marion County, West Virginia." *Amer. J. Epidemiol.*, **90**: 17–29.

McGILL, C. M. (1968). "Industrial back problems. A control program." *J. Occup. Med.*, **10**: 174–178.

McGREGGOR, D. (1970). "Daily inception of incapacity." *Trans. Soc. Occup. Med.*, **21**: 13–23.

MAGNUSON, P. B. (1932). "Backache from the industrial standpoint." *J. Bone Joint Surg.*, **14**: 165–169.

MAGORA, A. (1969). "An investigation of the problem of sick leave in the patient suffering from low back pain." *Industr. Med. Surg.*, **38**: 80–89.

MAGORA, A. (1970). "Investigation of the relation between low back pain and occupation." *Scand. J. Rehab. Med.*, **6**: 81–88.

MAGORA, A. (1970). "Investigation of the relation between low back pain and occupation." *Industr. Med. Surg.*, **39**: 465–471; 504–510.

MAGORA, A. (1972). "Investigation of the relation between low back pain and occupation. 3. Physical requirements: sitting, standing, and weight lifting." *Industr. Med. Surg.*, **41:** 5–9.

MAGORA, A. (1973). "Investigation of the relation between low back pain and occupation. 4. Physical requirements: bending, rotation, reaching and sudden maximal effort." *Scand. J. Rehab. Med.*, **5:** 187–190.

MAGORA, A. (1973). "Investigation of the relation between low back pain and occupation. 5. Psychological aspects." *Scand. J. Rehab. Med.*, **5:** 191–196.

MAGORA, A. (1974). "Investigation of the relation between low back pain and occupation. 6. Medical history symptoms." *Scand. J. Rehab. Med.*, **6:** 81–88.

MANTLE, M. J., GREENWOOD, R. M. & CURREY, H. L. F. (1977). "Backache in pregnancy." *Rheumatol. Rehab.*, **16:** 95–101.

MATTHEWS, J. (1964). "Ride comfort for tractor operators. I. Review of existing information." *J. Agric. Eng. Res.*, **9:** 3–31.

MATTHEWS, J. (1964). "Ride comfort for tractor operators. II. Analysis of ride variations in pneumatic-tyred tractors." *J. Agric. Eng. Res.*, **9:** 147–158.

MATTINGLY, S. (1970). "Rehabilitation of registered dock workers at Garston Manor." *Proc. Roy. Soc. Med.*, **64:** 757–760.

MAXWELL ROBERTSON, A. (1970). "The challenge of the painful back: an industrial and medical problem." *Trans. Soc. Occup. Med.*, **20:** 42–49.

MAY, J. & WRIGHT, H. B. (1961). "Heights and weights of business men." *Trans. Assoc. Indust. Med. Off.*, **11:** 143–149.

NACHEMSON, A. (1961). "Clinical observations of the spine in ejected pilots." *Acta Orthop. Scand.*, **31:** 135–145.

ONISHI, N. (1973). "Fatigue and strength of upper limb muscles of flight reservation system operators." *J. Human Ergon.*, **2:** 133–141.

OSANAI, H. (1966). "Lumbago in relation to occupational work." *J. Science of Labour*, **42:** 495–500.

PARTRIDGE, R. E. H. & ANDERSON, J. A. D. (1969). "Back pain in industrial workers." *Proc. XII Int. Rheum. Congr. Prague.* Abstract No. 284.

PARTRIDGE, R. E. H., ANDERSON, J. A. D. & DUTHIE, J. J. R. (1964). "Rheumatic disorders in industrial workers." *Med. et Hyg., Genéve*, **22:** 360.

PARTRIDGE, R. E. H., ANDERSON, J. A. D., McCARTHY, M. A. & DUTHIE, J. J. R. (1965). "Rheumatism in light industry." *Ann. Rheum. Dis.*, **24:** 332–340.

PARTRIDGE, R. E. H., ANDERSON, J. A. D., McCARTHY, M. A. & DUTHIE, J. J. R. (1968). "Rheumatic complaints among workers in iron foundries." *Ann. Rheum. Dis.*, **27:** 441–453.

PARTRIDGE, R. E. H. & DUTHIE, J. J. R. (1968). "Rheumatism in dockers and civil servants. A comparison of heavy manual and sedentary workers." *Ann. Rheum. Dis.*, **27:** 559–567.

PILLMORE, J. (1960). "The occupational low back hazard." *Indust. Med. Surg.*, **29:** 28.

RAMETTA, E. (1973). "Vertebral lesions in aviation medicine, especially in seat ejection and in parachuting." *Minerva Med.*, **64:** 3522–3549.

REDFIELD, J. T. (1971). "The low back X-ray as a pre-employment screening tool in the forest products industry." *J. Occup. Med.*, **13:** 219–226.

ROBERTSON, A. (1970). "The challenge of the painful back: an industrial and medical problem." *Trans. Soc. Occup. Med.*, **20:** 42–49.

ROTONDO, G. (1975). "Spinal injury after ejection in jet pilots: mechanisms, diagnosis, follow-up and prevention." *Aviat. Space Environ. Med.*, **46:** 842–848.

ROWE, M. L. (1969). "Low back pain in industry: a position paper." *J. Occup. Med.*, **11:** 161–169.

ROWE, M. L. (1971). "Low back disability in industry: updated position." *J. Occup. Med.*, **13:** 476–478.

SCHEIN, A. J. (1968). "Back and neck pain and associated nerve root irritation in the New York City Fire Department." *Clin. Orthop.*, **59:** 119–124.

SCHEIN, A. J. (1968). "Evolution and pathogenesis of discogenic spine pain and associated radiculitis as seen in the New York City Fire Department." *J. Mount Sinai Hosp.*, **35:** 371–389.

SEAGER, F. G. M. (1959). "Some observations on the incidence and treatment of back injuries in industry." *Ann. Occup. Hyg.*, **1:** 180–185.

SEMMENCE, A. (1971). "Rising sickness absence in Great Britain— a general practitioner's point of view." *J. Roy. Coll. Gen. Pract.*, **21:** 125–146.

SESSA, G. (1963). "Arthrosis of the vertebral column in sailors." *Folia Med., Naples*, **46:** 480–490.

SIMONS, G. R. & MIRABILE, M. P. (1972). "An analysis and interpretation of industrial medical data with concentration on back problems." *J. Occup. Med.*, **14:** 227–231.

STEEL, V. (1969). "Nurses' back injuries need not occur." *J. West. Aust. Nurses*, **35:** 4–7.

SWEETMAN, B. J., ANDERSON, J. A. D. & DALTON, E. R. (1974). "The relationships between little finger mobility, lumbar mobility, straight leg raising and low back pain." *Rheumatol. Rehab.*, **13:** 161–166.

TAUBER, J. (1970). "An unorthodox look at backaches." *J. Occup. Med.*, **12:** 128–130.

TAYLOR, P. J. (1967). "Shift and day work: a comparison of sickness absence, lateness and other absence behaviour in an oil refinery from 1962–1965." *Brit. J. Indust. Med.*, **24:** 93.

TAYLOR, P. J. (1967). "Individual variations in sickness absence." *Brit. J. Indust. Med.*, **24:** 169–177.

TAYLOR, P. J. (1968). "Personal factors associated with sickness and absence." *Brit. J. Indust. Med.*, **25:** 106–118.

TAYLOR, P. J. (1974). "Sickness absence: facts and misconceptions." *J. Roy. Coll. Phys. Lond.*, **8:** 315–354.

THOMSON, D. (1974). "Civil service experience of pre-employment examinations." *Proc. Roy. Soc. Med.*, **67:** 182–184.

TROISI, F. M. (1969). "Lumbago with changes of the spinal column caused by defective posture in sedentary work." *Med. Lavoro*, **60:** 21–27.

TROUP, J. D. G. (1965). "Relation of lumbar spine disorders to heavy manual work and lifting." *Lancet*, **1:** 857–861.

TROUP, J. D. G. (1969). "The spine of the tractor driver." *Rural Medicine*, **1:** 9–12.

TROUP, J. D. G. ROANTREE, W. B. & ARCHIBALD, R. (1970). "Industry and low back problem." *New Scientist*, **8:** 65–67.

ULRICH, S. P. (1974). "Incidence of backache in recruits." *Praxis*, **63:** 942–945.

UTTL, K. (1966). "On the incidence of discogenic disease (vertebrogenic disorders) with regard to work capacity. *Rev. Česk. Med.*, **12:** 116–122.

WALFORD, P. A. (1962). *Diseases of Bones and Organs of Movement*." In *Morbidity Statistics from General Practice. General*

*Register Office, Studies in Medical and Population Subjects.* **14:** 77–87.

WALKER, J. & DE LA MARE, G. (1971). "Absence from work in relation to length and distribution of shift hours." *Brit. J. Indust. Med.*, **28:** 36–4.

WILSON, P. D. (1962). "Low back pain: a problem for industry." *Arch. Environ. Hlth.*, **4:** 505–510.

WILSON, R. N. & WILSON, S. (1955). "Low backache in industry—a review of 1,163 cases." *Brit. Med. J.*, **11:** 649–652.

WOODHALL, B. (1947). 'Anatomicophysiological aspects of injuries to the intervertebral disc." A. Sensory patterns in the localization of disc lesions. B. Preliminary appraisal of army results." *J. Bone Joint. Surg.*, **29:** 470–475.

# 6

# TREATMENT

*(a) Medical (including Rehabilitation)*

ANDERSON, I. F. (1974). "Trial of a new antirheumatic agent." *Sth. Afr. Med. J.*, **48**: 899–903.

ASCHER, P. W. (1969). "Intrathecal cortisone management of lumbar radiculopathy." *Zbl. Chir.*, **94**: 1678–1679.

ASHOFF, H. (1966). "On the conservative treatment of lumbar intervertebral disk prolapse." *Zeit. Orthop.* **101**: 448–452.

BABB, F. S. (1968). "Stabilizing the spine to relieve low back pain." *Postgrad. Med.*, **43**: 248–250.

BAILEY, R. R. (1974). "Acute arthralgia after high-dose intravenous methylprednisolone." *Lancet*, **2**: 1014.

BARRETT, J. & GOLDING, D. (1972). "The management of low back pain and sciatica." *Practitioner*, **208**: 118–124.

BATTISTA, A. F. (1974). "Pain relief by subarachnoid hypothermic saline injection." *Amer. J. Surg.*, **128**: 662–667.

BELIVEAU, P. (1971). "A comparison between epidural anaesthesia with and without corticosteroid in the treatment of sciatica." *Rheumat. Phys. Med.*, **11**: 40–43.

BRÜGGER, A. (1977). *Disorders of the Locomotor Apparatus and Its Nervous System.* Stuttgart; Fischer.

BURN, J. M. B. & LANGDON, L. (1970). "Lumbar epidural injection for the treatment of chronic sciatica." *Rheumat. Phys. Med.*, **10**: 368–374.

BURROWS, R. (1973). "Warm baths and back trouble." *Lancet*, **2**: 913–914.

CHO, L. (1970). "Therapeutic epidural block with a combination of a weak local anaesthetic and steroids in management of complicated low back pain." *Amer. Surg.*, **36**: 303.

COHEN, A., NASELLI, F. P. & CRAIG, M. P. (1946). "Treatment of sciatica with alternating current." *Arch. Phys. Med.*, **27**: 219–222.

COLONNA, P. C. & FRIEDENBERG, Z. B. (1949). "The disc syndrome. Results of the conservative care of patients with positive myelograms." *J. Bone Joint Surg.*, **31A**: 614–618.

CONWELL, H. E. & ELLIS, J. D. (1940). *The Injured Back and Its Treatment.* Springfield, Illinois; Thomas.

COOK, K. (1972). "Treatment of whiplash injuries by nerve block." *Southern. Med. J.,* **65:** 572–574.

COOK, S. W. (1975). "Comments on ethical considerations in 'self-control techniques as an alternative to pain medication'." *J. Abnorm. Psychol.,* **84:** 169–171.

COOMES, J. (1961). "A comparison between epidural anaesthesia and bed-rest in sciatica." *Brit. Med. J.,* **1:** 20–24.

COOPER, A. L. (1961). "Trigger-point injection: its place in physical medicine." *Arch. Phys. Med. Rehab.,* **42:** 704–709.

COXHEAD, C. E. (1974). "A clinical trial of the management of sciatica with or without low back pain." *Physiotherapy,* **60:** 72–74.

CYRIAX, J. (1950). "Refresher course for general practitioners: the treatment of lumbar disc lesions." *Brit. Med. J.,* **2:** 1434–1438.

CYRIAX, J. (1958). "Lumbar disc-lesions: conservative treatment." *Sth. Afr. Med. J.,* **32:** 1–3.

CYRIAX, J. (1974). "Chiropractic." *Canad. Med. Assoc. J.,* **111:** 911; 1913.

CYRIAX, J. (1978). *Textbook of Orthopaedic Medicine.* 6th ed. London; Baillière.

DADONE, G. (1972). "Cervical arthrosis, cervicobrachalgia, physio-kinestherapy." *Minerva Ortop.,* **23:** 439–445.

DANDY, W. E. (1944). "Treatment of recurring attacks of low back pain without sciatica." *J. Amer. Med Assoc.,* **125:** 1175–1178.

DANIEL, J. W. (1969). "Rehabilitation and resettlement of patients suffering from rheumatical disorders." *J. Roy. Coll. Gen. Pract.,* **3** (Suppl.): 29–32.

DAVIDSON, J. T. & ROBIN, G. C. (1961). "Epidural injections in the lumbo-sciatic syndrome." *Brit. J. Anaesthesia,* **33:** 595.

DAVIS, R. (1974). "Transcutaneous nerve stimulation for treatment of pain in spinal-cord-injured patients." *Bull. Prosthet. Res.,* *(Fall issue)*: 298–301.

DAY, P. L. (1974). "Early, interim and long term observations on chemonucleolysis in 876 patients with special comments on the lateral approach." *Clin. Orthop.,* **99:** 64–69.

DEPARTMENT OF HEALTH AND SOCIAL SECURITY (1972). *Rehabilitation.* London; H.M.S.O.

DICKSON, J. H., HARRINGTON, P. R. & ERWIN, W. D. (1973). "Harrington instrumentation in the fractured, unstable thoracic lumbar spine." *Texas Med.*, **69:** 91–98.

DIETRICH, S. L. (1975). "Rehabilitation and nonsurgical management of musculo-skeletal problems in the hemophilic patient." *Ann. N.Y. Acad. Sci.*, **240:** 328–337.

DILKE, T. F. W., BURRY, H. C. & GRAHAME, R. (1973). "Extradural corticosteriod injection in management of lumbar nerve root compression." *Brit. Med. J.*, **2:** 635–637.

DONOFF, R. B. (1973). "Management of condylar fractures in patients with cervical spine injury." *J. Oral Surg.*, **31:** 130–135.

DUTHIE, J. J. R. (1952). "Medical treatment of the rheumatic diseases." *J. Bone Joint Surg.*, **34B:** 211–214.

DWYER, A. G. (1974). "Use of direct current in spine fusions." *J. Bone Joint Surg.*, **64A:** 1499.

EDWARDS, B. C. (1969). "Low back pain and pain resulting from lumbar spine conditions: a comparison of treatment results." *Austr. J. Physiotherapy*, **15:** 104–110.

EVANS, M. (1930). "Intrasacral epidural injection in the treatment of sciatica." *Lancet* **2:** 1225–1228.

EXTON-SMITH, A. N. (1974). "Rehabilitation of the elderly." *Update, (Sept.)*: 523–528.

FAHRNI, W. H. (1975). "Conservative treatment of lumbar disc degeneration: our primary responsibility." *Orthop. Clin. Nth. Amer.*, **6:** 93–103.

FEFFER, H. L. (1956). "Treatment of low-back and sciatica pain by the injection of hydrocortisone into degenerated intervertebral discs." *J. Bone Joint Surg.*, **46A:** 585–592.

FEFFER, H. L. (1969). "Therapeutic intradiscal hydrocortisone: a long-term study." *Clin. Orthop.*, **67:** 100–104.

FEFFER, H. L. (1975). "Regional use of steroids in the management of lumbar intervertebral disk disease." *Orthop. Clin. Nth. Amer.*, **6:** 249–253.

FERGUSON, V. (1975). "Pain and its alleviation: summary of a forum." *Arch. Phys. Med. Rehab.*, **56:** 172–173.

FINER, B. (1972). "The use of hypnosis in the clinical management of pain." In *Pain: Basic Principles, Pharmacology, Therapy*, pp. 168. Ed. by R. Janzen, W. D. Keidel, A. Herz and C. Steichele. Stuttgart; Thieme.

FISHER, A. G. T. (1923). "Some researches into the physiological principles underlying the treatment of injuries and diseases of the articulations." *Lancet*, **2**: 541–548.

FLANIGAN, S. & BOOP, W. C. (1974). "Spinal intrathecal injection procedures in the management of pain." *Clin. Neurosurg.*, **21**: 229–238.

FORD, D. E. & KRUSEN, E. M. (1957). "Conservative management of certain types of back injury: analysis and results." *Arch. Phys. Med. Rehab.*, **38**: 395–401.

FORD, L. T. (1969). "Clinical use of chymopapain in lumbar dorsal disk lesions: an end-result study." *Clin. Orthop.*, **67**: 81–87.

FRIEDENBERG, Z. B. (1953). "The results of nonoperative treatment of ruptured lumbar disks." *Surg. Clin. Nth. Amer.*, **33**: 1545–1549.

GAMMON, G. D. & STARR, I. (1941). "Studies on relief of pain by counter-irritation." *J. Clin. Invest.*, **20**: 13–20.

GARVIN, P. J. & JENNINGS, R. B. (1973). "Long-term effects of chymopapain on intervertebral disks of dogs." *Clin. Orthop.*, **92**: 281–295.

GILLY, R. (1970). "Trial of treatment of 50 cases of sciatica and lumbar radiculalgia by Celestene chronodose in pararadicular infiltrations." *Marseille Méd.*, **107**: 341–345.

GOFF, B. & ROSE, G. K. (1964). "The use of a modified spondylometer in the treatment of ankylosing spondylitis." *Rheumatism*, **20**: 63–66.

GOLDIE, I. & PETERHOFF, V. (1968). "Epidural anaesthesia in low-back pain and sciatica." *Acta Orthop. Scand.*, **39**: 20–26.

GOLOSKOV, J. & LE ROY, P. (1974). "Pain and suffering: use of the dorsal column stimulator." *Amer. J. Nursing*, **74**: 506–507.

GRAHAM, C. E. (1974). "Backache and sciatica: report of 90 patients treated by intradiscal injection of chymopapain." *Med. J. Austr.*, **1**: 5–8.

GRAY, F. J. (1969). "An assessment of body-weight traction on a polished inclined plane in the treatment of discogenic sciatica." *Med. J. Aust.*, **2**: 545–549.

GRAY, F. J. & HOSKING, H. J. (1963). "A radiological assessment of the effect of body weight traction on the lumbar disc spaces." *Med. J. Aust.*, **2**: 953–954.

GROGONO, P. (1969). "Backache: a conservative yet vigorous approach." *J. Canad. Physiotherapy Assoc.*, **21**: 31–35.

HARRINGTON, P. R. & TULLOS, H. S. (1969). "Reduction of severe spondylolisthesis in children." *Southern Med. J.*, **61:** 1–8.

HARTMAN, J. T. (1975). "A comparative study of five commonly used cervical orthoses." *Clin. Orthop.*, **109:** 97–102.

HENDERSON, R. S. (1952). "The treatment of lumbar intervertebral disc protrusion: an assessment of conservative measures." *Brit. Med. J.*, **2:** 597–598.

HILL, H. (1973). "Backache relieved by polystyrene mattress." *Lancet*, **1:** 36.

HINDLE, T. H. (1972). "Comparison of carisoprodol, butabarbital and placebo in treatment of low back syndrome." *Calif. Med.*, **117:** 7–11.

HINGORANI, K. (1968). "Oral enzyme therapy in severe back pain." *Brit. J. Clin. Pract.*, **22:** 209–210.

HINGORANI, K. & BISWAS, A. K. (1970). "Double blind controlled trial comparing oxyphenbutazone and indomethacin in the treatment of low back pain." *Brit. J. Clin. Pract.*, **24:** 120–123.

HIRSCHBERG, G. G. (1974). "Treating lumbar disc lesions by prolonged continuous reduction of intradiscal pressure." *Texas Med.*, **70:** 58–60.

HOGAN, J. T., MACEWEN, G. D. & SMITH, A. G. (1965). "A follow up of patients with low back pain treated without surgery." *Delaware Med. Journ.*, **37:** 53–55; 75.

HOOVER, R. M. (1938). "The treatment of sciatic pain." *Arch. Phys. Therap.*, **19:** 120.

HSU, J. (1973). "Orthopaedic management of spinal muscle atrophy." *J. Bone Joint Surg.*, **55B:** 663.

HUTSON, M. A. (1973). "Treatment of lumbo-sacral disc disorders." *Practitioner*, **210:** 415–417.

JACOBS, J. H. & GRAYSON, M. R. (1968). "Trial of an anti-inflammatory agent (indomethacin) in low back pain with and without radicular involvement." *Brit. Med. J.*, **3:** 158–160.

JENKINS, D. G. (1974). "The management of back pain." *Proc. Roy. Soc. Med.*, **67:** 496–498.

JENNETT, B. (1974). "Treatment of sciatica." *Lancet*, **1:** 132.

JONES, H. T. (1948). "Low back pain from the orthopedic standpoint." *Arch. Phys. Med.*, **29:** 186.

JURMAND, S. H. (1973). "Peridural injections of corticoids in the treatment of lumbar and sciatic pain of discal origin." *Rev. Rhum. Mal. Osteoartic.*, **40:** 461–464.

KAPSALIS, A. A., STERN, J. J. & BORNSTEIN, I. (1974). "The fate of chymopapain for therapy of intervertebral disc disease." *J. Lab. Clin. Med.*, **83:** 532–540.

KARK, W. (1972). "Low back injuries—results of treatment." *Sth. Afr. J. Surg.*, **10:** 89–95.

KENDALL, M. & JENKINS, P. (1968). "Exercises for backache: a double-blind controlled trial." *Physiotherapy*, **54:** 154.

KHVISIUK, N. I. (1974). "Devices for resetting of displaced vertebrae in spondylolisthesis." *Ortop. Trav. Matol. Preotez*, **12:** 66–67.

KNUTSEN, O. & YGGE, H. (1971). "Prolonged extradural anaesthesia with 'bupivacaine' in lumbago and sicatica." *Acta Orthop. Scand.*, **42:** 338–352.

KVIST, H., HARVINEN, M. & SORVARI, T. (1974). "Effect of mobilization and immobilization on the healing of contusion injury in muscle." *Scand. J. Rehab. Med.*, **6:** 134–140.

LANCET EDITORIAL (1973). "Physiotherapy or psychotherapy." *Lancet*, **2:** 1483.

LANDEN, B. R. (1967). "Heat or cold for the relief of back pain." *Phys. Ther.*, **47:** 1126–1128.

LEWIS, J. & McKIBBIN, B. (1974). "The treatment of unstable facture-dislocations of the thoraco-lumbar spine accompanied by paraplegia." *J. Bone Joint Surg.*, **56B:** 603–612.

LIDSTROM, A. & ZACHRISSON, M. (1970). "Physical therapy of low back pain and sicatica: an attempt at evaluation." *Scand. J. Rehab. Med.*, **2:** 37–42.

LODGE, T. (1963). "Radiology in the management of paraplegia." *Radiology*, **14:** 365–380.

LOGAN, T. (1958). "Counter-torque suspension." *Physiotherapy*, *March*: 71.

LOGAN, T. (1961). "The treatment of intervertebral disc protrusions with salt." *J. Coll. Gen. Pract.*, **4:** 96–100.

LONG, D. M. (1974). "Cutaneous afferent stimulation for relief of chronic pain." *Clin. Neurosurg.*, **21:** 257–268.

LOVETT, R. W. (1906). "The treatment of lateral curvature of the spine." *J. Amer. Med. Assoc.*, **46:** 1915–1922.

McKEE, G. K. (1957). "The treatment of backache and sciatica." *Med. Press*, **237:** 49–55.

MacNAB, I., McCULLOCH, J. A., WEINER, D. S., HUGO, E. P., GALWAY, R. D. & DALL, D. (1971). "Chemonucleolysis." *Canad. J. Surg.*, **14:** 280–288.

MAKOWSKI, J., BUCZYNSKI, A. Z. & KIWERSKI, J. (1972). "Clinical evaluation of depomedrol in acute backache syndromes." *Pol. Tyg. Lek.*, **28**: 261–263.

MARSHALL, C. M. (1974). "Teaching aid for mobilisation of the spine." *Physiotherapy*, **60**: 277.

MARSHALL, L. (1967). "Conservative management of low back pain: a review of 700 cases." *Med. J. Aust.*, **1**: 266–267.

MARSHALL, L. (1973). "Intradiscal enzyme for back pain." *Med. J. Aust.*, **2**: 616.

MATHEWS, J. A. (1969/70). "Dynamic discography: a study of lumbar traction." *Ann. Phys. Med.*, **9**: 275–279.

MATHEWS, J. A. & YATES, D. A. H. (1974). "Treatment of sciatica." *Lancet*, **1**: 352.

MATTMAN, E. VON, (1971). "Symptomatic pain therapy with intrathecal irrigation of warm hypertonic saline solution." *Arch. Neurol. Neurochir. Psychiat.*, **108**: 33–38.

MEDICAL RESEARCH COUNCIL WORKING PARTY ON TUBERCULOSIS OF THE SPINE (1973). "A controlled trial of ambulent out-patient treatment and in-patient rest in bed in the management of tuberculosis of the spine in young Korean patients on standard chemotherapy: a study in Masan, Korea." *J. Bone Joint Surg.*, **55B**: 678–697.

MELZACK, R. (1975). "Self-regulation of pain: the use of alpha-feedback and hypnotic training for the control of chronic pain." *Exp. Neurol.*, **46**: 452–469.

MILES, J. (1974). "Pain relief by implanted electrical stimulators." *Lancet*, **1**: 777–779.

MOLL, W. (1973). "Treatment of the acute lumbovertebral syndrome by optimal medical muscular relaxation with diazepam." *Med. Welt*, **24**: 1747–1751.

MORRISON, M. C. T. (1974). "Treatment of 'disc lesions'." *Physiotherapy*, **60**: 17–21.

MOTAMED, H. H. (1972). "Current orthopedic treatments in myelodysplasia." *Int. Surg.*, **57**: 951–956.

MOUNT, H. T. R. (1971). "Hydrocortisone in the treatment of intervertebral disc protrusion." *Canad. Med. Assoc. J.*, **105**: 1279–1280.

NACHEMSON, A. L. (1969). "Physiotherapy for low back pain patients." *Scand. J. Rehab. Med.*, **1**: 85–90.

TREATMENT

NACHEMSON, A. L. (1975). "Treatment of low back pain: a critical look at current methods." *J. Bone Joint Surg.*, **57B:** 262.

NASHOLD, B. S. & FRIEDMAN, H. (1972). "Dorsal column stimulation for control of pain." *J. Neurosurg.*, **36:** 590–597.

*New Zealand Medical Journal* (1975). "The management of lumbago." *N.Z. Med. J.*, **81:** 485–486.

NIEMINEN, R. (1974). "Conservative treatment of luxations and subluxations of the lower cervical spine." *Ann. Chir. Gynaecol. Fenn.*, **63:** 57–68.

NORDBY, E. J. & LUCAS, G. L. (1973). "A comparative analysis of lumbar disk disease treated by laminectomy or chemonucleolysis." *Clin. Orthop.*, **90:** 119–129.

NORDWALL, A. (1973). "Studies in idiopathic scoliosis relevant to etiology, conservative and operative treatment." *Acta Orthop. Scand., Suppl.* **150:** 1.

OSTERHOLM, J. L. (1973). "Successful treatment of severe experimental spinal cord injuries by intracisternal 3-alpha-dimethyl-tyrosine." *Surg. Forum*, **24:** 440–442.

PARISH, J. G. (1973). "The place of a rehabilitation centre in the treatment of low back pain." *Rehabilitation*, **84:** 15–19.

PARKINSON, D. & SHIELDS, C. (1973). "Treatment of protruded lumbar intervertebral discs with chymopapain (discase)." *J. Neurosurg.*, **39:** 203–208.

PARRY, C. B. (1974). "Rehabilitation of the inflammatory arthropathies." *Proc. Roy. Soc. Med.*, **67:** 494–496.

PARRY, J. (1970). "The use of external support in the treatment of low back pain." *Artif. Limbs*, **14:** 49–57.

PEARCE, J. & MOLL, J. M. H. (1967). "Conservative treatment and natural history of acute lumbar disc lesions." *J. Neurol. Neurosurg. Psychiat.*, **30:** 13–17.

PETERSON, T. H. (1963). "Injeection treatment for low back pain." *Amer. J. Orthop.*, **5:** 320–322.

PLEWES, M. (1948). "Rehabilitation in industry." *Lancet*, **2:** 699.

POTTER, J. (1974). "Treatment of sciatica." *Lancet*, **1:** 220.

PRIDIE, K. H. (1962). "Experience of discography in the treatment of cervical lesions." *J. Bone Joint Surg.*, **33B:** 440.

PROLO, D. J. (1974). "Pre-hospital management." *J. Kansas Med. Soc.*, **75:** 349–352.

RALSTON, E. L. (1971). "Conservative treatment for protrusion of the lumbar intervertebral disc." *Orthop. Clin. Nth. Amer.*, **2:** 485–491.

REED, J. W. (1967). "Rehabilitating the chronically ill." *J. Chron. Dis.*, **20:** 457–468.

RENIER, P. (1967). "Lumbago back pain and muscle relaxants." *Rehab. Phys. Med.*, **10:** 181.

RICHARDS, P., CHAMBERLAIN, M. J. & WRONG, O. M. (1972). "Treatment of osteomalacia of renal tubular acidosis by sodium bicarbonate alone." *Lancet*, **2:** 993–997.

ROBIN, J. P. (1973). "Comparative study of the value of diazepam and methocarbamol in the treatment of certain lumbosciaticas." *Vie Méd. Canad. Français*, **2:** 442–443.

ROBINSON, M. P. (1975). "Treatment of low back pain in general practice." *Brit. Med. J.*, **1:** 209.

ROSENTAHL, A. M. (1974). "Rehabilitation of the patient with chronic low back pain." *Illinois Med. J.*, **146:** 189–223.

ROTHMAN, R. H., MARVEL, J. P. & BAKER, R. (1971). "The conservative treatment of cervical disc disease." *Orthop. Clin. Nth. Amer.*, **2:** 435–441.

SAMSON, P. & HEYNS, M. (1972). "Relief of backache by abdominal decompression." *Med. Proc.*, **8:** 92–95.

SAVASTANO, A. A. & NAVACH, J. (1972). "Review of the conservative and operative management of spondylolisthesis in the lumbo-sacral spine." *Int. Surg.*, **57:** 571–576.

SAYLE-CREER, W. & SWERDLOW, M. (1969). "Epidural injections for the relief of lumbo-sciatic pain." *Acta Orthop. Belg.*, **35:** 728–734.

SCHOENDINGER, G. R. & FORD, L. T. (1971). "The use of chymo-papain in ruptured lumbar discs." *Southern Med. J.*, **64:** 333–336.

SCHUMAN, D. (1967). "Ambulation, osteopathic manipulative therapy, and joint sclerotherapy in the management of common low back disorders." *J. Amer. Osteopath.*, **67:** 104–111.

SCOTT, M. (1966). "Relief of nocturnal intractable low back and sciatic pain by chair sleep." *J. Amer. Med. Assoc.*, **195:** 150–151.

SENGUPTA, S. (1974). "Pain and its management." *J. Indian Med. Assoc.*, **63:** 312.

SHAEFFER, J. N. (1967). "Factors in a total rehabilitation program of low back pain." *J. Occup. Med.*, **9:** 12–15.

SHAW, B. H. (1944). "Treatment of sciatica." *Arch. Phys. Med.*, **25:** 312.

SHEALY, C. N. (1974). "Transcutaneous electrical stimulation for control of pain." *Clin. Neurosurg.*, **21**: 269–277.

SHIELD, B. S. & FRIEDMAN, H. (1972). "Dorsal column stimulation for control of pain." *J. Neurosurg.*, **36**: 590–597.

SIM, P. (1970). "Techniques for the lumbar spine." *N.Z. J. Physiotherapy*, **3**: 24–26.

SIMEONE, F. A. (1971). "The modern treatment of thoracic disc disease." *Orthop. Clin. Nth. Amer.*, **2**: 453–462.

SINGER, M. (1962). "Aspects of treatment of low back pain." *Sth. Afr. Med. J.*, **36**: 317–318.

SMITH, L. (1969). "Chemonucleolysis." *Clin. Orthop.*, **67**: 72–80.

SMITH, L. & BROWN, J. E. (1967). "Treatment of lumbar intervertebral disc lesions by direct injection of chymopapain." *J. Bone Joint Surg.*, **49B**: 502–519.

STAMM, J. (1955). "Manipulation and cervical spondylosis." *Lancet*, **1**: 355.

STUCKY, E. K. (1944). "Diagnosis and treatment of low back pain." *Arch. Phys. Therap.*, **25**: 34–40.

STURROCK, R. D. & HART, D. (1974). "Double-blind cross-over comparison of Indomethacin, Fluoribprofen and placebo in ankylosing spondylitis." *Ann. Rheum. Dis.*, **33**: 129–132.

SULLIVAN, C. R. (1961). "Diagnosis and treatment of pyogenic infections of the intervertebral disk." *Surg. Clin. Nth. Amer.*, **41**: 1077–1086.

SWART, H. A. (1973). "Treatment of injuries to the low back." *West Virginia Med. J.*, **69**: 55.

SWERDLOW, M. & SAYLE-CREER, W. (1970). "A study of extradural medication in the relief of the lumbosciatic syndrome." *Anaesthesia*, **25**: 341–345.

SWINSON, D. R. (1974). "Backache, II. The use of drugs in backache." *Gen. Pract.*, **June**: 17.

SYMONDS, G. (1975). "Treatment of sciatica." *Brit. Med. J.*, **2**: 38.

TITUS, N. E. (1931). "Treatment of sciatica by physical measures." *Arch. Phys. Therap.*, **12**: 662–665.

TRAVELL, W. & TRAVELL, J. (1946). "Therapy of low back pain by manipulation and of referred pain in lower extremity by procaine infiltration." *Arch. Phys. Med.*, **27**: 537.

VAN LEUVEN, R. M. & TROUP, J. (1969). "The instant lumbar corset." *Physiotherapy*, **55**: 499–502.

WEBER, H. (1970). "An evaluation of conservative and surgical treatment of lumbar disc protrusion." *J. Oslo City Hosp.*, **20:** 81–93.

WEINER, D. S. & MACNAB, I. (1970). "The use of chymopapain in degenerative disc disease: a preliminary report." *Canad. Med. Assoc. J.*, **102:** 1252–1256.

WEISFELDT, K. (1971). "Ambulatory approach to the treatment of low back pain." *J. Occup. Med.*, **13B:** 384.

WEITZMAN, G. (1971). "Treatment of stable thoracolumbar spine compression fractures by early ambulation." *Clin. Orthop.*, **76:** 116–122.

WILKINSON, M. C. (1959). "Treatment of tuberculosis of the spine." *Brit. Med. J.*, **1:** 280–282.

WILLIAMS, P. C. (1953). "The conservative management of lesions of the lumbosacral spine." *Amer. Acad. Orthop. Surg., Instructional Course Lect.*, **10:** 90–121.

WOLF, H. F. (1934). "Physical therapy of the sciatic syndrome." *Arch. Phys. Ther.*, **15:** 96–98.

WOLFF, H. D. (1972). "Relief of pain in the vertebral column: vertebral blocking and its manual therapy." *Verh. Dtsch. Ges. Rheumatol.*, **2:** 215–226.

WRIGHT, V. & ROBERTS, M. (1973). "Indomethacin in the treatment of rheumatic diseases." *Clin. Med.*, **Jan:** 12–15.

YATES, A. (1976). "Treatment of back pain." In *The Lumbar Spine and Back Pain*. pp. 341–353. Ed. by M. I. V. Jayson, London; Sector Publishing Co.

YOUNG, J. H. (1949). "The treatment of acute lumbago and acute low back strain in general practice." *Med. J. Aust.*, **2:** 596–600.

## (b) Manipulative (including Physiotherapy, Osteopathy, Chiropractic)

AUCHIN, E. E. (1974). "The place of manipulation of the back." *Aust. Fam. Phys.*, **3:** 276–280.

BEAUCHAMP, P. (1957). "Discussion of the present position of manipulative treatment." *Proc. Roy. Soc. Med.*, **50:** 137–144.

BELL, M. (1968). "Vertebral manipulation in chiropractic and physical medicine." *J. Can. Physiother. Assoc.*, **20:** 1.

BOURDILLON, J. (1955). "Manipulative methods in orthopaedics." *Brit. Med. J.*, **1:** 720.

BOURDILLON, J. (1970). "Spinal manipulation." *Lancet*, **2:** 1068.

BOURDILLON, J. (1973). *Spinal Manipulation*. 2nd ed. London; Heinemann.

BOURDILLON, J. (1974). "Manipulating the patient." *Lancet*, **2:** 587–588.

BREMNER, R. A. & EDIN, M. B. (1958). "Manipulation in the management of chronic low backache due to lumbosacral strain." *Lancet*, **1:** 20–21.

CHRISMAN, P. (1964). "Results following rotatory manipulation in the lumbar intervertebral disc syndrome." *J. Bone Joint Surg.*, **46A:** 517.

CHRISTIE, J. (1965). "Manipulation of the spine." *Ann. Phys. Med.*, **8:** 103–108.

COLDHAM, M. (1975). "Chiropractic." *Canad. Med. Assoc. J.*, **112:** 929–931.

COX, H. H. (1935). "Manipulation in low back conditions." *Arch. Phys. Therap.*, **16:** 36–38.

COYER, A. B. & CURWEN, I. (1955). "Low back pain treated by manipulation." *Brit. Med. J.*, **1:** 705–707.

CYRIAX, J. (1964). "The pros and cons of manipulation." *Lancet*, **1:** 572.

CYRIAX, J. (1967). "Manipulative medicine." *World Med.*, **2:** 15.

CYRIAX, J. (1971). "Manipulation by laymen or physiotherapists?" *J. Canad. Physiotherap. Assoc.*, **23:** 236.

CYRIAX, J. (1975). "Manipulation in treatment of low back pain." *Brit. Med. J.*, **2:** 334.

CYRIAX, J. (1975/78). *Textbook of Orthopaedic Medicine*. 2 Vols. London; Cassell.

DORAN, D. M. L. & NEWELL, D. J. (1975). "Manipulation in treatment of low back pain: a multicentre study." *Brit. Med. J.*, **2:** 161–164.

EBBETTS, J. (1964). "Spinal manipulation." *Lancet*, **2:** 1062.

EBBETTS, J. (1975). "Manipulation in treatment of low back pain." *Brit. Med. J.*, **2:** 393.

EWER, E. G. (1953). "Manipulation of the spine." *J. Bone Joint Surg.*, **35A:** 347–352.

449

EWERHARDT, F. H. (1941). "Rhythmic movements in chronic backache." *Arch. Phys. Med.*, **22:** 404–406.

FARFAN, H. F. (1973). *Mechanical Disorders of the Low Back.* Philadelphia; Lea and Febiger.

FICHERA, A. P. & CELANDER, D. R. (1969). "Effect of osteopathic manipulative therapy on autonomic tone as evidenced by blood pressure changes and activity of the fibrinolytic system." *J. Amer. Osteopath. Assoc.*, **68:** 1036–1038.

GIMLETT, D. M. (1972). "Osteopathic and allopathic medicine." *J. Occup. Med.*, **14:** 892.

GLOVER, J. R. (1966). "A clinical trial of rotational manipulation of the spine in back pain cases occurring in a factory." *Proc. Roy. Soc. Med.*, **59:** 847–848.

GLOVER, J. R. (1970). "Occupational health research and the problem of back pain." *Trans. Soc. Occup. Med.*, **21:** 2–12.

GLOVER, J. R., MORRIS, J. G. & KHOSLA, T. (1974). "Back pain: a randomized clinical trial of rotational manipulation of the trunk." *Brit. J. Indust. Med.*, **31:** 59–64.

GOLDIE, I. & LANDQUIST, A. (1970). "Evaluation of the effects of different forms of physiotherapy in cervical pain." *Scand. J. Rehab. Med.*, **2–3:** 117.

GOLDSTEIN, M. (Ed.). (1975). *The Research Status of Spinal Manipulative Therapy.* Bethesda, Maryland; N.I.H.

GRIEVE, G. P. (1979). *Mobilisation of the Spine.* 3rd ed. Edinburgh; Churchill Livingstone.

GRIFFIN, P. (1973). "Fringe medicine – osteopathy in general practice." *Proc. Roy. Soc. Med.*, **66:** 423.

GUTMANN, G. (1971). "Possibilities for objective assessment of the effects of chirotherapy." *Méd. Hyg.*, **29:** 1.

HARLEY, J. (1965). "Manipulation of the lumbar spine." *J. Gen. Pract.*, **102:** 189.

HICKLING, M. (1960). "Manipulation." *Physiotherapy*, **46:** 160.

JEANBLANC, P. (1970). "Indications and limitations of vertebral manipulation." *Ann. Méd. Nancy*, **9:** 117–122.

KALTENBORN, F. (1970). *Mobilisation of the Spinal Column.* Wellington; University Press.

LAMB, J. (1973). "Mobilization and manipulation." *Physiotherapy Canada*, **25:** 310–311.

LESCURE, P. (1968). "Cervical arthrosis and articular manipulations." *Ann. Med. Phys.*, **3**: 207.

LESCURE, P. (1968). "The place of articular manipulations in the treatment of cervico-brachial neuralgia." *Ann. Med. Phys.*, **3**: 213.

LIVINGSTON, J. (1968). "Spinal manipulation in medical practice: a century of ignorance." *Med. J. Aust.*, **2**: 552–555.

MCKENZIE, R. A. (1972). "Manual correction of sciatic scoliosis." *N.Z. Med. J.*, **76**: 194–199; 484.

MAIGNE, R. (1964). The concept of painlessness and opposite motion in spinal manipulation. *Amer. J. Phys. Med.*, **44**: 55.

MAIGNE, R. (1972). "*Pain of Vertebral Origin and Its Treatment by Manipulation.*" 2nd ed. Paris; Expansion Scientifique.

MAITLAND, G. D. (1961). "Lumbar manipulation: does it harm? A five year follow-up survey." *Med. J. Aust.*, **2**: 546.

MAITLAND, G. D. (1968). "Selection and assessment of patients for spinal manipulation." *N.Z. J. Physiotherap.*, **3**: 4–10.

MAITLAND, G. D. (1972). "Manipulation: individual responsibility." *Physiotherapy (Sth. Africa)*, **28**: 2–4.

MAITLAND, G. D. (1977). *Vertebral Manipulation.* 4th ed. London; Butterworth.

MATHEWS, J. A. & YATES, D. A. H. (1969). "Reduction of lumbar disc prolapse by manipulation." *Brit. Med. J.*, **3**: 696–697.

MENNELL, J. B. (1945). *Physical Treatment by Movement, Manipulation and Massage.* London; Churchill.

MENNELL, J. B. (1952). *Science and Art of Joint Manipulation (Spinal Column).* London; Churchill.

MENSOR, K. (1965). "Non-operative treatment, including manipulation, for lumbar intervertebral disc syndrome." *J. Bone Joint Surg.*, **47A**: 1073.

NACHEMSON, A. (1976). "A critical look at conservative treatment for low back pain." In *The Lumbar Spine and Back Pain.* pp. 355–365. Ed. M. I. V. Jayson. London; Sector Publishing.

NEWTON, P. (1958). "The place of manipulative treatment in lesions of the lumbar spine." *Postgrad. Med. J.*, **34**: 378.

NEWTON, P. (1962). "The scope of manipulative medicine." *J. Coll. Gen. Pract.*, **6** (Suppl. 3): 1–4.

NWUGA, V. C. (1976). *Manipulation of the Spine.* Baltimore; Williams and Wilkins.

PARIS, S. V. (1979). "Mobilization of the spine." *J. Amer. Phys. Therap. Assoc.*, **59**: 988–995.

PARSONS, W. B. & BOAKE, H. K. (1966). "Manipulation for backache and sciatica." *Appl. Therap.*, **8**: 954–961.

SCHAM, S. M. (1974). "Manipulation of the lumbosacral spine." *Clin. Orthop.*, **101**: 146–150.

SMITH, P. & ESTRIDGE, M. (1962). "Neurological complications of head and neck manipulations." *J. Amer. Med. Assoc.*, **182**: 528.

STODDARD, A. (1951). "Manipulative procedures in the treatment of intervertebral disc lesions." *Brit. J. Phys. Med.*, **May:** 101.

STODDARD, A. (1960). "Manipulation for low backache." *Rheumatism*, **16**: 20–24.

STODDARD, A. (1969). *Manual of Osteopathic Practice*. London; Hutchinson.

THIERRYMIEG, J. (1966). "Technics of vertebral manipulations used in the treatment of sciatica with discal hernia. Indications, contra-indications, and accidents." *Sém. Therap.*, **42**: 376–379.

TRAVELL, W. & TRAVELL, J. (1942). "Technic for reduction and ambulatory treatment of sacroiliac displacement." *Arch. Phys. Therap.*, **23**: 222.

TRAVELL, W. & TRAVELL, J. (1946). "Therapy of low back pain by manipulation and of referred pain in lower extremity by procaine infiltration." *Arch. Phys. Med.*, **27**: 537.

TUCKER, P. (1969). "Treatment of osteoarthritis by manual therapy." *Brit. J. Clin. Pract.*, **23**: 3.

VAN SCHAIJK, M. (1970). "Manipulative therapy in the Netherlands." *Nederlands Tijdschrift voor Fysiotherapie*, **April:** 189.

WARR, A. C., WILKINSON, J. A., BURN, J. M. B. & LANGOON, L. (1972). "Chronic lumbosciatic syndrome treated by epidural injection and manipulation." *Practitioner*, **269**: 53–59.

WILSON, P. (1962). "Manipulative treatment in general practice." *Lancet*, **1**: 1013.

### *(c) Surgical*

ALBEE, F. H., POWERS, E. J. & McDOWELL, H. C. (1945). *Surgery of the Spinal Column*. Philadelphia; Davis.

ALEXANDER, M. A. (1972). "Can experimental dorsal rhizotomy produce scoliosis?" *J. Bone Joint Surg.*, **54**: 1509–1513.

ALLEN, K. (1952). "Neuropathies caused by bony spurs in the cervical spine with special reference to surgical treatment." *J. Neurol. Neurosurg. Psychiat.*, **15**: 20–36.

ANDERSON, C. E. (1956). "Spondyloschisis following spine fusion." *J. Bone Joint Surg.*, **38A**: 1142–1146.

ARCT, W. A. (1974). "Intraspinal tuberculous abscess mimicking disc prolapse with compression of L5 and S1 nerve roots." *Arch. Orthop. Unfall-Chir.*, **80**: 13–19.

AUQUIER, L., GUIOT, G., ROUGERIE, J. & SIAUD, J. R. (1973). "Curettage of the disc in persistent lumbar disc pain: a preliminary series of 13 cases." *Rev. Rhum. Mal. Osteoartic.*, **40**: 9–18.

AUQUIER, L., HIRSCH, J. F., PAOLOGGI, J. B., ROUQUES, C. & GHOZLAN, R. (1970). "Stenosis of lumbar spinal canal and sciatic claudication: study of 29 cases, 13 of which were operated upon." *Ann. Rheum. Dis.*, **29**: 691–692.

BAKALIM, G. (1966). "Results of radical evacuation and arthrodesis in sacro-iliac tuberculosis." *Acta Orthop. Scand.*, **37**: 375–386.

BAKAY, L. (1973). "Postoperative myelography in spondylotic cervical myelopathy." *Acta Neurochirurg.*, **29**: 123–133.

BALAPARAMESWARA, R. A. (1970). "Lumbar disc prolapse: a study of 251 cases." *Neurol.*, **18**: 120–125.

BARASH, H. L., GALANTE, J. O., LAMBERT, C. N. & RAY, R. D. (1970). "Spondylolisthesis and tight hamstrings." *J. Bone Joint Surg.*, **52A**: 1319.

BEAMER, V. B., GARNER, J. T. & SHELDEN, C. H. (1973). "Hypertrophied ligamentum flavum: clinical and surgical significance." *Arch. Surg.*, **106**: 289–292.

BIRKELAND, I. W. & TAYLOR, T. K. F. (1969). "Major vascular injuries in lumbar disc surgery." *J. Bone Joint Surg.*, **51B**: 4–19.

BLAU, L. & KENT, L. (1974). "Conservative and surgical aspects of disc lesion management: follow-up review of 244 cases." *Western J. Med.*, **120**: 353–357.

BOCK, W. J. (1975). "Demonstration of cervical spine canal before and after fusion operation." *Neurochirurgica*, **18**: 12–15.

BOHLER, J. (1970). "Operative treatment of fractures of the dorsal and lumbar spine." *J. Trauma*, **10**: 1119–1122.

BOHLMAN, H. H. (1972). "Pathology and current treatment concepts of cervical spine injury." *A.A.O.S. Instructional Course Lectures*, **21**: 108–115.

Bossers, G. Th. M. (1972). "Columnotomy in severe Bechterew kyphosis." *Acta. Orthop. Belg.*, **38**: 47–54.

Bouchard, C., Tranier, J. & Chauvet, J. (1972). "Sciatica and surgical intervention: report of 458 cases." *Ann. Méd. Interne*, **123**: 587–591.

Brackett, C. E. (1973). "The posterior midline approach to a cervical disc." *J. Neurosurg.*, **38**: 668–671.

Bradford, F. K. & Spurling, R. G. (1945). *The Intervertebral Disc.* 2nd ed. Springfield, Illinois; Thomas.

Buck, J. E. (1970). "Direct repair of the defect in spondylolisthesis." *J. Bone Joint Surg.*, **52B**: 432–437.

Burns, B. H. & Young, R. H. (1951). "The results of surgery in sciatica and low back pain." *Lancet*, **1**: 245–249.

Chrostowska, T., Riwerski, J., Michalowska, B. & Makowski, J. (1972). "Results of treatment of lesions in the lower parts of the spine." *Chir. Narsadow Ruchu Ortop. Pol.*, **37**: 645–649.

Cloward, R. B. (1952). "Lumbar intervertebral disc surgery. Description of a new instrument, the vertebrae spreader." *Surgery*, **32**: 854–857.

Cloward, R. B. (1952). "The treatment of ruptured lumbar intervertebral disc by vertebral body fusion. III. Method of use of banked bone." *Ann. Surg.*, **136**: 987–992.

Cloward, R. B. (1953). "Treatment of ruptured lumbar intervertebral discs by vertebral body fusion. Indications, operative techniques, after care." *J. Neurosurg.*, **10**: 154–168.

Cloward, R. B. (1973). "Reduction of traumatic dislocation of the cervical spine with locked facets: technical note." *J. Neurosurg.*, **38**: 527–531.

Compere, E. L. (1932). "Excision of hemivertebrae for correction of congenital scoliosis." *J. Bone Joint Surg.*, **14A**: 555–562.

Connolly, R. C. & Newman, P. H. (1971). "Lumbar spondylotomy." *J. Bone Joint Surg.*, **53B**: 576–577.

Crock, H. V. (1976). "Observations on the management of failed spinal operations." *J. Bone Joint Surg.*, **58B**: 193–199.

Crue, B. C. & Felsoory, A. (1974). "Transcutaneous high vertical electronic cordotomy." *Minnesota Med.*, **57**: 204–209.

Curran, J. P. & McGraw, W. H. (1968). "Posterolateral spinal fusion with pedicle grafts." *Clin. Orthop.*, **59**: 125–129.

Darby, G. (1970). "Operative treatment of lumbar disc herniation." *J. Bone Joint Surg.*, **52B**: 189.

DAVIS, I. S. & BAILEY, R. W. (1972). "Spondylolisthesis – long term follow-up study of treatment with total laminectomy." *Clin. Orthop.*, **88:** 46–49.

DECKER, H. G. & SHAPIRO, S. W. (1957). "Herniated lumbar intervertebral disks. Results of surgical treatment without the routine use of spinal fusion." *Arch. Surg.*, **75:** 77–84.

DUBUC, F. (1975). "Knodt rod grafting." *Orthop. Clin. Nth. Amer.*, **6:** 283–287.

DU TOIT, J. G. (1954). "Anterior spinal fusion for spondylolisthesis." *J. Bone Joint Surg.*, **36B:** 342–343.

EMNEUS, H. (1968). "Wedge osteotomy of spine in ankylosing spondylitis." *Acta Orthop. Scand.*, **39:** 321–326.

ENSLIN, T. B. (1973). "Access to the ilio-lumbar angle for root clearance and lateral fusion of the spine from one side only." *J. Bone Joint Surg.*, **55B:** 440.

ENSLIN, T. B. (1975). "Debridement and fusion in the lumbosacral area through the iliolumbar approach." *Orthop. Clin. Nth. Amer.*, **6:** 291–297.

ESHOUGUES, J. R., DELCAMBRE, B., ASCHER, J. & WAGHEMACKER, R. (1974). "Introduction to radiological diagnosis and surgical treatment of lumbar pain: some important considerations." *Sem. Hôp. Paris*, **50:** 615–625.

EYRE-BROOK, A. L. (1952). "A study of late results from disk operations: present employment and residual complaints." *Brit. J. Surg.*, **39:** 289–296.

FAGER, C. A. (1973). "Results of adequate posterior decompression in the relief of spondylotic cervical myelopathy." *J. Neurosurg.*, **38:** 684–692.

FAIBURN, B. & STEWART, J. M. (1955). "Lumbar disc protrusion as a surgical emergency." *Lancet*, **2:** 319–321.

FARFAN, H. F. (1975). "Comment on debridement and fusion in the lumbosacral area through an iliolumbar approach." *Orthop. Clin. Nth. Amer.*, **6:** 297.

FARIN, I. & SPIRA, E. (1965). "The spinal fusion, our technique and its evaluation." *Acta Orthop. Scand.*, **36:** 265–273.

FERNSTROM, U. (1965). "Arthroplasty and intercorporal endoprosthesis in herniated disc and in painful disc." *Acta Orthop. Scand., Suppl.* **357:** 154–159.

FORD, L. T. (1968). "Symposium: complications of lumbar disc surgery, prevention and treatment." *J. Bone Joint Surg.*, **50A:** 418–428.

Fox, J. L. (1974). "Dorsal column stimulation for relief of intractable pain: problems encountered with neuropacemakers." *Surg. Neurol.*, **2:** 59–64.

Fox, J. L., Byrd, E. B. & McCullough, D. C. (1973). "Results of cervical laminectomy with dural graft for severe spondylosis with narrow canal." *Acta Neurol. Latinoamer.*, **18:** 90–95.

Freebody, D. (1964). "Treatment of spondylolisthesis by anterior fusion via the transperitoneal route." *J. Bone Joint Surg.*, **38B:** 485.

Freeman, L. W. (1961). "Surgical treatment of back and leg pain persisting after adequate disc surgery." *J. Indiana State Med. Assoc.*, **54:** 1265–1267.

Friberg, S. & Hirsch, C. (1946). "On late results of operative treatment of intervertebral disc prolapses in the lumbar region." *Acta Chir. Scand.*, **93:** 161.

Fried, L. C. (1973). "Atlanto-axial fracture-dislocations: failure of posterior C1 to C2 fusion." *J. Bone Joint Surg.*, **55B:** 490–496.

Gartland, J. J. (1971). "Orthopaedic versus neurosurgical approach to lumbar disc problems." *Orthop. Clin. Nth. Amer.*, **2:** 519–520.

Gerber, A. (1972). "The osteopathic orthopaedic surgeon and industrial back problems." *J. Occup. Med.*, **14:** 851–853.

Giles, W. M., Boop, W. C. & Flanigan, S. (1973). "Anterior decompression in cervical disc degeneration." *J. Arkansas Med. Soc.*, **69:** 285–290.

Gill, G. G., Manning, J. G. & White, H. L. (1955). "Surgical treatment of spondylolisthesis without spine fusion." *Arch. Phys. Med., Rehab.*, **36:** 788.

Goldner, J. L., McColum, D. E. & Urbaniak, J. R. (1968). "Anterior intervertebral discectomy and arthrodesis for treatment of low back pain with or without radiculopathy." *Clin. Neurosurg.*, **15:** 352–383.

Goutallier, D. & Debeyre, J. (1973). "Arthrodesis and discography in the surgical treatment of lumbar pain." *Rev. Rhum. Mal. Osteoartic.*, **40:** 763–765.

Graham, C. E. (1966). "Symposium on lumbar disc surgery. Lumbar discography." *J. Bone Joint Surg.*, **48B:** 595.

Gurdjian, E. S., Ostrowski, A. Z., Hardy, W. G., Lindner, D.

W. & THOMAS, L. M. (1961). "Results of operative treatment of protruded and ruptured lumbar disks." *J. Neurosurg.*, **18:** 783.

HAFT, K. (1966). "Herniated lumbar intervertebral disks with unilateral pain and midline myelographic defects: unilateral or bilateral excision." *Surgery*, **60:** 269.

HAFTEK, J. (1973). "Decompression of the cervical spine by removal of vertebral bodies and simultaneous stabilization using iliac or fibular bone grafts." *Chir. Narzad. Ruchu Ortop. Pol.*, **38:** 253–257.

HARMON, P. H. (1960). "Anterior extraperitoneal lumbar disc excision and vertebral body fusion." *Clin. Orthop.*, **18:** 169–184.

HARMON, P. H. (1961). "Practical application of non-myelographic methods of screening, diagnosis and localization of lumbar disc degenerations: special reference to injection of saline into the disc at operation." *Trans. Coll. Phys. Surg. Gynaec. Sth. Africa*, **5:** 29–42.

HARRINGTON, P. R. & TULLOS, H. S. (1971). "Spondylolisthesis in children: observations and surgical treatment." *Clin. Orthop.*, **79:** 75–84.

HARRIS, R. I. (1970). "Decompressive laminectomy for low back and sciatic pain." *Canad. Med. J.*, **102:** 1361.

HAVERLING, M. (1972). "Transsacral puncture of the arachnoidal sac: an alternative procedure to lumbar puncture." *Acta Radiol. (Diagn.)*, **12:** 1–6.

HEMMER, R. & PICK, S. (1971). "Laminectomy in metastases of the vertebral spine." *Arztliche Forsch.*, **25:** 1.

HENRY, M. O. (1932). "Tuberculosis of the fifth lumbar vertebra with spina bifida occulta: spinal fusion and cure." *J. Bone Joint Surg.*, **14:** 690–692.

HIBBS, R. A. & SWIFT, W. E. (1929). "Developmental abnormalities at the lumbosacral juncture causing pain and disability: report of 147 patients treated by the spine fusion operation." *Surg. Gynec. Obst.*, **48:** 604–612.

HIRSCH, C. (1947). "On lumbar facetectomies." *Acta Orthop. Scand.*, **17:** 240–252.

HIRSCH, C. (1958). "Exposure of ruptured lumbar discs." *Acta Orthop. Scand.*, **28:** 76–80.

HIRSCH, C. (1965). "Efficiency of surgery in low back disorders: patho-anatomical, experimental and clinical status." *J. Bone Joint Surg.*, **47A:** 991–1004.

HIRSCH, C. (1971). "Reflections on the use of surgery in lumbar disc disease." *Orthop. Clin. Nth. Amer.*, **2**: 493–498.

HIRSCH, C. & NACHEMSON, A. (1963). "The reliability of lumbar disc surgery." *Clin. Orthop.*, **29**: 189.

HIRSCH, C., WICKBOM, I., LINSTROM, A. & ROSENGREN, K. (1964). "Cervical disc resection: a follow-up." *J. Bone Joint Surg.*, **64A**: 1811–1821.

HITCHCOCK, E. (1974). "Stereotatic myelotomy." *Proc. Roy. Soc. Med.*, **67**: 771–772.

HOLSCHER, E. C. (1948). "Vascular complications of disc surgery." *J. Bone Joint Surg.*, **30A**: 968.

HUDGINS, W. R. (1974). "Should degenerated discs be removed?" *Surg. Forum*, **25**: 442–445.

HUDGINS, W. R. (1975). "Exposure of two interspaces for lumbar disc surgery." *J. Neurosurg.*, **42**: 59–60.

IRACI, G. (1972). "Intraspinal neurinomas and meningiomas." *Int. Surg.*, **56**: 289–303.

JACKSON, B. T. (1971). "The long term effects of wide laminectomy for lumbar disc excision." *J. Bone Joint Surg.*, **53B**: 609–616.

JOHNSON, R. W., HILLMAN, J. W. & SOUTHWICK, W. O. (1953). "The importance of direct surgical attack upon lesions of the vertebral bodies, particularly in Pott's disease." *J. Bone Joint Surg.*, **35A**: 17–25.

KAUFFMANN, E. A. (1971). "Use of autopolymerizing acrylic (methyl methacrylate) in fusion of the cervical-thoracic-lumbar column." *Acta Neurol. Latinoamer.*, **17**: 344–351.

KNUTSSON, B. (1962). "How often do the neurological signs disappear after the operation of a herniated disc?" *Acta Orthop. Scand.*, **32**: 352–356.

KUDELKA, P. (1968). "Laminectomy in lumbar disc syndrome." *Med. J. Aust.*, **1**: 1120–1122.

KUROIWA, A. (1973). "Clinical and roentgenological studies of anterior cervical body fusion for cervical disc lesion." *J. Jap. Orthop. Assoc.*, **47**: 769–792.

LAMOND, R. L., MORAWA, L. G. & PEDERSON, H. E. (1976). "Comparison of disk excision with combined disk excision and spinal fusion for lumbar disk rupture." *Clin. Orthop.*, **121**: 212–216.

LAURENT, E. (1959). "Experiences with operative treatment of spondylolisthesis." *Acta Orthop. Scand.*, **29**: 168–169.

LAW, W. A. (1969). "Osteotomy of the spine." *Clin. Orthop.*, **66:** 70–76.

LECUIRE, J., BRET, P., DECHAUME, J. P., DERUTY, R., BELLAVOIR, A. & BERGER-VACHON, C. (1973). "641 operations for sciatica." *Neurochirurgie*, **19:** 501–512.

LE VAY, D. (1967). "A survey of surgical management of lumbar disc prolapse in the United Kingdom and Eire." *Lancet*, **1:** 1211.

LEWIS, P. (1971). "Post-laminectomy syndrome." *J. Bone Joint Surg.*, **53A:** 389.

LINDAHL, O. (1966). "Resection of vertebral transverse processes in idiopathic scoliosis." *Acta Orthop. Scand.*, **37:** 342–347.

MACNAB, I. (1971). "Negative disc exploration: an analysis of the cause of nerve root involvement in 68 patients." *J. Bone Joint Surg.*, **53A:** 891.

MARTIN, N. S. & WILLIAMSON, J. (1970). "The role of surgery in the treatment of malignant tumours of the spine." *J. Bone Joint Surg.*, **52B:** 227.

MIXTER, W. J. (1937). "Rupture of the lumbar intervertebral disk: an etiologic factor for so-called 'sciatic' pain." *Ann. Surg.*, **106:** 777–787.

MIXTER, W. J. & BARR, J. S. (1934). "Rupture of the intervertebral disk with involvement of the spinal canal." *New Eng. J. Med.*, **211:** 210–215.

MURPHY, M. G. & GADO, M. (1972). "Anterior cervical discectomy without interbody bone graft." *J. Neurosurg.*, **37:** 71–74.

NAYLOR, A. (1974). "The late results of laminectomy for lumbar disc prolapse." *J. Bone Joint Surg.*, **56B:** 17.

NELSON, M. A. (1968). "A long term review of posterior spinal fusion." *Proc. Roy. Soc. Med.*, **611:** 558.

NELSON, M. A. (1976). "Surgery of the spine." In *The Lumbar Spine and Back Pain*. pp. 367–394. Ed. by M. I. V. Jayson. London; Sector Publishing.

NEWMAN, P. H. (1972). "Some special indications for operative treatment in mechanical derangement of the lumbar spine." *J. Bone Joint Surg.*, **54B:** 764.

NIELSEN, A. A. (1968). "Lumbago-ischias treated by sympathetic block." *Ugeskr. Laeg.*, **130:** 773–776.

OUDENHOVEN, R. C. (1974). "Articular rhizotomy." *Surg. Neurol.*, **2:** 275–278.

PAINE, K. W. E. (1976). "Results of decompression for lumbar spinal stenosis." *Clin. Orthop.*, **115**: 96–103.

PAWL, R. P. (1974). "Results in the treatment of low back syndrome from sensory neurolysis of the lumbar facets (facet rhizotomy) by thermal coagulation." *Proc. Inst. Med. Chir.*, **30**: 151–152.

PERVÈS, A. (1972). "Fracture of the dorsal and lumbar spine: operative indications and results." *Bull. Mém. Soc. Chir. Paris*, **62**: 364–371.

PERVÈS, A. & PIDHORZ, L. (1963). "Fractures of dorsal and lumbar spine: operative indications and results." *Rev. Chir. Orthop.*, **59**: 491–512.

PHILLIPS, D. G. (1973). "Surgical treatment of myelopathy with cervical spondylosis." *J. Neurol. Neurosurg. Psychiat.*, **36**: 879–884.

PIERRES, Y. LE & EVRARD, J. (1974). "Pott's disease – medical or surgical treatment? Study of 189 adult patients treated between 1960 and 1970." *Rev. Chir. Orthop.*, **60**: 401–413.

PROTHERO, S. R., PARKES, J. C. & STINCHFIELD, F. E. (1966). "Complications after low-back fusion in 1000 patients: a comparison of two series one decade apart." *J. Bone Joint Surg.*, **48A**: 57–65.

RAAF, J. (1970). "Removal of protruded lumbar intervertebral discs." *J. Neurosurg.*, **32**: 604–611.

RAND, R. W. & MOSSO, J. A. (1973). "Lumbar intervertebral body fusion without facet removal." *Bull. Los Angeles Neurol. Soc.*, **38**: 122–125.

RENS, T. J. G. VAN (1967). "Experiences with anterior lumbar spondylodesis in the treatment of low back pain." *Zeit. Orthop.*, **102**: 546–558.

RENS, T. J. G. VAN (1969). "The value and technique of anterior vertebral interbody fusion." *Acta Orthop. Belg.*, **35**: 752–762.

RIECHERT, T. (1973). "Operative relief of chronic pain by electrostimulation of the dorsal column." *Ger. Med.*, **3**: 144–145.

ROSEN, M. (1969). "Lumbar intervertebral disc surgery – review of 300 cases." *Canad. Med. Assoc. J.*, **101**: 317–323.

RUSSIN, L. A. (1971). "Lumbar disc surgery in geriatric patients." *J. Bone Joint Surg.*, **53**: 564.

SCOTT-CHARLTON, W. & ROEBUCK, D. J. (1972). "The significance of posterior primary divisions of spinal nerves in pain syndromes." *Med. J. Aust.*, **2**: 945–948.

SCOVILLE, W. B. (1966). "Types of cervical disk lesions and their surgical approaches." *J. Amer. Med. Assoc.*, **196:** 479.

SHAW, E. G. & TAYLOR, J. G. (1956). "The results of lumbo-sacral fusion for low back pain." *J. Bone Joint Surg.*, **38B:** 485.

SHENKIN, H. A. & HASH, C. J. (1976). "A new approach to the surgical treatment of lumbar spondylosis." *J. Neurosurg.*, **44:** 148–155.

SHUMACKER, H. B., KING, H. & CAMPBELL, R. (1961). "Vascular complications for disc operations." *J. Trauma*, **1:** 177.

SIMEONE, F. A. (1971). "The neurosurgical approach to lumbar disc disease." *Orthop. Clin. Nth. Amer.*, **2:** 499–506.

SMITH, G. W. & ROBINSON, R. A. (1958). "The treatment of certain cervical spine disorders by anterior removal of the intervertebral disc and interbody fusion." *J. Bone Joint Surg.*, **40A:** 607–624.

SMITH, H. T. (1970). "Trans-spinal ganglionectomy for relief of intercostal pain." *J. Neurosurg.*, **32:** 574–577.

SMITH, J. W. & WALMSLEY, R. (1951). "Experimental excision of the intervertebral disc." *J. Bone Joint Surg.*, **33B:** 612–625.

SMITH, M. J. & WRIGHT, V. (1958). "Sciatica and the intervertebral disc: an experimental study." *J. Bone Joint Surg.*, **40A:** 1410–1418.

SOUTHWICK, W. O. & ROBINSON, R. A. (1957). "Surgical approaches to the vertebral bodies in the cervical and lumbar regions." *J. Bone Joint Surg.*, **39A:** 631–643.

STAUFFER, R. N. (1971). "A rational approach to failures of lumbar disc surgery: an orthopedist's approach." *Orthop. Clin. Nth. Amer.*, **2:** 533–542.

STENER, P. (1971). "Total spondylectomy in chondrosarcoma arising from the seventh thoracic vertebra." *J. Bone Joint Surg.*, **53B:** 288–295.

STENER, P. & JOHNSEN, A. (1971). "Complete removal of three vertebrae for giant-cell tumour." *J. Bone Joint Surg.*, **53:** 3–12.

STERN, W. E. (1972). "Neurosurgical aspects of injuries of the thoracic and lumbar spine." *Surg. Clin. Nth. Amer.*, **52:** 769–781.

STRACHAN, W. E. (1972). "Surgical treatment of cervical spondylosis." *J. Bone Joint Surg.*, **54B:** 760.

TOAKELY, J. G. (1973). "Subcutaneous lumbar 'rhizolysis' – an assessment of 200 cases." *Med. J. Austr.*, **2:** 490–492.

TSUCHIYA, K. (1973). "A long-term follow-up study of transperitoneal anterior vertebral body fusion (Suzuki's method) for lumbar disc herniation: especially on the influence of vertebral body fusion upon the lumbar vertebral column." *J. Jap. Orthop. Assoc.*, **47**: 741–767.

VERBLEST, H. (1973). "Anterolateral operations for fractures or dislocations of the cervical spine due to injuries or previous surgical interventions." *Clin. Neurosurg.*, **20**: 334–366.

WEBER, H. (1970). "An evaluation of conservative and surgical treatment of lumbar disc protrusion." *J. Oslo City Hosp.*, **20**: 81–93.

WEBER, H. (1978). "Lumbar disc herniation." *J. Oslo City Hosp.*, **23**: 33–64; 89–120.

WHITE, J. C., & SWEET, W. H. (1969). *Pain and the Neurosurgeon: a Forty Year's Experience.* Springfield, Ill.; Thomas.

WHITE, W. A., PATTERSON, R. H. & BERGLAND, R. M. (1971). "Role of surgery in the treatment of spinal cord compression by metastatic neoplasm." *Cancer*, **27**: 558.

WILFLING, F. J., KLONOFF, H. & KOKAN, P. (1973). "Psychological, demographic and orthopaedic factors associated with prediction of outcome of spinal fusion." *Clin. Orthop.*, **90**: 153–160.

WILKINSON, M. C. (1969). "Tuberculosis of the spine treated by chemotherapy and operative debridement." *J. Bone Joint Surg.*, **51A**: 1331.

WILTBERGER, B. R. (1963). "Surgical treatment of degenerative disease of the back." *J. Bone Joint Surg.*, **45A**: 1509–1516.

WILTBERGER, B. R. (1964). "Resection of vertebral bodies and bone-grafting for chronic osteomyelitis of the spine." *J. Bone Joint Surg.*, **46A**: 1822–1823.

WOOD, J. P. (1974). "Lumbar disk surgery: complications." *J. Amer. Osteopath. Assoc.*, **74**: 234–240.

YAU, A. C. M. C., HSU, L. C. S., O'BRIEN, J. P. & HODGSON, A. R. (1974). "Tuberculous kyphosis: correction with spinal osteotomy, halo-pelvic distraction, and anterior and posterior fusion." *J. Bone Joint Surg.*, **56A**: 1419–1434.

### (d) Acupuncture

EDELIST, G., GROSS, A. E. & LANGER, F. (1976). "Treatment of low back pain with acupuncture." *Canad. Anesth. Soc. Journ.*, **23**: 303–306.

FERNANDEZ-HERLIHY, I. (1972). "Osler acupuncture and lumbago." *New Eng. J. Med.*, **287**: 314.

FOX, E. J. & MELZACK, R. (1976). "Comparison of transcutaneous electrical stimulation and acupuncture in the treatment of chronic pain." *Pain*, **2**: 141–148.

FROST, E. A. M., HSU, C. Y. & SADOWSKY, D. (1976). "Acupuncture therapy; comparative values in acute and chronic pain." *Advances in Pain Res. Therap.*, **1**: 823–829.

GHIA, J. N., MAO, W., TOOMEY, T. C. & GREFF, J. M. (1976). "Acupuncture and chronic pain mechanisms." *Pain*, **2**: 285–299.

KATZ, R. L., KAO, C. Y., EPIEGEL, H. & KATZ, G. J. (1974). "Pain, acupuncture, hypnosis." *Advances in Neurology*, **4**: 813–818.

LEE, P. K. Y., MODELL, J. H., ANDERSEN, T. W. & SAGA, S. A. (1976). "Incidence of prolonged pain relief following acupuncture." *Curr. Res. Anesth. Analg.*, **55**: 386.

LEVITT, E. E. & WALKER, F. D. (1975). "Evaluation of acupuncture in the treatment of chronic pain." *Chronic Dis.*, **28**: 311–316.

MANN, R., BOWSHER, D., MUMFORD, J., LIPTON, S. & MILES, J. (1973). "Treatment of intractable pain by acupuncture." *Lancet*, **2**: 57–60.

MURPHY, T. M. (1976). "Subjective and objective follow-up assessment of acupuncture therapy without suggestion in 100 chronic pain patients." *Advances in Pain Res. Therap.*, **1**: 811–815.

SATO, T. & NAKATANI, Y. (1974). "Acupuncture for chronic pain in Japan." *Advances in Neurol.*, **4**: 813–818.

SPOEREL, W. E., VARKEY, M. & LEUNG, C. Y. (1976). "Acupuncture in chronic pain." *Amer. J. Chinese Med.*, **4**: 267–279.

YAMAUCHI, M. (1976). "The results of therapeutic acupuncture in a pain clinic." *Canad. Anesth, Soc. J.*, **23**: 196–206.